FRED W.

McDARRAH

→ → →   →

the village Voice

WEEKLY NEWSPAPER OF NEW YORK

Vol. XIII, No. 35 • New York, N. Y. • Thursda

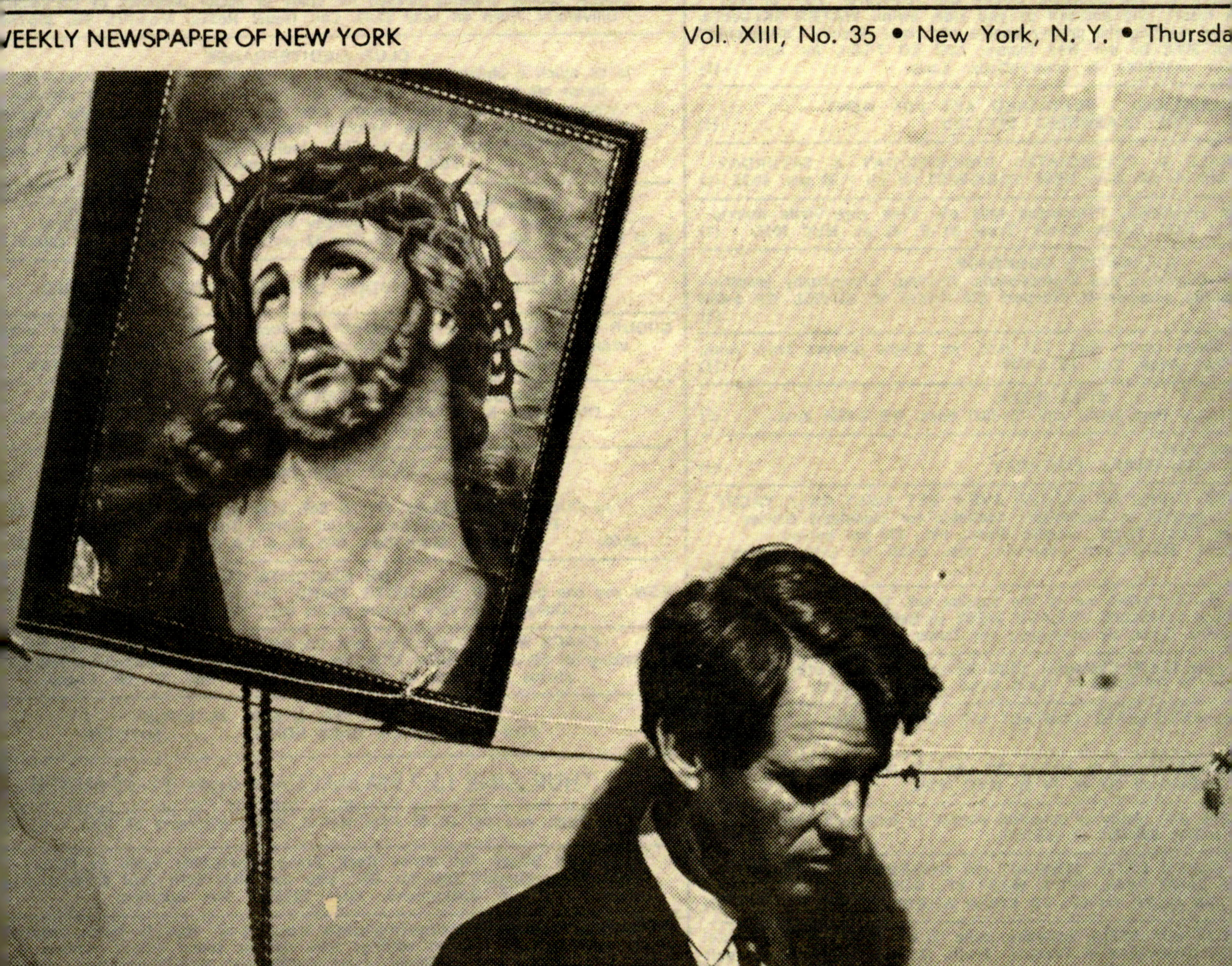

A SPECIAL SE

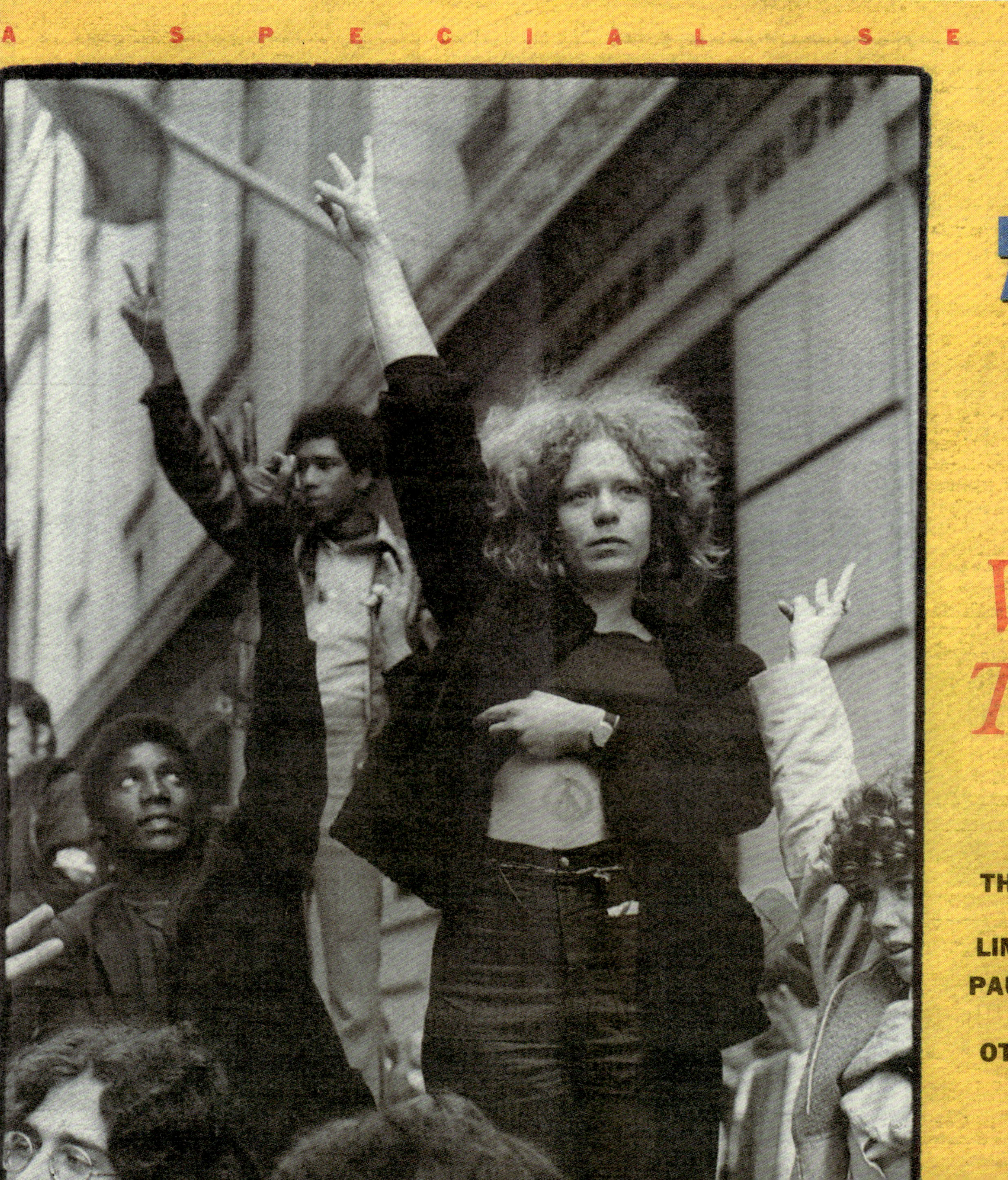

PER OF NEW YORK ● Vol. XV, No. 1 ● New York, N. Y. ● Thursday, Janu

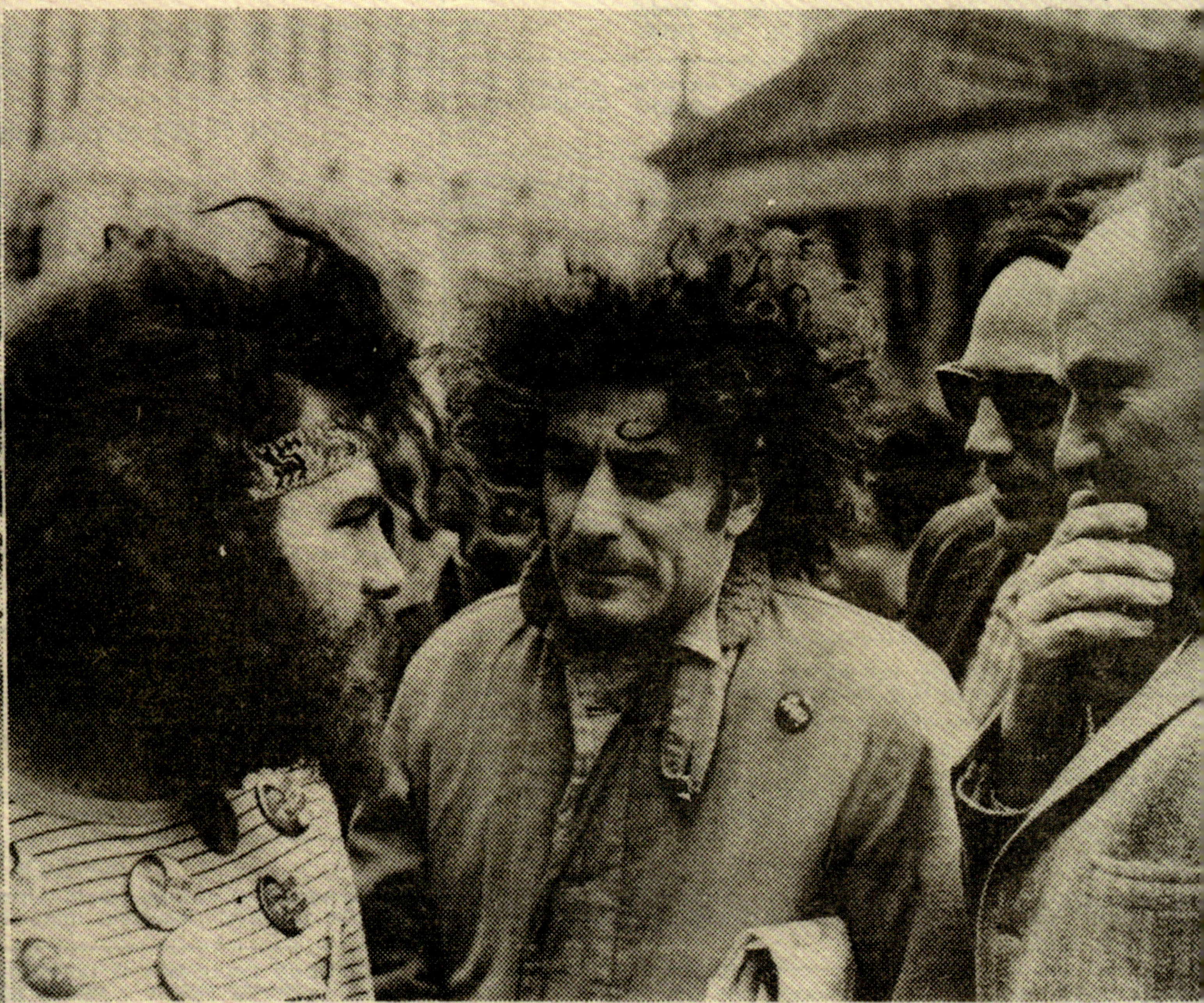

OICE

15¢

NEW YORK SCENES

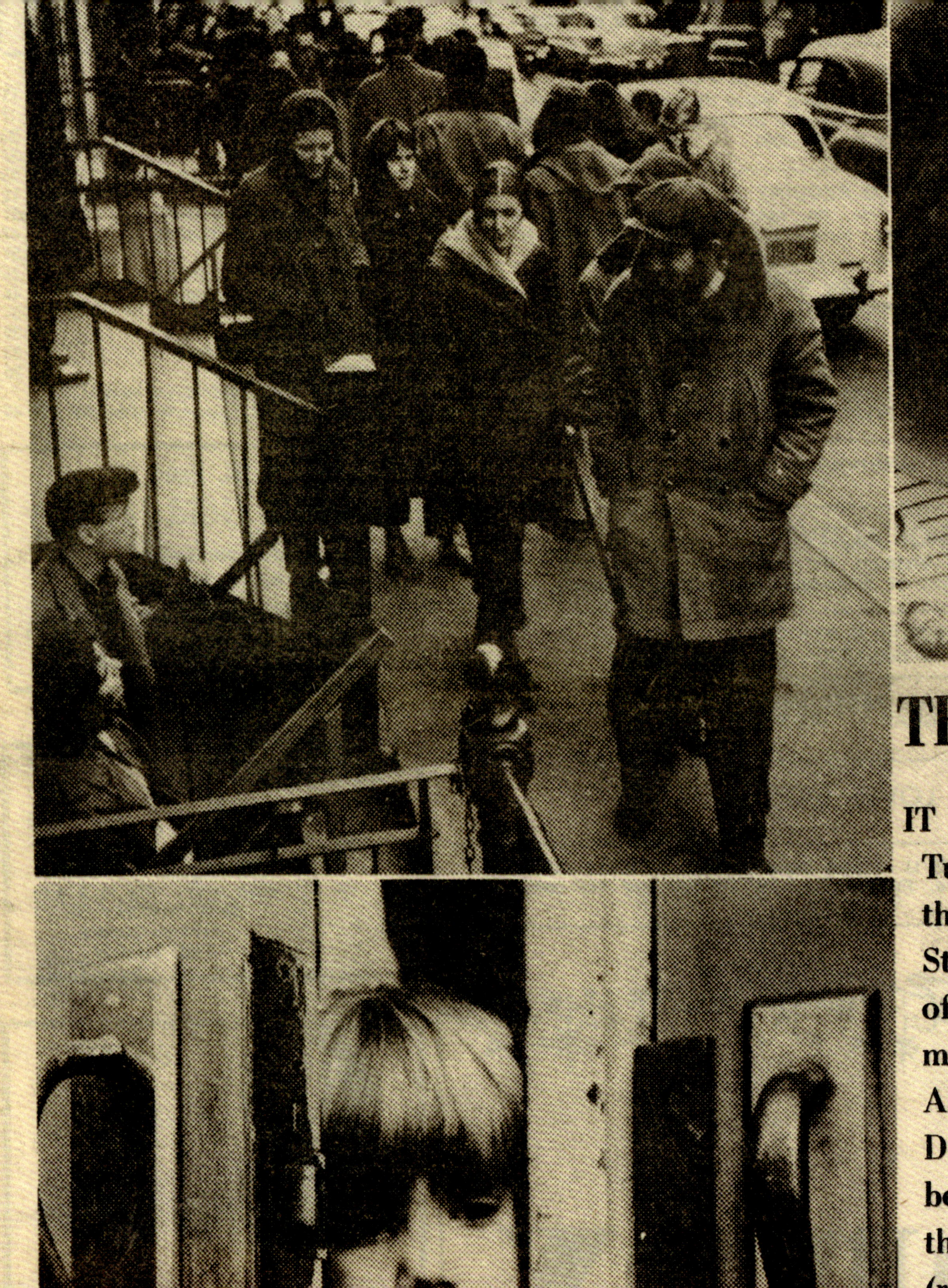

THI

IT BI
Tuli
the (
Stree
of tl
mili
Abbi
D ell
betw
there
(ri

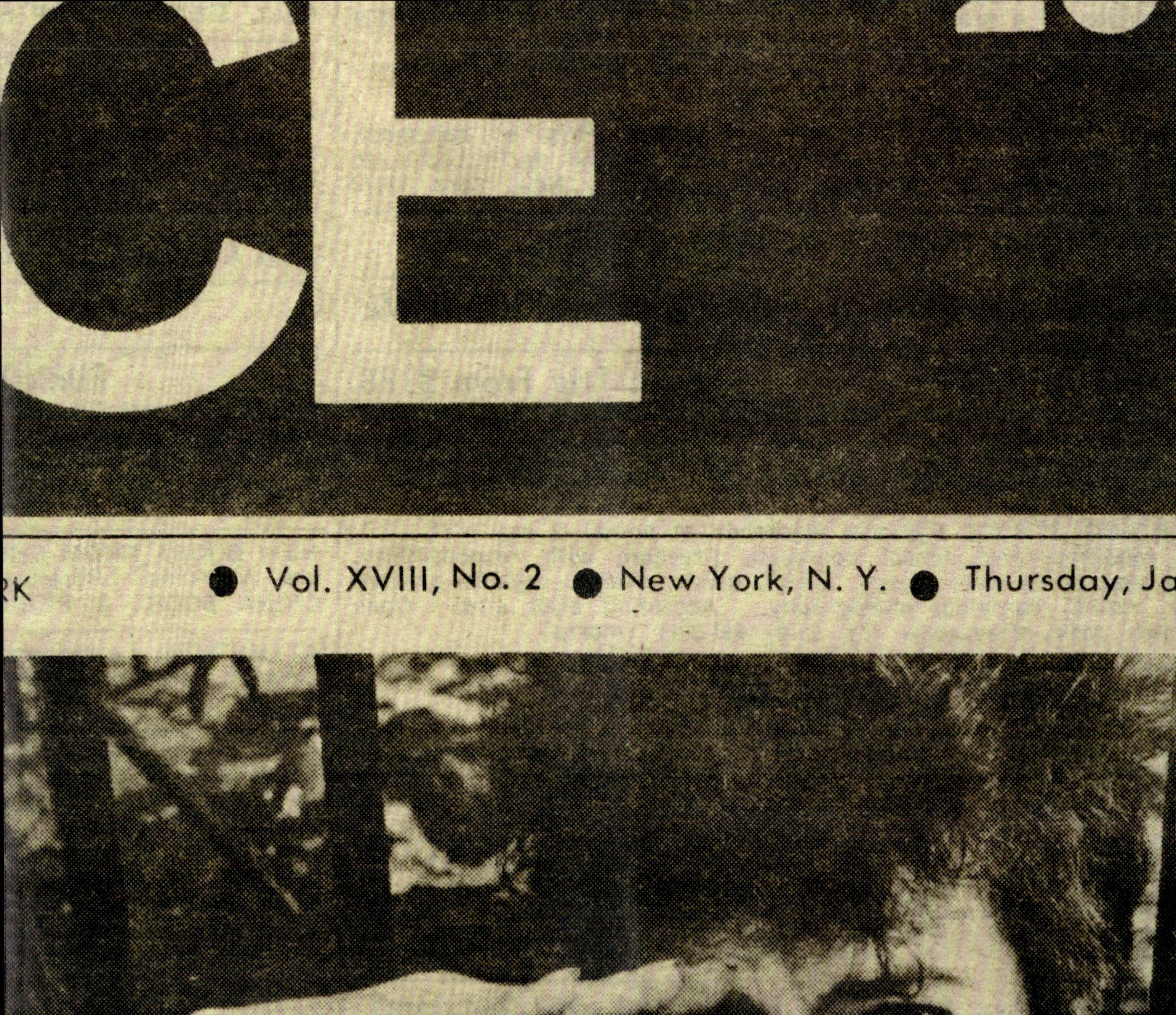

CE
RK
Vol. XVIII, No. 2 ● New York, N. Y. ● Thursday, Ja

ts:

of
gal
nd
he
in,
id
in
ut
erg
ke
art
y:

as
at
nn
ese
on
by

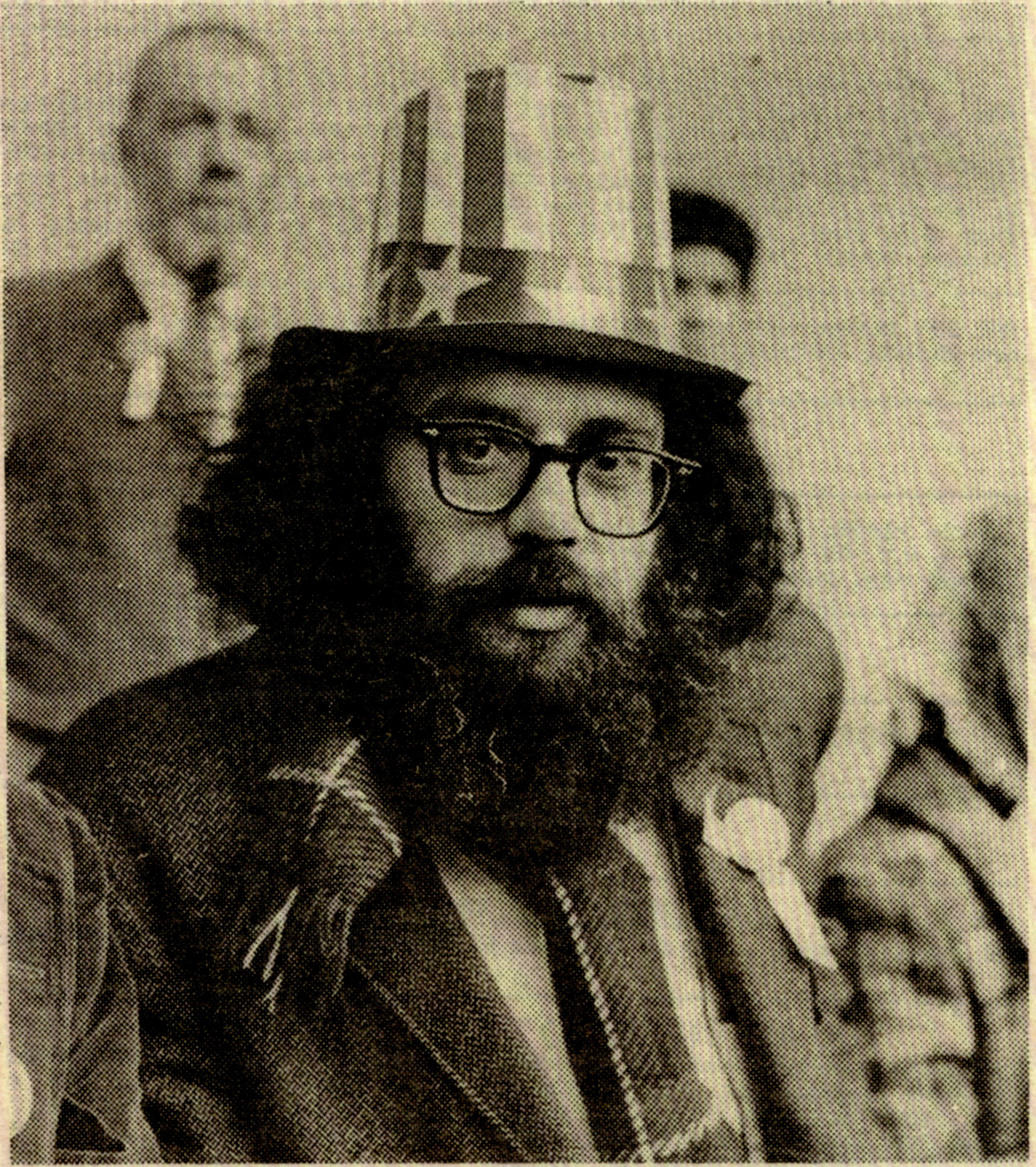

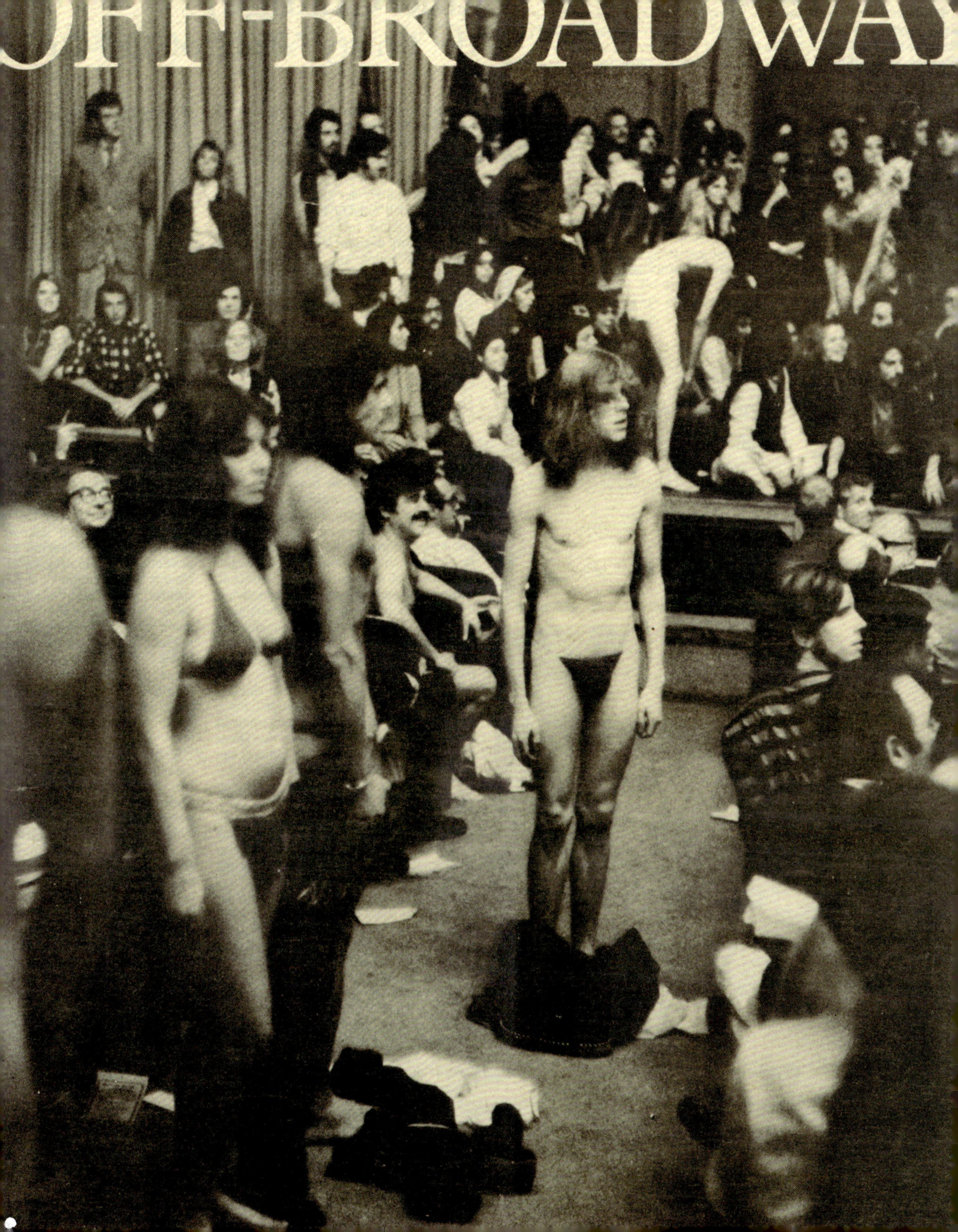

OFF-BROADWAY

FRED W.

NEW YORK

INTRODUCTION BY

ABRAMS, NEW YORK

McDARRAH

SCENES

SEAN WILENTZ

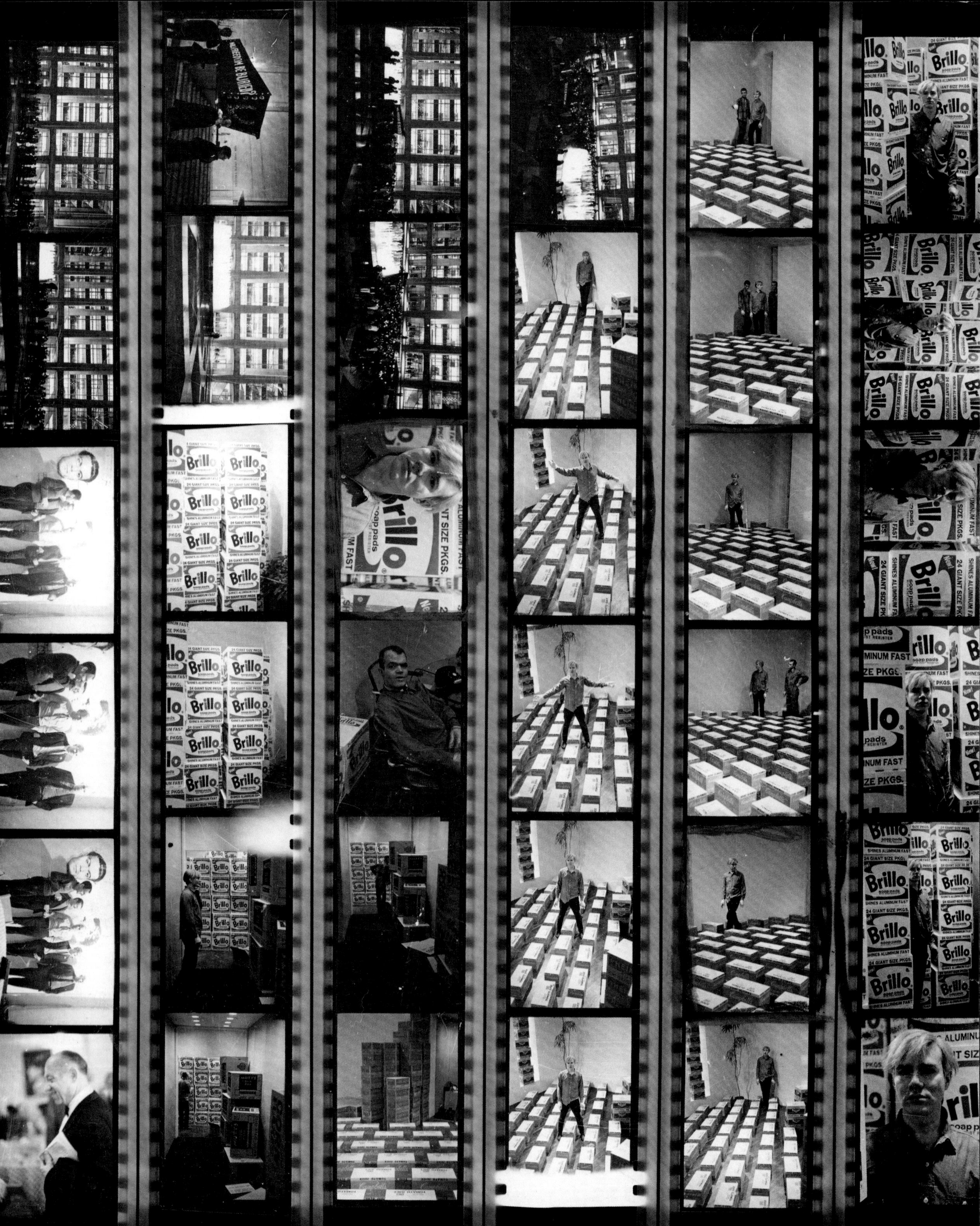

CONTENTS

Contact sheet of Pop artist Andy Warhol, from the night of
the opening of his exhibition, "The Personality of the Artist,"
at the Stable Gallery, 33 East 74th St., April 21, 1964.
Featured were his wooden sculptures of product boxes. The
beginning of the roll of film, left, records an event at Warhol's
Factory earlier that day (see pages 104–106).

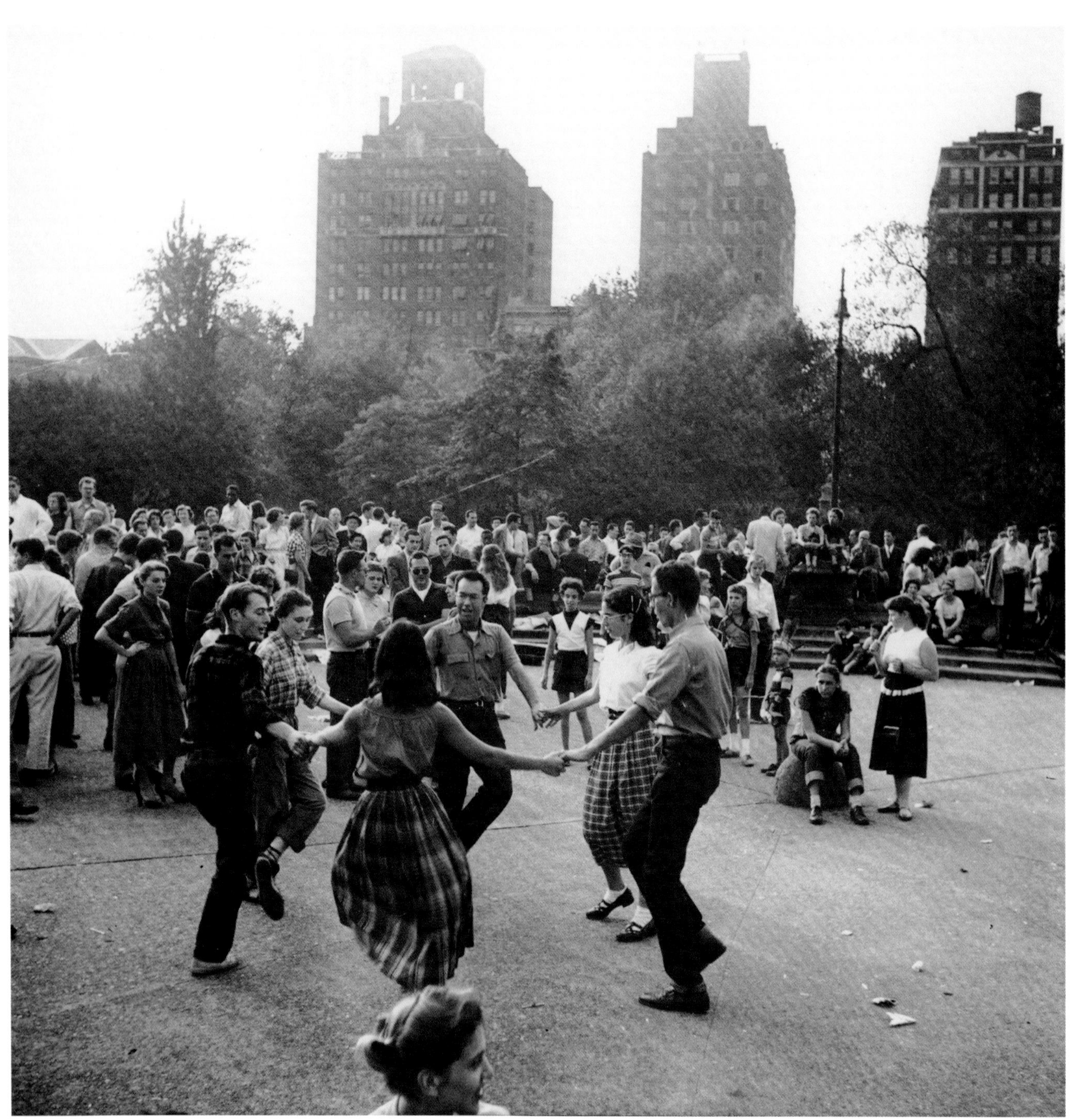

FRED W. McDARRAH'S BOHEMIAN CHRONICLE

BY SEAN WILENTZ

For half a century, Fred W. McDarrah was Greenwich Village's photographer in residence. He moved around a bit, from West Fourteenth Street to Thompson Street to LaGuardia Place, but he never left the neighborhood. His early work is a portfolio of the late fifties and early sixties Village, swirling with Beats, not-so-Beats, first- and second-generation Abstract Expressionists, theater and film avant-gardists, jazz musicians, folk musicians, and flocks of the simply curious. Over the succeeding decades, from his perch at the *Village Voice*, Fred captured what grew out of that place in time. But even though his later assignments sometimes took him far and wide, spiritually, he never traveled too far from home.

Near the beginning, in 1960, Fred collaborated with my father, Elias, on an anthology of poetry and Fred's pictures called *The Beat Scene*. In the book's introduction, Eli quoted from Herman Melville's *Pierre* about New York's "glorious paupers" of more than a century earlier: "They are mostly artists of various sorts; painters, or sculptors, or indigent students, or teachers of languages, or poets, or fugitive French politicians, or German philosophers. Their mental tendencies, however heterodox at times, are still very fine and spiritual upon the whole; since the vacuity of their exchequers leads them to reject the coarse materialism of Hobbes, and incline to the airy exaltations of the Berkelyan philosophy."

Folk dancers in Washington Square Park, Sunday, July 1, 1951.

The continuities between past and present were striking, and just as the bohemian spirit of Melville's time had persisted, so the Village Beat scene would help beget the sixties counterculture, which would beget punk. Until Fred, though, no photographer anywhere had had the imagination (let alone the equipment) to document that spirit and in doing so advance it. Some striking photographic portraits survive of nineteenth-century bohemians—Baudelaire by Étienne Carjat and Nadar, Walt Whitman by Mathew Brady and seemingly any other photographer the poet had time and money enough to visit. There is a picture of Verlaine, heavy-lidded in Le Procope in Paris, slumped behind a water pitcher and a glass of absinthe. From the Greenwich Village bohemia of the 1910s, alongside many, many portraits, there is a posed picture of the crowd inside Polly Holladay's restaurant hangout on MacDougal Street and a famous photograph of free-thinking Louise Bryant stretched out, perfectly nude, on the beach (though in Provincetown). But Fred, with his trusty Nikon, could enter places and do things his predecessors could not, and although he completed an abundance of portraits, he was supremely a photographer of everyday gatherings and readings and happenings, and he compiled the first full visual chronicle ever of bohemian kinetics and camaraderie. The scene was heterodox by the standards of the time, sometimes garishly exhibitionist, but also sometimes tweedily staid. And every once in a while, as in a couple of unposed pictures of Jack Kerouac, Fred's chronicle yielded rare images of energy and pathos.

Was Fred conscious of the historical dimension in his work? An unassuming and unpretentious (though fiercely proud) man, he probably would have shrugged all of that off: At bottom, he was a photojournalist, no more, no less. But there is a hint that he was well aware of the history, in a portrait taken in Allen Ginsberg's kitchen in 1960, with reproductions of Carjat's Baudelaire and a daguerreotype of Edgar Allan Poe taped to the refrigerator behind the poet. Ginsberg, who had had visitations from William Blake and poetized about picking up the "laurel tree cudgel" from Whitman, always dwelled on a historical plane, and he grandly wanted the world to know it. But that picture told about the photographer as well as his subject: McDarrah, too, in his un-grandiose way, was picking up something from photographers past and making of it something new, recording Greenwich Village illuminations of the 1950s and 1960s and the turbulence that followed, capturing bohemia and bohemians as never before.

A couple of Fred's pictures, made before this collection begins, set the scene: one of nighttime Eighth Street at the dawn of the 1950s (overleaf) and the other of folk dancers in Washington Square about eighteen months later (page 14). They are at once deceptive and telling. The bottom-heavy chunkiness of the automobiles, the fonts of the neon signs, the long, pleated skirts and bobby socks—these are of another era entirely from the one we've come to look at.

Yet embedded in those pictures, just out of Fred's range, things were already stirring and had been for a while.

In the nighttime picture, in the building above the Eighth Street Playhouse marquee on the right, Hans Hofmann, the great German-born Abstract Expressionist painter, may have been working in the studio which, along with his famous school, he had relocated there in 1938. (Three years before Hofmann moved in, near the horizon but still on the street, at 46 East Eighth, Jackson Pollack had rented a cheap floor-through apartment, where he would stay until he and Lee Krasner moved to Springs, Long Island, in 1945.) The Cedar Tavern, by now the painters' bar, was tucked away just off Eighth Street around the corner on University Place. At almost dead center, beneath and slightly to the right of a streetlamp's circular glow, at 32 West Eighth Street, the Eighth Street Bookshop, which my father and his brother had started in 1947, appears to be lit and open for business, even though it's New Year's; beneath the shop, there is a parked row of seven, maybe eight of the clunky cars, attracted most likely to the black and white, gay and straight cellar boîte Bon Soir, which had opened right there just three months earlier and was reputedly run by the mob.

As for Sunday in Washington Square, folk singers and dancers had begun congregating at the fountain around 1945, and just around the time Fred took this picture, maybe a little later, one of the younger people in the crowd could have been a teenage Mary Travers hanging out with her friends from the Little Red School House, a decade before she joined Peter, Paul and Mary.

Because of my father, the bookshop, and *The Beat Scene*, I've always associated Fred's early work with the literary side of the Village. Sure enough, near the start, there is a picture of Allen Ginsberg at the famed Artist's Club on Tenth Street, not exactly *howl*ing but hooting in the New Year of 1959. But Fred, a returned GI, had entered bohemia via the painters, and both before and after he accepted the offer of his friends Dan Wolf and Ed Fancher to join the fledgling *Village Voice* in 1954, he made many of his best pictures in studios and at art gallery openings. That same New Year's when Ginsberg hooted, also at the Artist's Club, a group including Franz Kline, the critic Harold Rosenberg, and a young Ted Joans (about to launch his literary career), posed for a memorable, playful shot, sartorially on the cusp, looking a little like hipster G-men (page 37). A couple of years later, Fred took one of his very best portraits in Kline's studio, the pint-size artist offsetting the scale and sweep of his art (page 88). A meticulous worker himself, Fred liked to show artists on the job, whether it be Norman Bluhm wrestling with a canvas (pages 82–83) or Diane Arbus shooting at the Whitney Museum (page 183).

Still, Fred seems to have had a special eye for writers, perhaps because they presented more of a challenge, as there was no obvious visual correlation to be made between the subject and the subject's work. One of the best-known

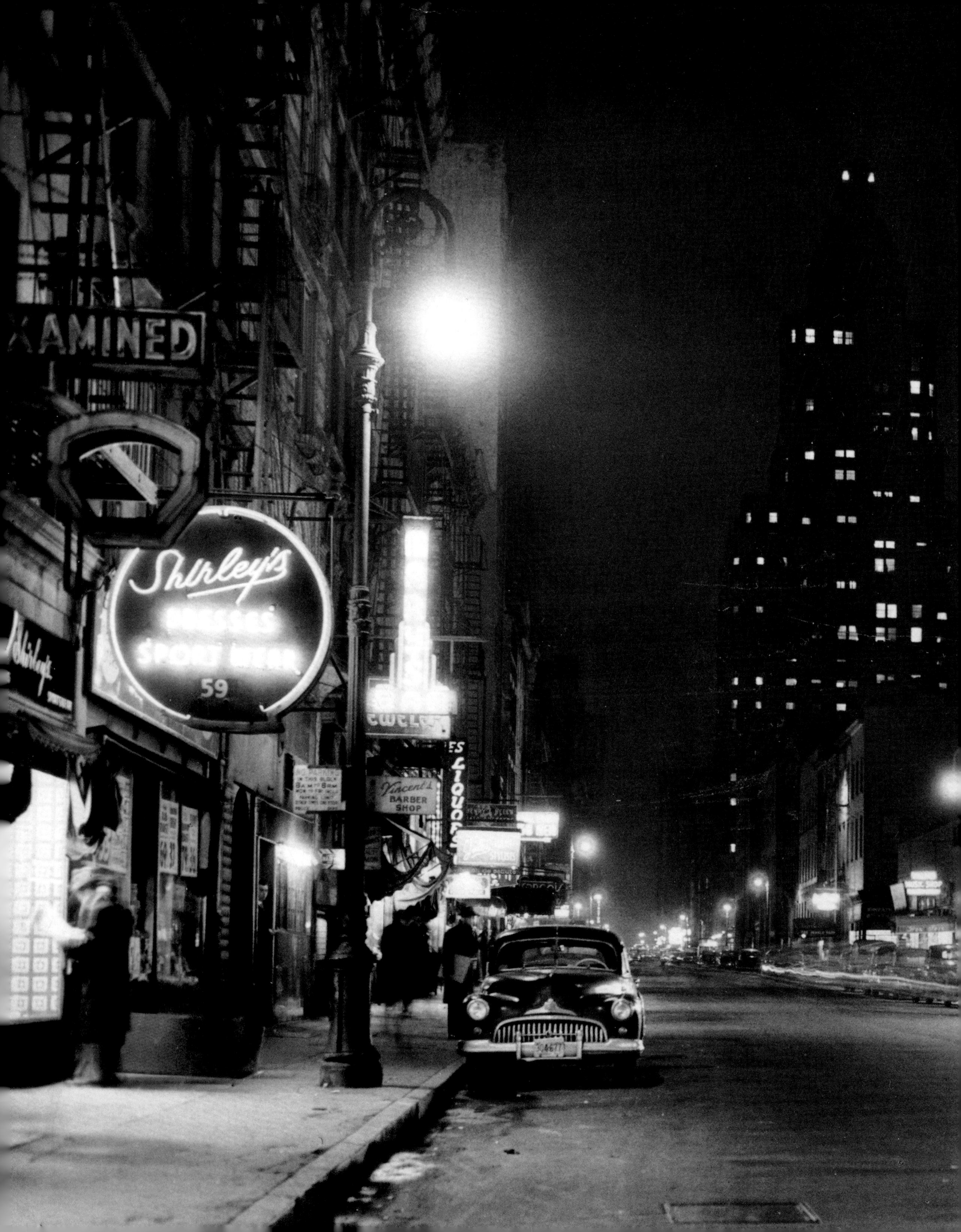
XAMINED
Shirley's
DRESSES
SPORT WEAR
59
Vincent's
BARBER
SHOP
LIQUORS

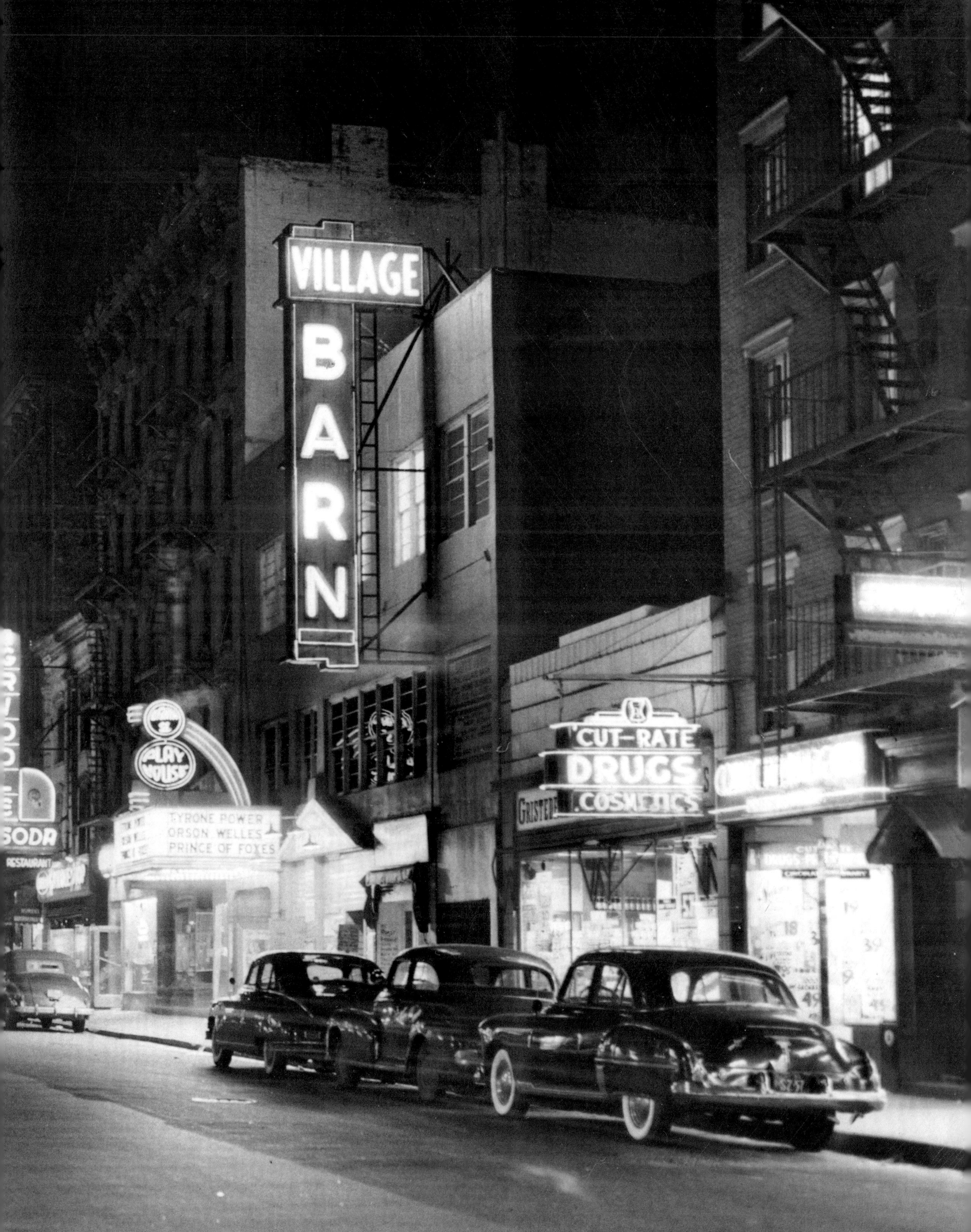

VILLAGE
BARN
PLAY HOUSE
TYRONE POWER
ORSON WELLES
PRINCE OF FOXES
CUT-RATE
DRUGS
COSMETICS
GRISTEDE
SODA
RESTAURANT

of Fred's pictures (it would become the cover of *The Beat Scene*) shows Jack Kerouac reading poetry in a checked lumberjack shirt rolled to the elbows, the gazes of his fellow poets onstage directed somewhere else (save Ted Joans, standing at the picture's left, transfixed by the performance). Kerouac declaims, his palms cupped and fingers curled in an animated instant that, at least in retrospect, looks like a kind of enacted crucifixion (page 41).

Even better is one of the most disturbing photographs I know, also of Kerouac—yet another picture taken at the Artist's Club on that busy New Year's 1959 (page 39)—about which a little background is useful. Although *On the Road* described events that occurred in 1947, it was not published until 1957, when its instant celebrity and notoriety turned Kerouac into a literary star with added bohemian glamour, a crushing fate. When Fred took this picture, Kerouac's fame was soaring: Suddenly it seemed that everybody wanted to hang out with him, drink with him, sleep with him, or else annihilate him. Kerouac was no doubt drunk, but his sweaty expression is that of a boxer in his corner, stunned by a right to the jaw and maybe a flurry of combinations, wondering what's just happened, well on the way to what the fight game knows as Queer Street. But he is not in a corner; he is about to cross a threshold, leaving the party, surrounded by faceless people scrounging in front and from behind through the narrow doorway, body parts not clearly attached to anybody, one disembodied hand grasping Kerouac's shoulder, and aloft in front of him there is a bone-white bisque baby doll's head, its lips puckered, eyes painted to glance off to one side, coquettish, but clutched at the throat— choked?—by one of the hands without an owner. Make of the symbolism what you will; to me, it is a tableau of dazed desolation.

(So, in a different way, is Fred's haunting picture [opposite], taken just a few weeks later, of Delmore Schwartz holding forth at his customary table at the White Horse Tavern to a woman who stares blankly, not at him, hand to her mouth. Schwartz was about to become the youngest poet ever honored with the Bollingen Prize, but he was also fraying, beginning the descent into alcoholism and mental illness that would kill him six years later.)

But then, about twenty pictures on and a few months later, here is Kerouac again, smiling and relaxed in soon-to-be-wed Fred McDarrah and Gloria Schoffel's apartment, co-composing a poem on the tongue, Gloria clacking it down on the typewriter, Fred snapping (page 57). It is Jack the charmer, at ease, just off the road from San Francisco, safe and seemingly centered, if only momentarily. Paired with the pictures taken in Ginsberg's apartment, this shows the unfrenzied, contemplative, even domestic side of bohemian life, not quite the stuff of either caricature or legend.

Apart from their various subjects and moods, I was struck, in looking again at these early photographs of Fred's, at how crossed-over the arts were even

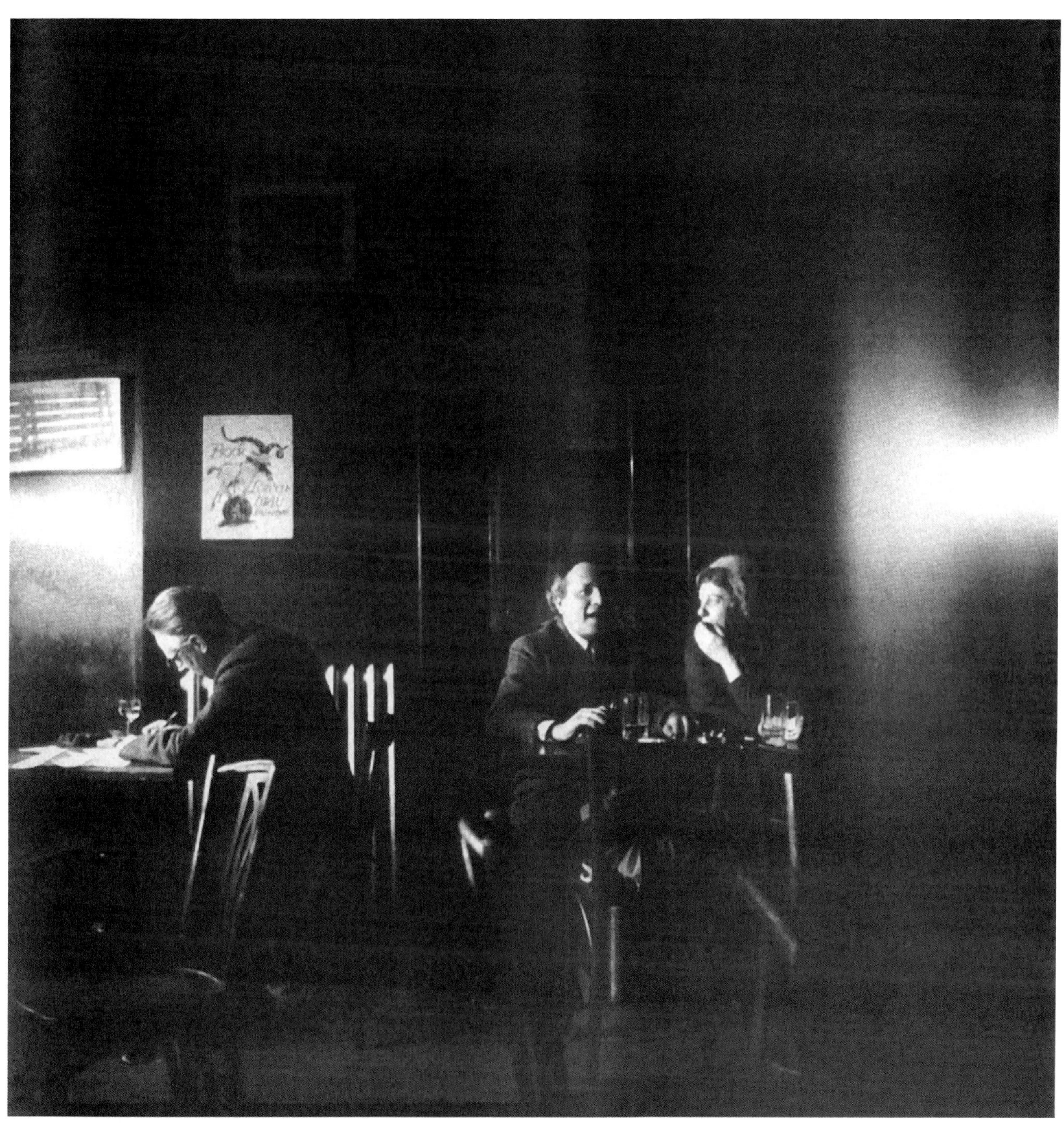

Delmore Schwartz (center) holding court in the back room of the White Horse Tavern, 567 Hudson St., February 22, 1959. The poet and short-story writer never lived up to his early promise—in his youth, he was heralded as the successor of Ezra Pound and T. S. Eliot. He was a spellbinding talker; in the fifties, his conversation pit was the White Horse Tavern, a gathering place for artists and writers, including Dylan Thomas.

sixty years ago. Painting, poetry, theater, filmmaking, and more all washed up against one another, breaching the barriers between them much as the first "happenings" dissolved the distance between actors and audience. The connections were personal as well as artistic. The painter Alice Neel, for example, a friend and frequent subject for McDarrah over the years (pages 80 and 227), would play a role in *Pull My Daisy*, the quintessential Beat film featuring the poets Ginsberg, Gregory Corso, and Peter Orlovsky, another painter (Larry Rivers), a composer (David Amram), and more, based on a script by Kerouac (who narrates) and directed by the photographer Robert Frank and the filmmaker Alfred Leslie, all of whom also populate McDarrah's photographs. (Leslie's loft just outside the Village would be the setting for one of Fred's pictures, pages 66–67.) One could draw many circuits like that among Fred's subjects, including the musicians whose genres actually blended if you thought about them hard enough. I am reminded of a story that Bob Dylan tells in *Chronicles: Volume One*, about how, when he was starting out performing at Gerde's and the Gaslight, he spotted Thelonious Monk off-hours in a Village jazz club and introduced himself, explaining that he was playing folk music up the street. To which Monk replied, as Dylan tells it, "We all play folk music."

There were politics, too, in the Village, although the poets' and painters' relations to them (the left-wing Ginsberg and a few others aside) were at best oblique. There were protesters like Dave McReynolds of the War Resisters League—my father and uncle would allow him to set up his soapbox beside the bookshop and address little crowds about the doomsday nuclearized war machine. There was enormous support in the Village for the civil rights movement; whole busloads of Villagers journeyed to the Lincoln Memorial for the March on Washington, to hear Martin Luther King Jr. but also the day's folk-singer reinforcements, including, from the Village, Dylan, Joan Baez, and Peter, Paul and Mary (page 101).

The Village politics I remember best, though, because of my father's involvement in them, were the largely successful local efforts to halt the disastrous social and architectural vandalism that masqueraded as "slum clearance" and "urban renewal"—above all the plan to build an auto expressway along Broome Street, which would have obliterated what later became known as SoHo. The devil in each of those dramas was Robert Moses, every inch the arrogant manipulator described brilliantly by Robert Caro in *The Power Broker*; the saint was Jane Jacobs, who not only theorized about the soul of neighborhoods like the Village but also fought like hell to protect them, depicted here happily demonstrating against some looming desecration (page 99). Ed Koch was another shining light, the insurgent reform hero of the Village Independent Democrats who, in 1963, upset the odds and thwarted a comeback attempt by the last of the old Tammany Hall bosses, Carmine DeSapio. At more or less that moment, Koch posed for Fred, vigilant and triumphant, amid the clutter of the VID office (page 99).

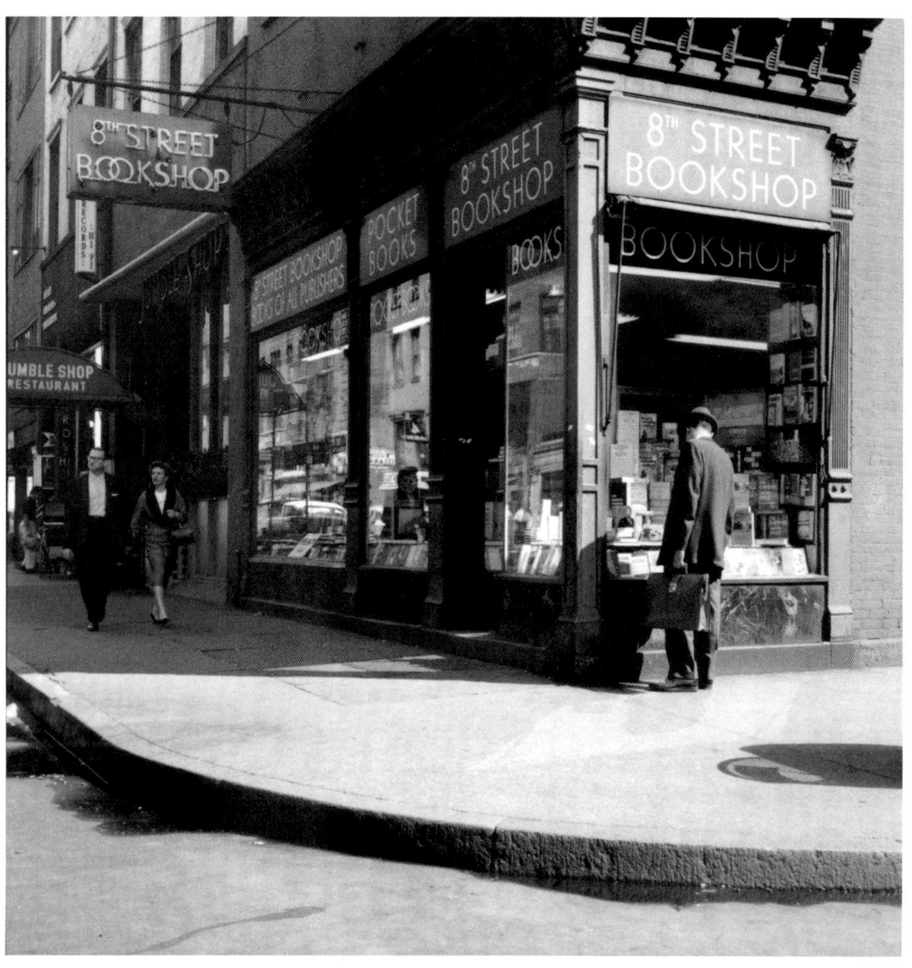

The Eighth Street Bookshop, 32 West Eighth St., May 16, 1959. The bookstore, on the corner of West Eighth St. and MacDougal St., was a gathering place of poets, artists, novelists, and other intellectuals, and it spawned Corinth Books, an adventurous publishing company; both enterprises often helped out struggling writers. Late in 1963, Bob Dylan met Allen Ginsberg in co-owner Ted Wilentz's third-floor apartment, where Ginsberg and Peter Orlovsky, recently returned from overseas, were living temporarily. The corner is now home to a chain coffee store.

I lived through all of this as a child and early teenager almost exclusively from the vantage point of the bookshop (above). My Brooklyn-born mother refused to leave her native borough (or so we children were told), so my parents got about as close to the Village as they could by purchasing a semi-ruined, wood-frame house on Brooklyn Heights, which they put back together again. Hence, my two siblings and I did not have proper Village childhoods; our cousin Kathy, who lived with her mother and father above the shop, was by far the sophisticate of the younger generation. Still, I spent a lot of time on weekends noodling around the bookshop, complaining about the lack of history books for younger readers, but also absorbing the hum of what was by now a literary crossroads. I have, on a shelf in my study in Princeton, double-framed, a remnant from those times, a postcard that Jack Kerouac sent in 1964 from Brittany to "Avrum Ginsberg and Élias Wilentz," care of the shop, likening its picture of the Breton coast to Big Sur, and pledging caritas. It came postage due—which all the more evokes the sense of literary insiderdom that I picked up on very early. The problem was that I thought it all was normal, creating expectations and presumed entitlements I've had to spend a good deal of my life overcoming.

Something happened, though, to crack open what I remember as a kind of idyll, something that split the 1960s in two and that shows up starkly in Fred's photographs. People who were alive then recognize the changes in tone, priorities, politics, and art, as the hopeful, even earnest early sixties lurched into a late sixties that sometimes felt like living on the edge of apocalypse. I can date precisely when the crack came—it was February 21, 1965—although that timing is of course deeply personal, bound up with the Village, the Eighth Street Bookshop, and, as it happens, Fred McDarrah.

My father and uncle did well for themselves and by the beginning of 1965 they were in a position to get out from under their landlord and move the shop to a building of their own, across the street to the north side of Eighth and a little to the east, at number 17. The move came in mid-February and Fred photographed the old shop just before we schlepped an entire store's worth of stock from one place to the other. (As I was about to turn fourteen, eligible for working papers, Pop put me to work hauling as much as I could lift.) Coincidentally, the date selected for the grand party to celebrate the new shop's opening was the day after my birthday, February 21, a Sunday.

It was a pretty lavish affair for a Village bookshop launch, with (as I remember) a huge wheel of cheese, plenty of champagne and other fine wine, and, as entertainment, a way, way avant-garde free jazz trio led by the alto and tenor saxophonist Giuseppi Logan. I can't recall if Ed Koch was there, but the Village's charismatic congressman, John V. Lindsay, sure was, about to mount his first run for the New York City mayoralty. The place was stuffed with novelists, playwrights, poets, book clerks who were also poets, publishing company muck-a-mucks, NYU professors, and the most loyal of the shop's loyal customers. The *New York Times* covered the event, and the next day, a picture ran in the paper; if you look hard enough, you can see me drinking (or at least carrying) my first-ever glass of champagne. Fred McDarrah was there too, a close friend of the shop but also on assignment for the *Voice*. One of his pictures from that day is here, of the calm before the storm, my dad and uncle chatting with what look like some of the muck-a-mucks (page 117).

Suddenly, around the time Lindsay showed up, word began circulating that Malcolm X had been murdered in Harlem. (There was no social media then, and nobody had been listening to the radio amid the party.) It was (for a literary event at the time) a racially integrated crowd, and a tense confusion hit the room, not enough to halt the festivities but discomfiting all the same. What I remember most distinctly is LeRoi Jones grimly and swiftly departing the scene, presumably headed uptown. Jones was a longtime Eighth Street friend and regular, but nobody saw him in the shop after that for a very long time, and by the time he showed up, his name was Amiri Baraka. Things had utterly changed.

The changes were everywhere, not just in racial politics, and Fred recorded
them as no other press photographer did. The present collection might even be
read as a before and after tale. Look, for example, at the photograph of LeRoi
Jones with Diane di Prima at the Cedar in 1960 (page 67)—Beat poets, inti-
mates, tenderly young (both twenty-five), soon to launch their little magazine,
The Floating Bear. Then look at the photograph taken seven years later of
the black arts cultural nationalist Baraka, chained and bloodied outside the
station house where he had been beaten amid the Newark riots (page 153).
Compare the photograph of Ted Joans's Le Sang des Poetes birthday party in
1959, or for that matter the one of Alfred Leslie's loft party a year later, with
any of those taken of the gatherings at Andy Warhol's Factory or at Warhol's
Exploding Plastic Inevitable shows: Bohemia turned into pop spectacle (pages
122–123 and 129). Gentle Tuli Kupferberg grinning outside the Gaslight in
1959 looks like an immigrant not long off the boat—in fact, for a moment,
MacDougal Street appears to be transformed into the Orchard Street of fifty
years earlier—but by mid-1966, crowds crammed along the same MacDougal
Street going to hear Tuli and Ed Sanders and the rest of the Fugs (pages 42
and 133).

One aspect of the later sixties in which Fred had a direct hand was the rise
of a new kind of photographic celebrityhood. Directly across the street from
the new bookshop, for many years, there was a store called Postermat, which
specialized in selling oversize poster portraits of the countercultural heroes
(mostly) and heroines of the day, perfect for papering over dull dorm-room
walls. The posters became, for a swelling generation of college students, an
affordable statement of allegiance and an accessible talisman of hipness.
(The other talismans were buttons, buttons with all kinds of slogans, political
and whimsical and often dopily sexual.) The taped-up pictures of Poe and
Baudelaire on Allen Ginsberg's refrigerator had morphed into an entire subcul-
ture of decoration and display. I remember one poster in my dorm at Columbia
of a smiling Ho Chi Minh, to which someone had slyly affixed a slogan of the
time, advertising a popular brand of rye bread: "You Don't Have to Be Jewish
to Love Levy's!"—or maybe somebody just joked about it.

Postermat sold enough of those posters to stay in business for a pretty long run.
The most popular of them included one of Allen Ginsberg at a peace rally in a
cardboard Uncle Sam hat, putting his "queer shoulder to the wheel," as he had
written ten years earlier in his poem "America," and a second of Bob Dylan in
Sheridan Square, either mock saluting or shielding his eyes from the sun (and
sorely in need of a ChapStick). Both were McDarrah pictures (pages 127 and
115), which made sense given Fred's centrality. I only hope he got a decent cut
of the royalties.

More than anything, the Vietnam War and the protests against it changed everything in the mid-sixties by politicizing the already politicized Village more than at any time in recent memory. The protests started at more or less the same moment as I remember time cracking open inside the bookshop. On February 13, 1965, President Johnson ordered the commencement of what became Operation Rolling Thunder, the bombing campaign against communist North Vietnam that would continue until 1968. On March 8, the first American combat troops, 3,500 marines, landed at China Beach near Da Nang. The very next day, Villagers were out in force to demonstrate against it all, among them the brilliant short-story writer Grace Paley, who would also become one of the most energetic and eloquent of antiwar activists (page 118). A week later, an even larger demonstration at Washington Square featured the soon-to-be-famous Bread and Puppet Theater of the Lower East Side, their outsize figures and masked musicians blending religious imagery with a kind of Brechtian satire (page 119). Of course, on both occasions, Fred was there—as he was when the demonstrations grew and spread around the country to become the largest American antiwar protest movement since at least World War I, and possibly in the nation's history.

(As a side note, I can't help remarking on Fred's photograph of beautiful Grace Paley in her tam-o'-shanter. Of all of the writers and artists I was privileged to meet as a kid—and this is the first time I've admitted it—Grace was the one I came closest to loving palpably, long before I came to love her work. I could not have been alone, for she seemed to me to embody the beloved community that the Village could be at its finest, so deeply respectful and attentive and warm to her friends, who included her friends' children—the young as well as the old.)

The war and the movement against it punctuated Fred's work for years to come, at times showing how deeply the New York literary world—what might be called greater Greenwich Village—shaped and was shaped by the conflict. The March on the Pentagon in October 1967 was the subject of the finest piece of prose to come out of the protests, Norman Mailer's *The Armies of the Night*— and on the back of the book's dust jacket appeared one of Fred's photographs of Mailer and his literary compatriots (allies at least for that day) setting off on the procession across the Potomac, among them Robert Lowell and Dwight Macdonald (overleaf, left). Mailer and Macdonald turn up again in a picture Fred took less than a year later in Macdonald's apartment, sitting alongside George Plimpton and other literati and listening intently to the radical leaders of Columbia's Students for a Democratic Society (SDS) explain their protests that had shut down the university (overleaf, right). In 1962, Susan Sontag posed for Fred at a Bleecker Street symposium on sex, an intimidating intellectual femme fatale; five years later he photographed her, composed and smiling slightly, as a cop led her by the arm to be booked after an anti-draft protest at the Whitehall Street induction center (pages 93 and 157).

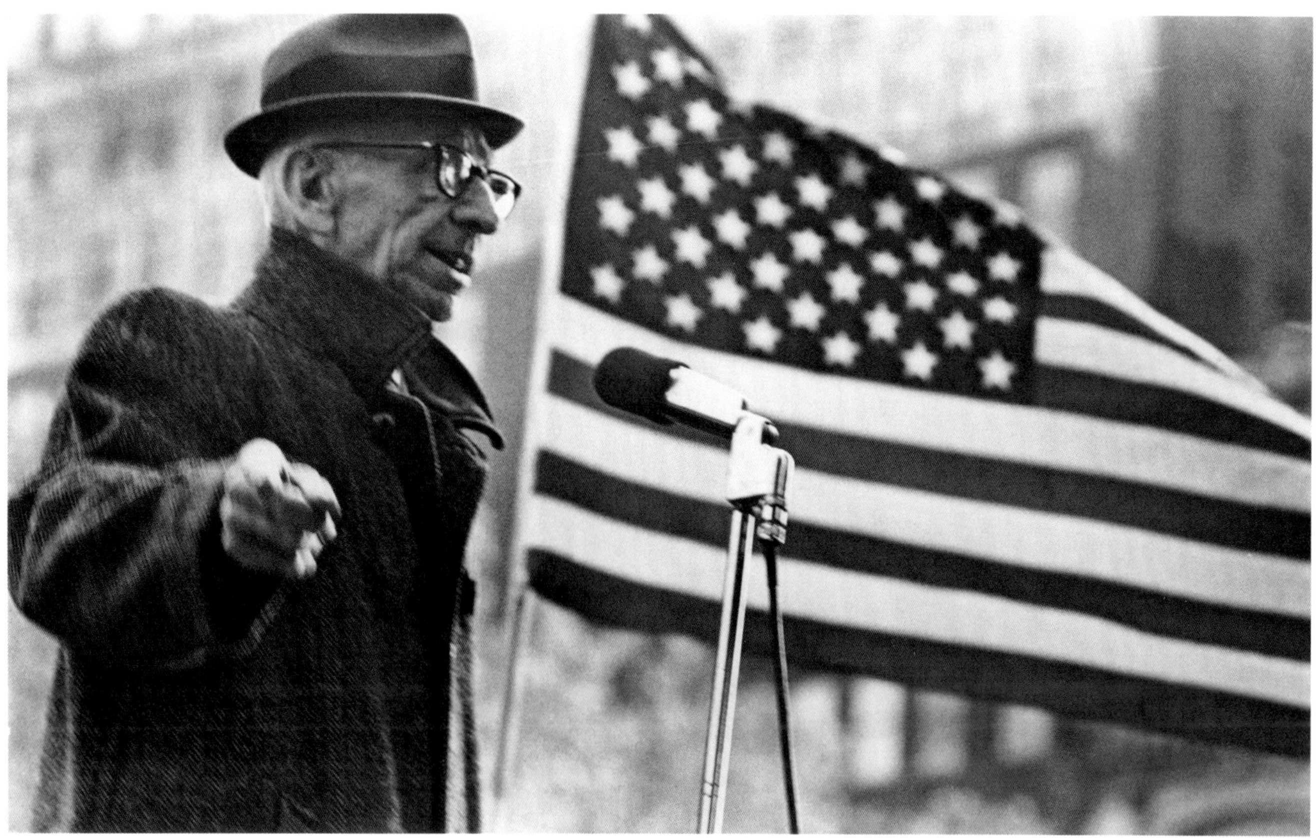

Fred also photographed the venerable pacifist A. J. Muste addressing a New York rally, a human bridge connecting the radicalism of the 1910s and 1920s with the anti–Vietnam War protests (above). At a later demonstration, Fred photographed Martin Luther King Jr. trying to build a different kind of bridge between the civil-rights and antiwar movements, despite harsh resistance. Fred's pictures of the demonstrations at the Democratic National Convention in Chicago in August 1968 have become iconic, above all the beautifully composed and darkroom-edited shot of a pyramid of protesters in Grant Park, the day before the police riot that blew the lid off the convention—and that in the end, ironically, probably contributed to the election of Richard M. Nixon to the presidency that fall (pages 172–173).

My favorite of Fred's Vietnam protest pictures is one he took a little earlier, at a draft-card burning outside the federal building in Foley Square (page 168). Like the picture in Grant Park, this one forms a pyramid, here of people reaching upward. And as I see it, the picture is a striking counterpoint to the one that Fred took ten years earlier of the dazed Jack Kerouac at the Artist's Club. Once again, there is a confusing thrust of disembodied hands and arms, obscuring almost all of the faces—but instead of a baby doll held aloft, there is a trio of draft cards, two of them aflame. Both pictures convey the same discomfort of being crowded, jostled, pushed and shoved—but the second one, with some of

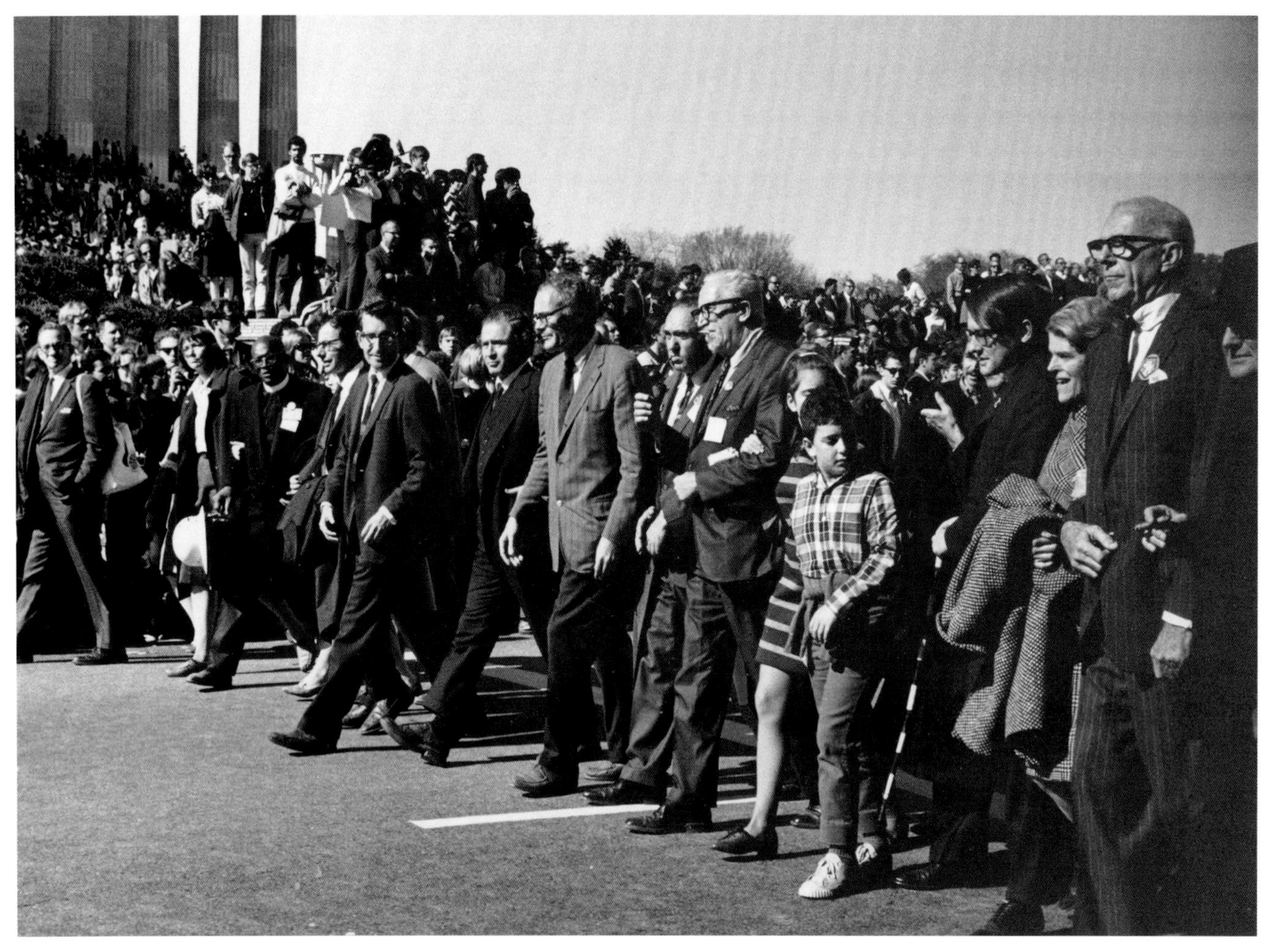

Demonstrators passing the Lincoln Memorial during the March on the Pentagon in Washington, D.C., October 21, 1967. Among the activists on the front line at the largest rally against the Vietnam War up to that time are, from right, Dr. Benjamin Spock (with lapel badge), author of the bestselling *Baby and Child Care* (1946), and his wife, Jane; literary and social critic Dwight Macdonald; union organizer and antinuclear author Sidney Lens; poet Robert Lowell; Norman Mailer (whose "nonfiction novel" *The Armies of the Night*, about the march, bagged the Pulitzer Prize and the National Book Award the following year); theoretical linguist Noam Chomsky; and scholar and social critic Marcus Raskin.

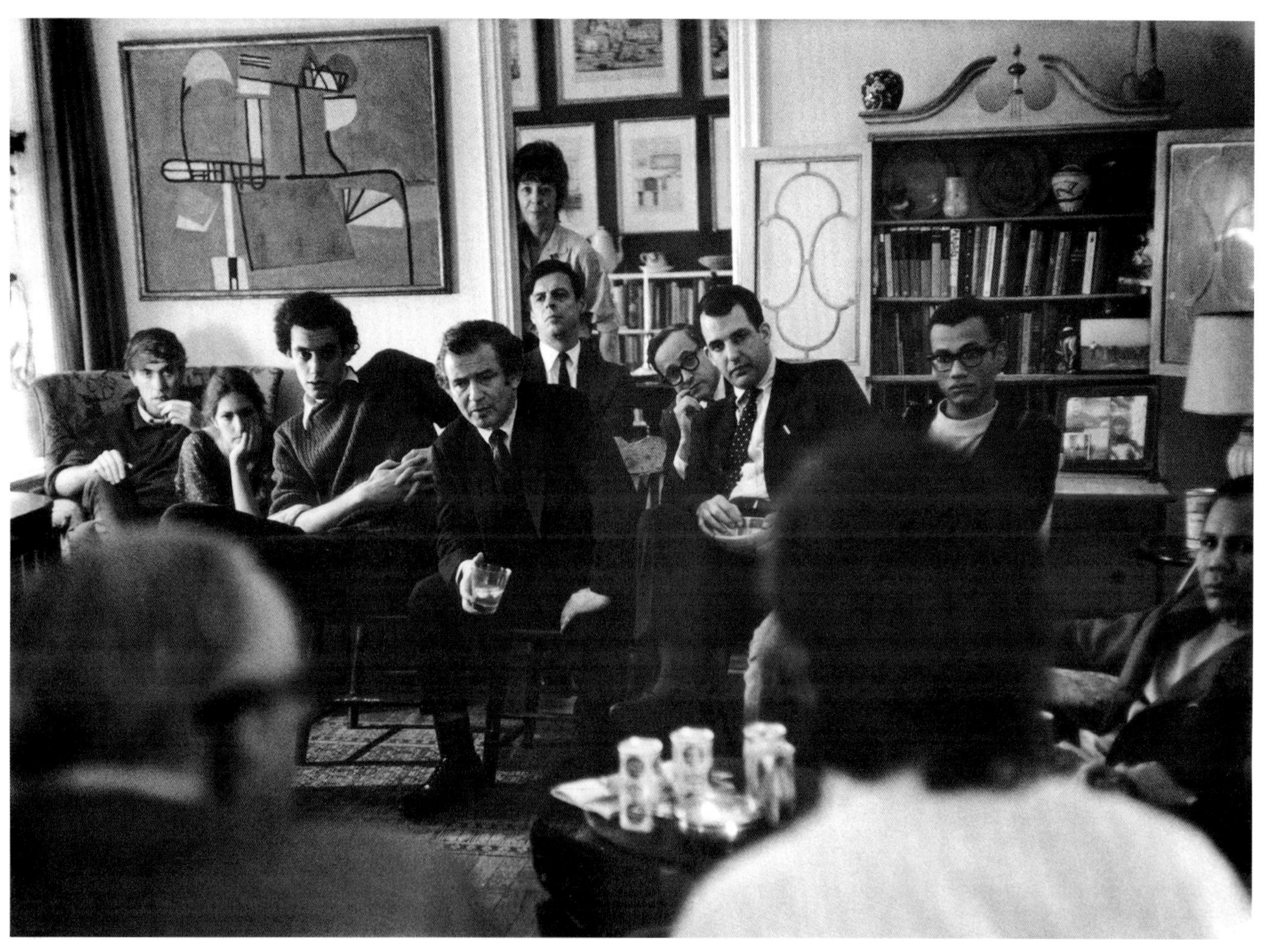

The New York literary establishment meets with the Students for a Democratic Society (SDS) at the apartment of critic and political activist Dwight Macdonald, May 24, 1968. Macdonald is seated at the lower left (back to camera). Also at the meeting are Columbia University SDS leader Mark Rudd (rear, far left), Norman Mailer (center, with drink in hand), George Plimpton (directly behind Mailer), and author and former light heavyweight boxing champion José Torres (far right). The meeting was held in the aftermath of student protests at Columbia University in April and May that ended in police actions.

the fingers shaped into the V sign for peace, shows a protest, not a party. And whereas Kerouac's bewildered drunken visage is the human focal point in the first picture, in the second, that point rests at the bottom of the image in the half-hidden face of the short woman beneath the pyramid. Staring up at the burning draft cards with a brow furrowed in agitation, she emanates what might be fearful concern or purposeful determination or both, a combination well aligned with those times. And although it is cut off in the picture, that face is as instantly recognizable to students and veterans of the period as Jack Kerouac's is in the earlier photograph: It is Grace Paley's face.

The antiwar protests and the emerging counterculture fed off each other, both charged by an unresolved alienation from and adoration of America itself that continues half a century later. The Beat Village had always shared a bond with San Francisco, including a bond between the Eighth Street Bookshop and Lawrence Ferlinghetti's City Lights bookstore in North Beach. So it did not take long for the Bay Area hippie explosion of 1966–67 to arc into the Village, and for St. Marks Place to become an approximation of Haight-Ashbury.

With Ginsberg acting as a kind of go-between and impresario, the East Village, especially, became an epicenter for consciousness expansion of every kind, chemical and purely mystical. In time, Bill Graham bought the old Village Theater on Second Avenue and turned it into the Fillmore East, where the rock music and psychedelia pioneered in San Francisco flourished (page 166). On another hook entirely, Andy Warhol had already been staging his multimedia Exploding Plastic Inevitable shows at the Polish National Home (Polski Dom Narodowy, or the Dom for short) on St. Marks, with the Velvet Underground as the house band (pages 126 and 128–129). Flower power and decadence mingled—but in New York as in San Francisco, the mixture could be destructive, especially when the nastier drugs, chiefly speed and heroin, took hold.

In late March 1967, ten thousand New York hippies and fellow travelers turned up at the Sheep Meadow in Central Park for their own version of a Human Be-In, as staged two months earlier in Golden Gate Park. The crowd was tiny compared to the San Francisco gathering, but the New York parks department and police were cooperative—John Lindsay was now the mayor—and the event continued on into the evening without trouble, despite all of the pot. Fred took a sheaf of photographs that day of the painted and glittered bodies of clowns and troubadours and ersatz gauchos, flowers in people's hair (page 145). I was there too, but not even as a fellow traveler, just a spectator, really, with a group of my Brooklyn friends, wanting to see what the fuss was all about. Though never much of a drug-taker—my vices would run to the more traditional and perfectly legal—I loved the music and I eventually got to know my way around the Fillmore pretty well. But that day, I was startled to see my sophisticated cousin Kathy in the middle of a circle, obviously high, performing some kind of dervish-y dance. Our fathers had grown deeply estranged, and she and I had not kept in touch, and I was now too embarrassed (for her? for me?) to say hi; but she looked so wild and free. She had just turned sixteen, younger by one day than I. I never saw her again, and a few years later she died, a casualty of the counterculture. So thinking about that whole part of the sixties still makes me ache and still makes me mad.

As does one of the strongest pictures of Fred's career, taken six weeks or so after the Be-In. The fracturing that I've dated to early 1965 was in fact set in motion with the assassination of President Kennedy in 1963—still the most shattering event in the nation's political and cultural history since the end of World War II. At Kennedy's death, his brother Robert instantly became a repository for liberal dreams, and he somewhat stiffly stepped up and won a Senate seat from New York. (Fred caught up with him during that 1964 campaign, Kennedy speaking from a flatbed truck near the corner of Eighth Street and Sixth Avenue, his stiffness reflected in that of the two men beside him, a local state assemblyman and district leader Ed Koch; page 108.)

But after the fracture, once he had turned against the Vietnam War and spoke up for the blacks and the browns and the poor of all colors without losing his Irish toughness and his Catholic appeal, Kennedy became something far greater, what some of us began to think of then (and may well do until our dying day) as the last true tribune for justice in America who could unite the country and lift it out of the hole it was in. And one day in a Stanton Street tenement in 1967, while the senator was campaigning for nothing, Fred, hidden from view, took a picture of *this* Robert Kennedy that would never be surpassed (pages 148–149). Kennedy's face is a mask of agony and empathy for whomever he and his companions are talking with, set off by the homely portrait of Christ suffering on the cross, askew on the wall just above his head. Inside of Fred's work, there is the faintest echo here of the Kerouac Christ picture from 1959, but just the faintest. Move any object in it, or add one more touch of symbolism, and the picture would be ruined. Given what we all know happened a year later, and all that proceeded from what happened, it is devastating.

Thereafter, madness, idealism, creativity, and decay chased each other around: The apocalypse did not come, but the old spheres were no longer reliable. Out of the civil rights movement came the igniting of second-wave feminism, its champions ranging from Betty Friedan to Germaine Greer. Inspired by both of these movements and also by the hardening militancy of antiwar protests—but mostly just fed up with being shaken down, beaten up, and otherwise bullied by the police—the customers of the Stonewall Inn on Christopher Street fought back one summer's night in 1969, which became the impetus for forming the Gay Liberation Front (page 184). The antiwar militancy, meanwhile, became lethal with the emergence of the self-proclaimed terrorist Weatherman faction of SDS, one cell of which turned a West Eleventh Street townhouse into a bomb factory, which they accidentally blew up, themselves along with it (page 191), although two of them survived. Rock became more performative and self-consciously decadent, preparing the way for the punk uprising to come (page 207). Nixon—his awkwardness captured by Fred at a Madison Square Garden rally just prior to the 1968 election (page 177)—finally self-destructed in the Watergate scandal, and the Vietnam War was finally abandoned, but nothing was redeemed.

The Village I knew was completely destroyed late one night in March 1976, when someone—we thought we knew who, but couldn't prove anything—threw a blazing trash barrel through the front display window of the bookshop and started a fire that gutted the place in minutes. (My sister, who was helping to run the shop by then and was living upstairs, escaped in the nick of time.) When the firefighters had finally departed, we were left with row upon row upon row of books turned to cinder, as sickening to look at as to smell (opposite). Fred, on assignment but also as a lover of the shop and an old friend of my father's, recorded the scene; above all, he photographed my father in an upstairs office that was spared, at the worst moment in his life (below). As I remember it, Fred didn't look much better, but we were all in a haze.

The Village rallied 'round. There was an artists' benefit where Ginsberg delivered an extemporaneous poem, "The Burning of the Eighth Street Bookstore," which, to his chagrin, nobody had the good sense to tape-record. And so my father—as much out of pride and defiance for his attackers as anything else—rebuilt the place and reopened for business. But the times, by now, really had changed. The big book chains had started moving into the neighborhood, making commercial prospects murky, and as I had just started teaching at Princeton and my brother and sister also wanted to move on, Eli had less and less to look forward to. In 1979, he closed the place for good. Forty years later, people still bemoan to me its loss.

The Village, of course, remained, but Fred's pictures from the very late 1970s, at least the ones that are here, get darker and in hindsight portentous. Celebrity became everything—celebrity as celebrated uptown in the exclusive, cocaine-fueled confines of Studio 54. Fred's picture of John Belushi partying there is scary in retrospect (though at least, we can be thankful, Jann Wenner survived to tell the tale; page 221). Writers like Mailer and Truman Capote became celebrities, too (page 220). Robert Mapplethorpe was beautiful and Charles Ludlam absurdly funny and ridiculously well-endowed—and nobody had yet heard of AIDS (pages 228 and 215). Perhaps nobody outside of the high-roller loop knew much about the obnoxious real-estate developer Fred Trump, but Fred McDarrah's camera clearly sensed he had something in store and that it was barking mad. It would take his son, still the smug dauphin in 1978, to turn the family name into a cognomen for a kind of racketeering culture of narcissism (pages 224–225). I'm only happy, in a way, that our Fred didn't live to see where it was all headed, because it might well have killed him.

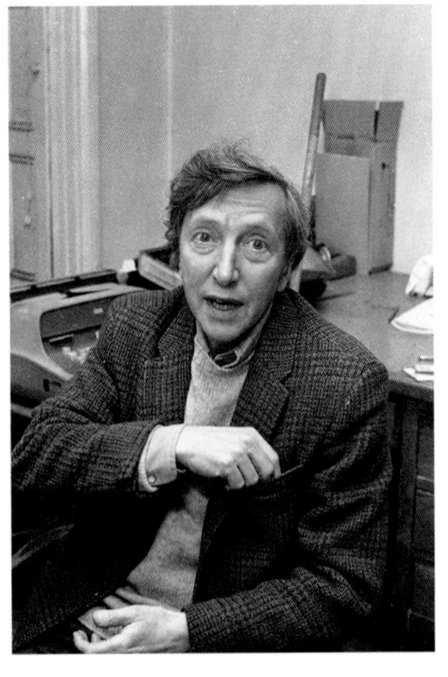

Eli Wilentz in his office in
the Eighth Street Bookshop,
March 10, 1976.

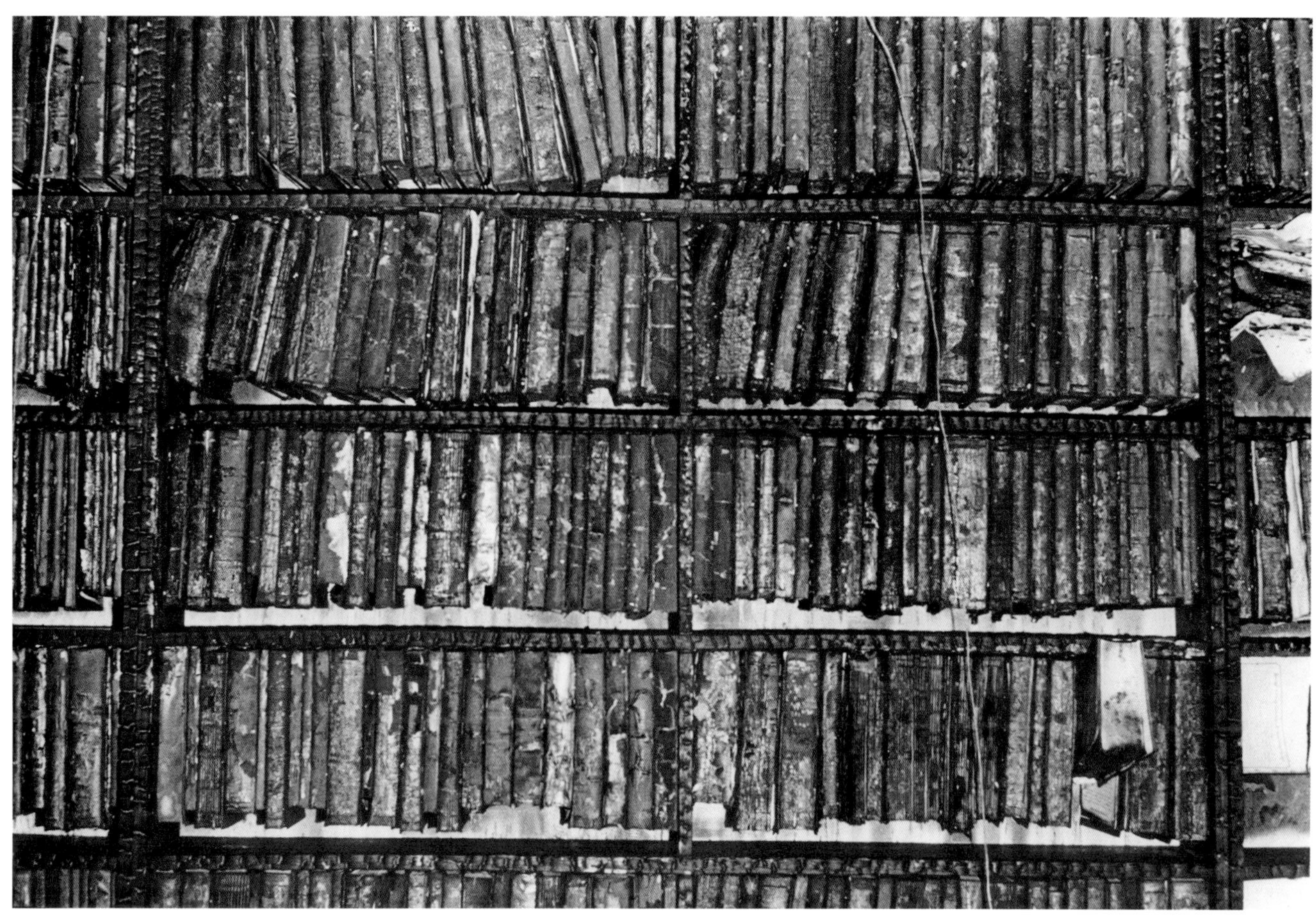

View of books, still shelved, in the aftermath of a fire at the Eighth Street Bookshop, March 10, 1976. After the fire, the city's leading poets, writers, and editors held a fund-raiser and the store reopened, but in 1979, when it became apparent that his children had no interest in continuing with it, owner Eli Wilentz closed it.

Bohemia has been described as a formless but inevitable site within modern society, its borders permeable, built out of youth and poverty with a tinge of criminality, devoted above all to turning life into art. By that reckoning, the death of bohemia—which, in the case of the Beat Generation, was proclaimed as early as 1961, with Fred McDarrah and his camera in the room—would signify the death of capitalist democracy itself, a prospect that under the current circumstances is too frightening to think about for too long. But come what may, Fred left behind an unprecedented body of work from inside that movable site as it existed in mid-century Greenwich Village, when, for a while anyway, it shook the nation and the world. Nobody had ever come close to depicting what Fred did, and any future bohemian chronicle is bound to be shot differently from the way Fred did it. He was in the right place at the right time, and when the chance came for him to make the most of it, he didn't blow it. So as long as there are those who will pay attention, Fred W. McDarrah's spirit, the spirit inside these pictures, will tell its magical stories.

THE
PHOTOGRAPHS

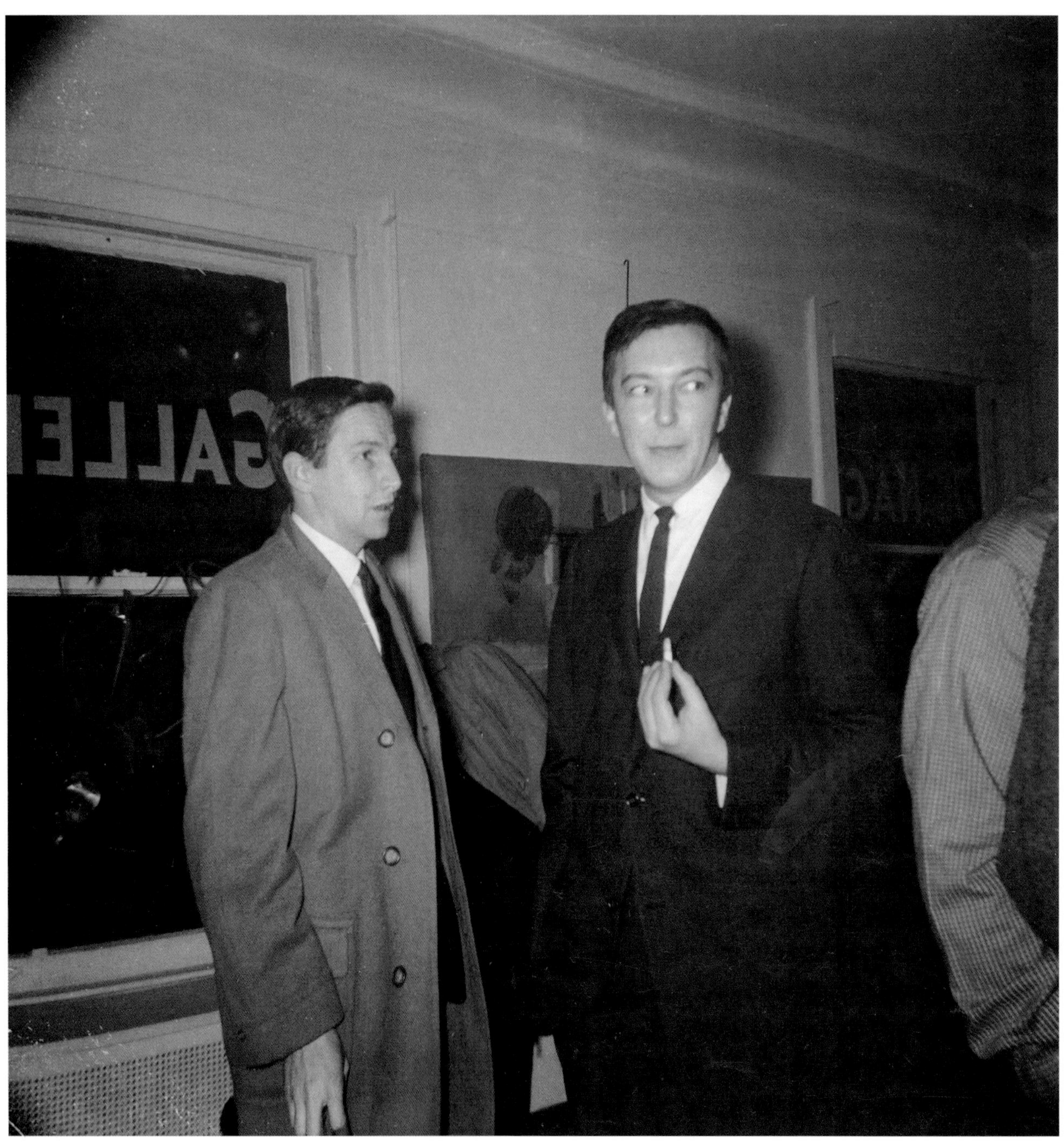

Artists Robert Rauschenberg (left) and Jasper Johns at the Tibor de Nagy Gallery, December 1, 1958. They were thirty-three and twenty-eight, respectively, and this was the year of Johns's first solo show, at the Leo Castelli Gallery (where Rauschenberg also had one of his first solo exhibitions, shortly after Johns's).

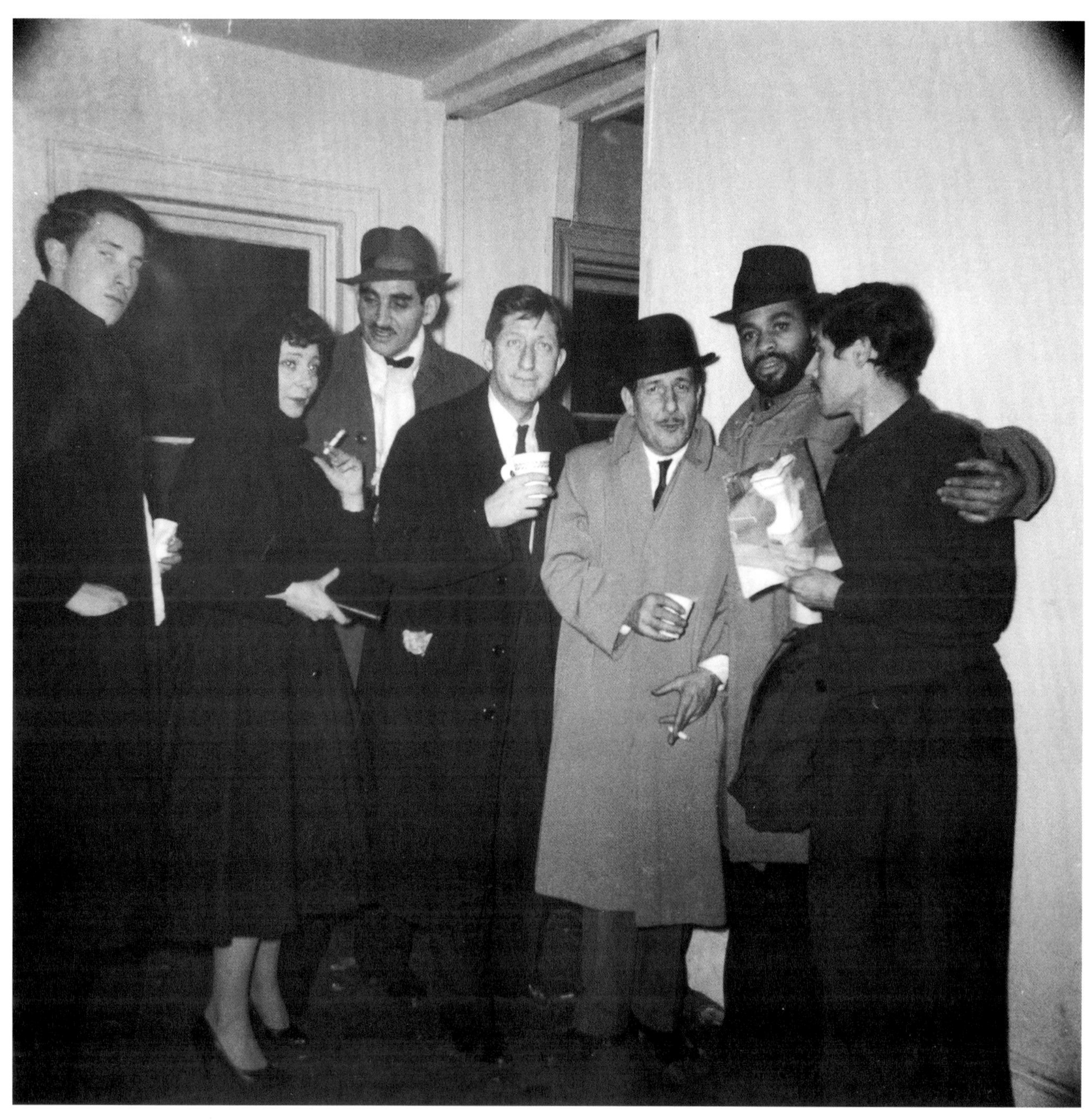

Revelers in trench coats pose together at the Artist's Club's New Year's Eve party, December 31, 1958.
From left, critic Michael C. D. Macdonald; artist Nancy Ward; art critic Harold Rosenberg; Peter D.
Martin, cofounder of the San Francisco bookstore City Lights; Abstract Expressionist painter Franz Kline;
Beat poet, painter, and jazz trumpeter Ted Joans; and artist Jimmy Cuchiara.

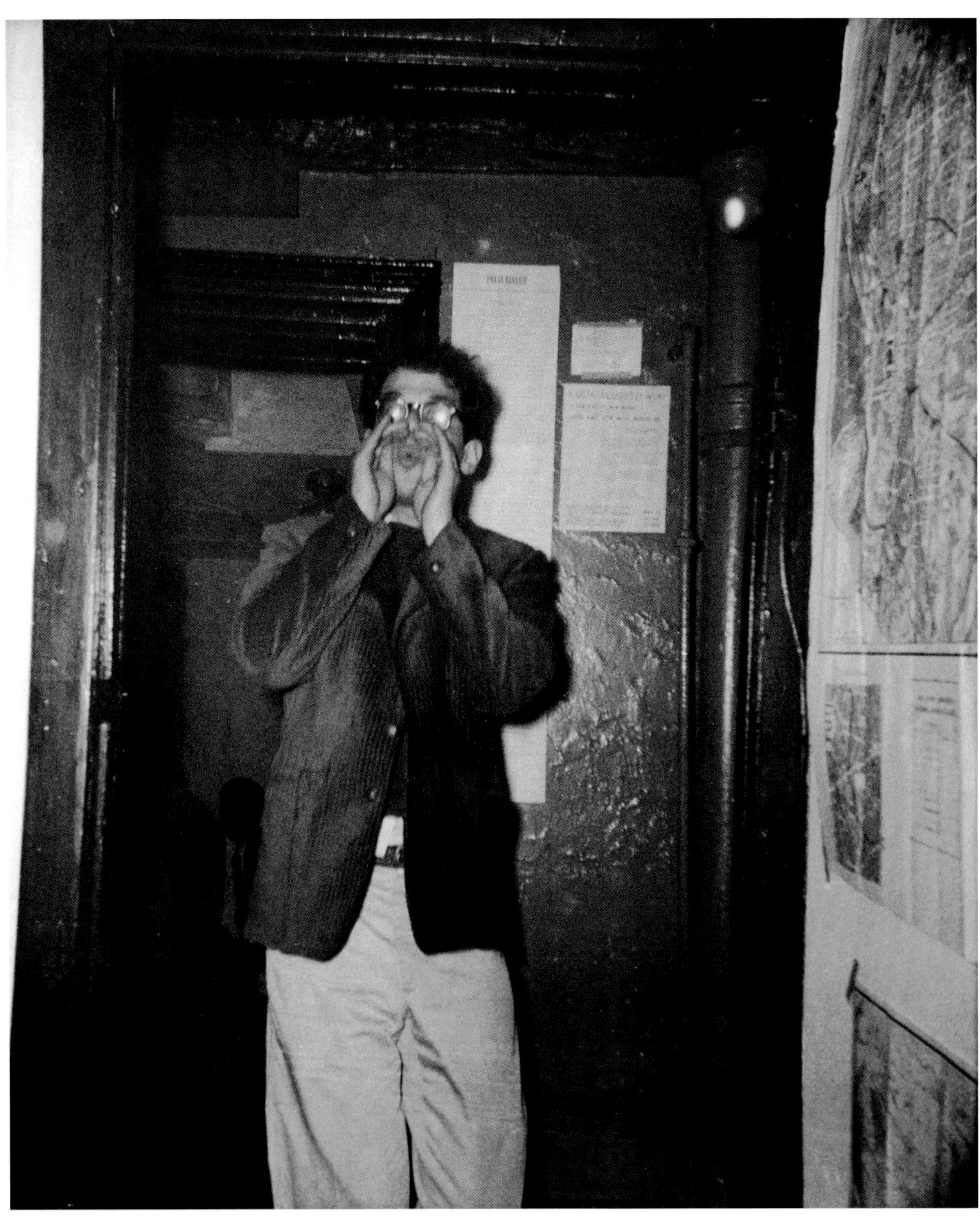

Allen Ginsberg holds his hands to his mouth and howls as he stands in a doorway at the Artist's Club during New Year's Eve celebrations, December 31, 1958. His poem "Howl" had been published two years earlier. Along with Kerouac's *On the Road* (1957), "Howl" was a foundational document of the Beat movement.

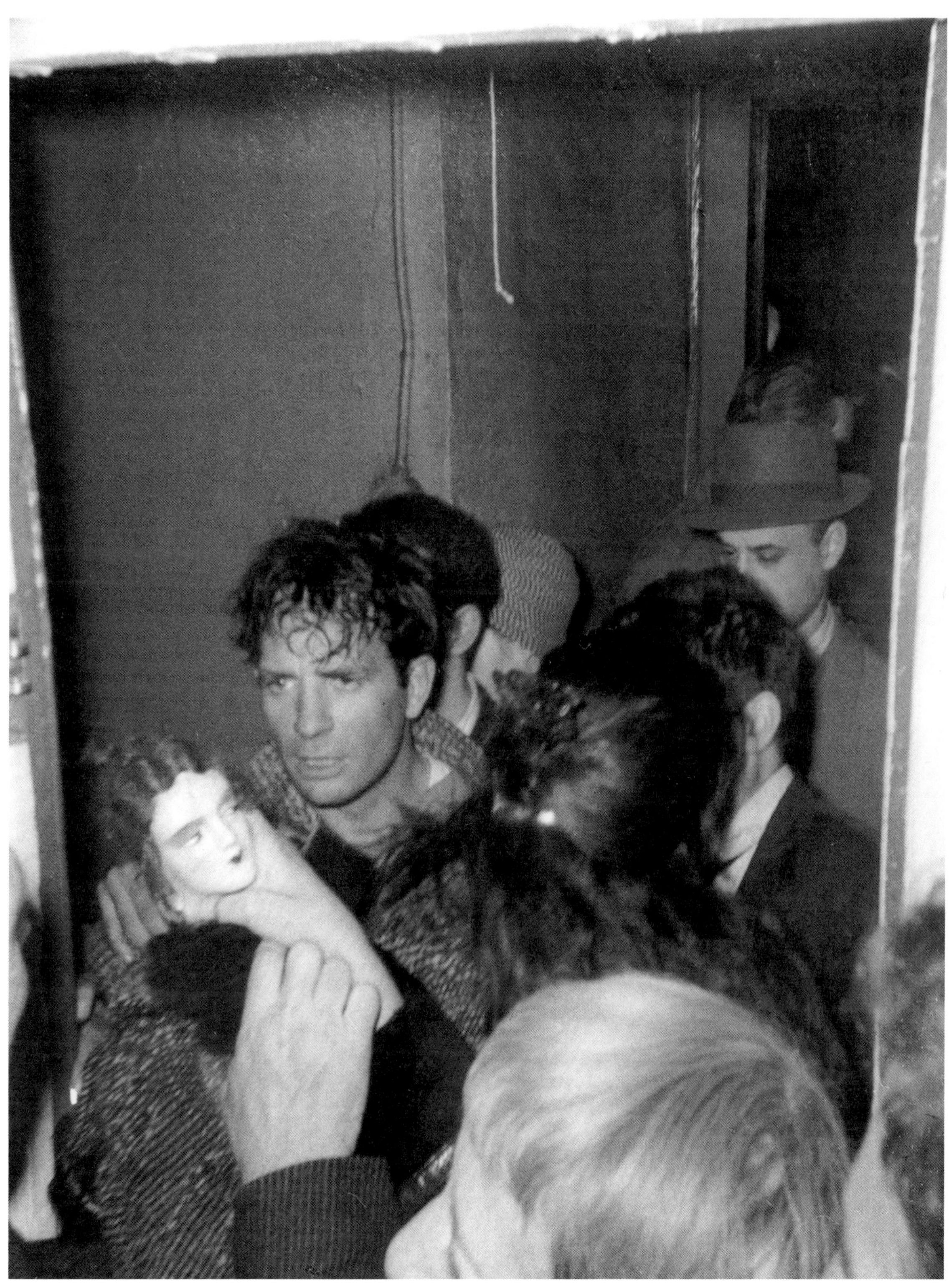

Jack Kerouac as he leaves the Artist's Club, 73 Fourth Ave. at East Tenth St., after a New Year's Eve party, January 1, 1959. Mostly obscured are Kerouac's new girlfriend, artist Dody Muller, art dealer Richard "Dick" Bellamy, and Beat Generation poet Gregory Corso. In addition to the new year, the party celebrated the Robert Frank and Alfred Leslie film *Pull My Daisy*, written and narrated by Kerouac, which featured many of the other Beat artists who attended. The club and its seminars, panels, parties, talks, readings, and other events were central to the creation of the Abstract Expressionist movement and the New York School.

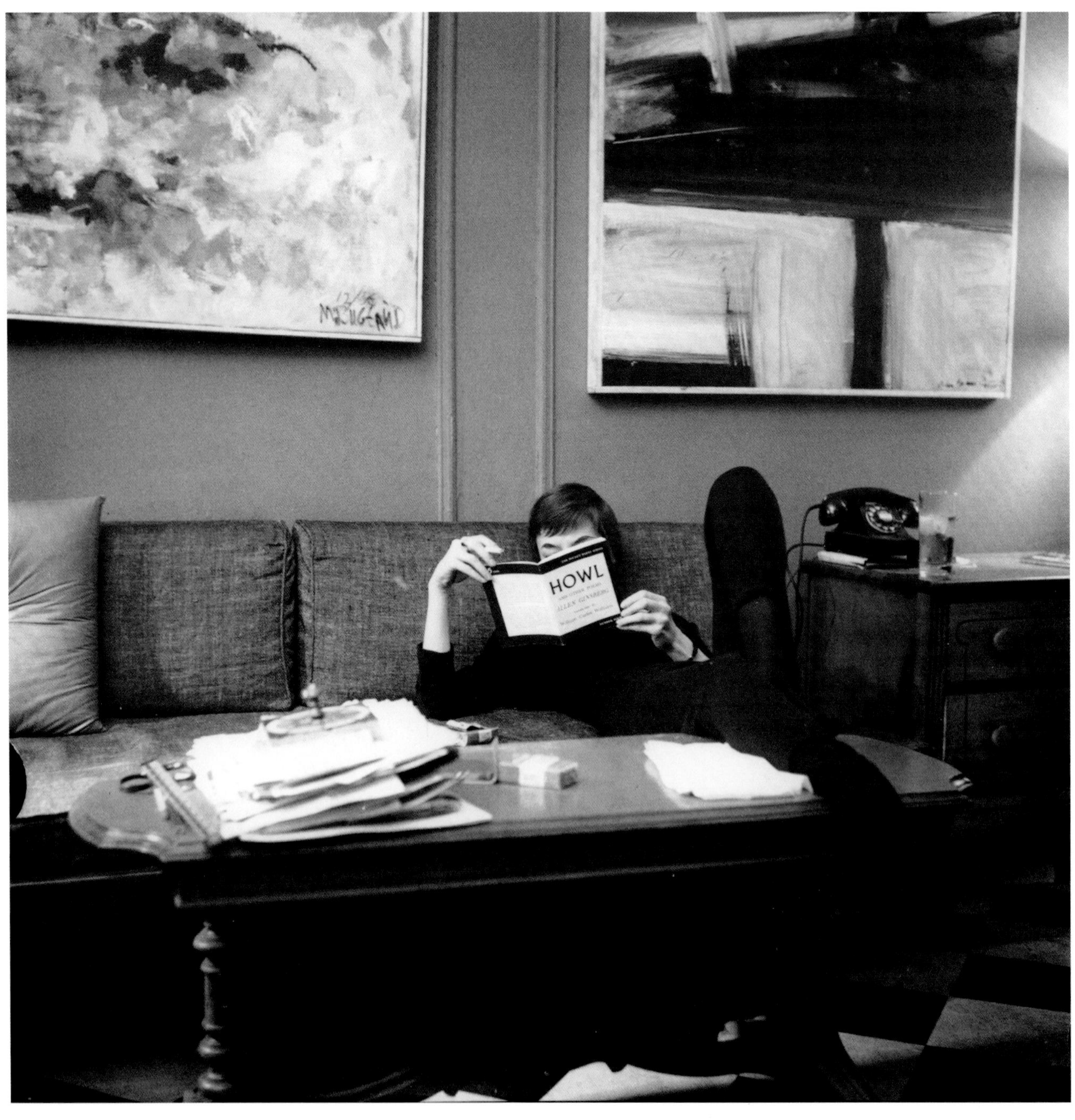

Reading a copy of Allen Ginsberg's "Howl" on the couch at
Fred W. McDarrah's apartment, 304 West Fourteenth St.,
February 14, 1959.

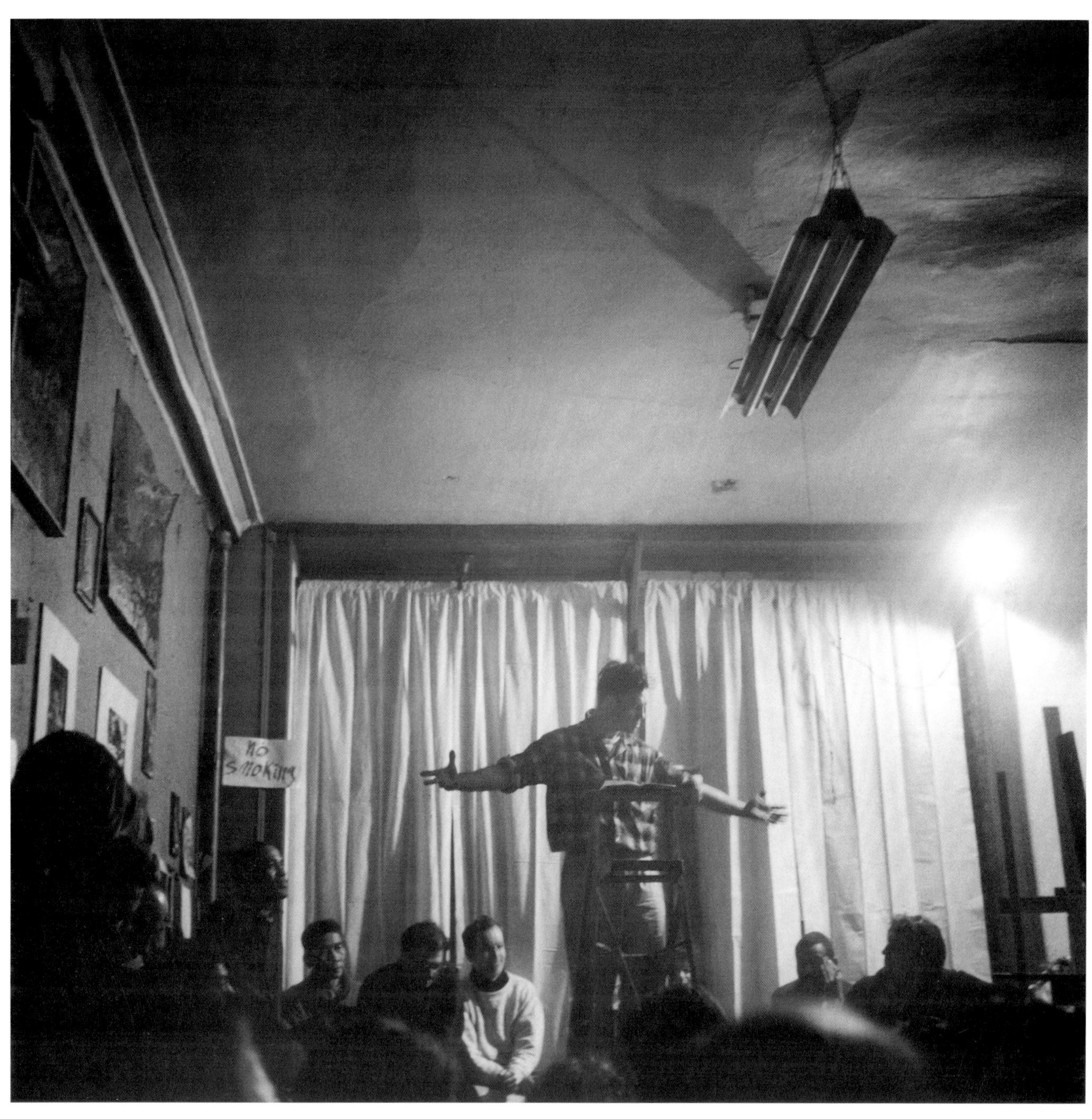

Jack Kerouac reads poetry at the Artist's Studio, 48 East Third St., February 15, 1959. Seated to Kerouac's right on the stage are poets Edward Marshall and Allen Ginsberg. The Artist's Studio met in the home of George Nelson Preston, a scholar of African art (consecrated as an Akan chief in Ghana), curator, poet, and later the founding director of the Museum of Art and Origins in Harlem.

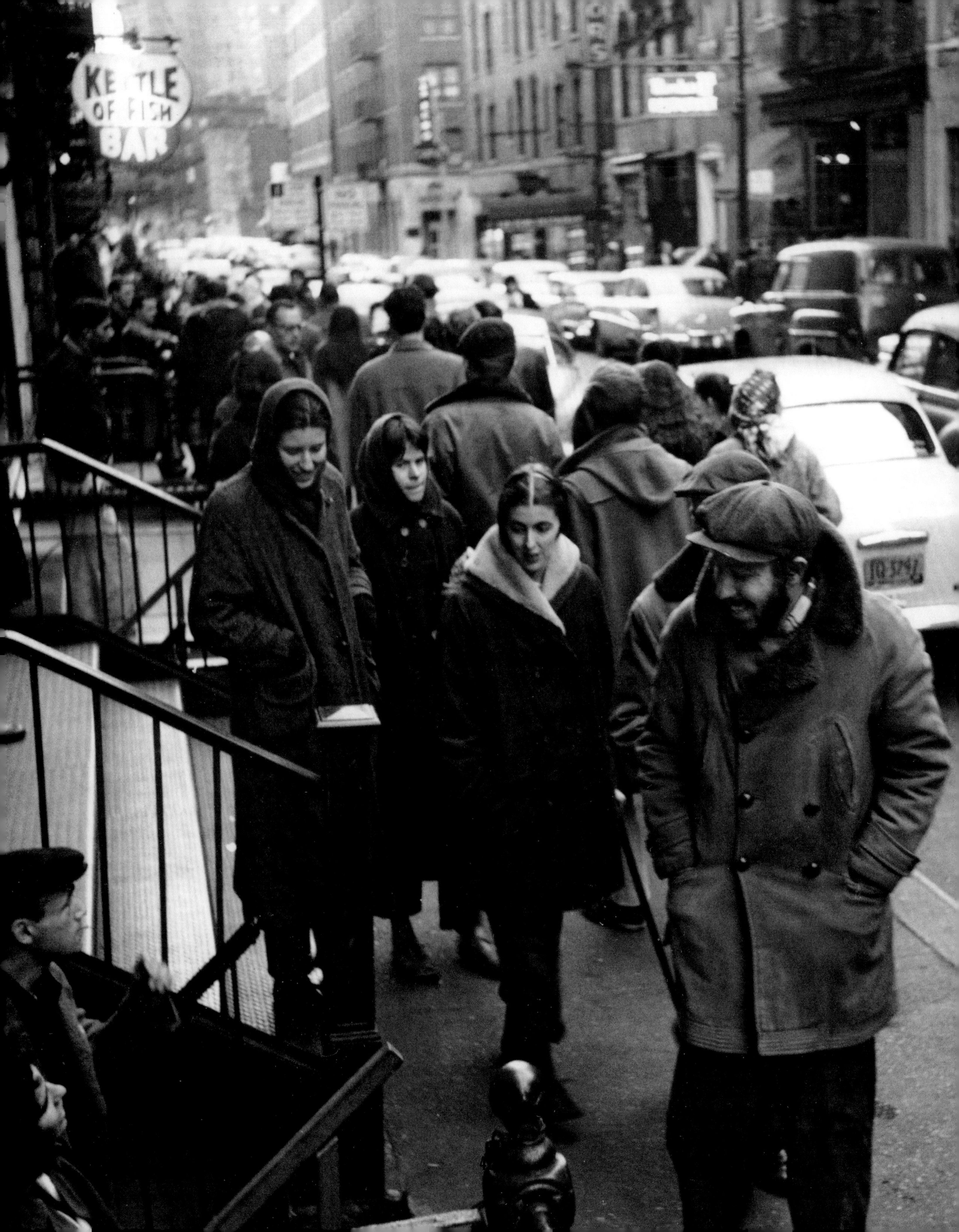
KETTLE
OF FISH
BAR

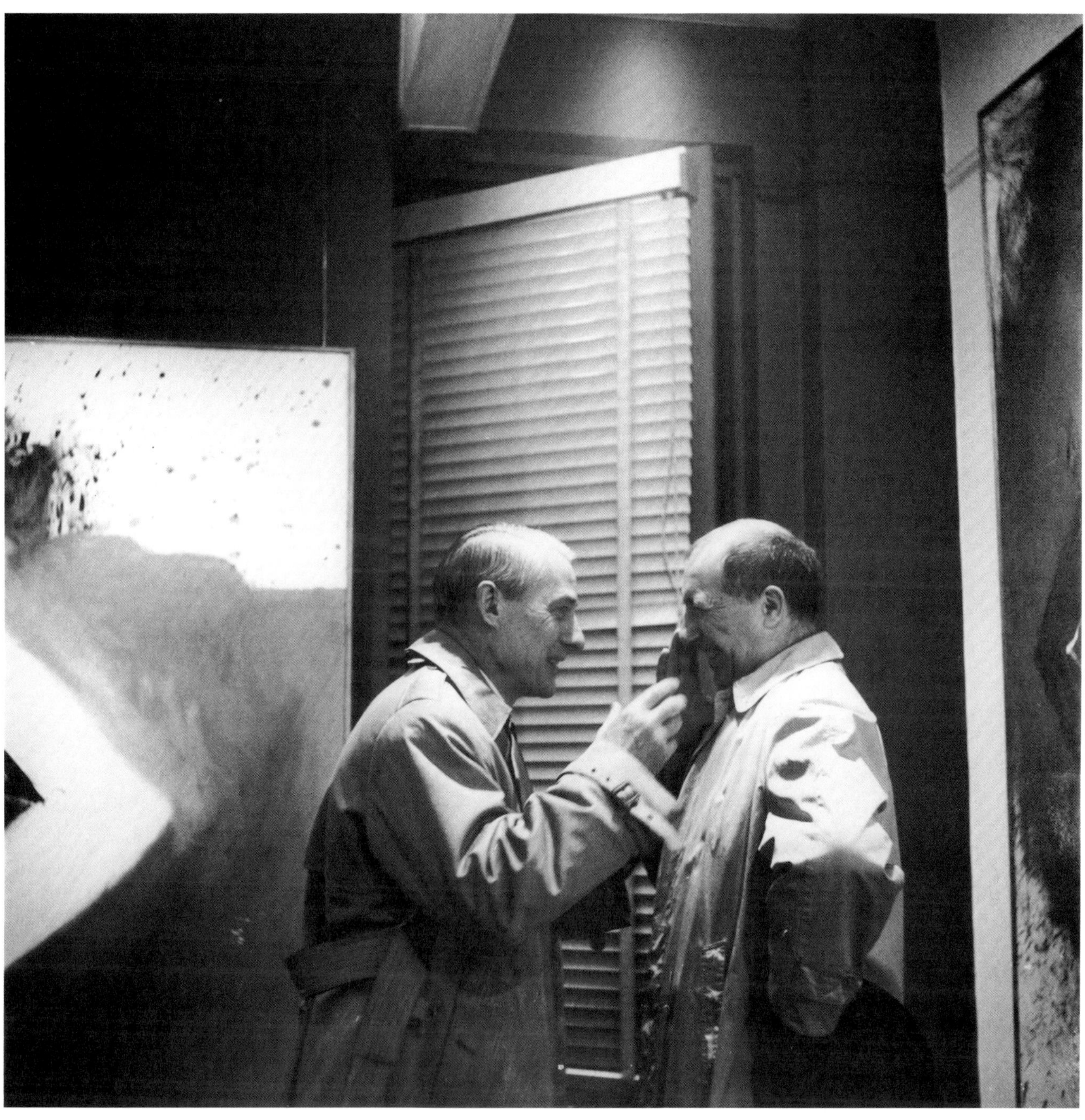

Poet, musician, and activist Tuli Kupferberg (right, hands in pockets) and his wife, writer Sylvia Topp, walk past the steps that lead down to the Gaslight Cafe (116 MacDougal St.), a folk music venue in Greenwich Village, March 8, 1959. Visible behind them is the sign for the Kettle of Fish bar (114 MacDougal St.), frequented by Jack Kerouac and Bob Dylan. Kupferberg, memorialized in Ginsberg's "Howl" for jumping off the Brooklyn Bridge—in reality, the Manhattan Bridge, at a moment of great unhappiness—and surviving, went on to cofound the satirical, political, and lyrically uncensored Lower East Side rock group the Fugs in 1964.

Artists Willem de Kooning (left) and Jack Tworkov share a laugh at the Sidney Janis Gallery, March 9, 1959. They were attending the opening of an exhibition of Robert Motherwell's paintings. De Kooning was to be a frequent subject of McDarrah's camera. Tworkov was also an Abstract Expressionist painter and a fellow founder of the New York School. Motherwell, educated as a philosopher, was one of the movement's theorists and spokesmen.

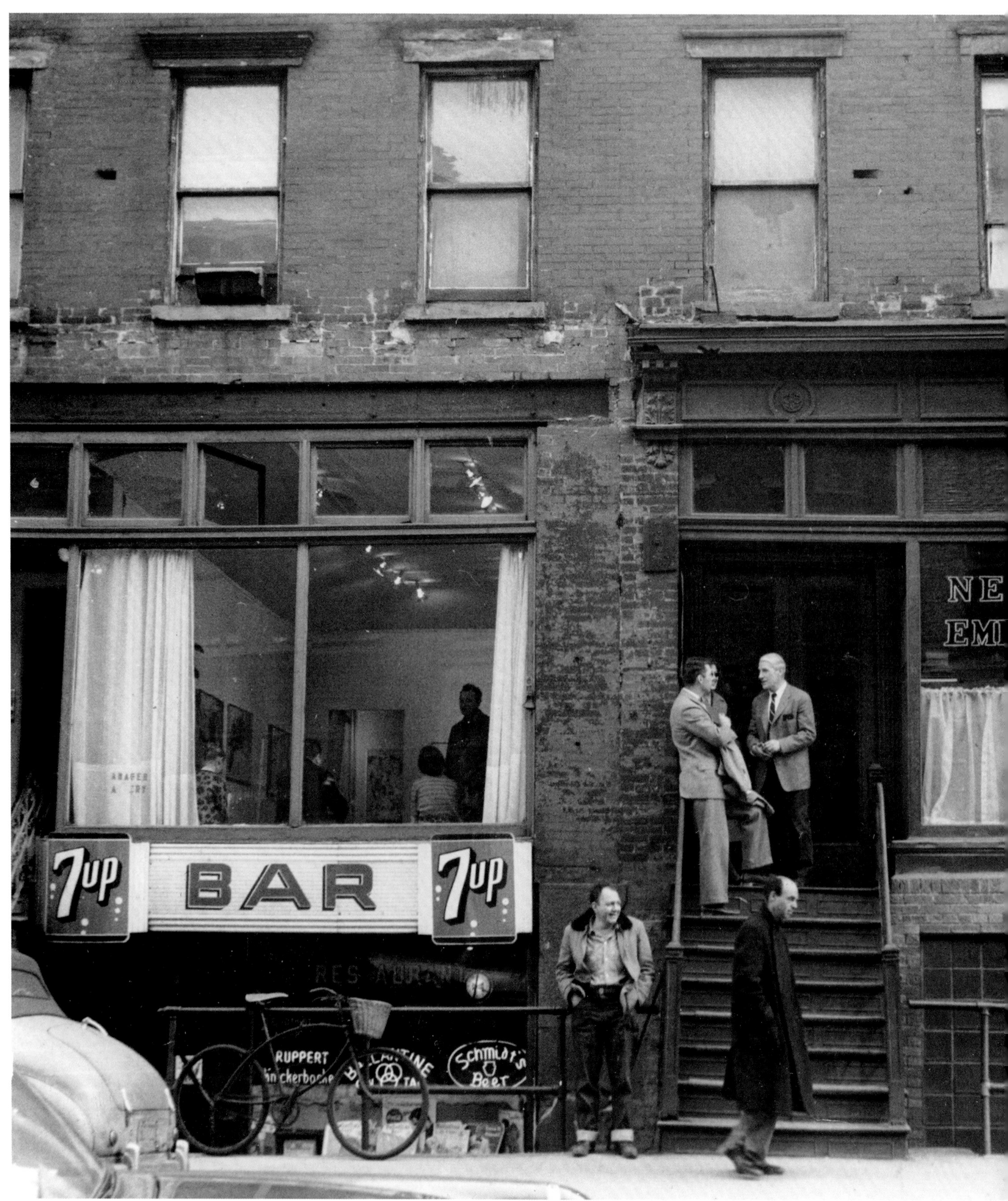

7UP
BAR
7UP
NE
EM
RUPPERT
Schmidt's
Beer

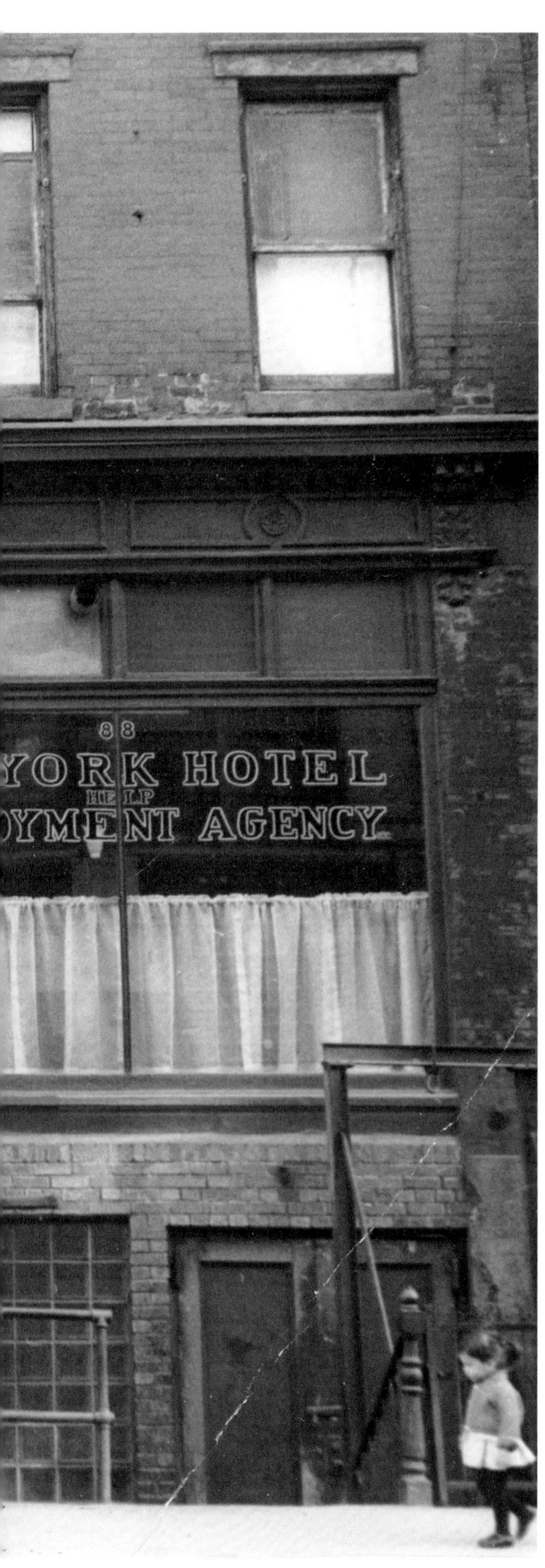

Willem de Kooning (center, with light hair) speaks with novelist Noel Clad and his wife, Jean, at the top of the stoop, 88 East Tenth St., April 5, 1959. De Kooning's home and studio were on the top floor of the three-story building. Next door, the glass-windowed storefront above the "Bar" sign is the Tanager Gallery, one of eight cooperative, artist-run galleries in the area that were collectively known as the "10th Street Galleries" and were incubators of new talent.

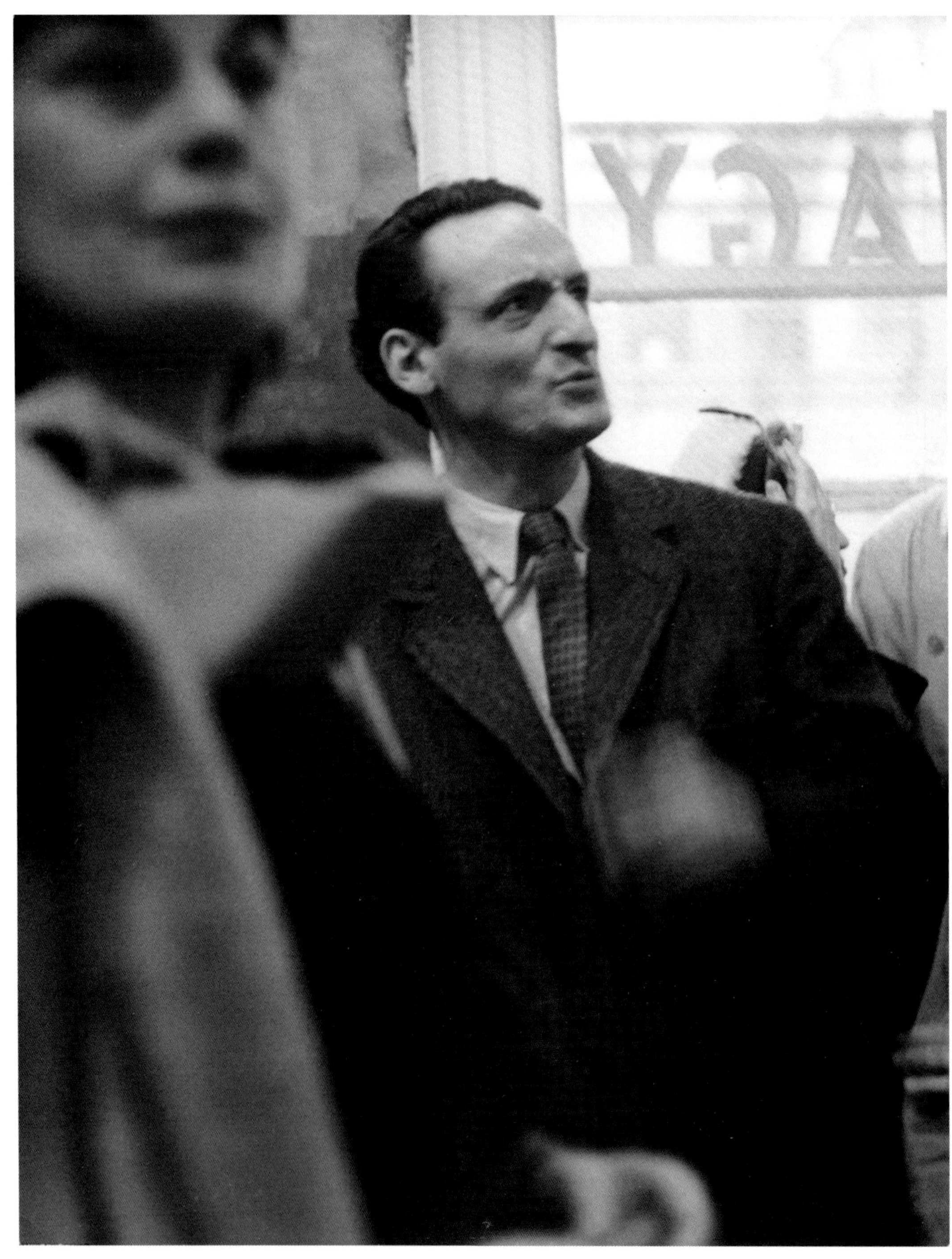

Larry Rivers at the opening of a Grace Hartigan exhibition at the Tibor de Nagy Gallery, April 28, 1959. A precursor of Pop art, Rivers was not only a painter and sculptor but also a poet, jazz saxophonist, teacher, filmmaker, and occasional actor.

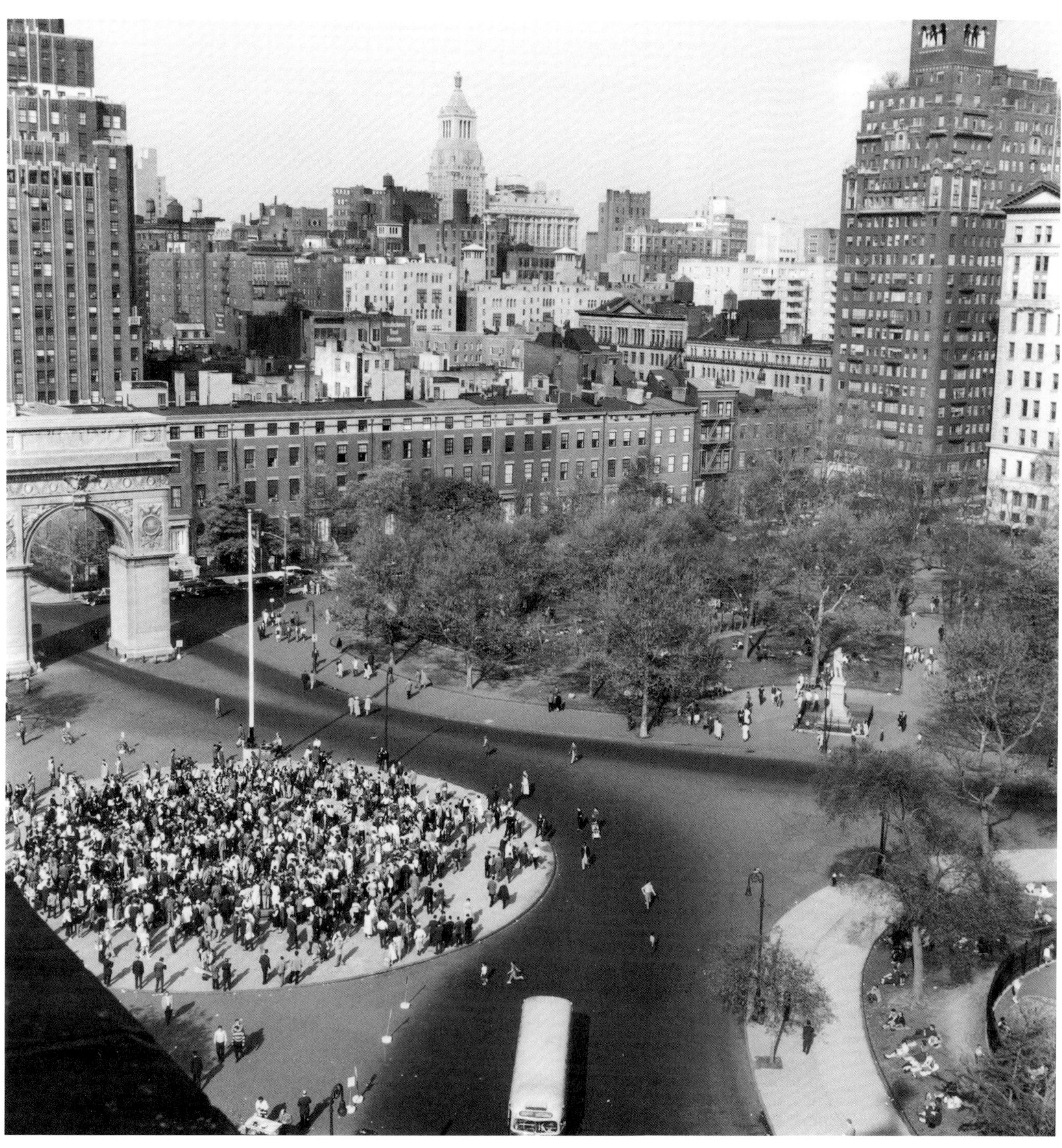

View of Washington Square Park from the bell tower of the Judson Memorial Church, with a large gathering of people around and in the fountain to hear folksingers, May 3, 1959. After World War II, musicians came here to perform informally on Sundays. A few months after this photograph was taken, in August 1959, the park was permanently closed to traffic.

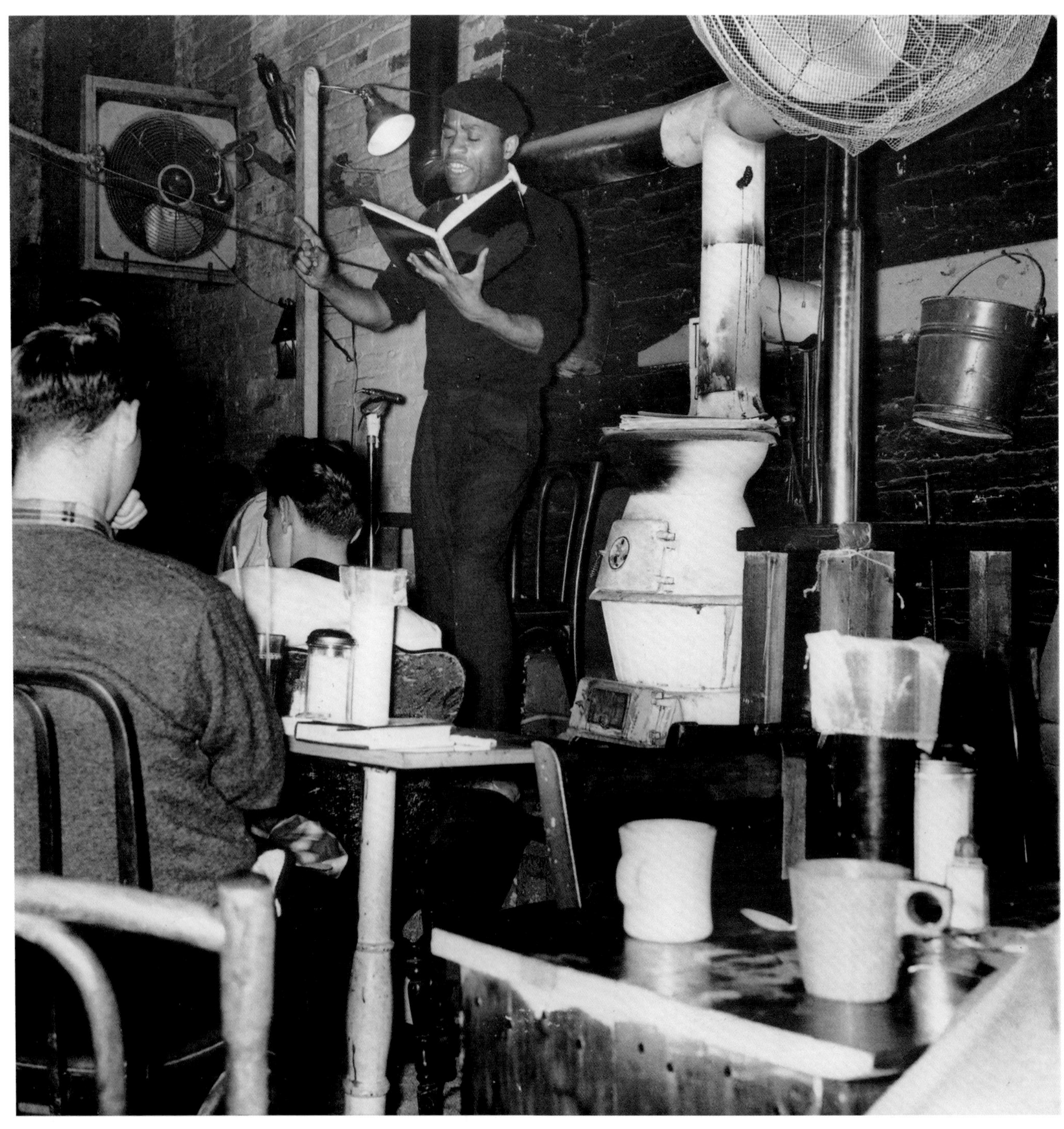

Poet Ted Joans reading from his work in the Gaslight Cafe,
May 24, 1959. The multitalented Joans was a Surrealist
whose writings were also inspired by jazz rhythms like those
he played on the trumpet.

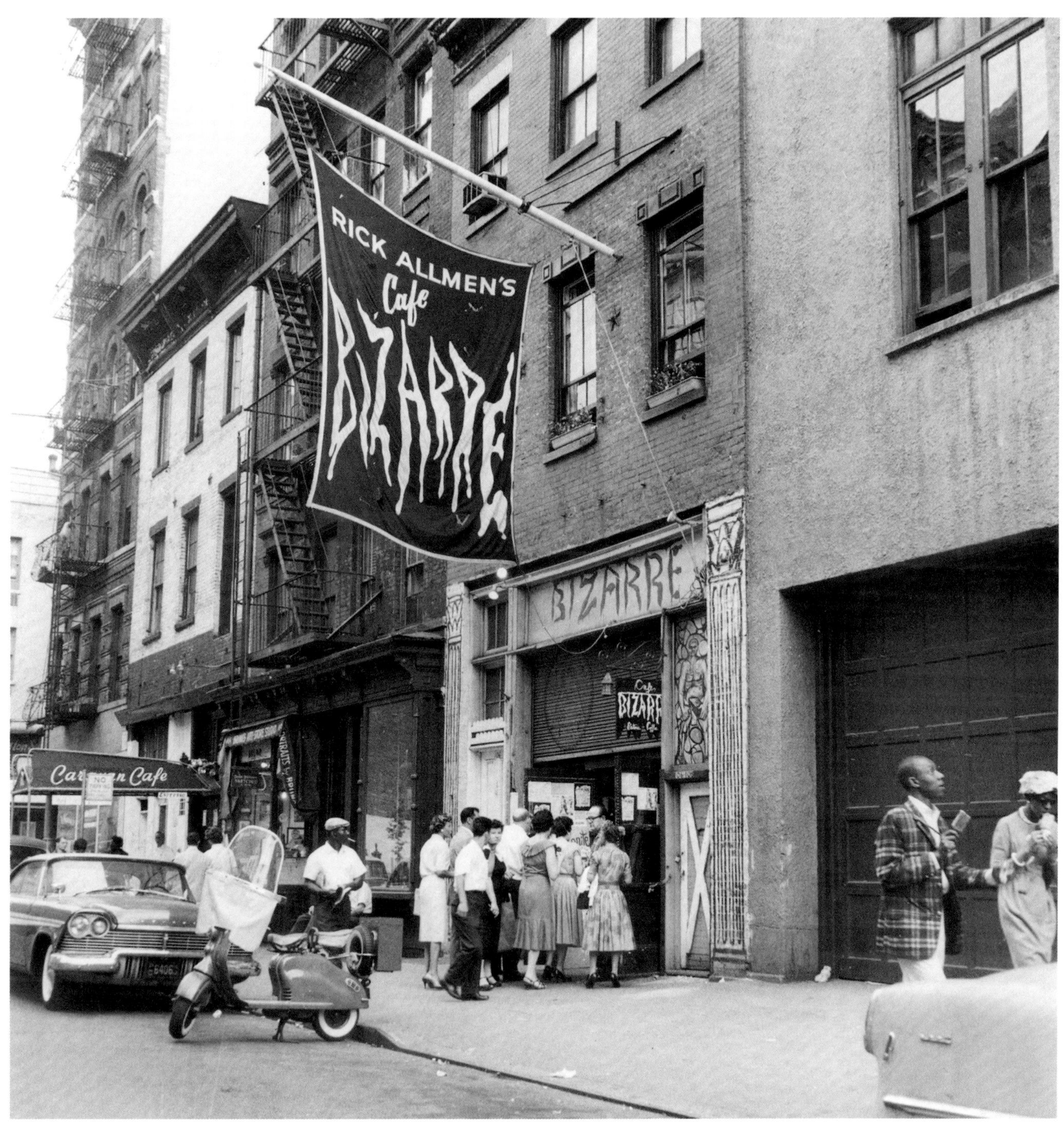

The Cafe Bizarre, 106 West Third St., June 7, 1959. The club was a crossroads for Beat writers and jazz musicians. The headliner the night it opened, in 1957, was singer and civil rights activist Odetta. Others who played there included the Velvet Underground (Andy Warhol first saw them there), the Gerry Mulligan Quartet, George Shearing, and Charlie Parker. Beats including Jack Kerouac, Allen Ginsberg, Gary Snyder, and Diane di Prima were regulars.

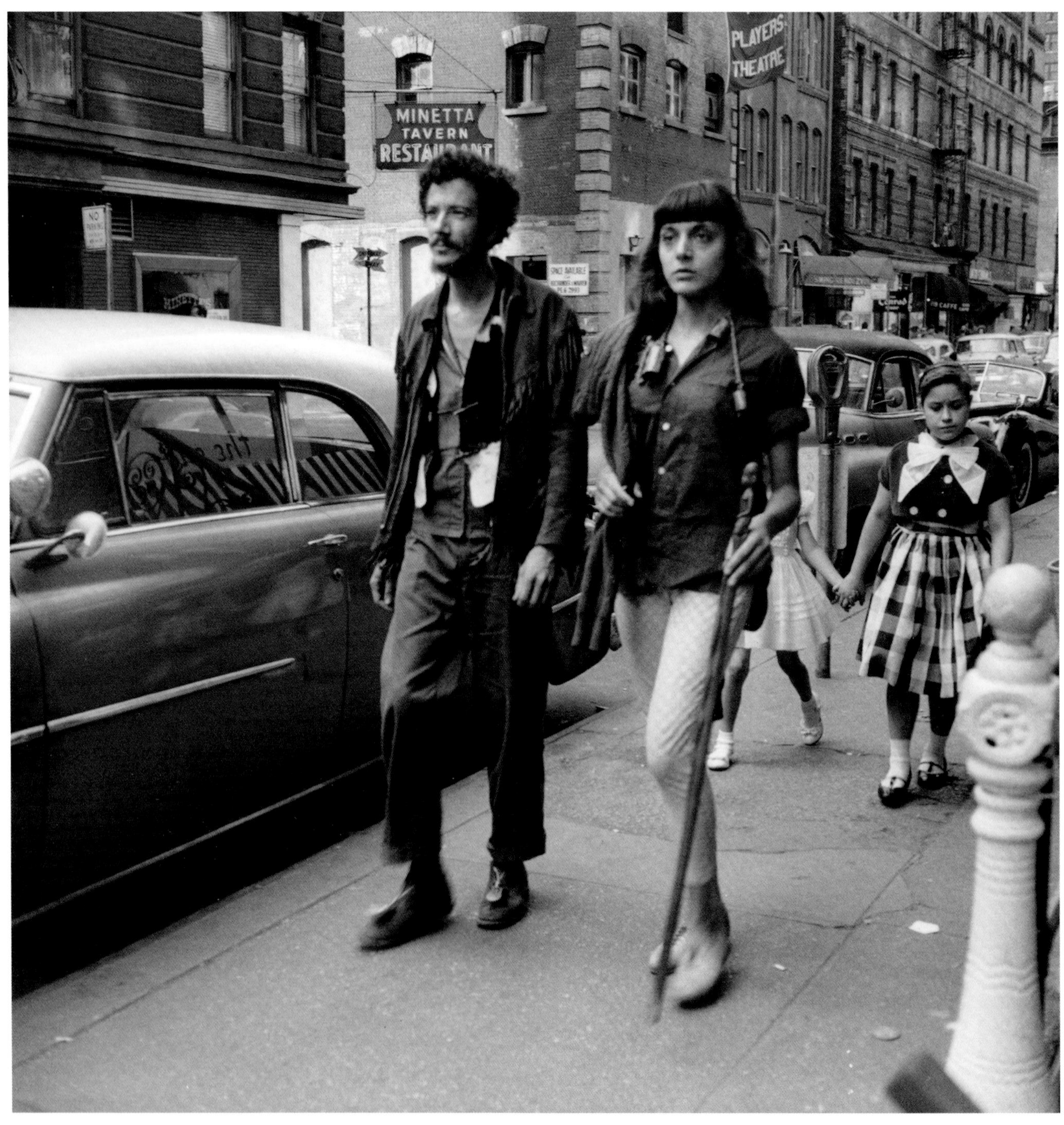

Author Ambrose Hollingworth Redmoon (born James Neil Hollingworth) and his wife, Dakota (born Louise Durham), walk along MacDougal Street, just past the intersection with Minetta Lane, June 21, 1959. Redmoon later managed the San Francisco psychedelic rock group Quicksilver Messenger Service and, after a car crash left him in a wheelchair, became a writer. Visible in the background are the Minetta Tavern, a Beat hangout, and the Players Theatre, home to one of the oldest Off-Broadway stages.

People gather on the roof of 164 Henry St., with the Manhattan and Brooklyn Bridges in the background, August 30, 1959.

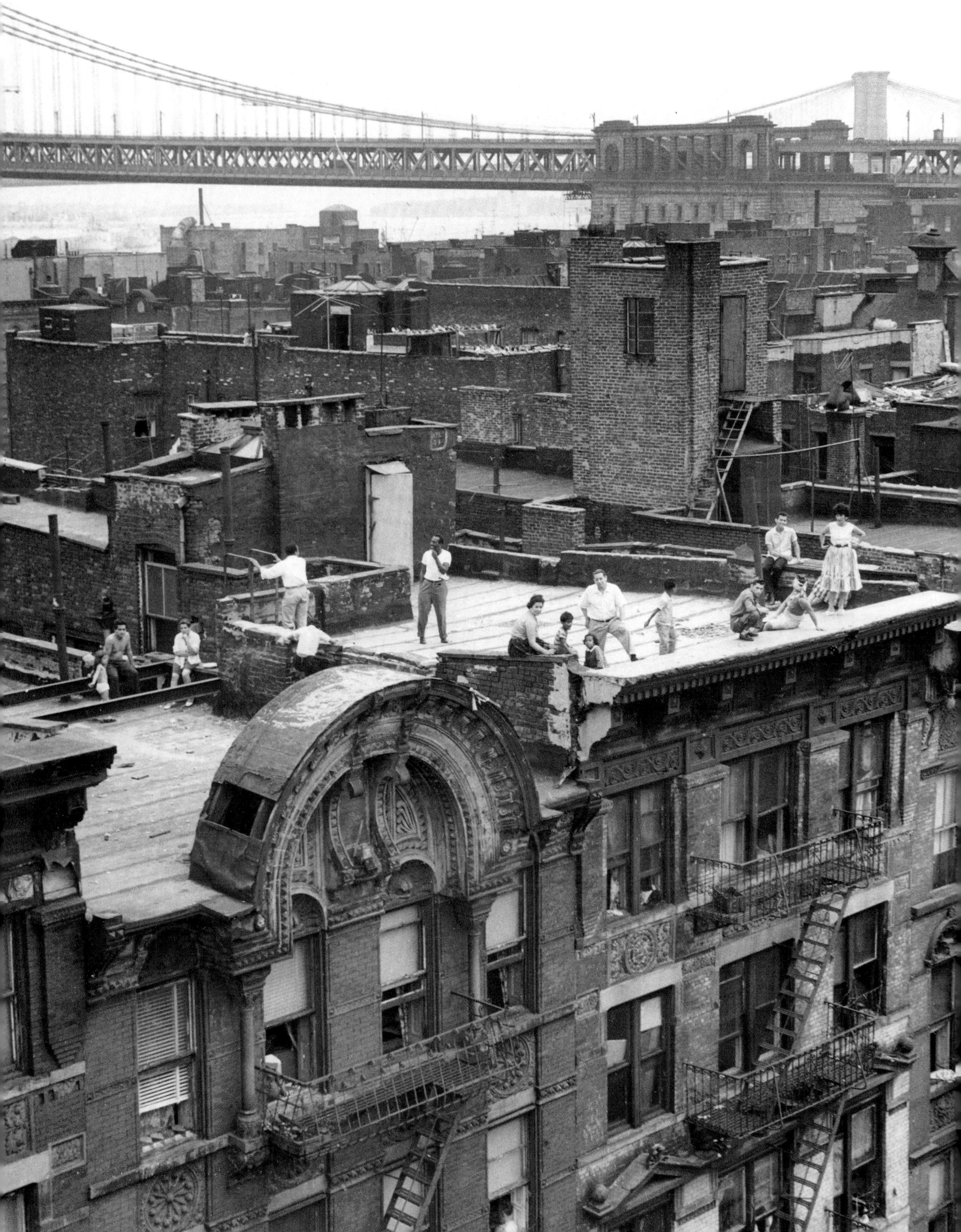

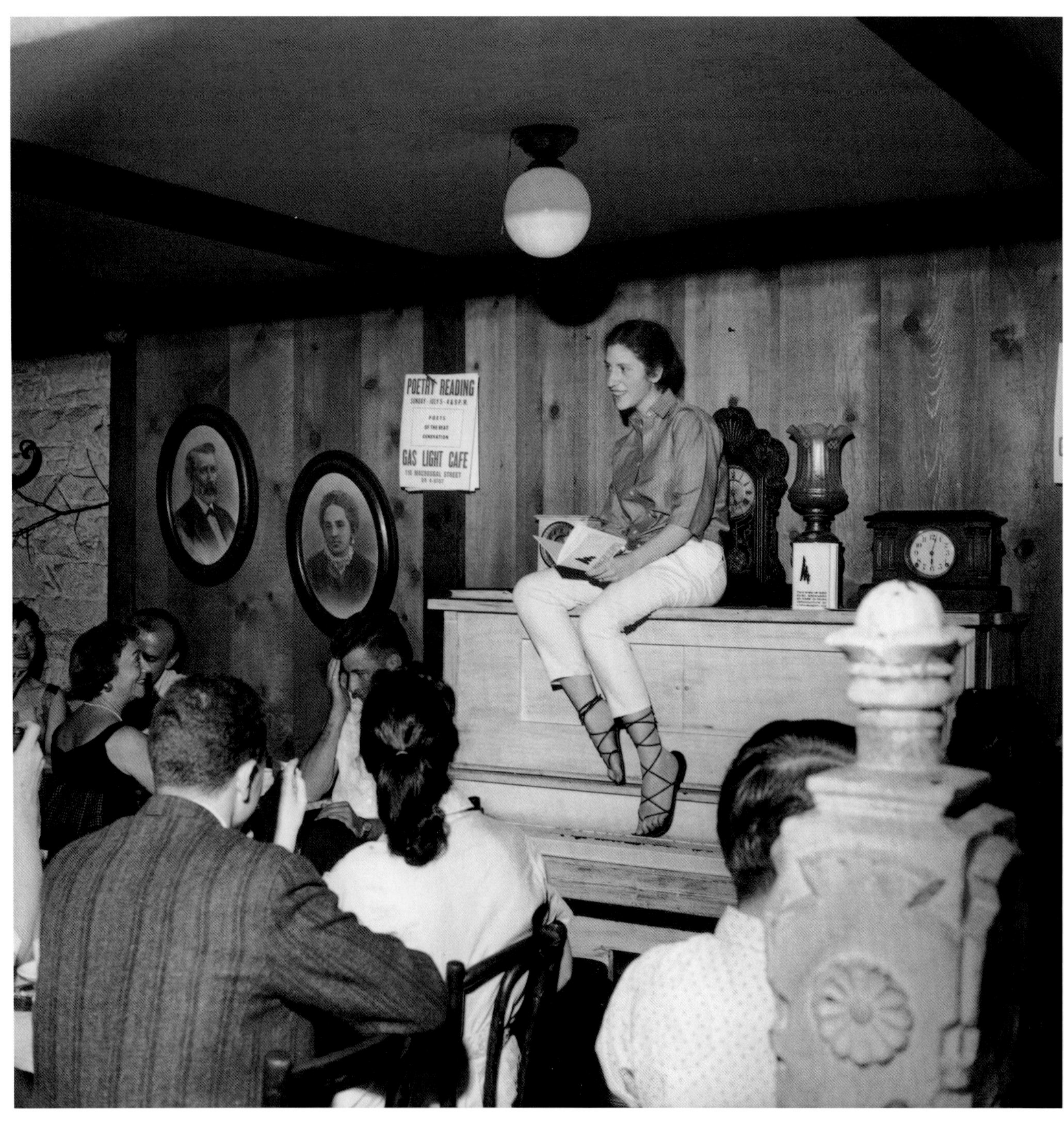

Poet Diane di Prima sits atop a piano and reads from her first
published collection, *This Kind of Bird Flies Backward* (1958),
at the Gaslight Cafe, 116 MacDougal St., June 28, 1959.

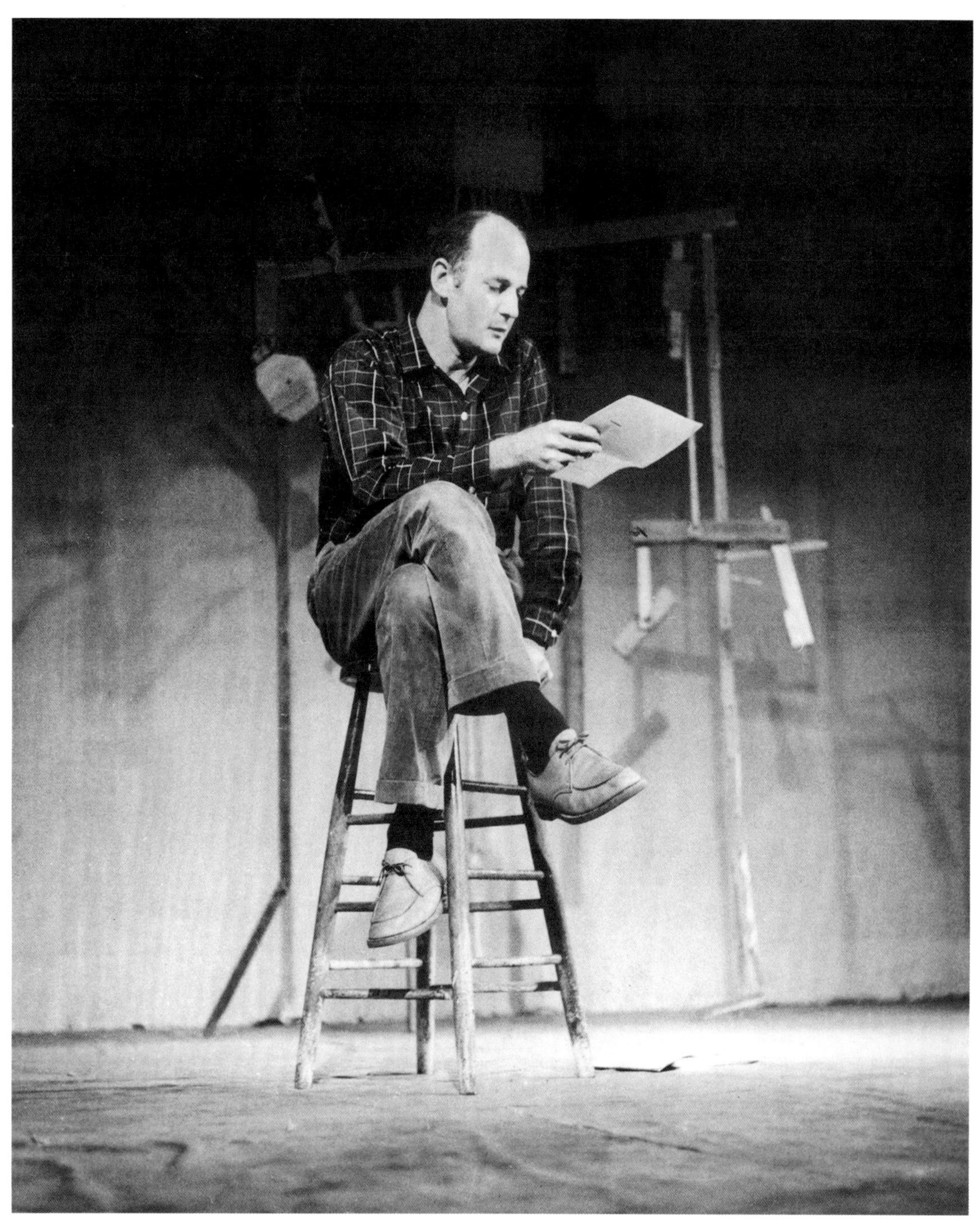

Poet and City Lights bookstore cofounder Lawrence Ferlinghetti reads from his poetry collection *A Coney Island of the Mind* (1958) at the Living Theatre, 69 West Fourteenth St., October 5, 1959. The Living Theatre was a radical theater company founded by Judith Malina and Julian Beck in 1947.

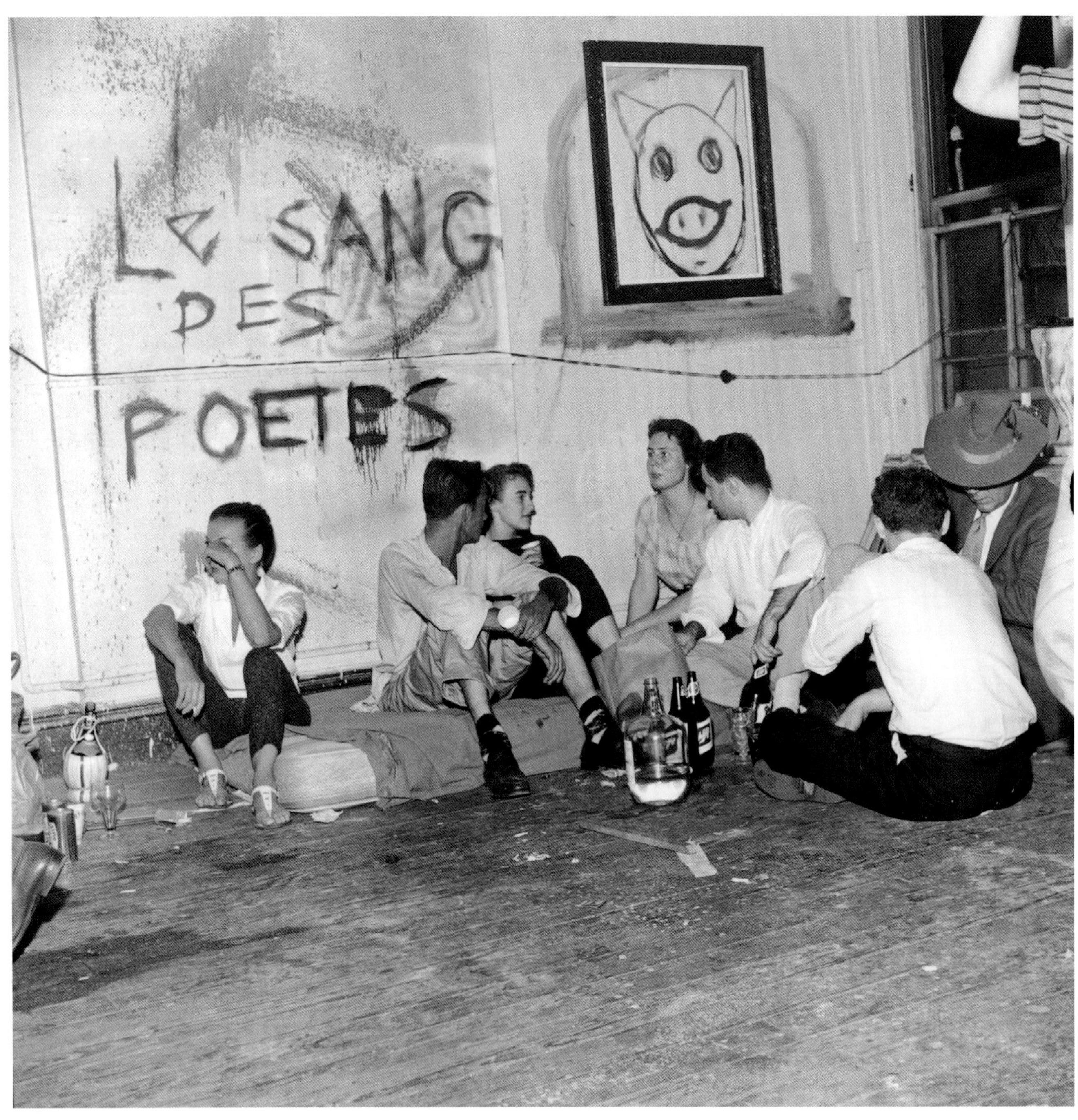

Guests sit on a mattress and on the floor at a birthday party for Ted Joans (not pictured), July 25, 1959. The graffito on the wall reads "Le Sang des Poetes" ("The Blood of the Poets"), after the 1930 Surrealistic film *The Blood of a Poet* directed by Jean Cocteau.

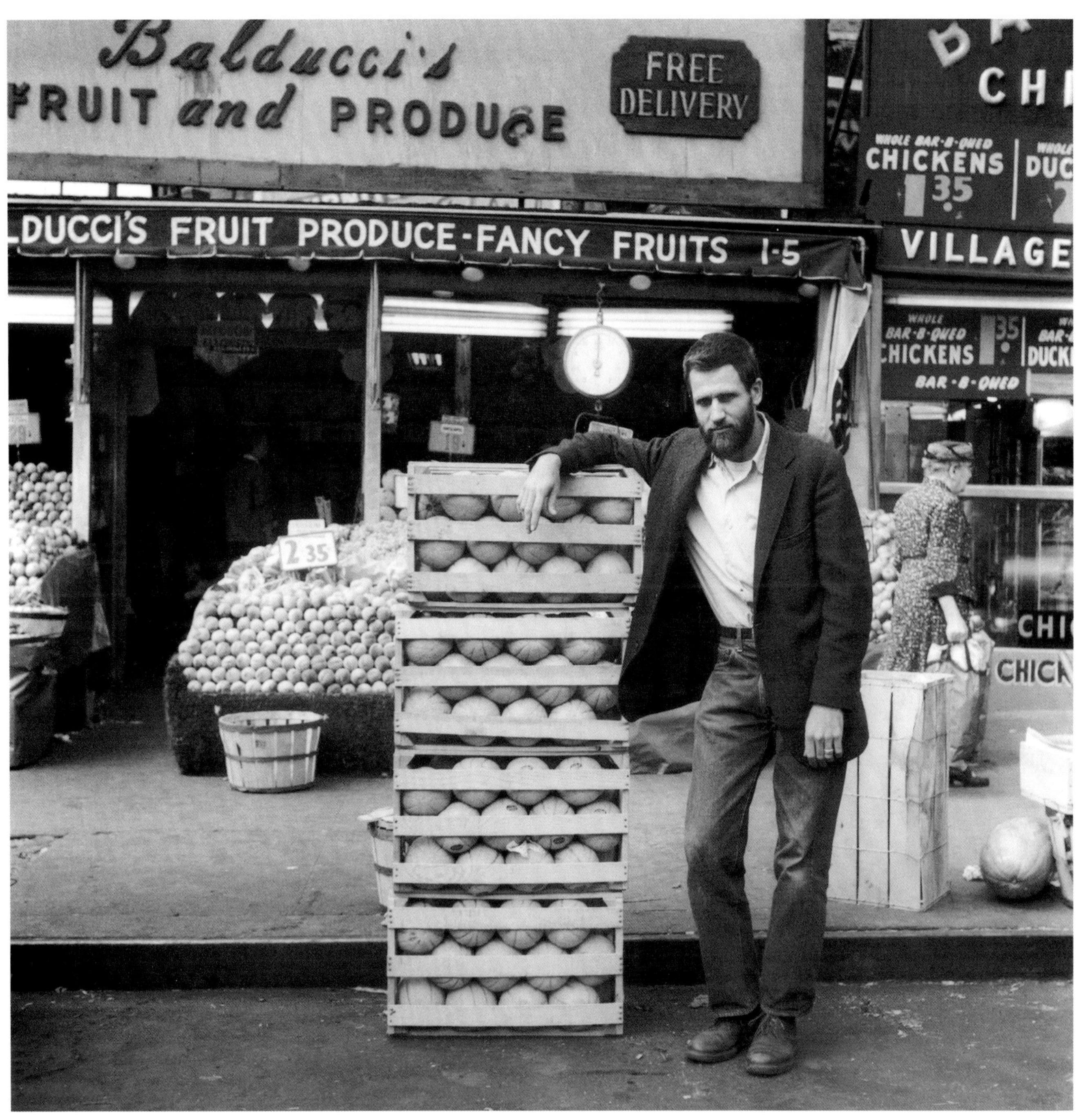

Artist Allan Kaprow, credited with coining the term "happenings" for audience-participation performances of the late fifties and sixties, leans on a stack of melon crates outside Balducci's market, then at the intersection of West Eighth St., Sixth Ave., and Greenwich Ave., September 15, 1959. His *Eighteen Happenings in Six Parts*, presented `at the Reuben Gallery in 1959, included a woman squeezing oranges.

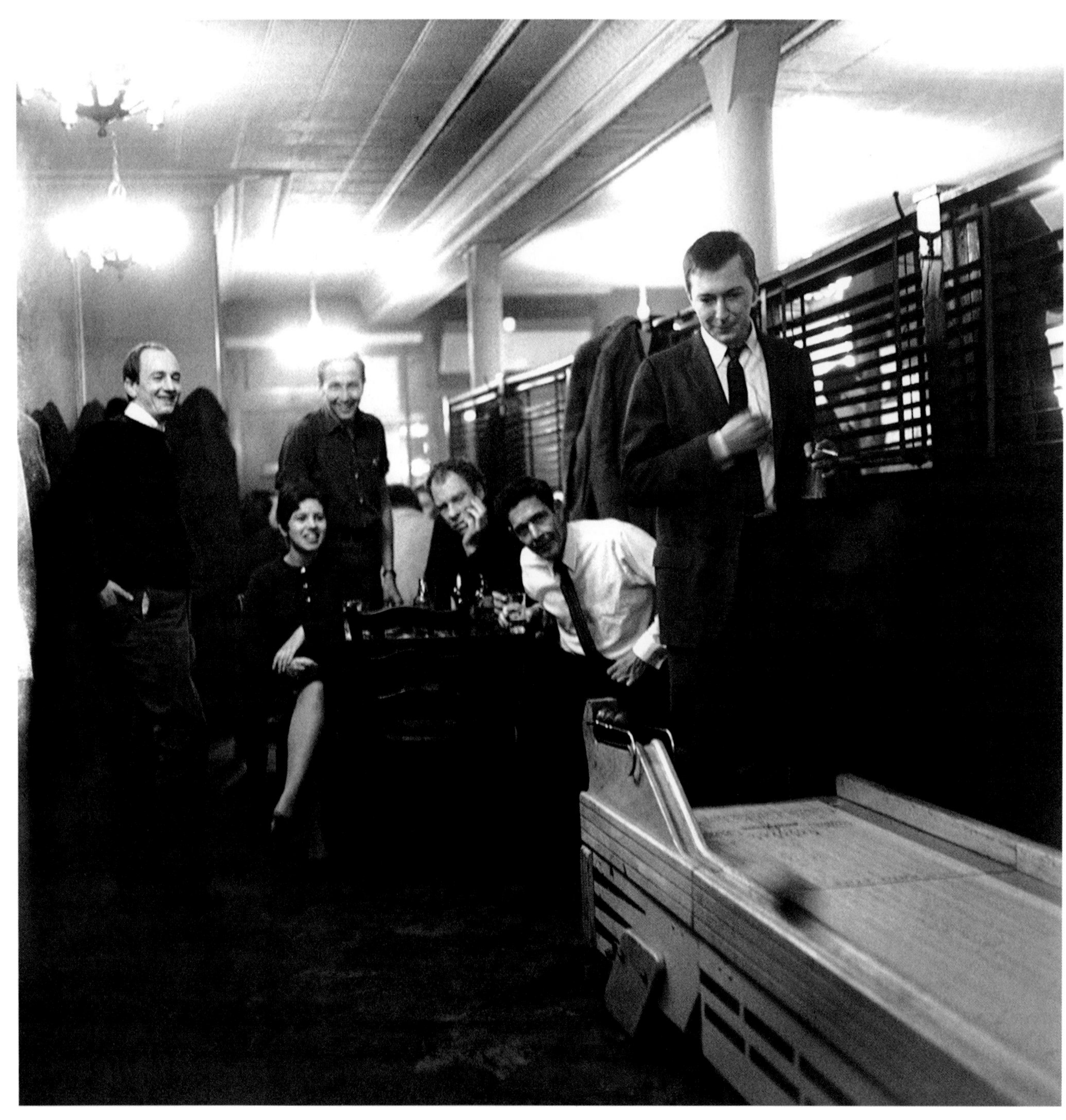

From left, artists William Giles, Anna Moreska, and Robert Rauschenberg; dancer-choreographer
Merce Cunningham; and composer John Cage watch artist Jasper Johns play Skee-Ball in Dillon's Bar,
80 University Place, November 10, 1959. Cunningham and Cage were lovers for nearly a half century, as
were Rauschenberg and Johns during the fifties. Along with the Cedar Tavern, Dillon's was a major artists'
hangout of the time. In the seventies, the building housed the offices of the *Village Voice*.

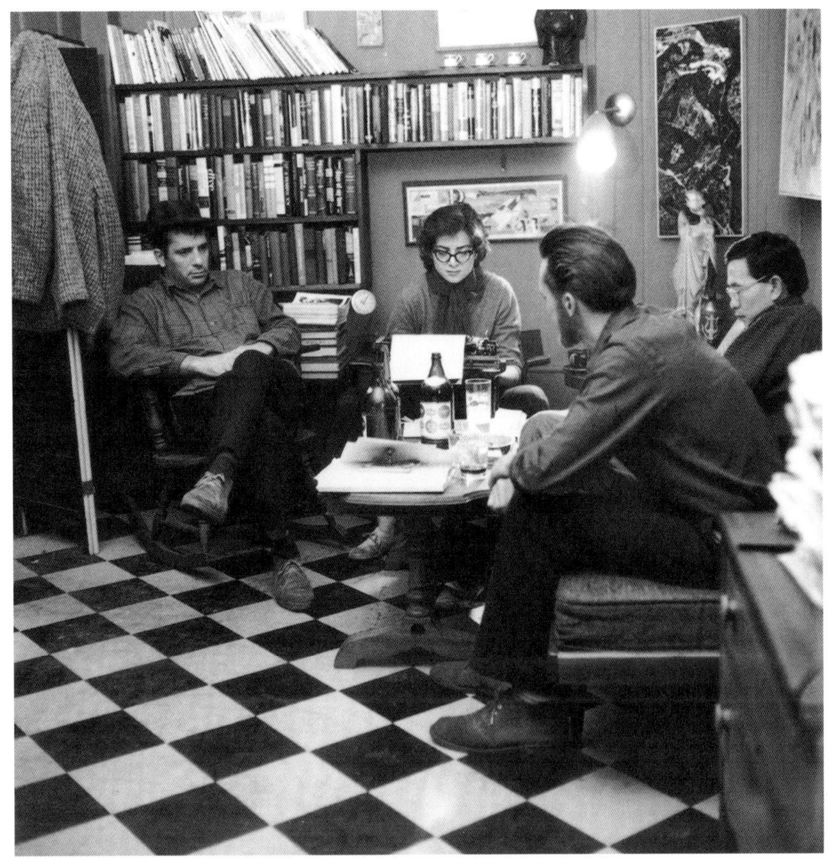

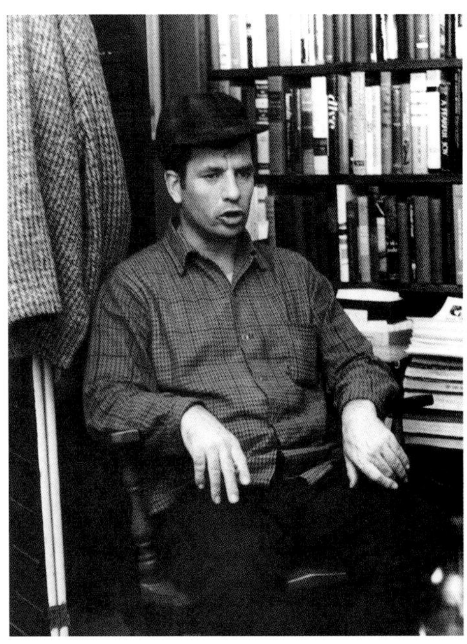

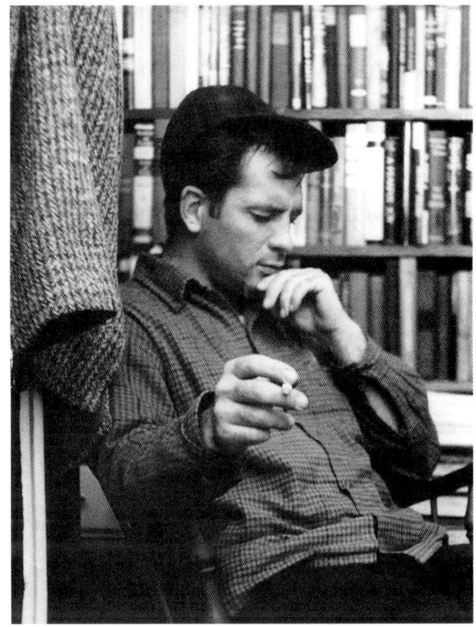

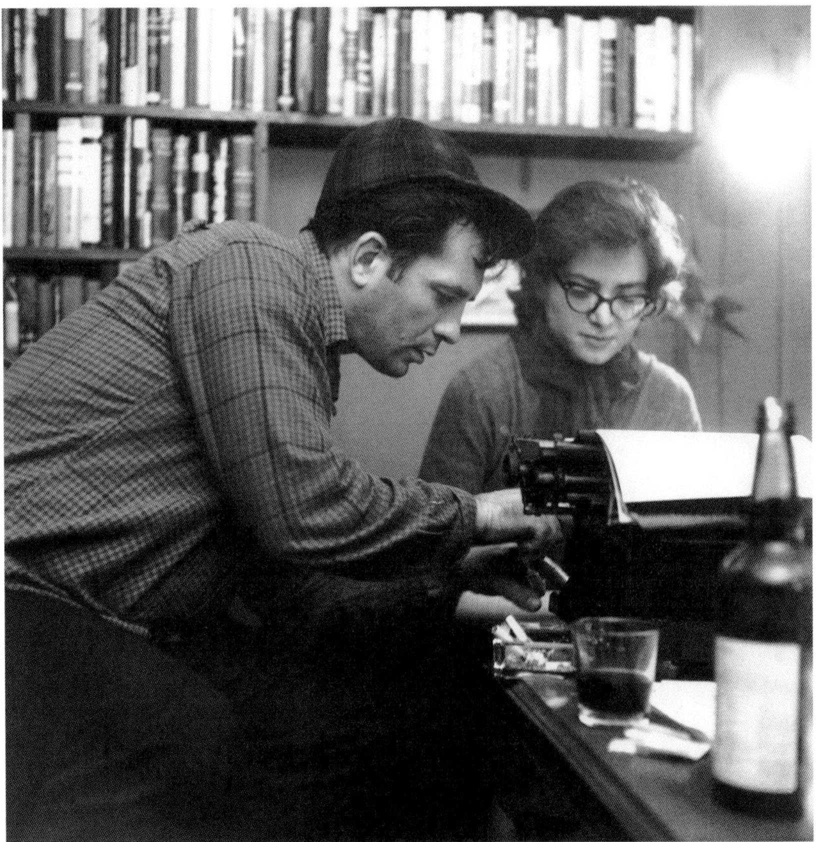

Jack Kerouac and Beat poets Lew Welch and Albert Saijo sit around a low table as they collaborate on a poem, which is being typed by Gloria Schoffel in the apartment of her soon-to-be husband, photographer Fred W. McDarrah, at 304 West Fourteenth St., December 10, 1959. The work was titled "This Is a Poem by Albert Saijo, Lew Welch, and Jack Kerouac" (later published as *Trip Trap*) and was based on the trio's just-completed journey from San Francisco to New York in Welch's car.

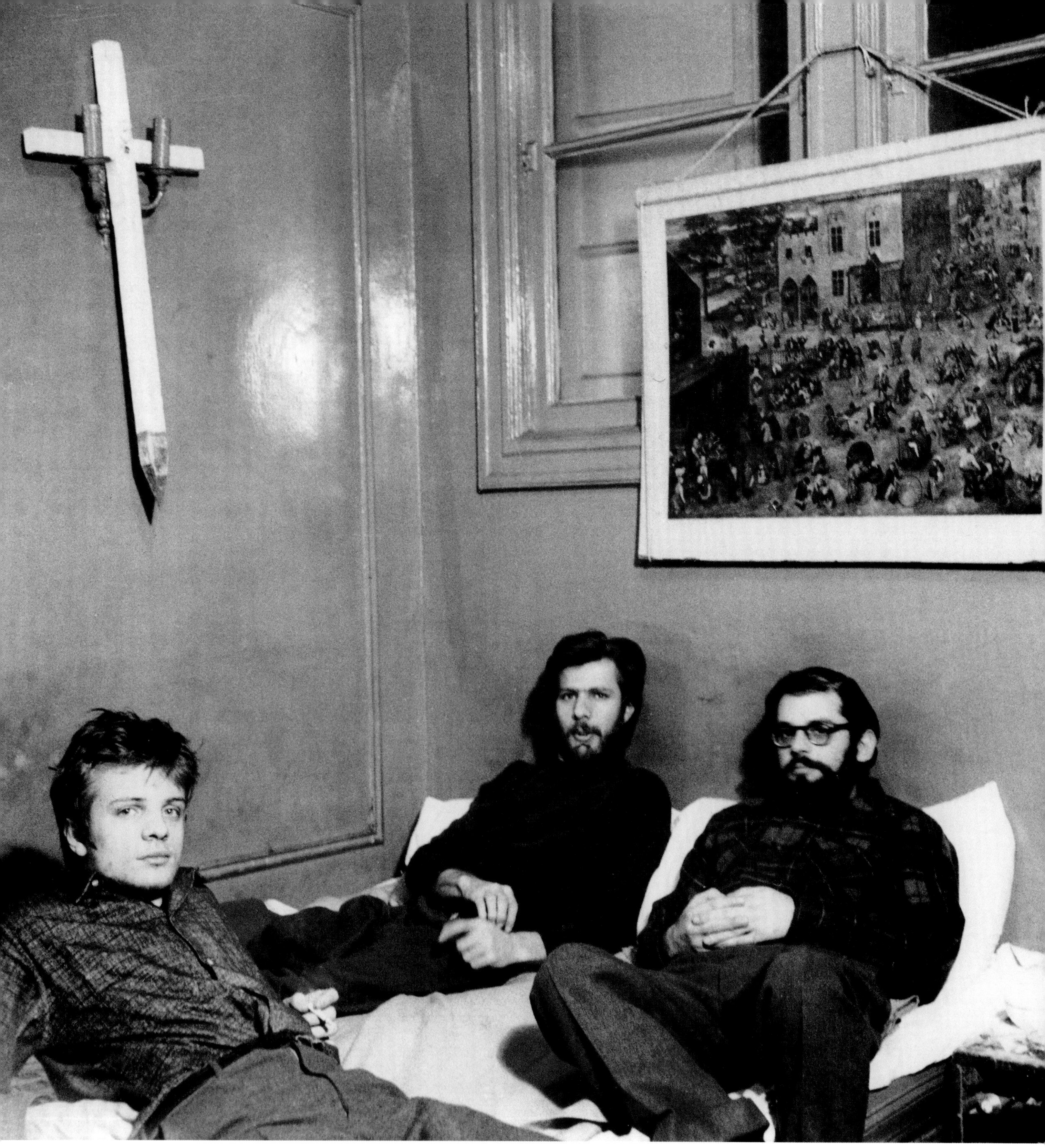

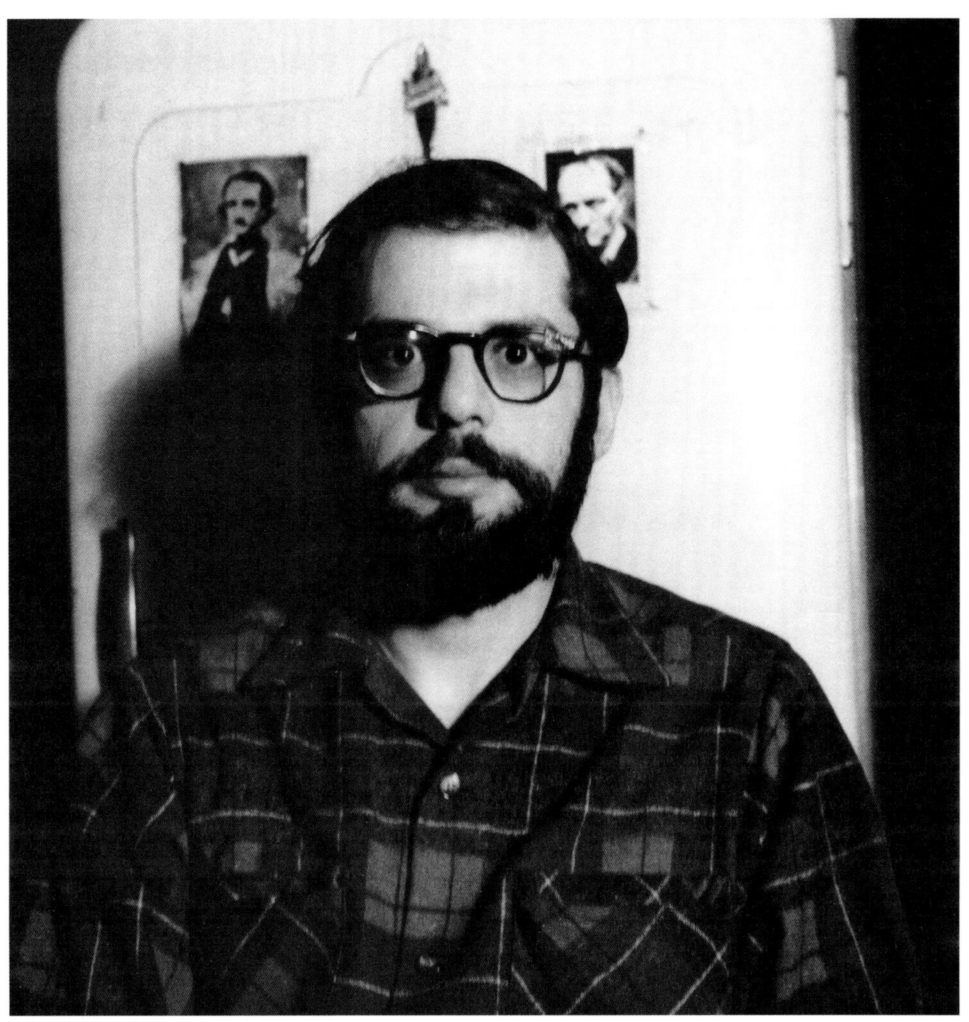

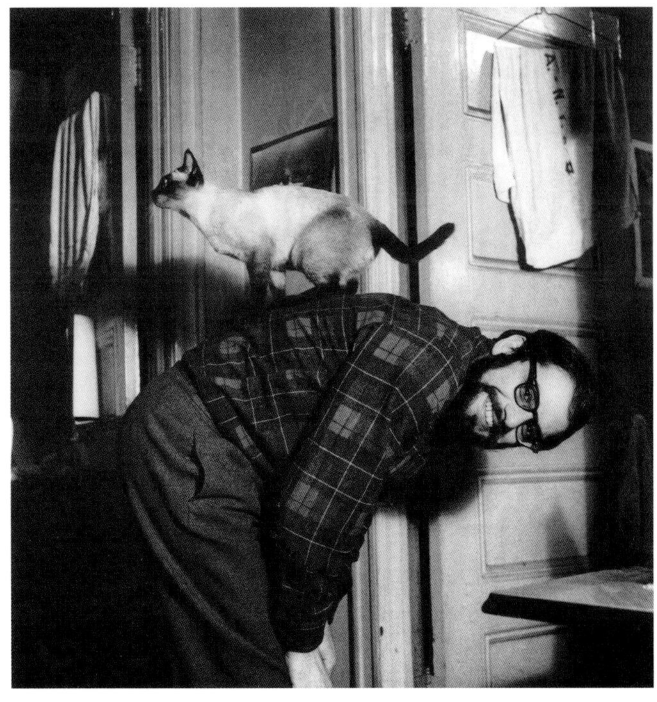

Opposite page: From right, Allen Ginsberg, his longtime companion
Peter Orlovsky, and Orlovsky's brother Lafcadio relax in their apartment
at 170 East Second St., January 9, 1960. Above: The photos taped to
the refrigerator door are of Edgar Allan Poe (left) and Charles Baudelaire.
Left: Ginsberg spent his entire adult life in the East Village.

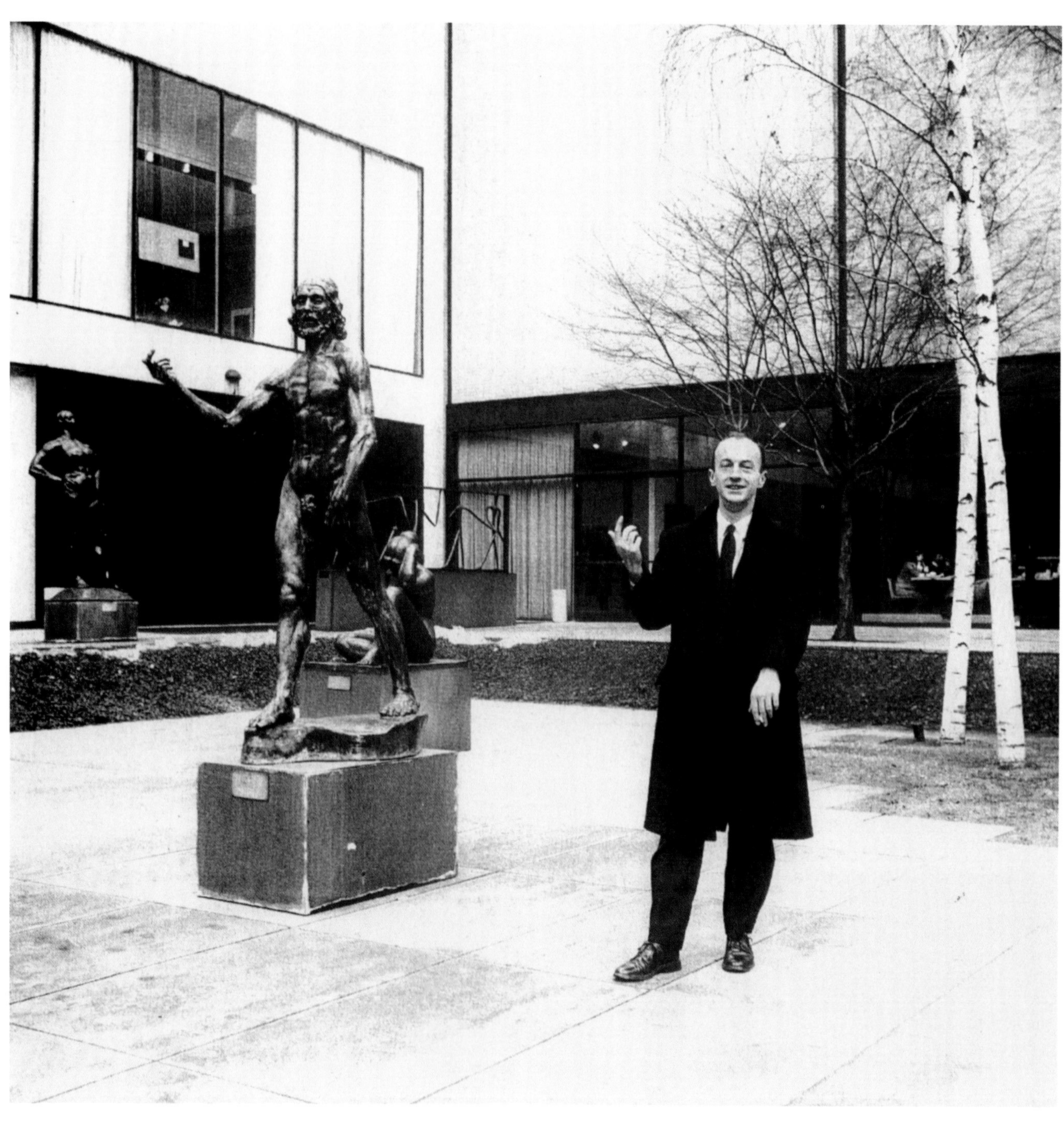

Poet Frank O'Hara, a curator at the Museum of Modern Art, poses with
Auguste Rodin's *St. John the Baptist Preaching* in the museum's garden,
January 20, 1960. O'Hara bridged many of the city's creative communities
until his accidental death on a Fire Island beach in 1966.

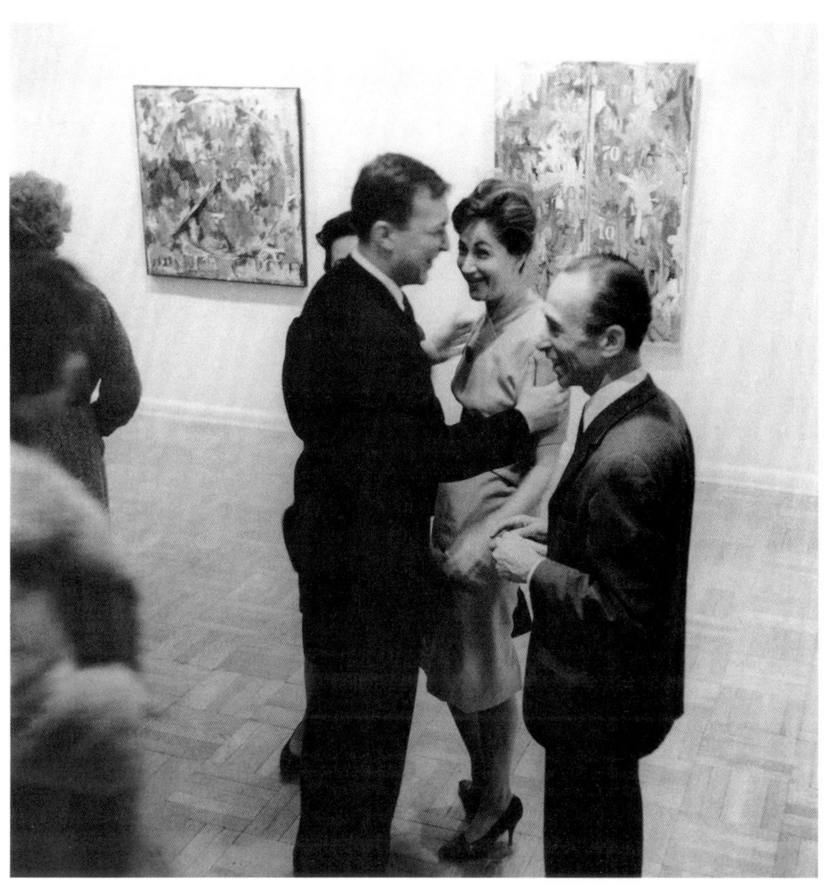

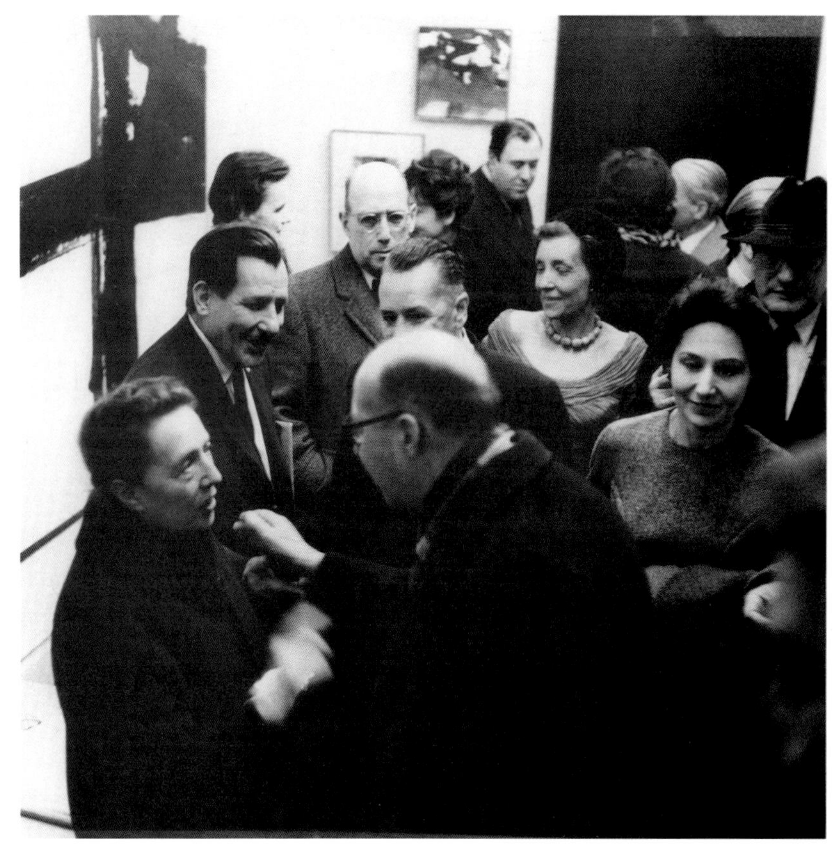

Jasper Johns greets collector Ethel Scull at the opening of Johns's exhibition at the Leo Castelli Gallery, 4 East Seventy-Seventh St., February 15, 1960. Leo Castelli, a leading dealer of contemporary art for five decades, is standing next to Scull. With her husband, taxi baron Robert Scull, Ethel was an important collector of Pop art in the sixties.

Painter Franz Kline (left, in dark suit) smiles at his Sidney Janis Gallery opening, March 7, 1960. Also visible are Janis's wife, writer and collector Harriet Grossman Janis (to his right); fellow Abstract Expressionist William Baziotes (center, partially obscured behind an unidentified balding man); his wife, Ethel (right, in sweater); painter Mark Rothko (far right, in hat and looking toward camera); sculptor Louise Bourgeois (with large necklace); and her husband, Robert Goldwater (to her right), an art historian and first director of the Museum of Primitive Art. At the back of the crowd are British art critic and curator David Sylvester (far left) and Willem de Kooning (far right).

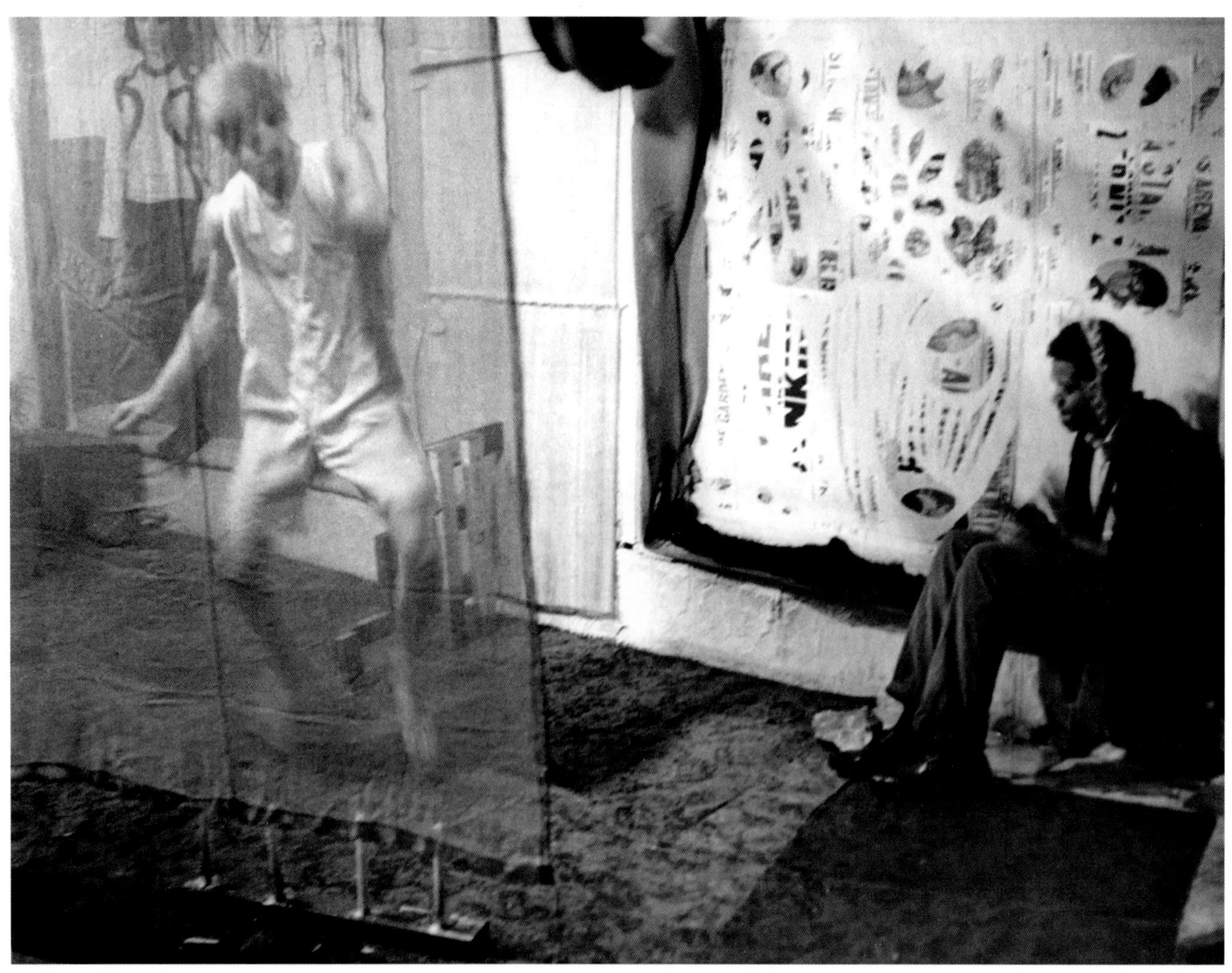

Pop artist Red Grooms (born Charles Rogers Grooms), accompanied by artist Bob Thompson on bongos, performs in an early happening by figurative painter Marcia Marcus, titled *In the Garden: A Ballet*, at the Delancey Street Museum, 148 Delancey St., February 6, 1960.

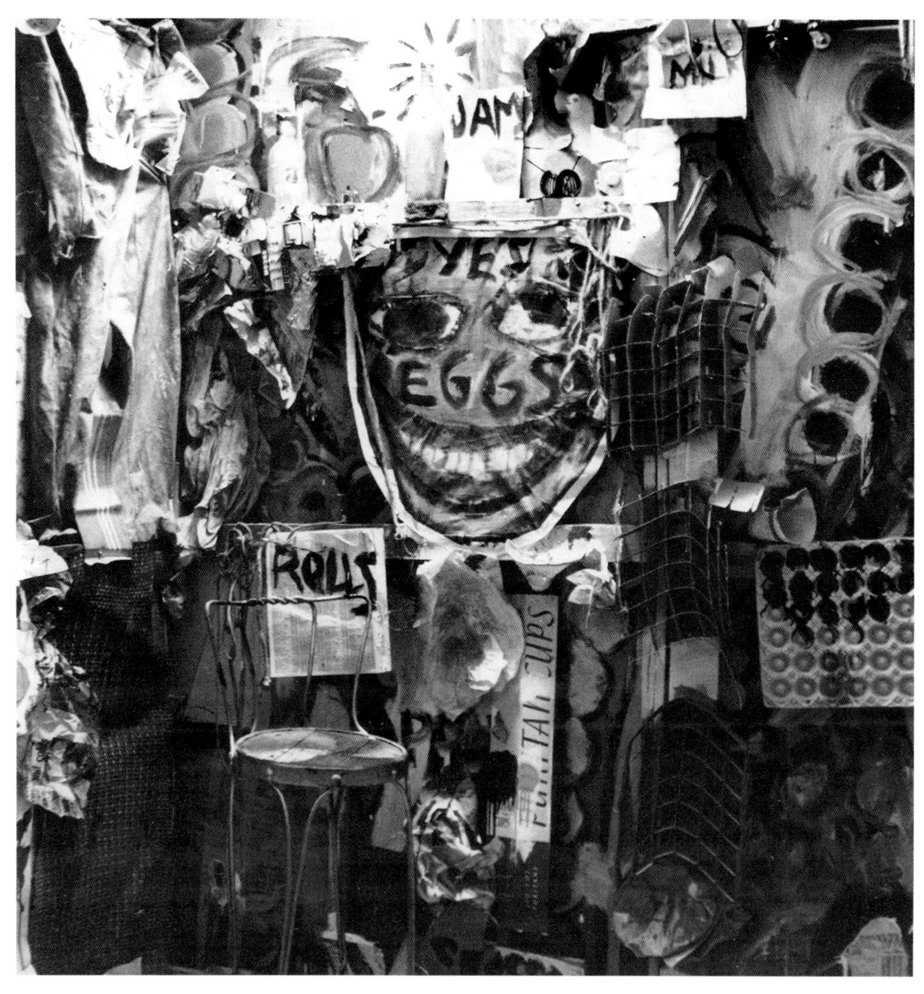

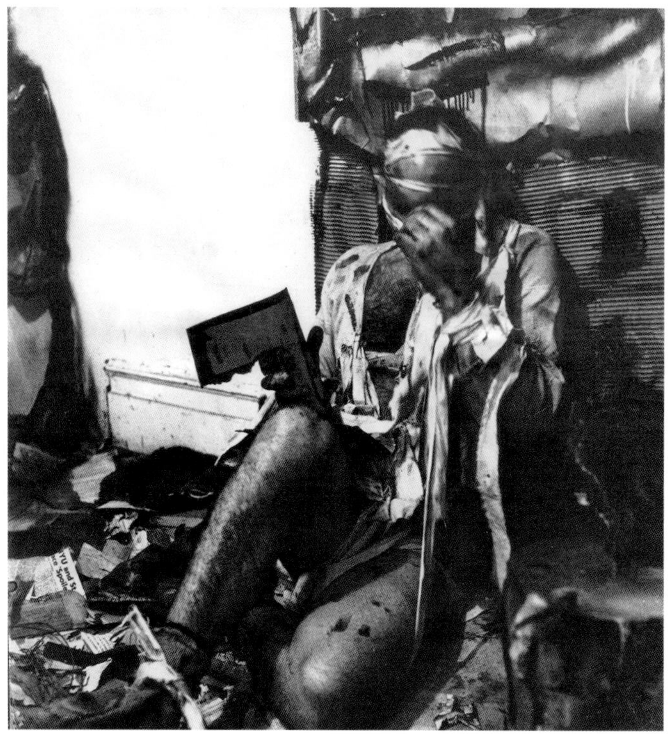

Ray Gun Specs (also known as *Ray Gun Spex*) was a collaborative happening at the Judson Gallery in the Judson Memorial Church created by Claes Oldenburg, Jim Dine, and others, featuring performances, painting, sculpture, and even an auction for the audience. The performances were a precursor to Oldenburg's own *Ray Gun Theater* shows in 1962. Top: The gallery was set up for the performances, February 20, 1960. Bottom: Oldenburg appears in a scene from "Snapshots from the Street," March 1, 1960. *Ray Gun Specs* ran from February 29 to March 2.

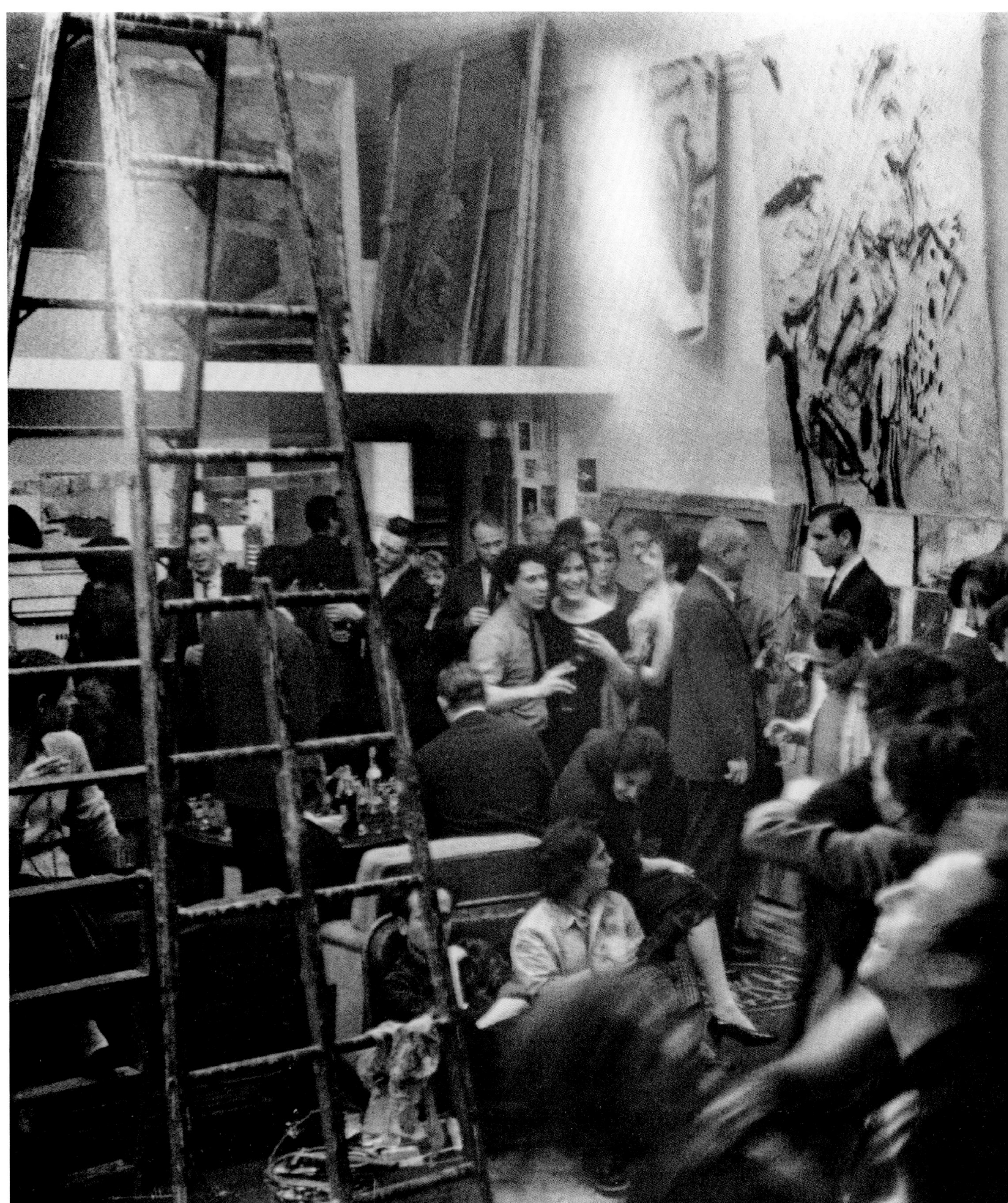

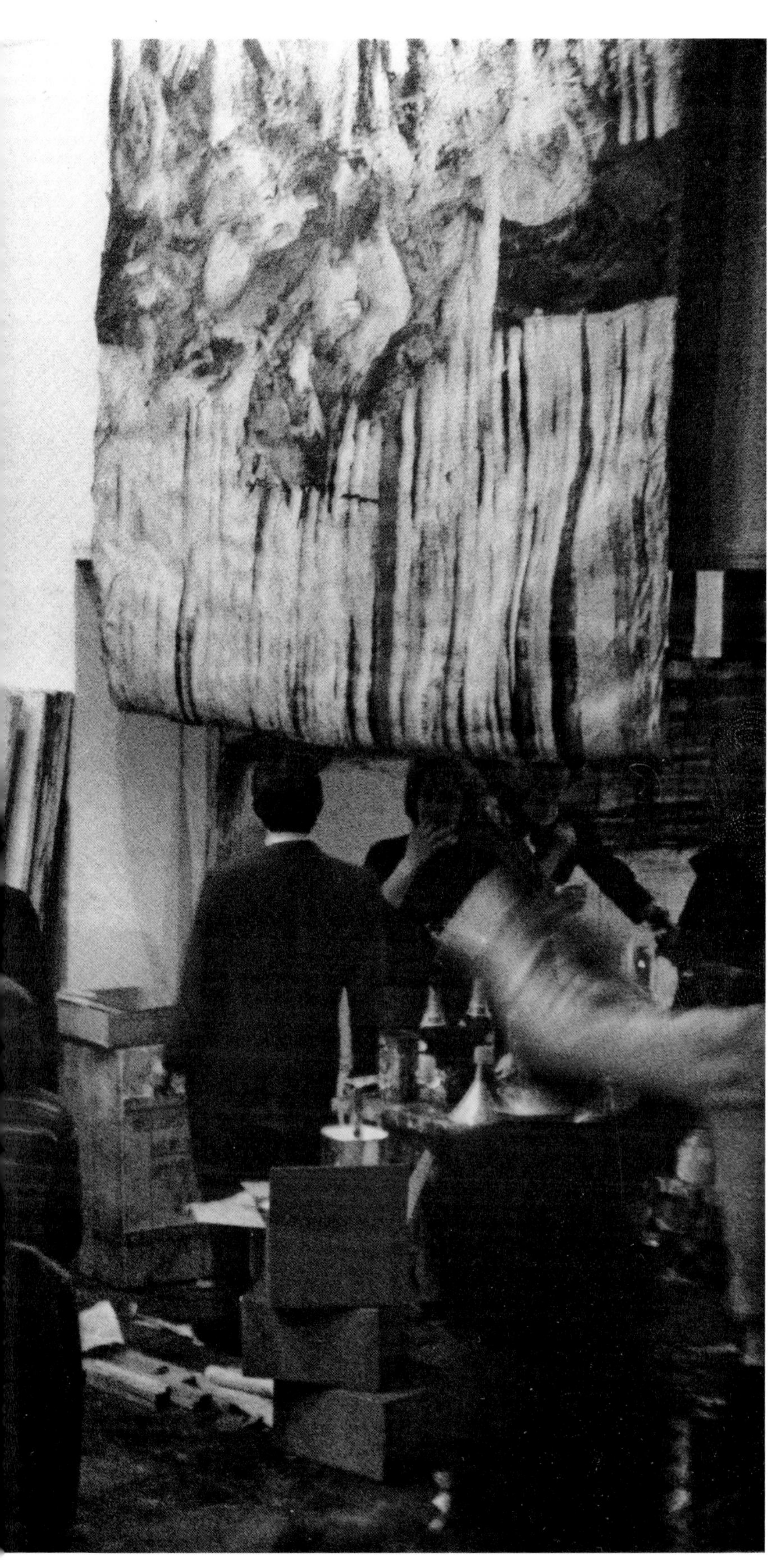

Artist and filmmaker Alfred Leslie (center, in light shirt and dark tie), who codirected the short film *Pull My Daisy*, talks to guests at his loft party, West Twenty-Second St., March 28, 1960.

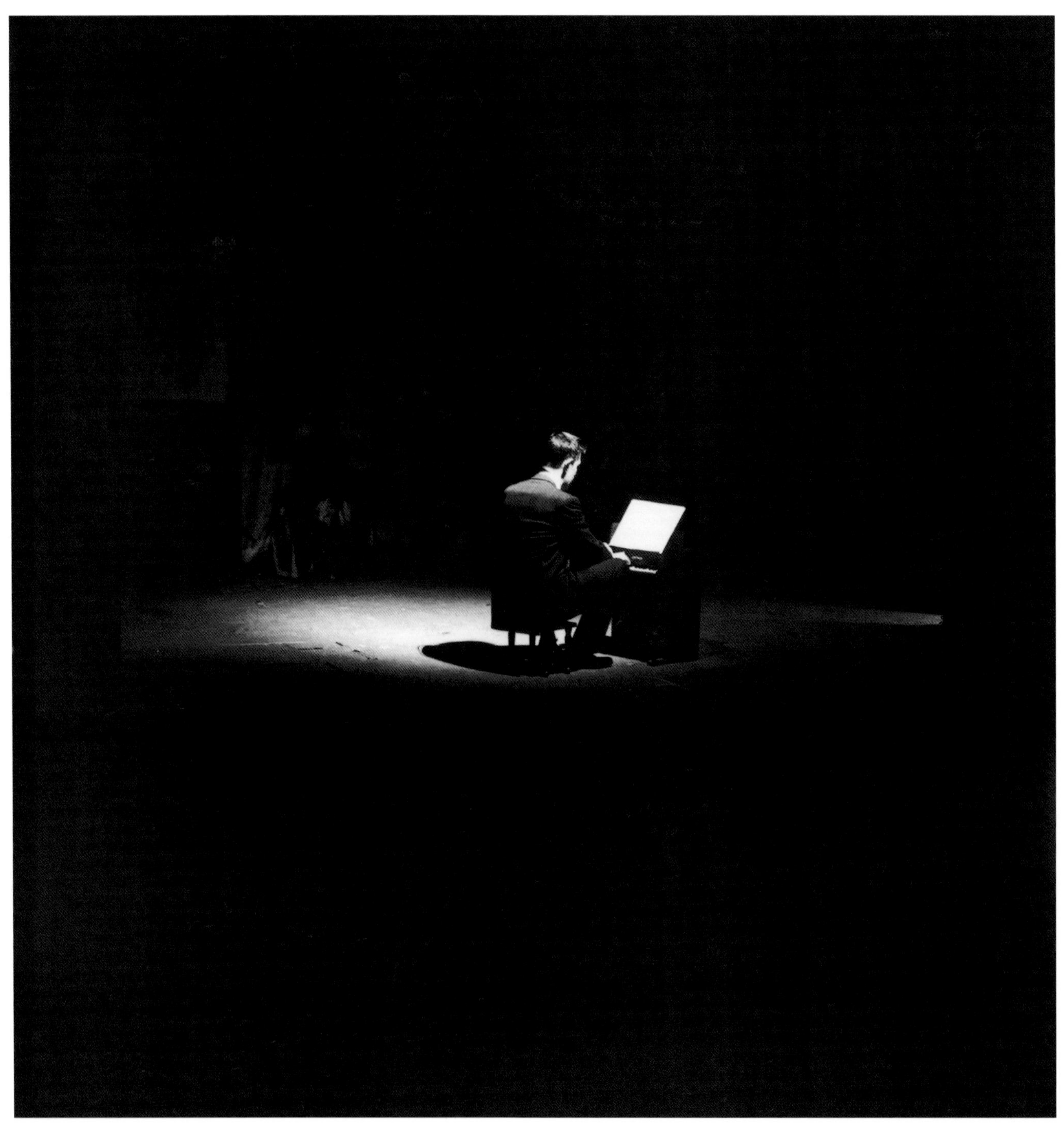

The composer John Cage, illuminated by a single spotlight,
performs his Suite for Toy Piano at the Living Theatre, 69 West
Fourteenth St., March 14, 1960.

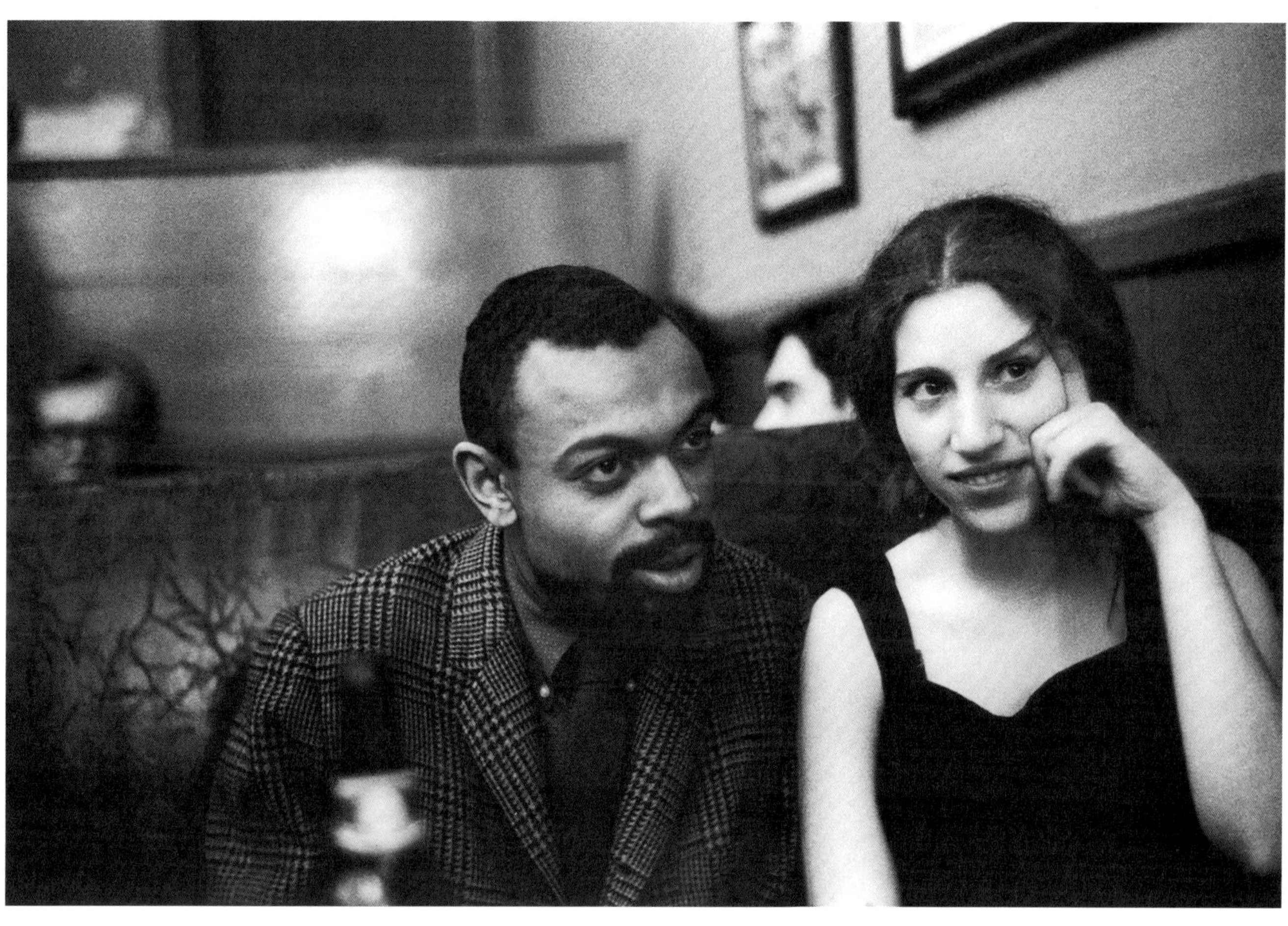

Poet, playwright, and activist LeRoi Jones (later known as Amiri Baraka) and poet Diane di Prima sit together in a booth at the Cedar Tavern, then at 24 University Place, April 5, 1960. The following year, the close friends would begin the publication of a literary magazine titled *The Floating Bear*.

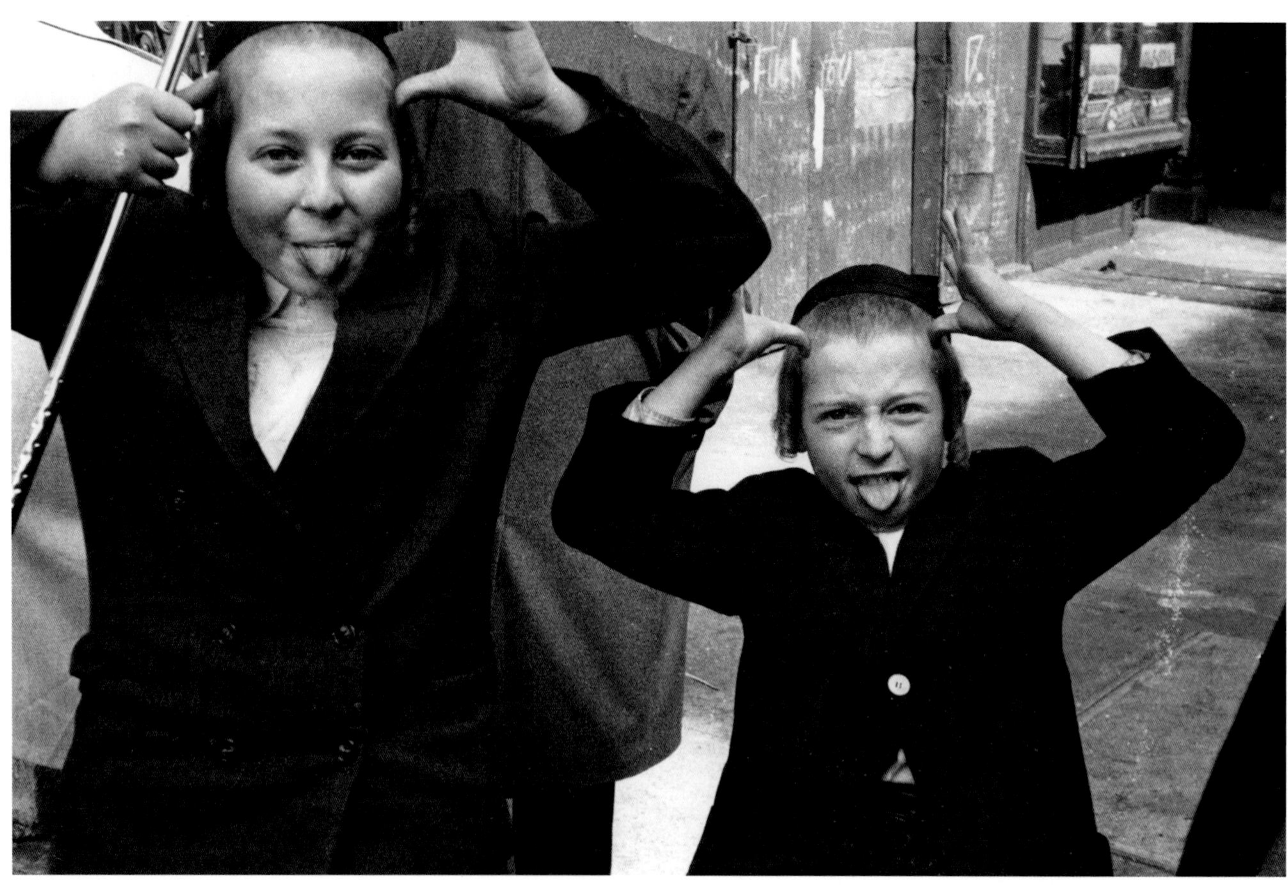

Orthodox Jewish boys make faces on East Tenth St., April 13, 1960. The
East Village and the Lower East Side were home to a large population of
Eastern European Jews from the late nineteenth century, though most had
left by the sixties, with only a small Orthodox community remaining.

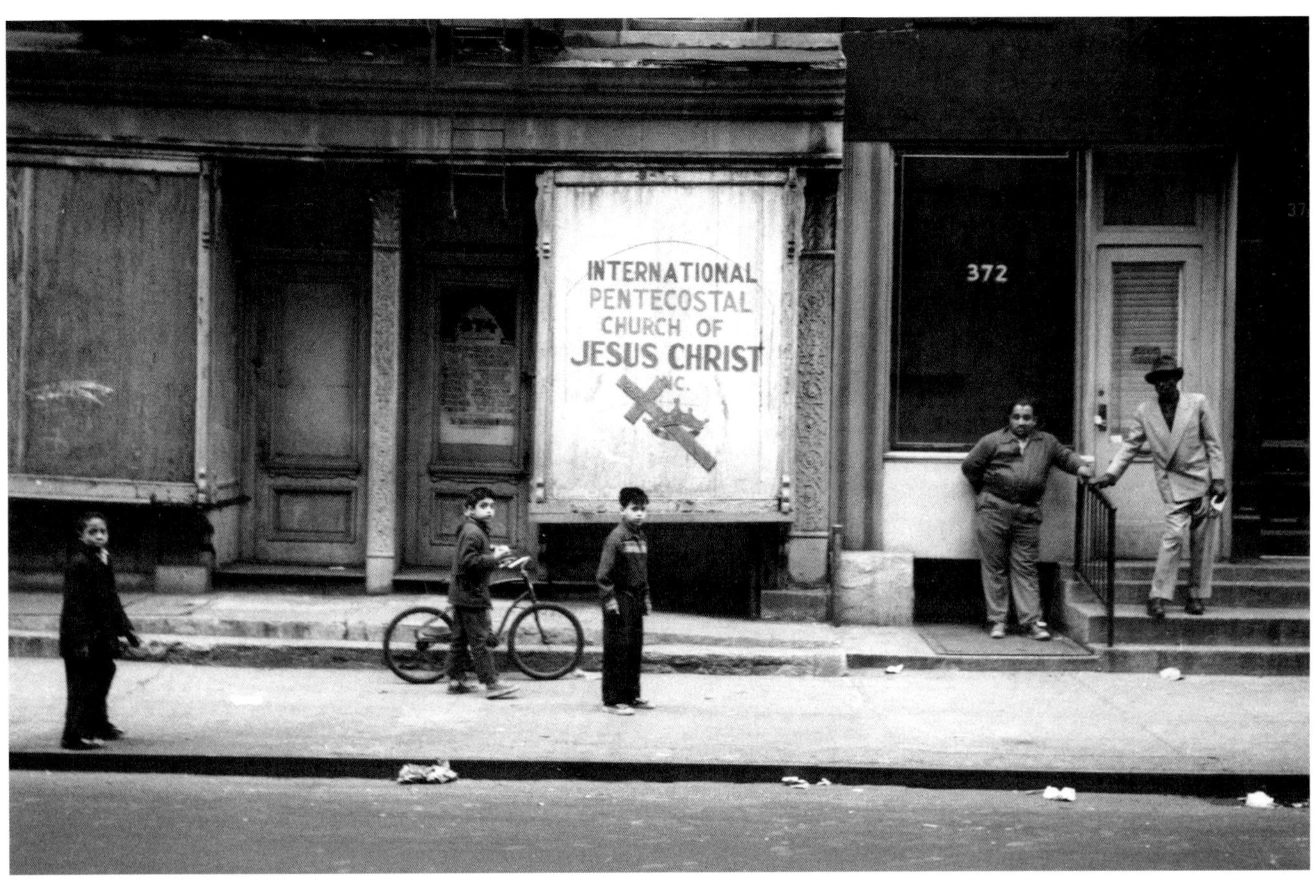

People in front of a church on East Tenth St., between Avenues B and C, April 15, 1960. By then, earlier immigrant populations of Germans and Eastern European Jews had largely moved away, and the Alphabet City neighborhood, named for Avenues A through D, was gaining a largely Puerto Rican population and a new nickname, "Loisaida" (Spanglish—a mix of Spanish and English—for the broader Lower East Side area).

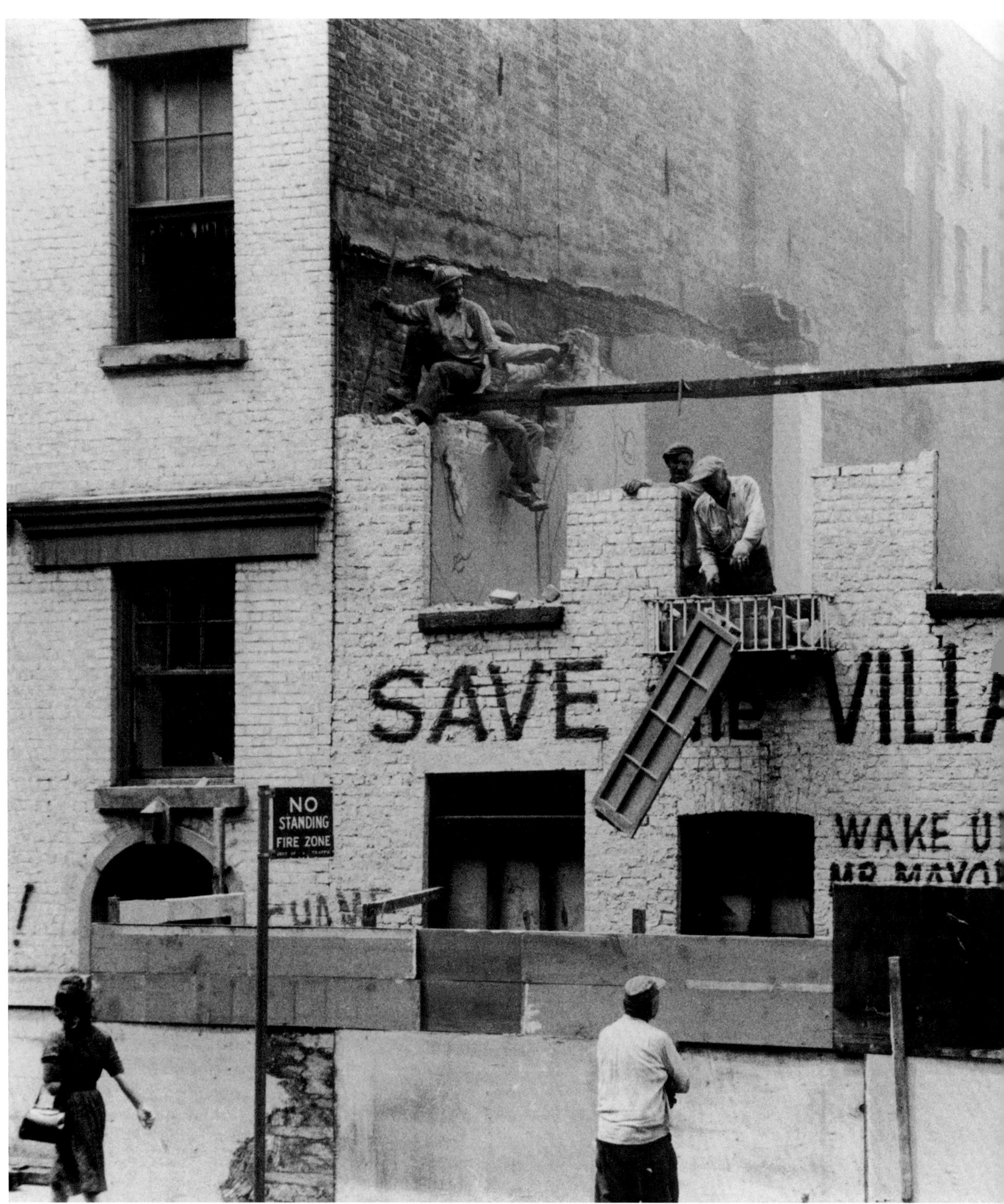

NO STANDING FIRE ZONE
SAVE THE VILLA
WAKE U
MR MAYO

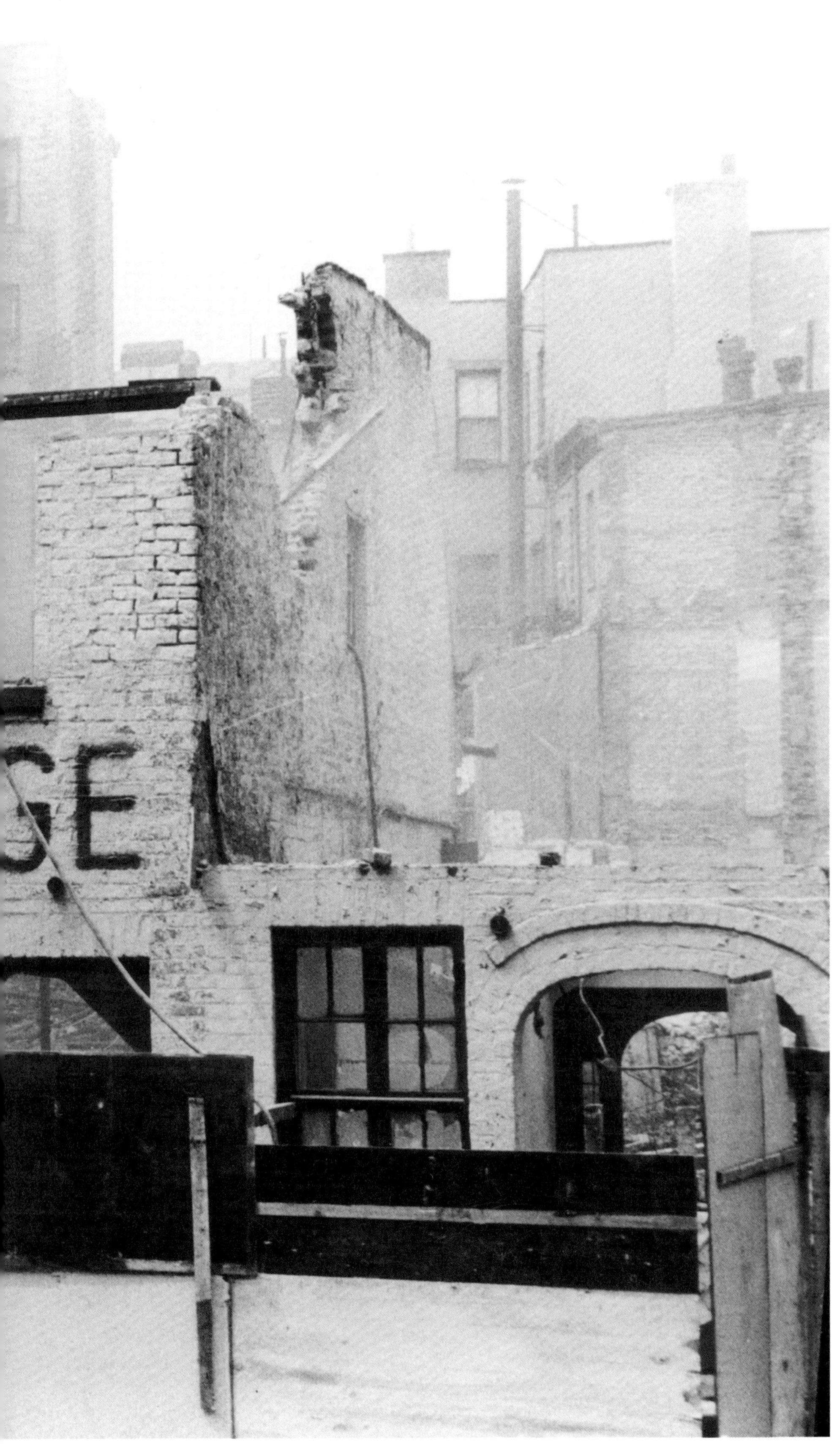

Workers demolish the former studio of sculptor
Arnold Henry Bergier, the facade of which is
painted with the slogans "Save the Village" and
"Wake Up Mr. Mayor!," 33 Greenwich Ave.,
at West Tenth St., May 19, 1960. Bergier was
a founder of the Save the Village Committee
in 1959 and fought high-rise development.
McDarrah passed the corner on a regular basis as
the *Village Voice* offices at the time were across
the street at 22 Greenwich Ave.

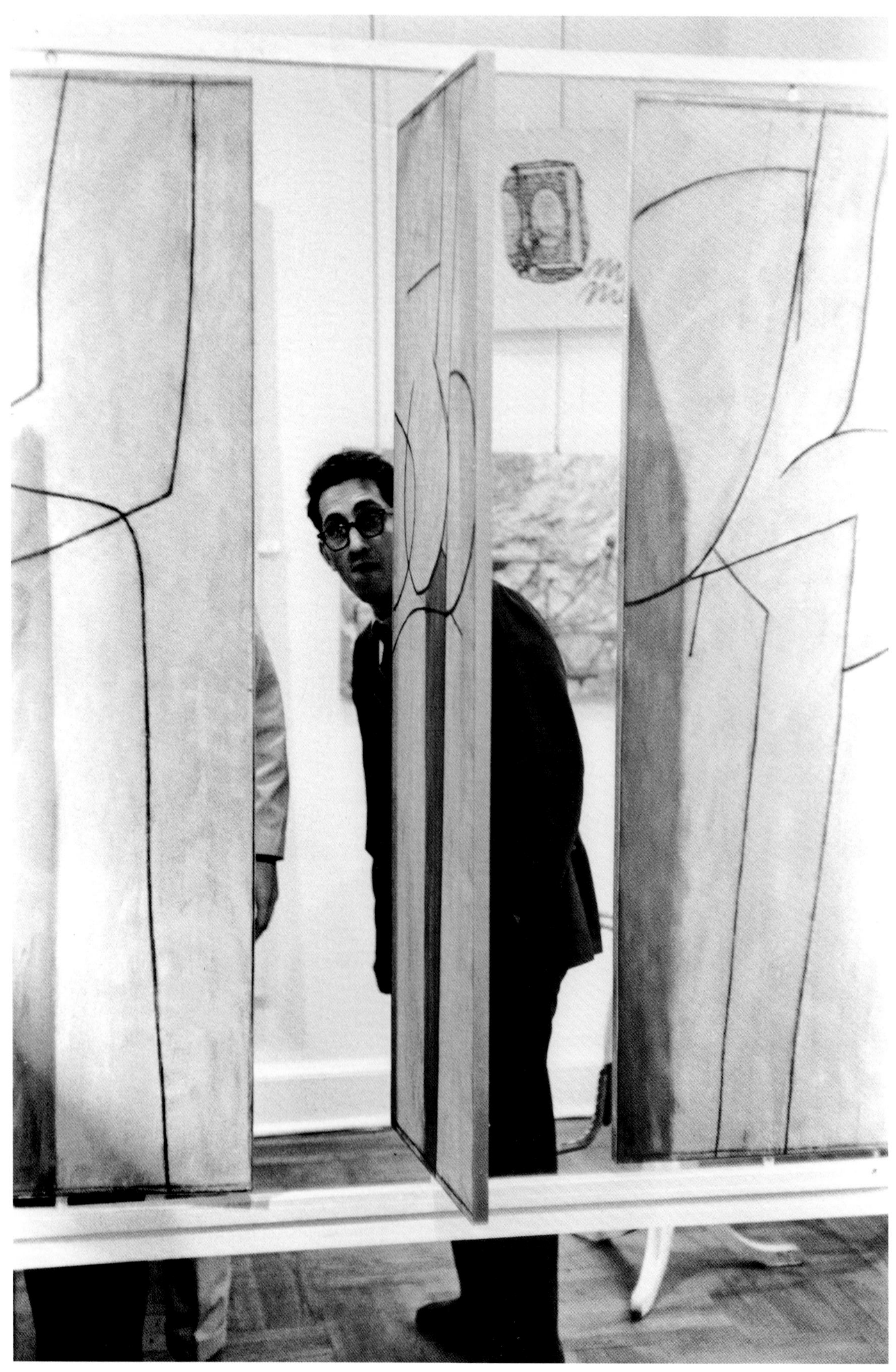

72

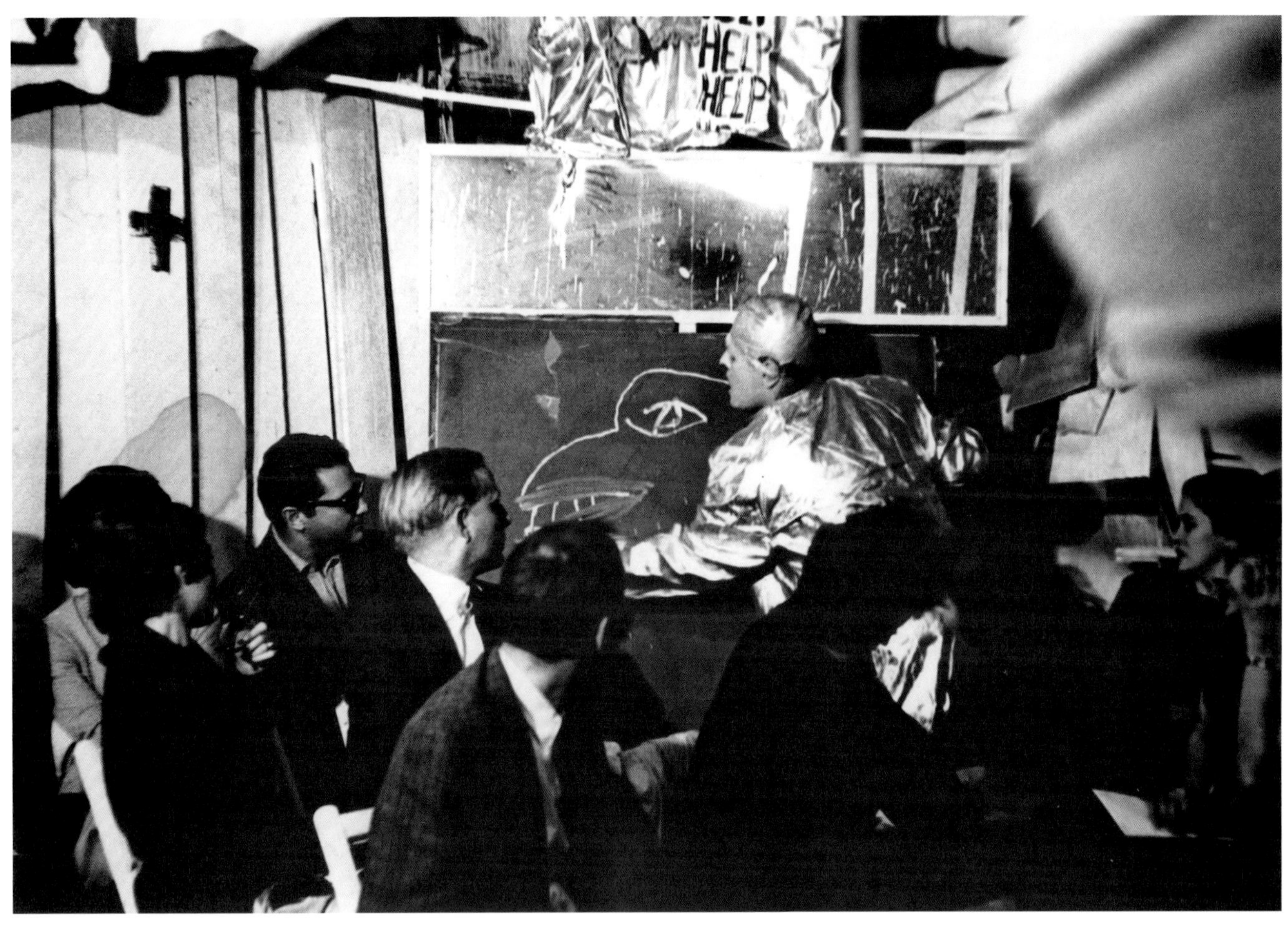

Artist Frank Stella peeks around his work in the *New Media* exhibition, which showcased art made from discarded objects and garbage, at the Martha Jackson Gallery, 32 East Sixty-Ninth St., September 28, 1960. Stella's pursuit of the picture-as-object led to a life of exploring three-dimensionality in mostly wall-mounted works.

Pop artist Jim Dine in his performance piece *Car Crash*, Judson Gallery, November 1, 1960.

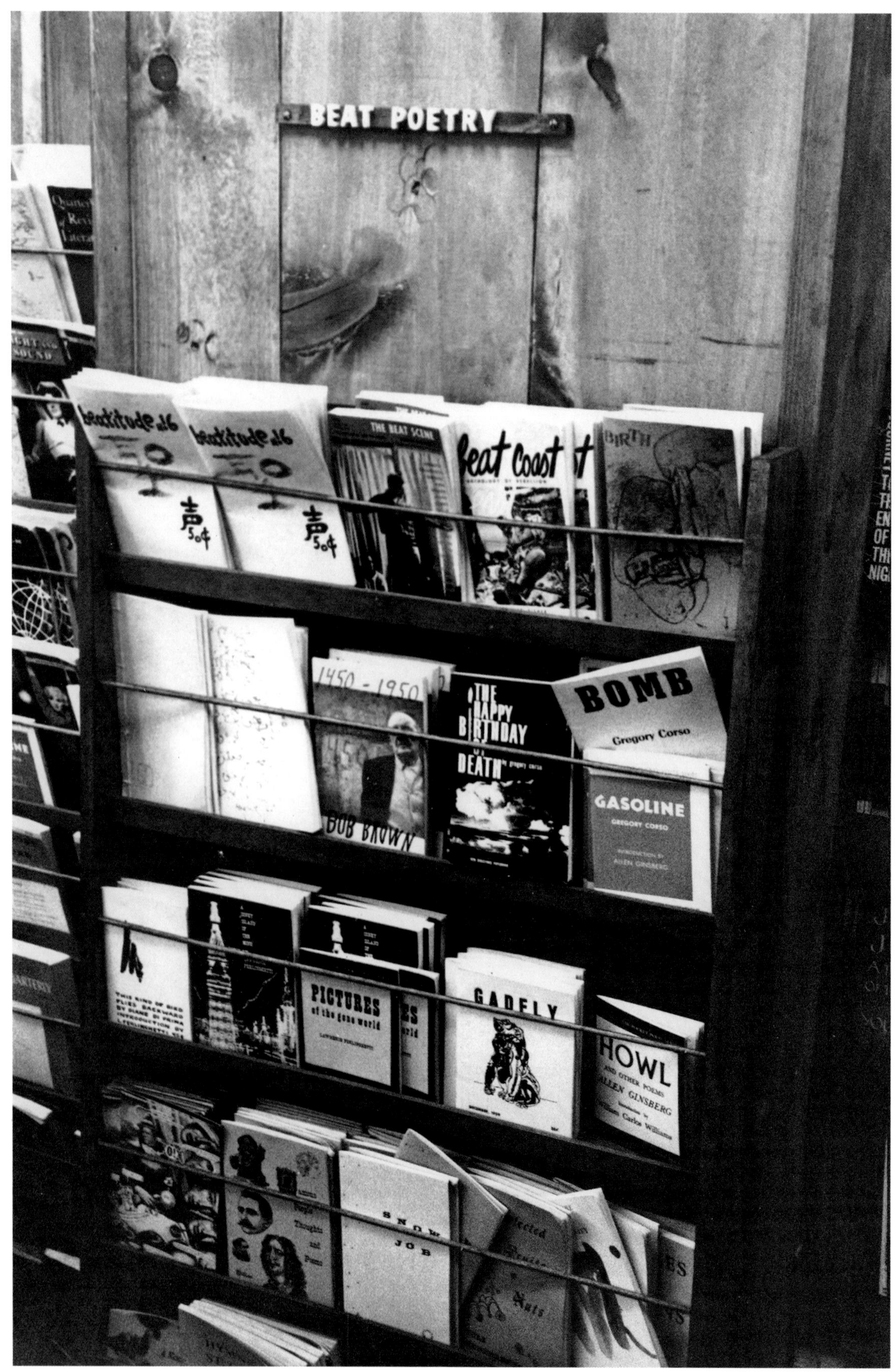

BEAT POETRY
beatitude #6
beatitude #6
THE BEAT SCENE
beat coast
BIRTH
1450 - 1950
THE HAPPY BIRTHDAY OF DEATH
BOMB
Gregory Corso
BOB BROWN
GASOLINE
GREGORY CORSO
PICTURES
of the gone world
GADFLY
HOWL
AND OTHER POEMS
ALLEN GINSBERG
SNOW JOB

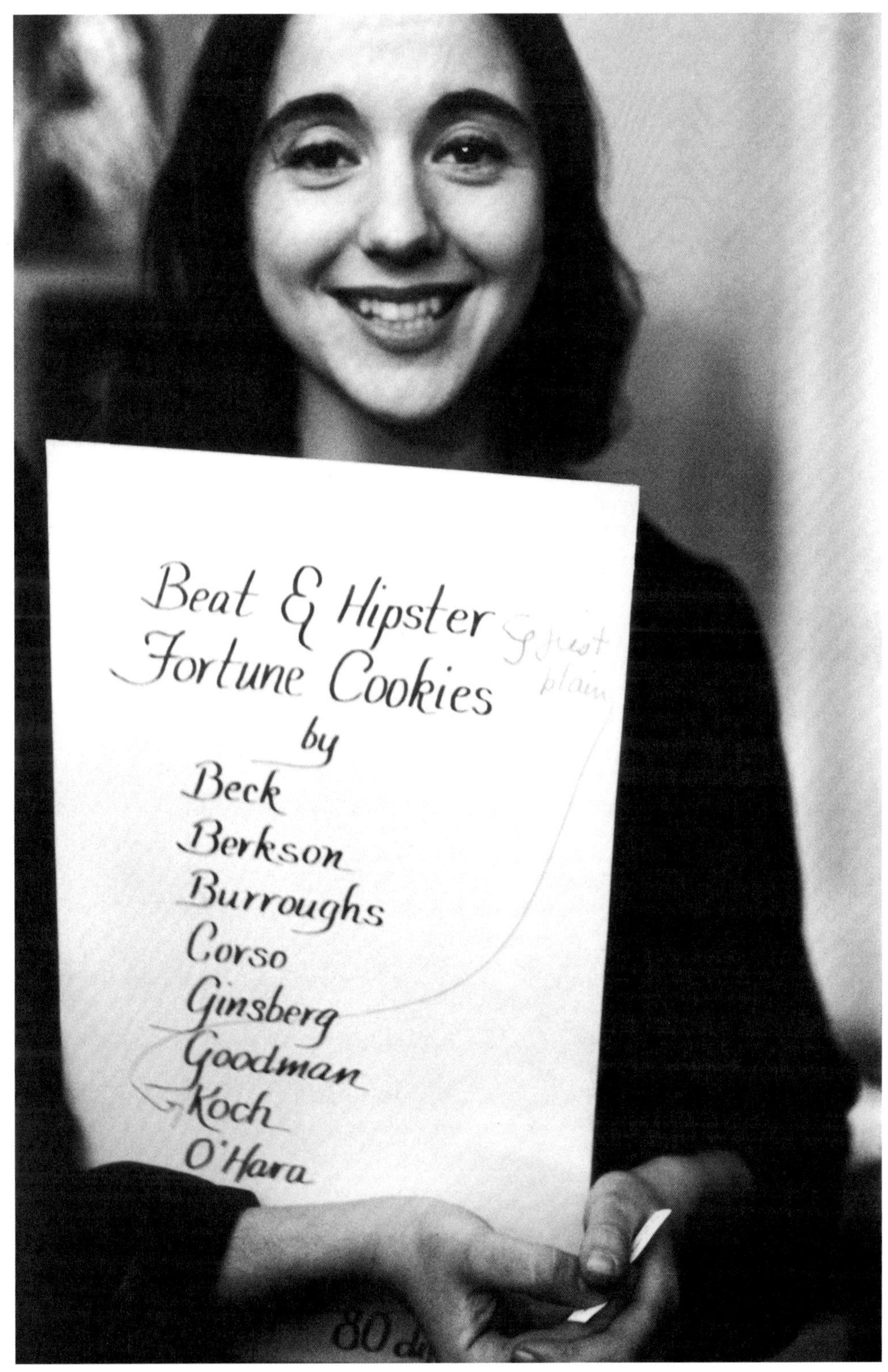

A rack of "Beat Poetry" at the Paperback Book Gallery, 90 West Third St., November 19, 1960. Independent bookstores were ubiquitous in sixties New York, especially in Greenwich Village.

Actress Cynthia Robinson as she poses with a menu of "Beat & Hipster Fortune Cookies" in the lobby of the Living Theatre, 69 West Fourteenth St., November 28, 1960.

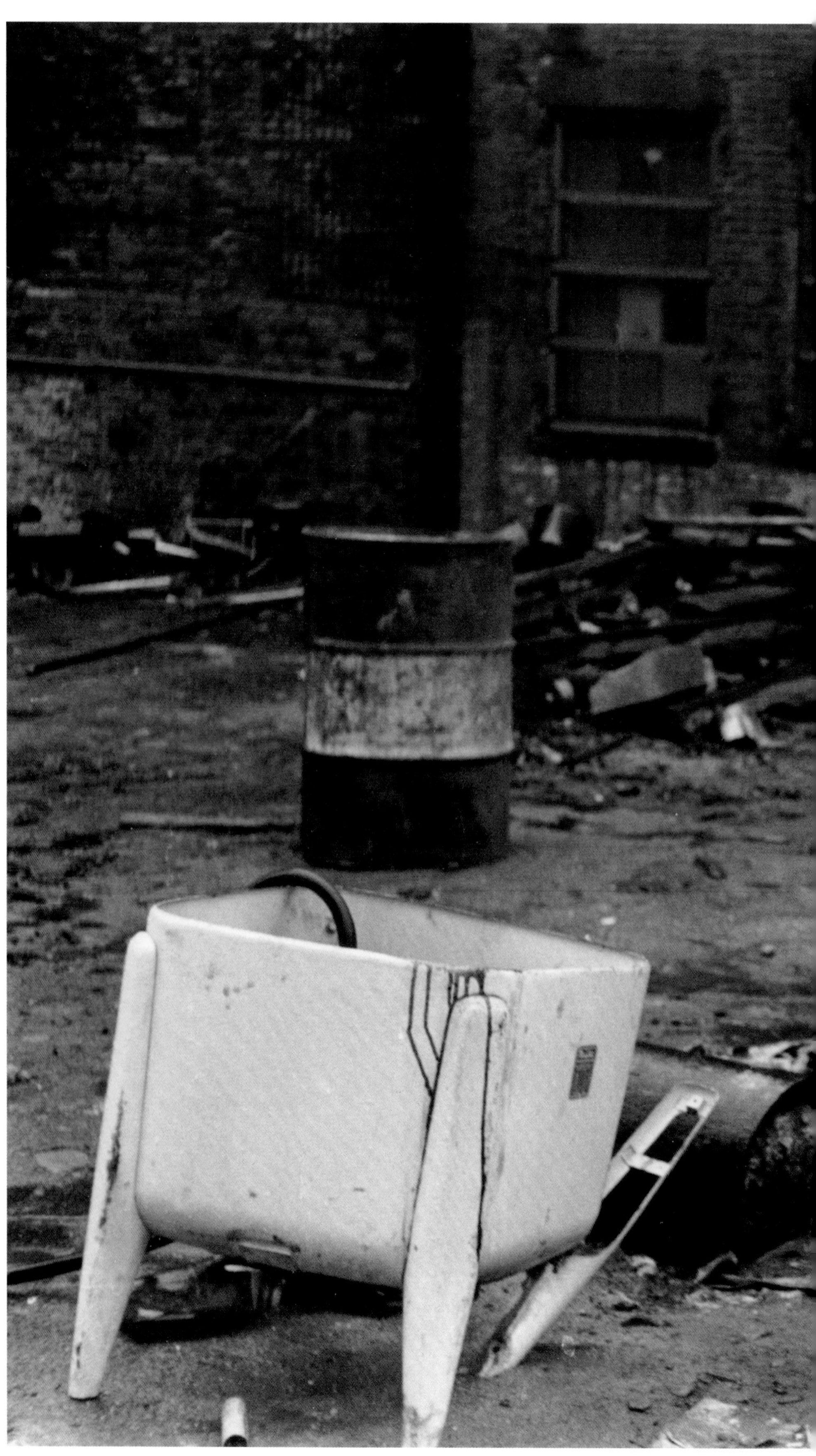

Robert Rauschenberg, who often integrated trash
and other everyday objects into his artwork, reads
a newspaper in a vacant lot near his Front Street
studio, January 15, 1961.

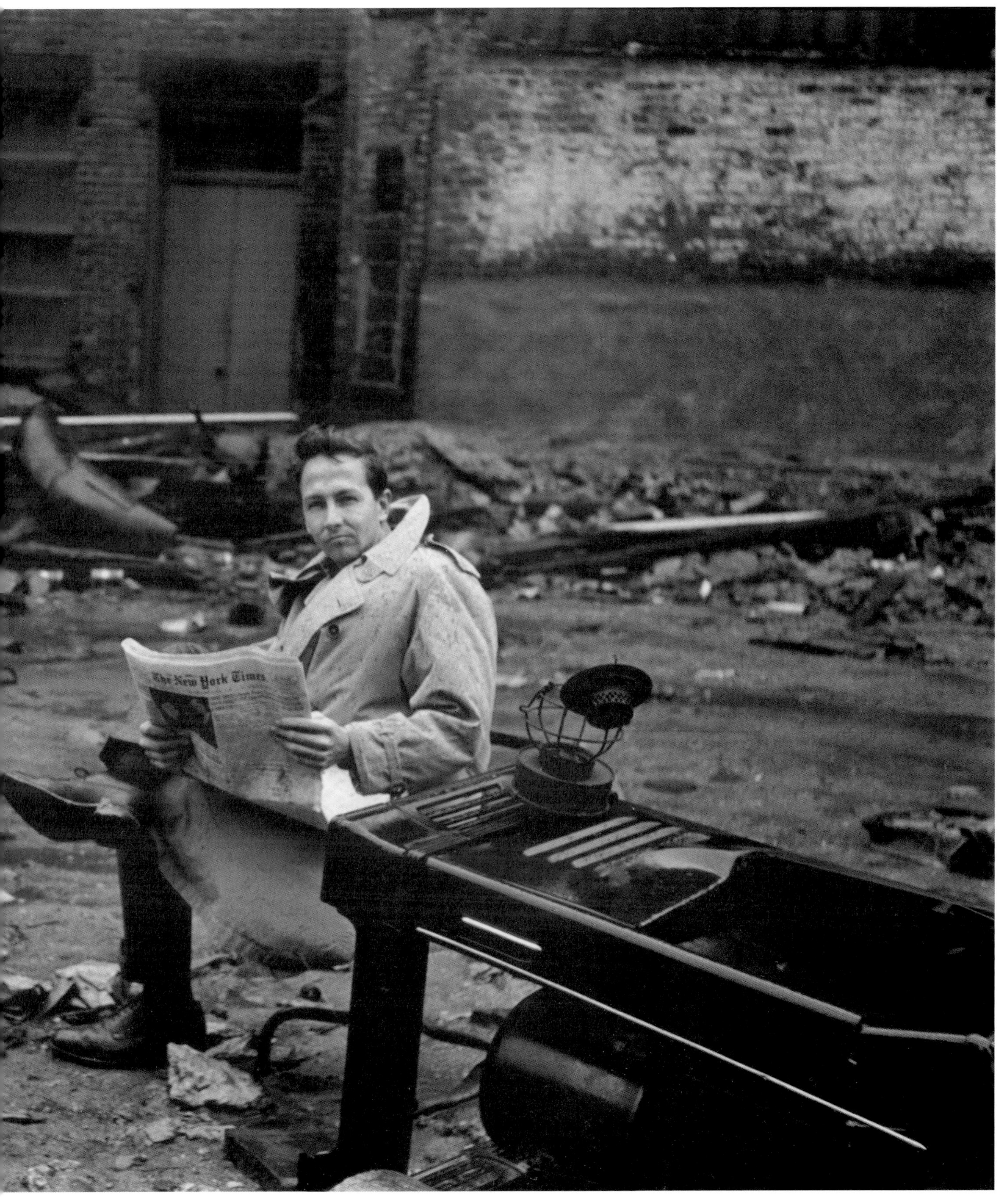
The New York Times

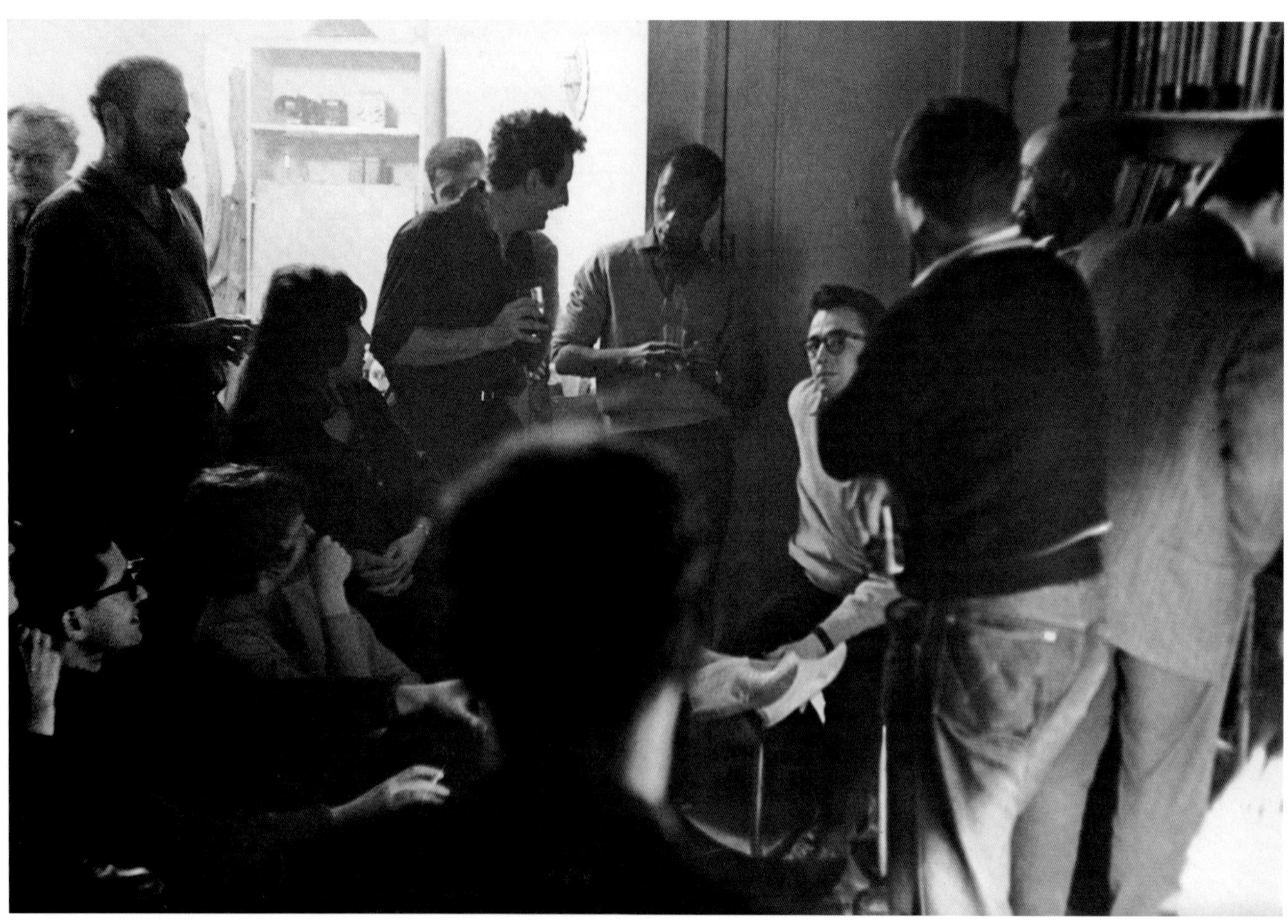

In the apartment of theater director Robert Cordier (center, in dark shirt with glass in hand, looking to his left), guests gather to discuss—and, for some, to celebrate—"the Funeral of the Beat Generation," 85 Christopher St., January 23, 1961. Among them are writer James Baldwin (looking at Cordier), painter De Hirsh Margules; poet, singer-songwriter, and children's book author Shel Silverstein; Sylvia Topp; Gloria Schoffel McDarrah; poet Howard Hart; writer Norman Mailer; Ted Joans; and poet and art collector Lester Blackiston.

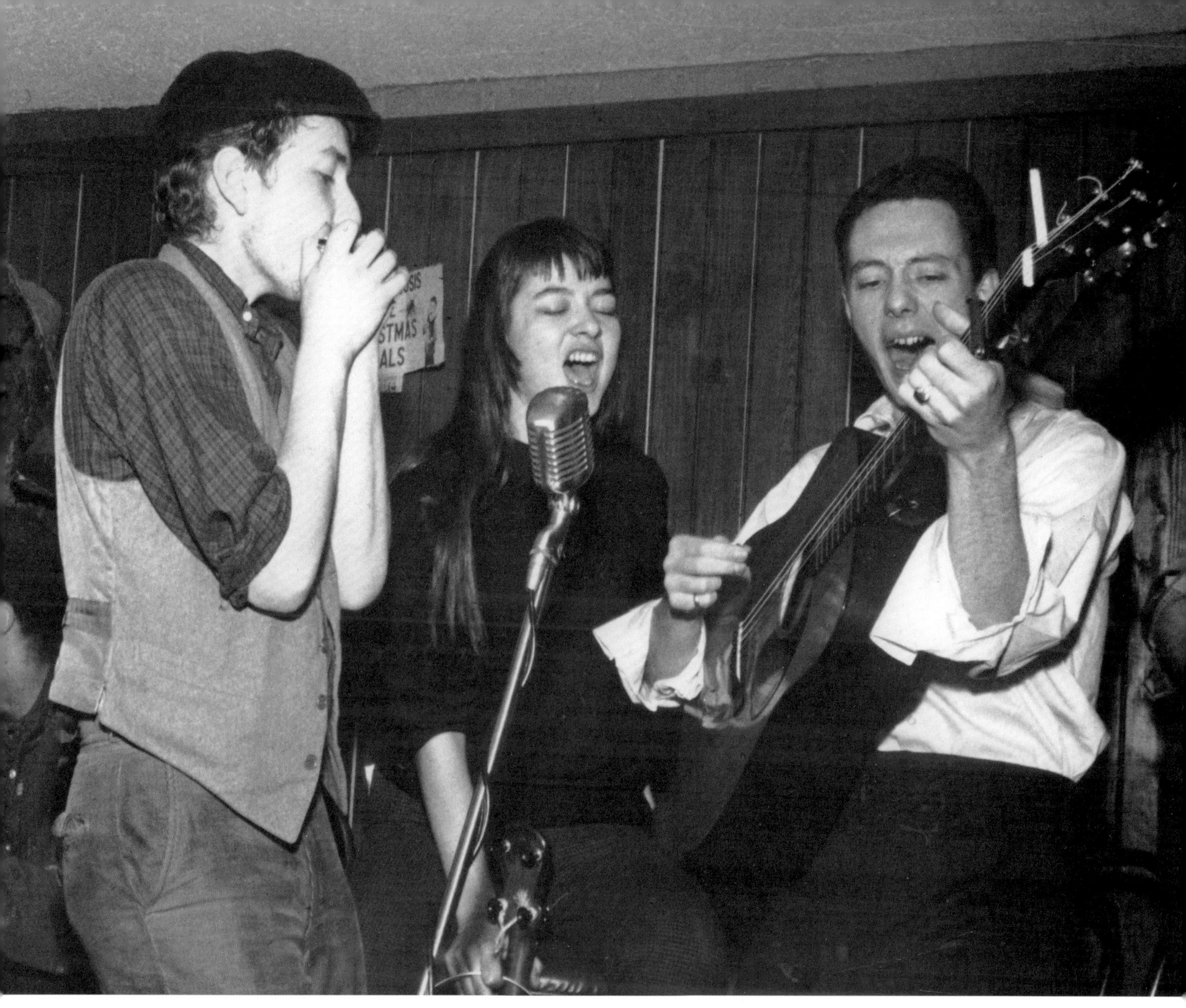

Nineteen-year-old newcomer Bob Dylan (left), Karen Dalton, and Fred Neil (who later wrote the hit song "Everybody's Talkin'") perform at Cafe Wha?, 115 MacDougal St., February 6, 1961. Dylan had arrived in New York from the Midwest less than two weeks earlier, on January 24; since it was a "hootenanny night," he was allowed to play a few Woody Guthrie songs—and found someone to offer him a couch to sleep on. In the basement of the Players Theatre, Cafe Wha? later hosted Jimi Hendrix, Bruce Springsteen, and Richard Pryor en route to stardom.

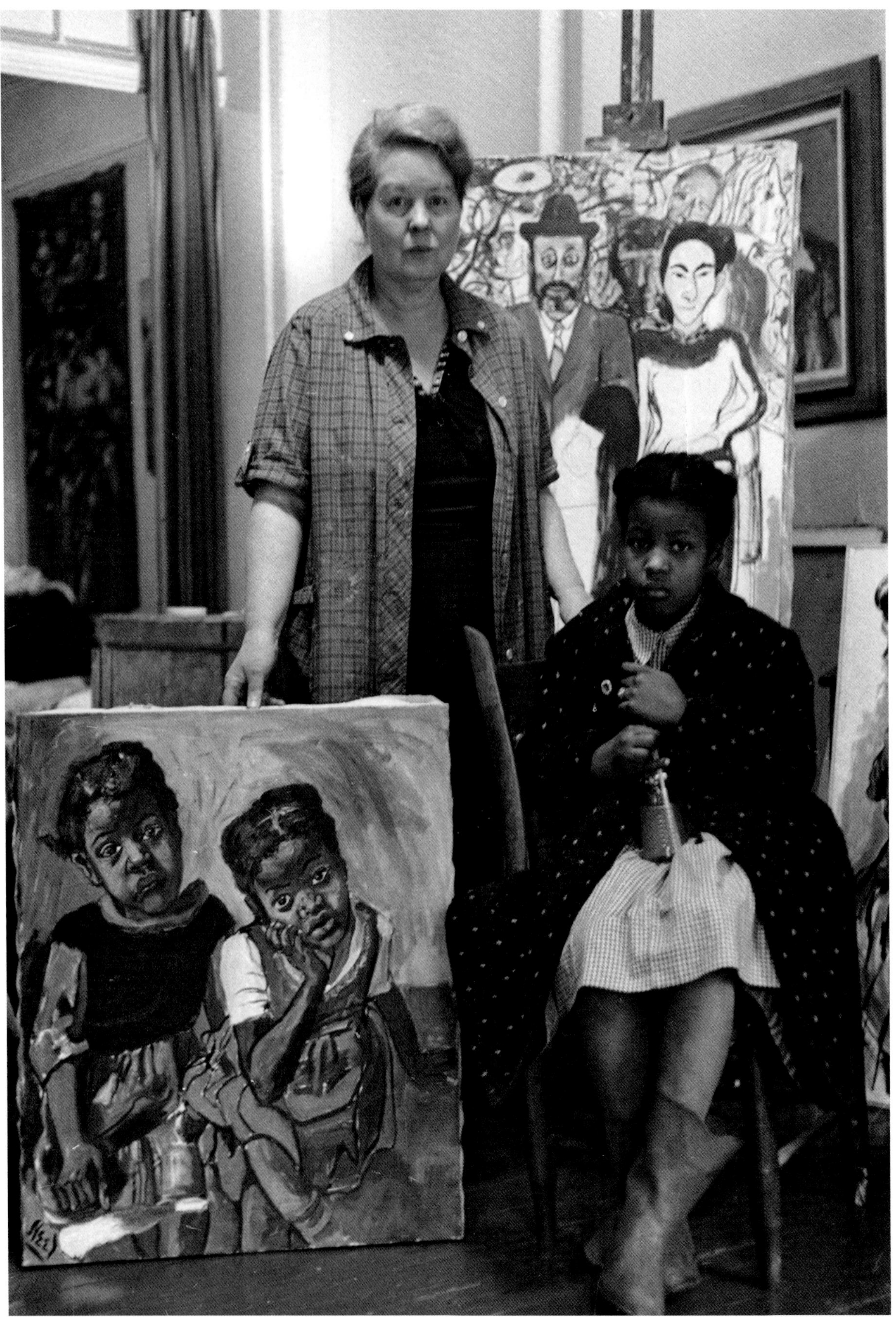

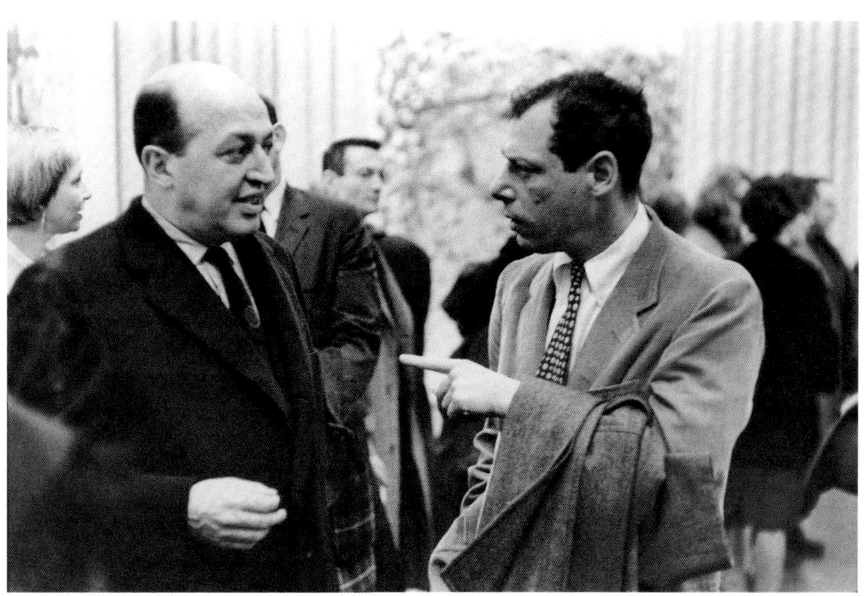

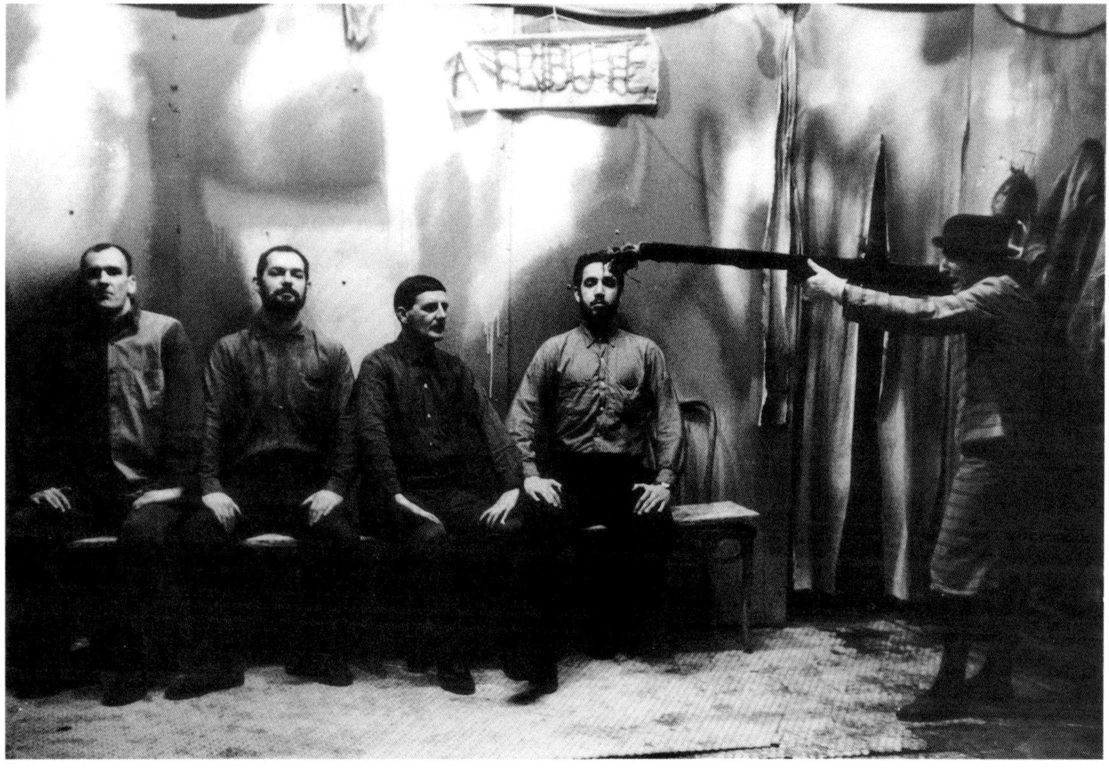

Painter Alice Neel poses in her East Harlem home and studio, 21 East 108th St., February 10, 1961. Seated is her neighbor Antonia Encarnacion, next to *Two Black Girls (Antonia and Carmen Encarnacion).* Neel, whose long engagement with portraiture dated back to the twenties, was the epitome of the Bohemian New York artist. McDarrah befriended her, and he went uptown to shoot her with her paintings numerous times over the years.

Art critic Clement Greenberg (left) speaks with *ARTnews* executive editor (later managing editor) Thomas Hess at the opening of an exhibition by abstract painter Herman Cherry at the Poindexter Gallery, 21 West Fifty-Sixth St., February 20, 1961. Despite propounding sharply divergent theories of art criticism, both men were influential in championing Abstract Expressionist artists, especially Jackson Pollock in Greenberg's case and Willem de Kooning in Hess's.

From left, Tom Wesselmann, Clifford Smith, Edgar Blakeney, Carl Lehmann-Haupt, and Judith Tirsch (with gun) in Claes Oldenburg's *Ironworks/Fotodeath*, Reuben Gallery, 61 Fourth Ave., February 25, 1961.

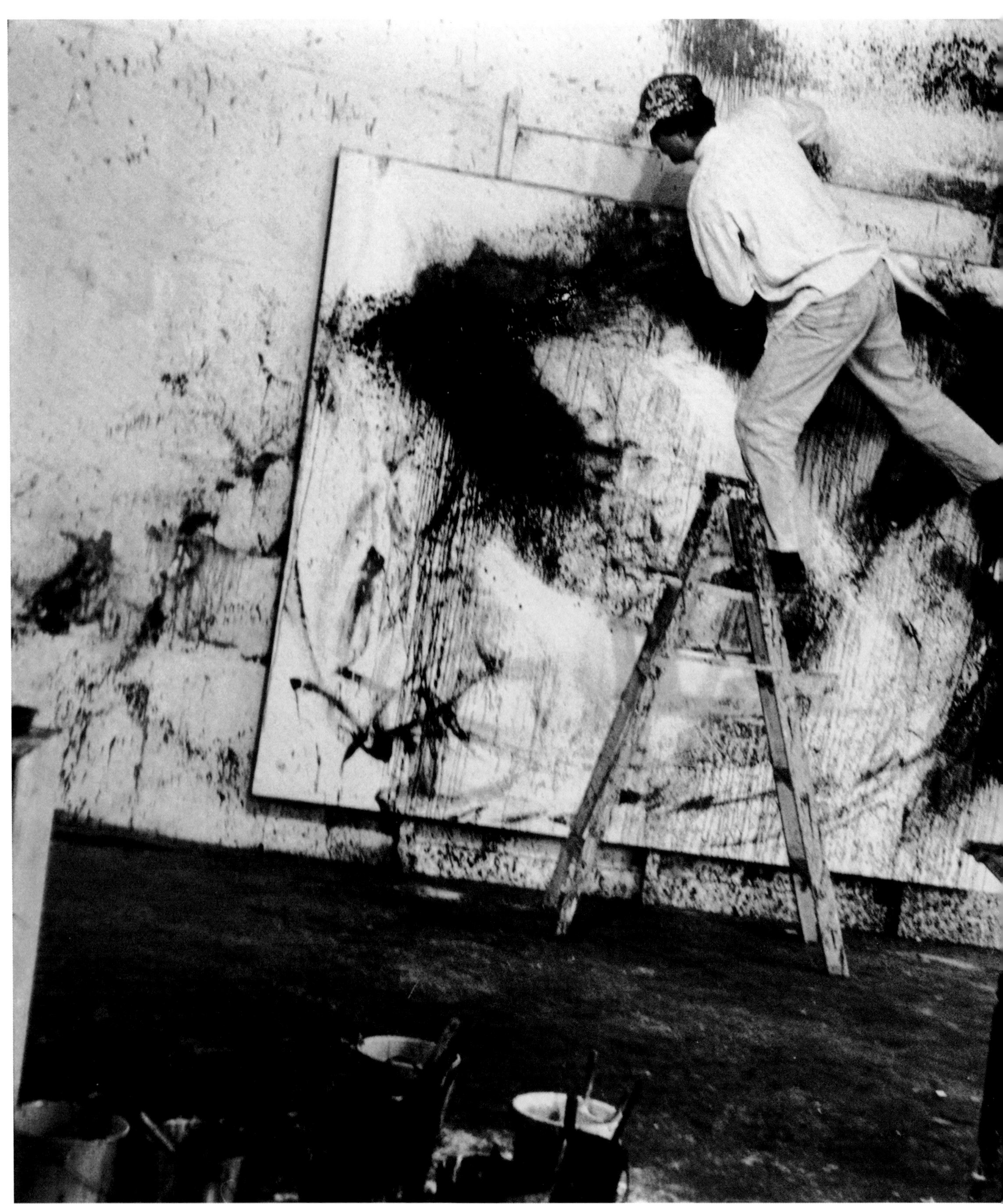

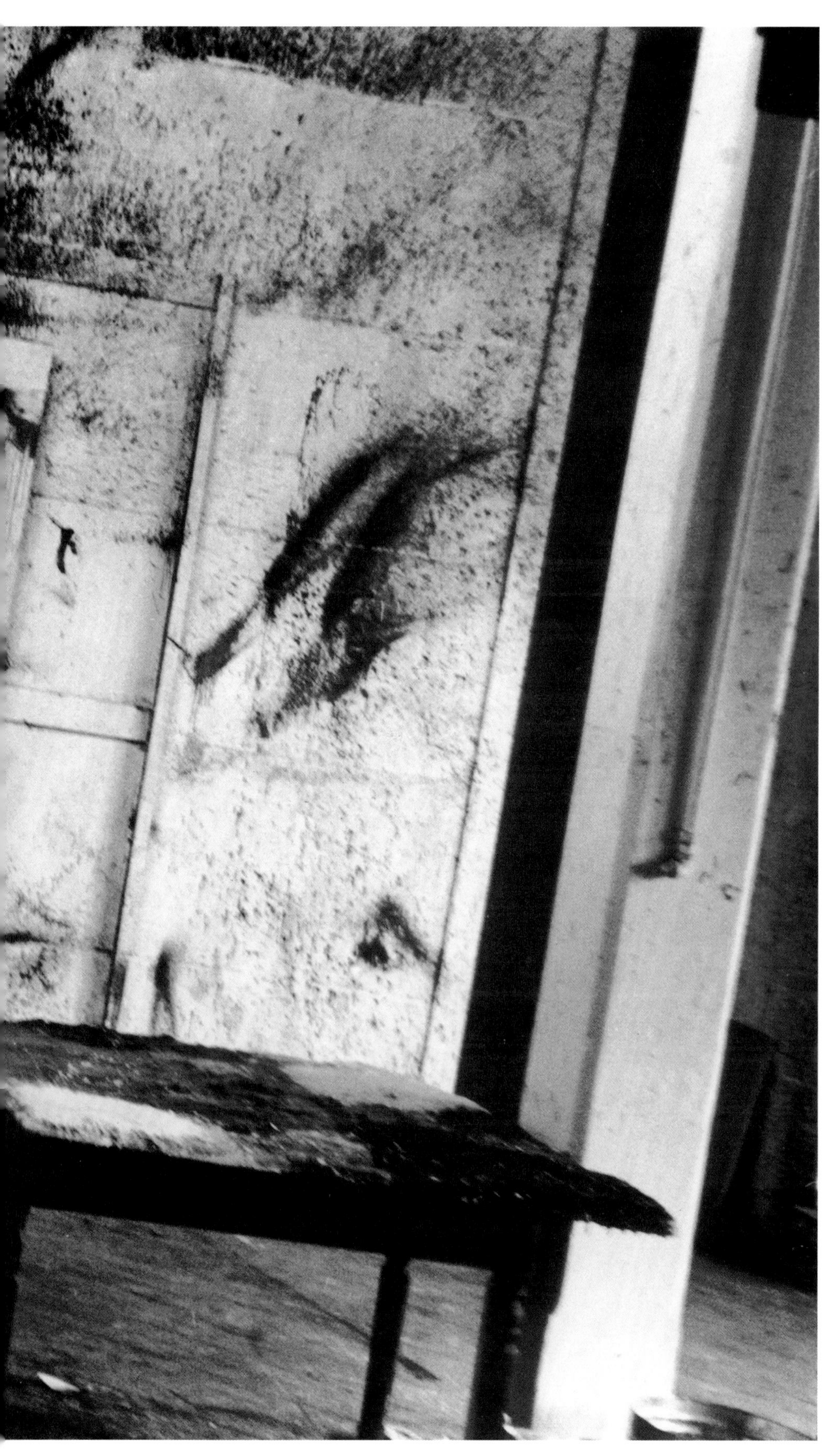

Norman Bluhm works on the oversize canvas of one of his action paintings in his studio, 333 Park Ave. South, February 22, 1961. This spontaneous style of dripping, splashing, or smearing paint onto canvases, best known in the work of Jackson Pollock, was one of several abstract styles Bluhm explored during his career.

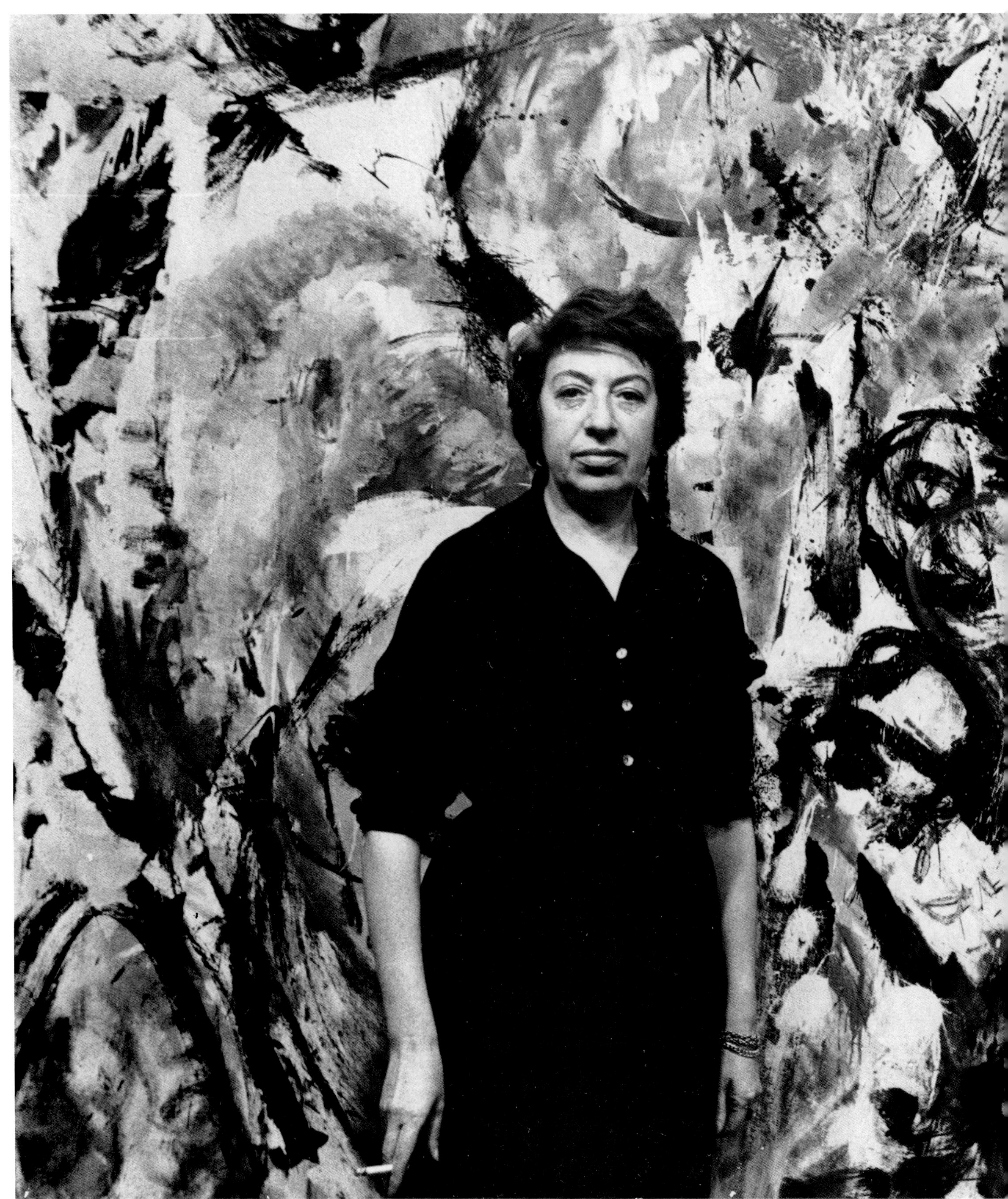

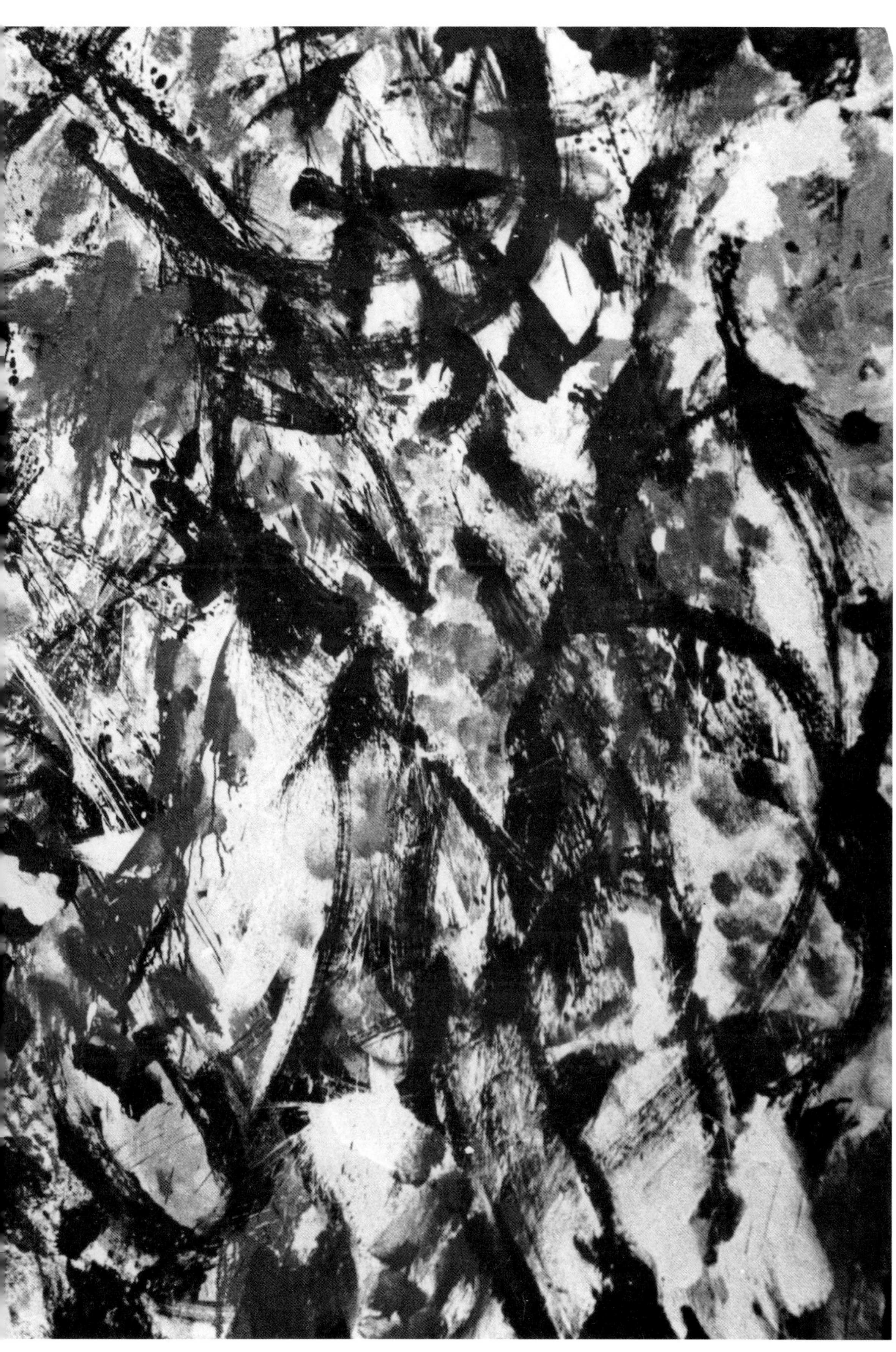

Abstract Expressionist
artist Lee Krasner, who
was married to Jackson
Pollock, in front of
one of her paintings,
February 26, 1961.
Krasner liked this portrait
so much that she acquired
it, and it now hangs in the
Pollock-Krasner House in
East Hampton, New York.

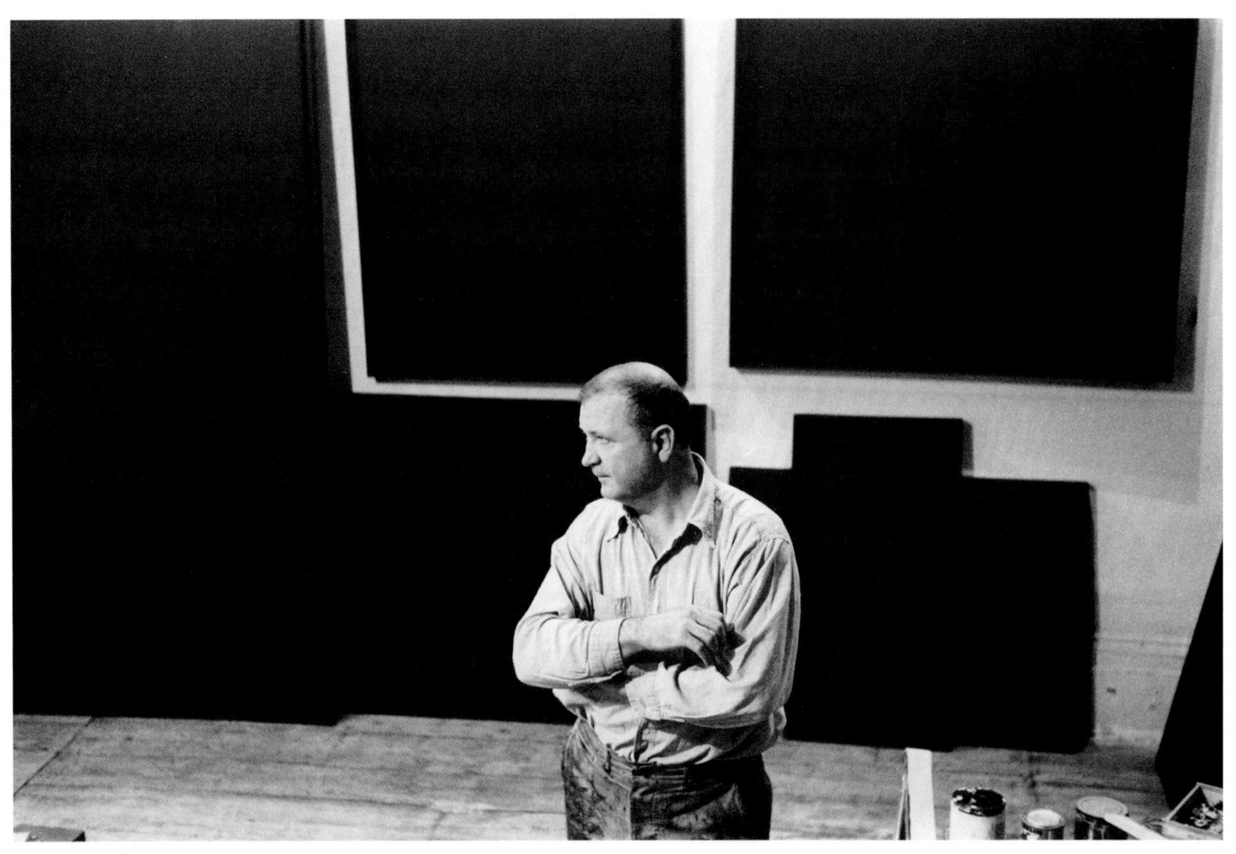

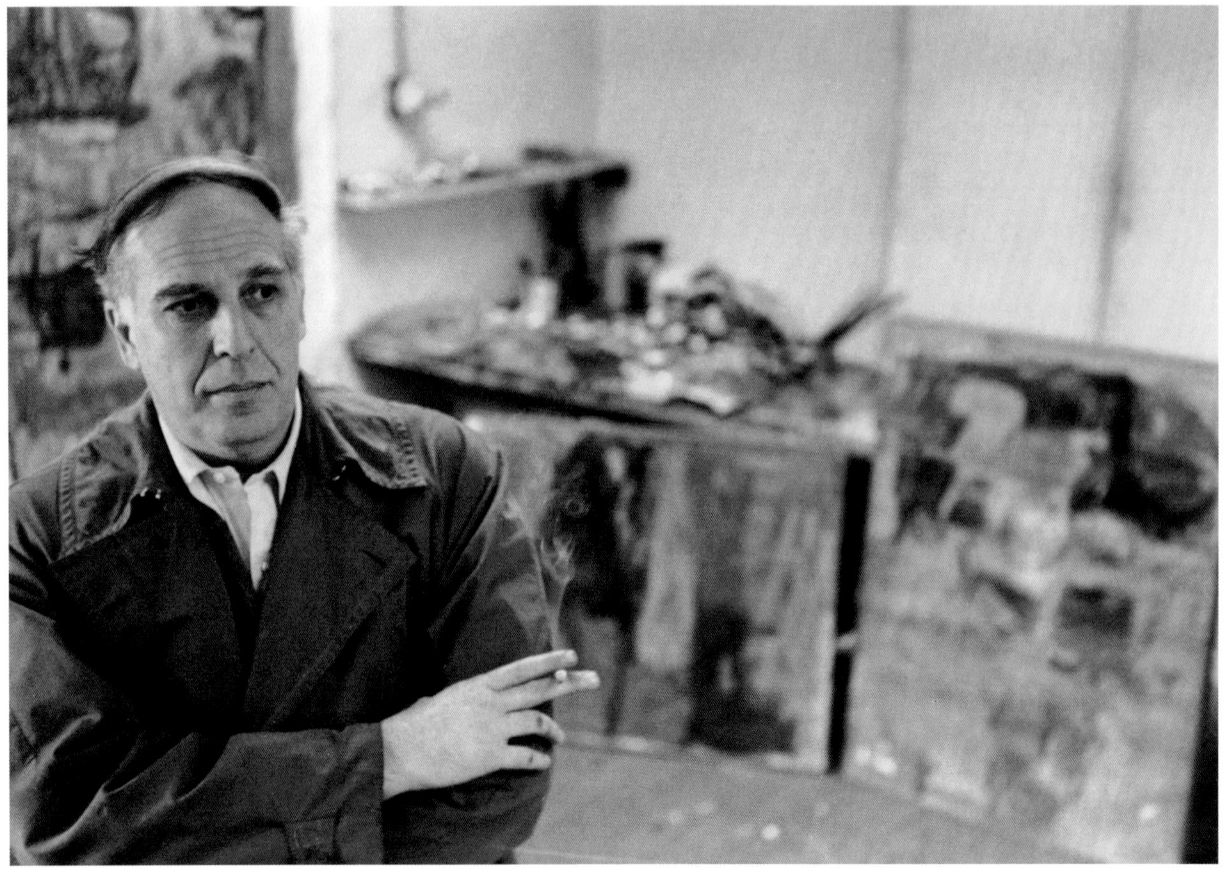

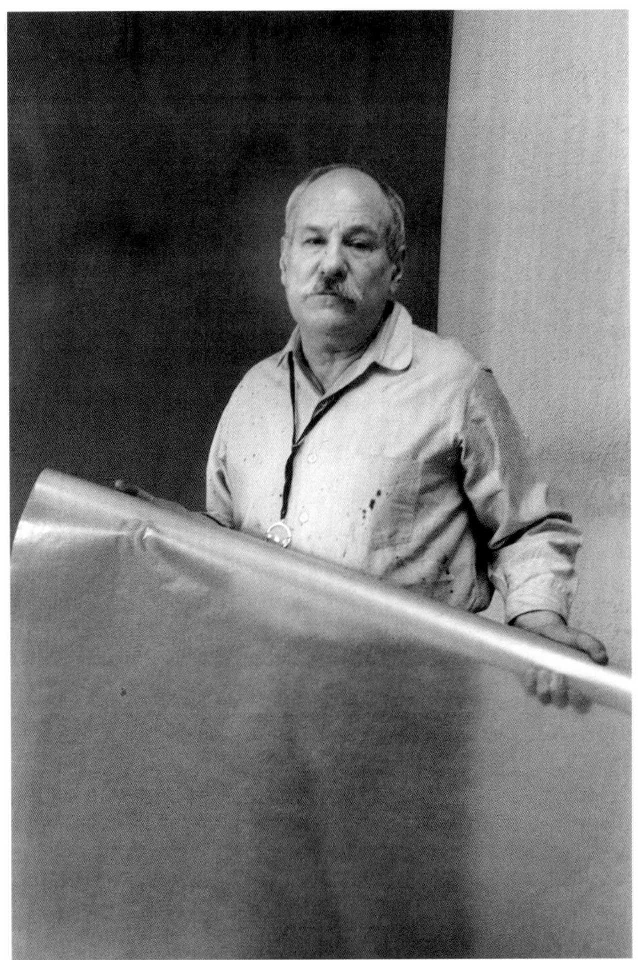 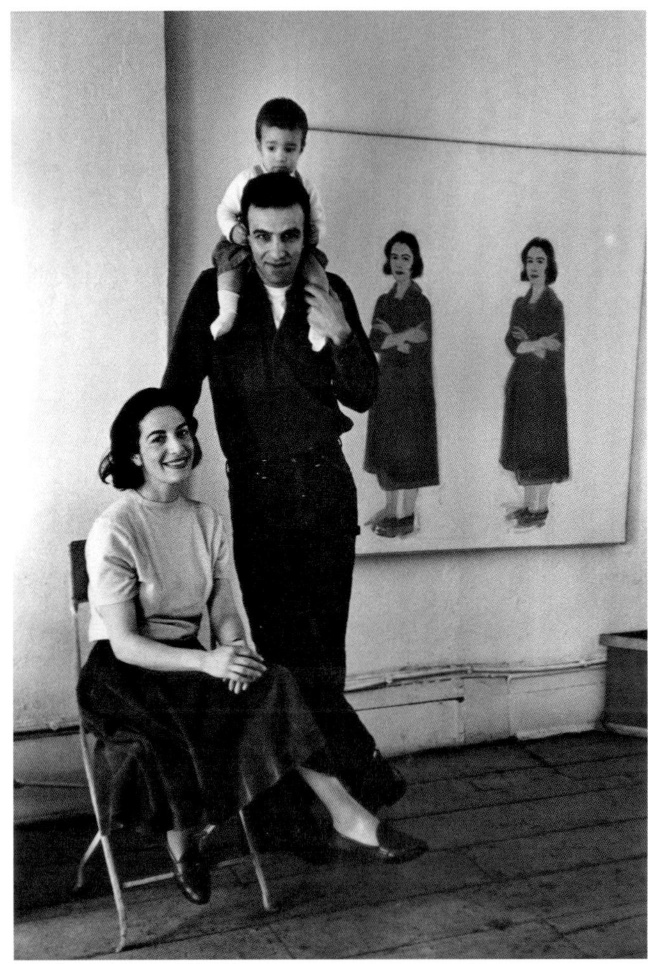

Opposite: Ad (short for Adolph) Reinhardt, April 1, 1961. An Abstract Expressionist painter and critic, Reinhardt was an uncompromising advocate of abstract art.

Painter Philip Guston in his studio on East Eighth Street, April 14, 1961. Later in the sixties, he would turn away from two decades of Abstract Expressionism and to a personal style of representational painting.

This page: Abstract Expressionist artist Barnett Newman at his studio, 100 Front St., April 2, 1961. Newman was a precursor to Color Field and Minimalist art, and an important figure for many younger New York artists in the sixties.

Figurative artist Alex Katz, his wife, Ada, and their son pose in his studio in front of his painting of Ada, April 6, 1961. His diverse work included collages, large-scale paintings of faces, groups of people, and landscapes, but he was best known for his portraits of Ada.

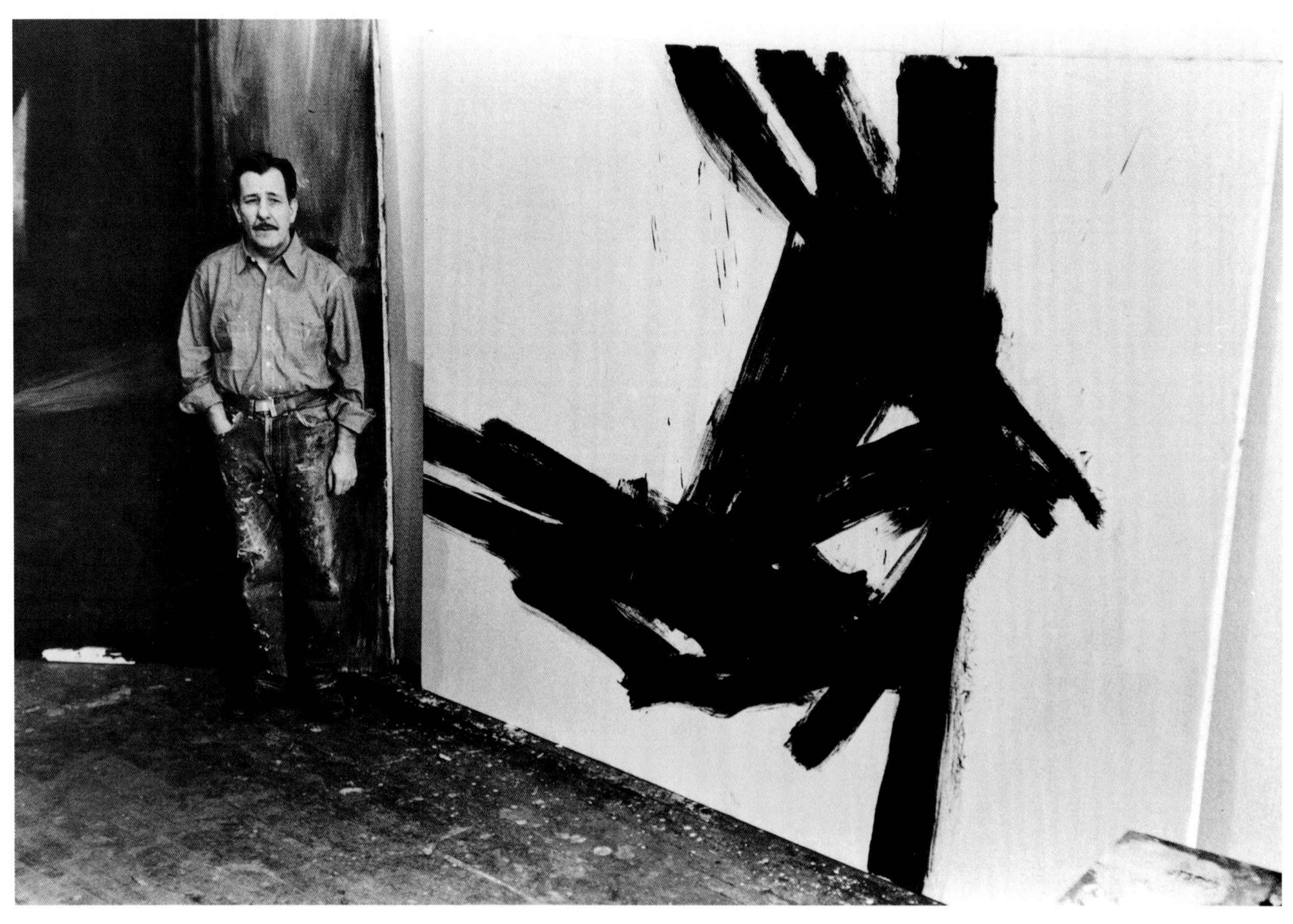

Abstract Expressionist artist Franz Kline with his painting *Corinthian II* (1961) in his home and studio, 242 West Fourteenth St., April 7, 1961. McDarrah, living just down the block at 304 West Fourteenth St., was his friend and photographed him often.

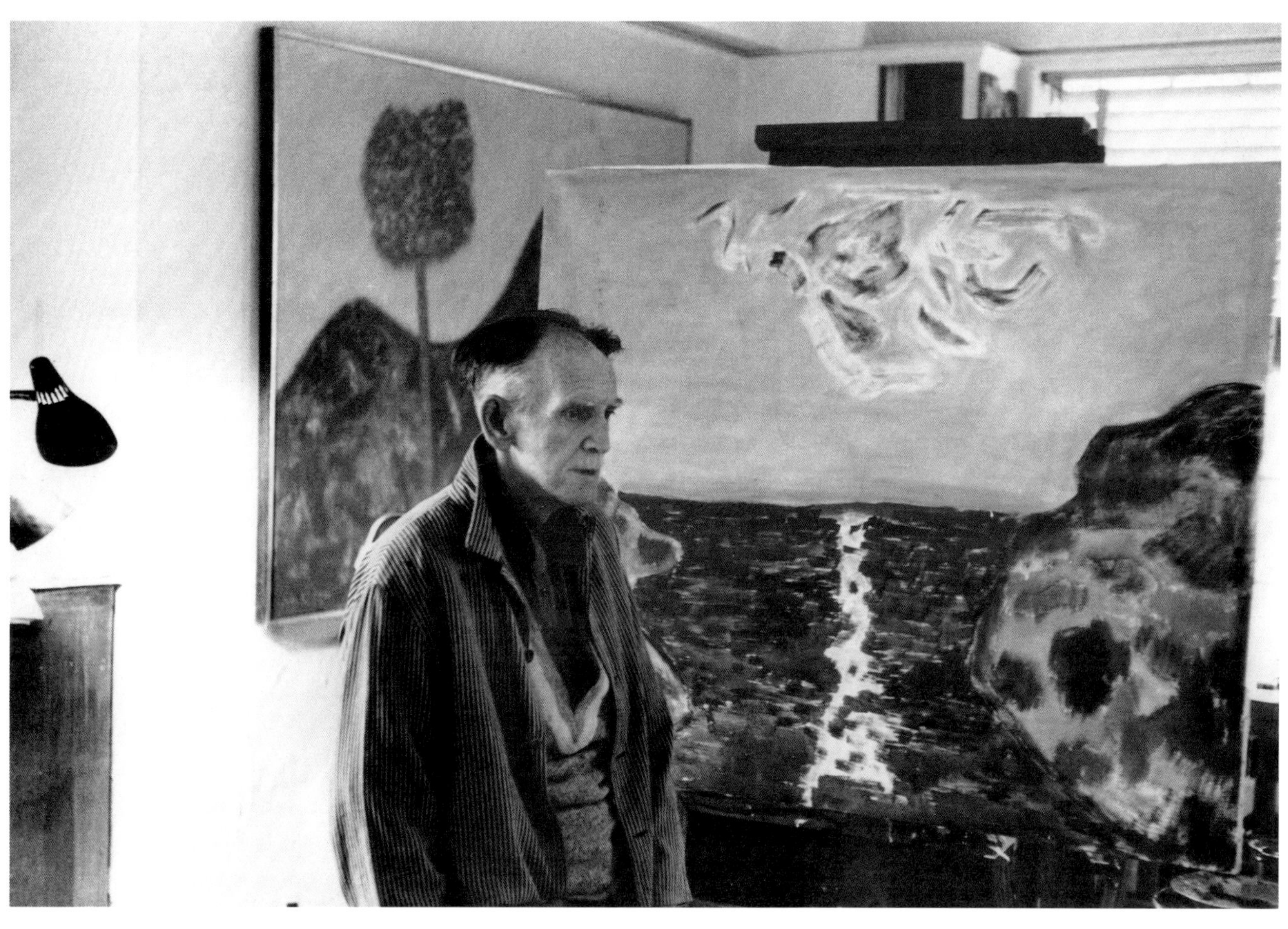

Artist Milton Avery, February 19, 1962. Avery, whose career began long
before World War II, was the rare prewar representational painter who found
a welcome among the New York School painters of the fifties.

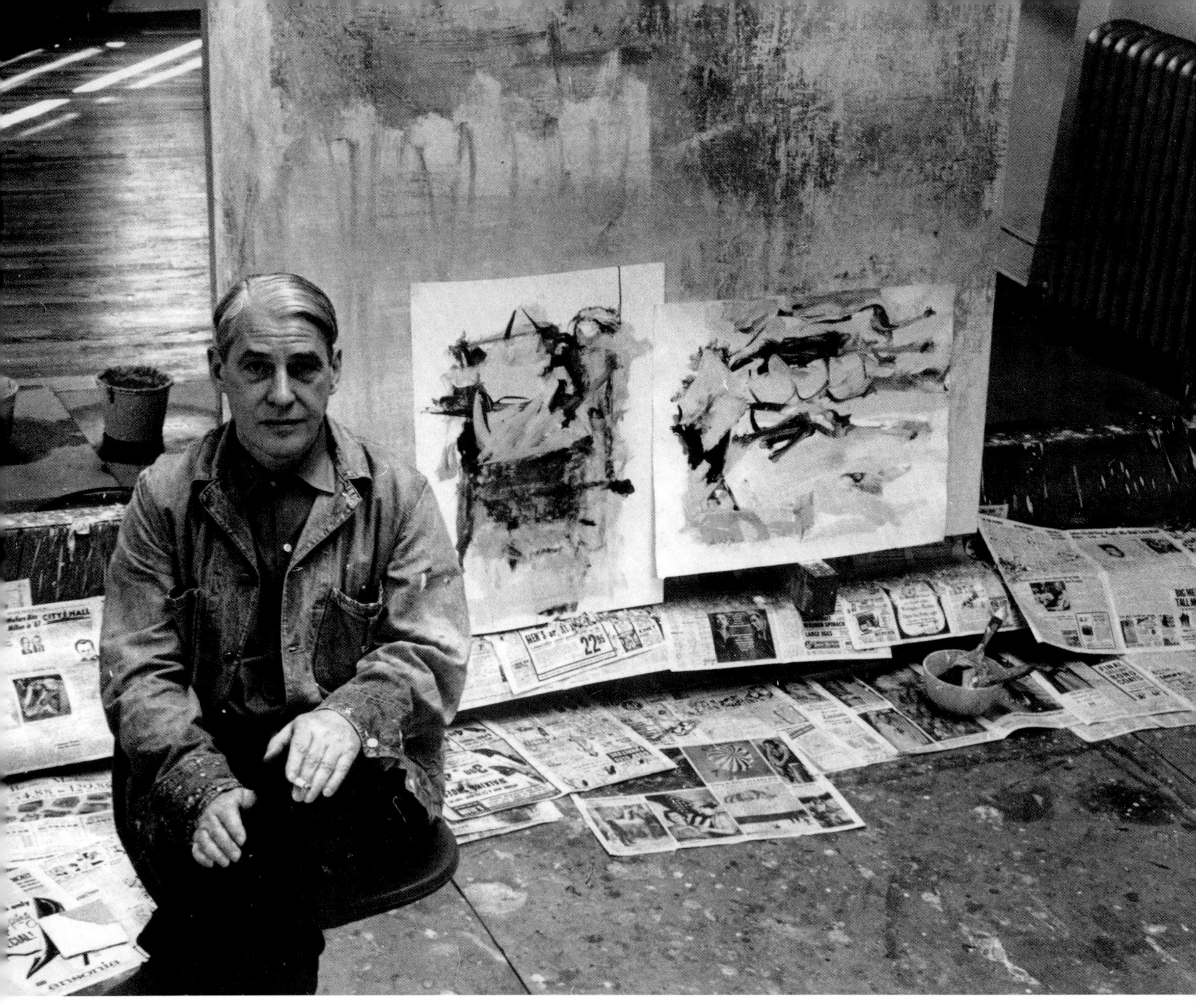

Willem de Kooning in his studio, 827–831 Broadway,
March 23, 1962. Just ten days earlier, the Dutch-born
artist—who arrived in the United States in 1926 as a
twenty-two-year-old stowaway on a British freighter—
became an American citizen.

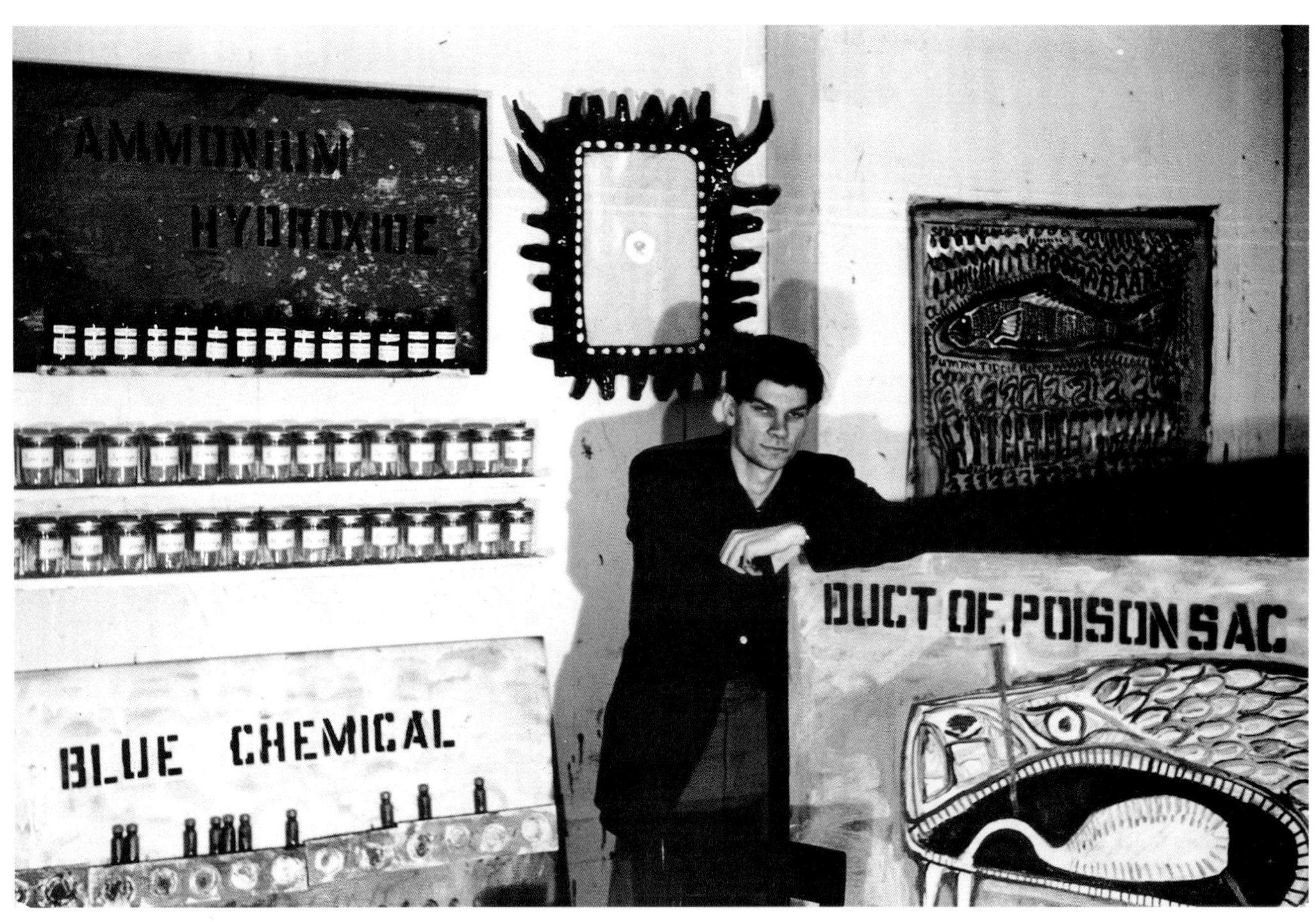

Robert Smithson poses with a selection of his works,
October 24, 1962. He later changed mediums and became
far better known for his site-specific land art, or Earthworks,
especially *Spiral Jetty* on the Great Salt Lake in Utah.

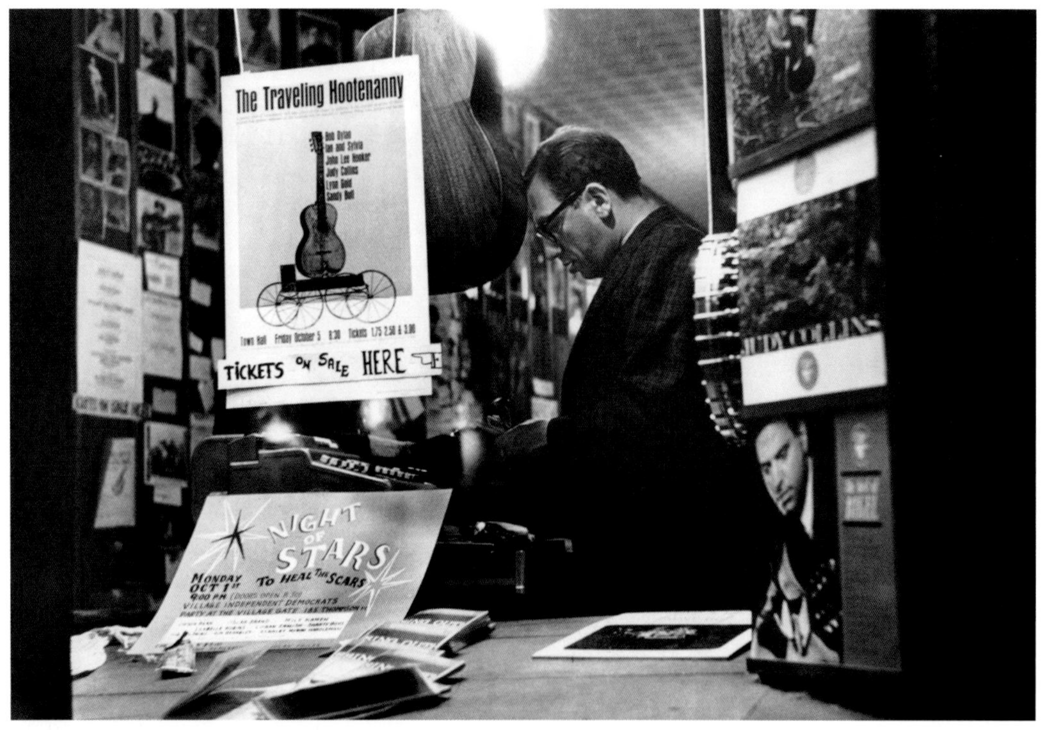

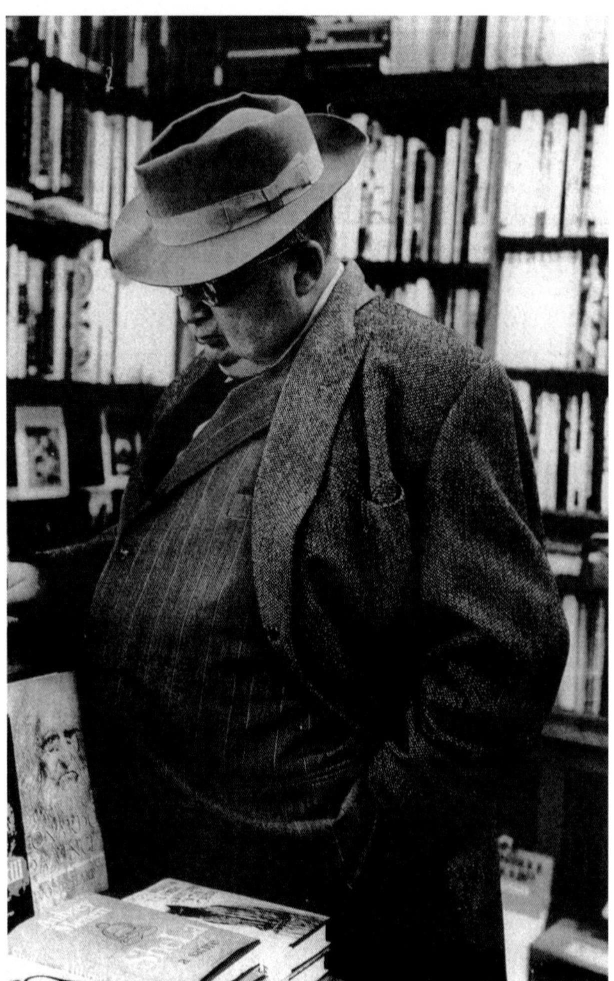

Izzy Young in his music store, the Folklore Center,
110 MacDougal St., September 26, 1962.
The store was filled with everything to do with
folk music: books, records, magazines—and
folksingers and songwriters who hung out there,
met one another, and even had concerts arranged
by Young. He moved to Stockholm in 1973 to
open the Folklore Centrum.

Journalist and critic A. J. Liebling browsing at the
Eighth Street Bookshop, October 24, 1961. His
widely praised essays and other writings, primarily for
the *New Yorker* from 1935 until his death at the end
of 1963, cover a range of subjects including World
War II, boxing, and food.

Writer and critic Susan Sontag, New York intellectual
and political activist for four decades, at the
Mills Hotel (originally called Mills House No. 1),
160 Bleecker St., during a symposium on sex,
December 2, 1962.

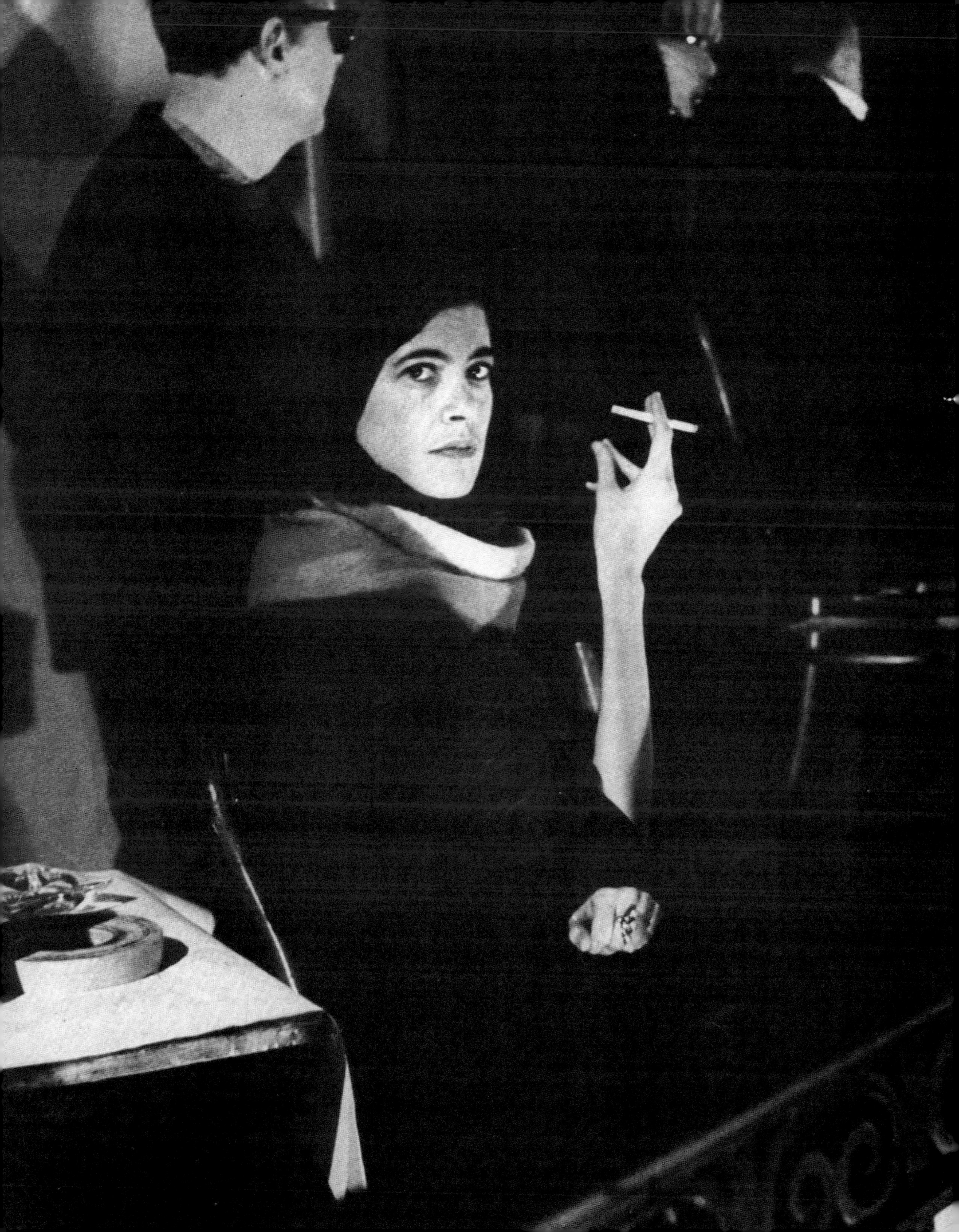

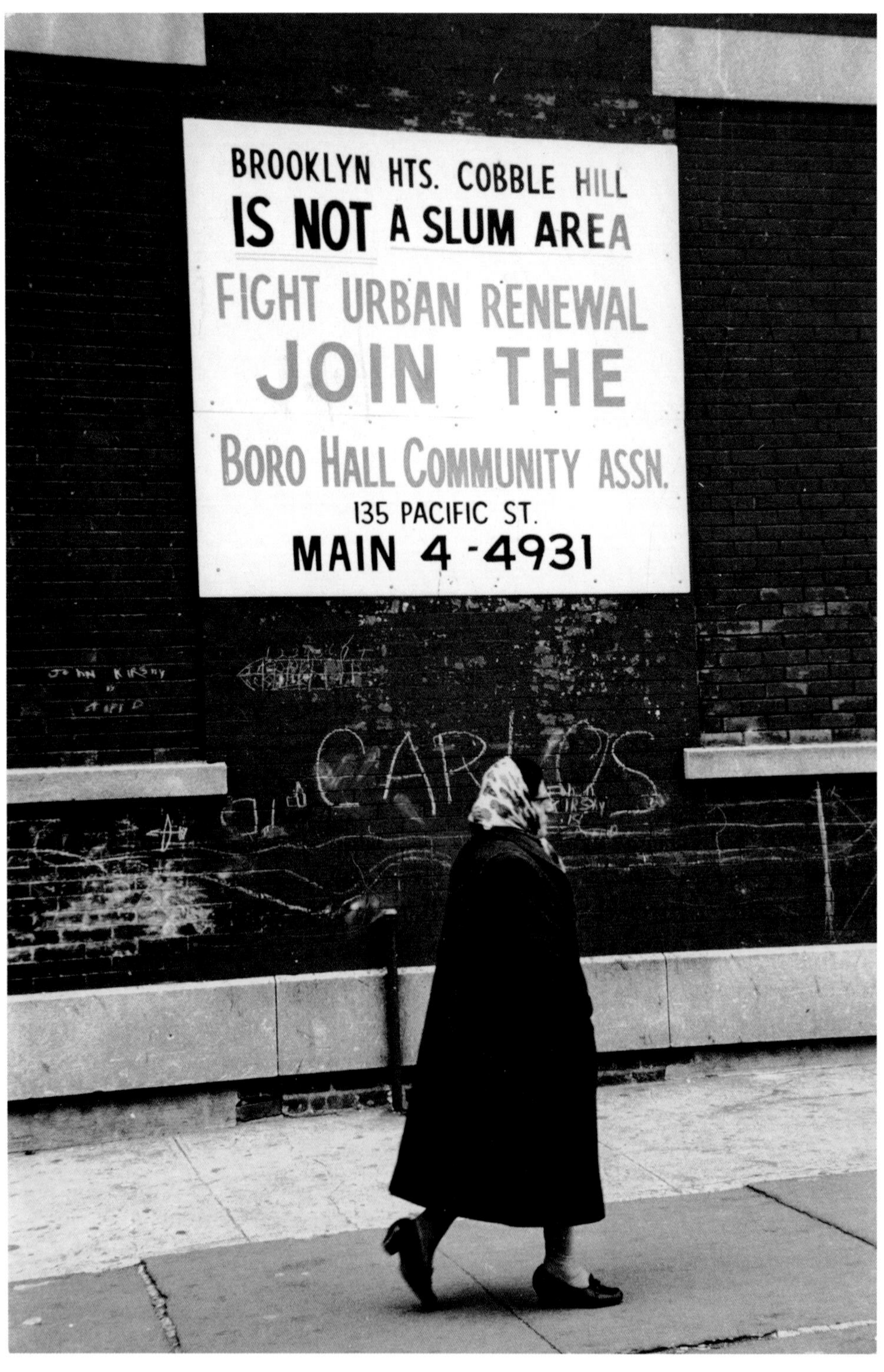

A woman walks along Atlantic Ave. past a sign, mounted on a brick wall, that reads in part, "Brooklyn Hts. Cobble Hill is NOT a Slum Area; Fight Urban Renewal," November 2, 1962. The protesters battled to preserve older, often historic—and frequently rent-controlled—buildings from an onslaught by developers seeking to tear them down and replace them with modern high-rises and public housing projects.

In the vernacular of the day, a "Bowery Bum" walks on a snowy, trash-strewn sidewalk near East Houston St. and the Bowery, February 3, 1963. A torn, giant poster on the wall behind him advertises a musical titled *Stop the World—I Want to Get Off*.

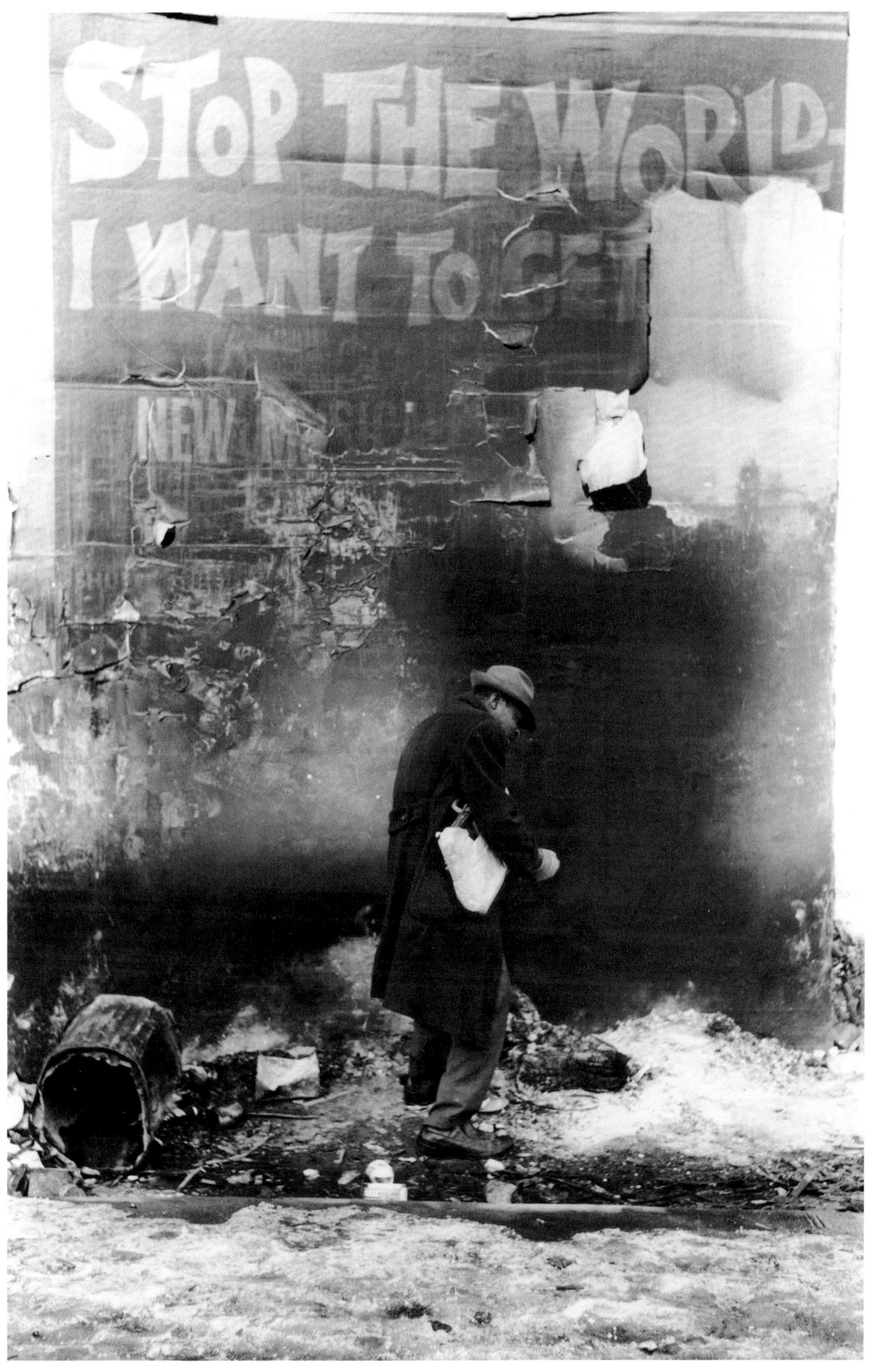

STOP THE WORLD
I WANT TO GET
NEW MUSICAL

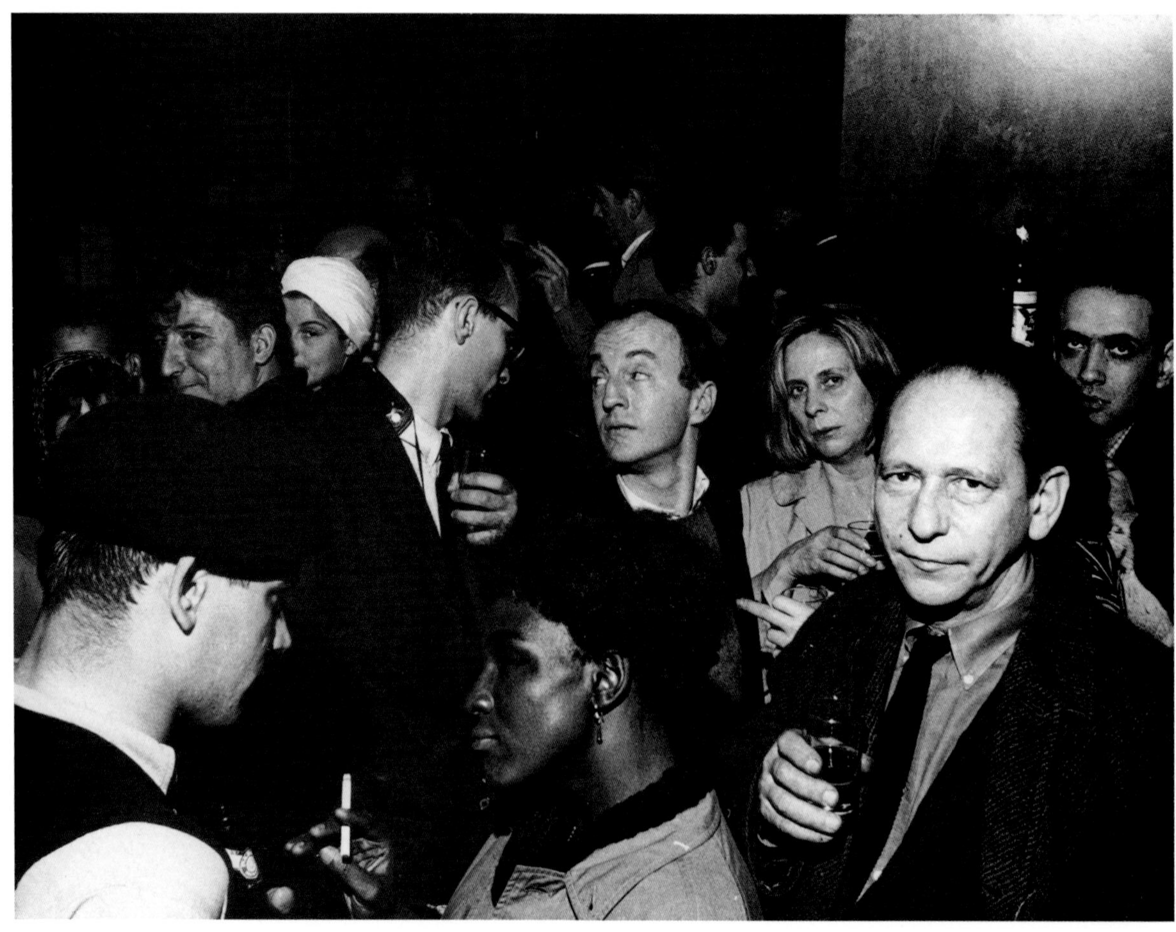

The crowded interior of the Cedar Tavern, 24 University Place, on its closing night, March 30, 1963. Among those visible are poets Jack Micheline (left, smiling toward camera), Frank O'Hara (center, looking toward Micheline), and Barbara Guest (looking at camera, in a light-colored jacket), as well as abstract sculptor Abram Schlemowitz (in front of Guest, with glass in hand). The bar reopened a year later a few blocks away, at 82 University Place.

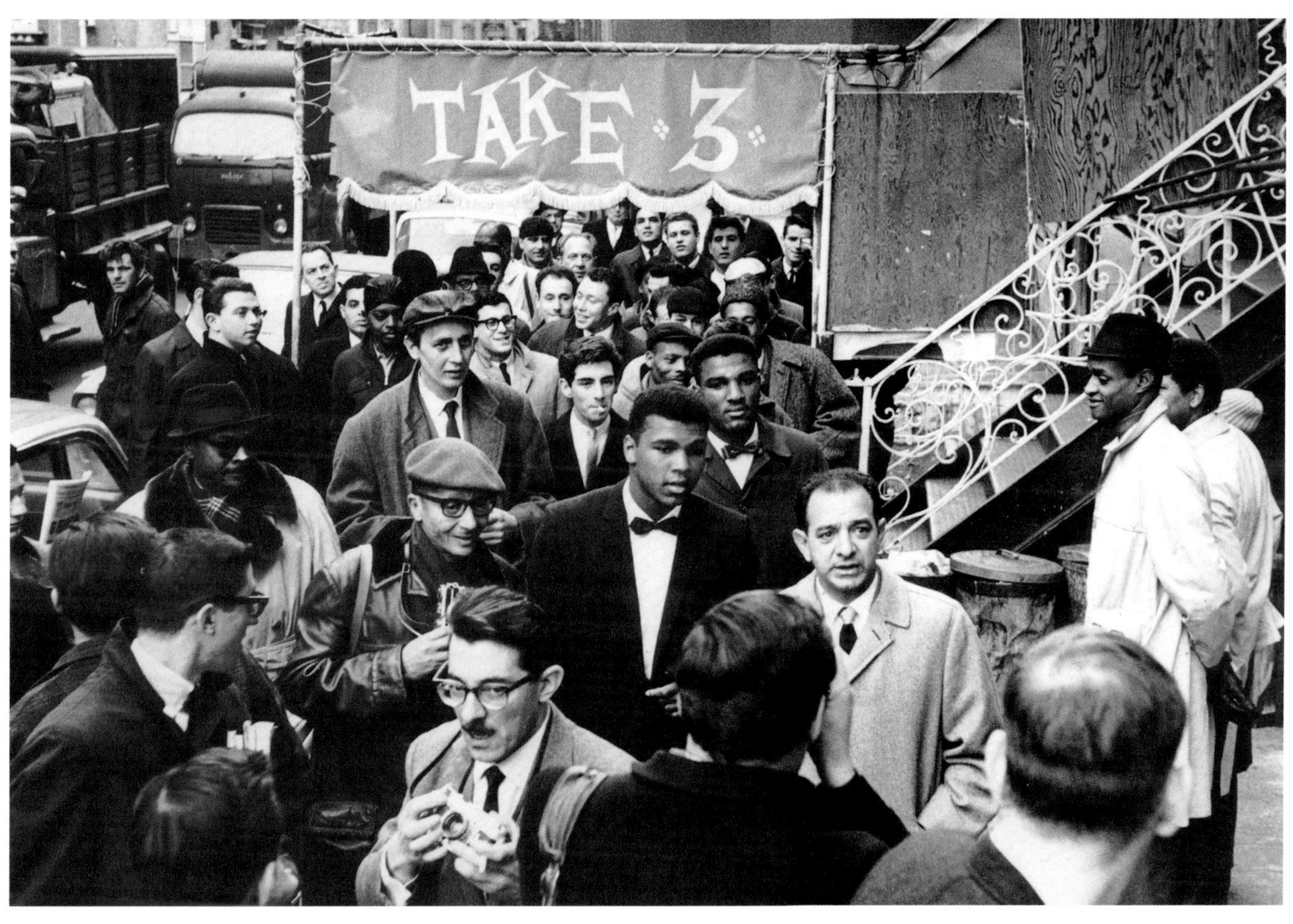

Surrounded by fans and journalists, Muhammad Ali (then known by his birth name, Cassius Clay) arrives at the Bitter End, 147 Bleecker St., to participate in a poetry reading with Village poets Howard Ant, Jill Castro, Kathleen Fraser, Diane Wakoski, Betty Taub, Ree Dragonette, and Doe Lindell, March 12, 1963. The twenty-one-year-old boxer read an original work called "'Ode to a Champion: Cassius Marcellus Clay,' by Cassius M. Clay." He would win a unanimous decision against Doug Jones the following night in Madison Square Garden and, in a major upset, take away the heavyweight title from Sonny Liston on February 25, 1964.

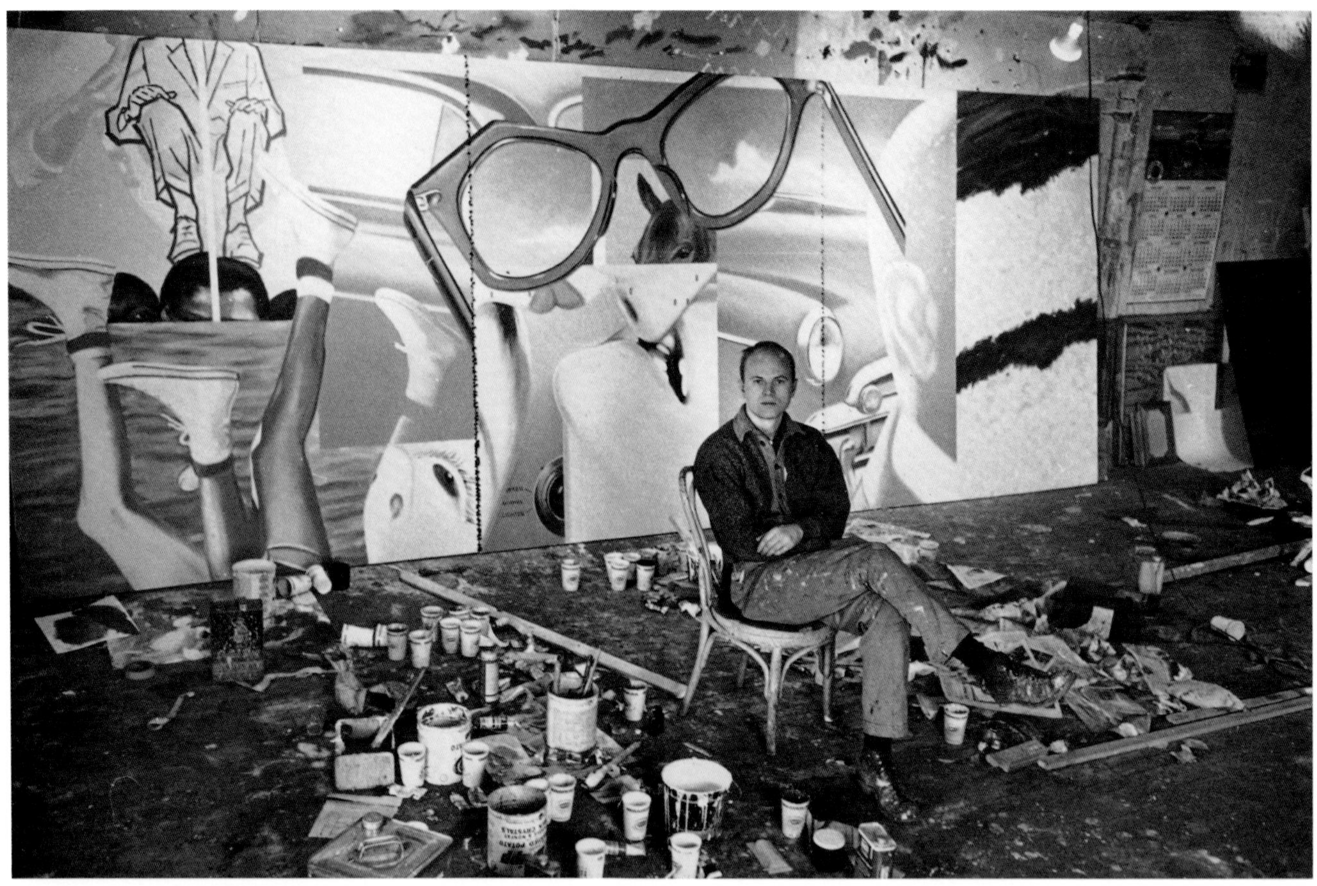

Pop artist James Rosenquist sits
in front of his *Painting for the
American Negro* (1962–1963)
in his studio, 3–5 Coenties
Slip, March 30, 1963. For
about a decade starting in
the mid-fifties, several artists,
including Ellsworth Kelly, Robert
Indiana, and Agnes Martin, also
occupied abandoned sail-making
lofts in this two-block area of
Lower Manhattan between Pearl
and South Sts.

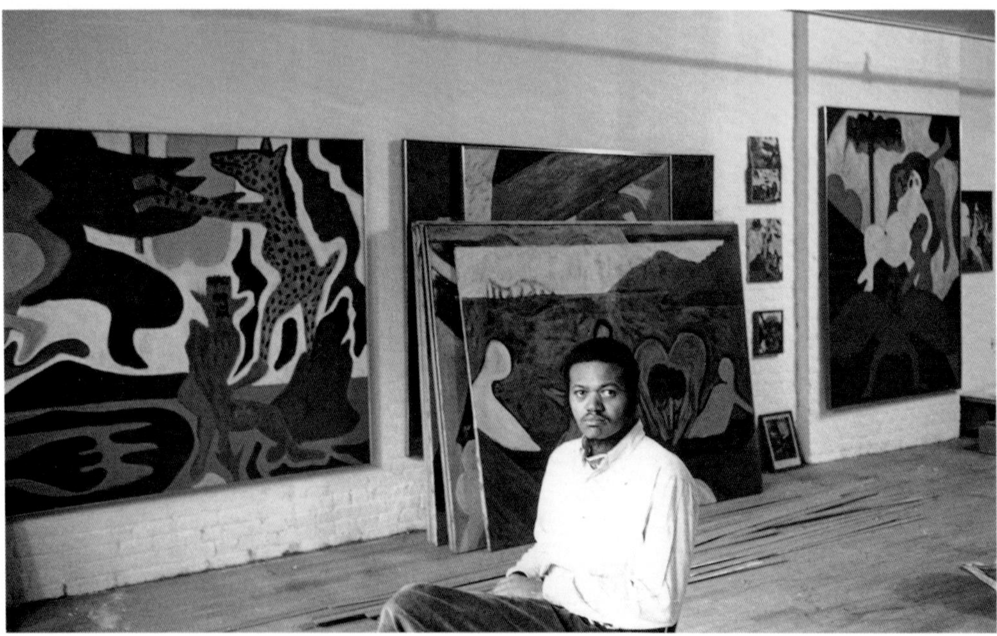

Artist Bob Thompson in his East Village loft, November 30, 1963. The painter
was known for colorful figurative works, sometimes derived from the compositions
of Old Masters. Thompson was not quite twenty-nine when he died in May 1966,
not long after emergency gallbladder surgery in Rome.

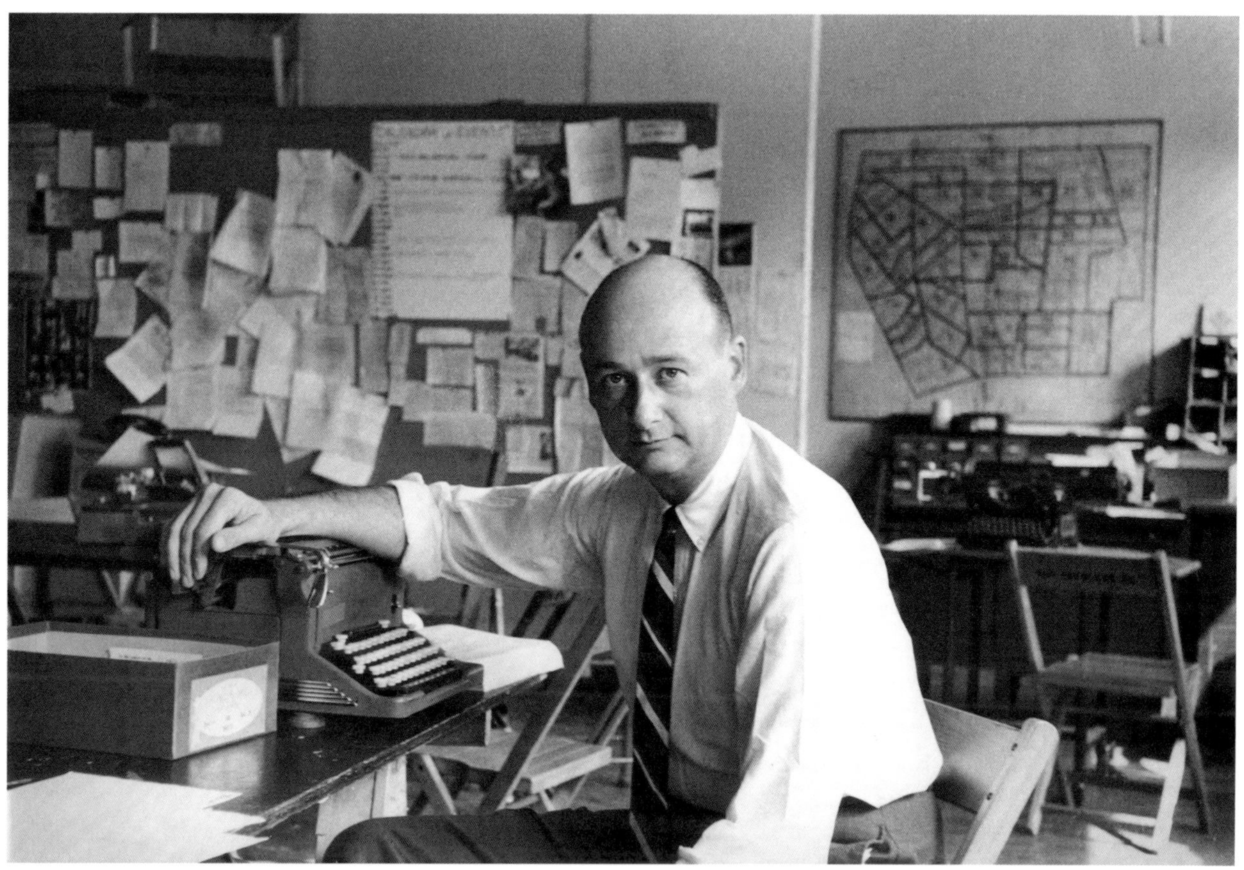

Edward I. Koch in the Village Independent Democrats office, August 24, 1963. Backed by the reform organization, Koch won an upset victory that year as Democratic Party leader of the district including Greenwich Village, thwarting Carmine DeSapio, the last powerful boss of the longtime Democratic political machine called Tammany. Then a political maverick, Koch would serve as a member of the city council, a US representative, and a three-term mayor of New York, from 1979 through 1989.

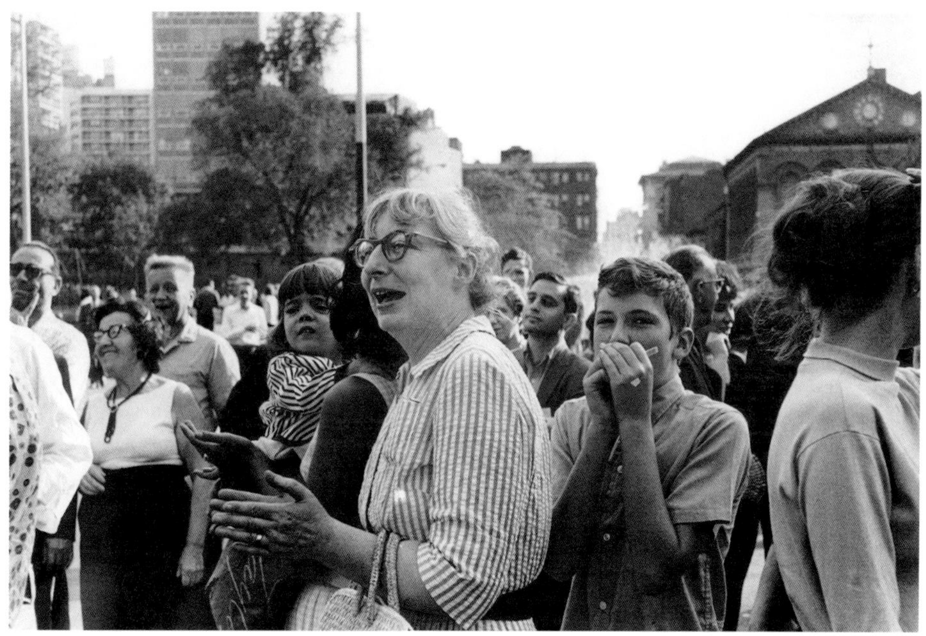

Activist and author Jane Jacobs in a demonstration in Washington Square Park, August 24, 1963. The author of *The Death and Life of Great American Cities* (1961) was a champion of preservation and an ardent foe of wholesale destruction of neighborhoods in the name of urban renewal, including attempts by the almost all-powerful "master builder" Robert Moses to run a new highway through Washington Square Park and surrounding neighborhoods.

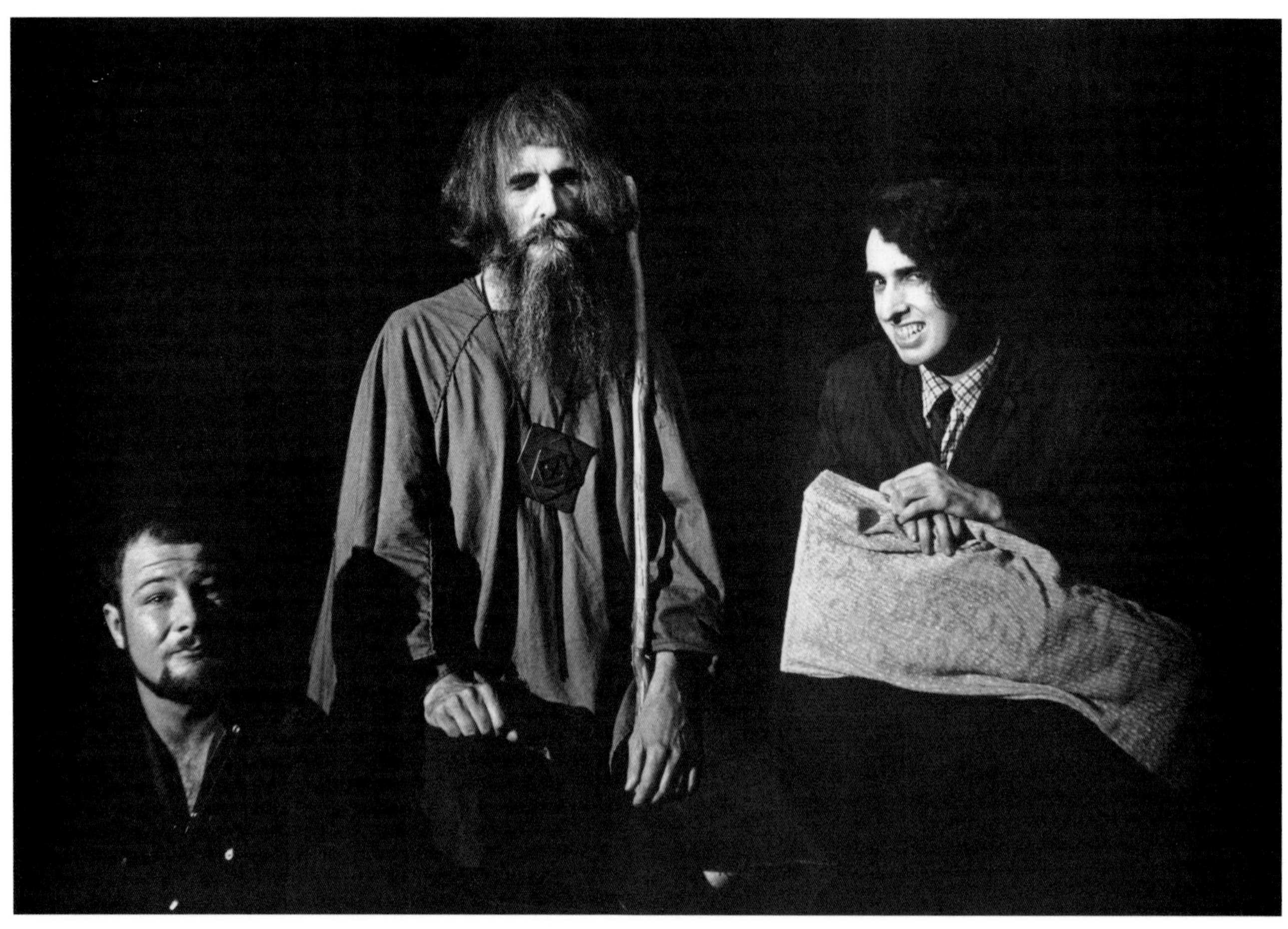

From left, Hugh Romney (later known as Wavy Gravy), Moondog, and Tiny Tim, July 2, 1963, at the Fat Black Pussycat Theatre, 11–13 Minetta St. During the day, the space was a coffee shop called the Commons; Bob Dylan wrote "Blowin' in the Wind" and other songs there. Wavy Gravy, a lifelong peace activist who often dressed as a clown, cofounded the famed hippie commune called the Hog Farm. Moondog (born Louis Hardin) was a musician, composer, poet, and inventor of musical instruments. Blind from the age of sixteen, he was known, from the forties until 1972, as the "Viking of Sixth Avenue" for the cloak and horned helmet he wore. Tiny Tim (born Herbert Khaury) would take his falsetto, heavy with vibrato, and his ukulele to national fame for the rest of the sixties, with renditions of old popular songs.

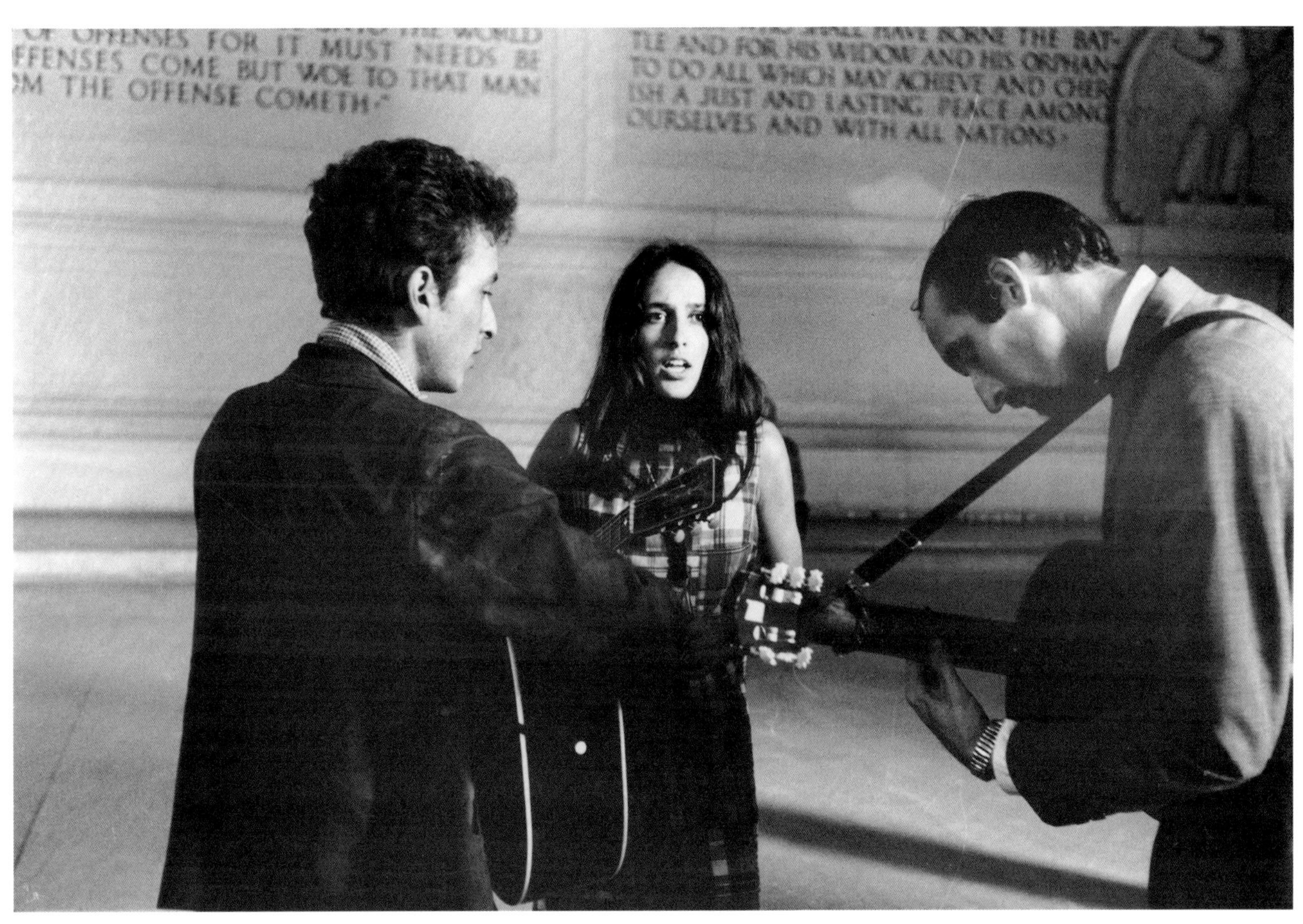

From left, folksingers Bob Dylan, Joan Baez, and Noel Paul Stookey (of Peter, Paul and Mary) warm up
at the Lincoln Memorial before performing at the March on Washington for Jobs and Freedom,
August 28, 1963. Afterward, the huge crowd heard speeches—among them, Martin Luther King Jr.'s
landmark "I Have a Dream" speech.

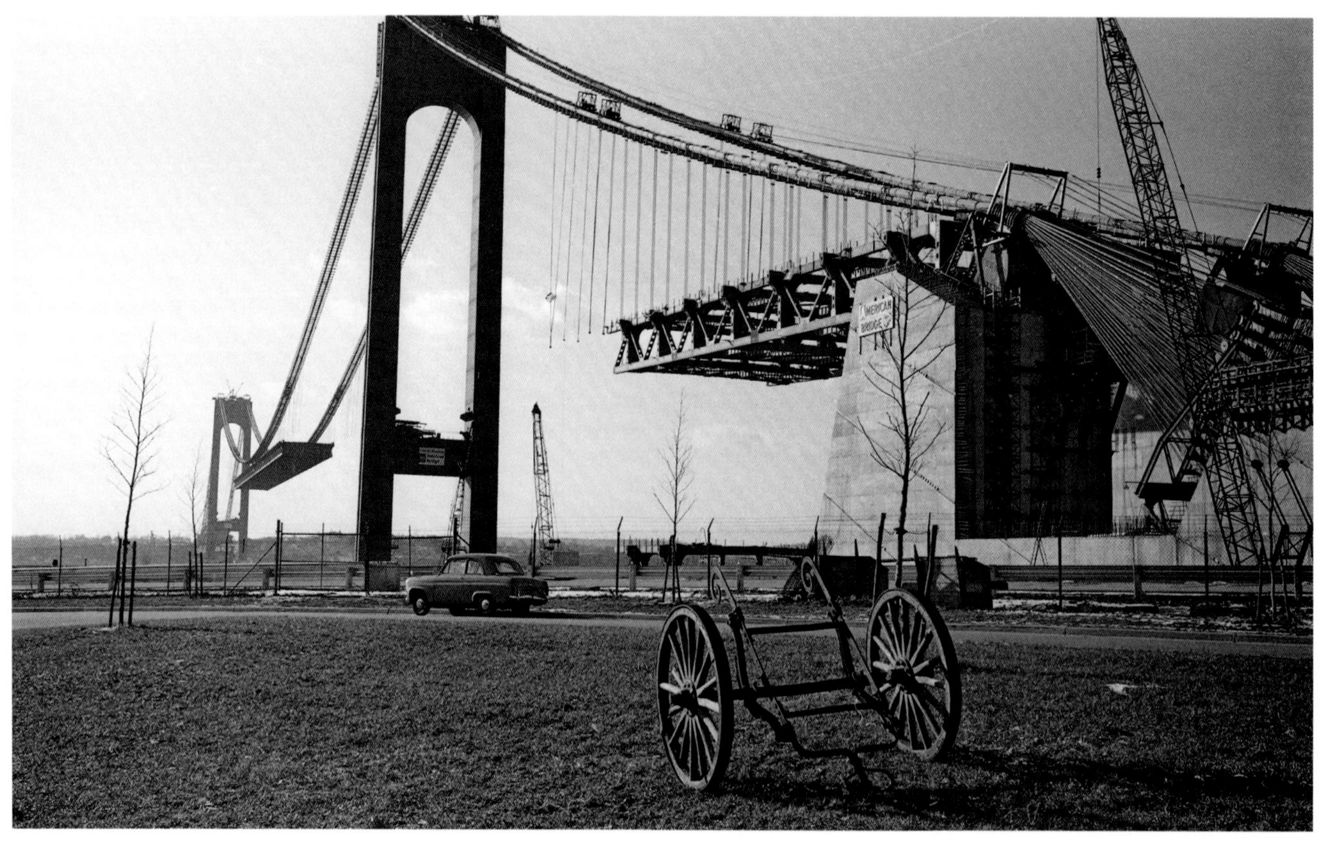

The Verrazano-Narrows Bridge linking Staten Island to Brooklyn, under construction, December 19, 1963. From its opening the following November until 1981, it was the longest suspension bridge in the world, with a central span of 4,260 feet. The bridge was named—but misspelled—in honor of Italian explorer Giovanni da Verrazzano and the Narrows, a tidal strait connecting Upper and Lower New York Bay.

Looking northeast in winter over Tompkins Square Park, East Seventh St. and Avenue A, February 13, 1964. The park would be the scene of protests in the eighties related to police actions to remove drug dealers and encampments of homeless people, with one demonstration on August 6–7, 1988, resulting in dozens of injuries.

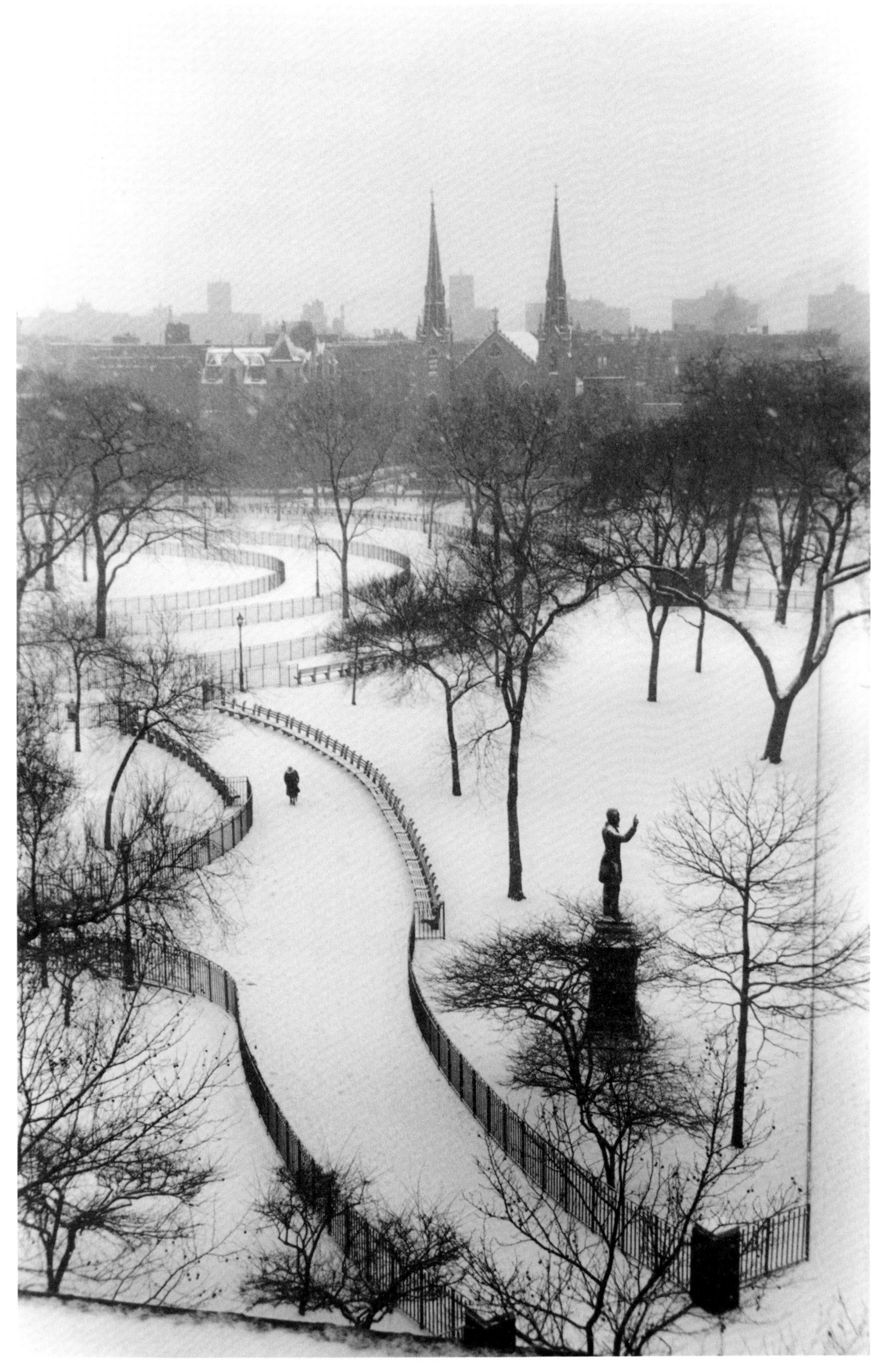

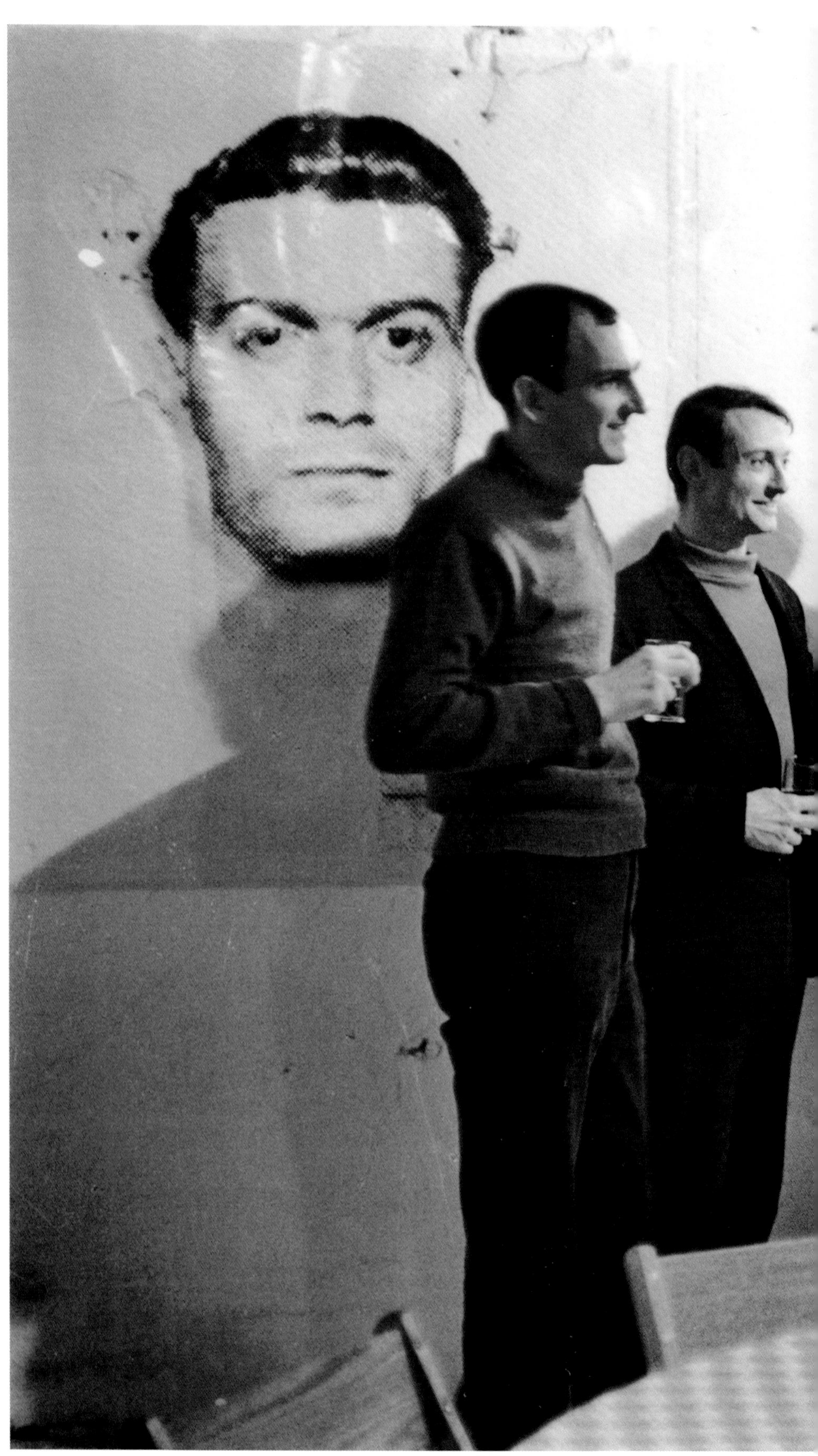

From left, Pop artists Tom Wesselmann, Roy
Lichtenstein, James Rosenquist, Andy Warhol,
and Claes Oldenburg at Warhol's Factory,
231 East Forty-Seventh St. (its first location,
until 1967), April 21, 1964. The occasion
was a party celebrating Warhol's soon to be
censored mural, *Thirteen Most Wanted Men*,
at the New York World's Fair.

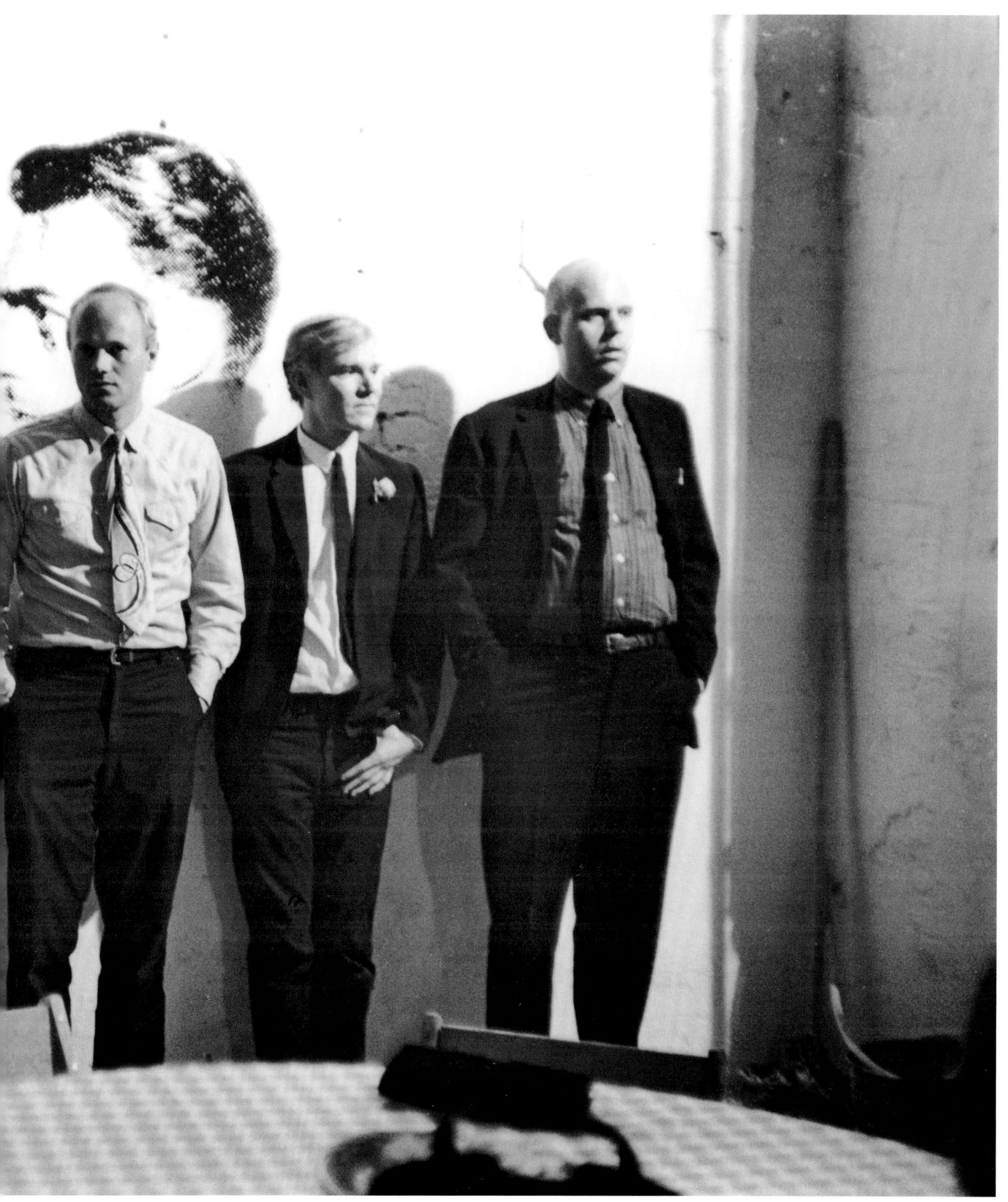

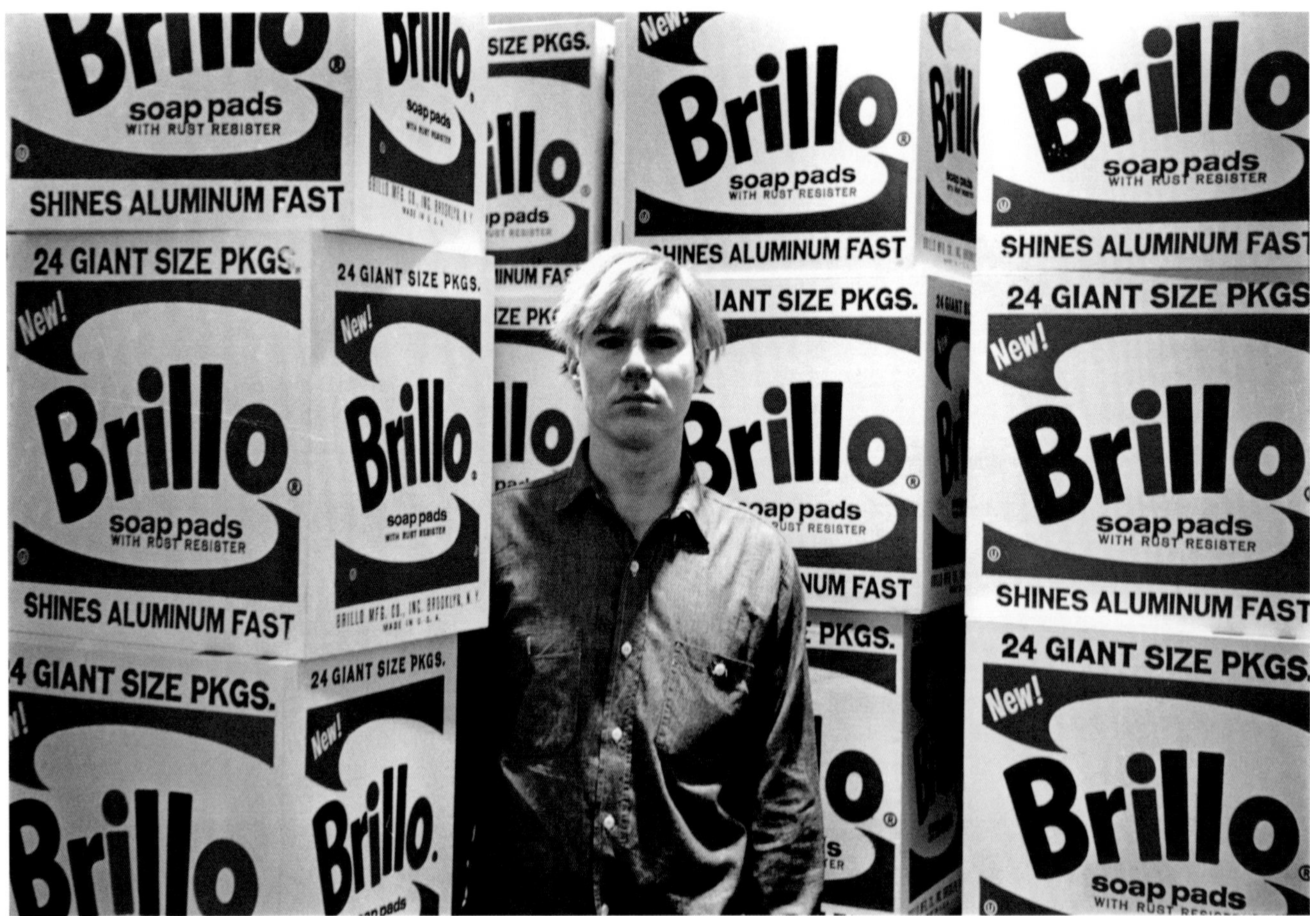

Andy Warhol at the opening of his exhibition, "The Personality of the Artist," at the
Stable Gallery, 33 East 74th St., April 21, 1964.

Warhol adjusts his viewfinder as poet Taylor Mead, who appeared in several of Warhol's
films, stands naked with back to camera, to be filmed in *Camp*, September 4, 1964.

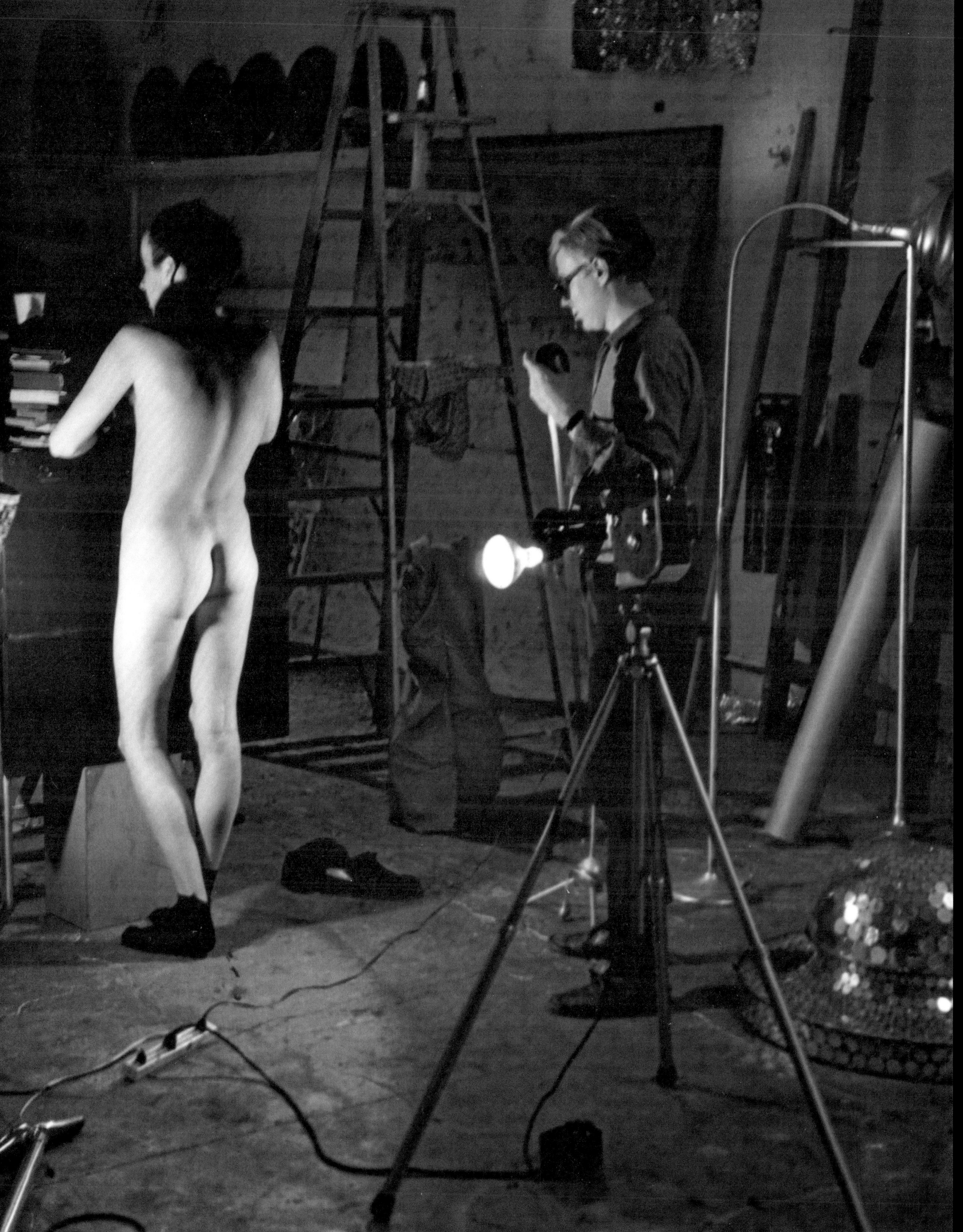

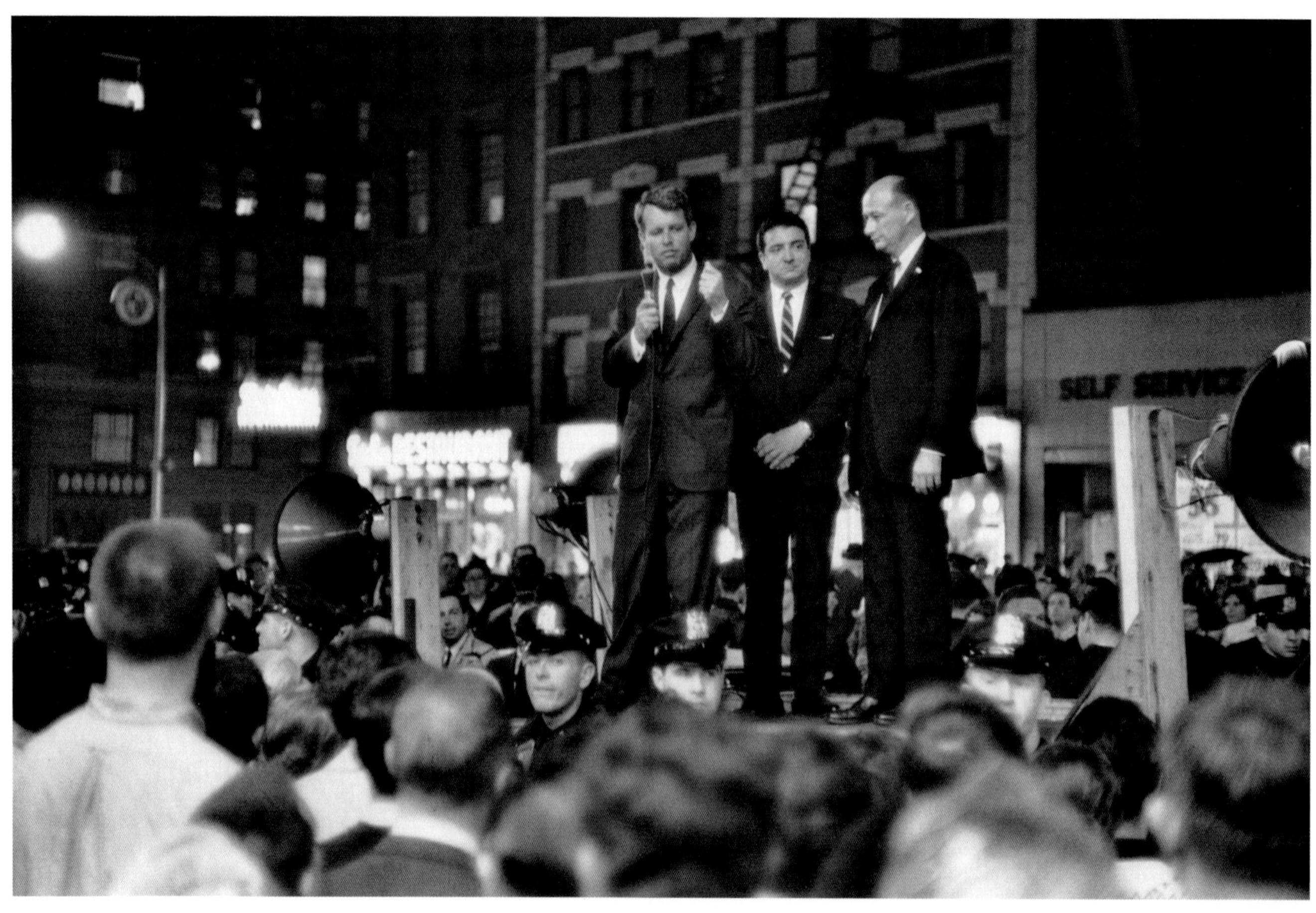

From left, US Senate candidate Robert F. Kennedy, New York State Assemblyman William
Passannante, and reform Democratic district leader Ed Koch—the future mayor of New York City—
stand on a truck flatbed at Sixth Ave. and West Eighth St. in Greenwich Village, October 2, 1964.
Despite accusations of being a carpetbagger from Massachusetts, Kennedy would defeat incumbent
Republican Kenneth Keating on November 3 by more than seven hundred thousand votes.

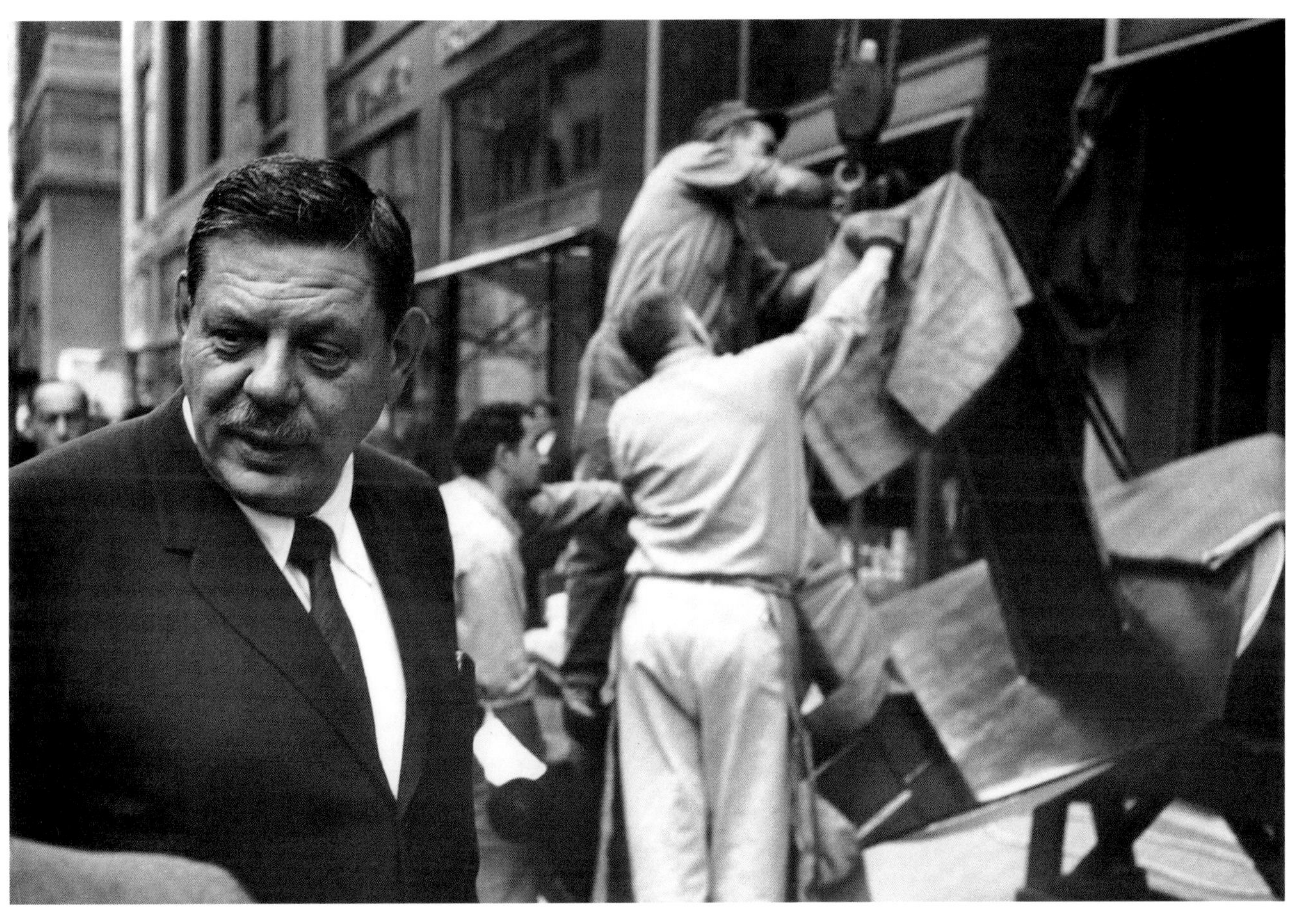

Sculptor David Smith oversees the hoisting and installation of his artwork for an exhibition at the Marlborough-Gerson Gallery, 41 East Fifty-Seventh St., October 17, 1964. Smith created abstract welded metal sculptures.

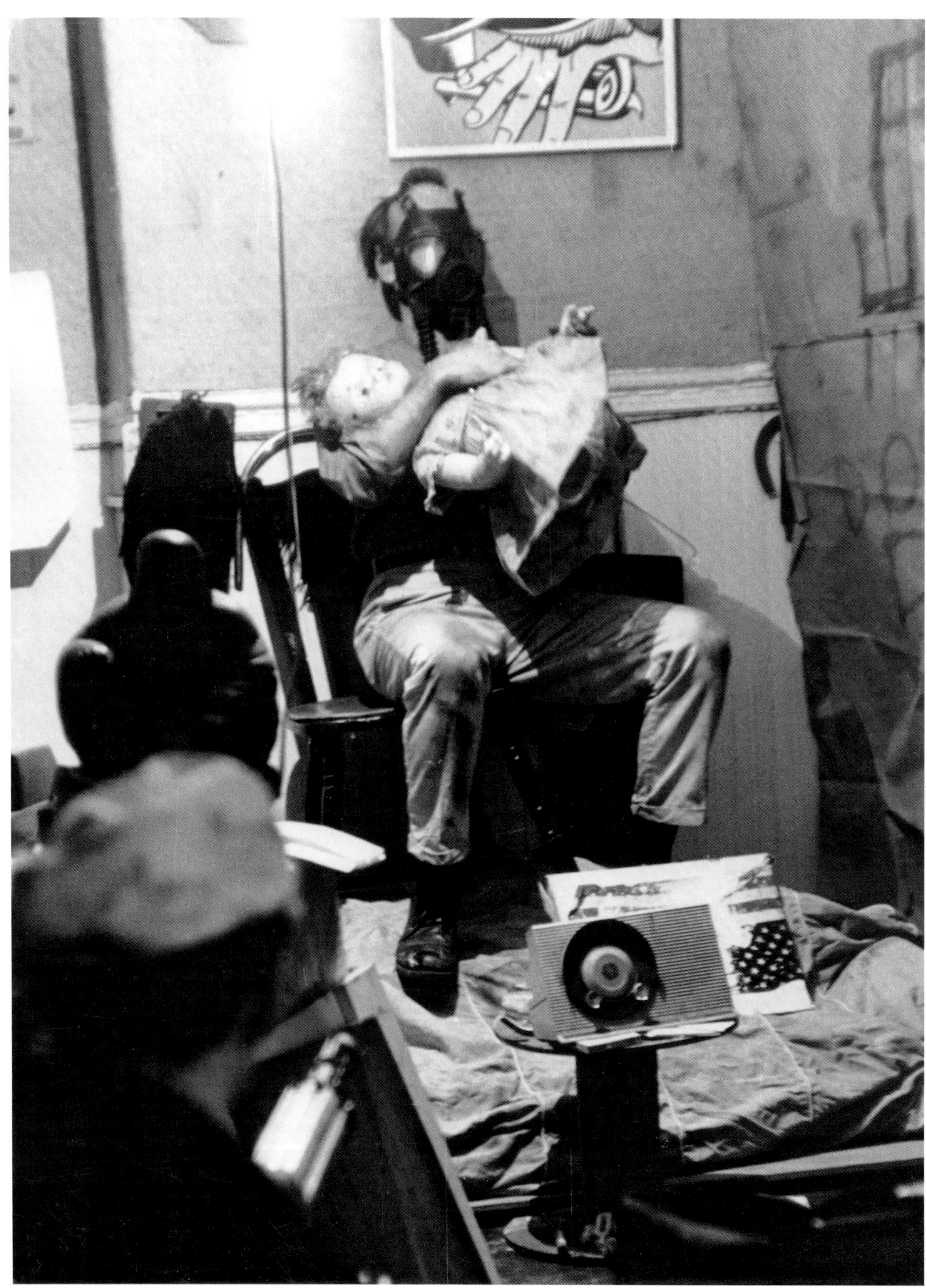

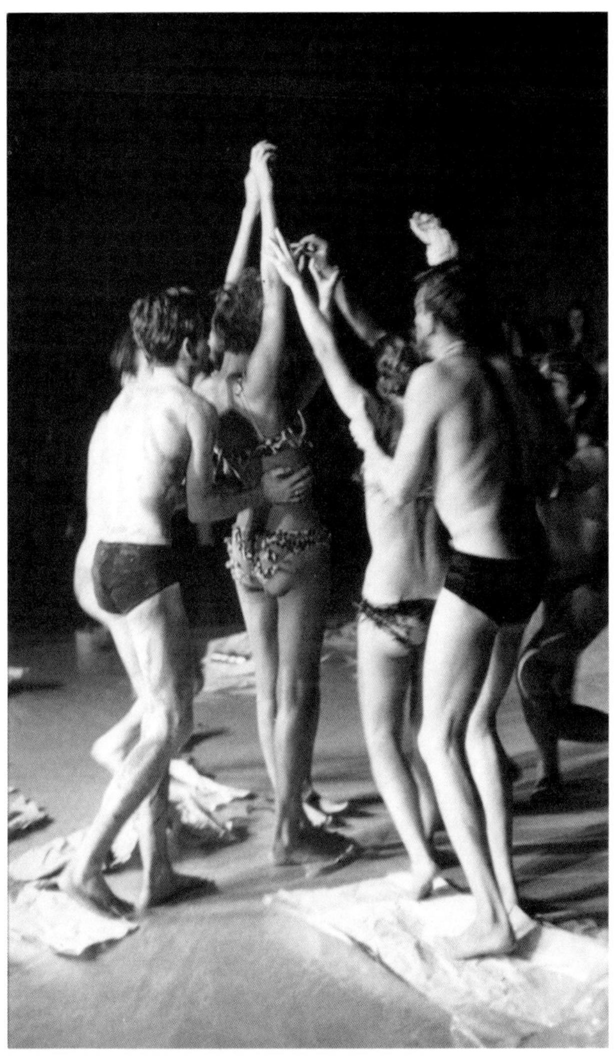

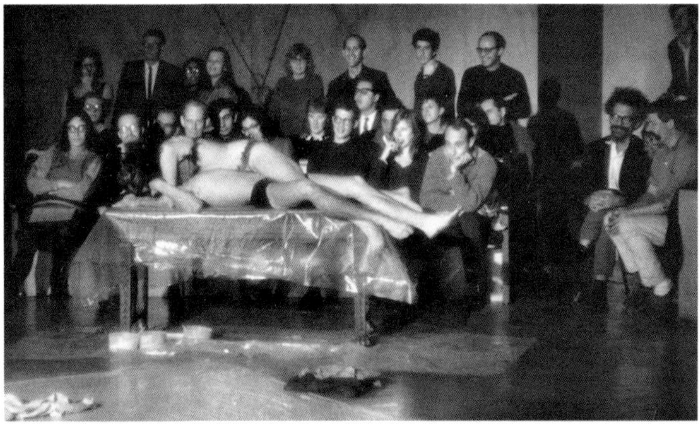

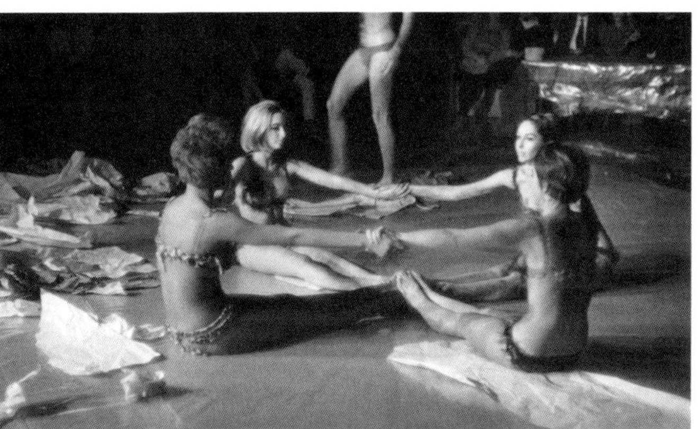

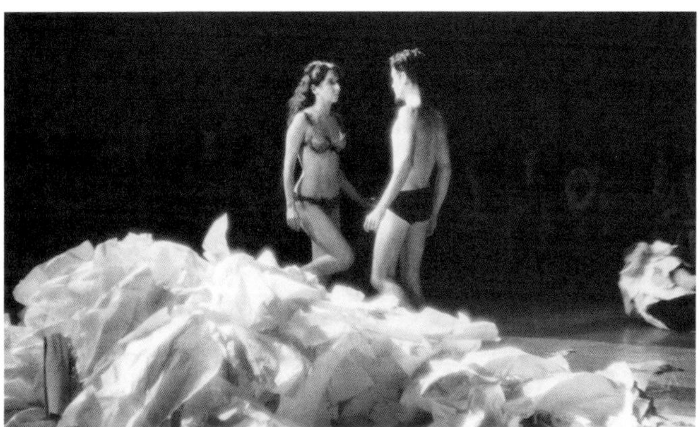

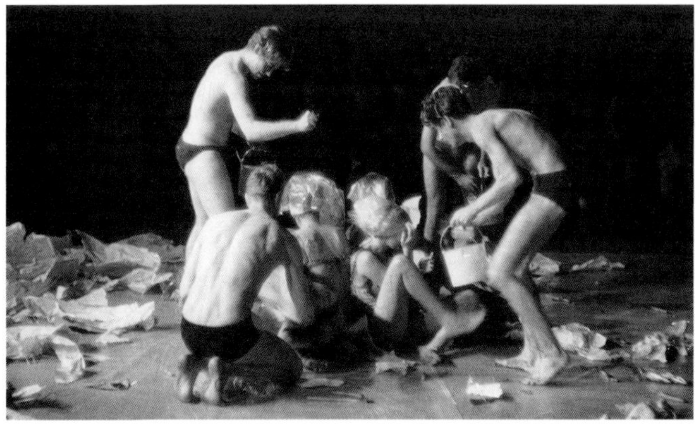

Performance artist Al Hansen, a member of the group of experimental multimedia artists known as Fluxus, in a loft performance piece, October 30, 1964. He was a grandfather of rock musician Beck.

Actors in Carolee Schneemann's Kinetic Theater group present the performance art piece *Meat Joy*, which she described as "celebration of flesh as material," in the Judson Memorial Church auditorium, November 16, 1964. Schneemann explored issues involving the female body and sexuality in happenings, on film, and through other media.

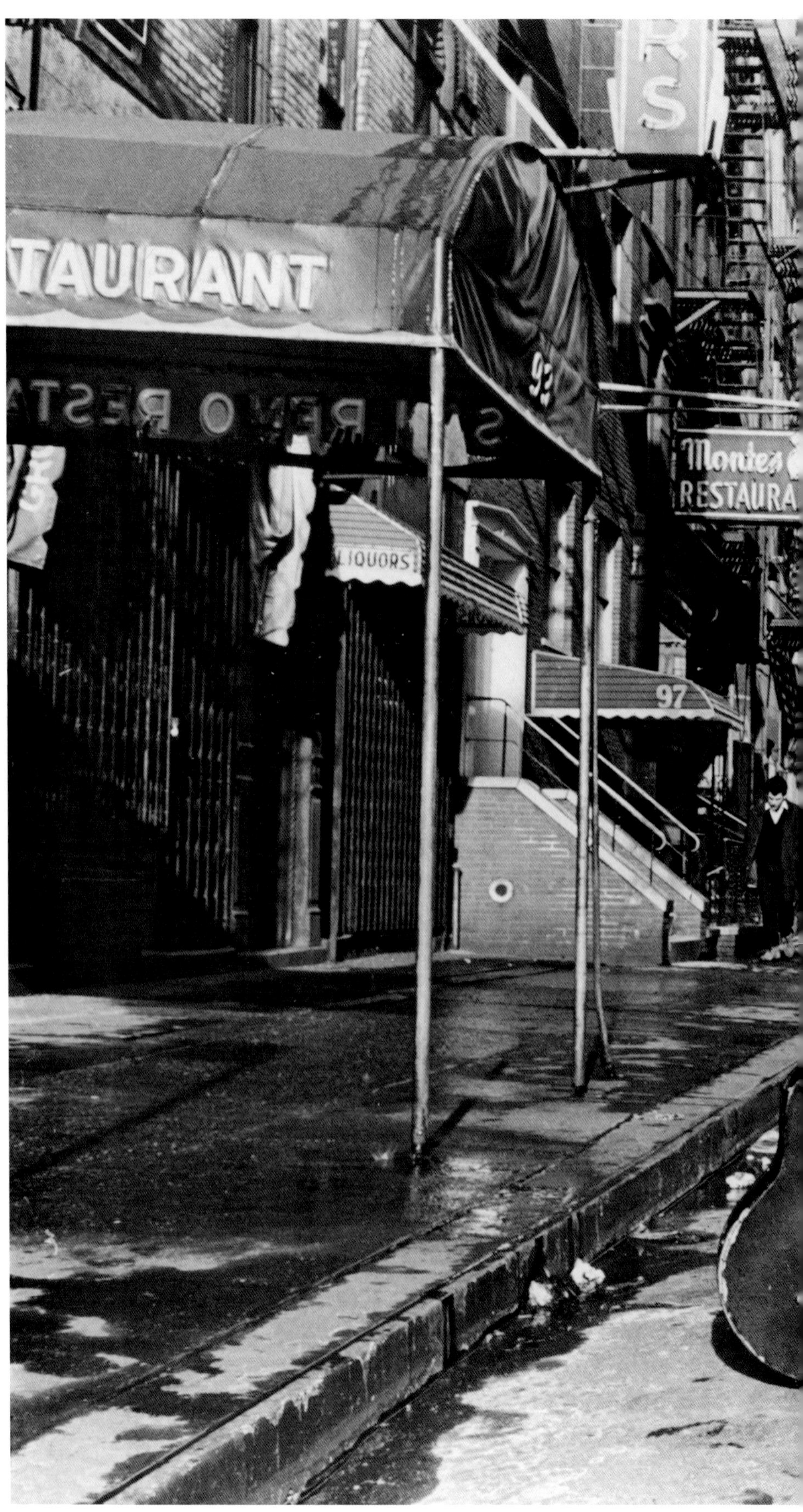

Folksinger, songwriter, and political activist Phil Ochs poses with his guitar on MacDougal St. in Greenwich Village, January 3, 1965. His often sharply pointed antiwar and other topical songs (as he called them) included "I Ain't Marching Anymore," "Draft Dodger Rag," the scathing "Love Me, I'm a Liberal," and "Outside of a Small Circle of Friends." His years of serious drug, alcohol, and mental health problems would end in suicide on April 9, 1976.

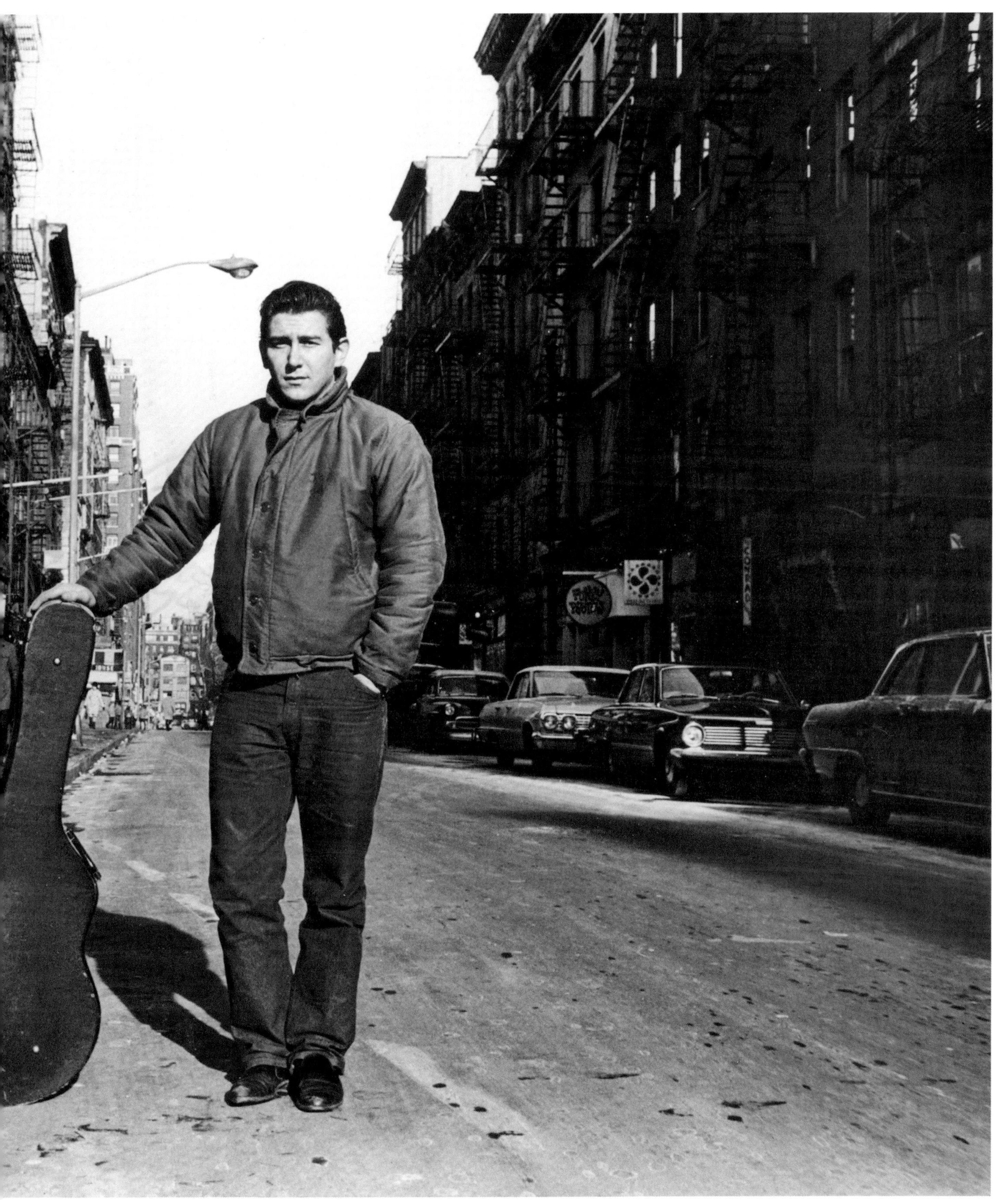

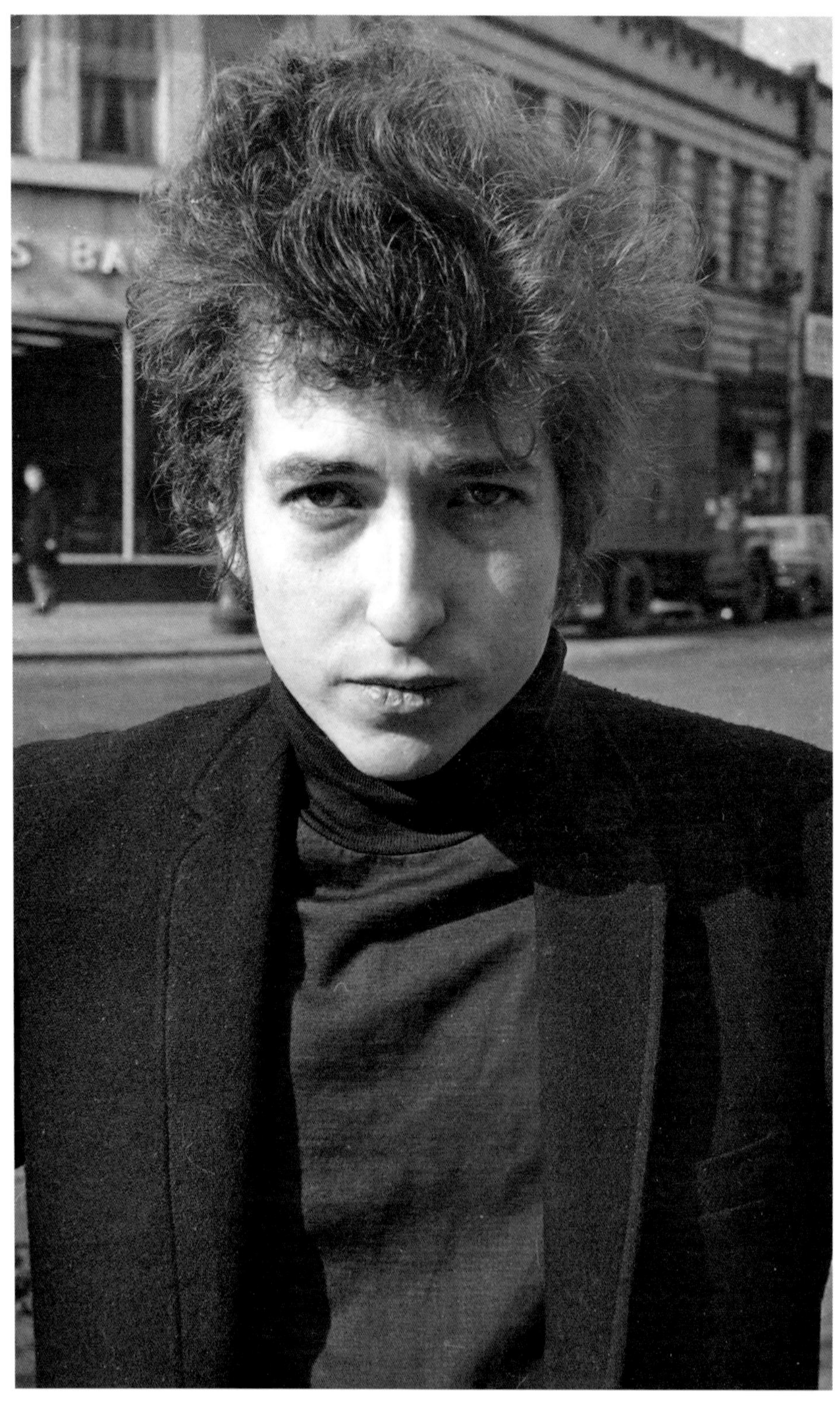

Bob Dylan outside the offices of the *Village Voice*, 61 Christopher St. at Seventh Ave. South,
January 22, 1965.

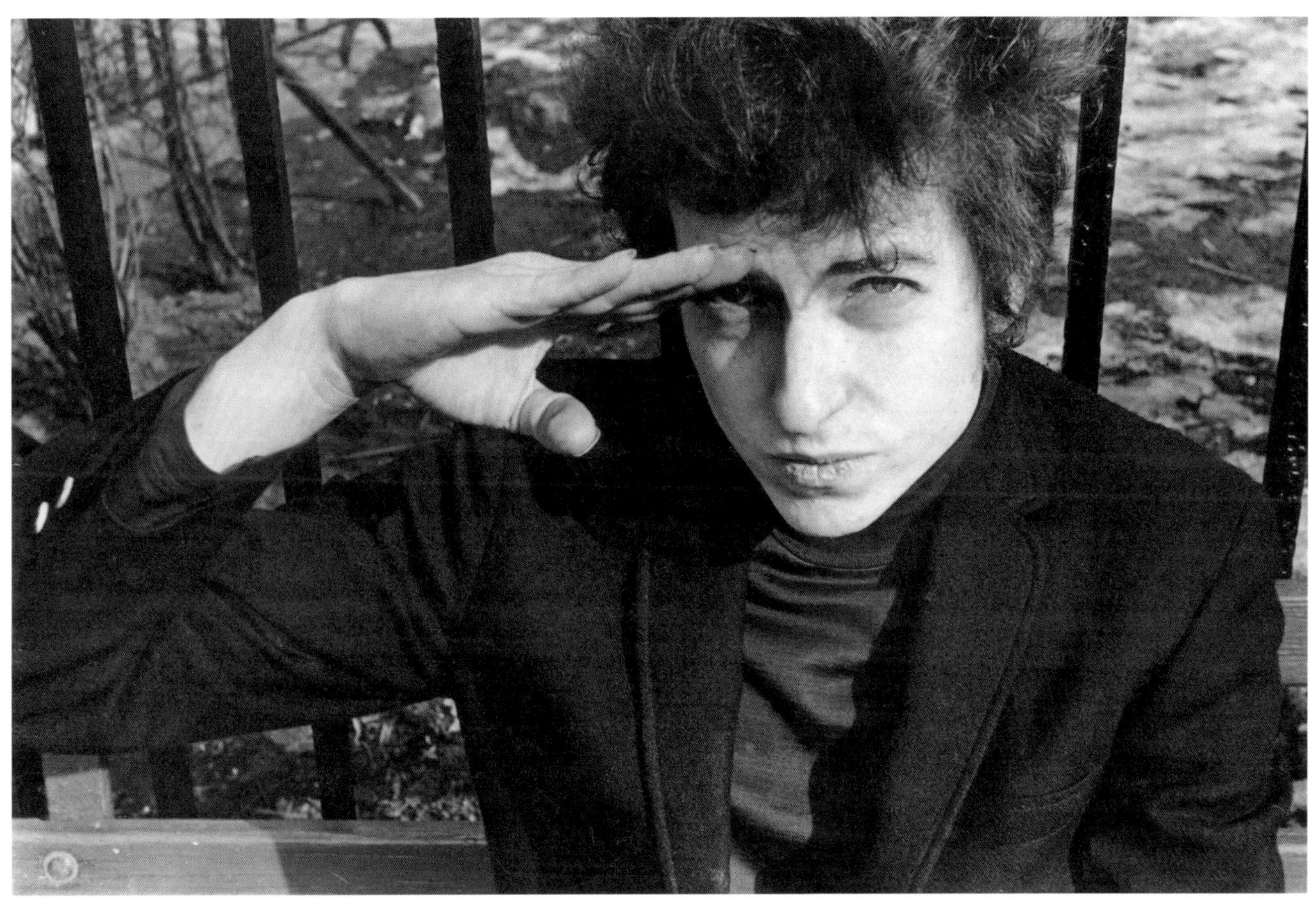

Bob Dylan, sitting on a bench in Christopher Park (across the street from the offices of the *Village Voice* since 1960), either salutes or shields his eyes from the sun, January 22, 1965. Taken the week he recorded the album *Bringing It All Back Home*, this photograph was used by Dylan on the cover of 2013's *Complete Album Collection Vol. One*.

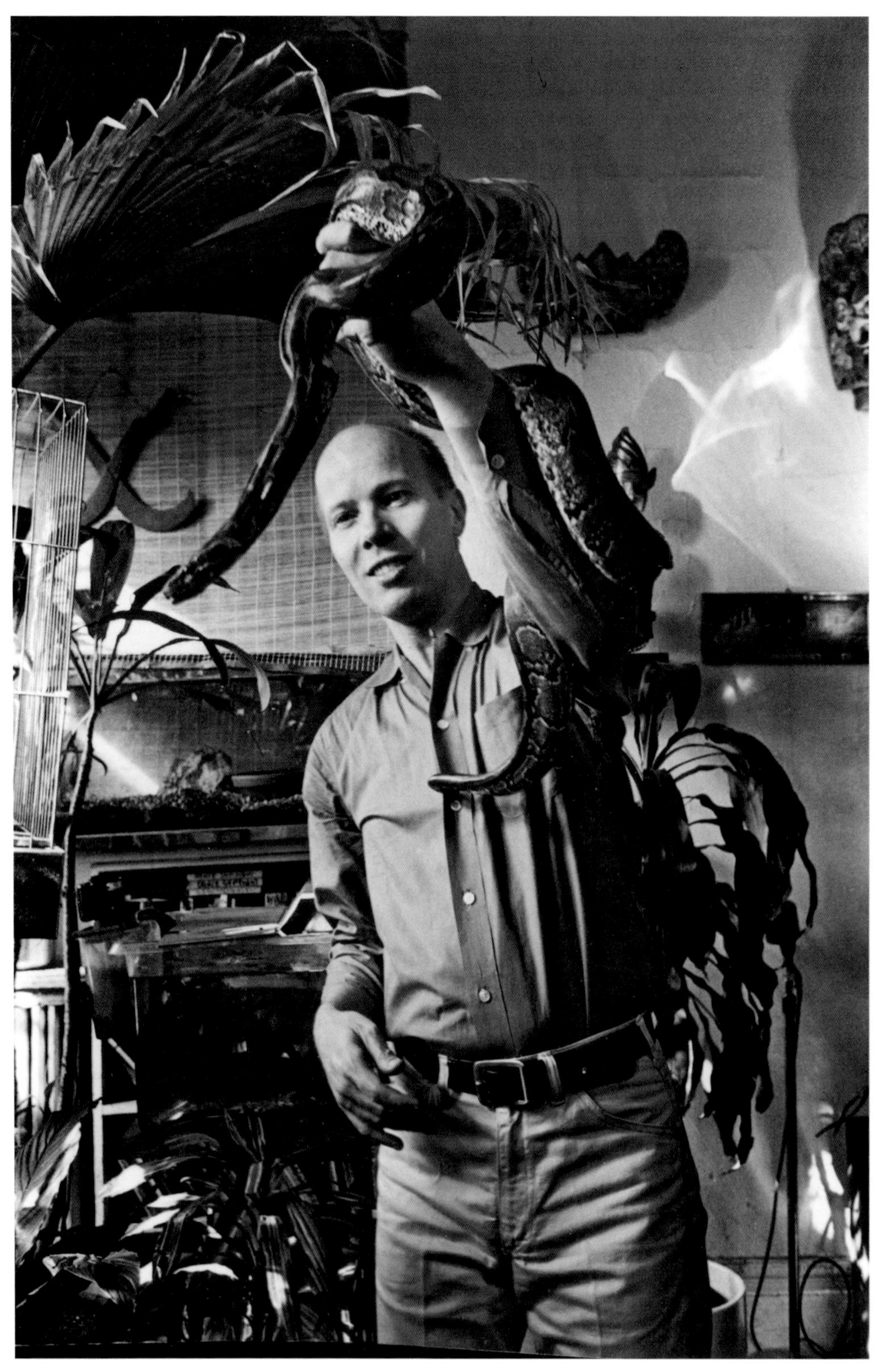

Artist Ray Johnson, a Neo-Dada and Pop artist known for his mail art, holds up a snake in composer George Kleinsinger's studio in the Chelsea Hotel, 222 West Twenty-Third St., February 10, 1965. Kleinsinger, who kept exotic animals, wrote the music for the opera *Archy and Mehitabel*, the Broadway musical adaptation *Shinbone Alley*, and the hit song "Tubby the Tuba."

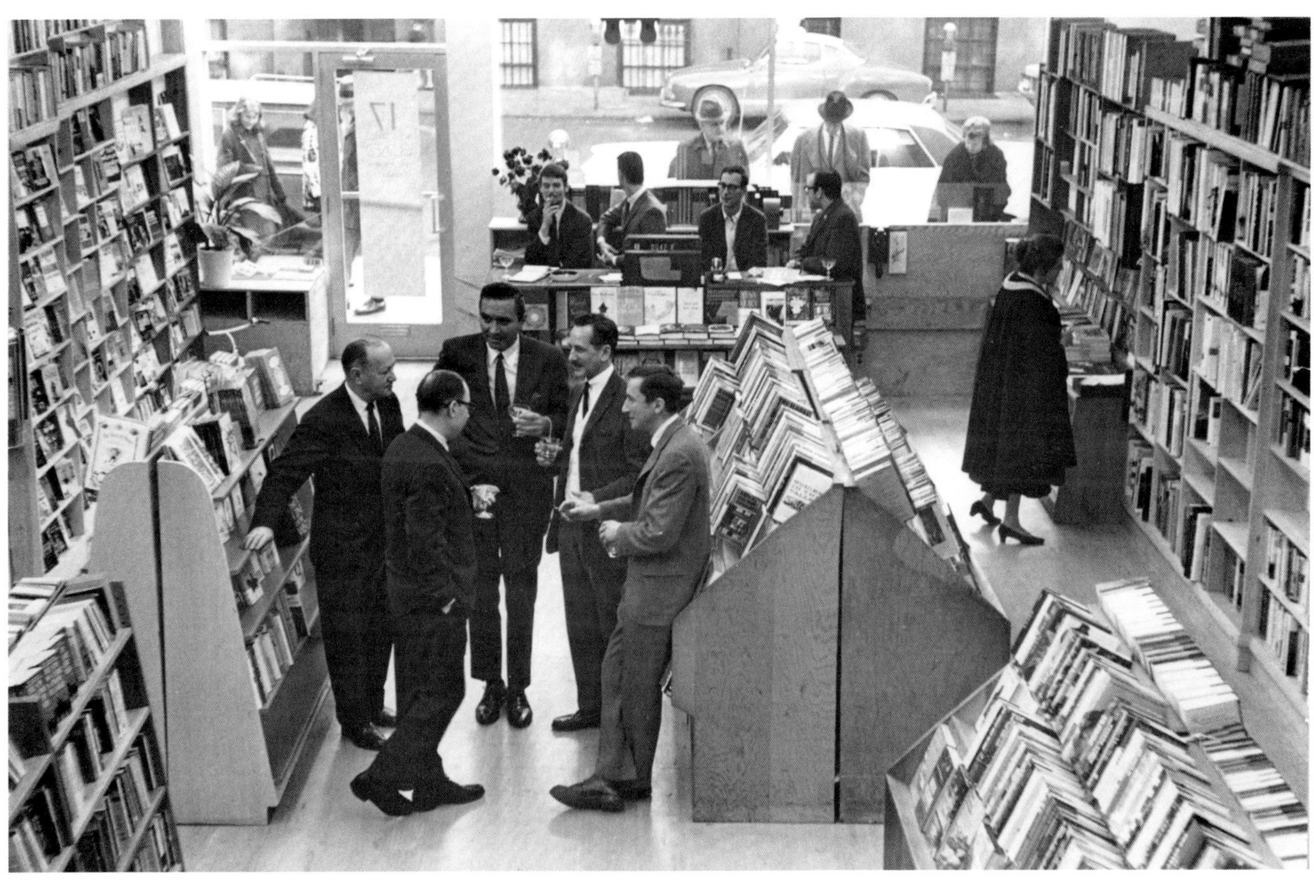

The Eighth Street Bookshop opens its new, second home at 17 West Eighth St., across from its original location,
February 21, 1965. Brothers Eli and Ted Wilentz were the owners of the Village institution: Eli is at right in the central group,
leaning against a bookcase, and Ted—who would sell his share in the store to his brother in 1967—stands to Eli's right.

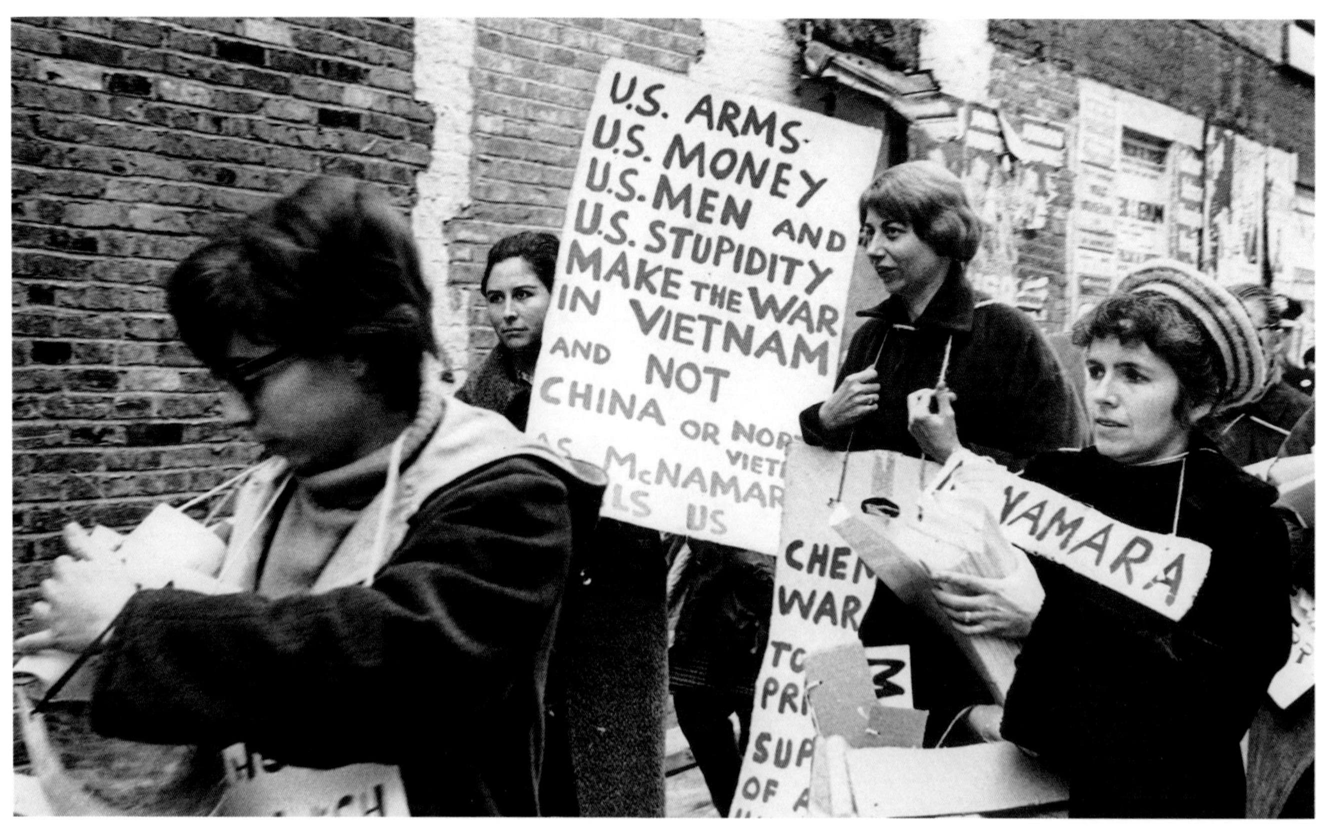

Short-story writer, poet, and antiwar activist Grace Paley (right) is demonstrating against the Vietnam War, March 9, 1965. The partially obscured sign around her neck reads "McNamara," referring to the leading architect of the war from 1961 to 1968, Secretary of Defense Robert S. McNamara.

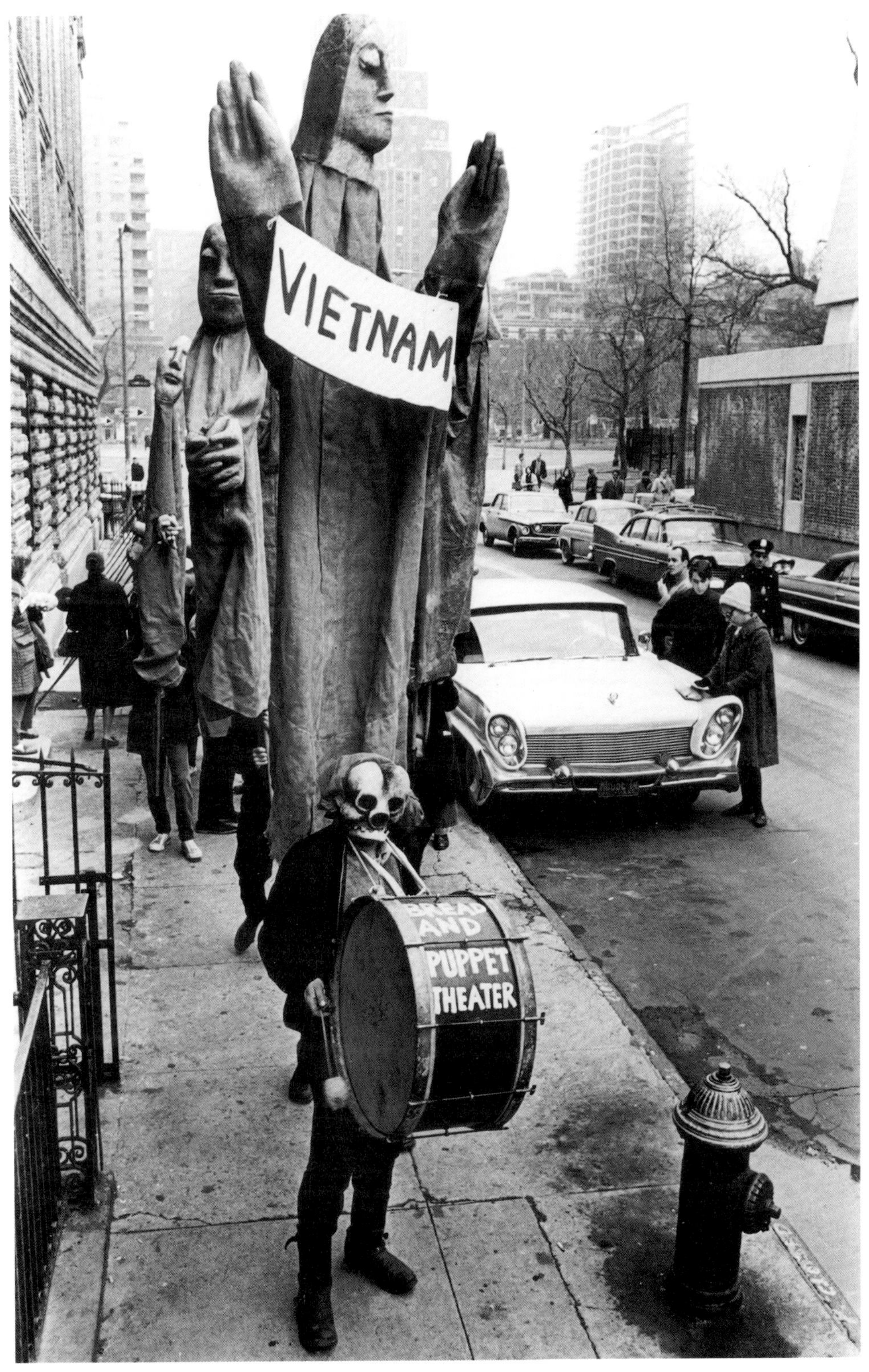

In one of the first protests in New York City against the Vietnam War, masked members of the Bread and Puppet Theater, led by artist, writer, and director Peter Schumann, march down Thompson St. from Washington Square, March 15, 1965. Schumann launched the group in 1963 on the Lower East Side, and he continues to bake bread that he distributes at Bread and Puppet Theater performances around the world.

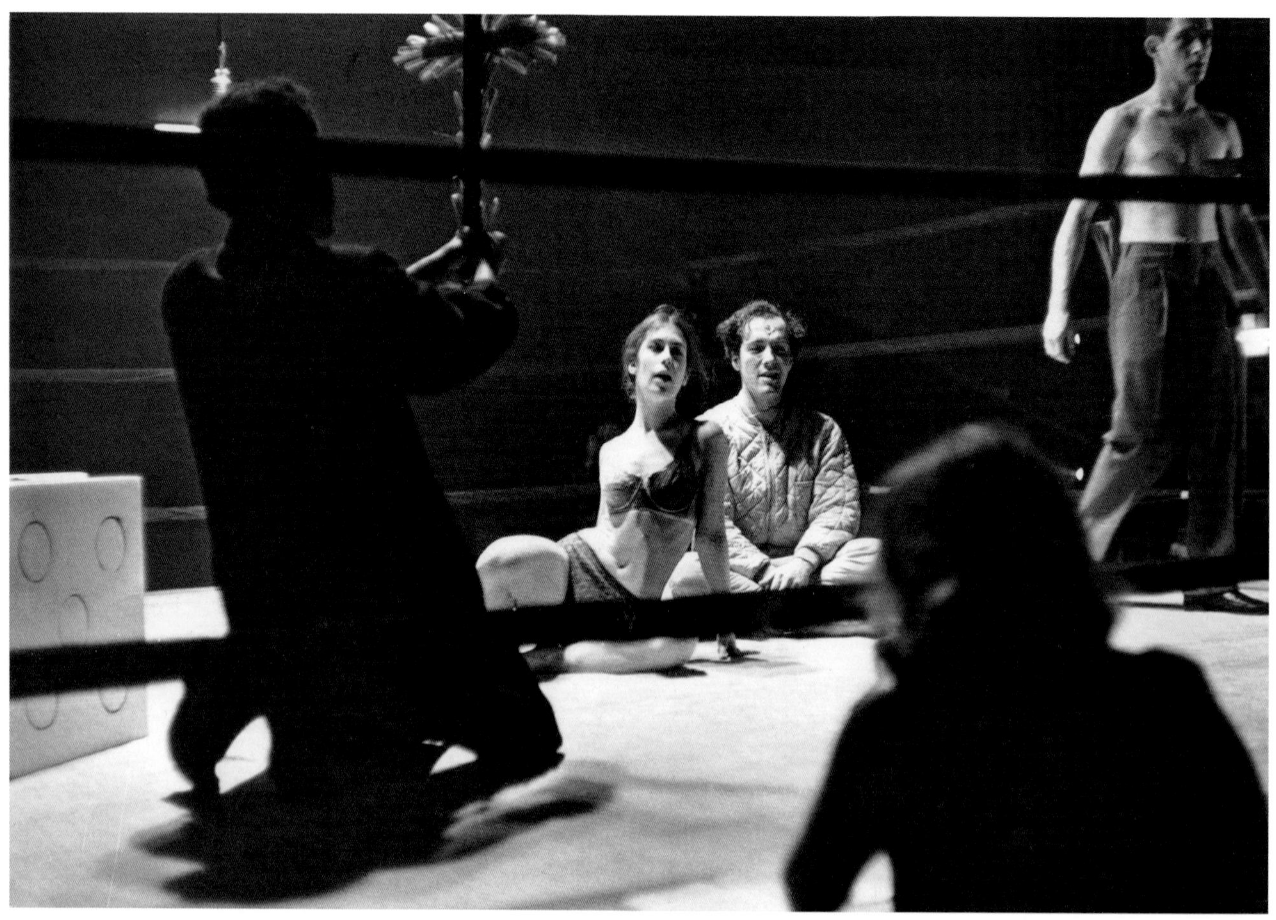

Scene from *The Tart*, a happening by artist and writer Dick Higgins, performed in a boxing ring
in Sunnyside, Queens, April 17, 1965. Higgins, a cofounder of the Fluxus movement, coined the
term "intermedia" to describe combinations of theatricality, visual art, and music.

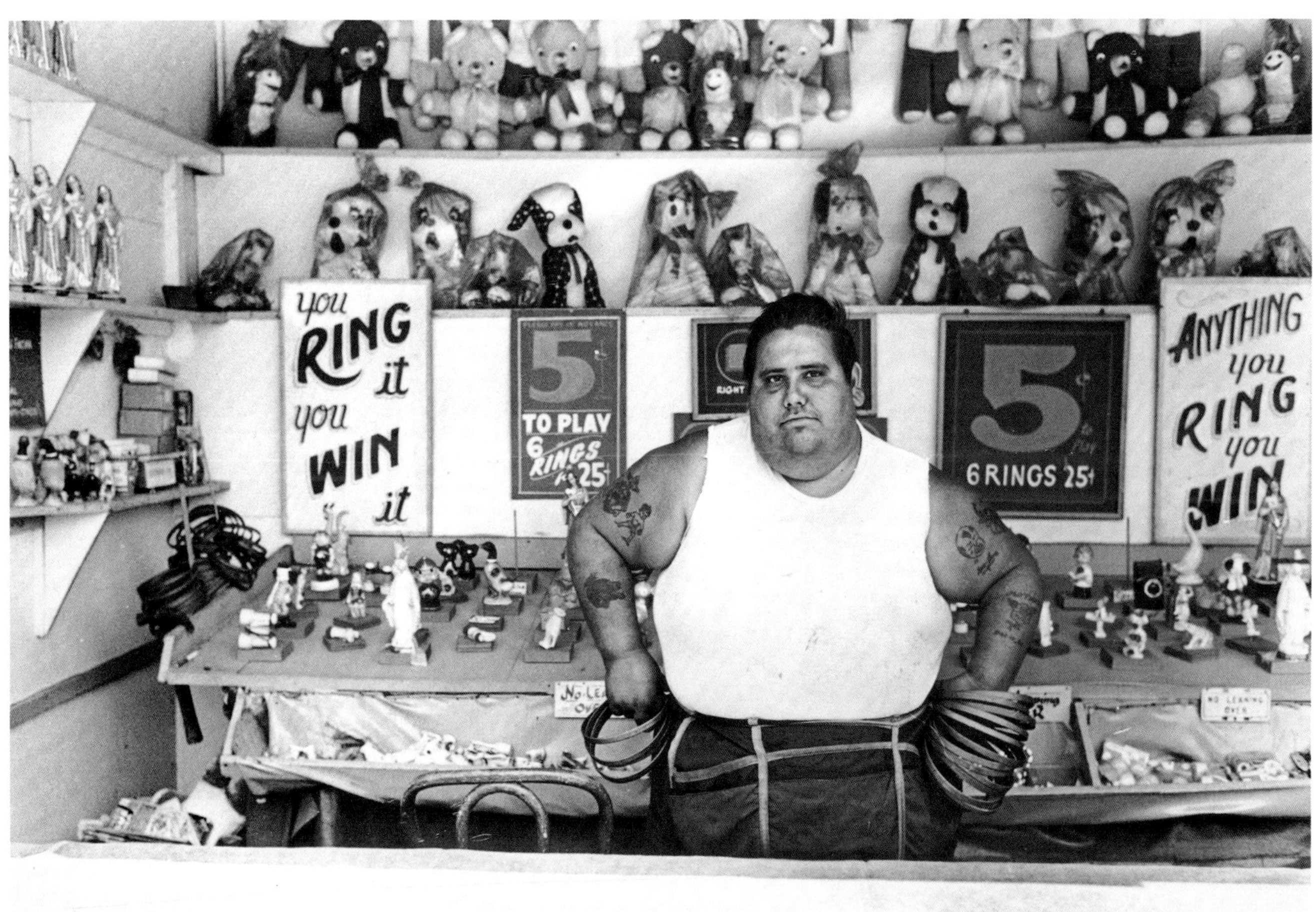

Waiting for a customer at a Coney Island ring toss booth, June 13, 1965. Steeplechase Park had closed the year before, two decades after Luna Park, ending a nearly century-long era in which Coney Island was the largest amusement area in the United States, with millions of visitors a year. But the games of chance, the boardwalk, the Cyclone, and Nathan's hot-dog stand remain.

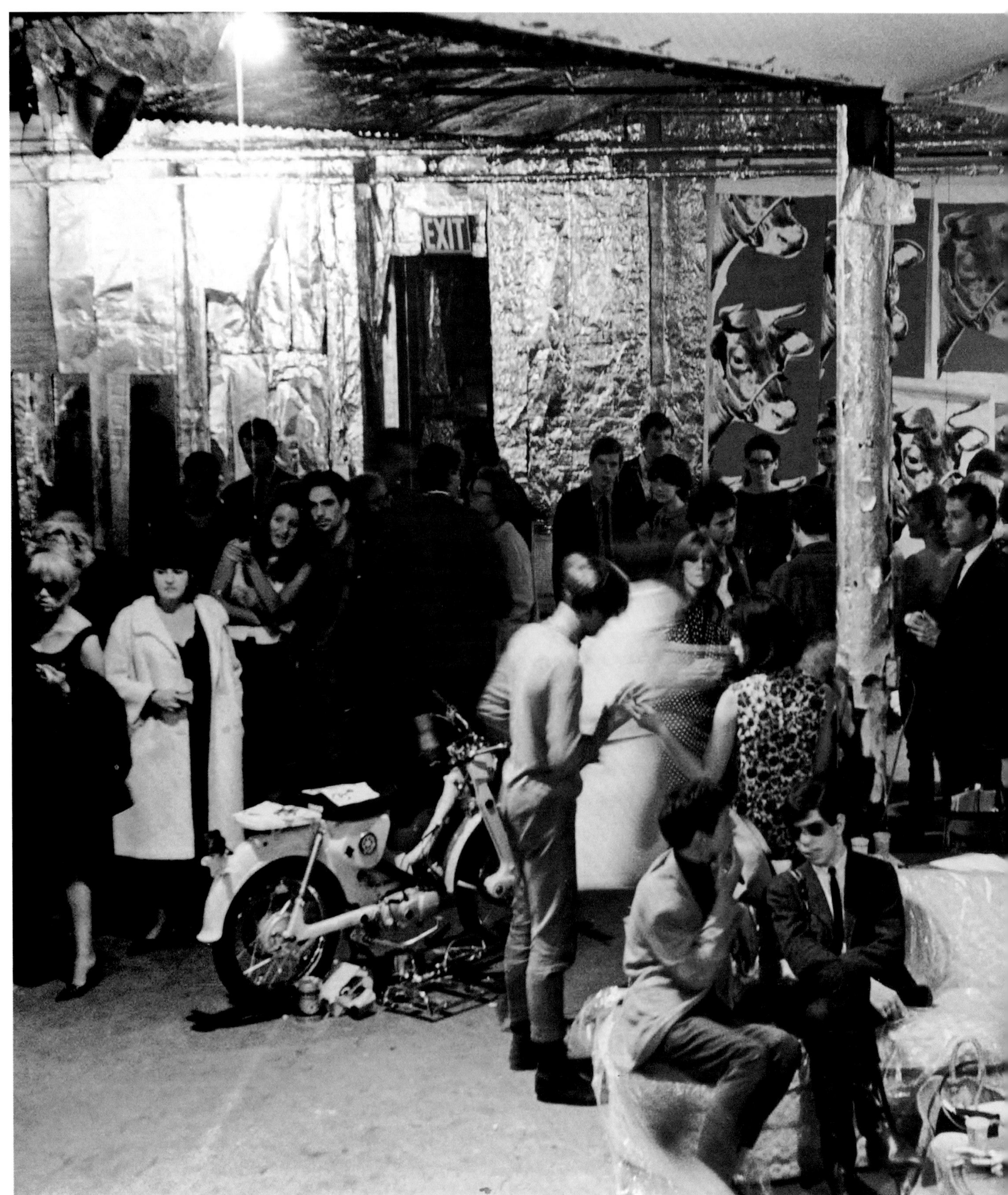
EXIT

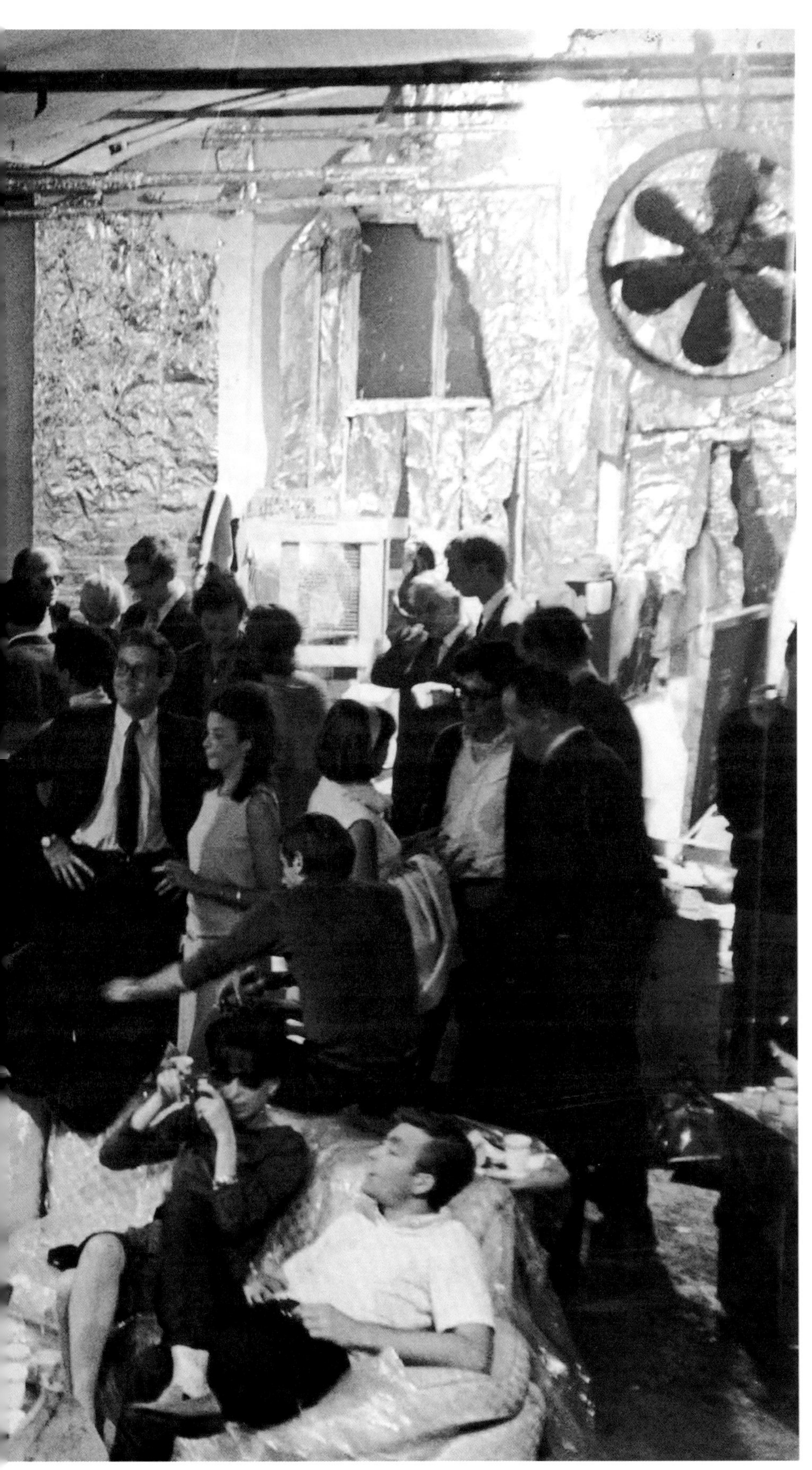

A party in full swing at Andy Warhol's Factory, 231 East Forty-Seventh St., August 31, 1965. The loft, including the toilet, was decorated with silver vinyl paper. Photographer Stephen Shore, in sunglasses, is seated on the couch, and an early version of Warhol's Cow Wallpaper is on the back wall.

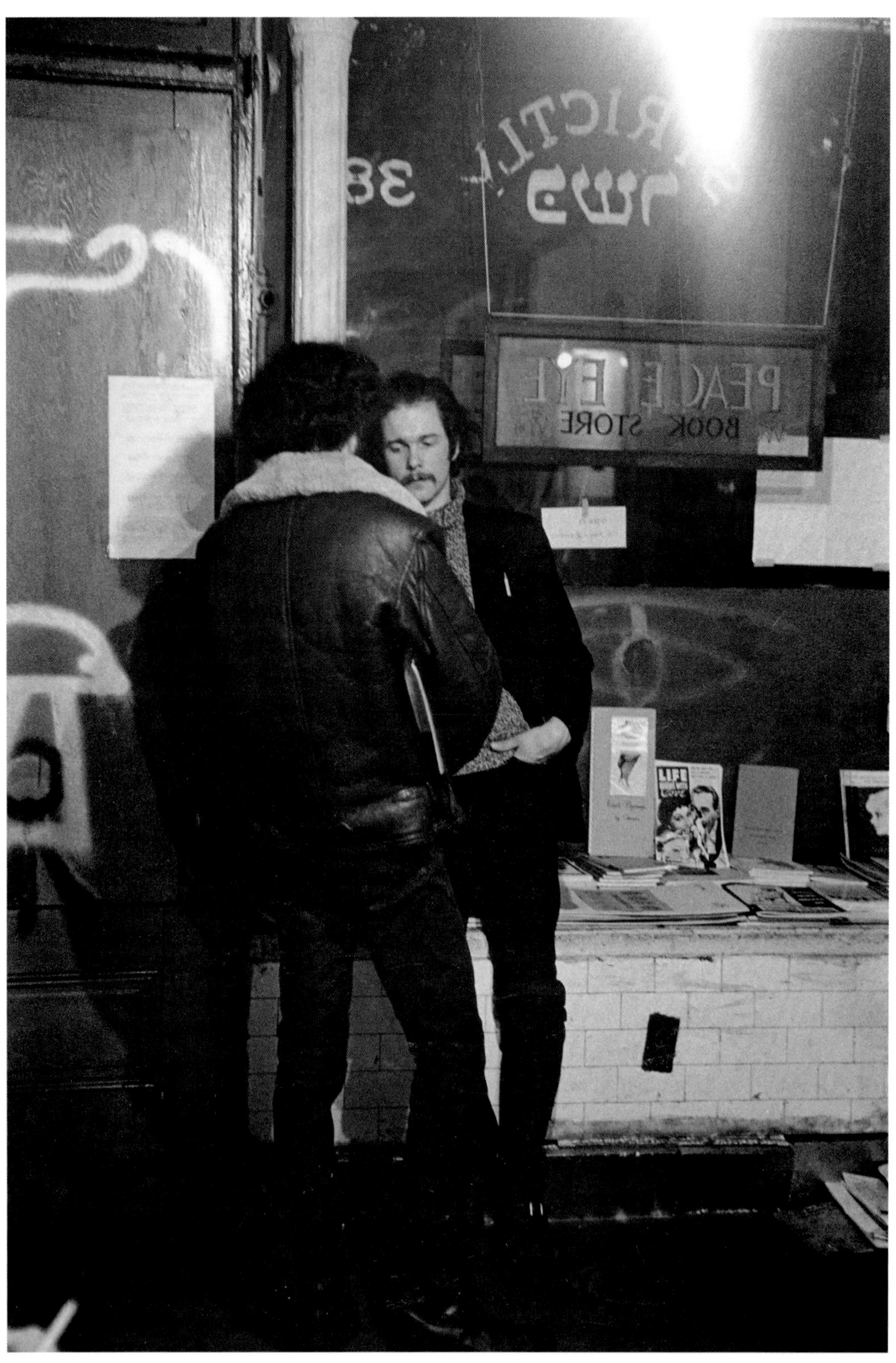

Musician, poet, and activist Ed Sanders (facing camera), who cofounded the Fugs with Tuli Kupferberg in late 1964, speaks with a customer inside his Peace Eye Bookstore and cultural center, 383 East Tenth St., January 14, 1966. (The "Strictly Kosher" sign, in English and Hebrew, is from its previous incarnation as a butcher shop.) Sanders was an early promoter of legalized marijuana and underground comic art; two weeks before this photo was taken, he had been arrested in a police raid and charged with obscenity for distributing his mimeographed magazine, *Fuck You: A Magazine of the Arts.*

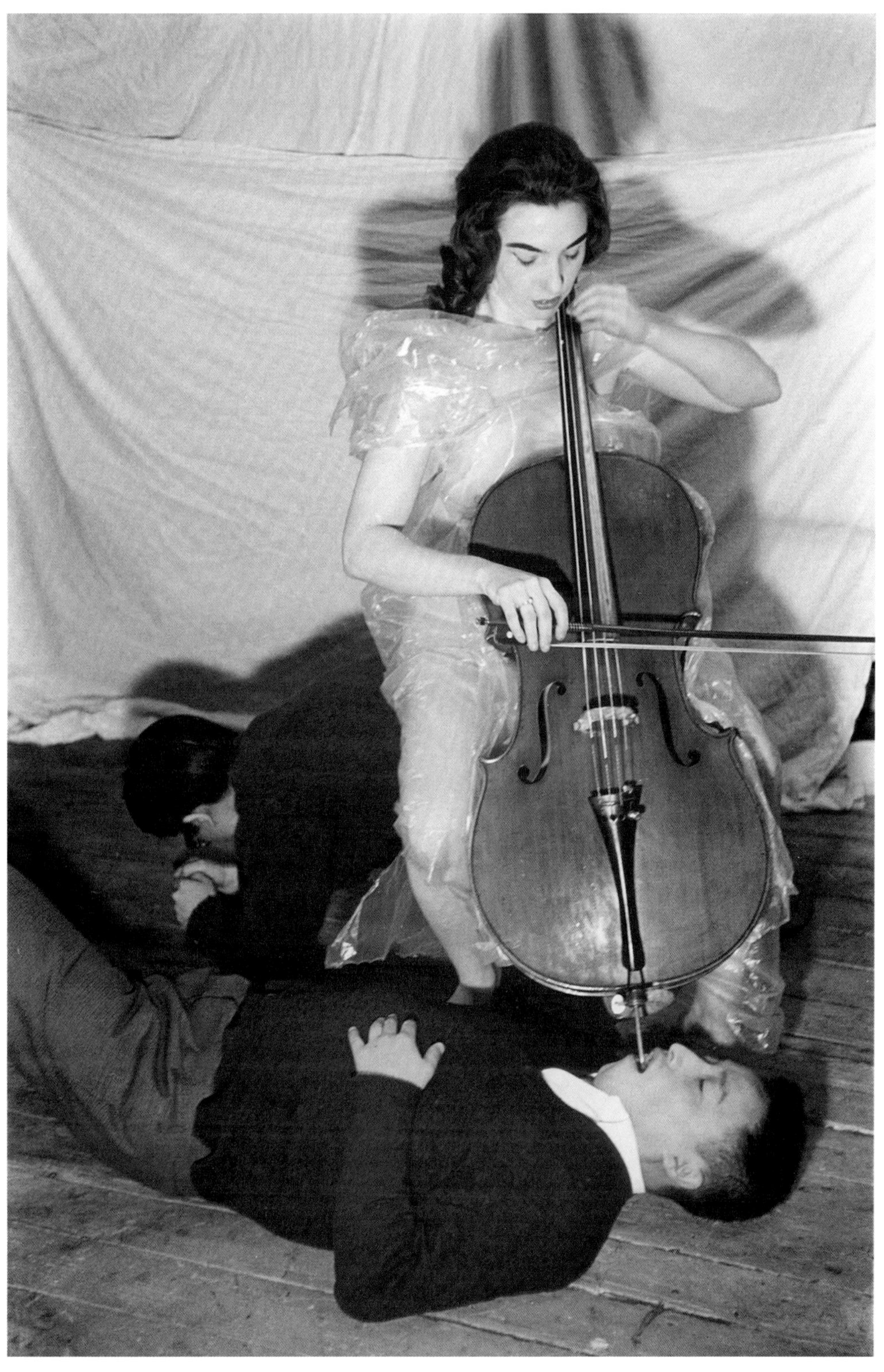

Performance artist Charlotte Moorman sits on the back of Japanese composer and violinist Takehisa Kosugi and plays a cello held between the teeth of artist and composer Nam June Paik, January 18, 1966. Moorman founded the Avant Garde Festival of New York in 1963, and it took place annually (with three exceptions) through 1980. She collaborated with Paik—best known as the founder and leading innovator of video art—on multimedia performance pieces for decades.

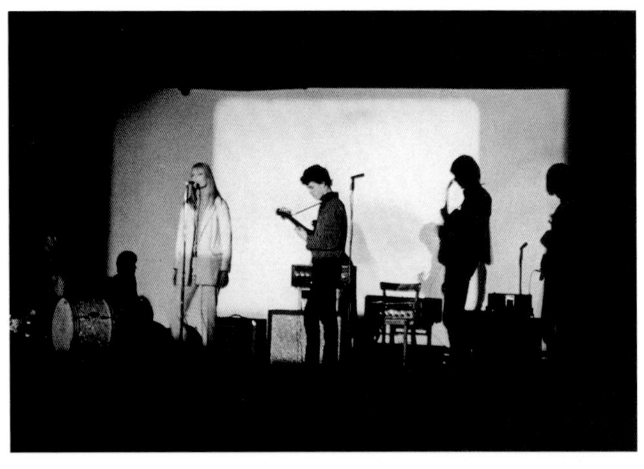
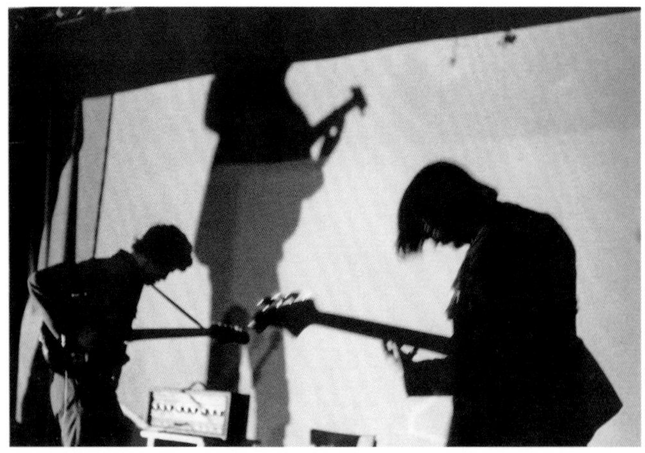

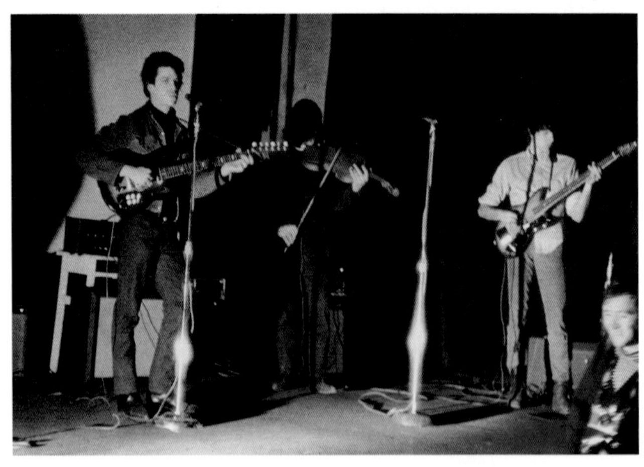
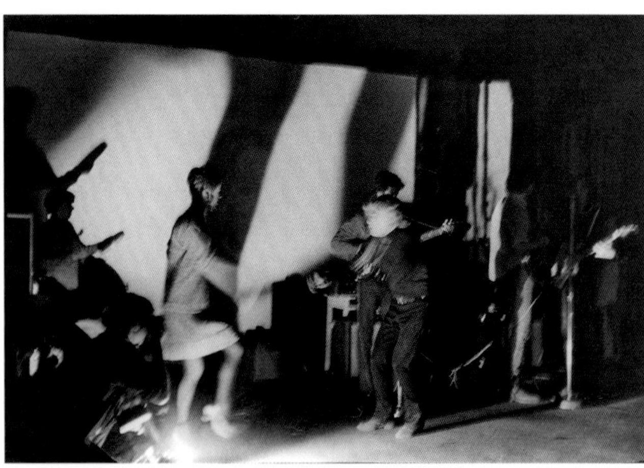

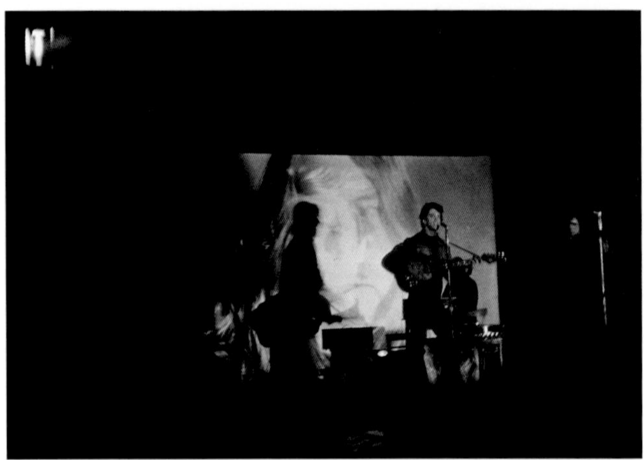
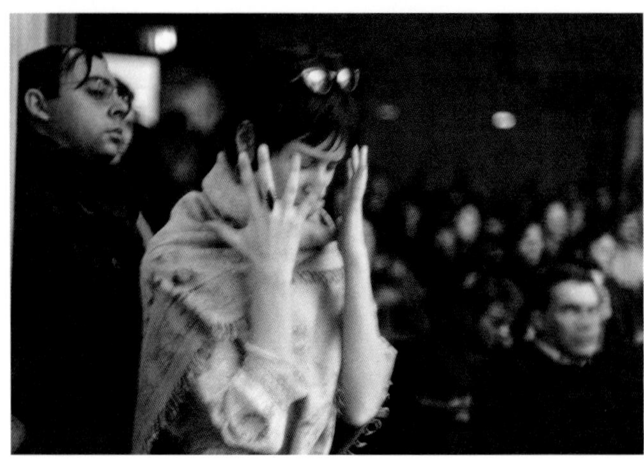

The Velvet Underground performs with Nico at the Film-Makers' Cinemateque 125 West Forty-First St., February 8, 1966. The band—Lou Reed, John Cale, guitarist Sterling Morrison, and drummer Maureen "Moe" Tucker—came together in 1965 and was soon being managed, loosely, by Andy Warhol. Rolling Stones' guitarist Brian Jones had introduced Nico, a German singer, model, and actor, to Warhol, who pressed her on the band. In one frame, Warhol assistant Gerard Malanga and muse, model, and actress Edie Sedgwick dance onstage; in another, an audience member reacts.

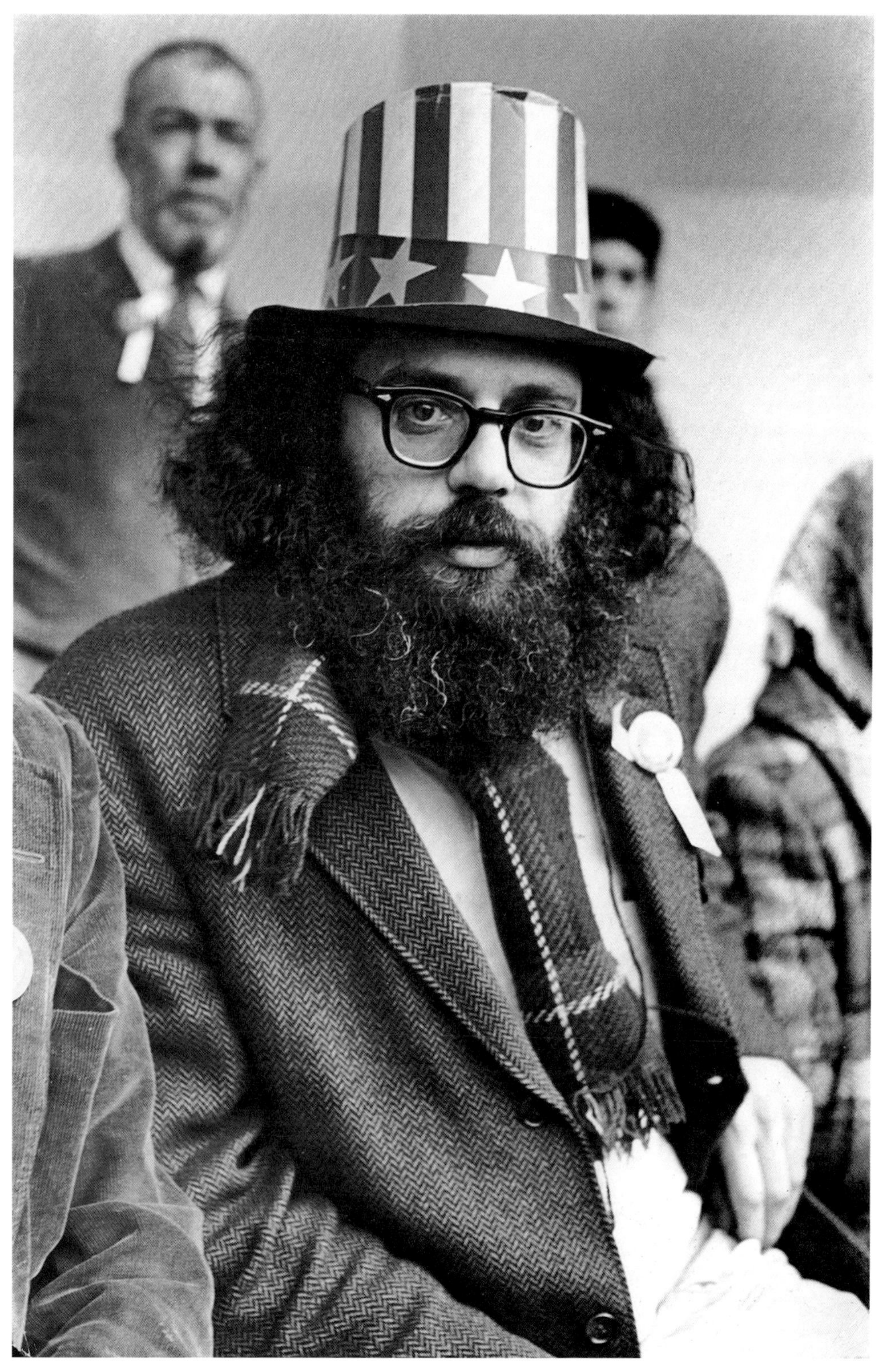

Allen Ginsberg, wearing a paper "Uncle Sam hat," as he called it, sits at the Naumburg Bandshell in Central Park during an anti–Vietnam War rally following a mile-long march from Bryant Park at Forty-Second St., March 26, 1966. The event was part of two days of antiwar demonstrations in more than a dozen cities around the United States and overseas.

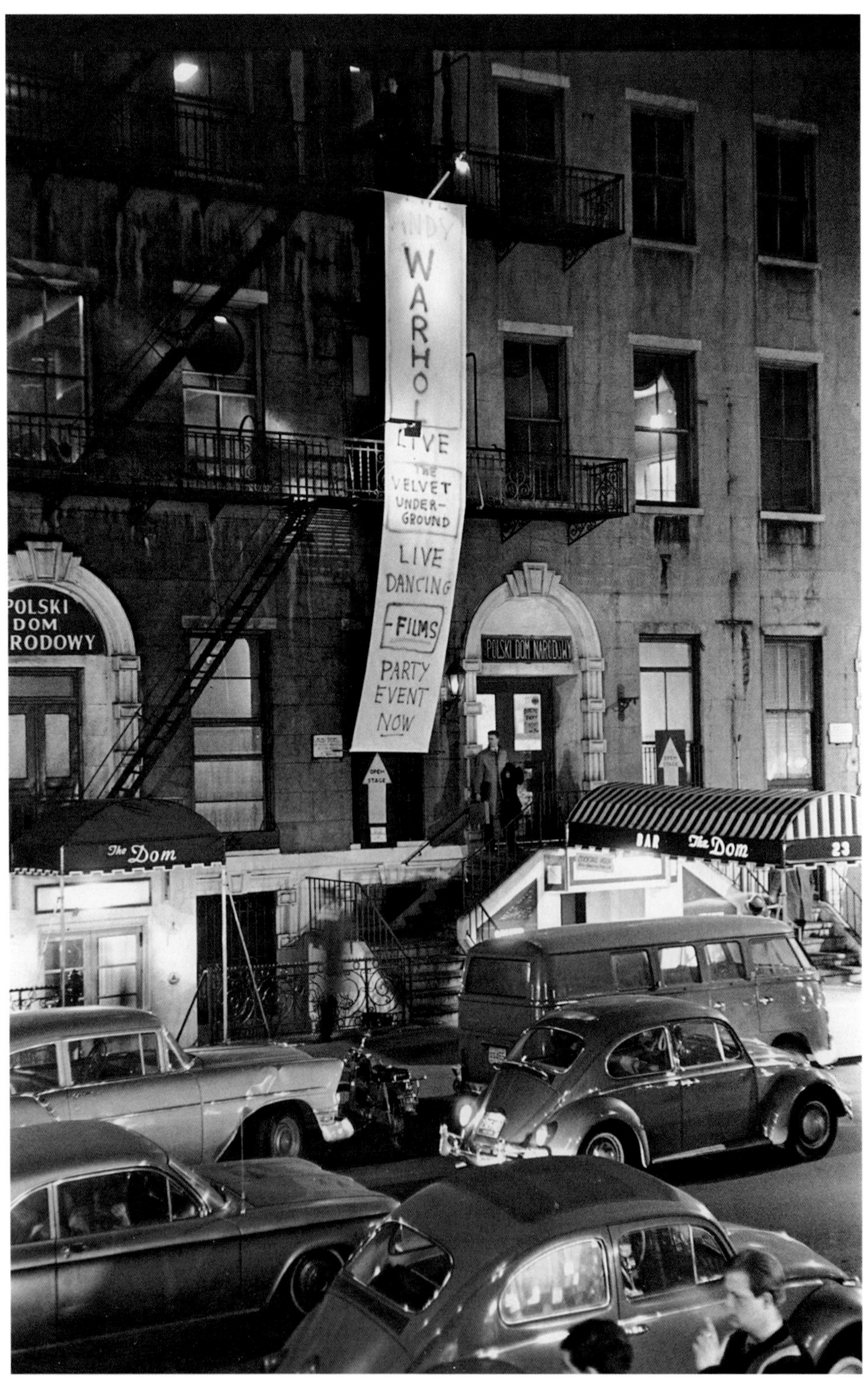

The entrance to the Dom—short for Polski Dom Narodowy, or "Polish National Home"—at 23 St. Marks Place, site of Andy Warhol's Exploding Plastic Inevitable multimedia events, March 31, 1966. Warhol and his frequent film director, Paul Morrissey, sublet the large ballroom—created in the twenties by the Polish National Home out of interior space in four adjacent buildings—and turned it into a nightclub. Inside, Warhol stands behind the spotlights on the balcony inside the Dom during the evening's performance. A day later, McDarrah returned and got a shot of the Velvet Underground in front of a projected eye. In 1967, the building would become home of the psychedelic club the Electric Circus, until 1971.

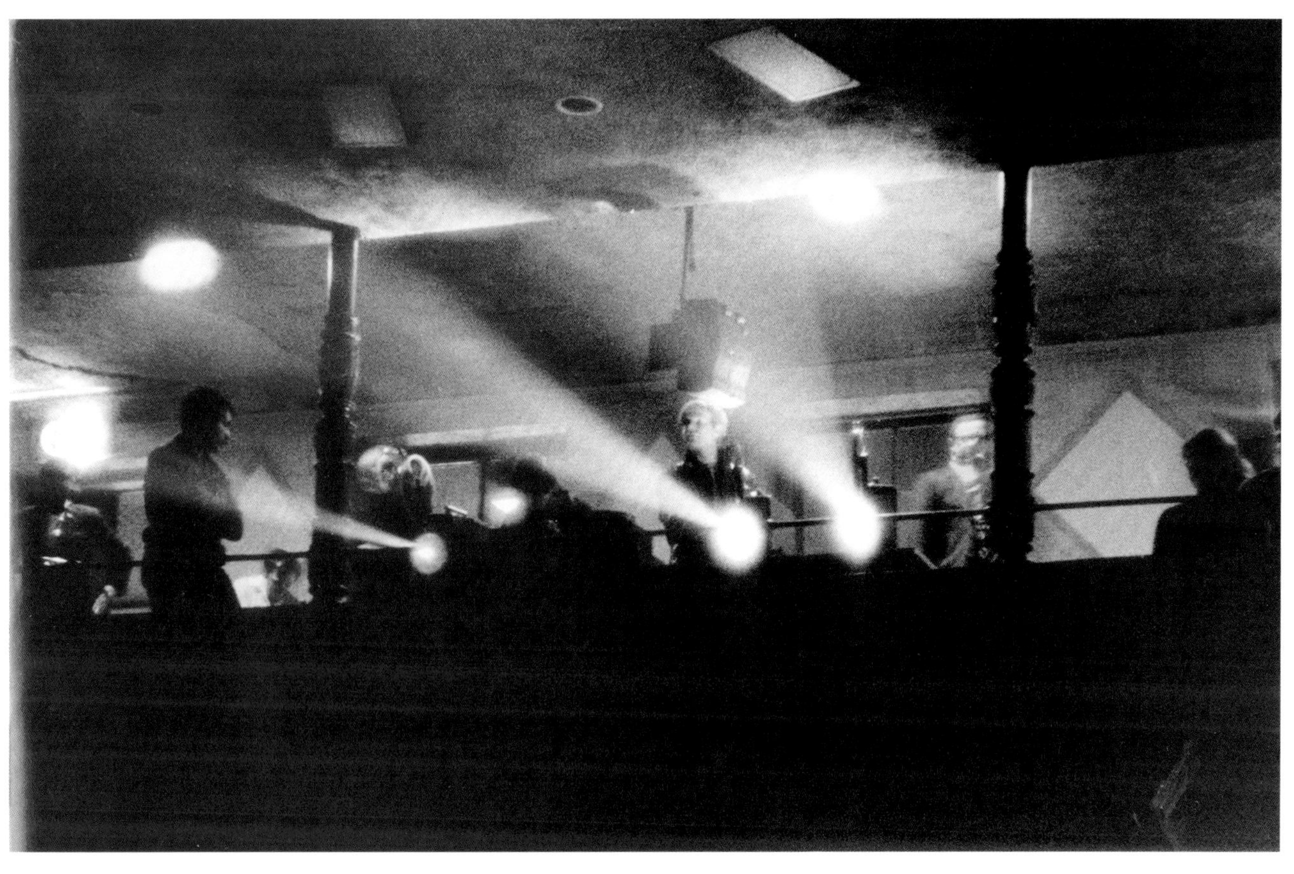

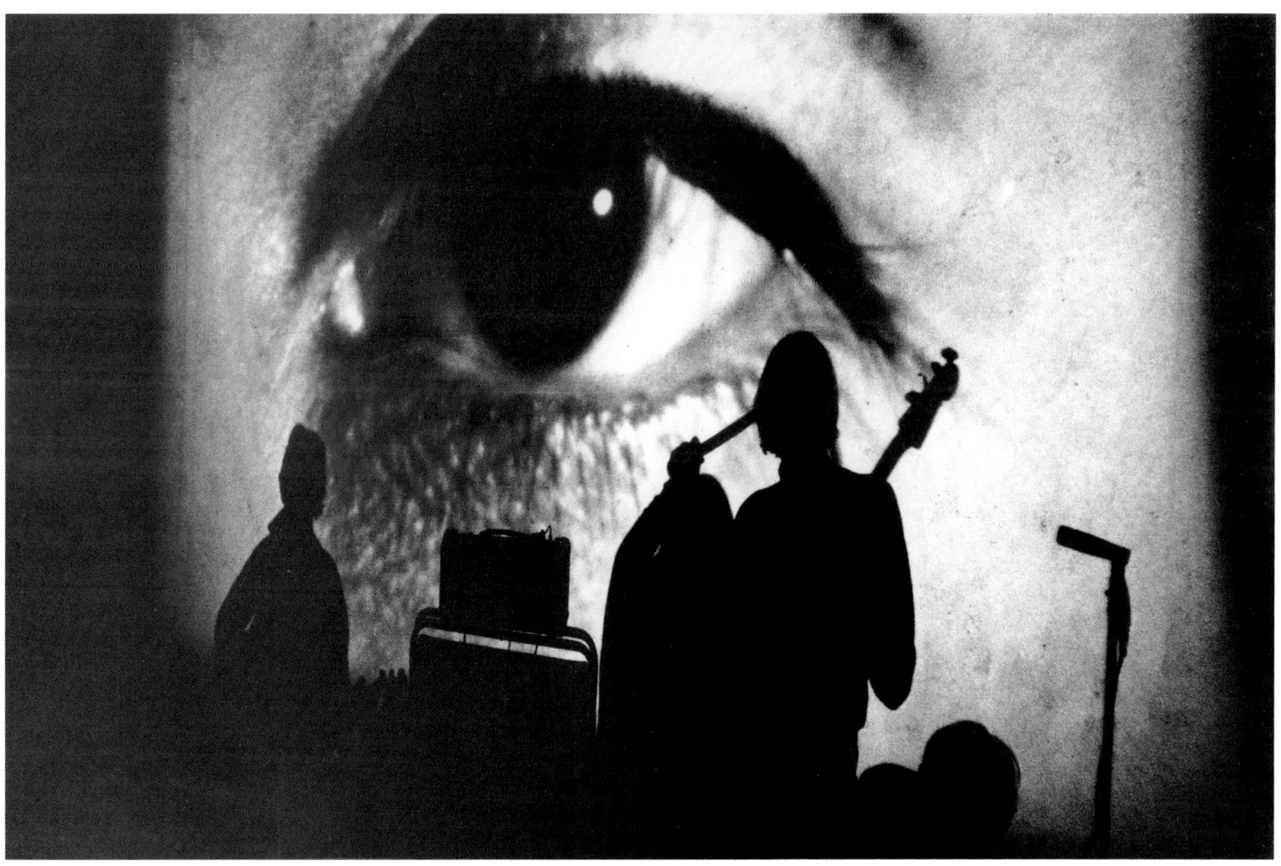

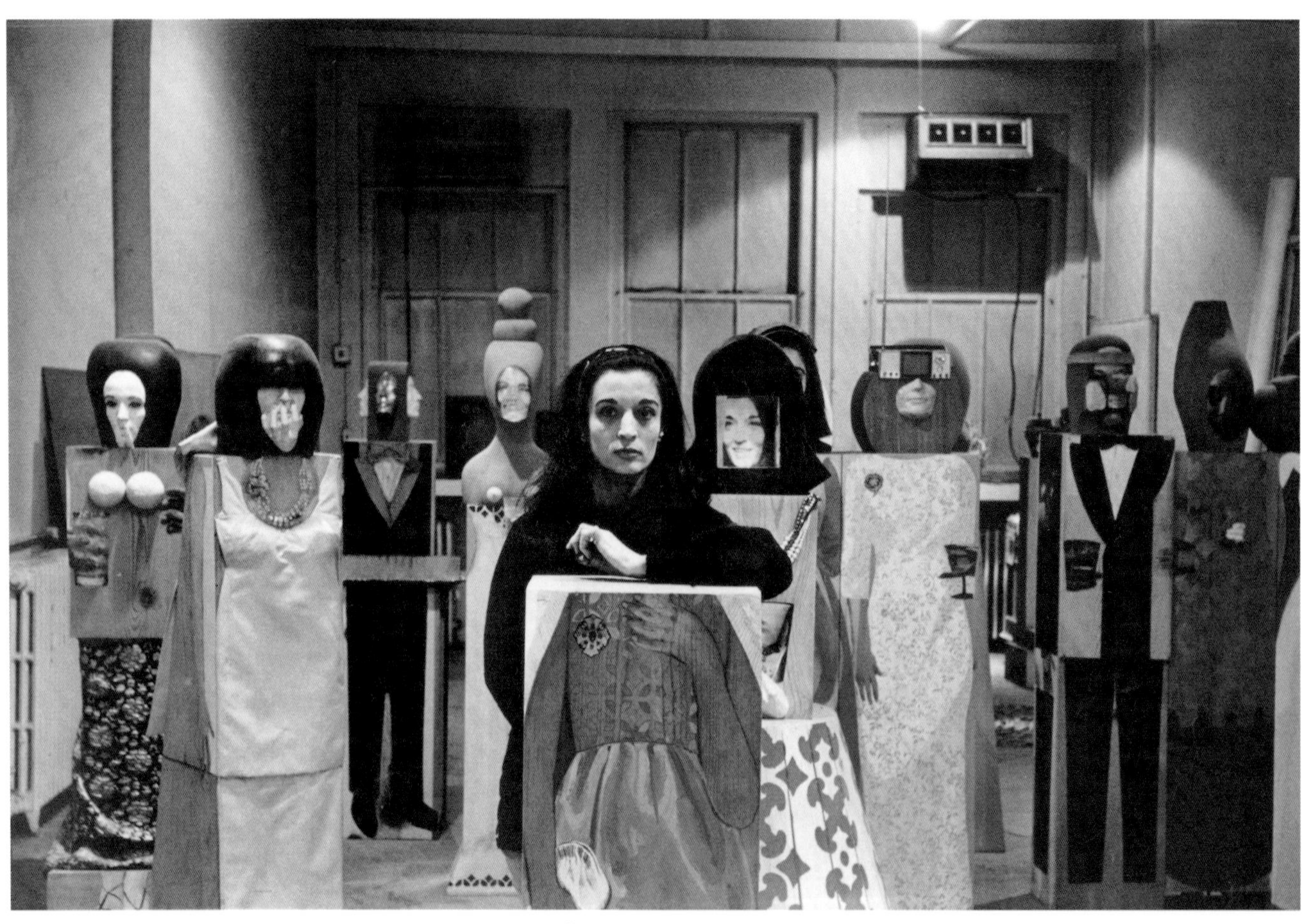

Artist Marisol Escobar, generally known simply as Marisol, poses amid her group of fifteen freestanding wood sculptures, titled *The Cocktail Party*, a blend of Pop and folk art combining photography, woodcarving, plaster-casting, painting, and collage, April 14, 1966.

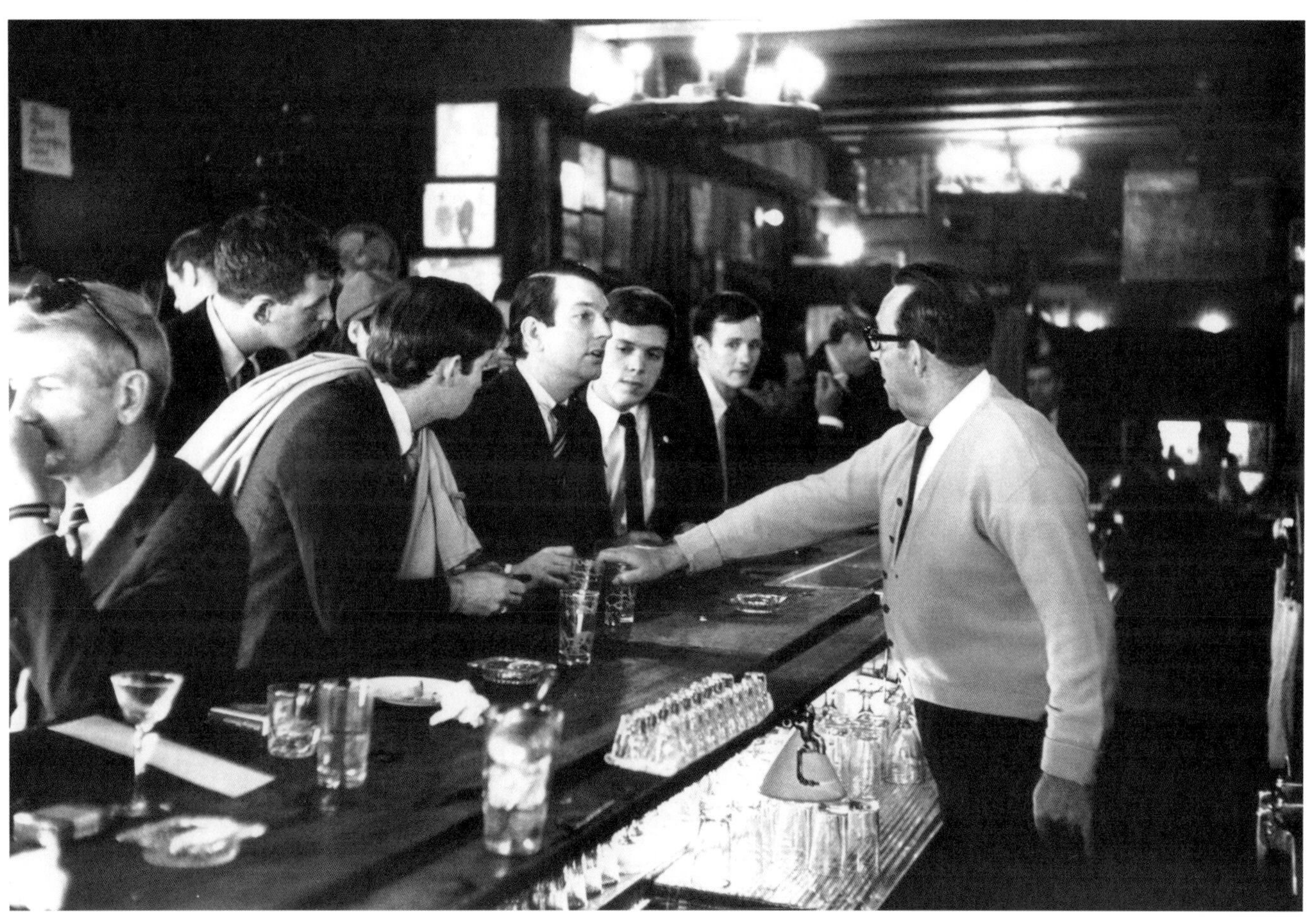

A bartender at Julius' Bar, 159 West Tenth St., refuses to serve members of the Mattachine Society—an early American gay rights group, who were protesting New York liquor laws that prohibited serving gay customers—including (from left) John Timmins, group president Dick Leitsch, Craig Rodwell (who went on to found the Oscar Wilde Memorial Bookshop, selling literature by gay authors, the following year), and Randy Wicker, April 21, 1966. The carefully orchestrated "Sip-In," inspired by civil rights protests, was a precursor to the Stonewall uprising in 1969. The group eventually sued the New York State Liquor Authority, and in 1972 the "deviant" laws were finally struck from the books. Julius' now promotes itself as a gay bar.

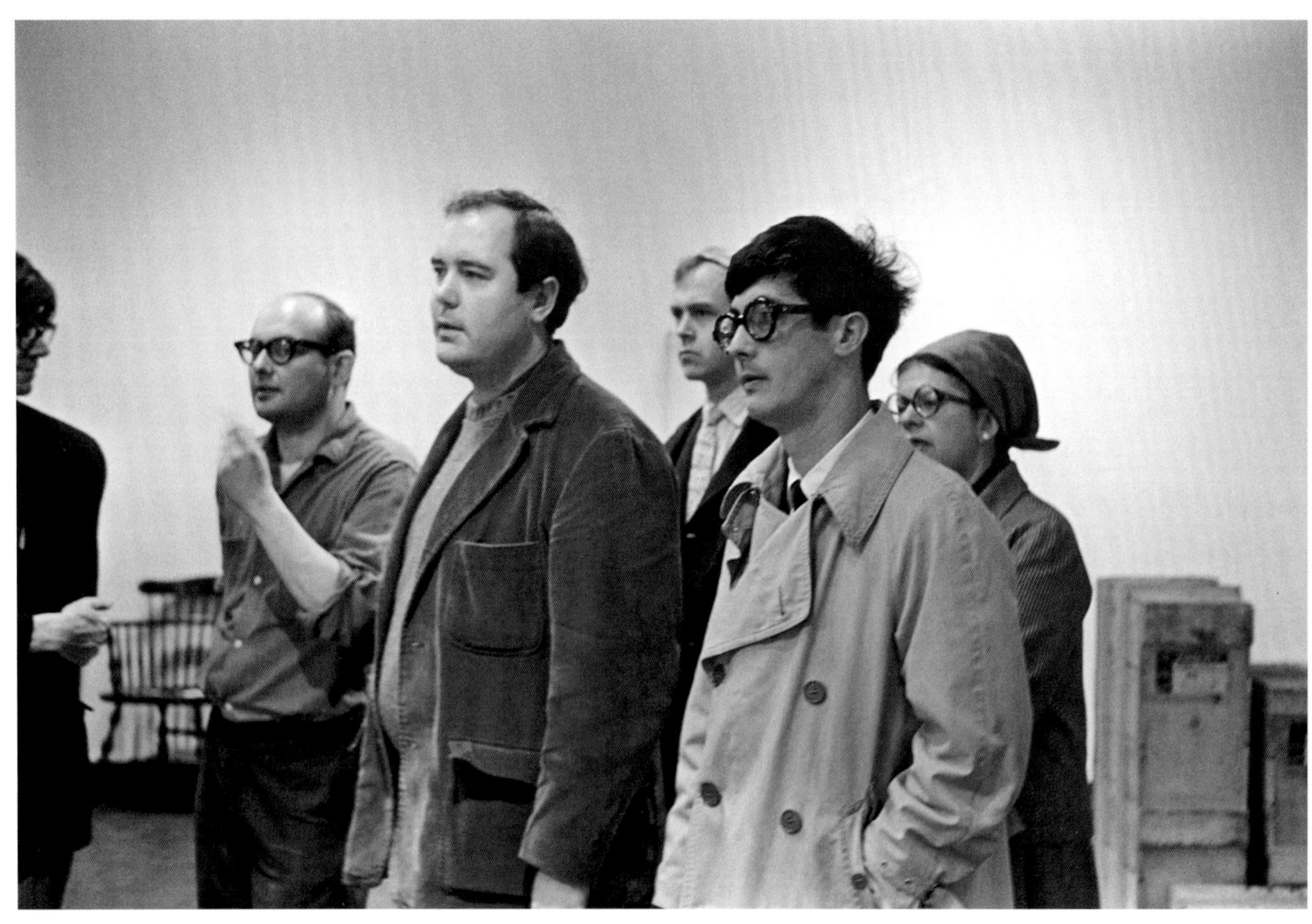

A group of art-world figures observing the installation of the *Primary Structures* exhibition at the Jewish Museum, April 26, 1966, includes gallerist Richard Bellamy (front row, right), standing next to artist Dan Flavin, and artists Robert Smithson (far left) and Sol LeWitt. In the back are curator David Whitney (with necktie) and gallerist Jill Kornblee. The exhibition of younger American and British sculptors, organized by curator Kynaston McShine, was credited with introducing Minimalism to a wider audience. Among the many other artists in the show were Ellsworth Kelly, William Tucker, Donald Judd, and Larry Bell.

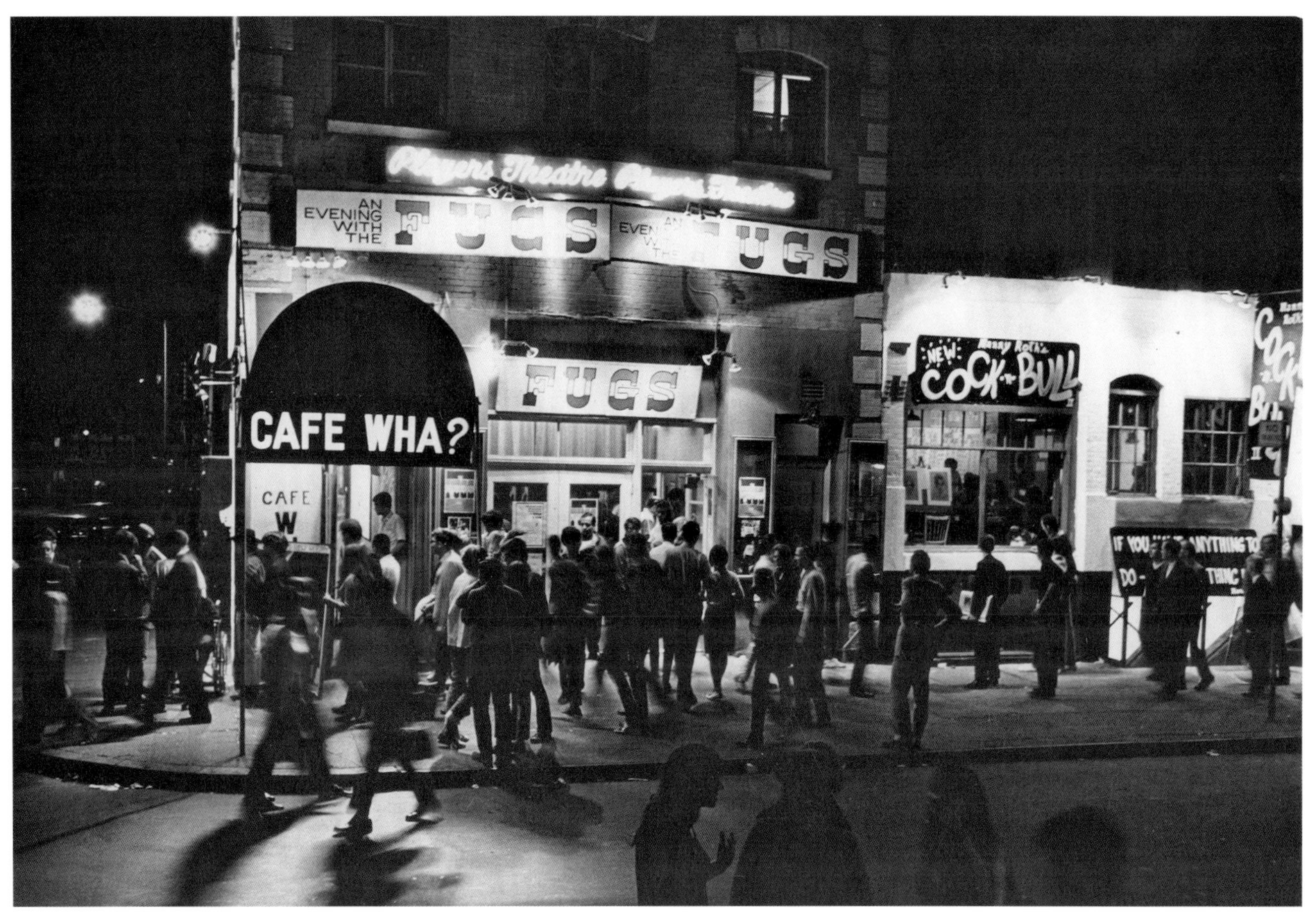

People wait to get into Cafe Wha?, 115 MacDougal St., for a performance by the Fugs, May 22, 1966. The band's name came from the euphemism for "fuck" foisted on Norman Mailer by the publisher of his first novel, *The Naked and the Dead*.

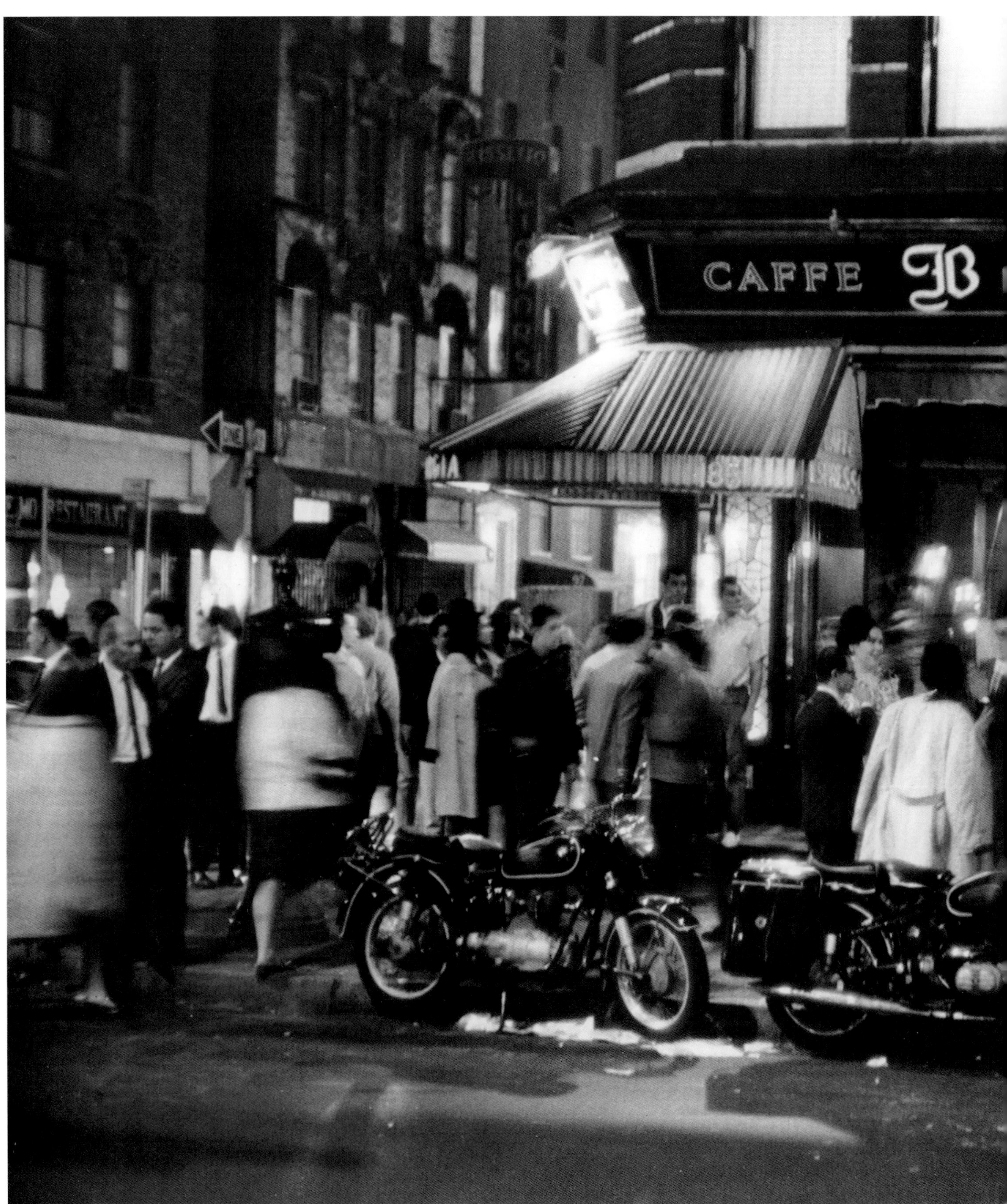

CAFFE B
ONE WAY
RESTAURANT

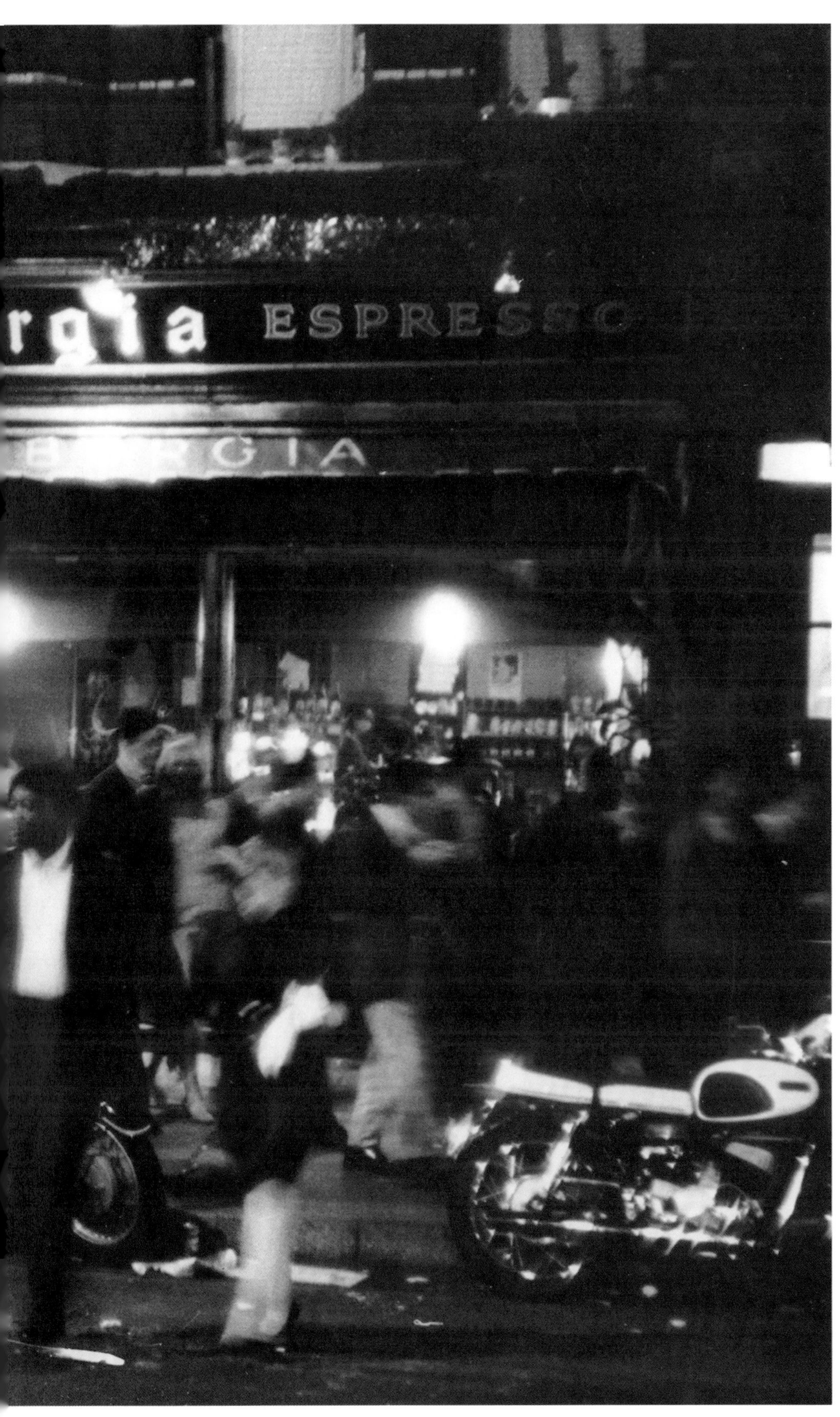

A balmy Tuesday evening outside the
Caffe Borgia, at the corner of MacDougal
and Bleecker Sts., May 24, 1966. The busy
intersection also had the Cafe Figaro across
Bleecker St. and the San Remo across
MacDougal, all of them gathering places
for writers, artists, and other Bohemian
denizens of the Village. The San Remo
closed in 1967, the Figaro in 1969, and
the Borgia in 2001.

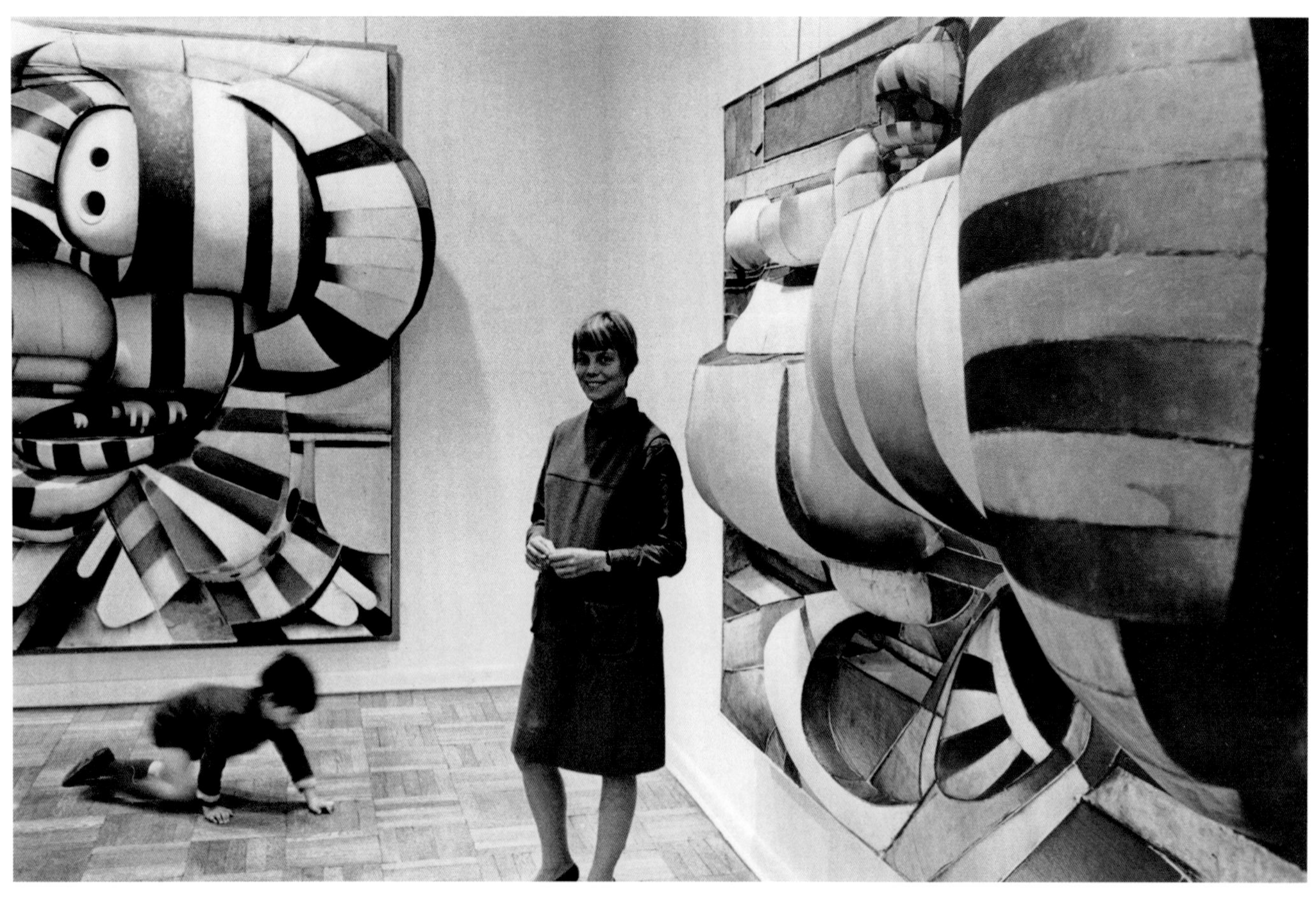

Artist Lee Bontecou stands among her wall-mounted sculptures on exhibit at the Leo Castelli Gallery a few days before the opening, October 4, 1966. Her works incorporated steel, canvas, conveyor belts, mailbags, and other found objects. The photographer's son Timothy is on the floor behind her.

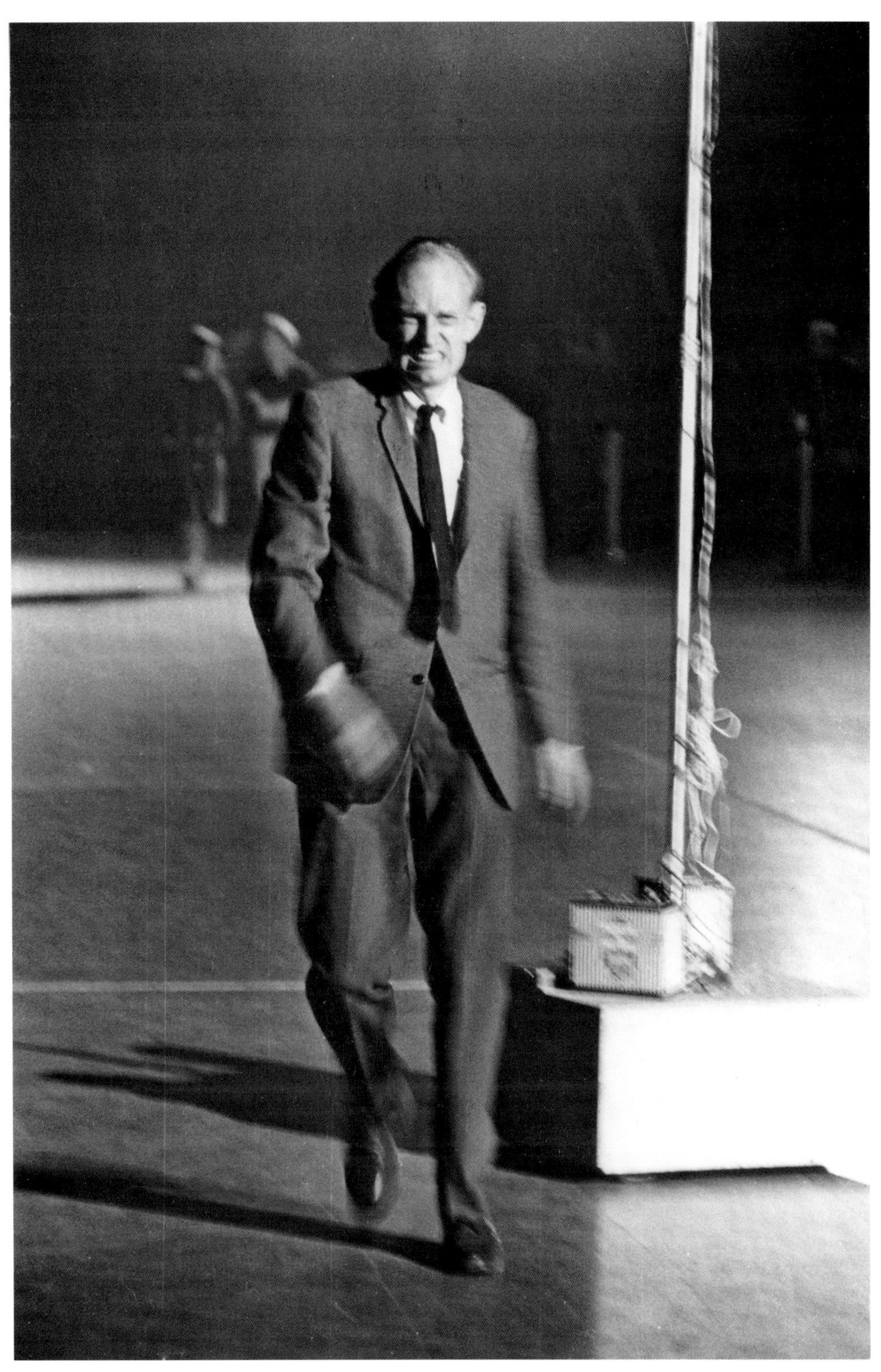

Billy Klüver at *9 Evenings: Theatre and Engineering*, 69th Regiment Armory, 68 Lexington Ave., October 18, 1966.
An engineer who worked on laser systems for Bell Laboratories, he founded Experiments in Art and Technology (EAT),
a nonprofit organization that encouraged artists and engineers to create interdisciplinary art projects, with engineer
Fred Waldhauer and artists Robert Rauschenberg and Robert Whitman. The group's initial enterprise, *9 Evenings:
Theatre and Engineering* brought together forty engineers and ten contemporary artists for ten multimedia pieces.

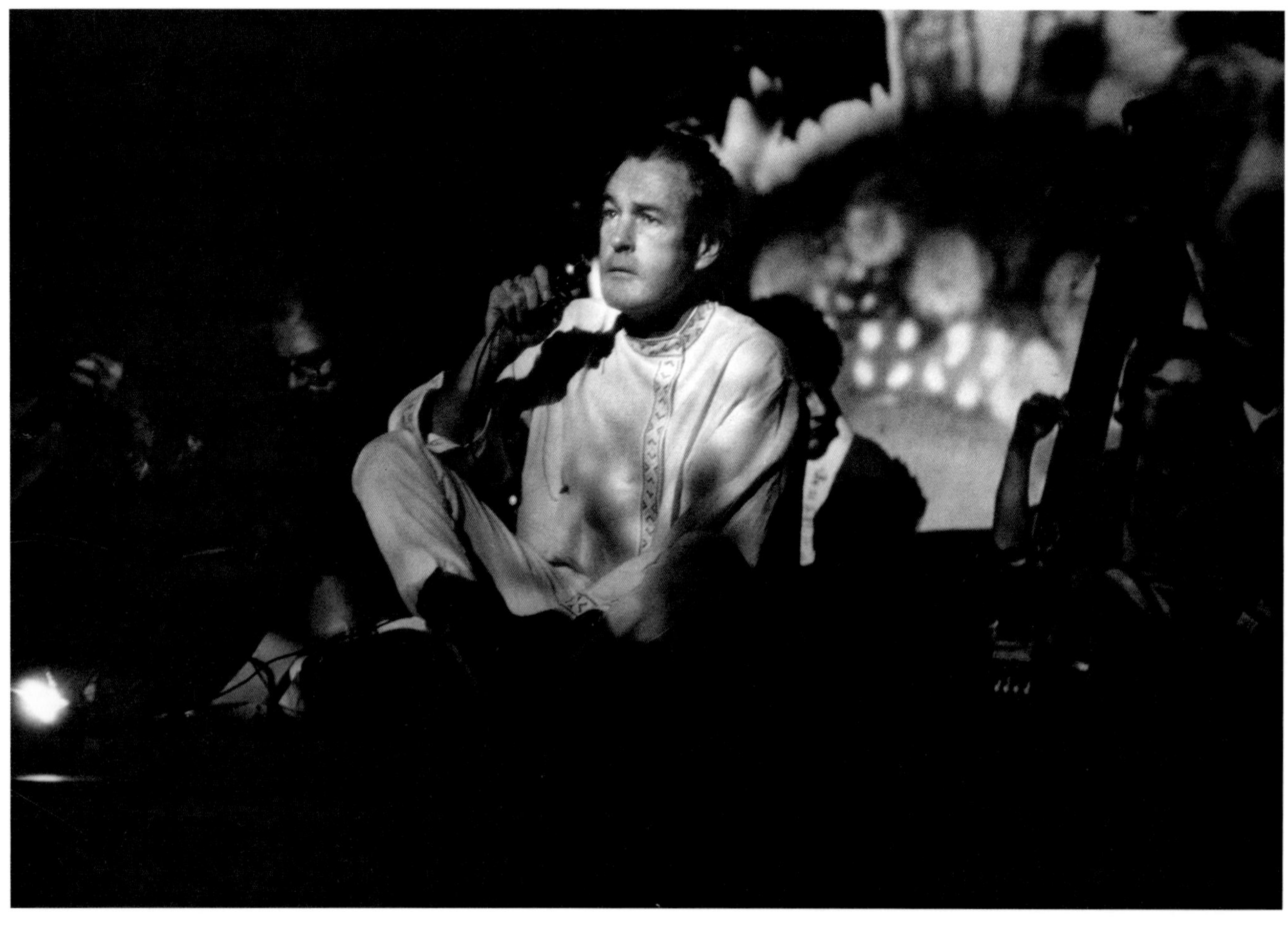

Timothy Leary sits on the stage at the Village Theater, 105 Second Ave., as he hosts his multimedia presentation *Illumination of the Buddha*, December 6, 1966. At left is Allen Ginsberg (in glasses). Leary's newly founded League for Spiritual Discovery, advocating the legal use of hallucinogenic drugs in ceremonies modeled after the Native American Church's peyote rituals, sponsored his "Psychedelic Religious Celebrations." From 1968 to 1971, the Village Theater would become the Fillmore East, promoter Bill Graham's East Coast venue for some of the biggest rock acts of the day.

Contact sheet of Japanese artist Yayoi Kusama posing in a fur coat, Bolero hat, and boots, her body (and the backdrop) painted with polka dots, June 7, 1967. The polka dots (which she said signified the sun, moon, and earth) and nudity were frequent elements in her performance pieces.

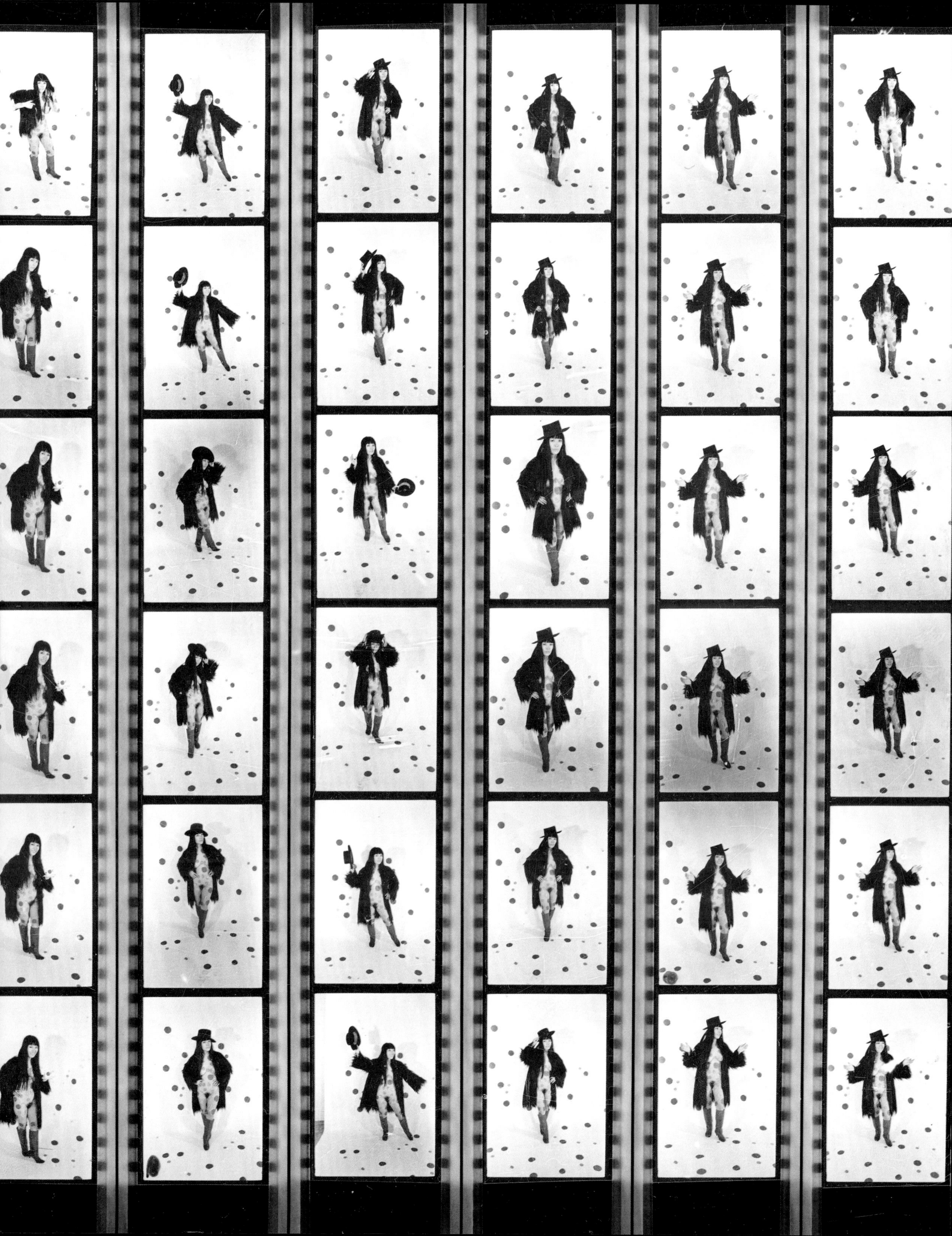

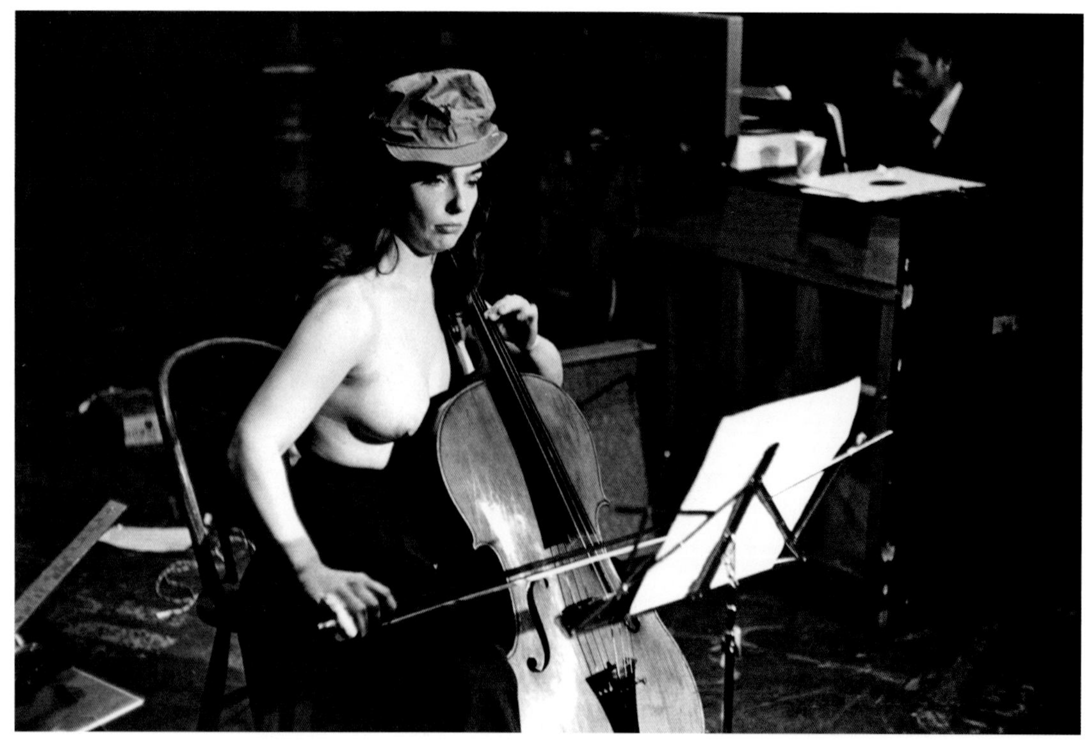

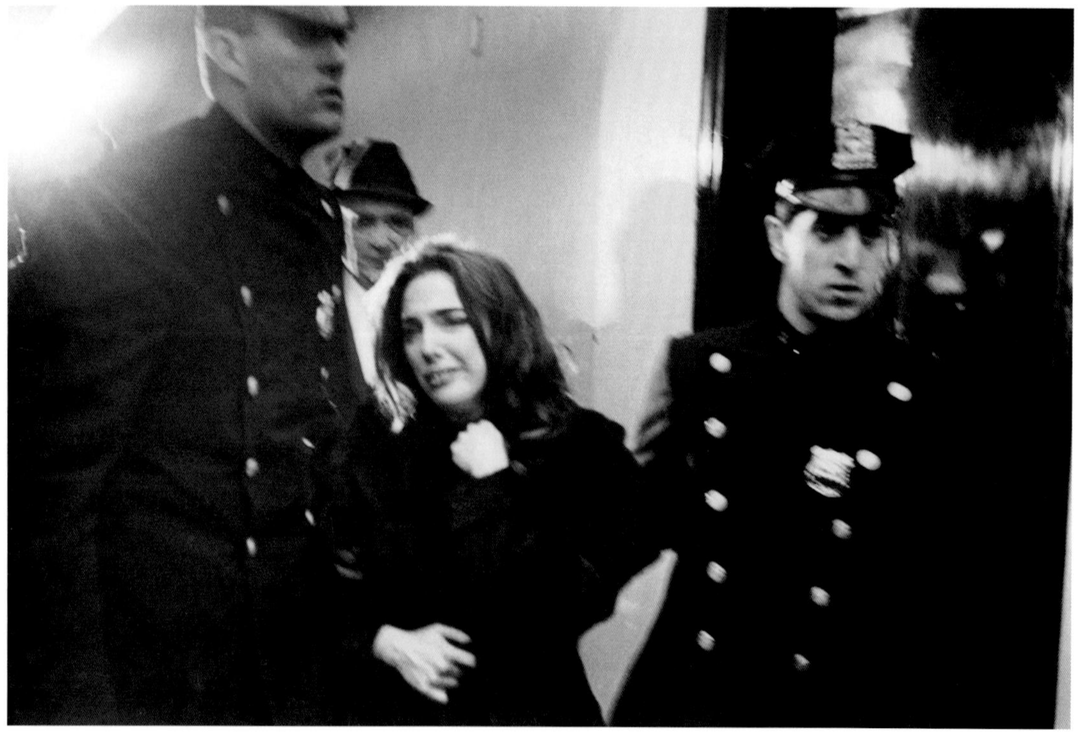

Charlotte Moorman and composer Nam June Paik perform his *Opera Sextronique* at the Film-Makers' Cinematheque, 125 West Forty-First St., February 9, 1967. Moorman was arrested for indecent exposure in the middle of the piece's second movement, halting the performance. The charges were later dropped, but afterward she was often referred to as "the topless cellist." Had she been allowed to continue, the third movement would have been performed bottomless and the fourth movement nude.

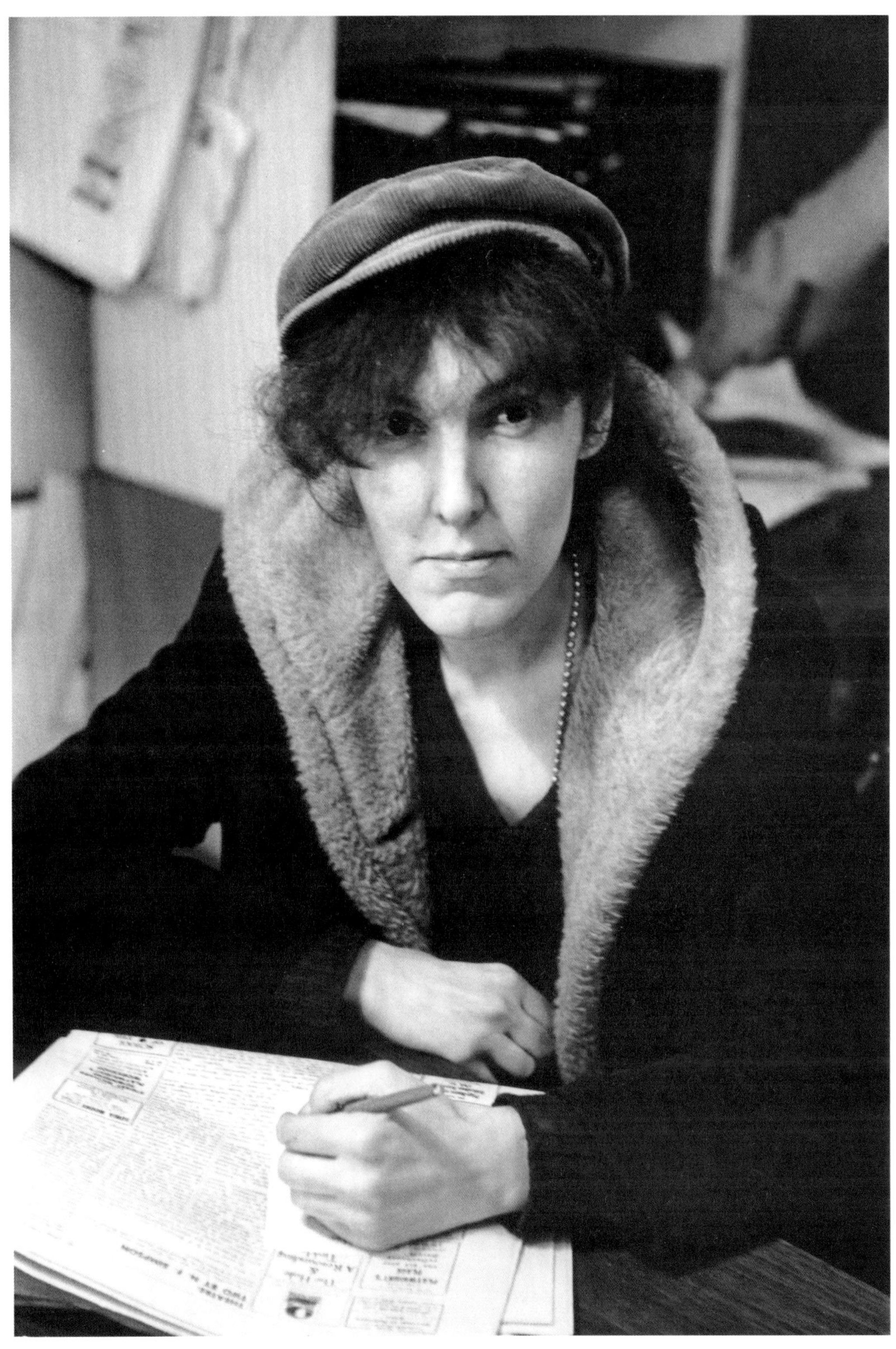

Valerie Solanas as she sits in the offices of the *Village Voice*, February 16, 1967. Solanas had recently self-published the infamous *SCUM Manifesto*, calling on women to "overthrow the government…and eliminate the male sex." On June 3 of the following year, she shot artist Andy Warhol (and also slightly wounded art critic Mario Amaya), whom she accused of stealing or losing a script she had given him. Warhol barely survived; Solanas served a three-year prison sentence, including psychiatric treatment. Like many fame seekers, artists, writers, politicians, and others looking for publicity, she simply wandered into the *Voice* offices to cajole someone into writing about her. Often McDarrah would snap a single frame of the visiting passerby, because you never knew, he thought, what would become of them.

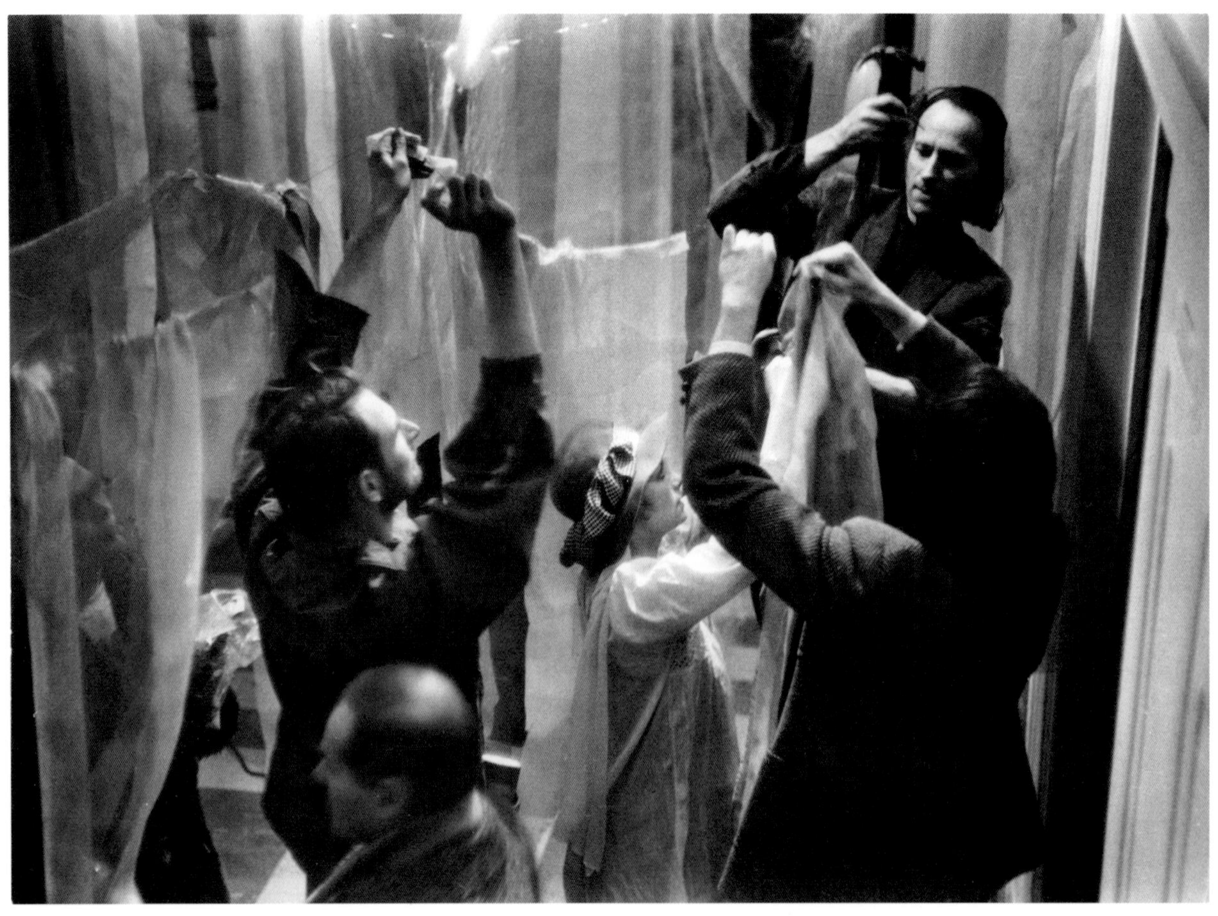

In the lobby of the Film-Makers' Cinematheque, 125 West Forty-First St., film director Jack Smith (center left), filmmaker and performance artist Barbara Rubin (center, in hat), and Jonas Mekas (rear, right) drape clear plastic sheets over wires (to be used as screens) for a film and mixed-media happening, February 18, 1967. Smith is best known for *Flaming Creatures* (1963), a satirical tribute to B movies, and Rubin for the sexually explicit *Christmas on Earth* (1963).

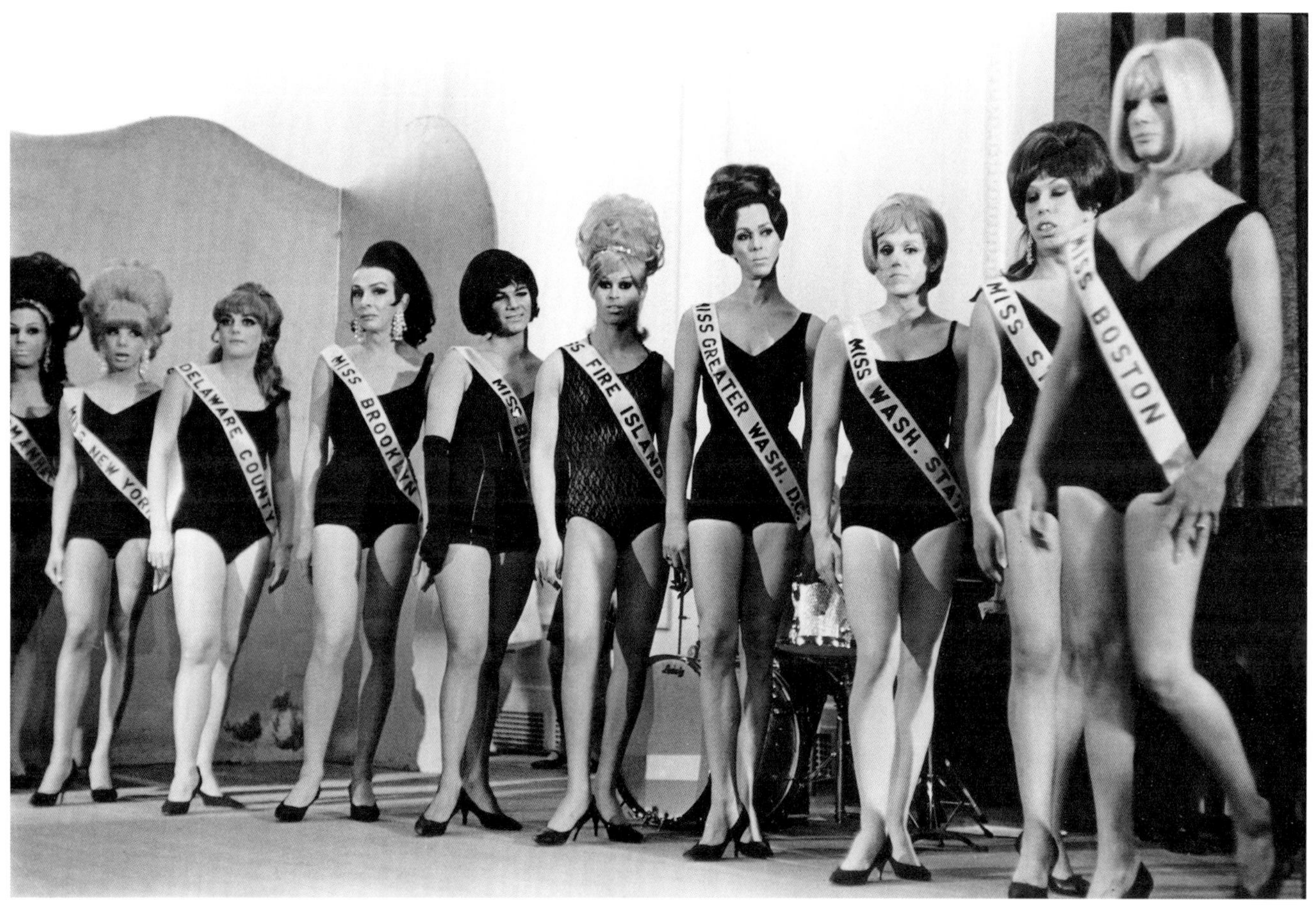

Drag queens compete in the Miss All-America Camp Beauty Pageant at Town Hall,
123 West Forty-Third St., February 20, 1967. Artists Andy Warhol, Larry Rivers, and
Jim Dine, and writers Terry Southern, Bruce Jay Friedman, and George Plimpton were
among the judges; Miss Philadelphia, Richard Finochio (aka Harlow), was the winner.
A well-regarded documentary about the pageant, *The Queen*, was released in 1968.

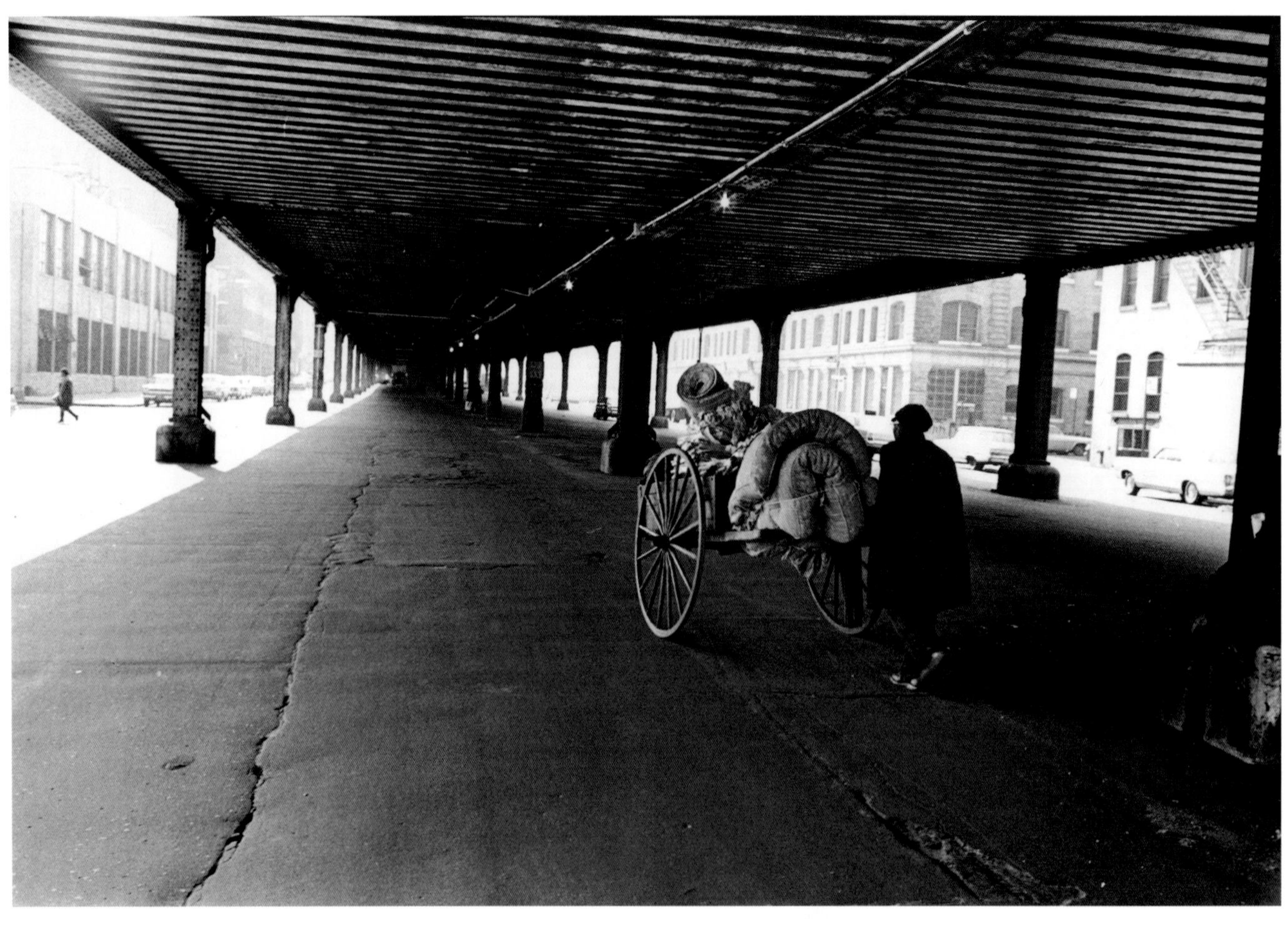

A man pushes a cart under the elevated train tracks on Park Ave.
(looking south at East 131st St.), March 9, 1967.

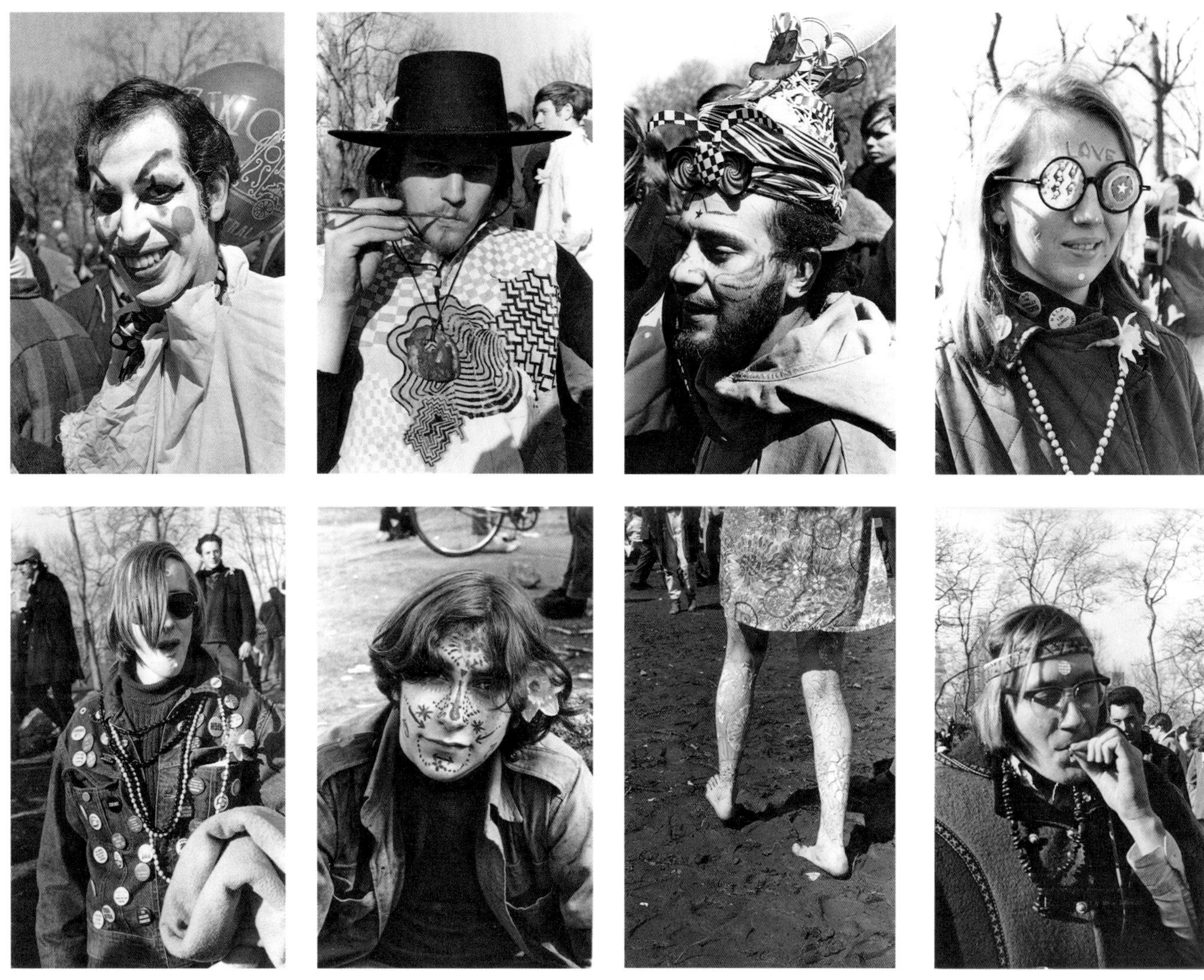

Painted hippie faces—and legs—in the crowd at the "Easter Be-In" in Central Park's Sheep Meadow, March 26, 1967. Inspired by an event in January that drew about one hundred thousand people in San Francisco, the New York gathering attracted more than ten thousand people and lasted into the evening, with the cooperation of the police and parks department.

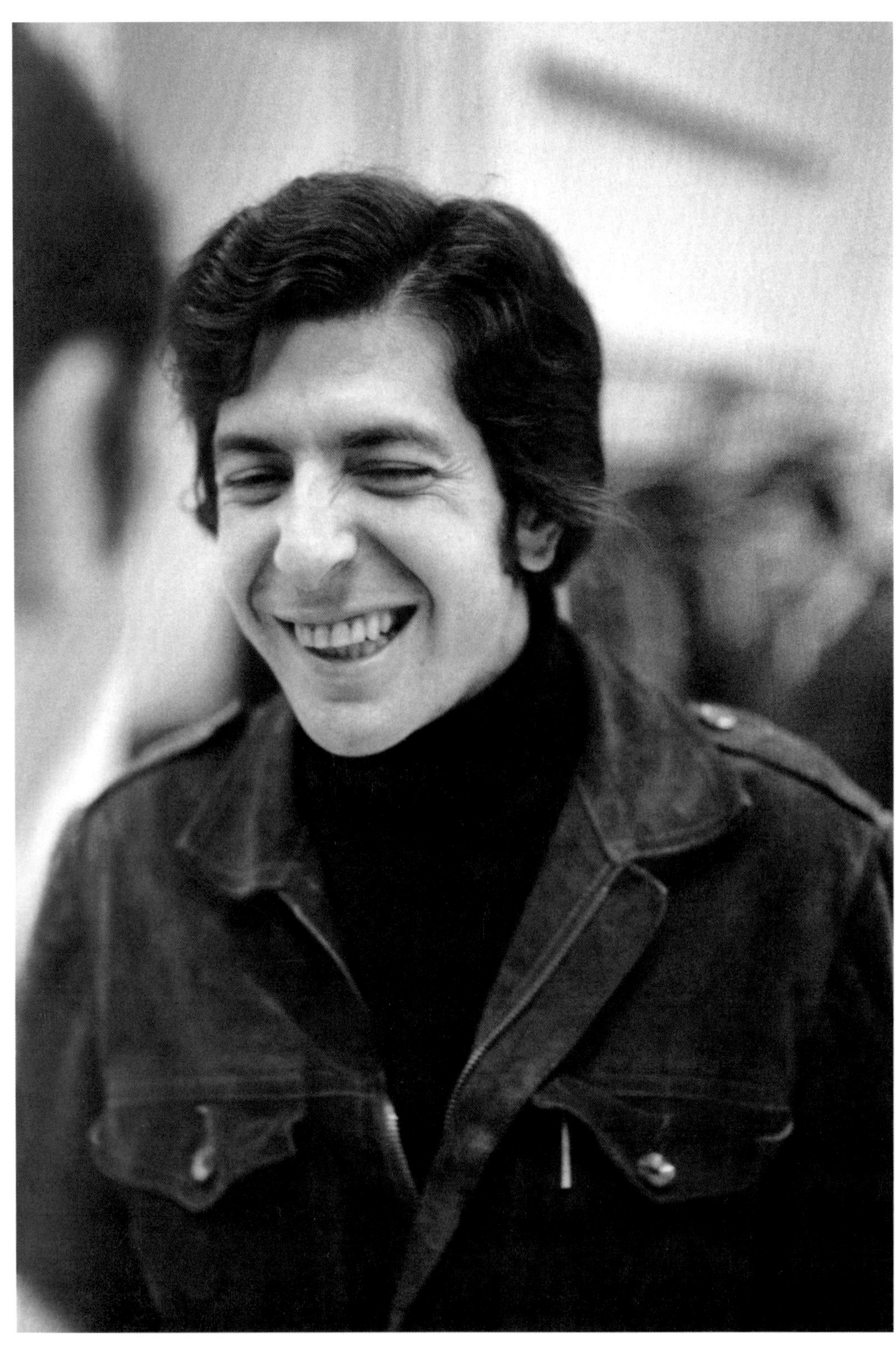

Canadian poet, songwriter, and musician Leonard Cohen, April 20, 1967, ten days
before he sang, nervously, at Town Hall. Cohen arrived in New York in 1966; his debut
album, *Songs of Leonard Cohen*, was released at the end of 1967.

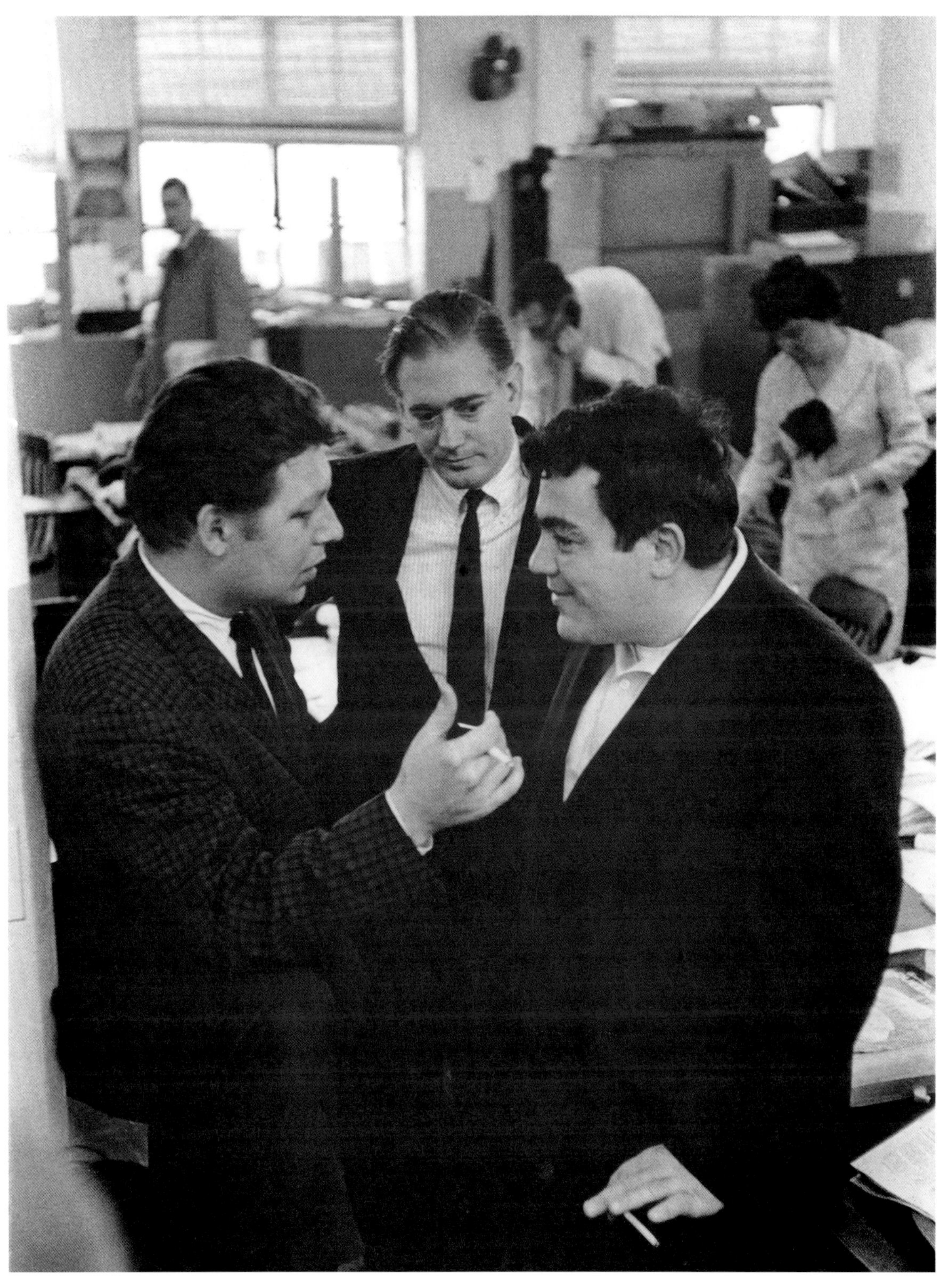

From left, journalists Pete Hamill, Clay Felker, and Jimmy Breslin talk in the *New York World Journal Tribune*'s newsroom on the paper's last day, May 5, 1967. The evening broadsheet was an eight-month failed attempt to survive the economic struggles of the city's many papers. Its name gives only a hint of its heritage: a merger of the *World-Telegram & Sun* (once three separate papers), the *Journal-American* (two), and the *Herald Tribune* (two). Hamill and Breslin were associated with the New Journalism, a term that Hamill is said to have coined. Editor Felker went on to launch *New York* magazine in 1968; it had been a Sunday supplement for the *Herald Tribune* and its short-lived successor.

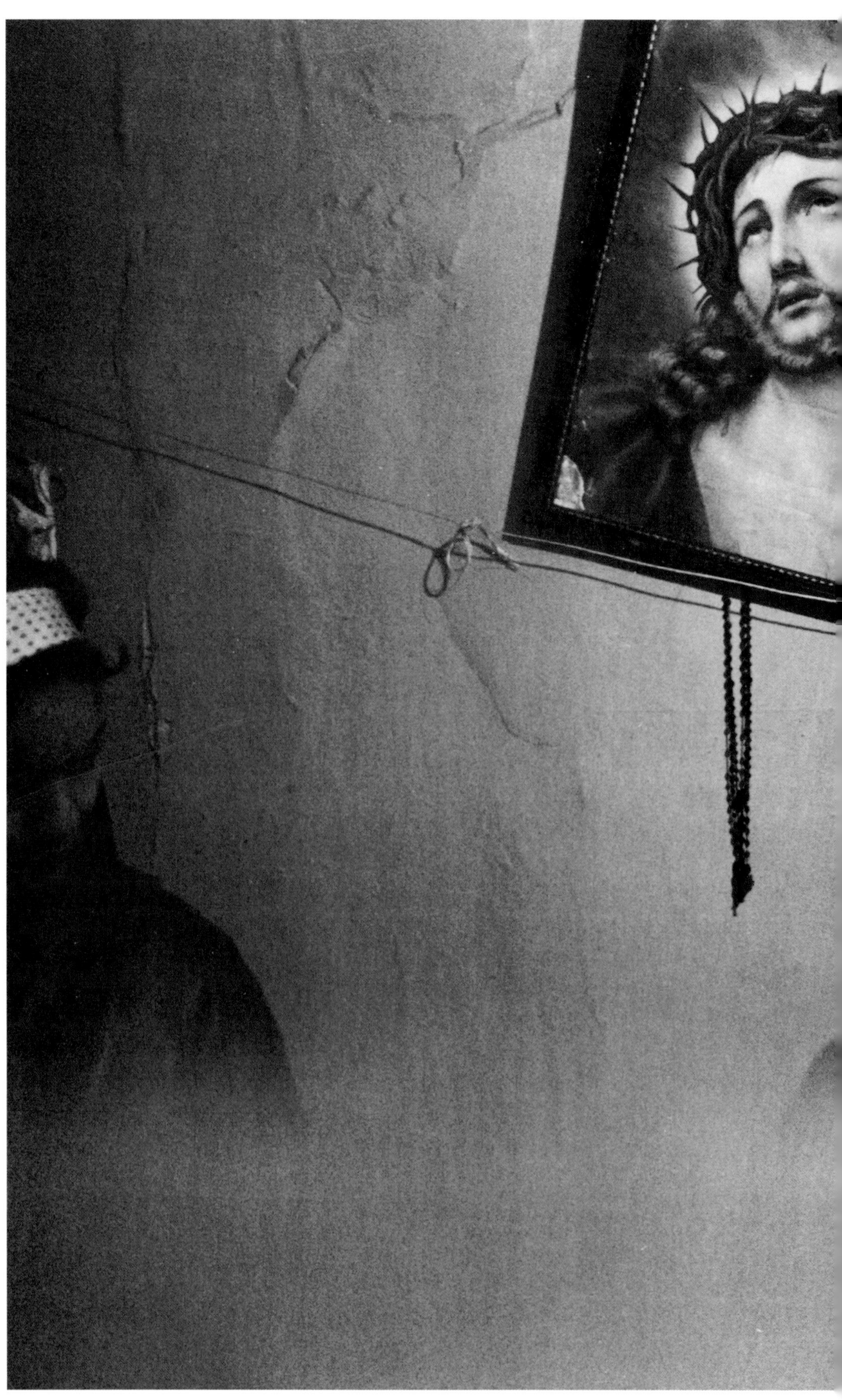

Senator Robert F. Kennedy during
a tour of a tenement apartment on
Stanton St. on Manhattan's Lower East
Side, May 8, 1967. Despite his family's
wealth, Kennedy developed empathy for
the poor and minorities, especially as
a senator visiting impoverished areas.
While campaigning for the presidency
a year later, Kennedy was assassinated
right after winning the California
primary on the night of June 4–5.
He died on June 6.

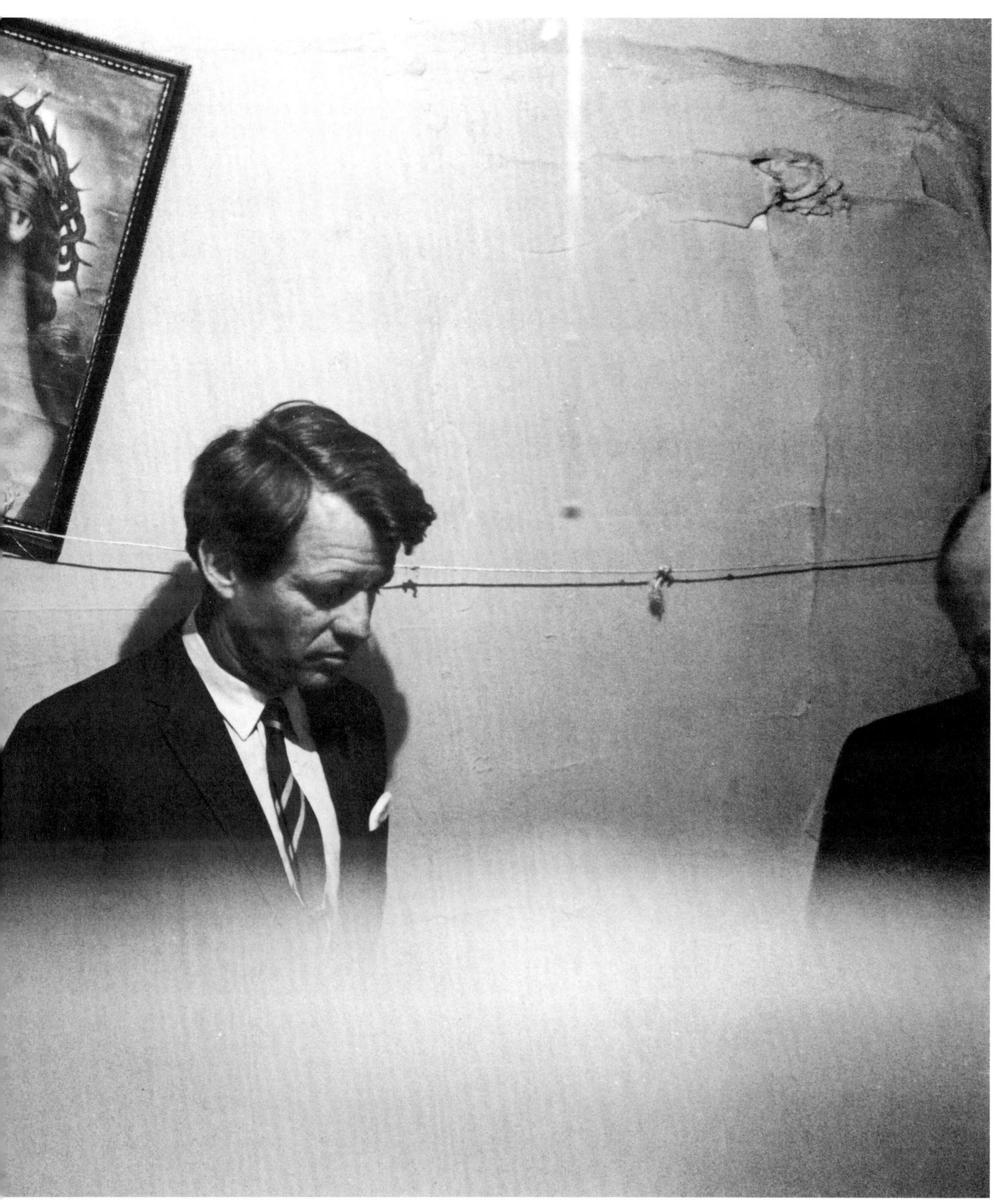

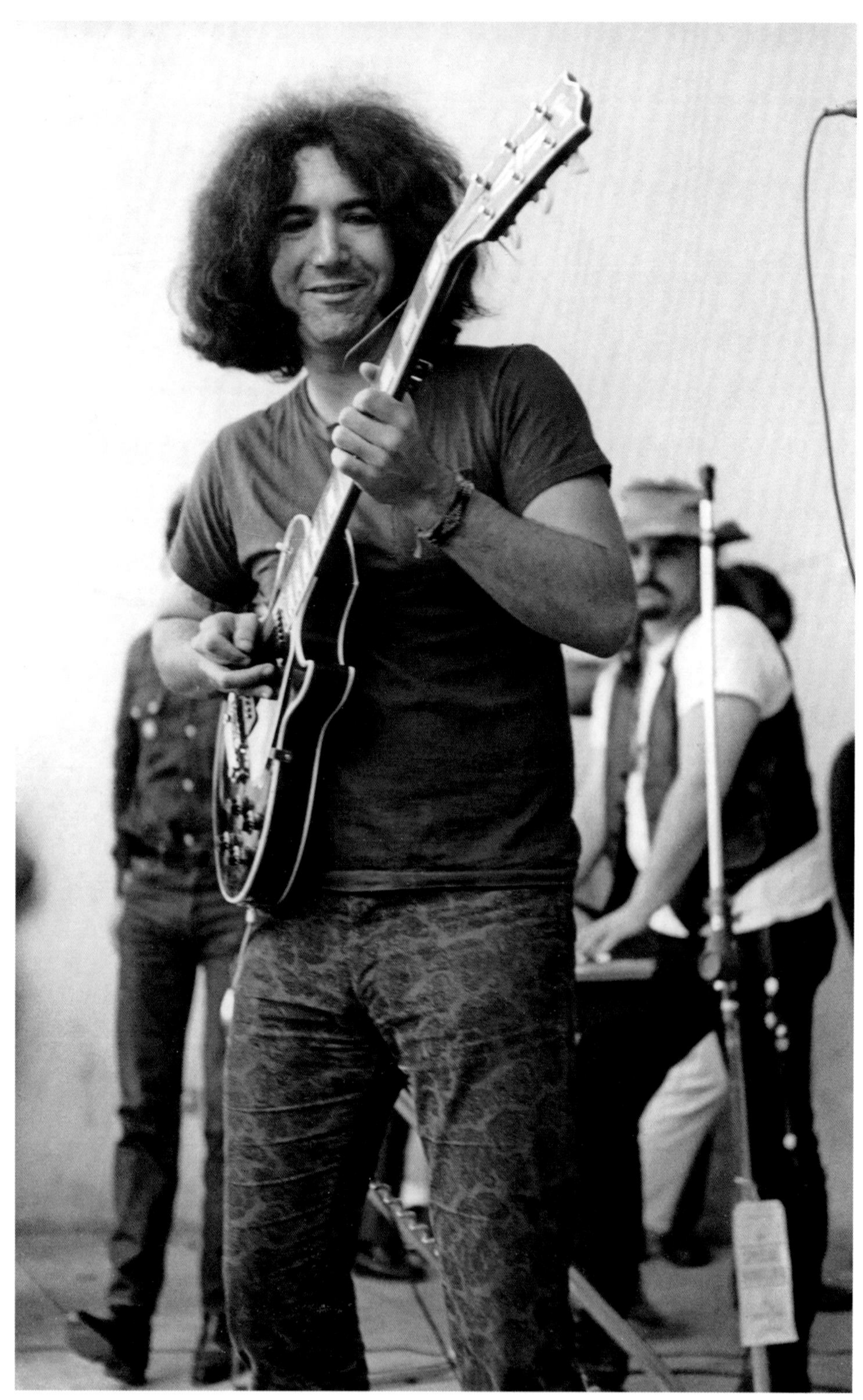

Jerry Garcia at a free Grateful Dead concert in the bandshell in Tompkins Square Park, June 1, 1967. The San Francisco band's first appearance in the East officially began with several nights at the Cafe au Go Go, 152 Bleecker St., in early June, but before that the Dead, known for giving free shows, appeared in this outdoor afternoon concert—until they stopped when someone lodged a noise complaint.

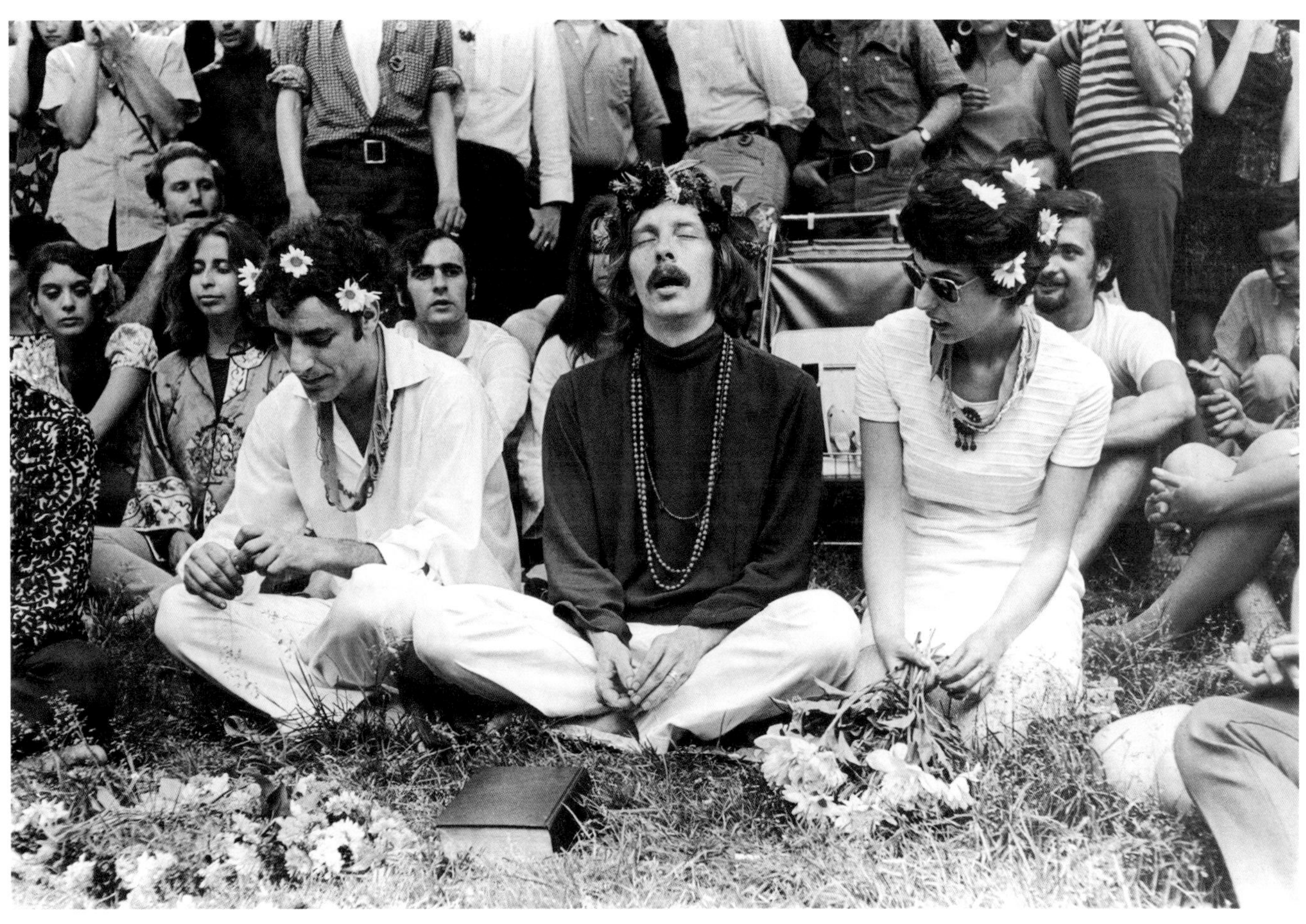

Activist Abbie Hoffman (left, in white) and Anita Kushner sit on either side of Linn House, the Boo Hoo (self-styled priest) of the satirical, psychedelic Neo-American Church, who is performing their wedding ceremony in Central Park, June 10, 1967. The public hippie wedding was followed by a "proper" wedding in a synagogue to appease the bride's parents. Ardent practitioners of street theater to protest the Vietnam War and other targets, the couple and others would found the mock Youth International Party, or Yippies, at the end of the year and take it to the ill-fated Democratic National Convention in Chicago in 1968.

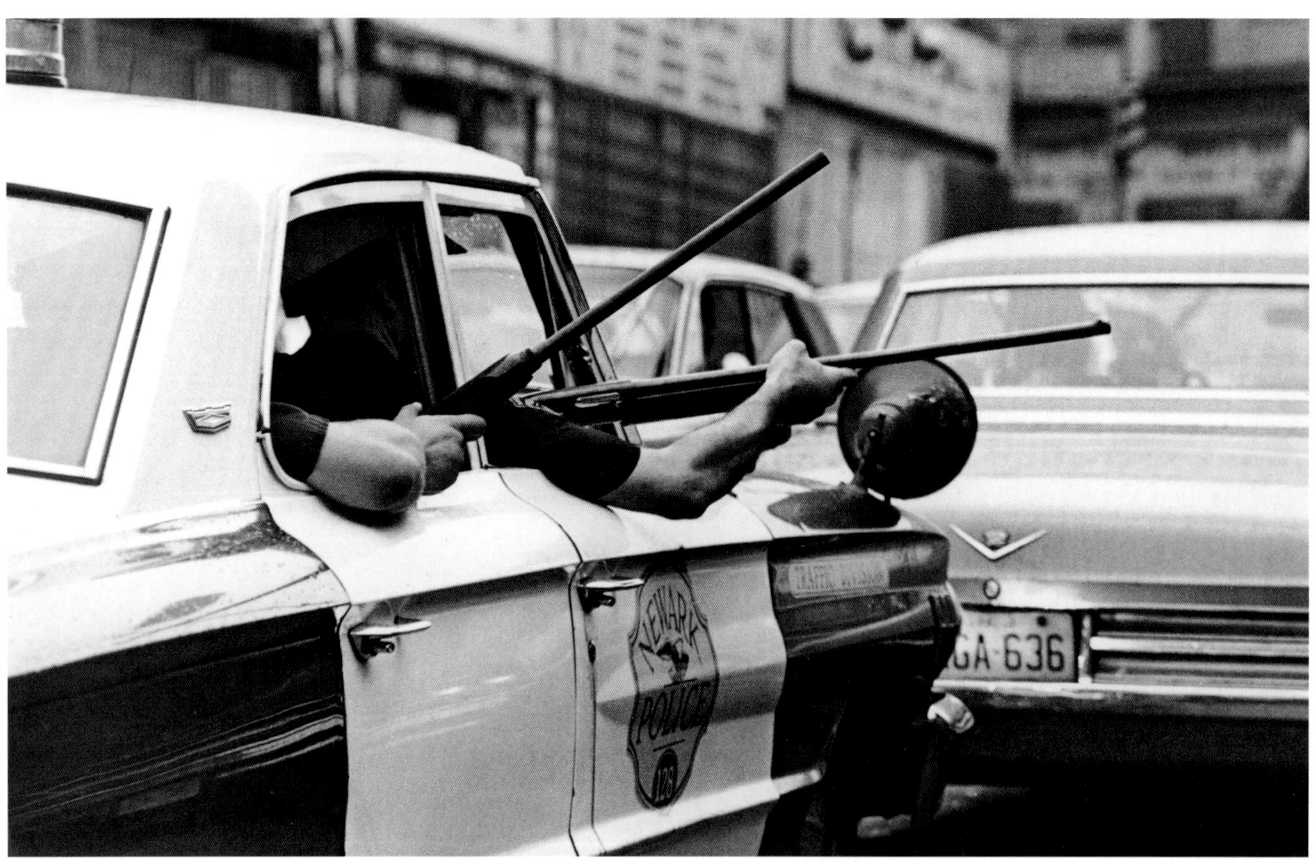

A Newark, New Jersey, police car on Springfield Ave. during the Newark riots, July 14, 1967. After two white officers arrested and beat a black cab driver, rumors that he had been killed led to demonstrations and five days of rioting, on July 12–16. The Newark riot—one of scores around the country in 1967—resulted in twenty-six deaths, more than seven hundred injuries, and millions of dollars in property damage.

LeRoi Jones (later known as Amiri Baraka) leaves a police station bloodied and in chains during riots in Newark, New Jersey, July 14, 1967. Jones had been arrested for allegedly carrying concealed weapons and was beaten while in custody; his conviction was later overturned. His son Ras Baraka was elected mayor of Newark in 2014.

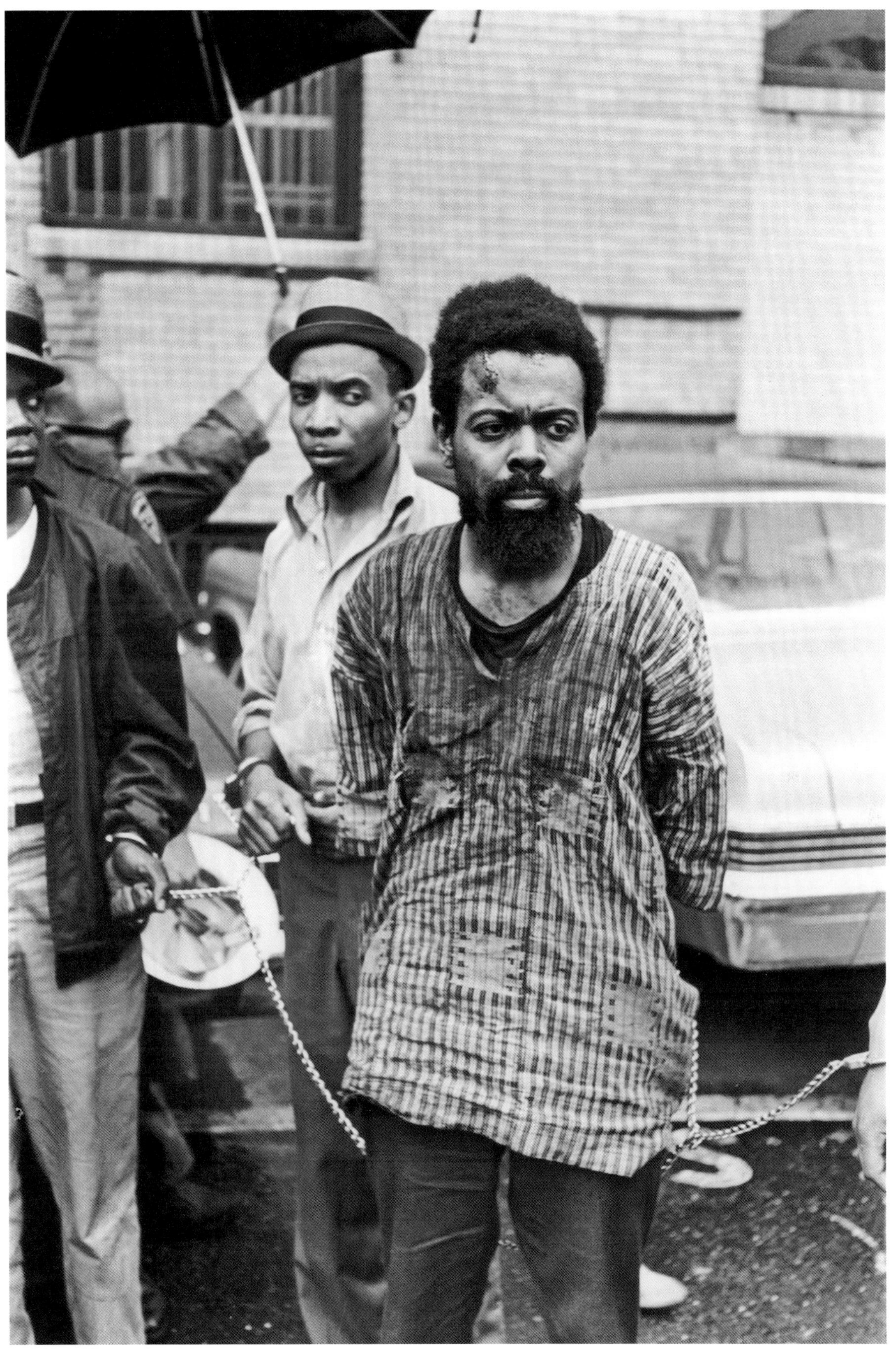

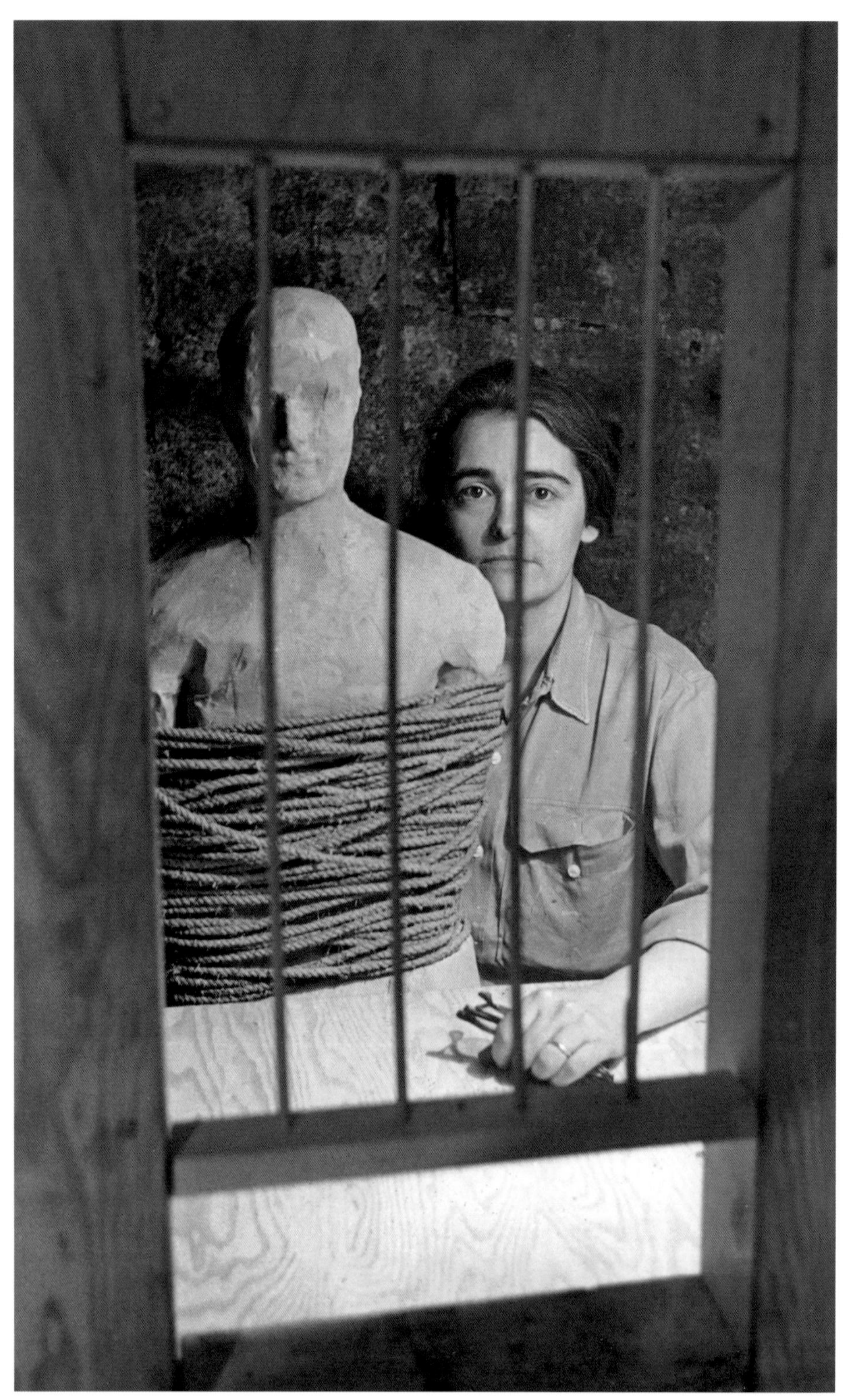

Kate Millett, author of *Sexual Politics* (1970) and primarily an artist at the start of her career, poses with one of her sculptures in her studio, 295 Bowery, July 7, 1967. Even as Millett increasingly turned to feminist activism, she continued to create and exhibit art—reflecting her political and social concerns—through the nineties and again in a group show in 2009.

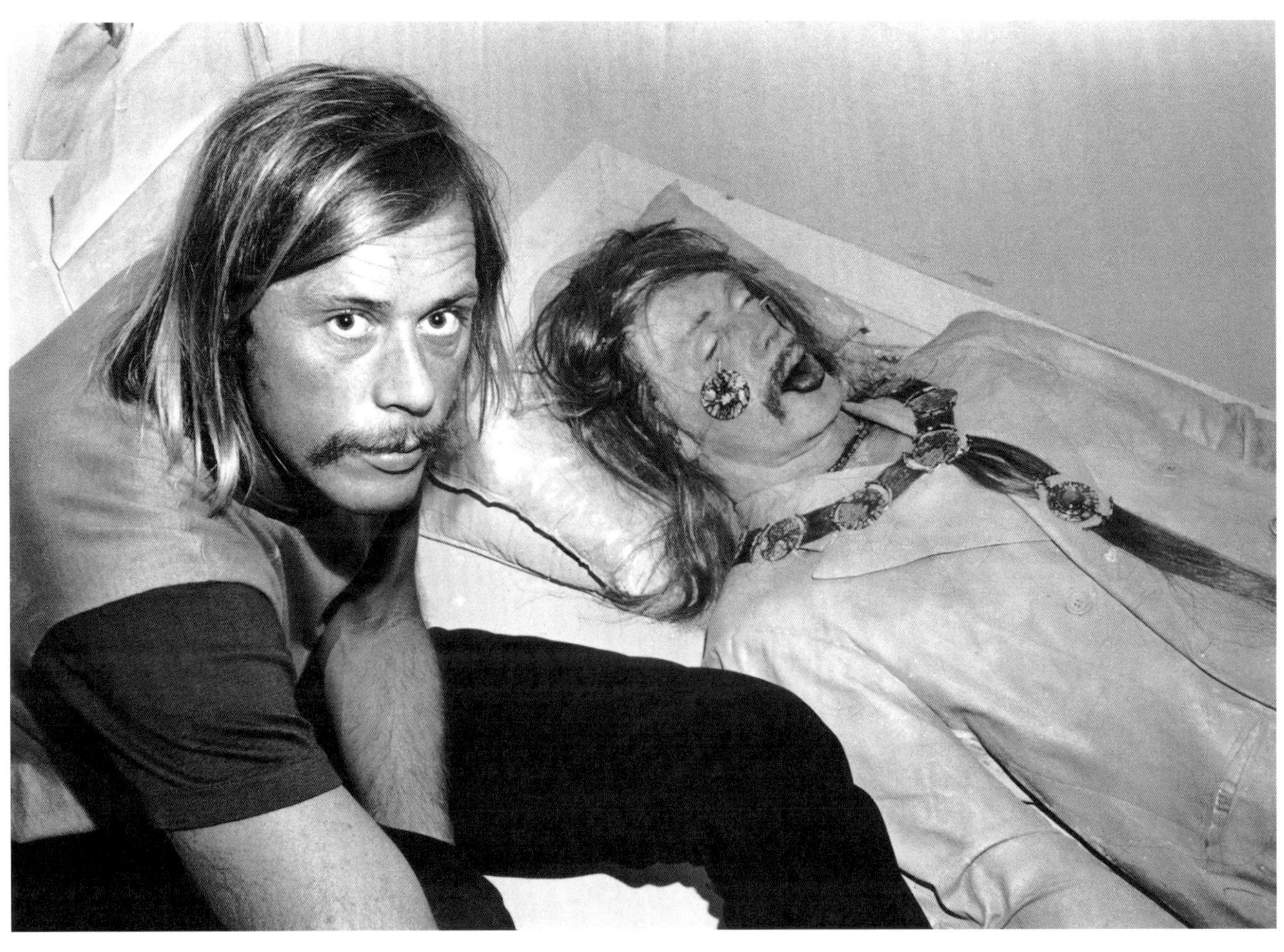

Artist Paul Thek poses beside a life-size wax effigy of himself, September 16, 1967. It was shown on the floor of a wooden ziggurat, viewed from above, in the exhibition *The Tomb* at the Stable Gallery, 33 East Seventy-Fourth St. Thek's effigy traveled around the United States and Europe for more than a decade before being damaged in transit back to New York.

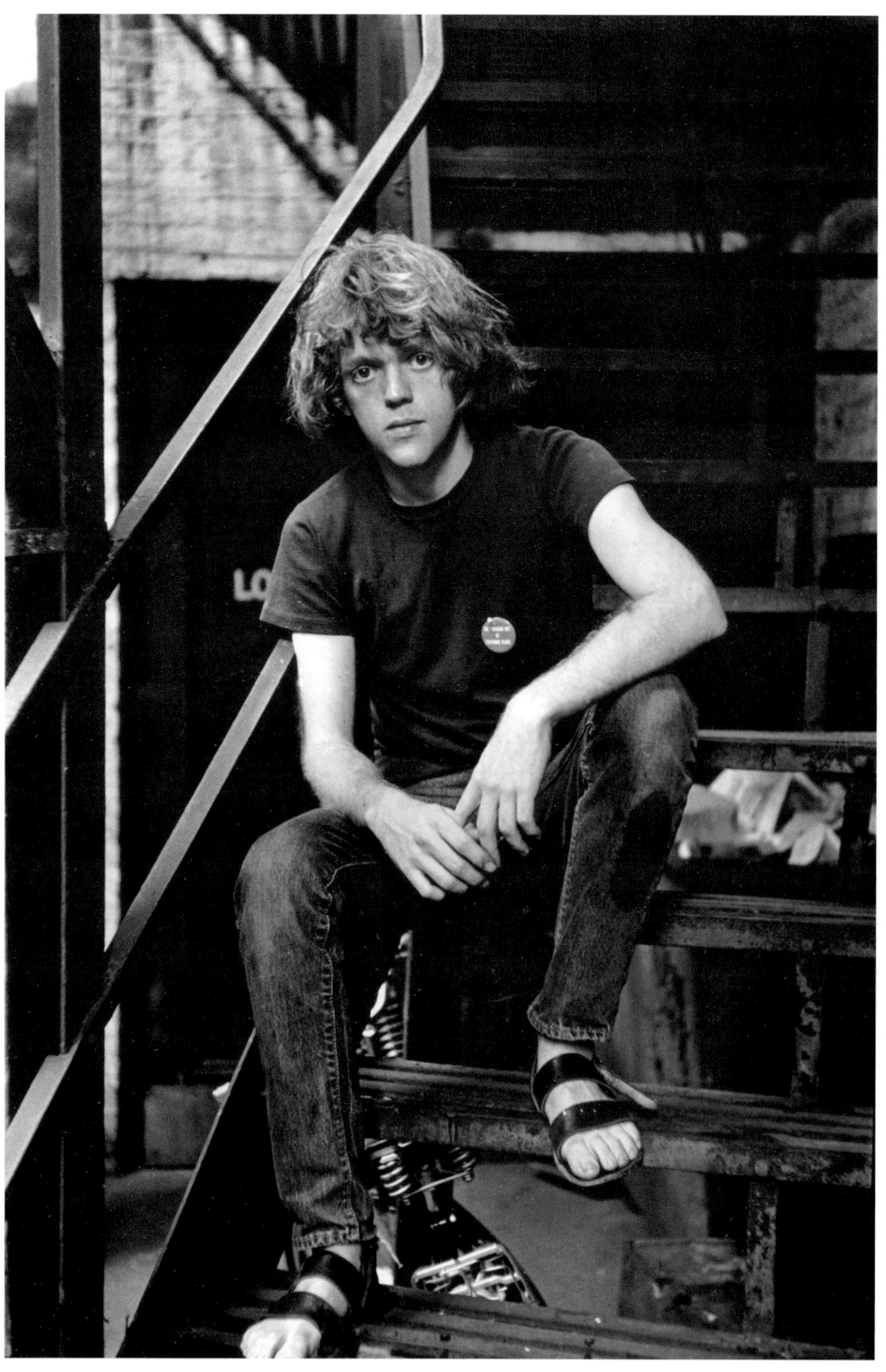

Gay rights activist Jim Fouratt, October 16, 1967. Fouratt was the ringleader, with Abbie Hoffman, of a group that flung dollar bills onto the floor of the New York Stock Exchange from the visitors' balcony on August 24, 1967, and later he participated in the Stonewall riots and helped organize the Gay Liberation Front.

Police arrest author and activist Susan Sontag during a draft protest at the Whitehall Army Induction Center, 39 Whitehall St., December 5, 1967. Allen Ginsberg and Dr. Benjamin Spock were also among more than 250 antiwar protesters arrested when a group about ten times that size marched on the facility.

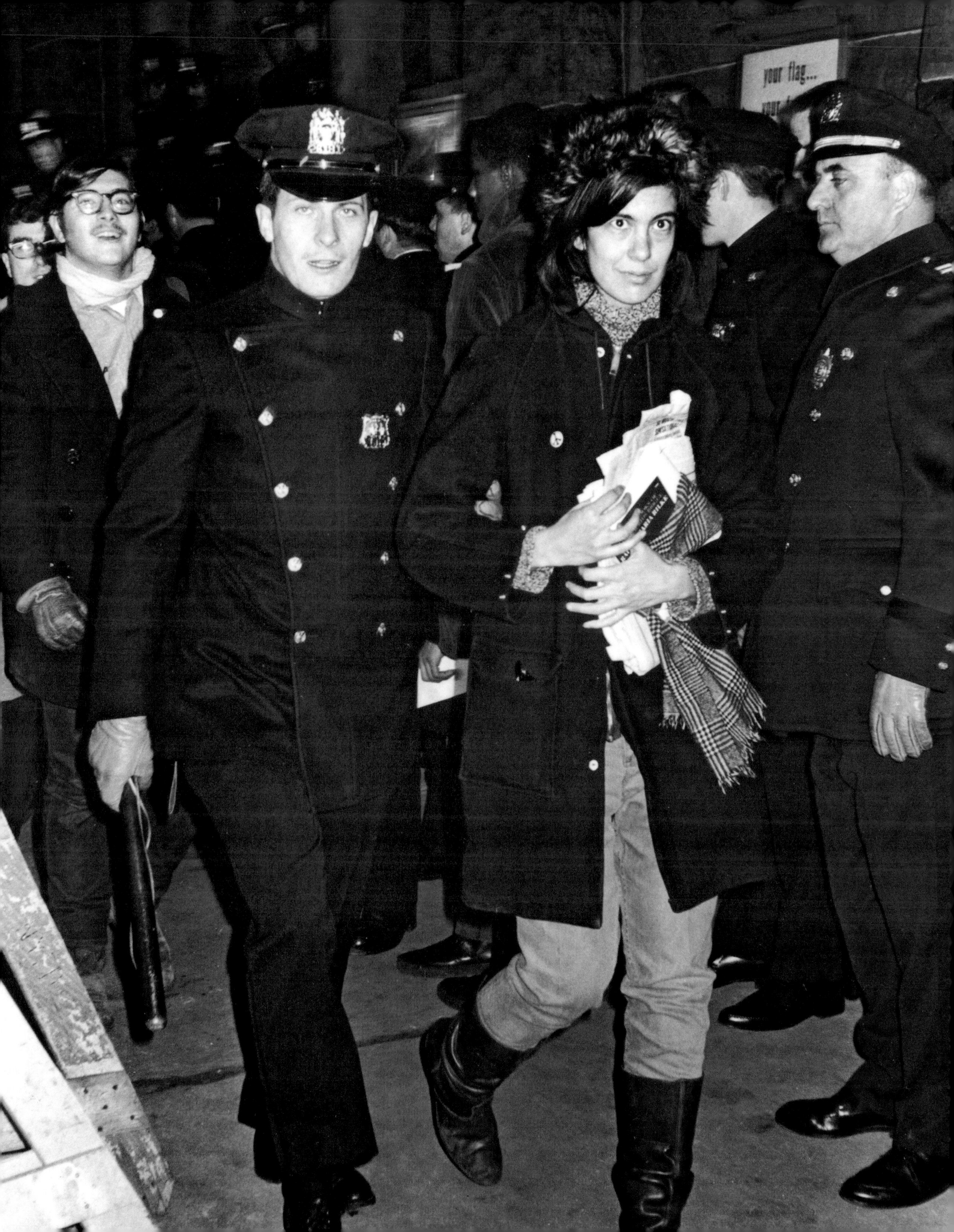

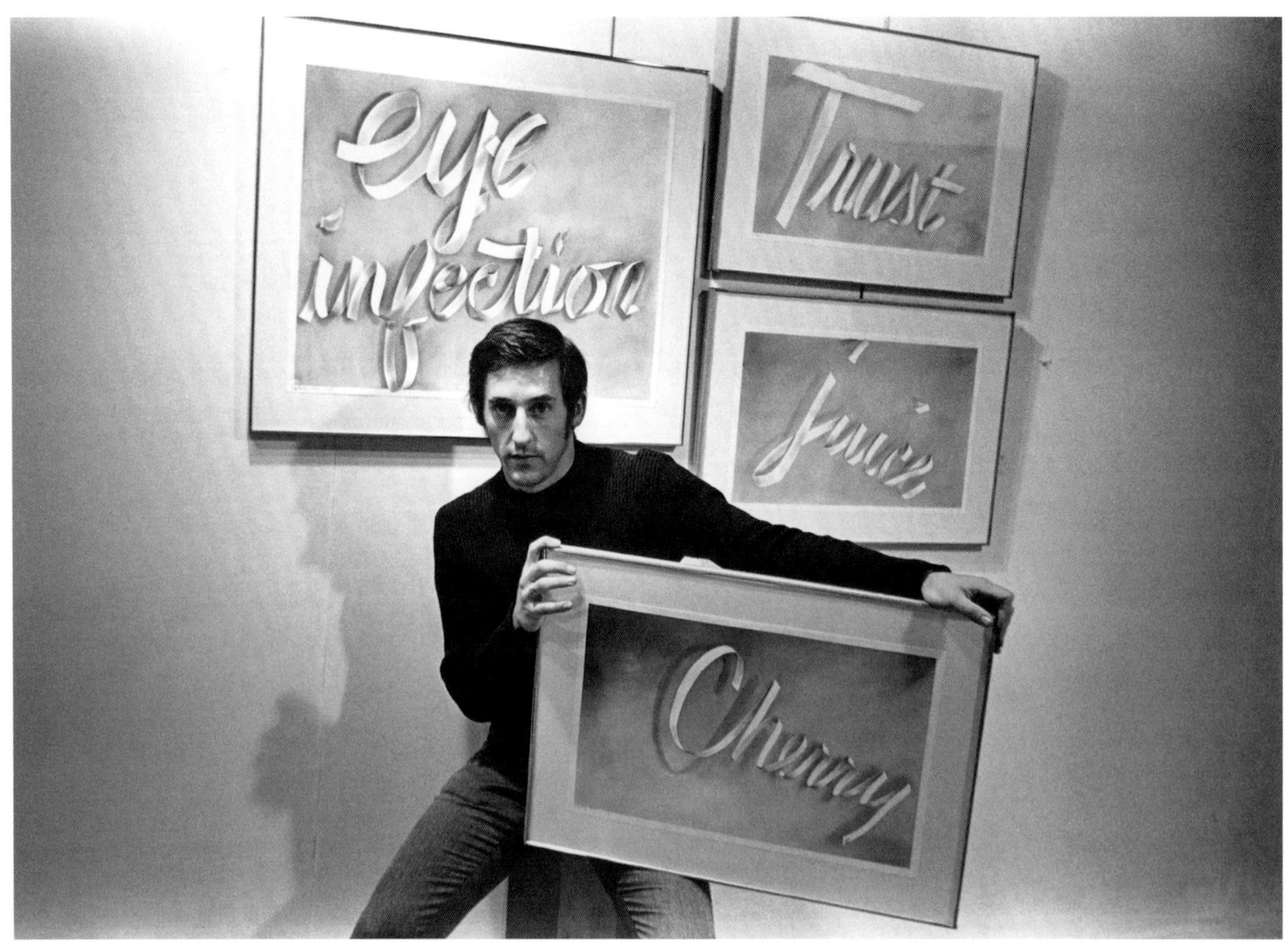

Artist Ed Ruscha with some of his "gunpowder ribbon drawings," December 9, 1967. A California-based Pop artist, Ruscha often used unusual materials like gunpowder for his paintings.

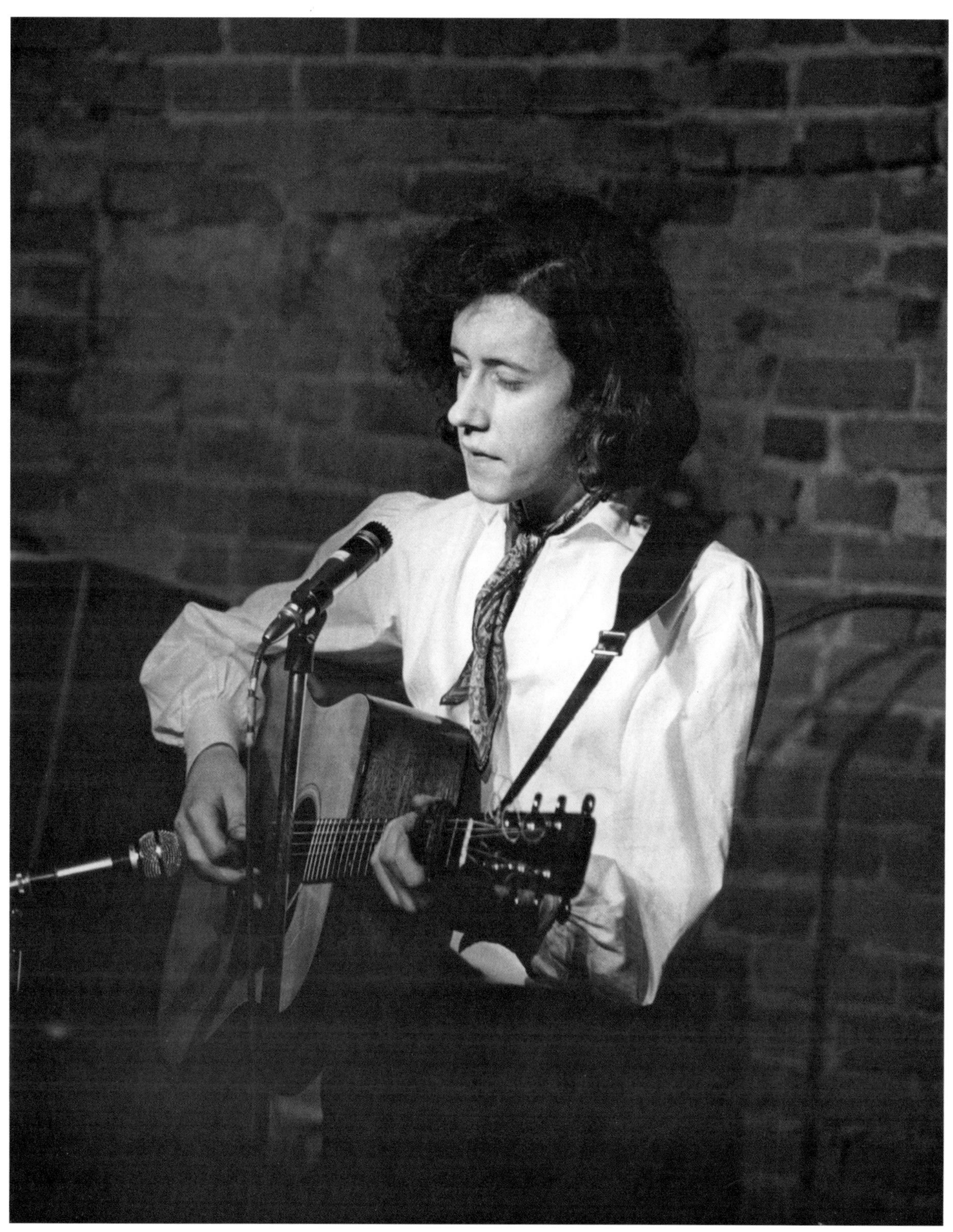

Arlo Guthrie at the Bitter End cafe, 147 Bleecker St., December 20, 1967. Two months earlier, his father, folksinger Woody Guthrie, died and Arlo released his first album, *Alice's Restaurant*, with the entire A side devoted to his eighteen-minute, thirty-four-second satirical talking blues hit about the draft, the war, and littering, "Alice's Restaurant Massacree."

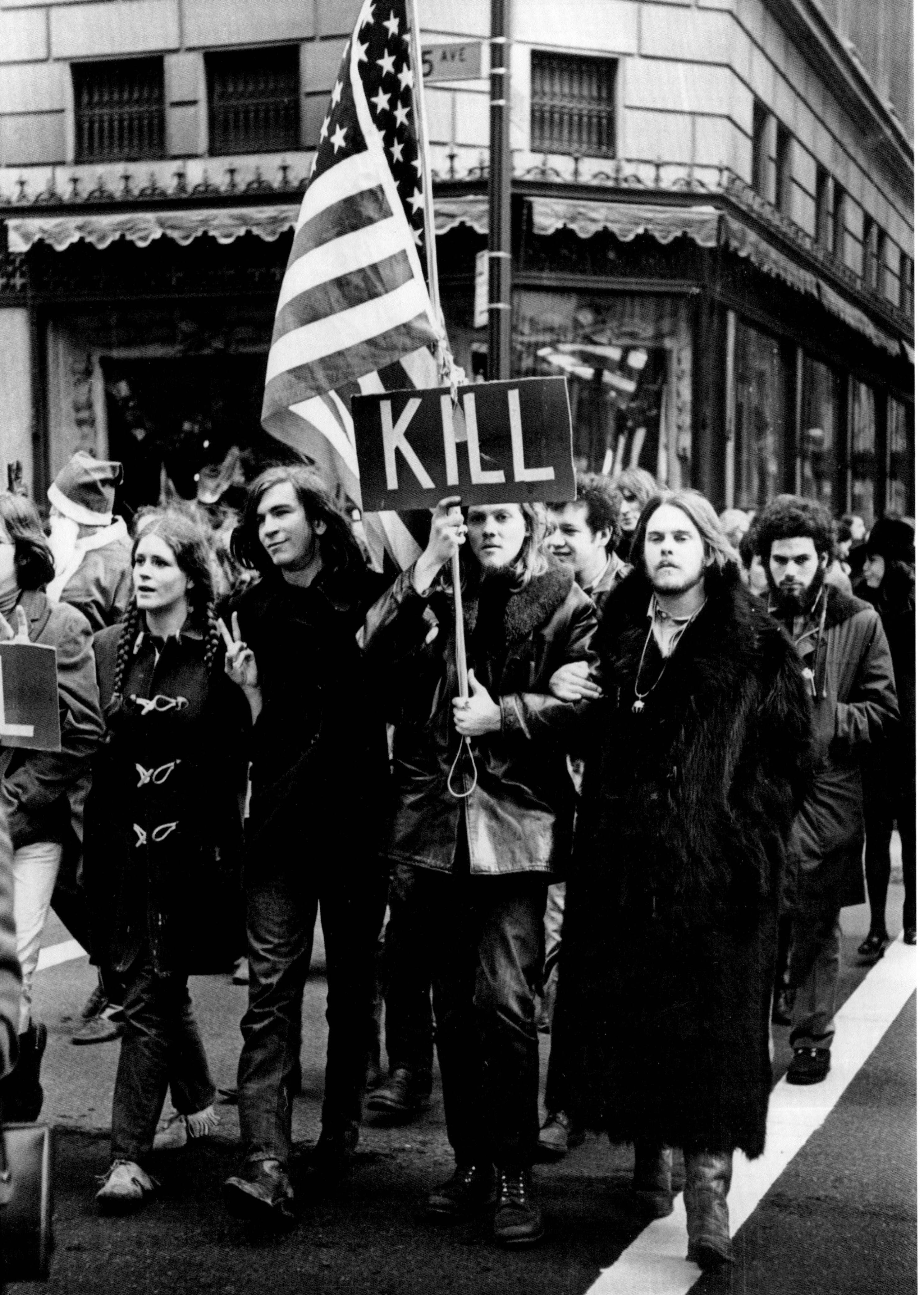

5 AVE
KILL

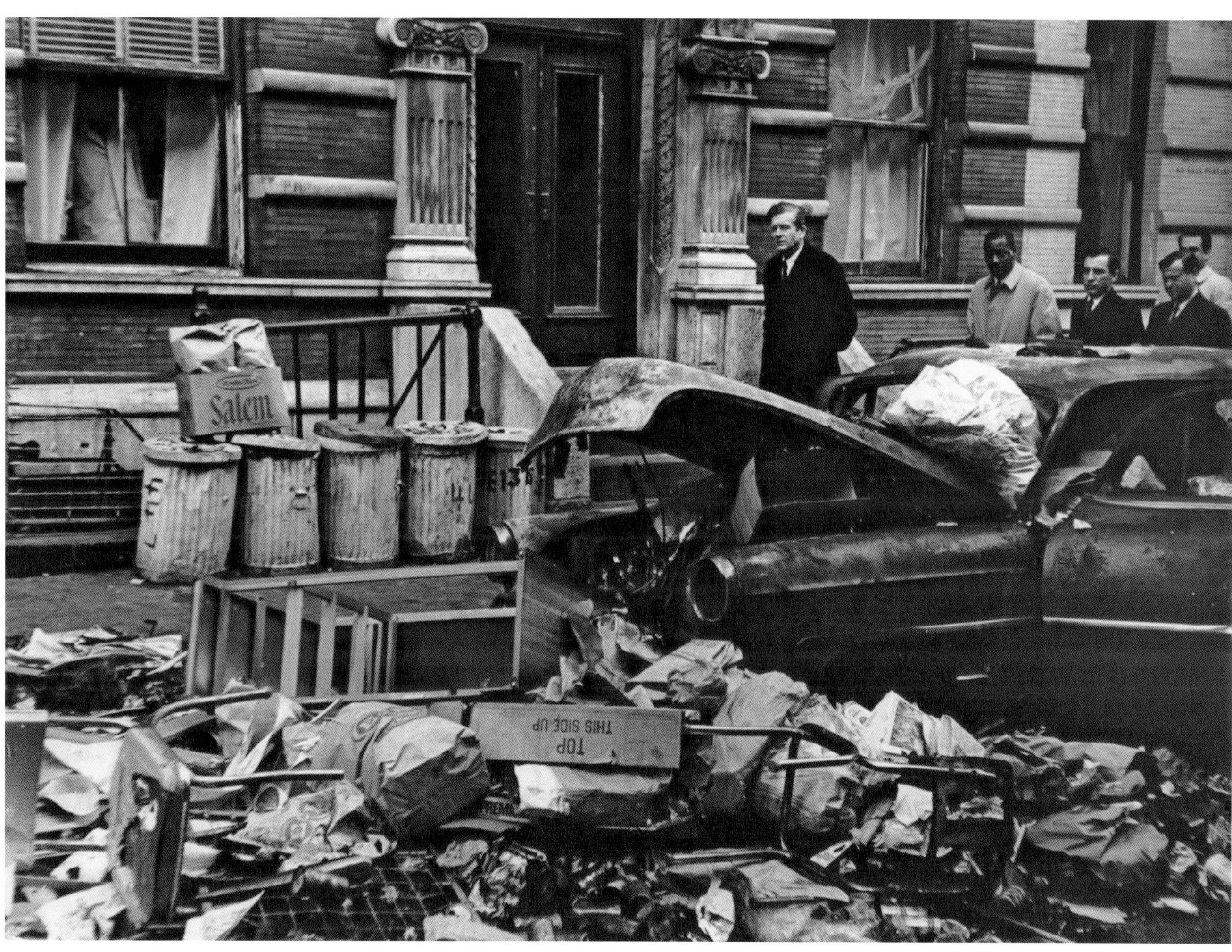

Antiwar protesters, crossing
Fifth Ave. at 49th St.,
December 23, 1967.

Mayor John V. Lindsay tours a Brooklyn street during a citywide sanitation strike, February 9, 1968. On
February 2, after working for six months without a contract, the ten thousand New York sanitation workers
had called a strike—which violated the 1967 state Taylor Law, forbidding public workers from striking. The
union leader was jailed, but one hundred thousand tons of garbage had piled up all over the city by the time
Governor Nelson Rockefeller called a health emergency on February 10, seized state control of the sanitation
department—and essentially gave the union what it wanted. Inspired by the strike, sanitation workers in
Memphis called one on February 12—and it was in support of them that Martin Luther King Jr. was in
Memphis on April 4, when he was assassinated.

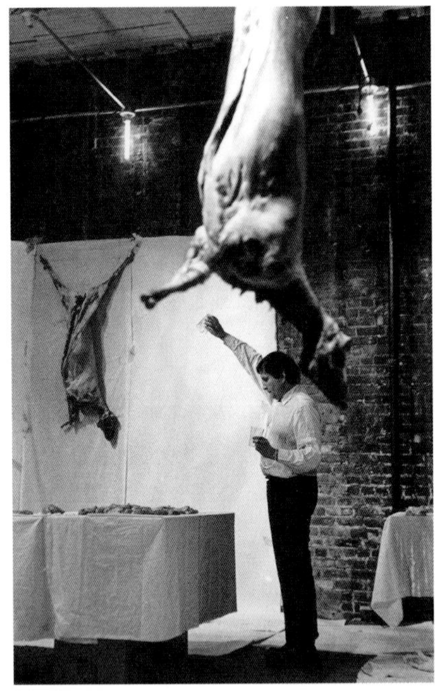
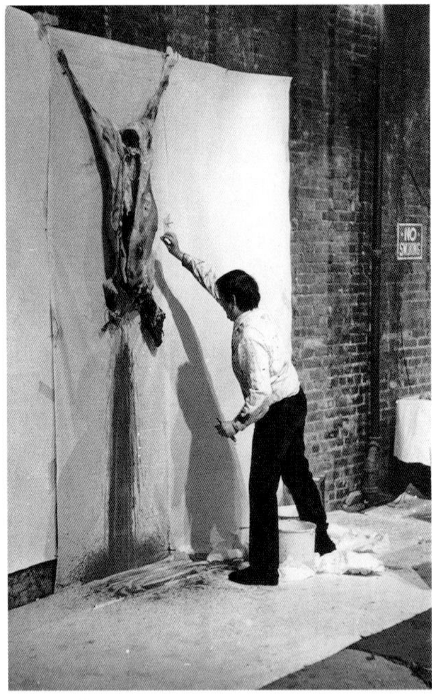
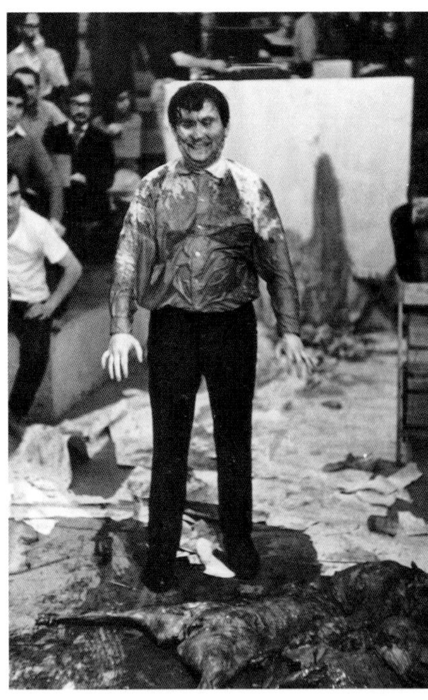
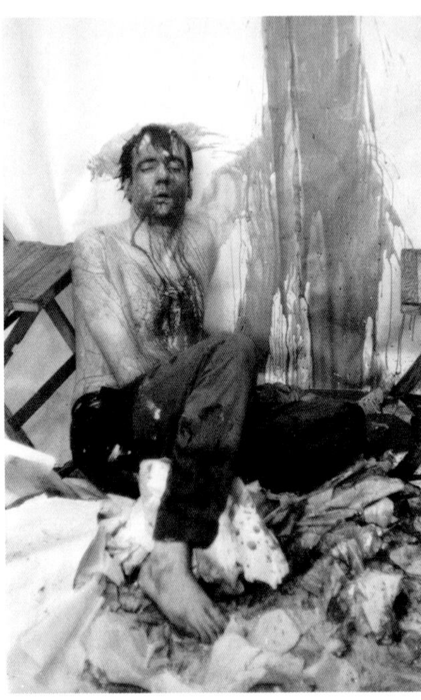
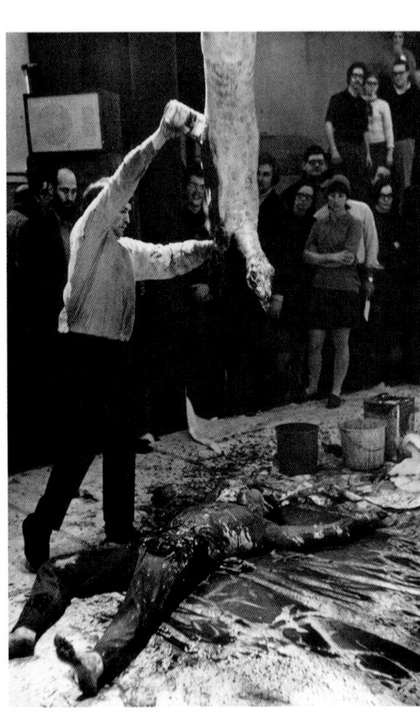
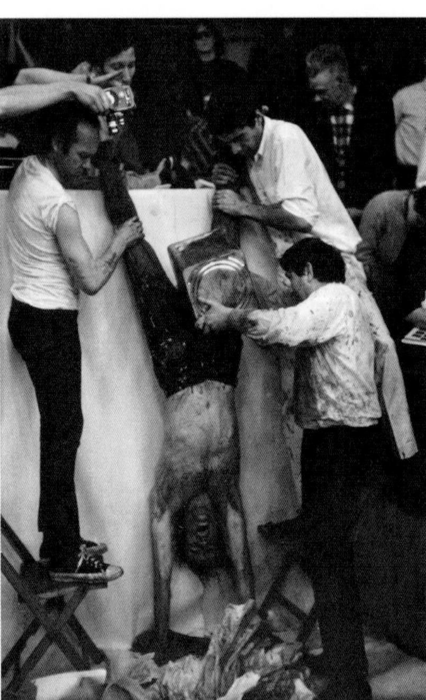

Austrian artist Hermann Nitsch performs his Orgy Mystery Theater at the Film-Makers' Cinematheque, 80 Wooster St., March 2, 1968. Over the next three decades, he would stage nearly one hundred performances, ritualistically incorporating animal carcasses, music, dance, and audience participation, which led to repeated trials for indecency and protests by animal rights groups.

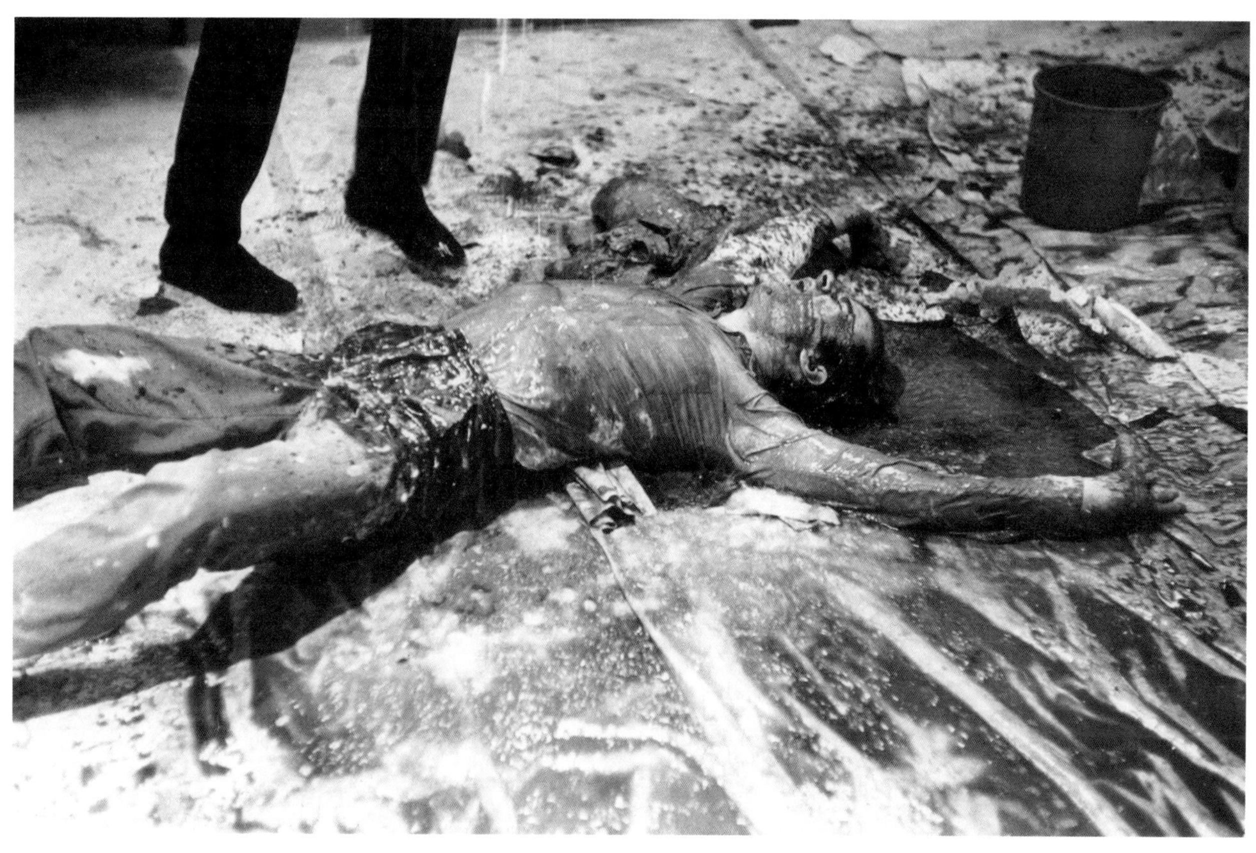

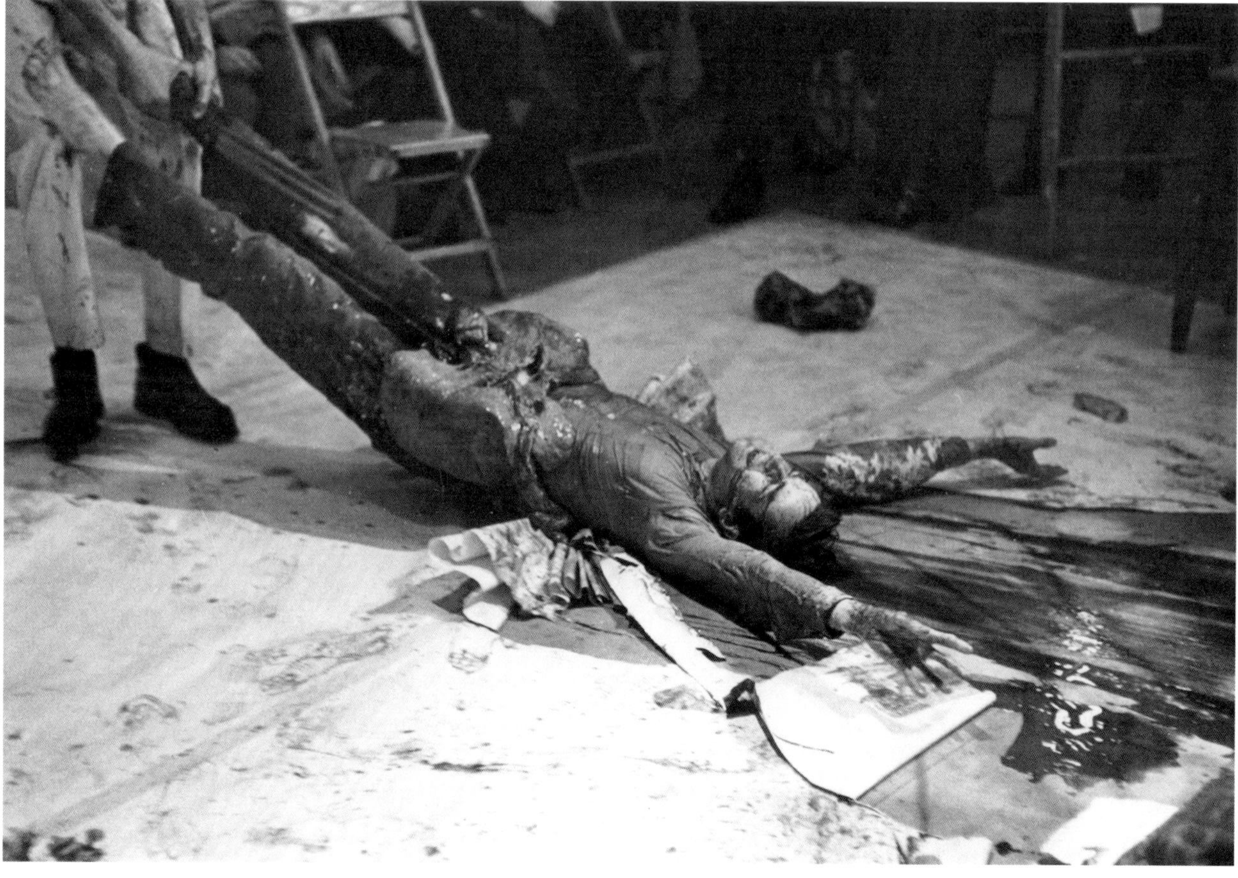

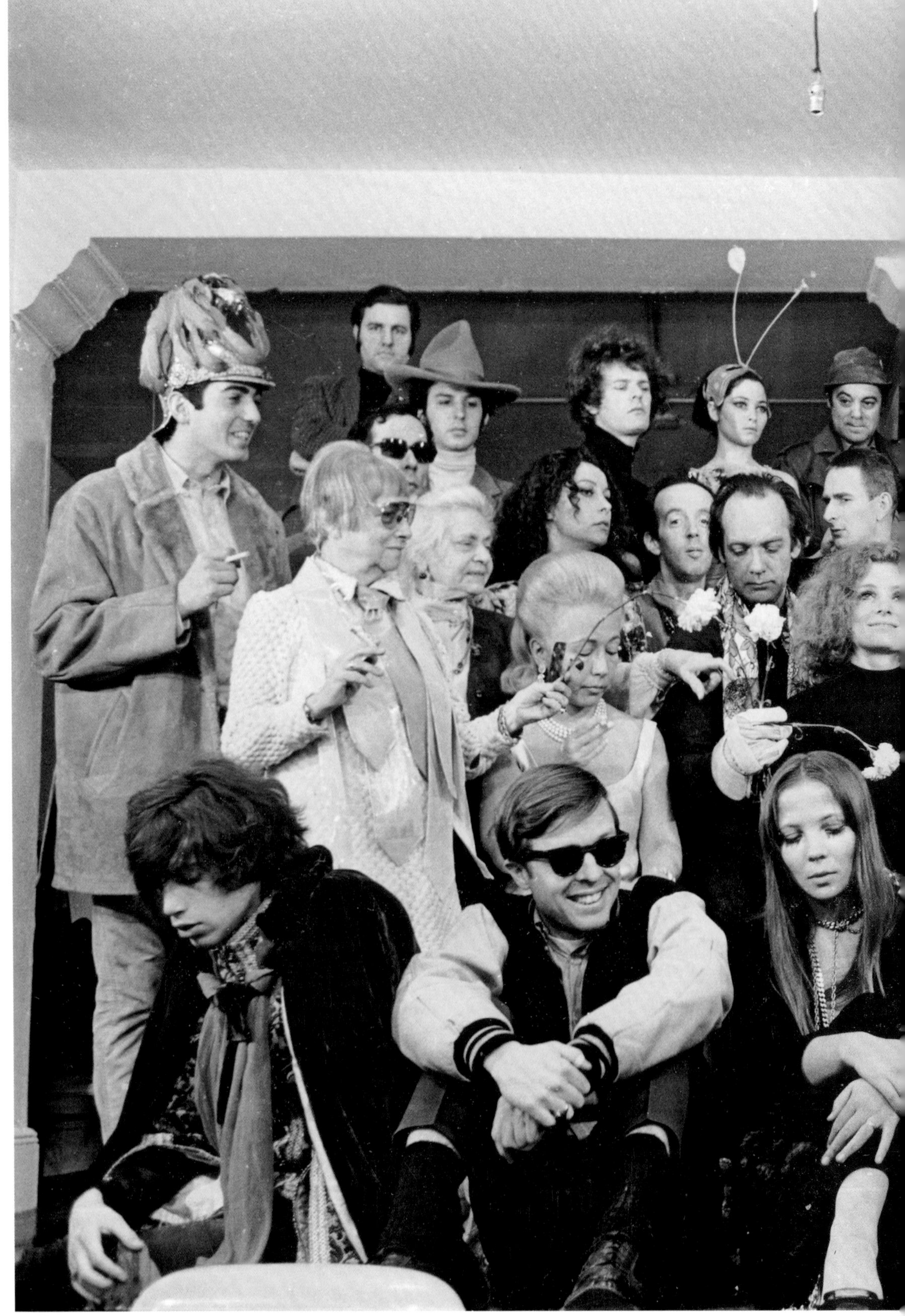

The underground film family and other friends of Andy Warhol posing for a photo to celebrate publication of Charles Henri Ford's book of poetry *Silver Flower Coo*, the Factory (at its second location), 33 Union Square West, March 6, 1968.
From left, bottom row: Jonathan Lieberson, Andreas Brown, Penelope Tree, Andy Warhol, Catherine Milinare, and Jason Fishbein.
Second row: Lil Picard, Frances Steloff, Lita Hornick, Al Hansen, Viva, Charles Henri Ford, Kenneth King, and Ruth Ford.
Third row: Bruce Miller, Buddy Wirtschafter, Ultra Violet, Taylor Mead, Jack Smith, Sally Chamberlain, Wynn Chamberlain, Ron Zimardi, Ken Jacobs, Florence Jacobs, and Maurice Hogenboom.
Back row: Bob Cowan, Fred Hughes, Paul Morrissey, Donna Kerness, John Wilcock, and Willoughby Sharp.

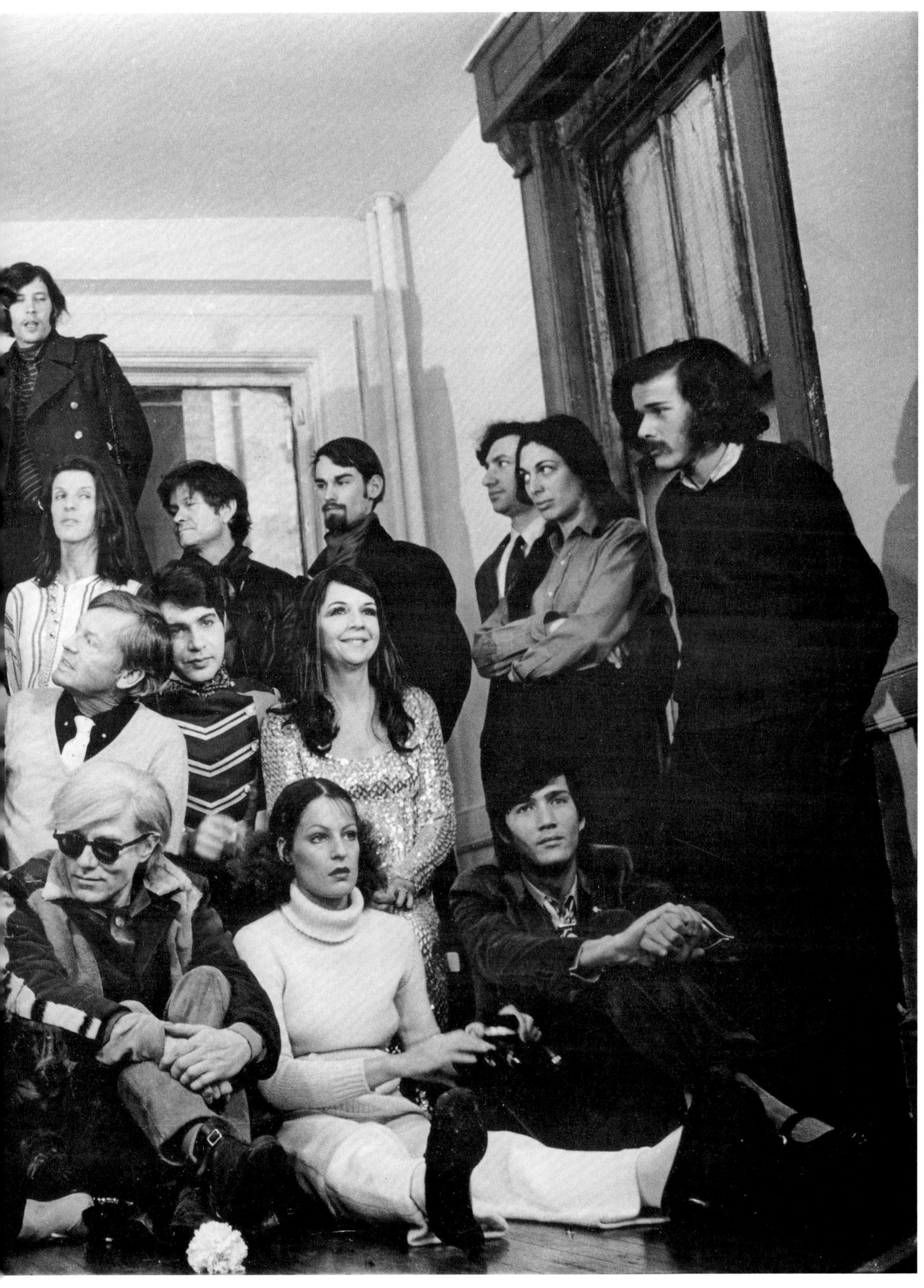

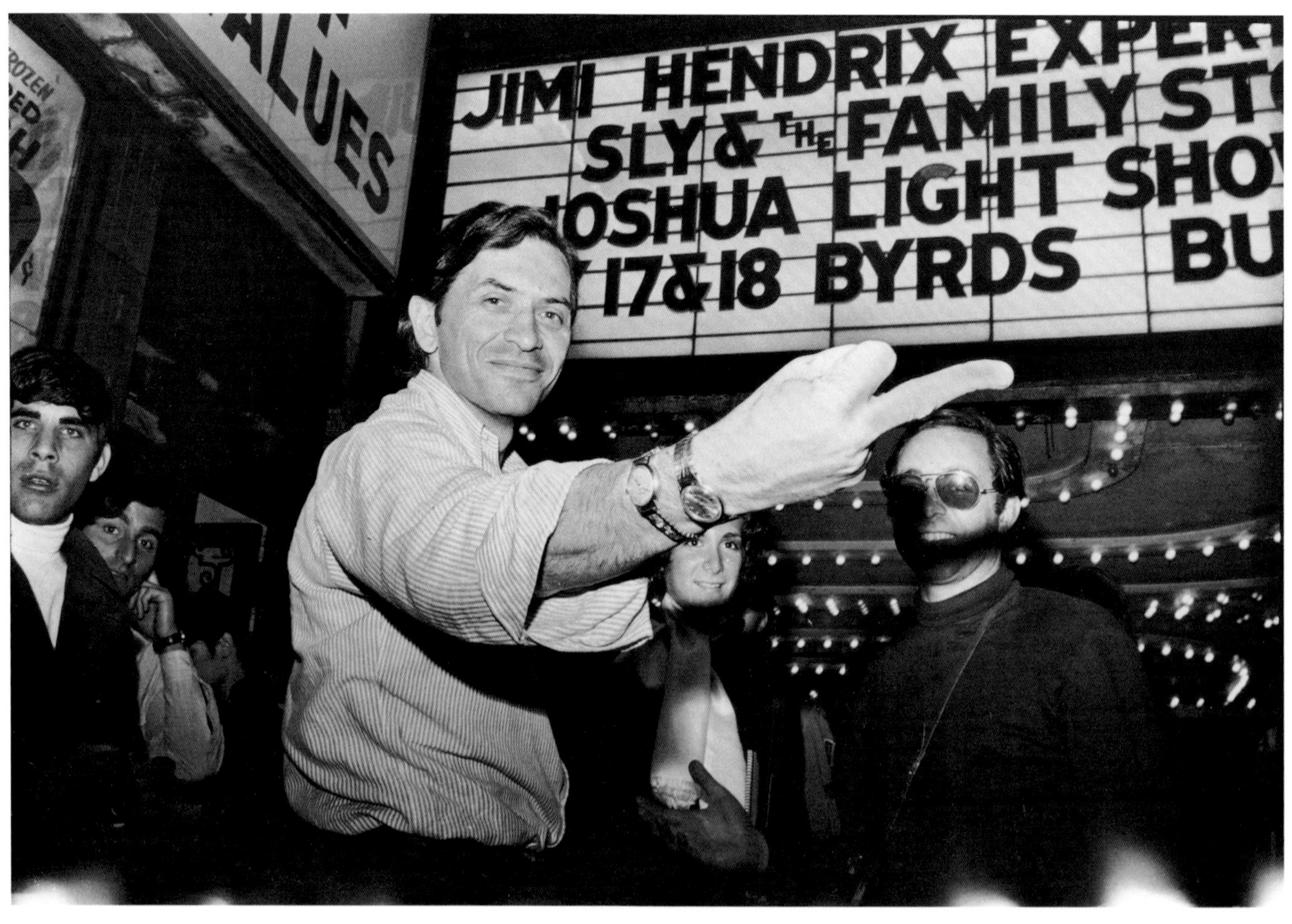

Rock promoter and Fillmore operator Bill Graham stands with concertgoers under the marquee and gives a finger to the camera at his Fillmore East, 105 Second Ave. at East Sixth St., May 11, 1968. Visible under his wrist is *Village Voice* writer Blair Sabol. Graham always wore two watches, one with New York time and one with the time in San Francisco, where his original Fillmore Auditorium was located. Both venues closed in 1971.

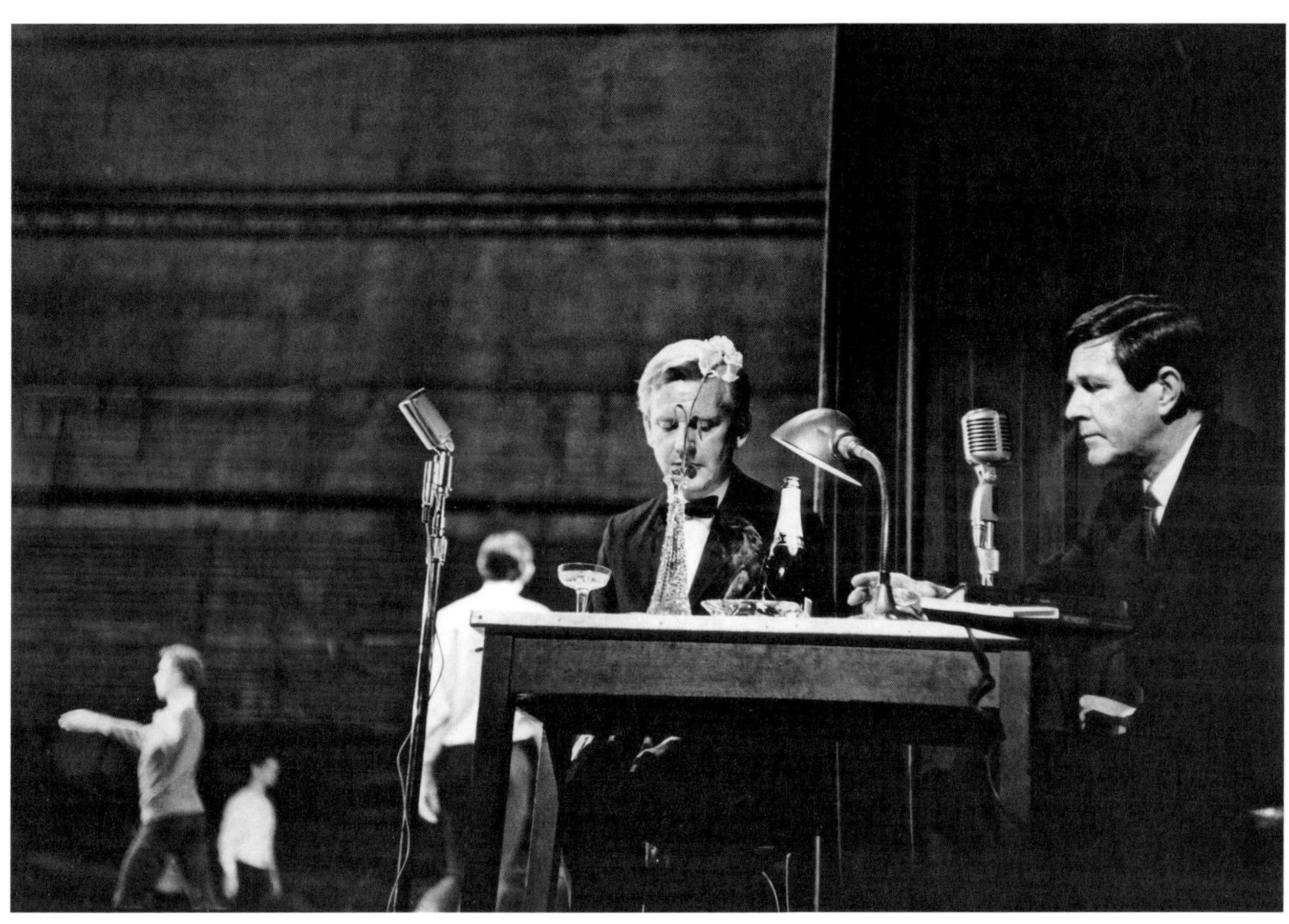

John Cage (right) and writer, dancer, choreographer, and actor David Vaughan (center, at table)
performing in *How to Pass, Kick, Fall and Run* at the Brooklyn Academy of Music, May 15, 1968.
Merce Cunningham dances, arms outstretched, at lower left. Vaughan was the longtime secretary
of the Merce Cunningham Dance Company and would become its archivist and historian.

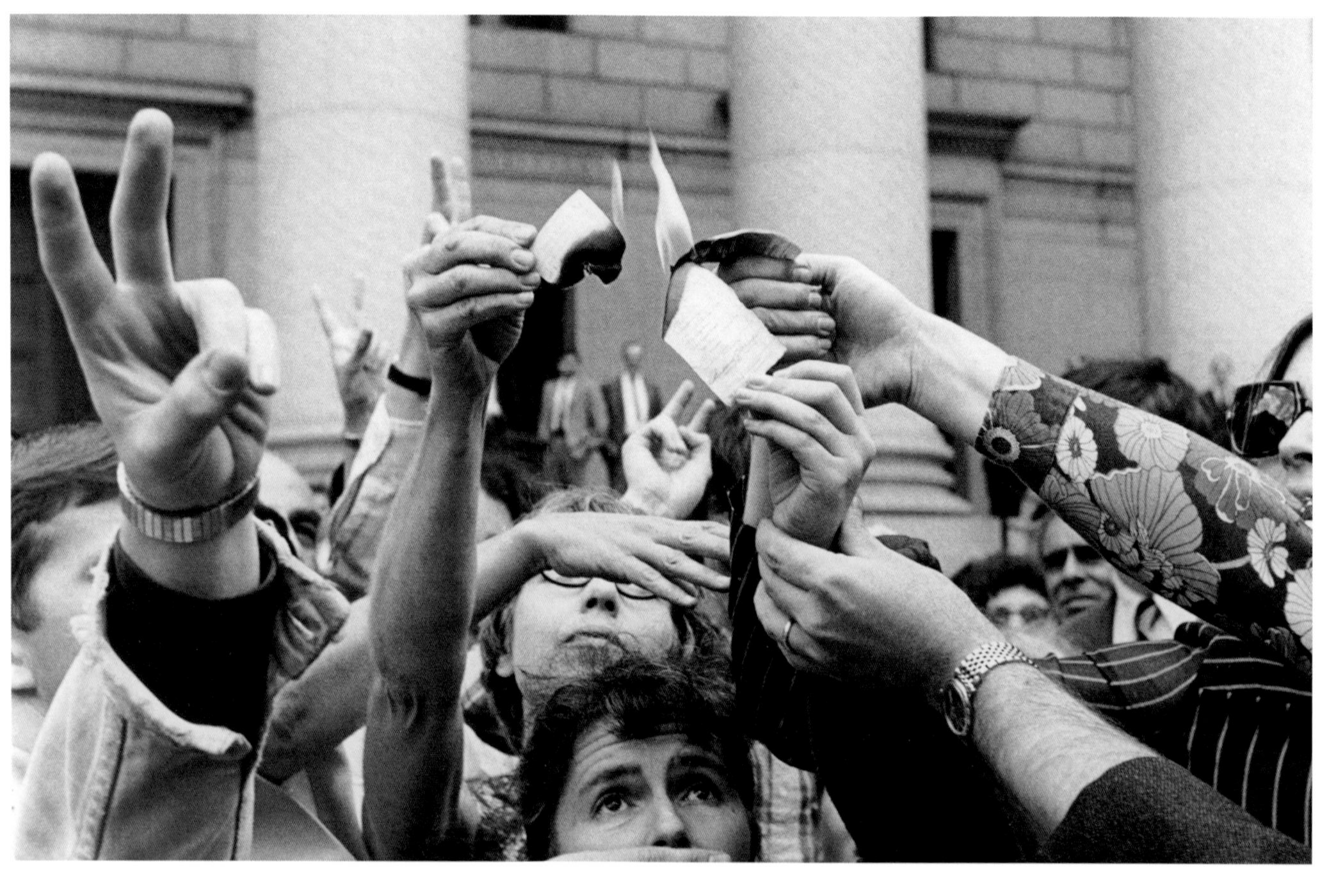

Antiwar protest outside the Federal Courthouse, Foley Square, June 18, 1968.
Grace Paley is partially visible at the bottom of the frame (center). The women
are holding up the burning draft cards of their husbands and sons to symbolize
their opposition to the war.

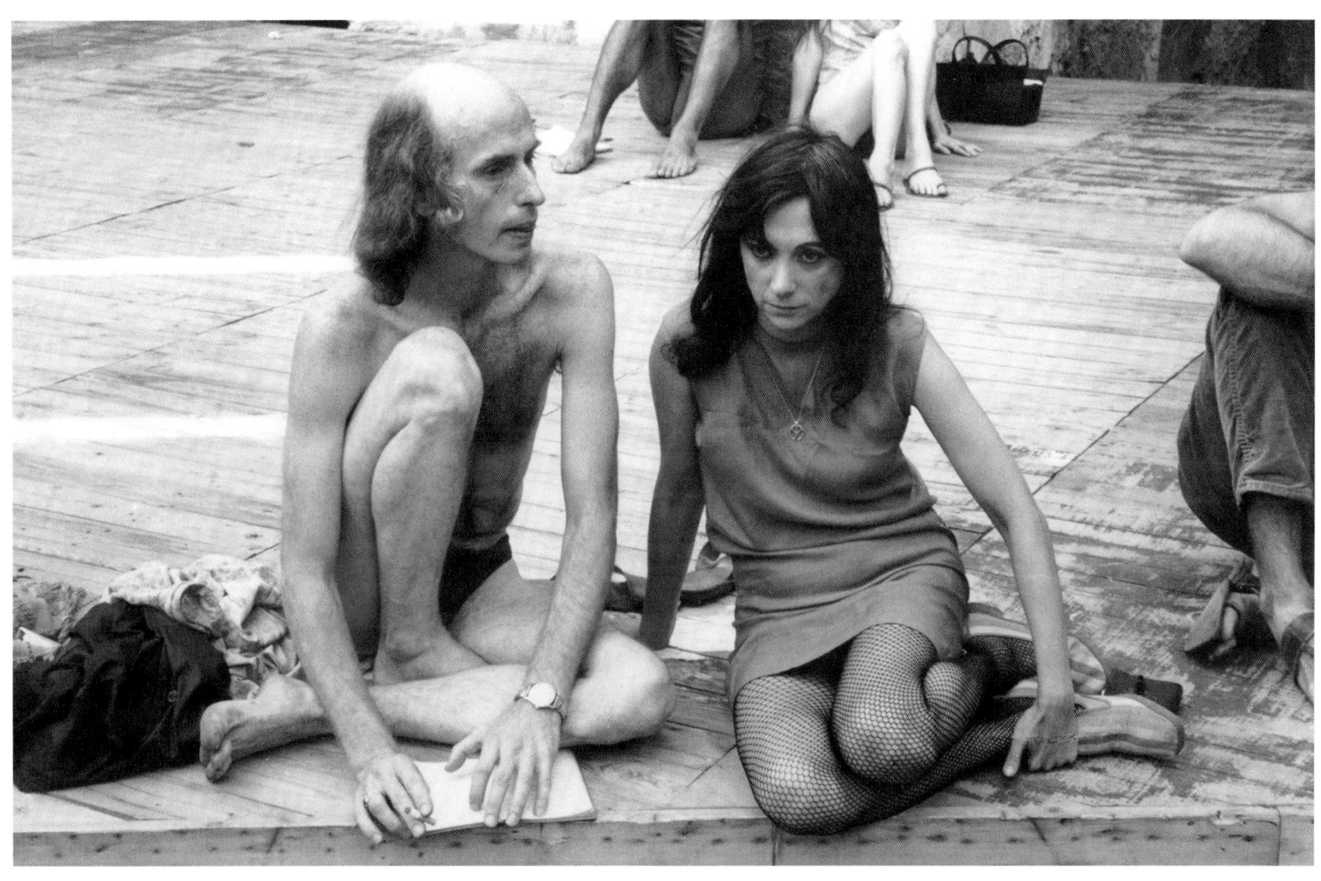

Julian Beck and Judith Malina, founders of the Living Theatre, at a rehearsal in Avignon, France, after the troupe left the United States as a result of a tax dispute, July 15, 1968. Launched in 1947, it remains America's oldest experimental theater group.

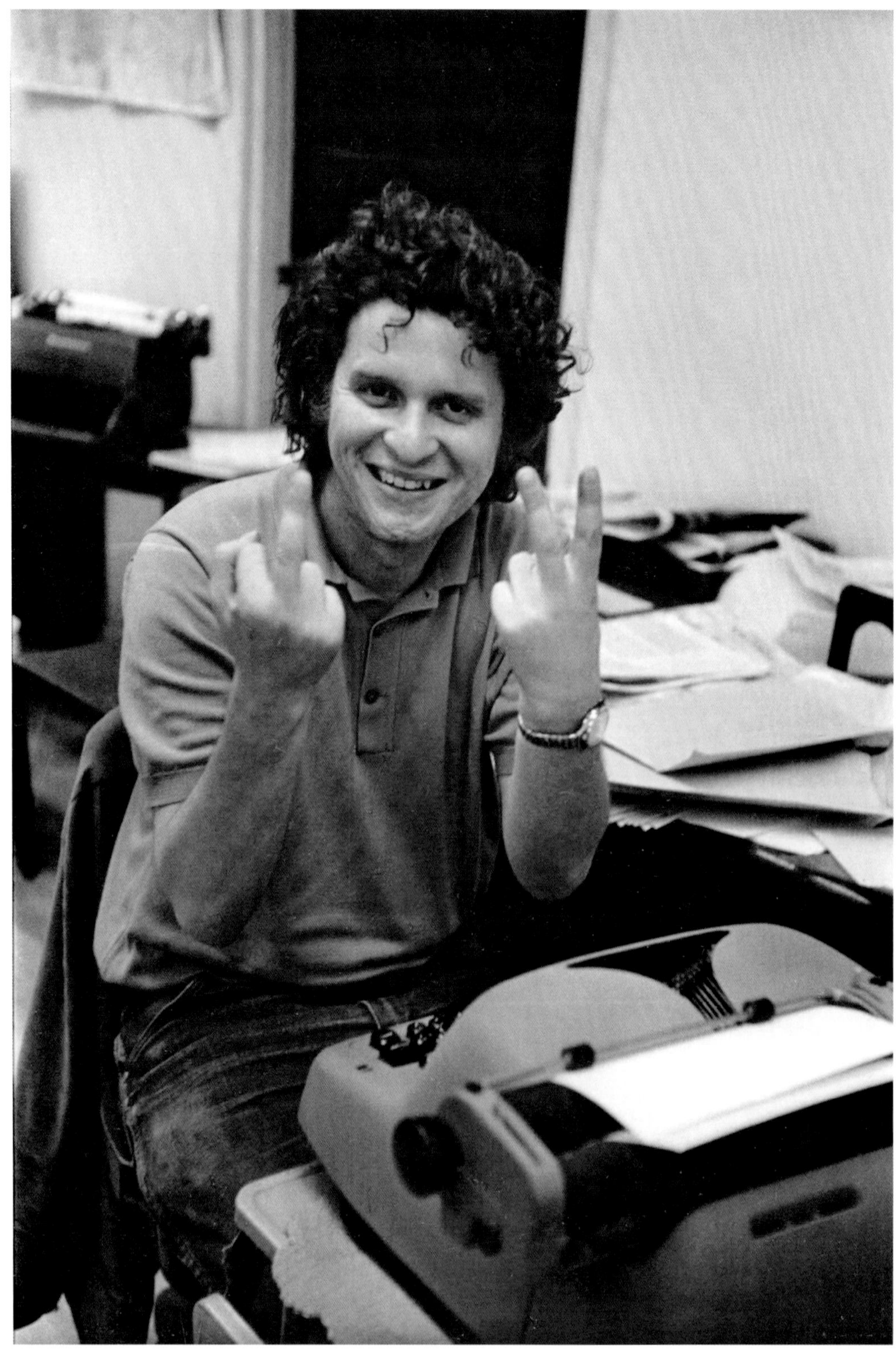

Author and editor Paul Krassner is seen here a few days before the Democratic National Convention in Chicago, August 23, 1968. Krassner founded *The Realist*, a pioneering counterculture magazine of "social-political-religious criticism and satire," in 1958.

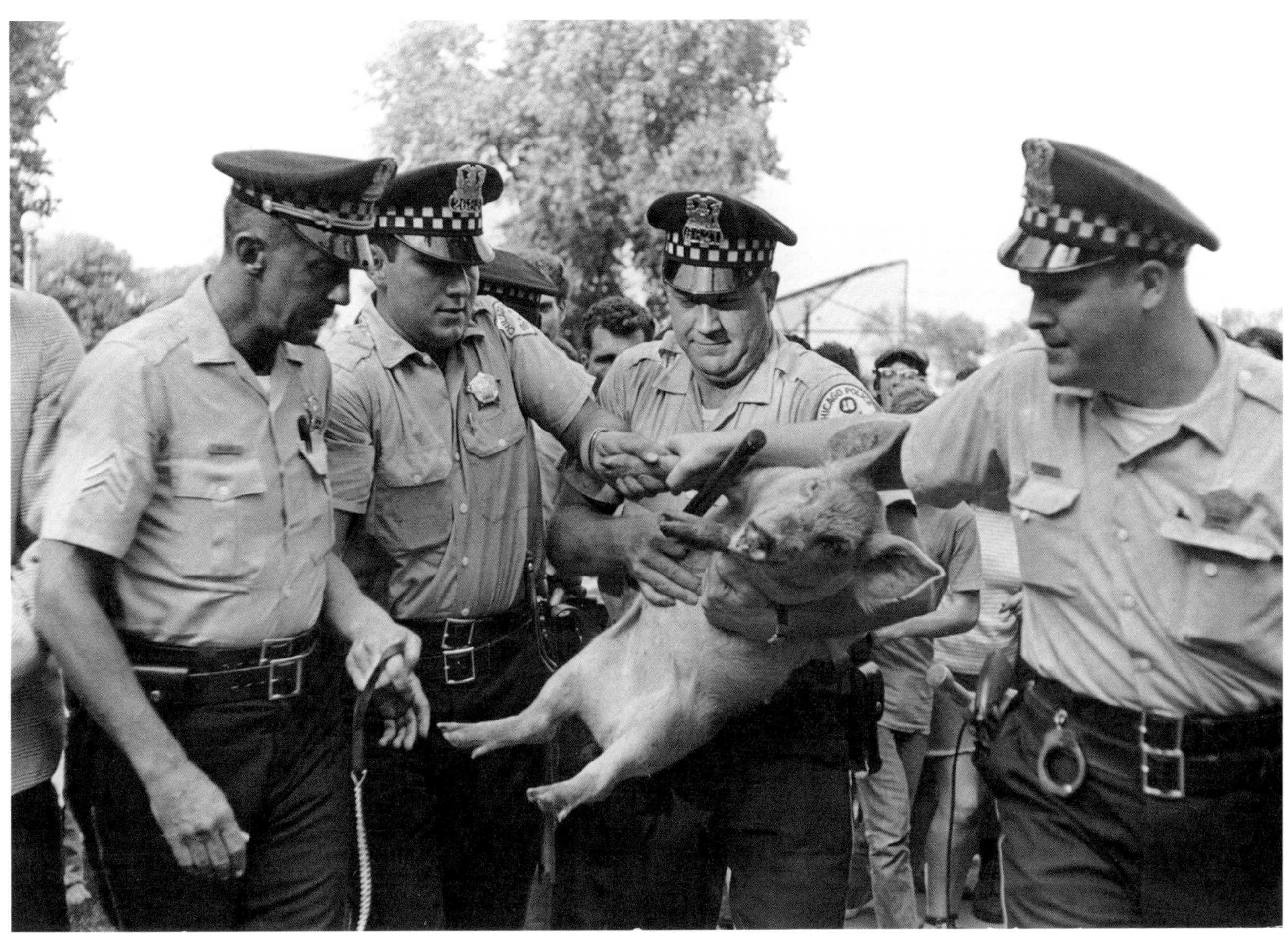

During the days of mass demonstrations before the Democratic National Convention in Chicago, police officers "arrest" Pigasus, the Youth International Party (Yippie) mock nominee for president, outside the Chicago Civic Center, August 23, 1968. Seven Yippies, including Jerry Rubin (in the middle of reading the pig's acceptance speech) and singer Phil Ochs (who had bought the candidate from a farmer), were arrested and briefly held, while the nominee was taken to the Chicago Anti-Cruelty Society and ended up back at a farm.

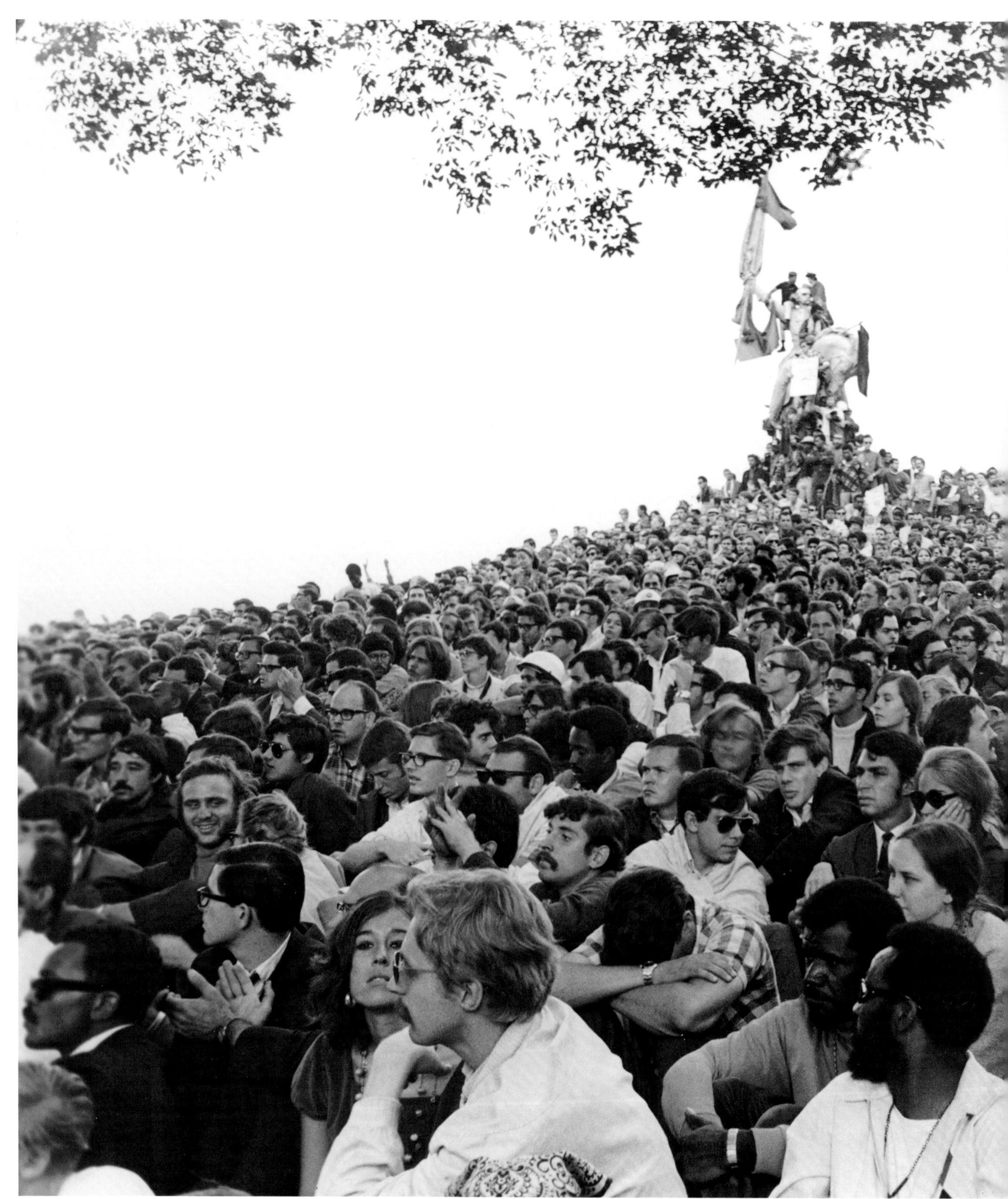

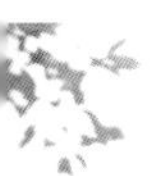

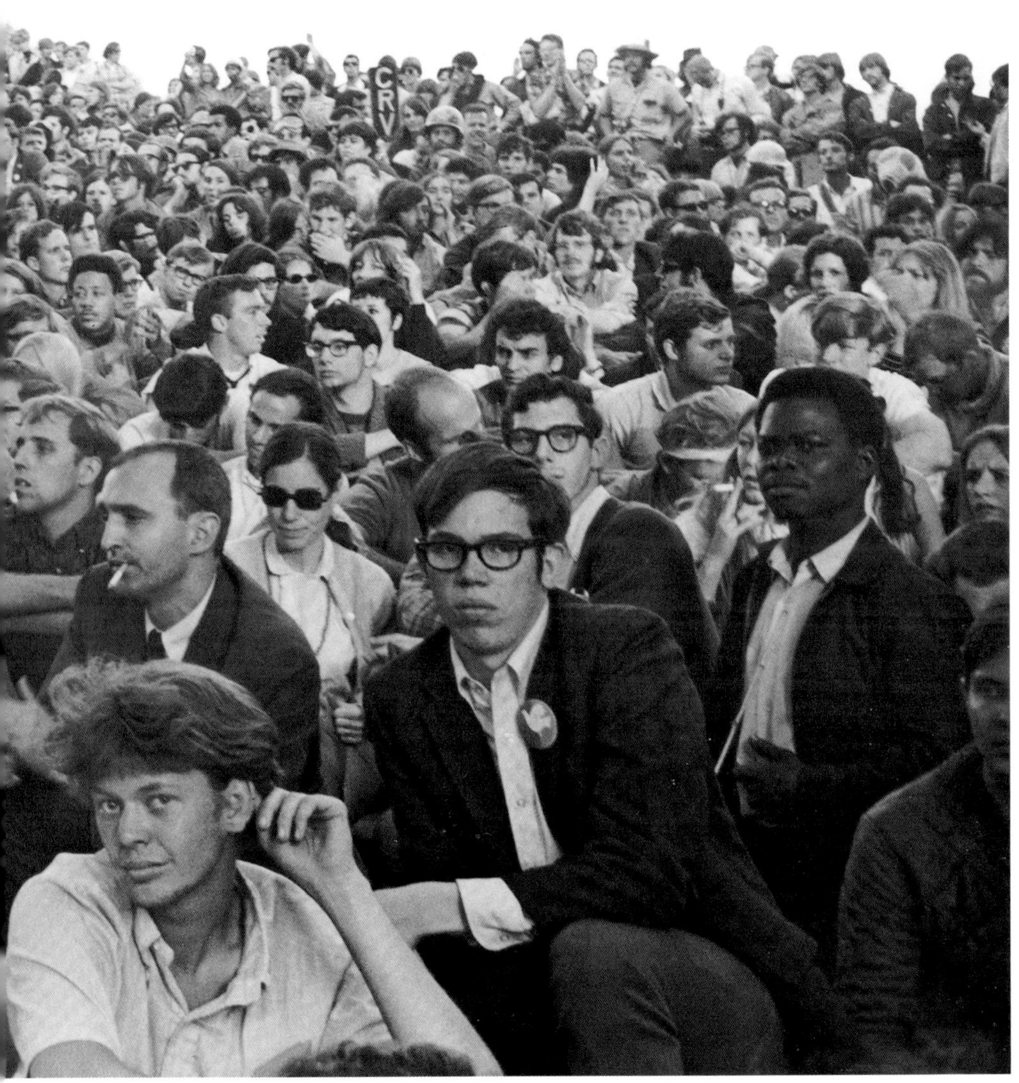

A crowd of demonstrators in Chicago's
Grant Park during the Democratic National
Convention, sitting around a hill topped
by a statue of Union General John Logan,
August 27, 1968. On the following day, the
"Battle of Michigan Avenue" resulted in what a
government-funded study later concluded was
a police riot.

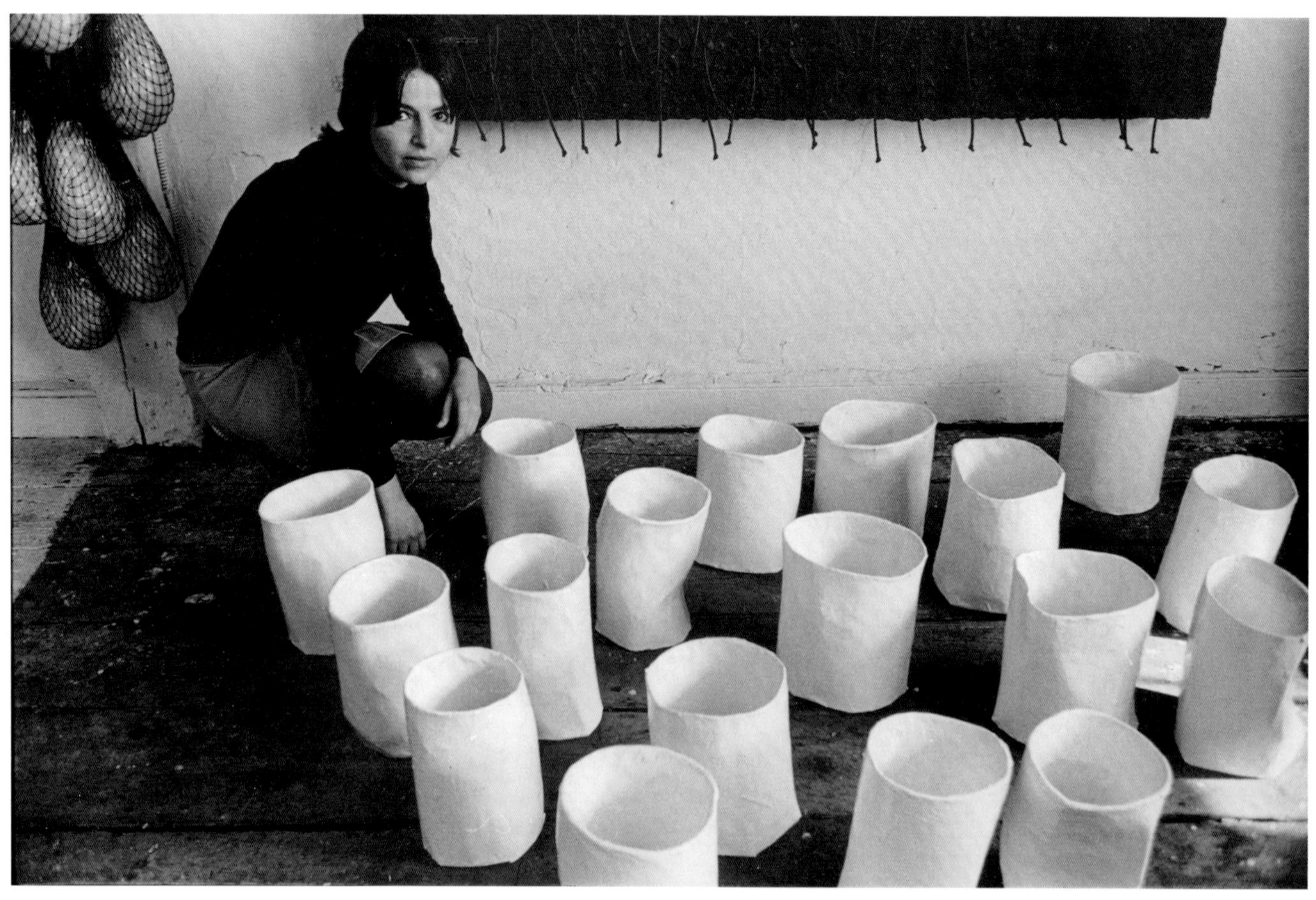

Artist Eva Hesse posing next to her sculpture *Repetition Nineteen III* in her Bowery studio, September 14, 1968. Hesse was a pioneer Post-Minimalist artist.

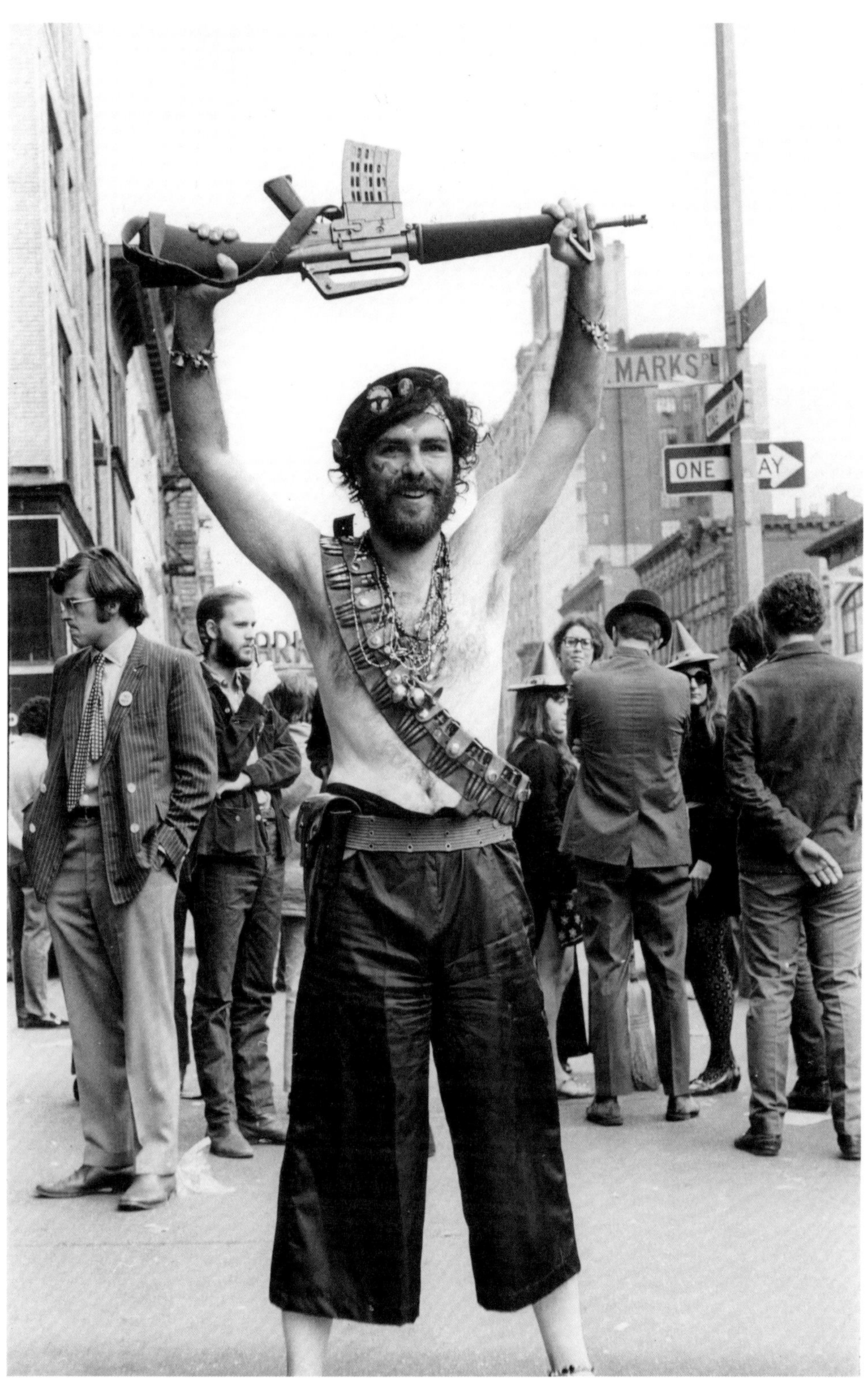

Political and social activist Jerry Rubin stands shirtless as he holds an M16 assault rifle above his head at the intersection of St. Marks Place and Second Ave. (view is looking north), September 28, 1968. His pal Abbie Hoffman lived steps away at 30 St. Marks Place.

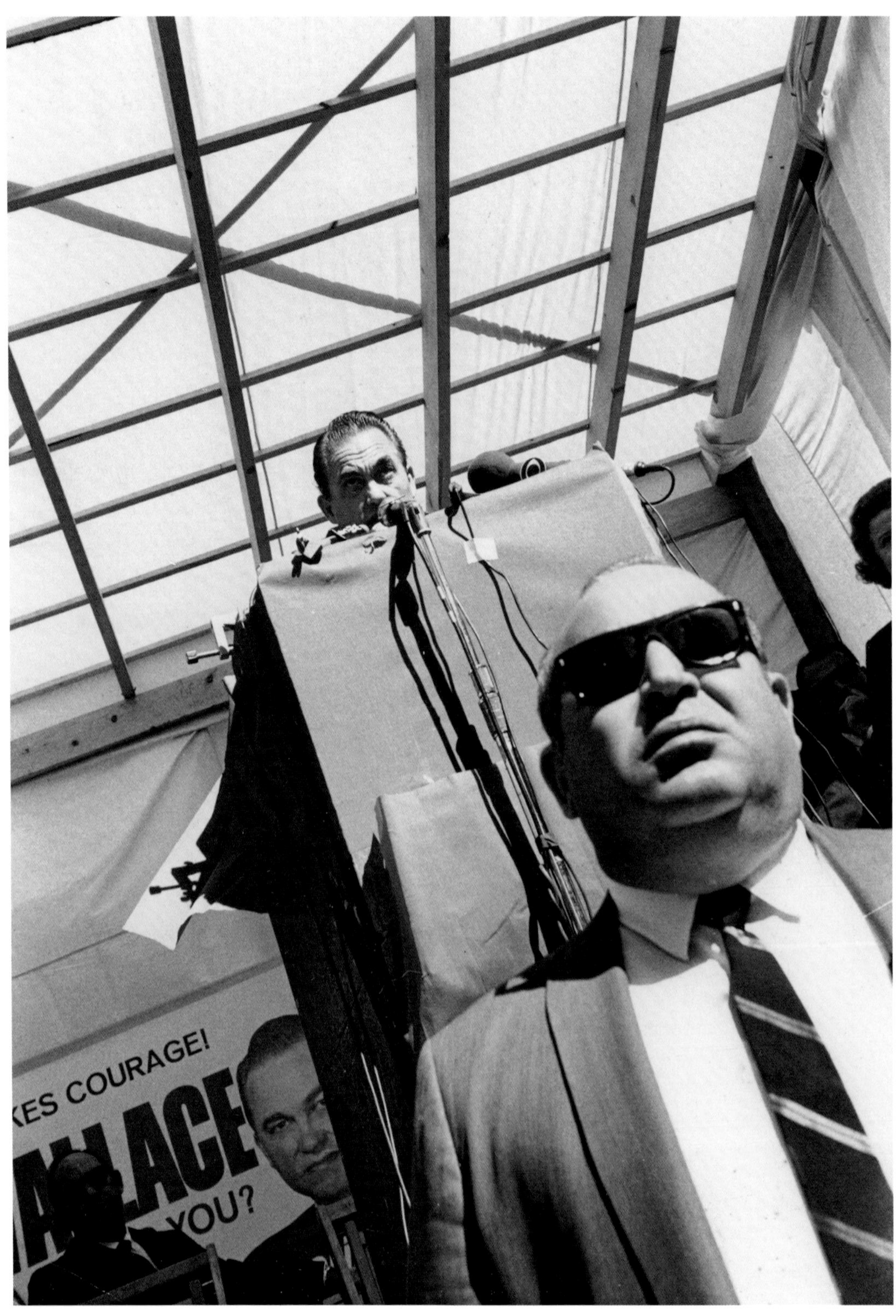

Governor George A. Wallace of Alabama at the lectern, October 5, 1968, behind a bodyguard in sunglasses. Wallace was campaigning in Newark, New Jersey, as a candidate for president on the ticket of the segregationist American Independent Party. On October 24, he would address about sixteen thousand supporters at a rally in Madison Square Garden, and he went on to win five Deep South states and forty-six electoral votes in the November election.

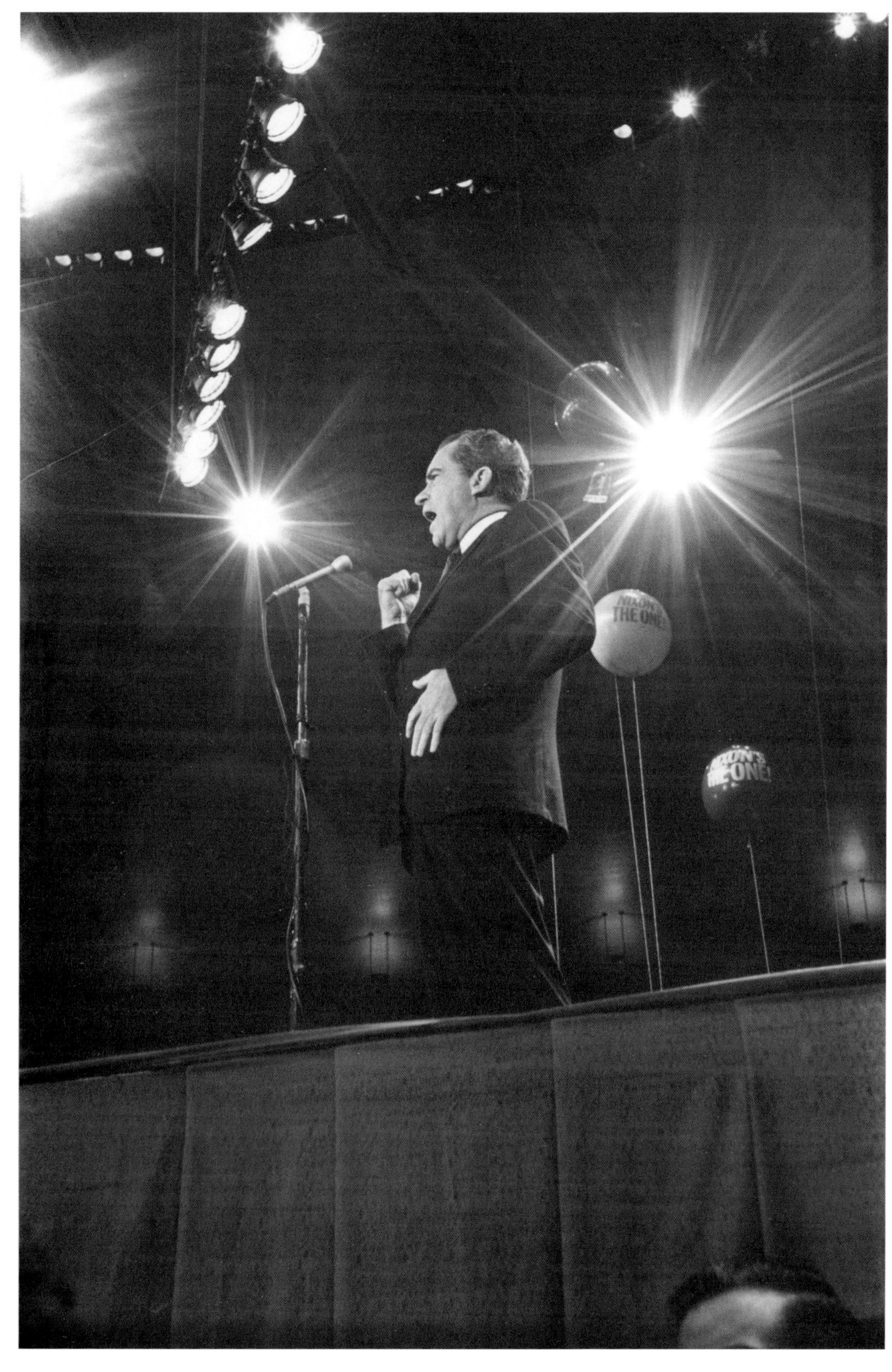

Republican presidential nominee Richard M. Nixon making a point with his fist during a campaign rally in Madison Square Garden, October 31, 1968. His election—narrow in the popular vote, not in the electoral vote—over Democrat Hubert H. Humphrey followed on November 5.

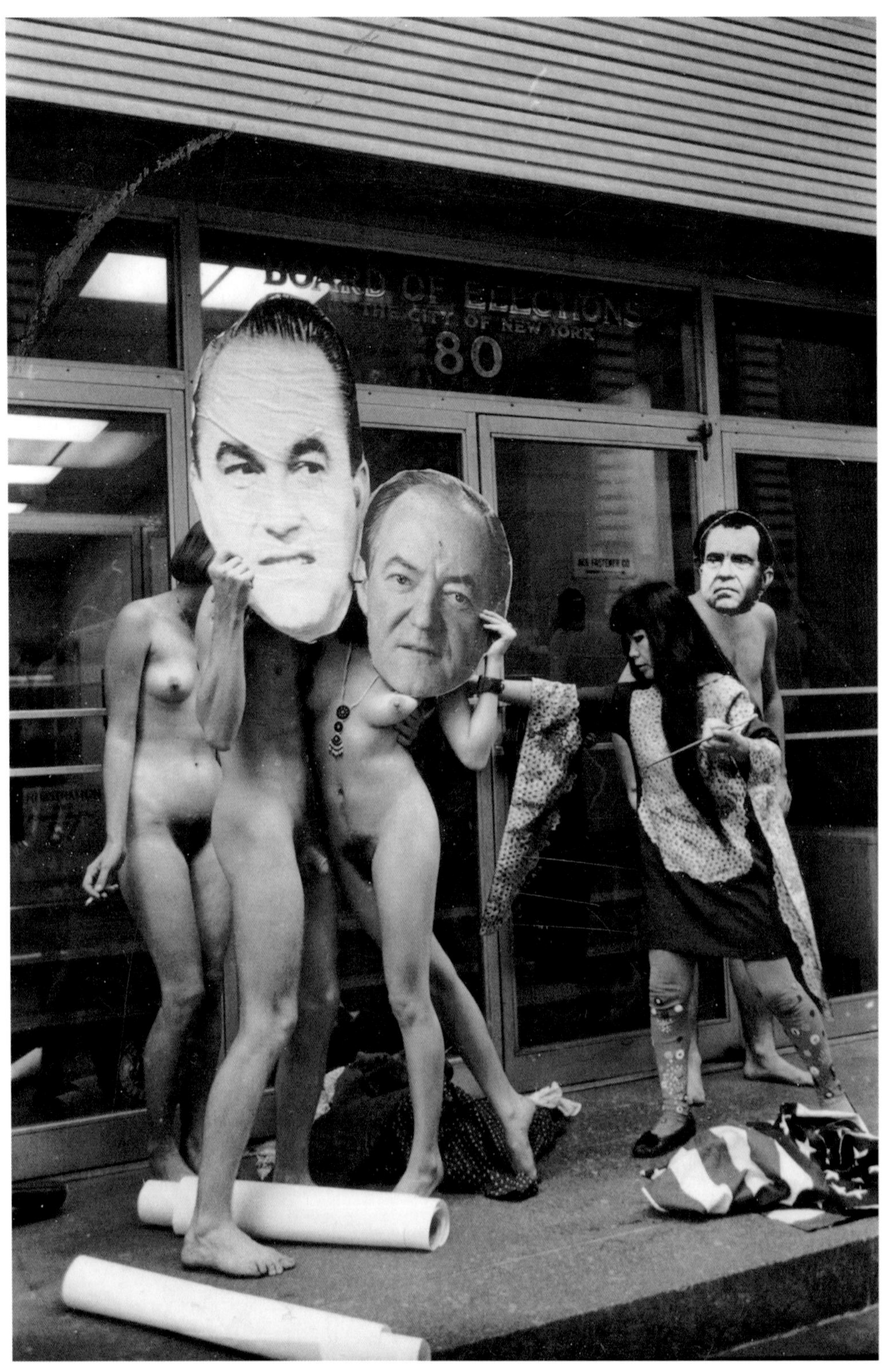

Japanese artist Yayoi Kusama and performers outside the New York City Board of Elections, November 3, 1968. That year, Kusama staged a series of *Anatomic Explosion* events in New York City, culminating with this one, two days before the presidential election, where performers display outsize face masks of the nominees: George Wallace, Hubert H. Humphrey, and Richard Nixon.

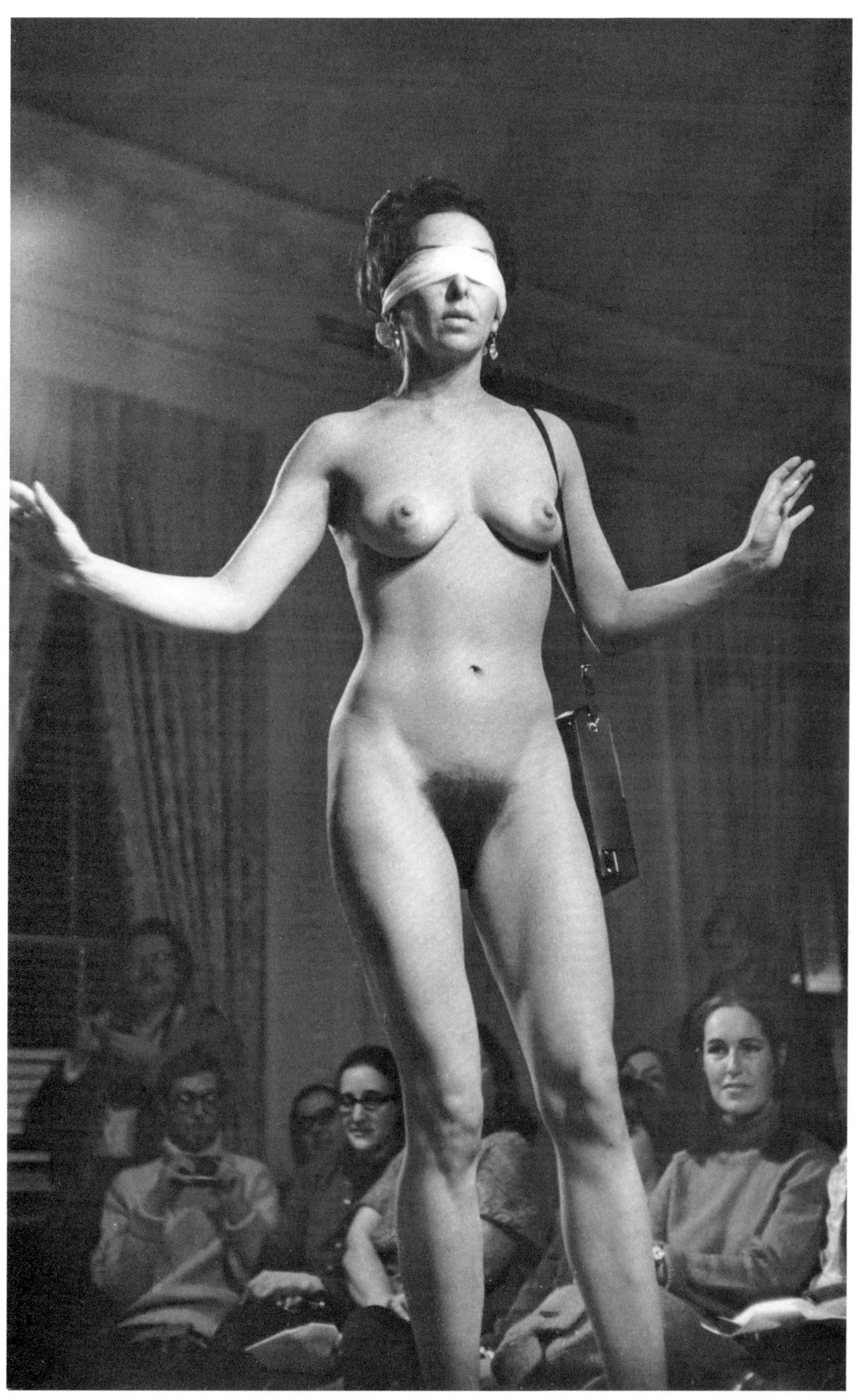

Artist Carolee Schneemann, wearing only a blindfold, in a performance staged by Claes Oldenburg for a Fashion Show Poetry Event at the Center for Inter-American Relations, 680 Park Ave., January 14, 1969. She is carrying a tape recorder that played a recording of Oldenburg describing a wedding dress. According to the event's program, "The poets will provide her clothes."

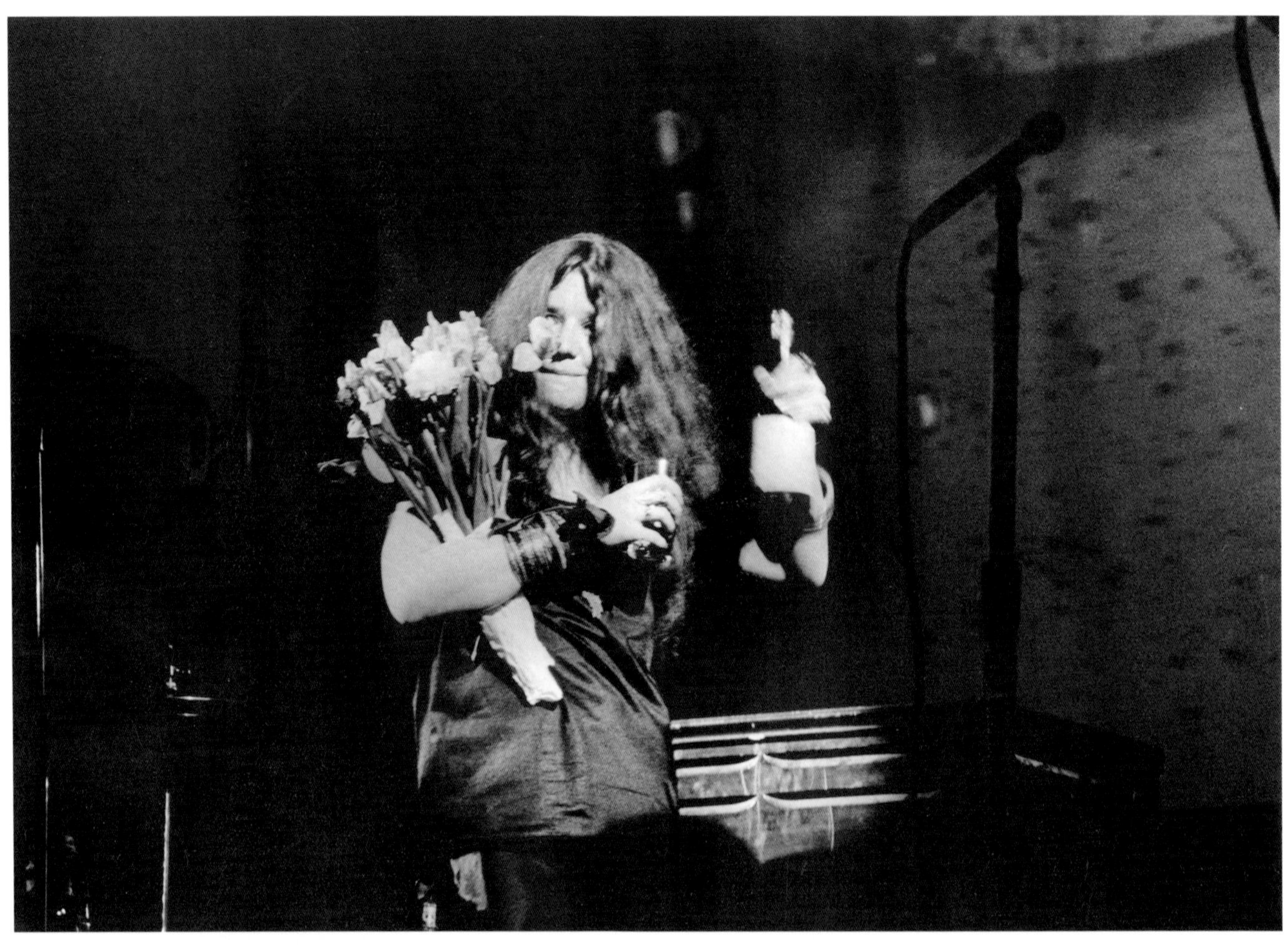

Janis Joplin at the Fillmore East, February 10, 1969. This was one of the singer's first bookings with her new backup group, the Kozmic Blues Band, after two and a half years with Big Brother and the Holding Company.

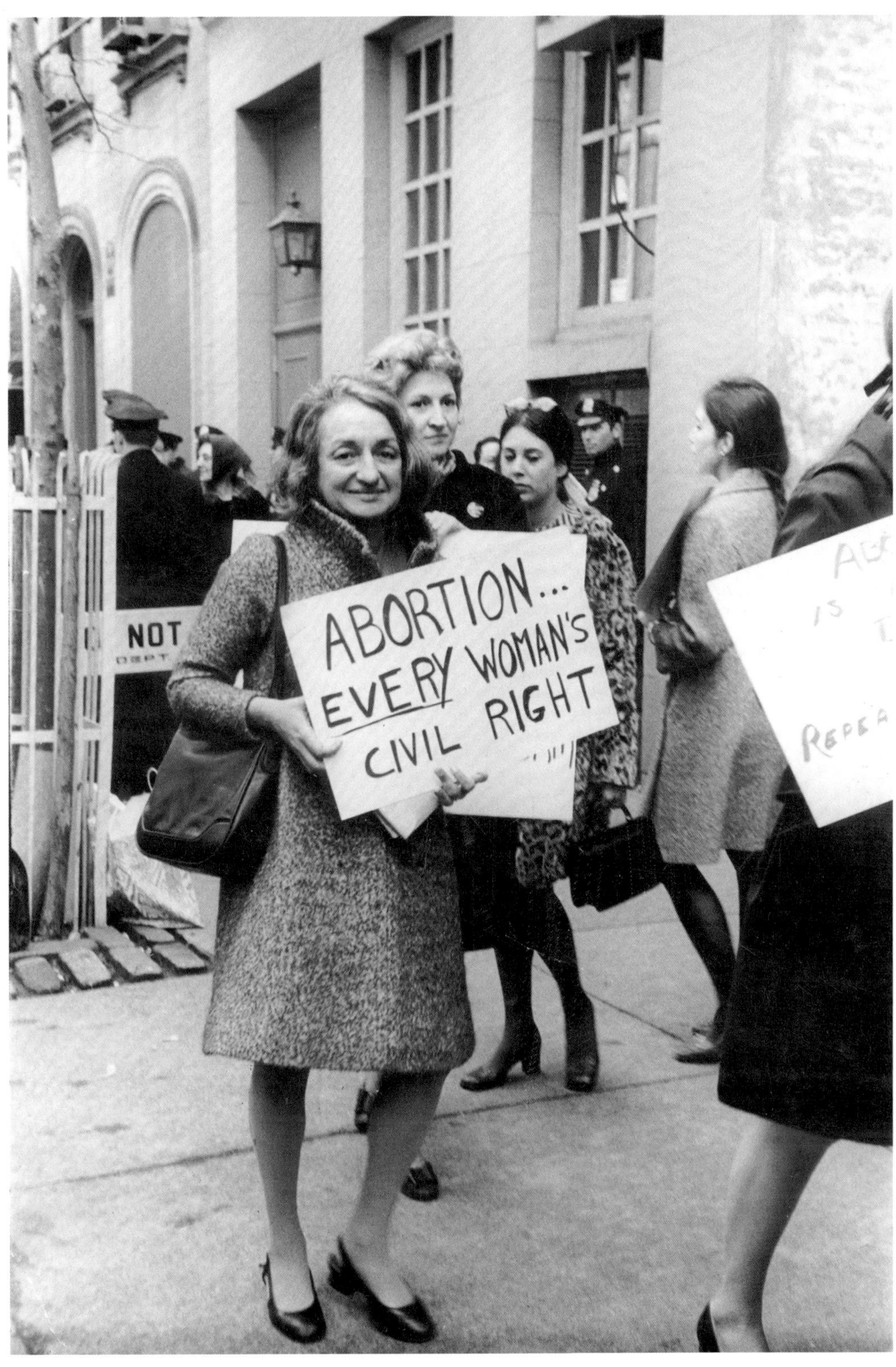

Betty Friedan at an abortion rights rally in front of Governor Nelson Rockefeller's New York office on West Fifty-Fourth St., March 21, 1969. Author of *The Feminine Mystique* (1963), in 1966 she cofounded and became first president of the National Organization for Women (NOW).

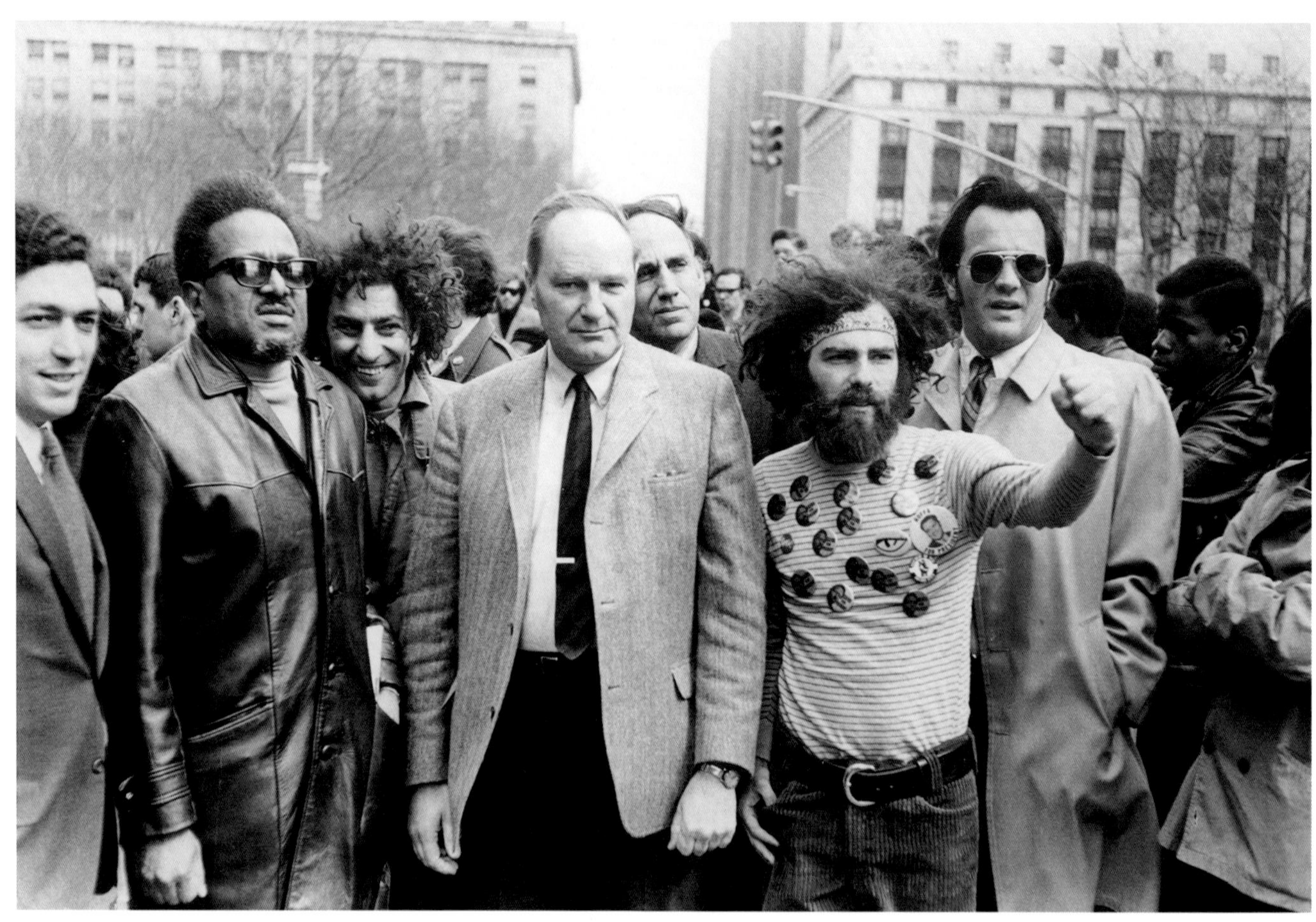

At a rally organized by the Black Panther Party, Abbie Hoffman (grinning, third from left), David Dellinger (in tie), attorney William Kunstler (behind Dellinger), and Jerry Rubin (in beard and buttons, at right) gather outside the Federal Courthouse on Foley Square, March 22, 1969. Two days previously, Dellinger, Hoffman, and Rubin had been indicted with five others for conspiracy to cross state lines with intent to incite a riot at the 1968 Democratic National Convention; Kunstler was one of their attorneys. Complex court battles followed; all of the so-called Chicago Eight were eventually cleared of the original charge, although some were found to be in contempt of court—at the very least, they had been memorably outspoken in the courtroom.

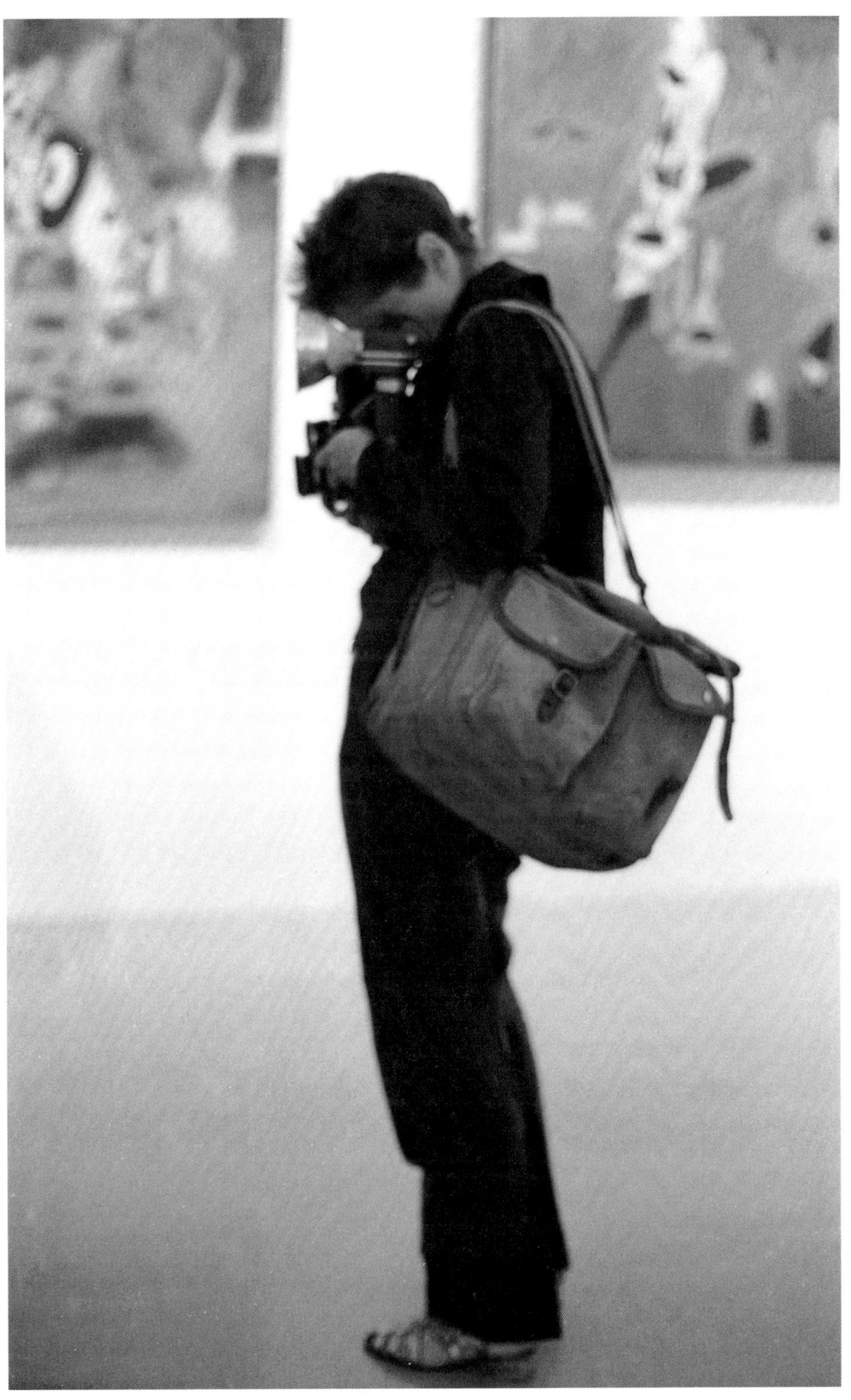

Photographer Diane Arbus (born Diane Nemerov) takes a picture at the Whitney Museum of American Art, June 16, 1969. Arbus was celebrated for her portraits of people considered to be on the outskirts of society.

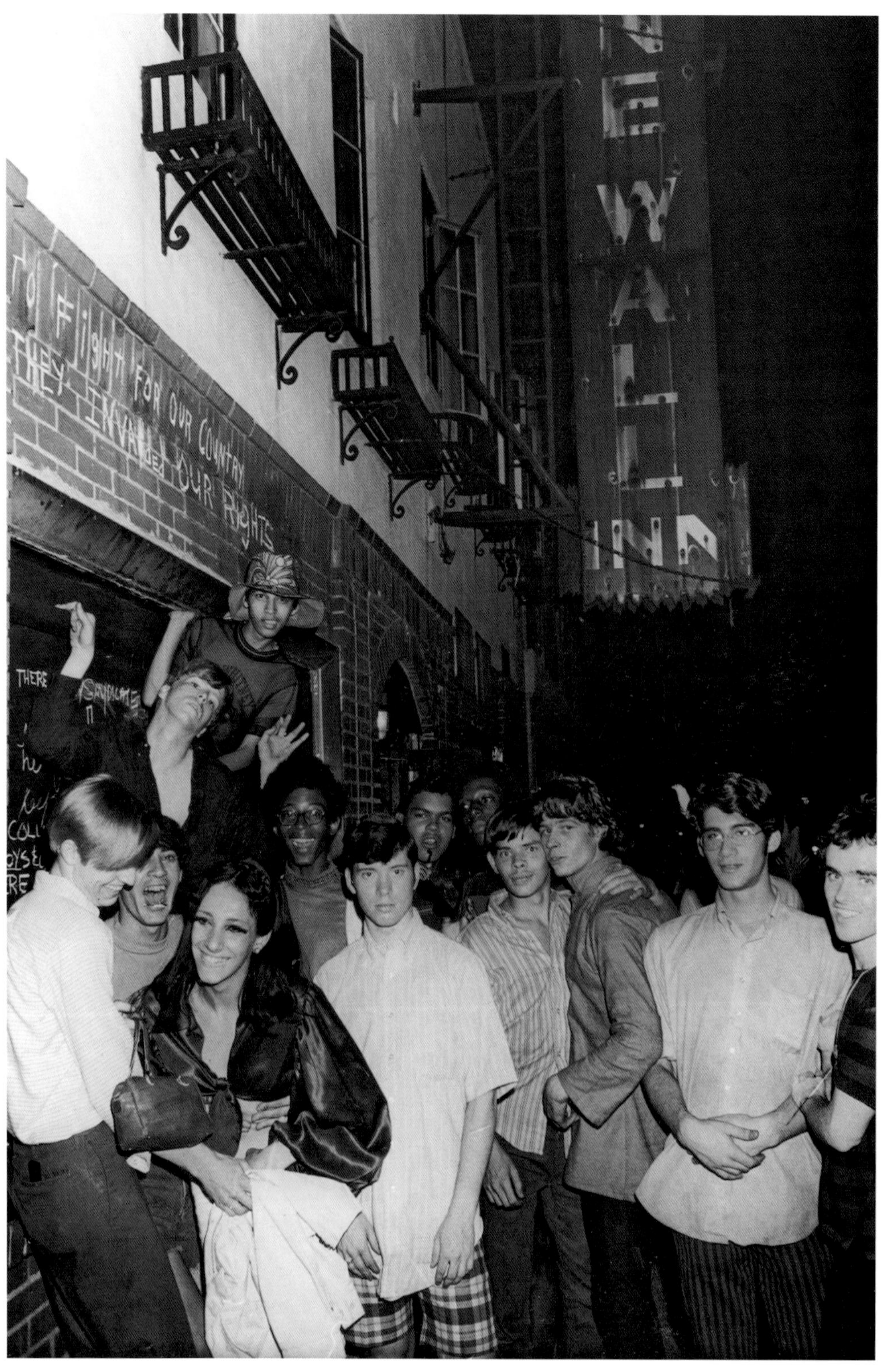

Young people outside the Stonewall Inn, 51–53 Christopher St., June 28, 1969. The group includes artist Tommy Lanigan-Schmidt (far right), still an activist and who later identified some of the others in the photo; Roger Davis (hands clasped); Miss Boston and Miss Boston's husband (embracing); Sylvia (behind and to the left of the embracing couple); Nelly (aka Betsy Mae Koolo, rear, above the crowd); Drag Queen Chris (laughing, open mouth); and in front, in a black blouse, Michelle. A gay bar since early 1967, popular because dancing was allowed, the Stonewall had been subjected to regular police raids like all gay bars at the time. After a police raid at about 1:30 a.m. on the June 28, patrol wagons were delayed, the growing crowd outside grew unruly, and suddenly the police outside and still in the bar found themselves under attack. Confrontations continued off and on for days in the area.

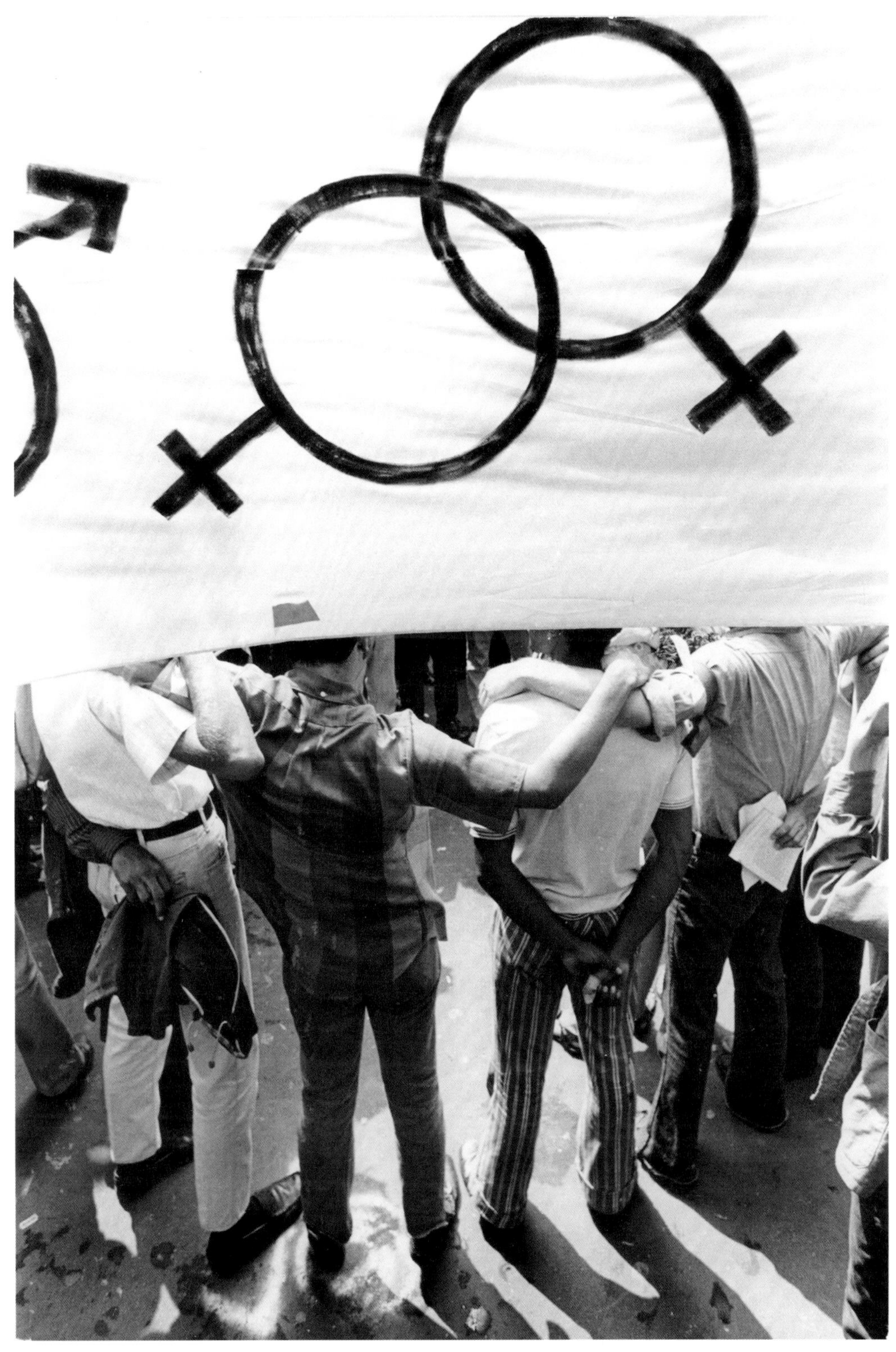

First gay liberation rally, Washington Square Park, July 27, 1969. After Stonewall, meetings took place to organize forceful activist groups. On July 24, younger and more militant gay activists split off from the more mainstream and cautious Mattachine Society, choosing the name Gay Liberation Front a week later. Meanwhile, on July 27, several hundred people attended this rally, where they listened to speeches by Marty Robinson, Jim Fouratt, and Martha Shelley. In November, a conference of "homophile organizations" agreed to plan the first gay pride march, which took place on June 28, 1970, the first anniversary of the Stonewall riots, when thousands marched from Washington Place up Sixth Ave. to a "Gay-In" at Central Park's Sheep Meadow.

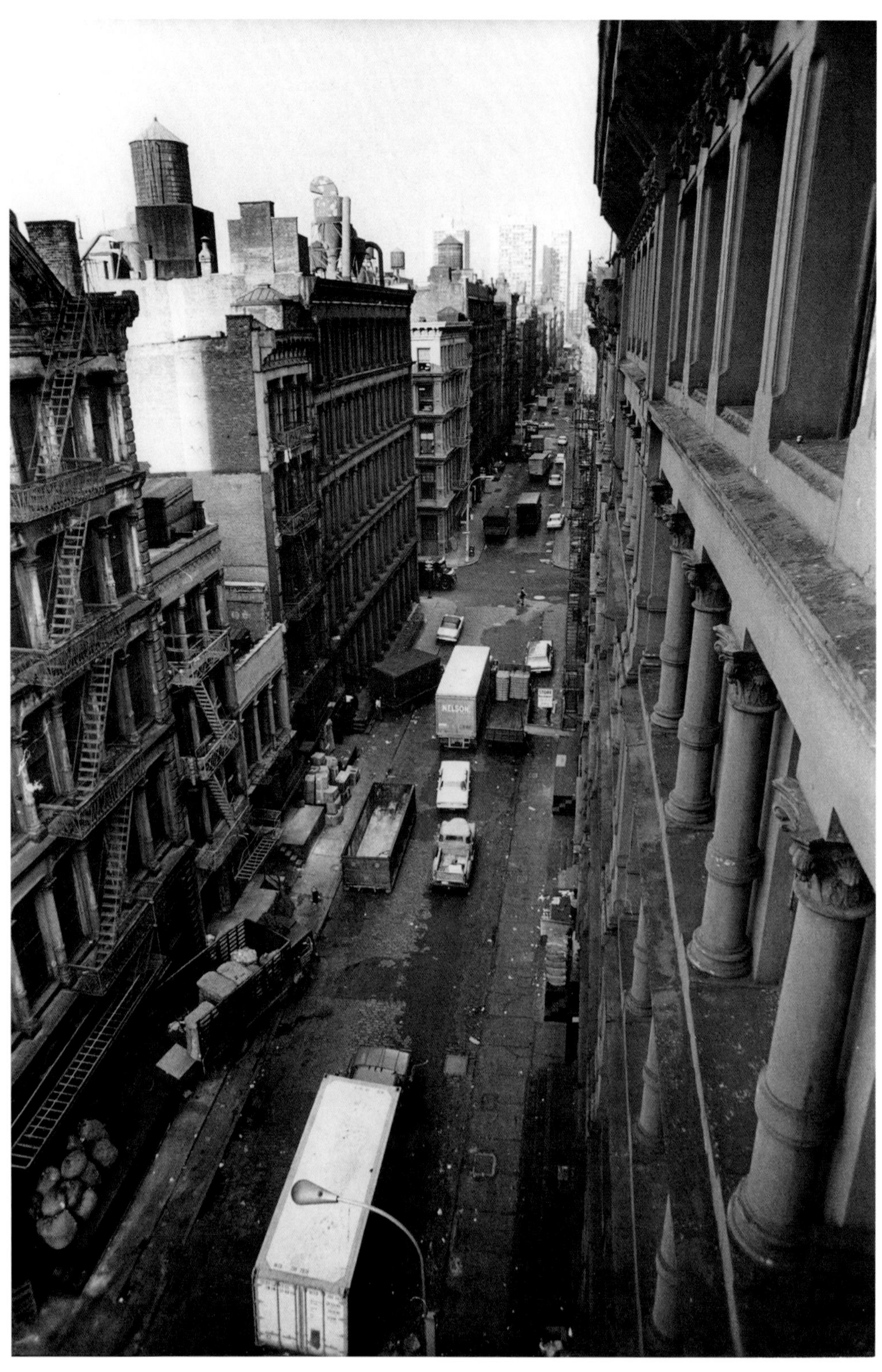

Cast-iron buildings dating back to the late nineteenth century line Greene St., October 9, 1969. This run-down industrial area of sweatshops and small factories, empty at night, attracted many artists to live illegally in its large lofts, to the point that it was rezoned in 1971 to permit artists to live where they worked. Two years later, the district was designated a landmark based on those historic buildings. Once called Hell's Hundred Acres, the area morphed into SoHo, the area south of Houston St.

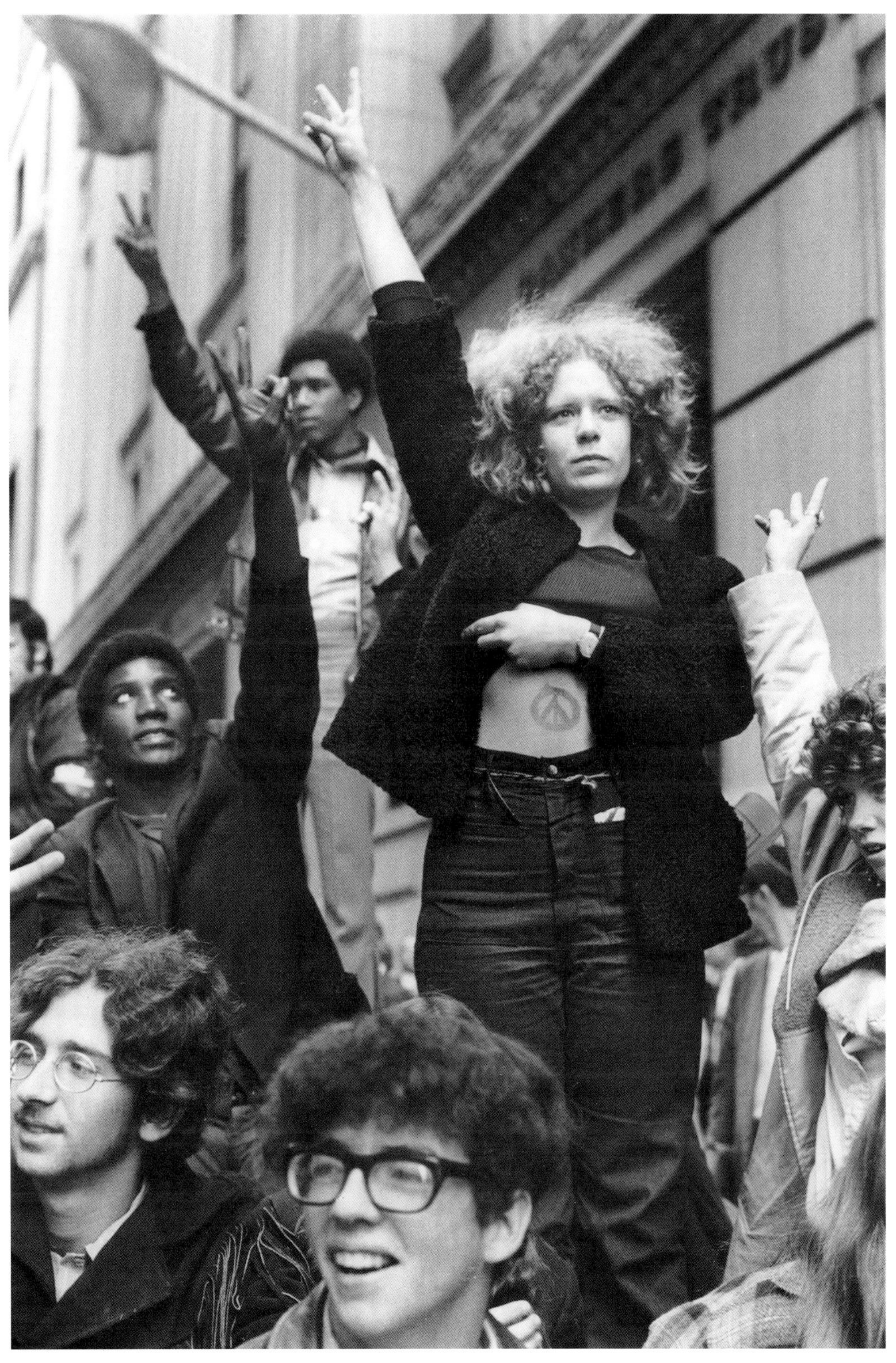

Protesters on Wall St. during the massive nationwide antiwar protest under the name Moratorium to End the War in Vietnam, October 15, 1969. A group supporting the war shouted slogans and tried to intimidate the protesters.

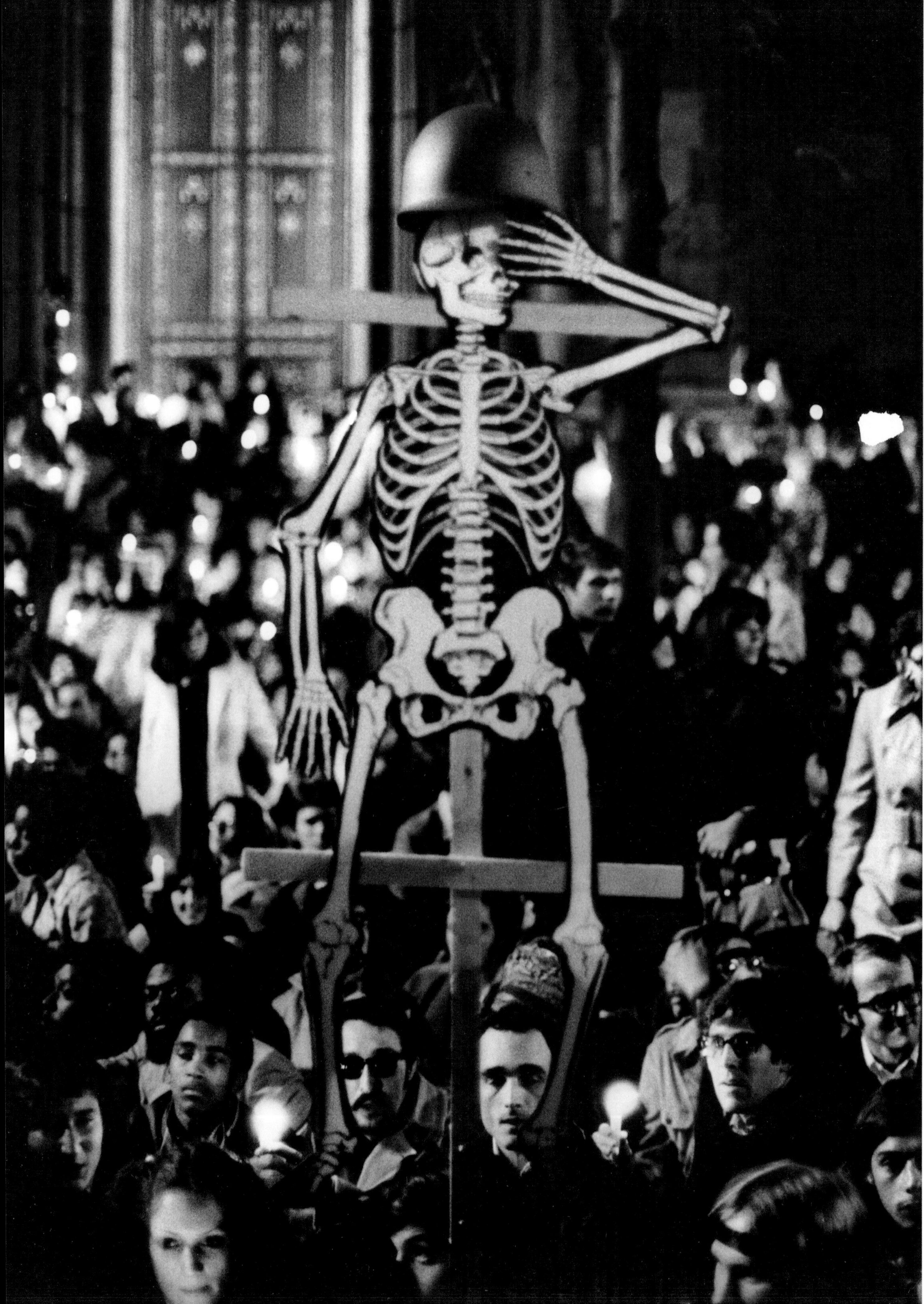

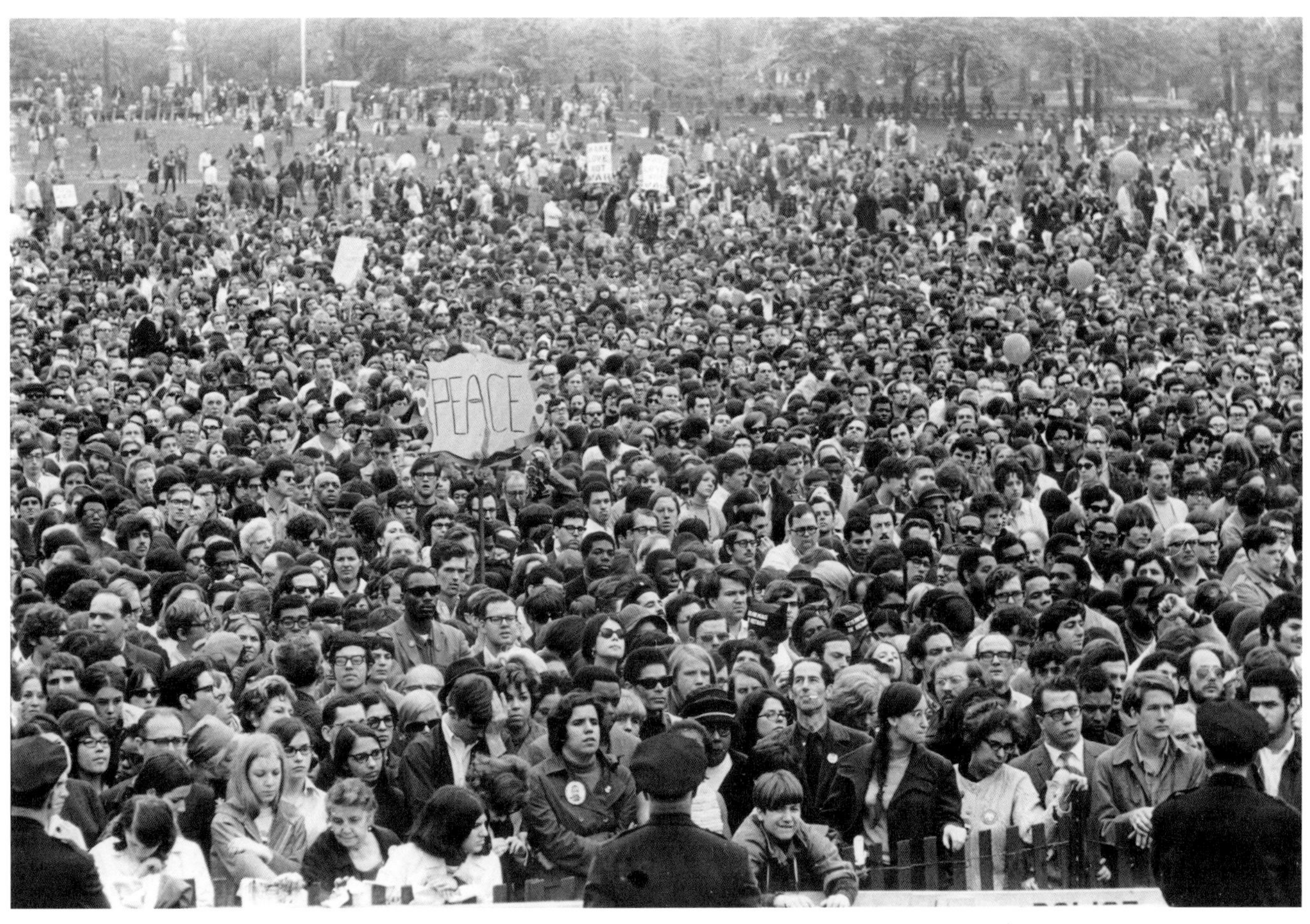

Antiwar protest on the steps of St. Patrick's Cathedral, October 15, 1969. Well over one hundred thousand demonstrators were estimated to have taken part in Moratorium Day in New York, including a march from the United Nations to Bryant Park. In the evening, after many speeches, several thousand protesters held candles and walked to the cathedral, singing antiwar songs.

Peace demonstration, Central Park, November 15, 1969. A few thousand people gathered in the park, as simultaneously up to a half-million demonstrators marched in Washington, D.C.

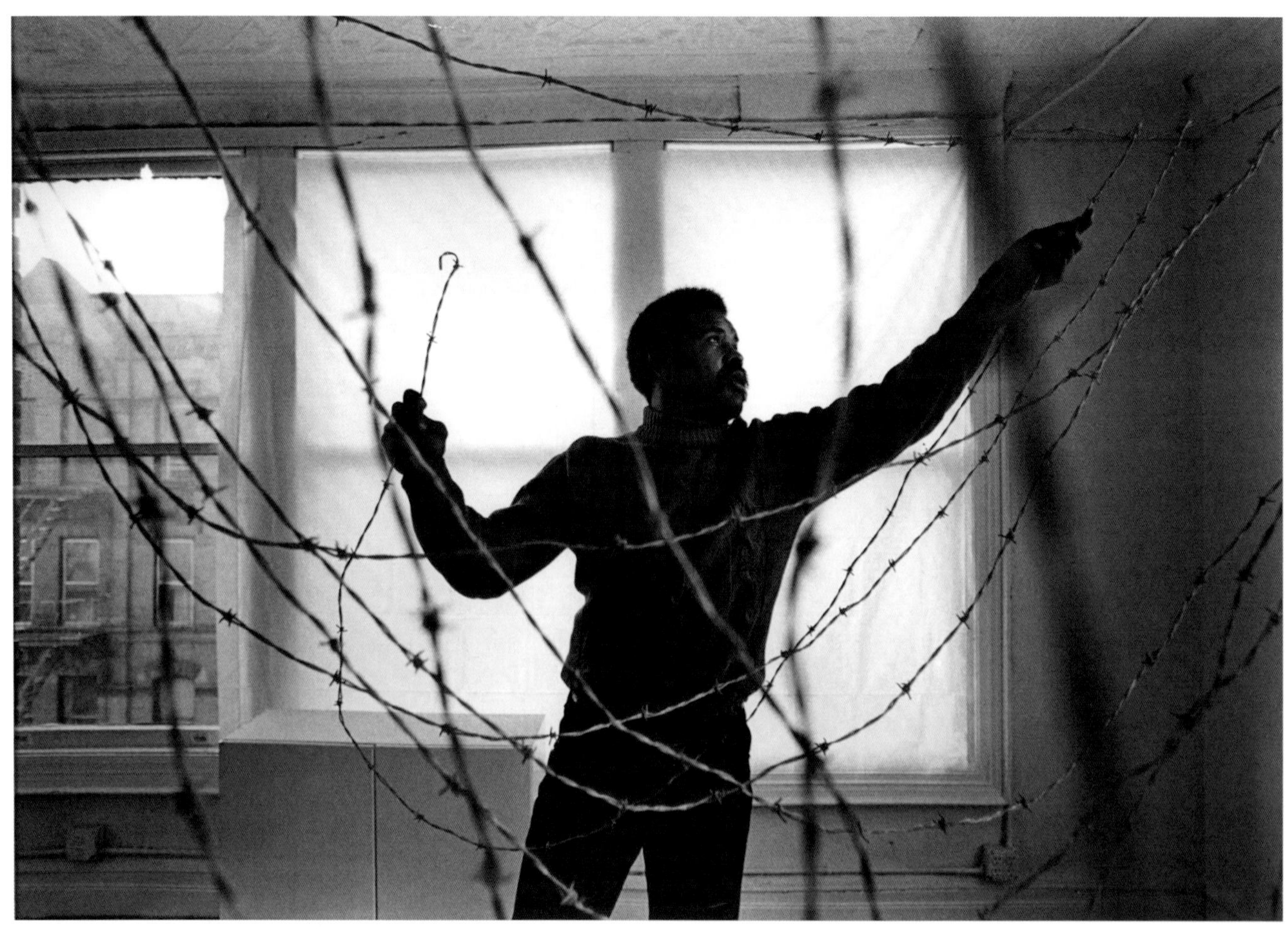

Artist Melvin Edwards constructs a sculpture with barbed wire in an empty studio space, February 20, 1970. The following month he would become the first African American sculptor to have a solo exhibition at the Whitney Museum.

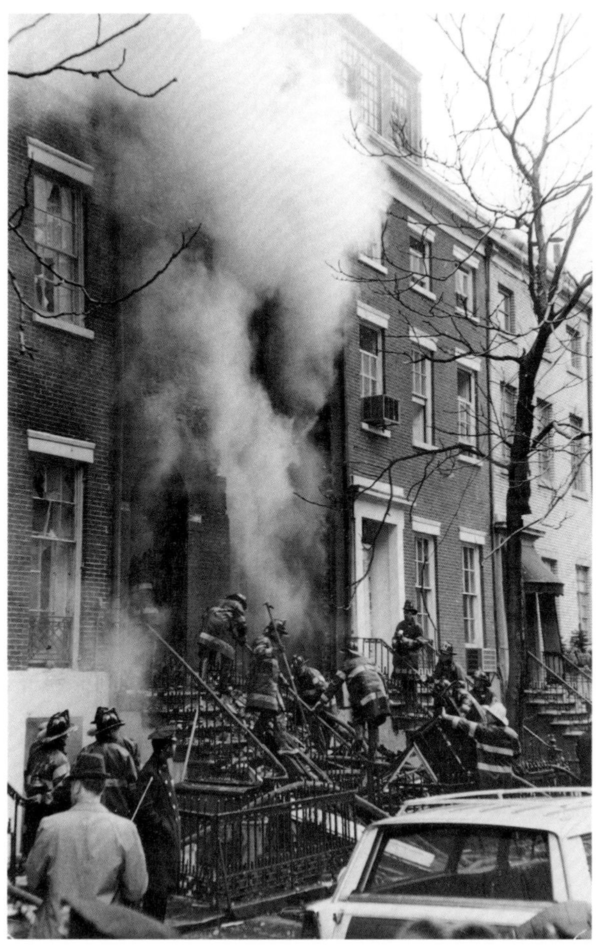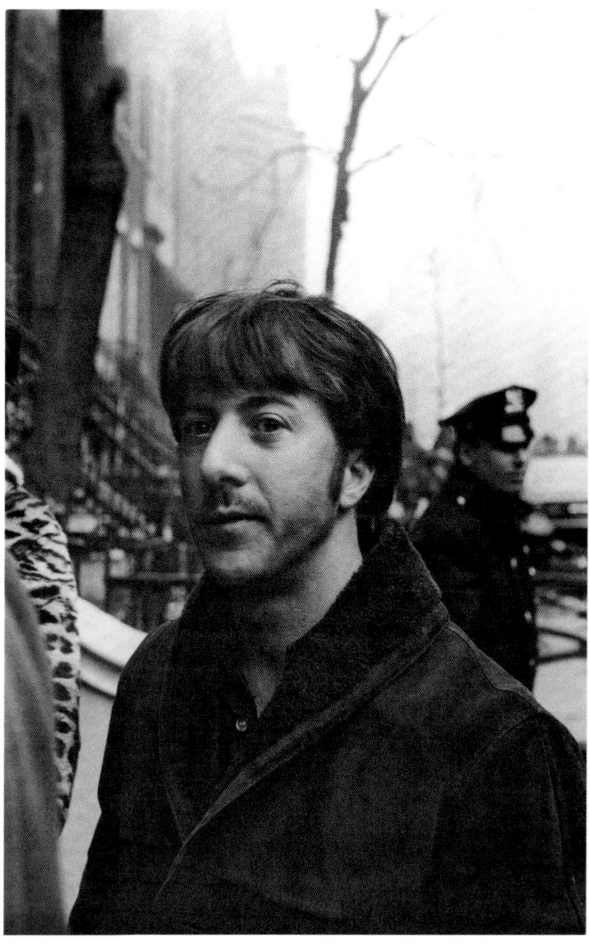

Firefighters battle smoke and flames from an explosion in the basement of 18 West Eleventh St., March 6, 1970. The Greenwich Village town house was being used by members of the radical political group the Weathermen, and the explosion, caused by the accidental detonation of a bomb, reduced the building to rubble. The bomb makers, Diana Oughton and Terry Robbins, were killed, as was Ted Gold, who was just walking into the town house. Kathy Boudin and Cathy Wilkerson were injured but received aid and then fled, remaining on the run for a decade. Actor Dustin Hoffman was living at 16 West Eleventh St., next door to the blast scene. McDarrah was alerted to the scene by a call from his son Patrick's nursery school, which was three doors down. "Please come and take your child home, there has been an incident on the block," he was told.

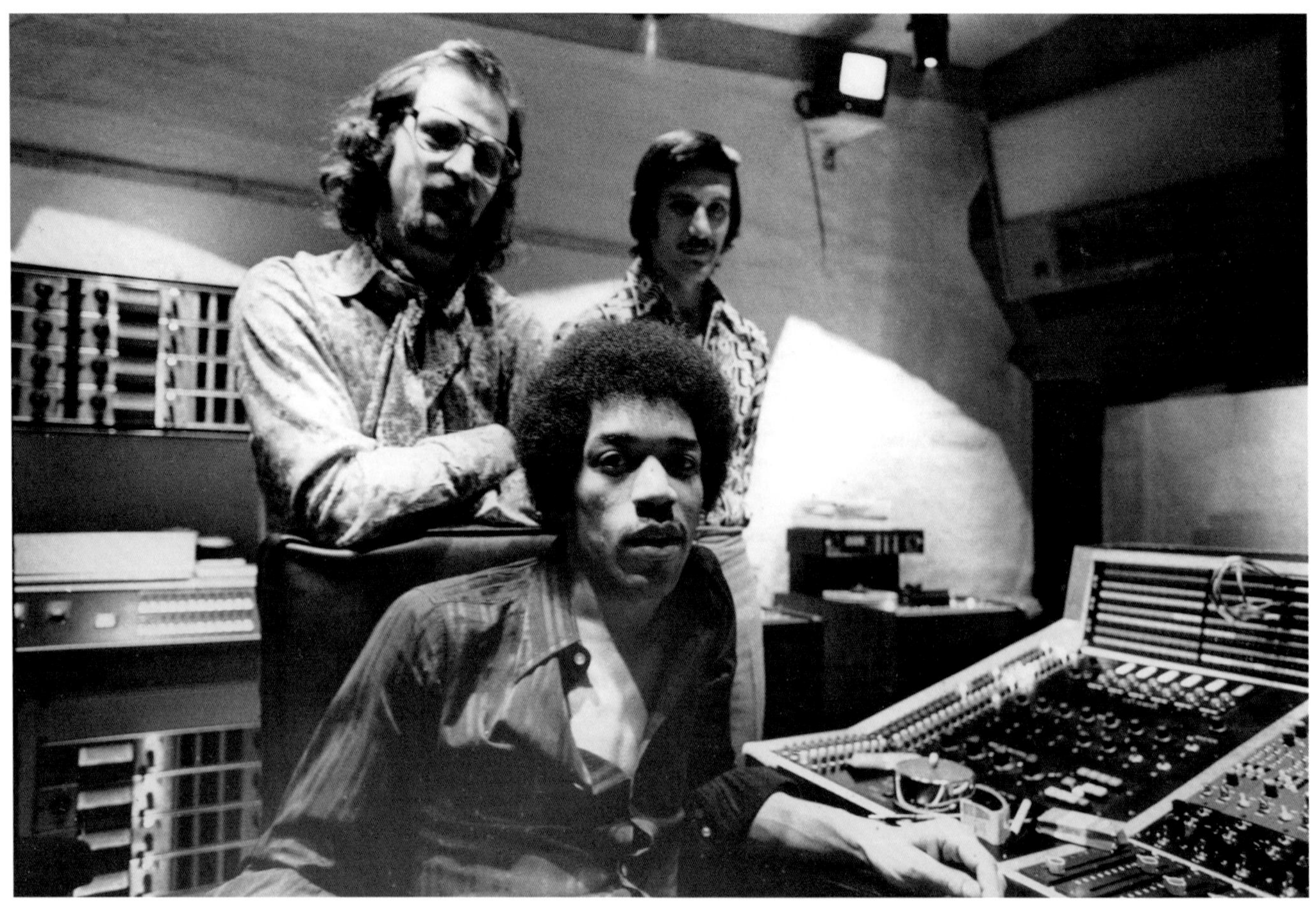

From left, producer and engineer Eddie Kramer, musician Jimi Hendrix, and studio manager Jim Marron in the control room of Hendrix's Electric Lady Studios, then still under construction at 52 West Eighth St. June 17, 1970. Hendrix died on September 18, almost exactly three months after this photo was taken, at age twenty-seven. McDarrah took the only photos of Hendrix at the soundboard, which he barely got to use before his death—though dozens of notable musicians have recorded there since then. He lived nearby at the time, in an apartment at 59 West Twelfth St.

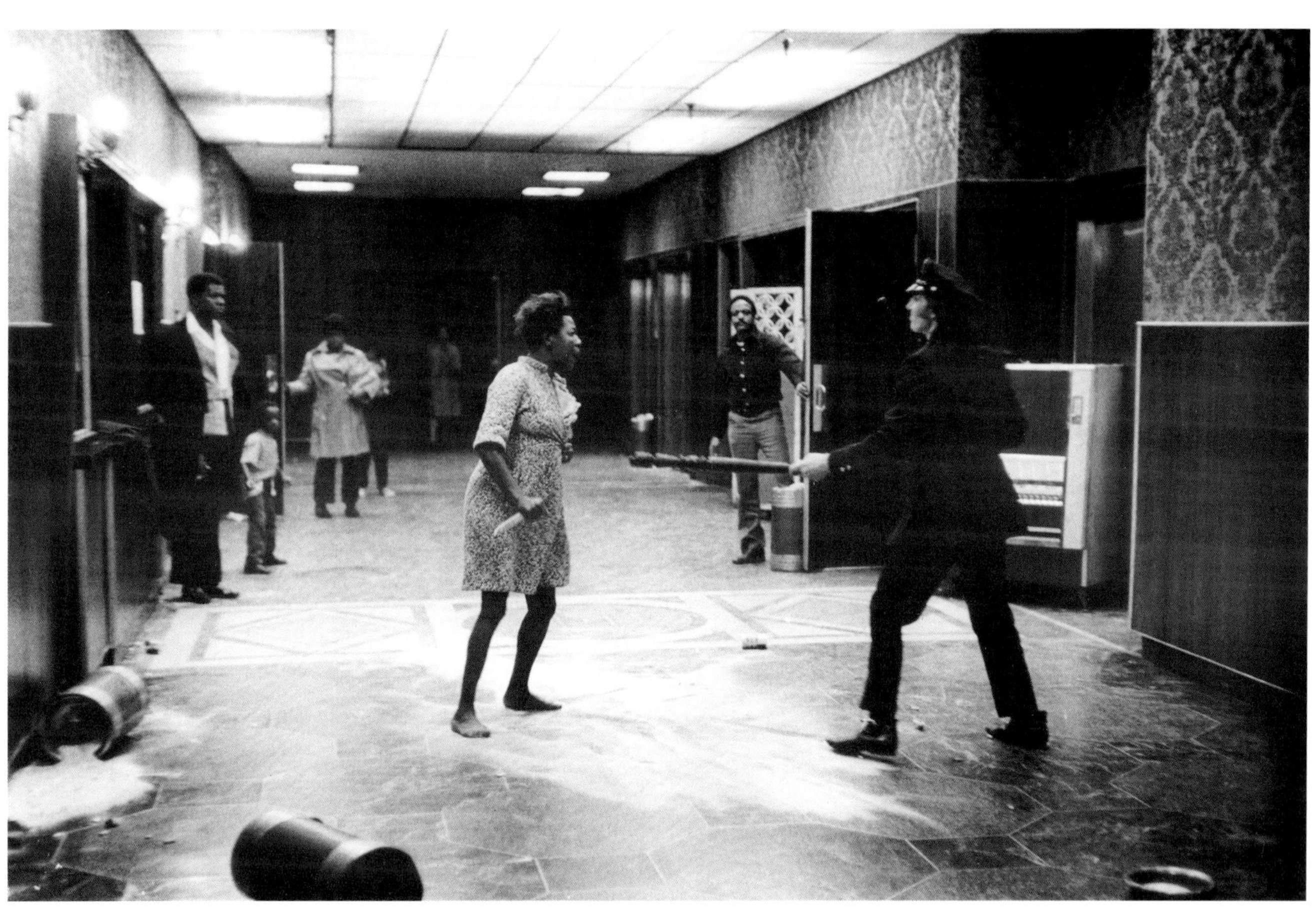

A security guard at the Broadway Central Hotel, 673 Broadway near Bond St., faces off against a knife-wielding resident, November 18, 1970. Once one of New York's grandest facilities, by the sixties it had become a troubled welfare hotel. In the early seventies, it was known for its ground-floor Mercer Arts Center, which was a beloved downtown performance space. On August 3, 1973, the building collapsed. New York University then built a twenty-two-story law school dormitory on the site.

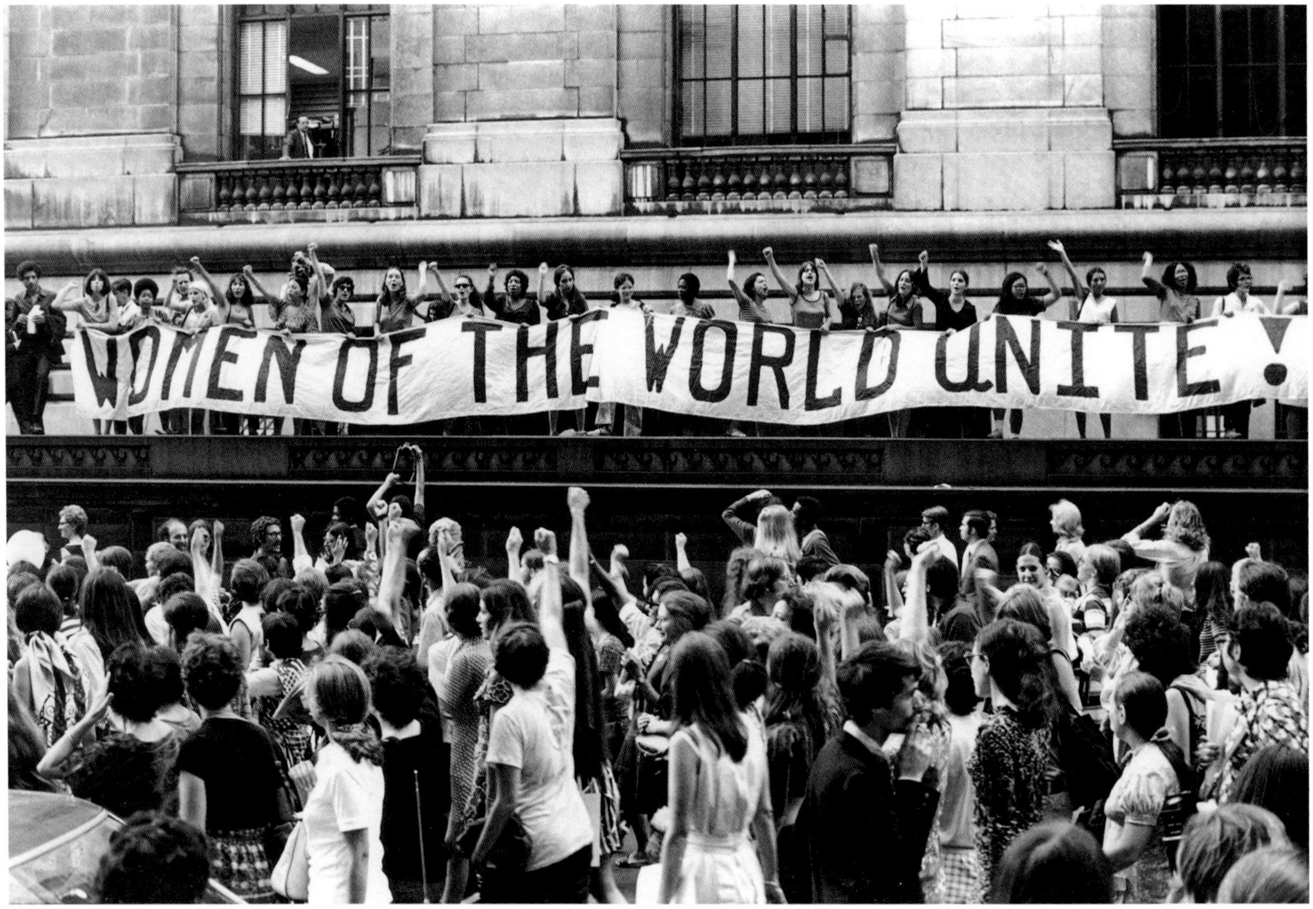

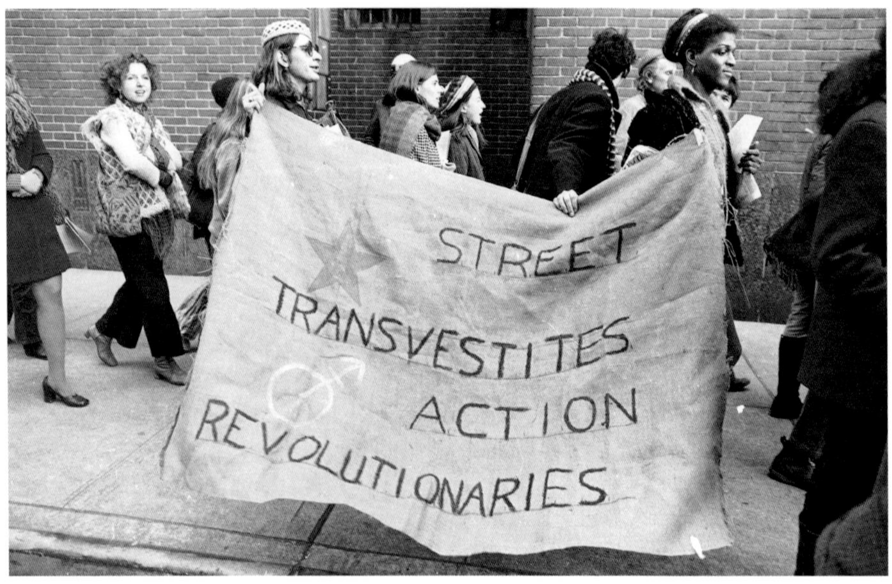

To commemorate the fiftieth anniversary of women's suffrage in the United States, an estimated twenty thousand women march along Fifth Ave., here past a banner that reads, "Women of the World Unite!," August 26, 1970. In March, the National Organization for Women (NOW) called for a nationwide women's strike and marches to mark Equality Day. There were demonstrations of various sizes in about ninety cities nationwide. NOW's main demands were the repeal of antiabortion laws, the establishment of child-care centers, and equal opportunity in jobs and education.

Activists Sylvia Rivera (with beret and sunglasses) and Marsha P. Johnson (with hairband) carry a sign that reads, "Street Transvestites Action Revolutionaries," December 20, 1970. They cofounded that group, called STAR, to help homeless trans women of color and young drag queens. In 1992, Johnson's body was found in the Hudson River, with a wound to her head. Some friends insisted it was murder; police promptly dismissed it as suicide.

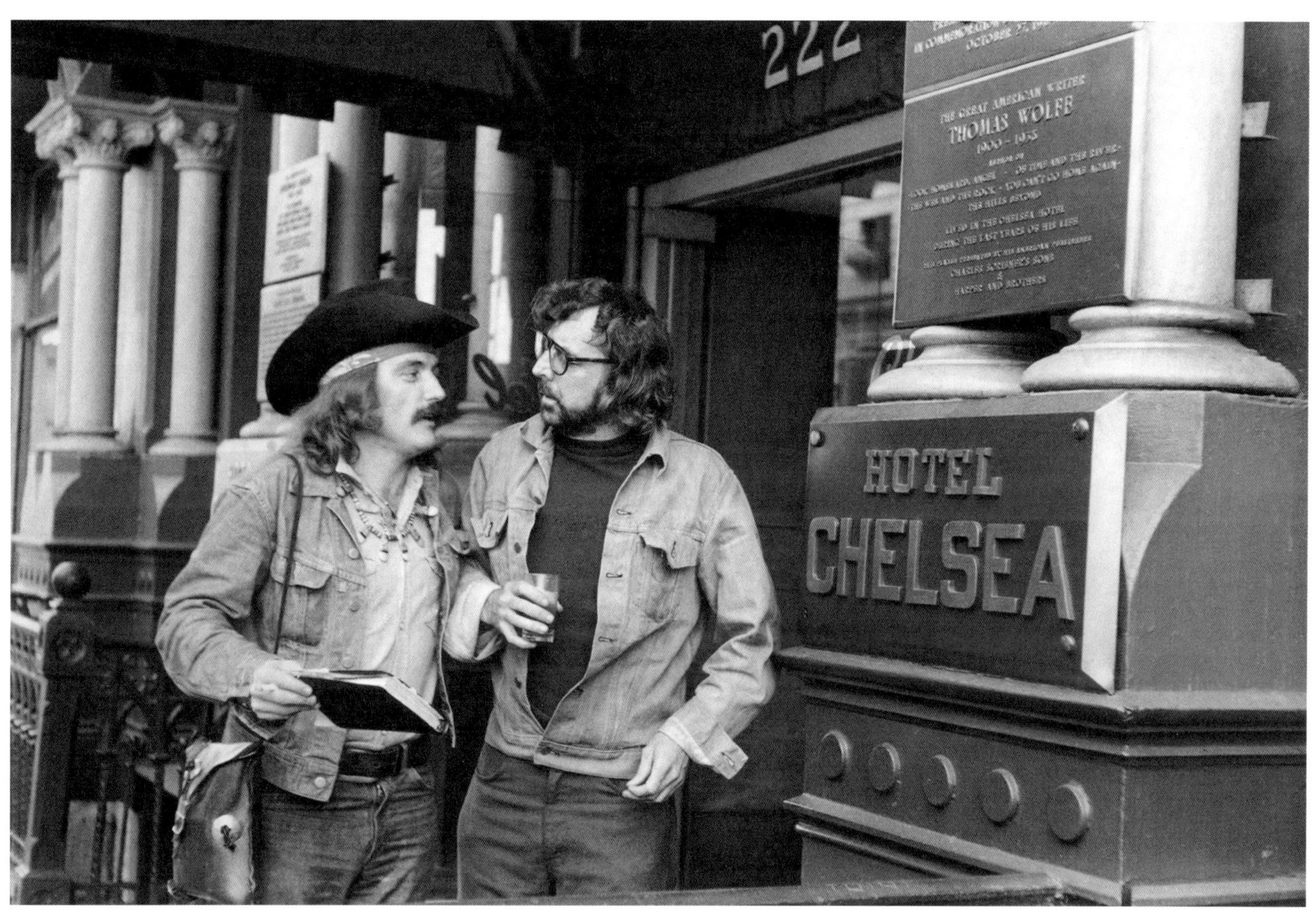

Actor Dennis Hopper (left) and author Terry Southern in front of the Chelsea Hotel, 222 West Twenty-Third St., September 30, 1971. Hopper and Southern, along with Peter Fonda, shared writing credit on the sixties classic film *Easy Rider* (1969), which Hopper also directed and costarred in. They are just two of the dozens of famous (and sometimes infamous, or just eccentric) writers, artists, musicians, actors, directors, fashion designers, and others who lived in the hotel since it opened in 1884, and the Chelsea has been the subject of many books, songs, and films.

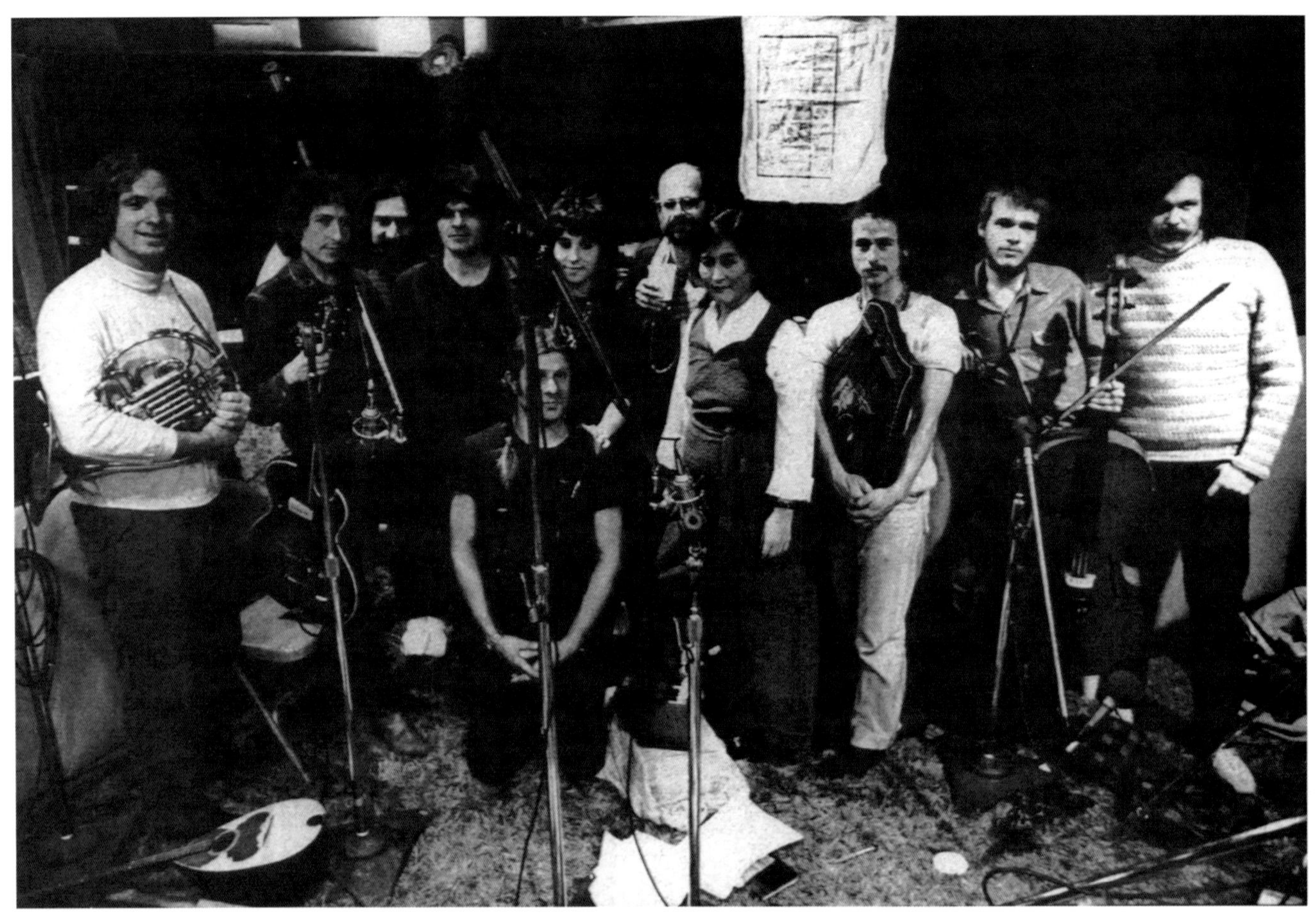

Posing at a recording session at the Record Plant, 321 West Forty-Fourth St., from left, musicians and poets David Amram, Bob Dylan, Happy Traum, Gregory Corso, Peter Orlovsky (kneeling in front), Denise Mercedes, Allen Ginsberg, Sadi Kazi, Jon Sholle, Arthur Russell, and Ed Sanders, November 13, 1971. The session was hastily thrown together by Ginsberg, who called McDarrah to document it. The album that emerged from the session, *Holy Soul Jelly Roll*, was not released until 1994. Throughout, Ginsberg takes lead vocals with Dylan on guitar, harmonica, and backing vocals.

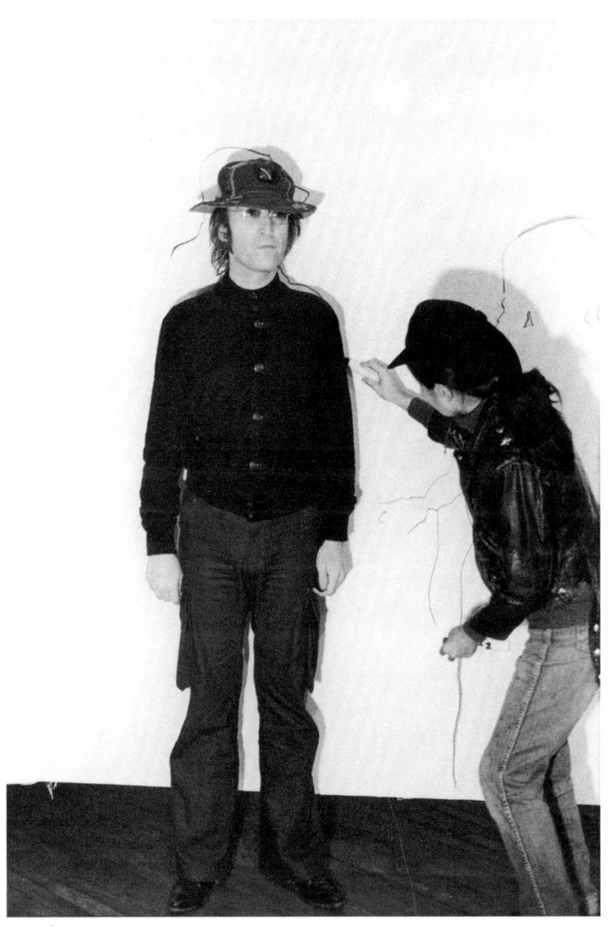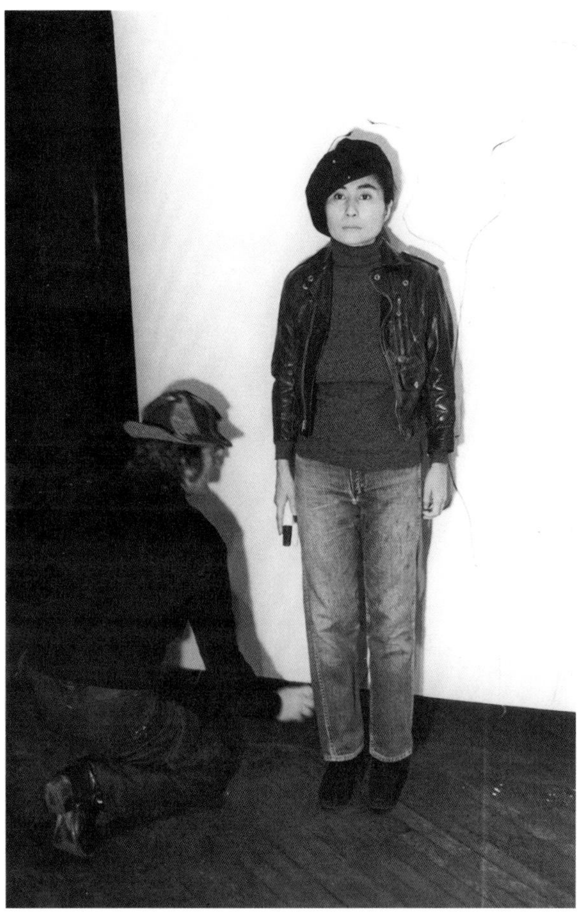

Yoko Ono traces John Lennon, and vice versa, during the Eighth Avant Garde Festival in the 69th Regiment Armory on Lexington Ave. off East Twenty-Fifth St., November 19, 1971. Ono had been part of the New York art scene for many years before she met and married the Beatle, and the pair were often low-key participants or audience members at downtown performances. They submitted eight works to this festival, including *Wind Peace*, in which musicians played whatever pages of notes randomly appeared thanks to a battery of fans.

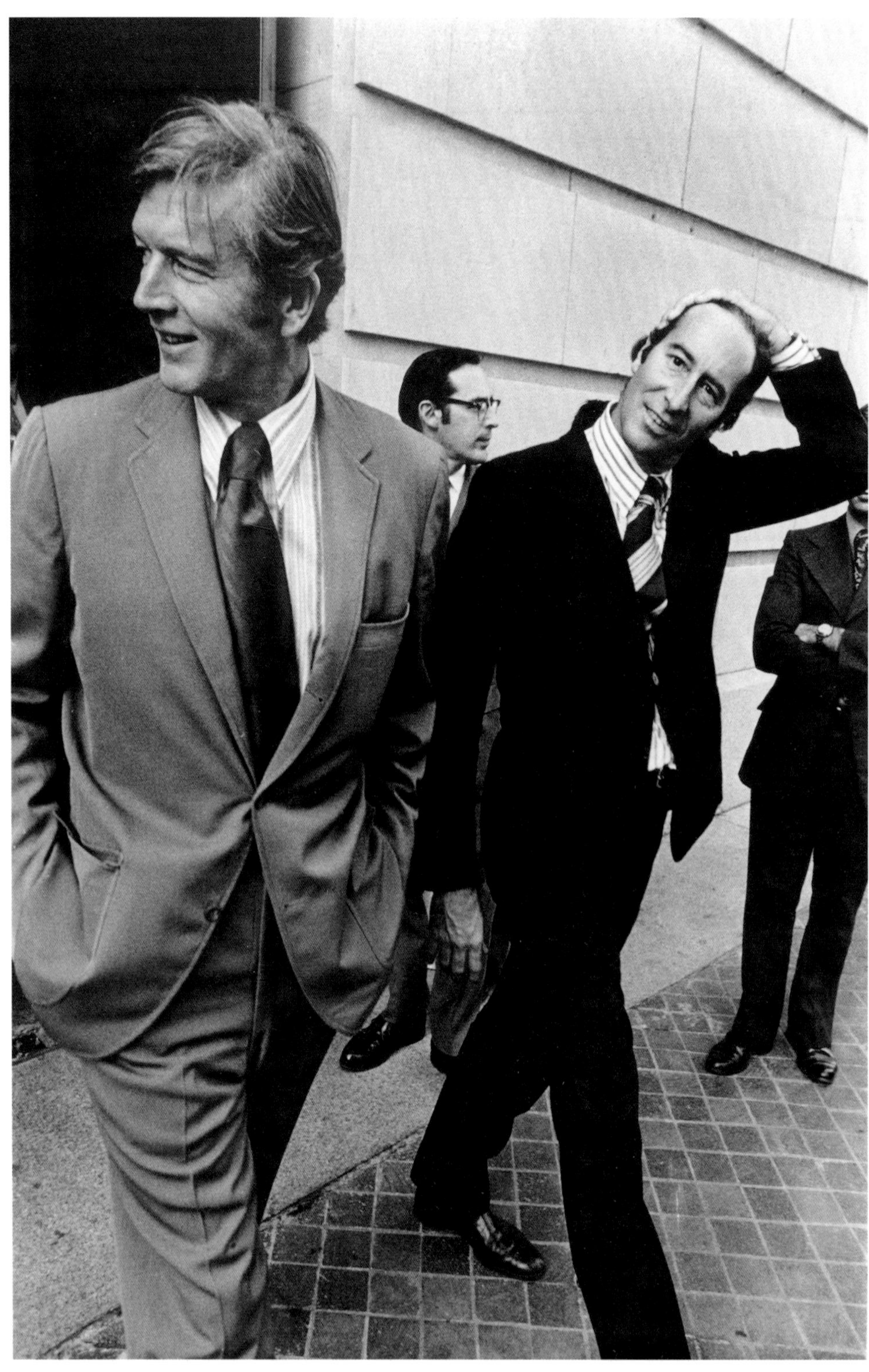

Mayor John V. Lindsay (left) and Metropolitan Museum of Art director Thomas Hoving (smoothing back his hair) leave the inaugural exhibition of the museum's Costume Institute, October 21, 1971. Hoving had been director of the Met since 1967, after a short stint as Lindsay's parks commissioner. During his ten years in the post, he expanded both the museum's physical space and its collections. Lindsay, a liberal Republican, was elected mayor in 1965 and again in 1969. In 1971, he became a Democrat and launched a short-lived attempt to win the party's presidential nomination in 1972.

Abandoned buildings across a vacant lot full of debris in the Brownsville section of Brooklyn, December 18, 1971. When this photograph was taken, Brownsville was a national symbol of urban decline: a neighborhood where 29 percent of the residents were impoverished that was gradually being burned down by arsonists. Conditions slowly began to improve after the seventies.

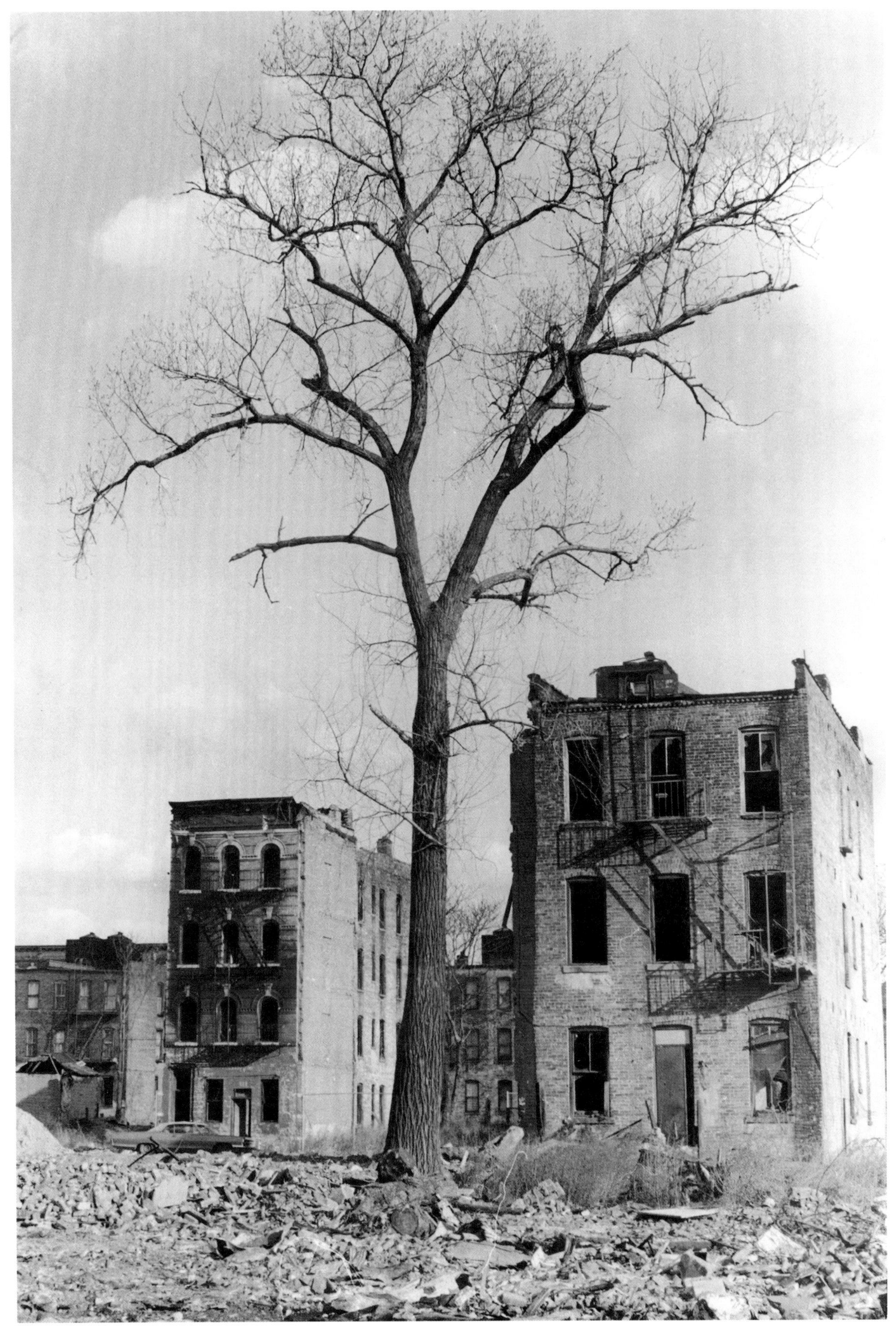

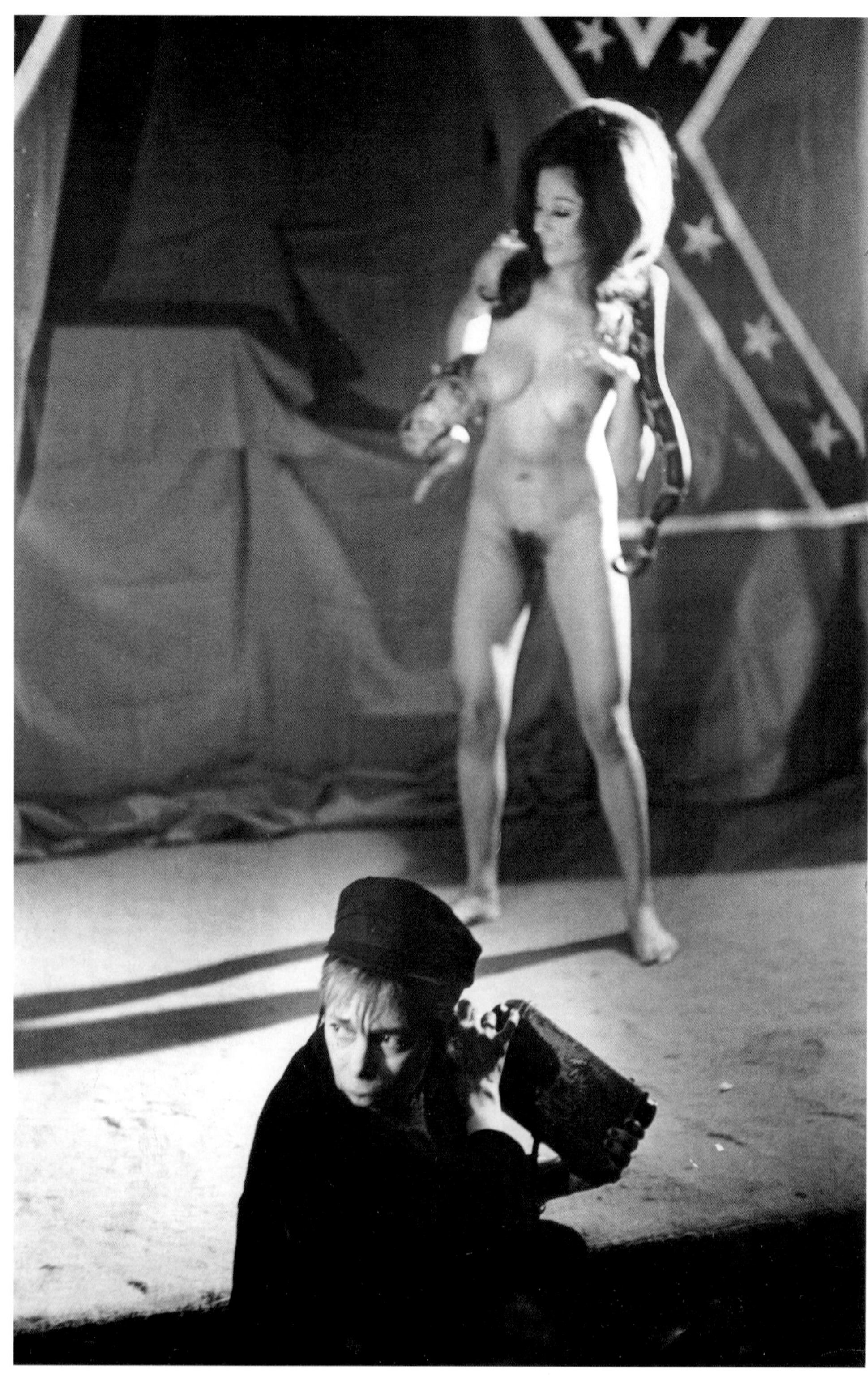

Shirley Clarke, February 6, 1972. The filmmaker formed the Teepee Video Space Troupe in her Chelsea Hotel home and experimented with this medium in the seventies and into the eighties. Clarke made numerous short films starting in the early fifties but was best known for her feature *The Connection* (1961), from Jack Gelber's play about jazz musicians waiting for their heroin dealer to show up.

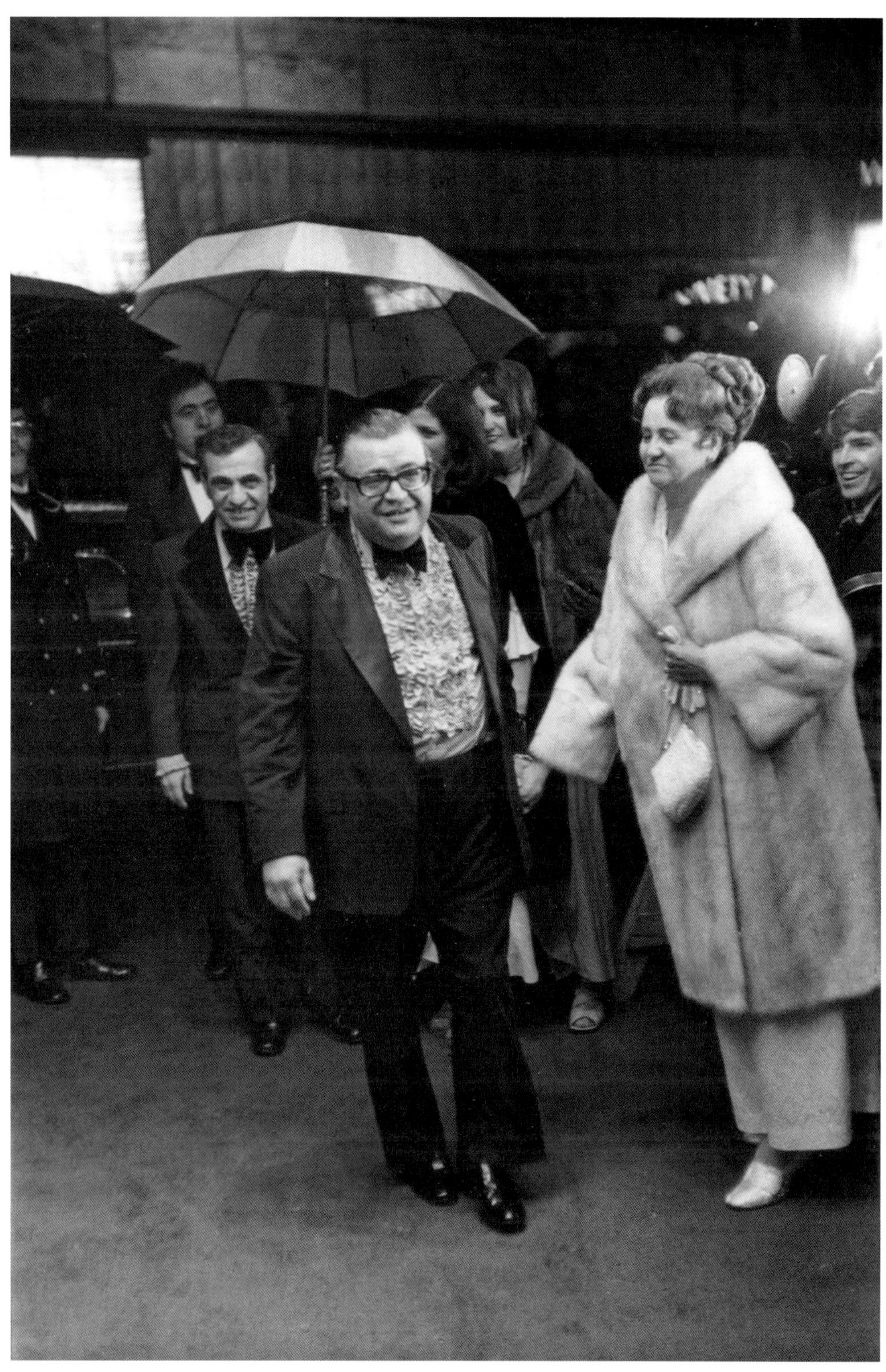

Writer Mario Puzo at the premiere of *The Godfather*, February 14, 1972. A struggling writer well into his forties, Puzo decided to write about the Mafia and came up with a number-one bestseller that topped the charts for months, and then won an Academy Award for the best adapted screenplay when Francis Ford Coppola turned his novel into a film—and then a trilogy.

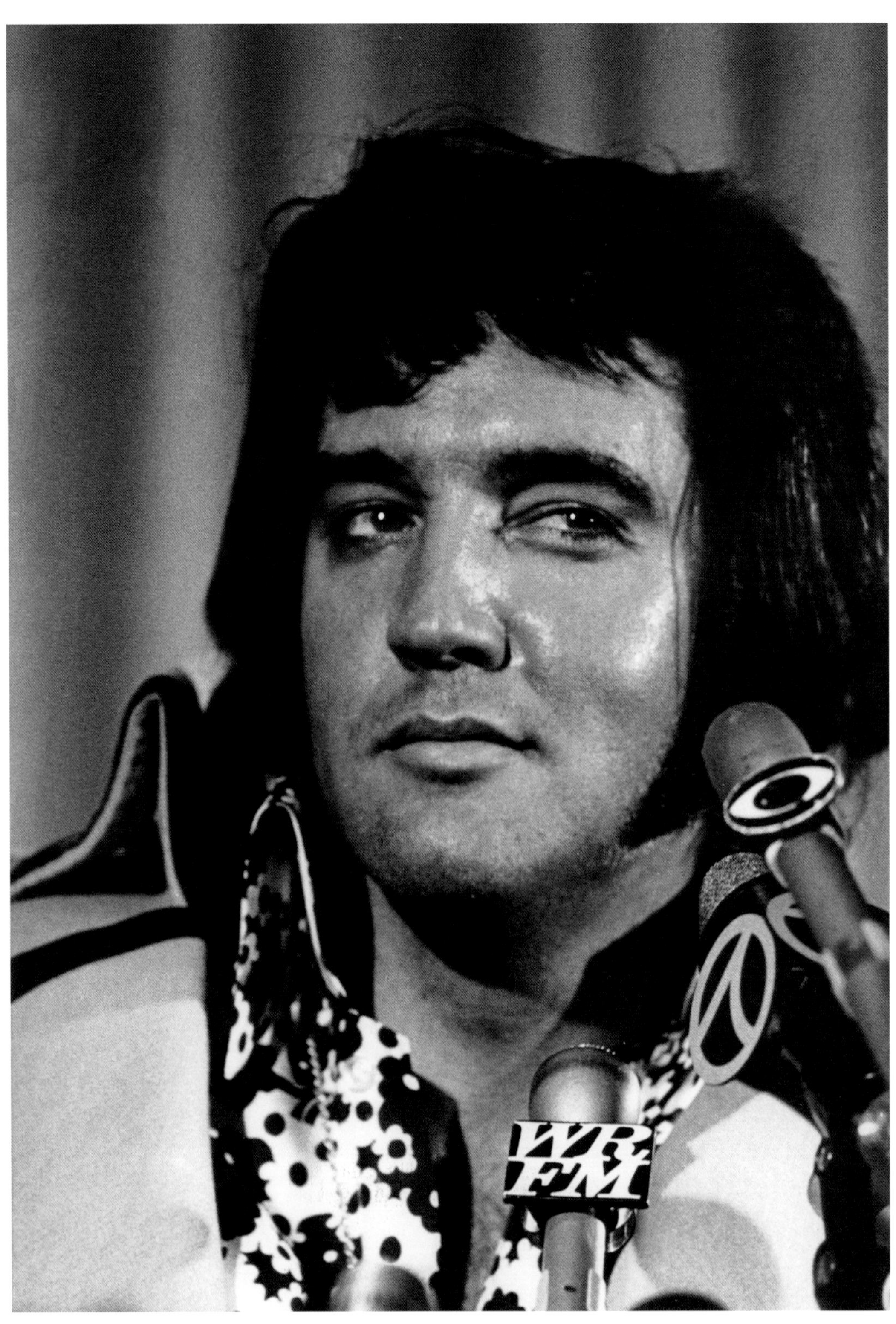

Elvis Presley at a press conference at the New York Hilton to discuss his forthcoming performance at Madison Square Garden, June 9, 1972. His four consecutive sold-out shows there—a first for that venue—on June 9–12 were his first performances before a live audience in New York since appearances on TV shows in 1957. The four concerts, before a total of eighty thousand fans, received rave reviews, and a live album was released only nine days after they ended.

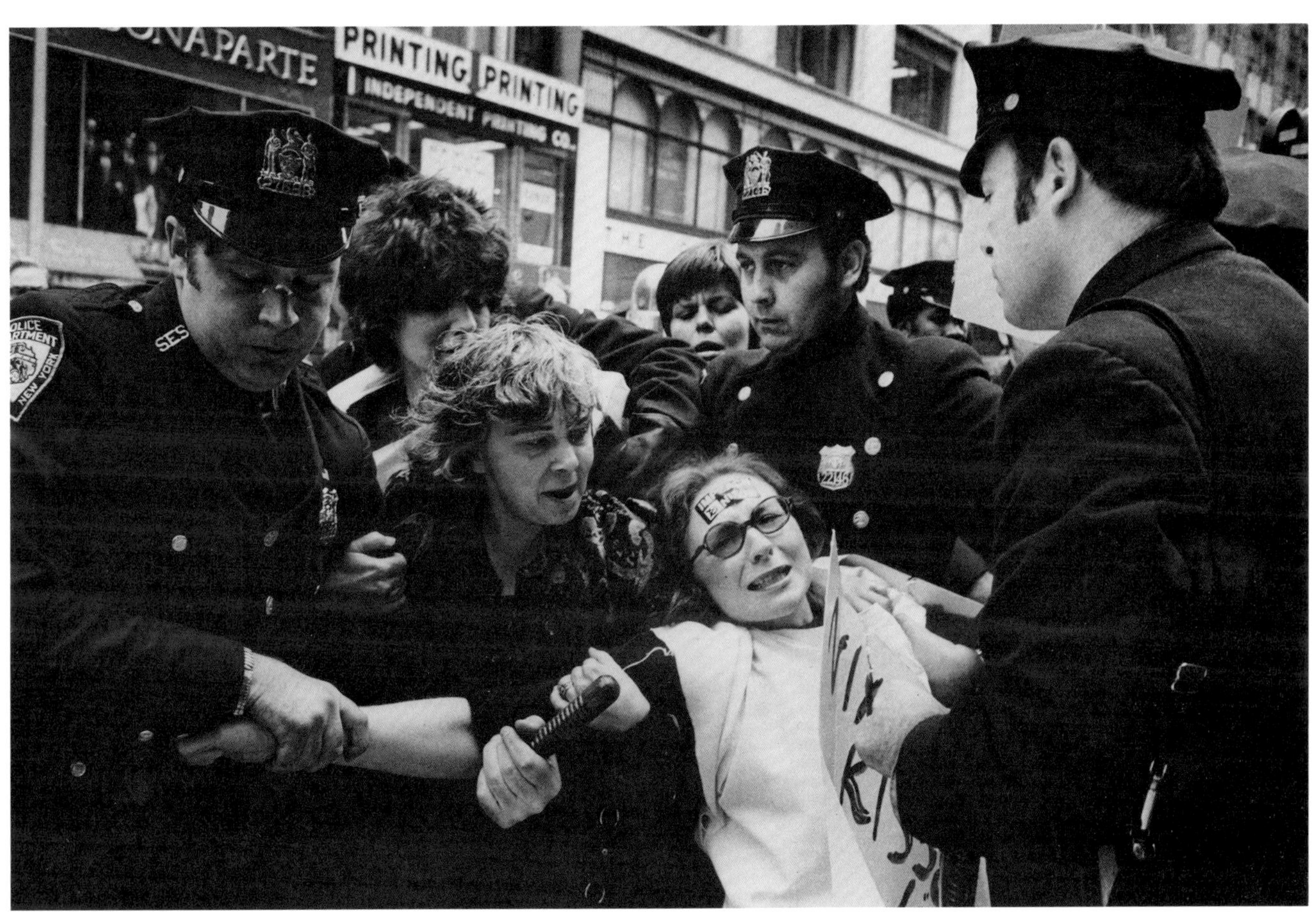

Activist and writer Ti-Grace Atkinson being arrested—as were several others—at the Women Against Richard Nixon (WARN) "Kiss-Off Nixon" demonstration in front of the "Nixon Now" reelection headquarters on Madison Ave. and Fifty-Third St., October 23, 1972. She left her leadership role in the National Organization for Women in 1968 to found a more radical group, the October 17th Movement, later called The Feminists.

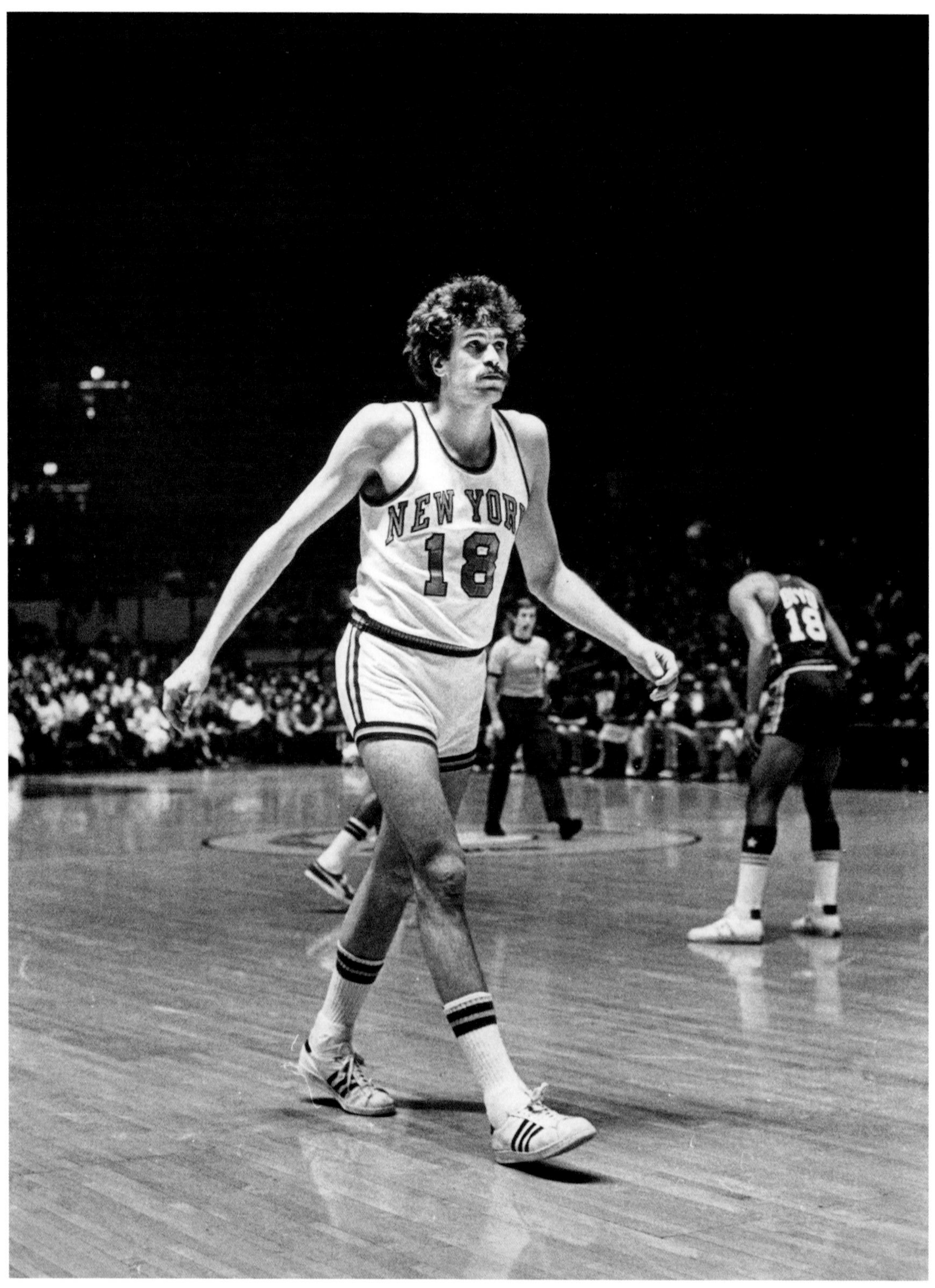

New York Knicks forward Phil Jackson on the hardwood at Madison Square Garden, February 19, 1973. He saw limited playing time in that NBA title season and would retire as a player in 1980. He later was a championship coach with Chicago and Los Angeles, influenced by Eastern philosophy as channeled through Robert Pirsig's bestseller *Zen and the Art of Motorcycle Maintenance* (1974), and then a less successful front-office executive with the Knicks.

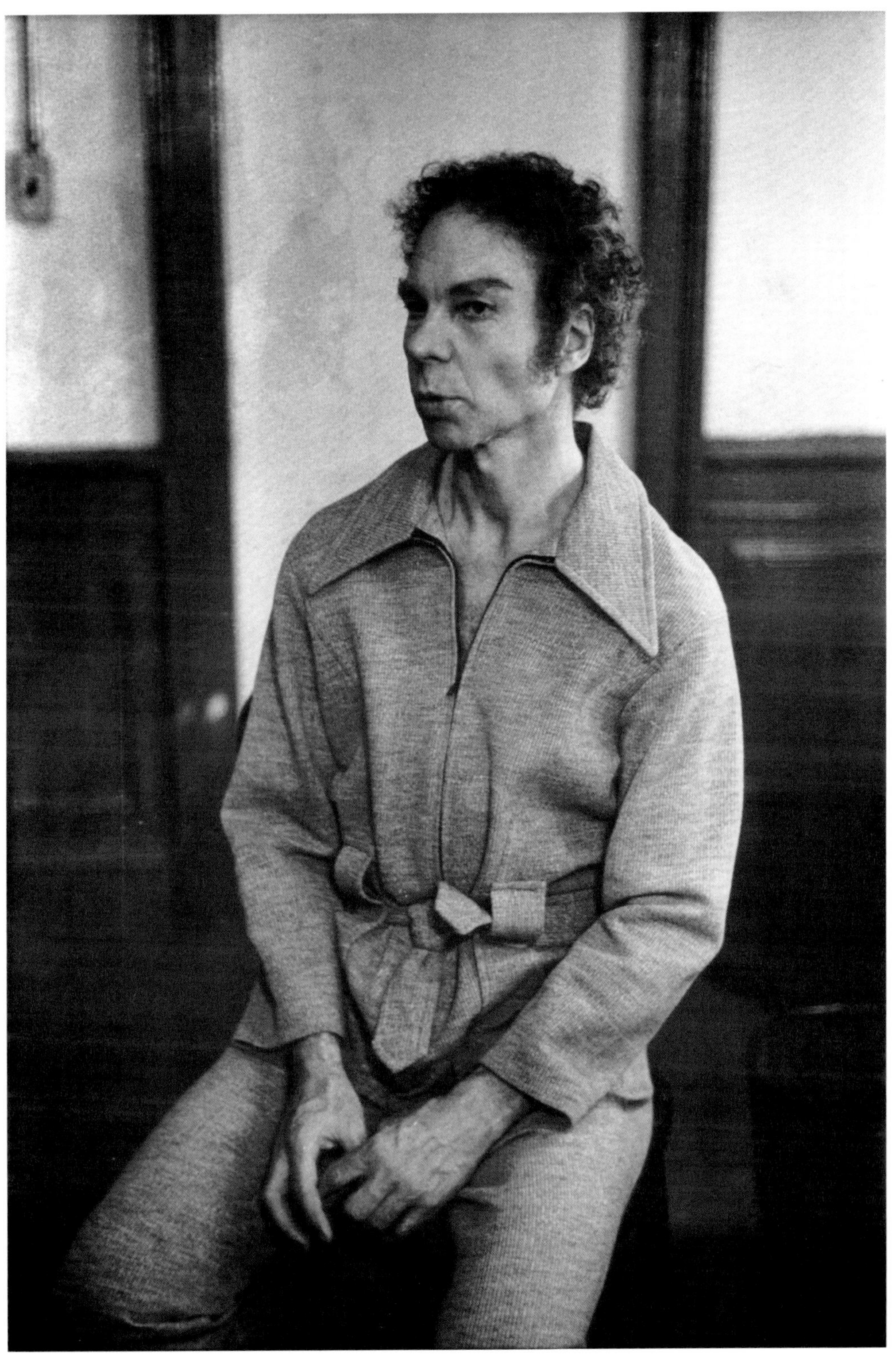

Merce Cunningham, March 22, 1973. A leading figure of modern dance for more than a half century, Cunningham also influenced avant-garde art through his frequent collaborations with musicians and artists, including John Cage and Robert Rauschenberg. His company lasted from 1953 to 2012.

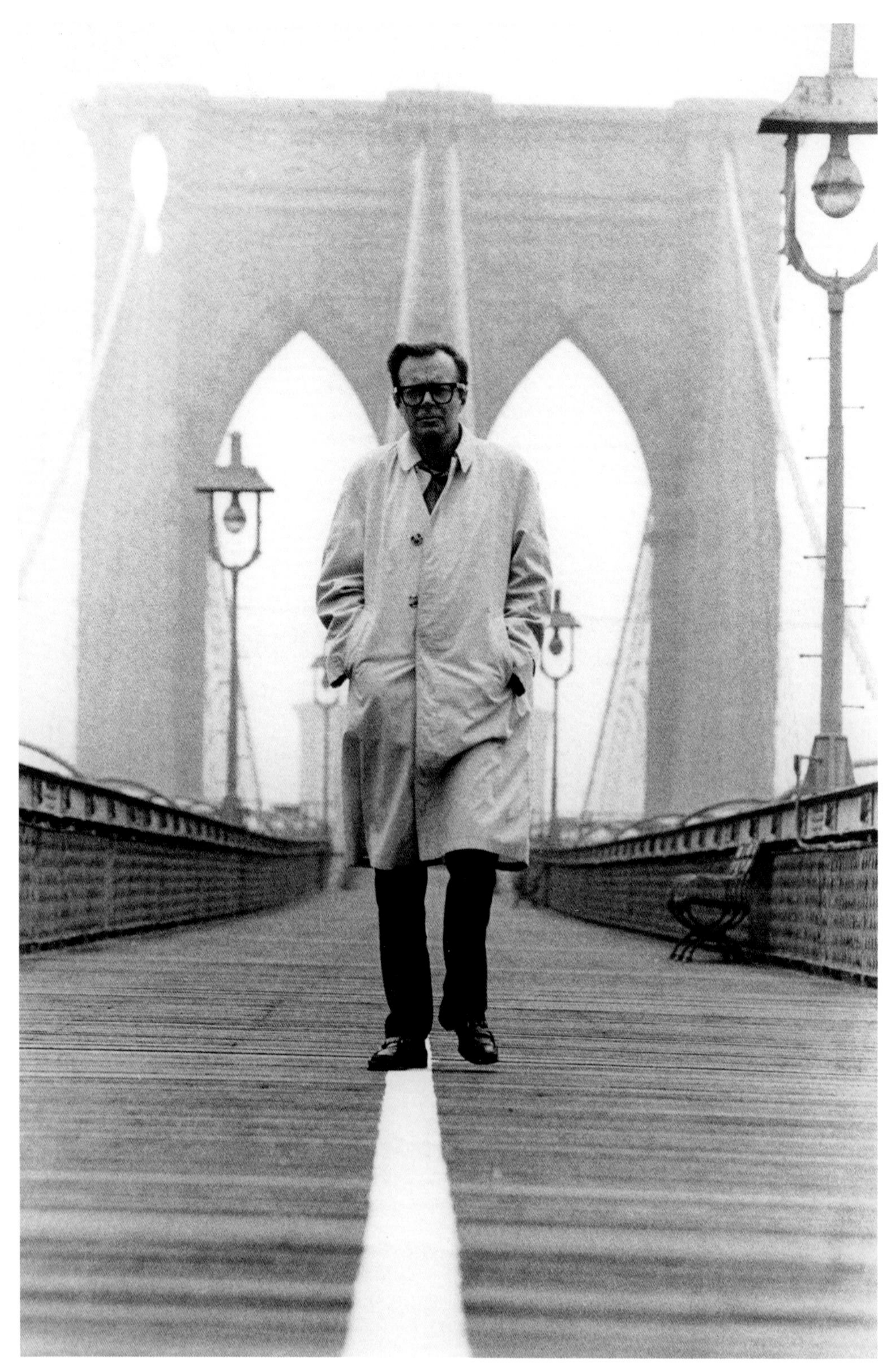

Hubert Selby Jr., author of the novel *Last Exit to Brooklyn*, on the Brooklyn Bridge, May 11, 1973. A cult classic blending drugs, sexuality, and violence, it was later made into a film, as was Selby's 1978 novel, *Requiem for a Dream*, about an informal extended family of drug abusers spiraling downward.

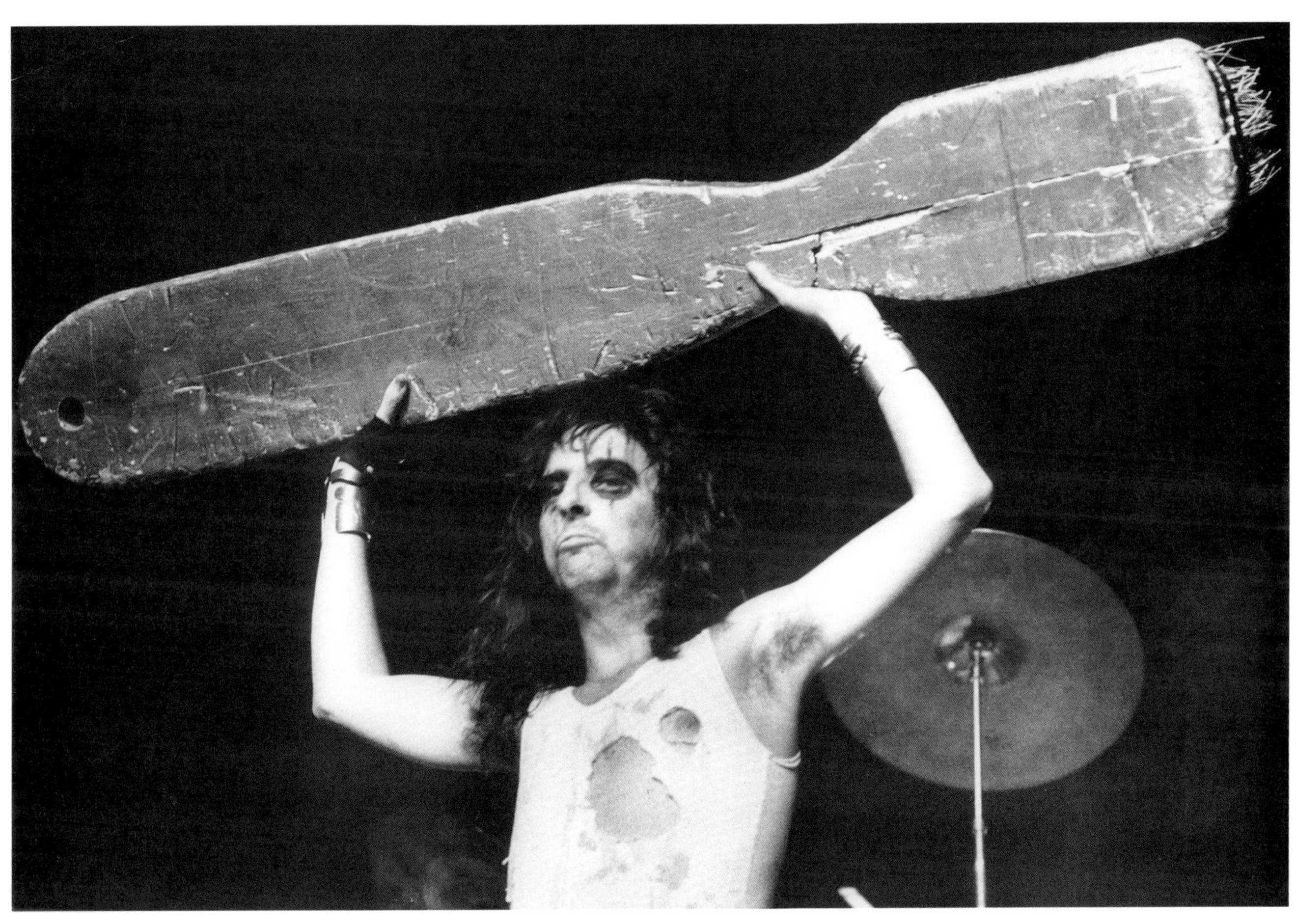

Alice Cooper at Madison Square Garden, June 3, 1973. Called "the Godfather of Shock Rock,"
Cooper has thrived for decades on stage shows that are not unlike some of the more extreme
performance art pieces of the sixties.

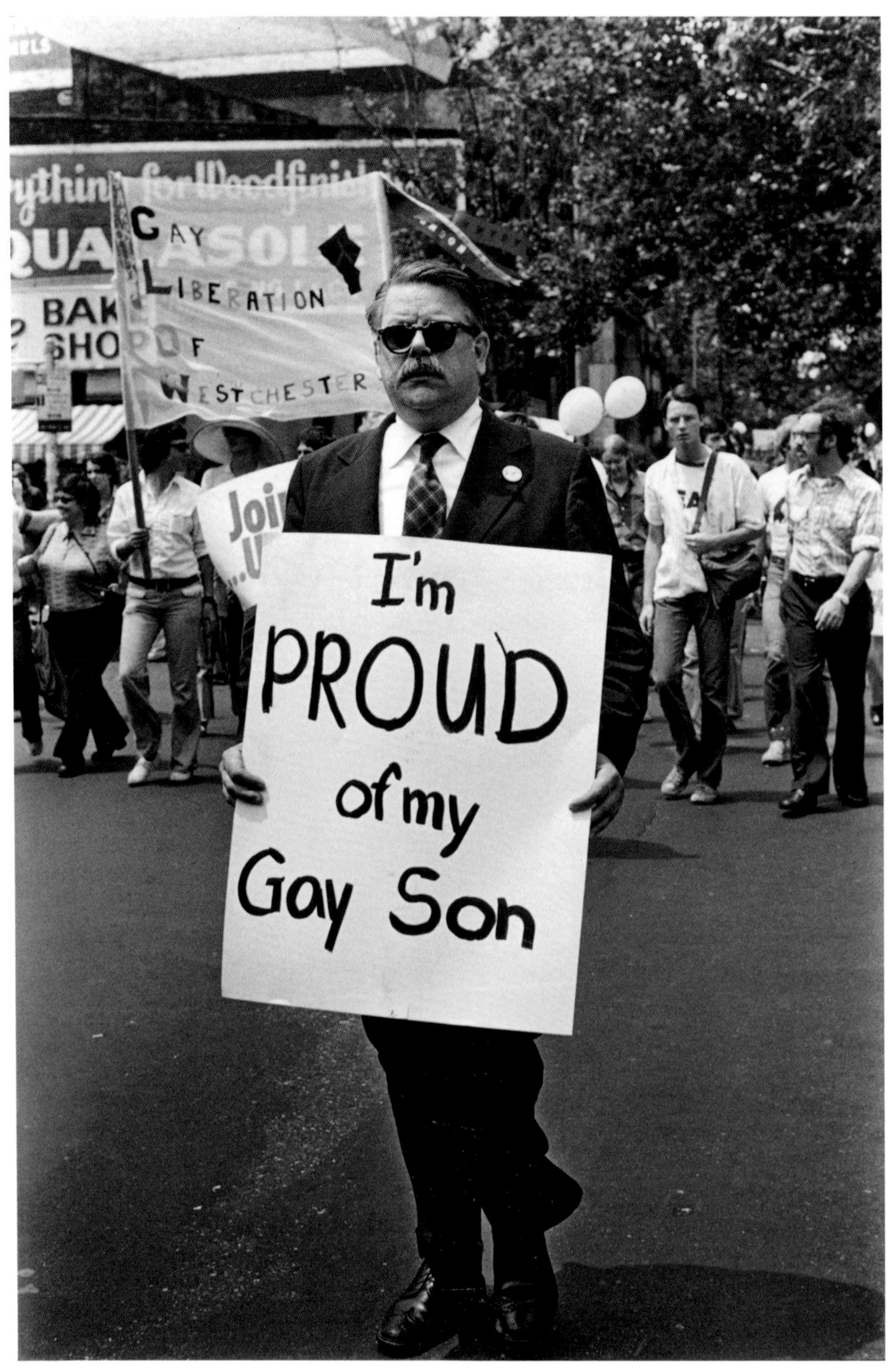

Dick Ashworth, a cofounder of Parents of Gays (now PFLAG, which originally stood for Parents and Friends of Lesbians and Gays), at the Gay Pride March, Sixth Ave. at Ninth St., June 30, 1974. He and his wife, Amy, were regulars on talk shows and helped create the Hetrick-Martin Institute, which provides support to LGBTQ youth in the New York metropolitan area. Two of their three sons were gay, and died of AIDS.

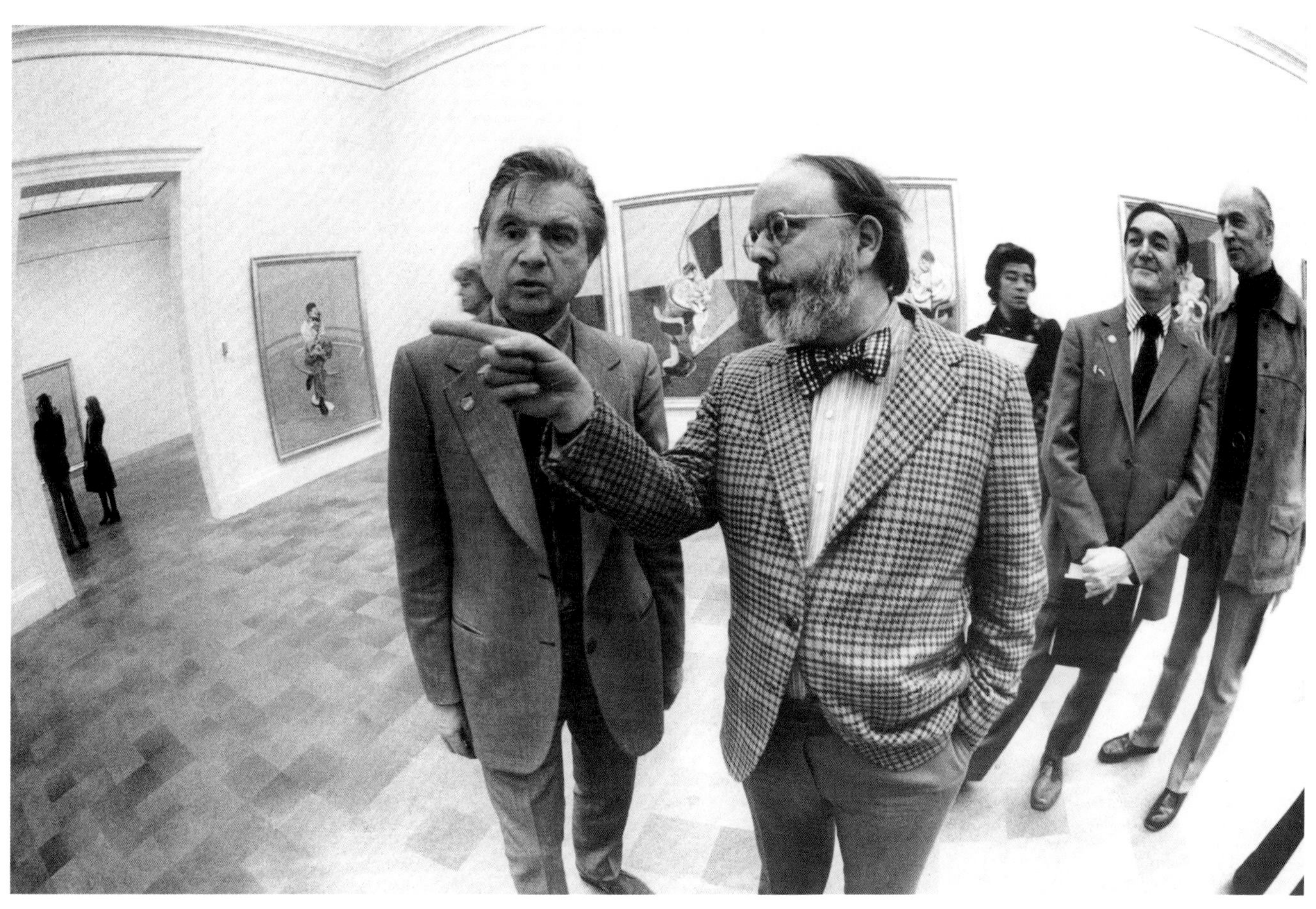

Curator and art critic and historian Henry Geldzahler makes a point with Irish painter Francis Bacon at the opening of a retrospective of his work at the Metropolitan Museum of Art, March 19, 1975. A force in New York's art world, Geldzahler was the Met's first curator for twentieth-century art. From 1977 to 1982, he served as city commissioner of cultural affairs.

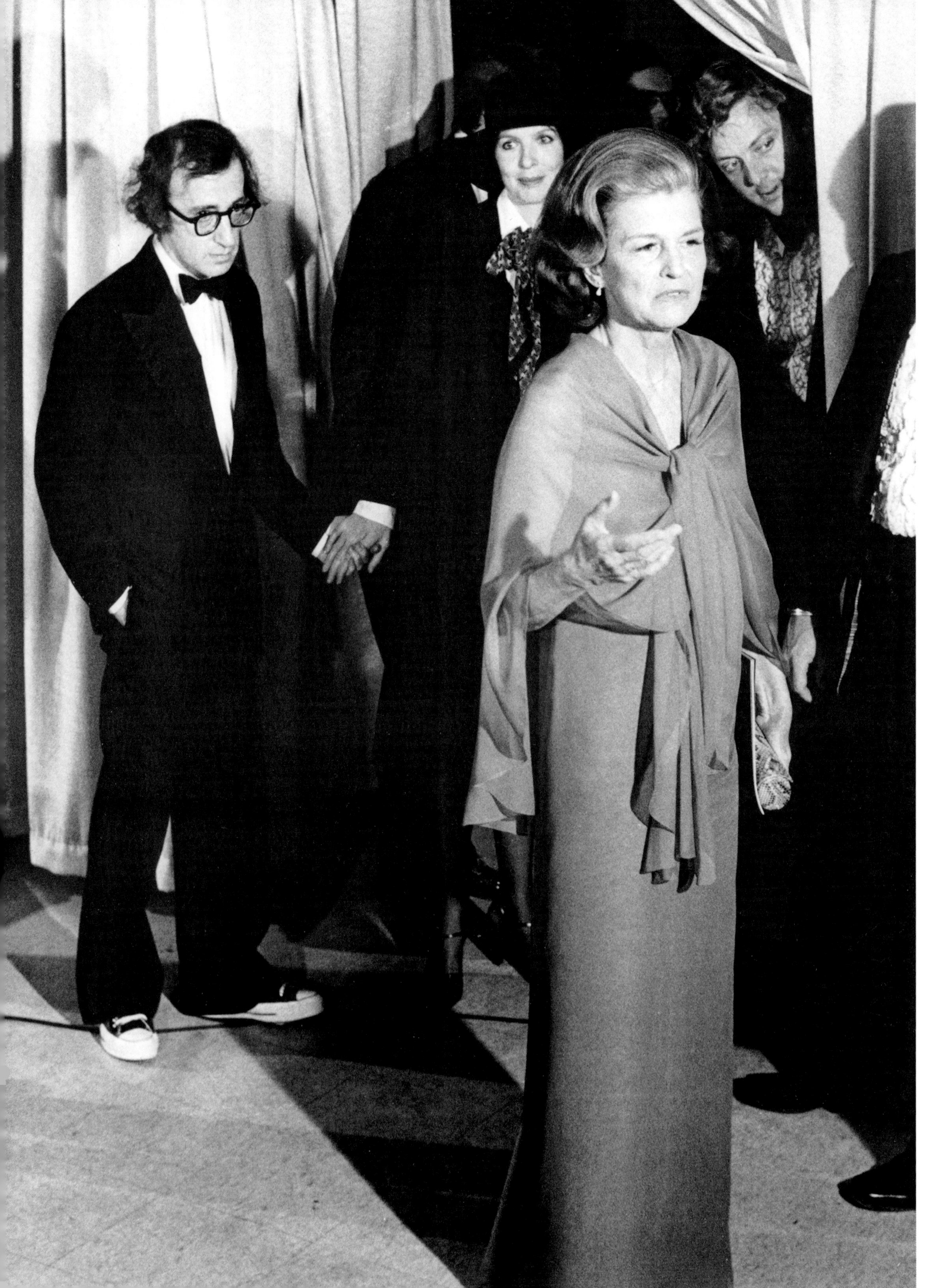

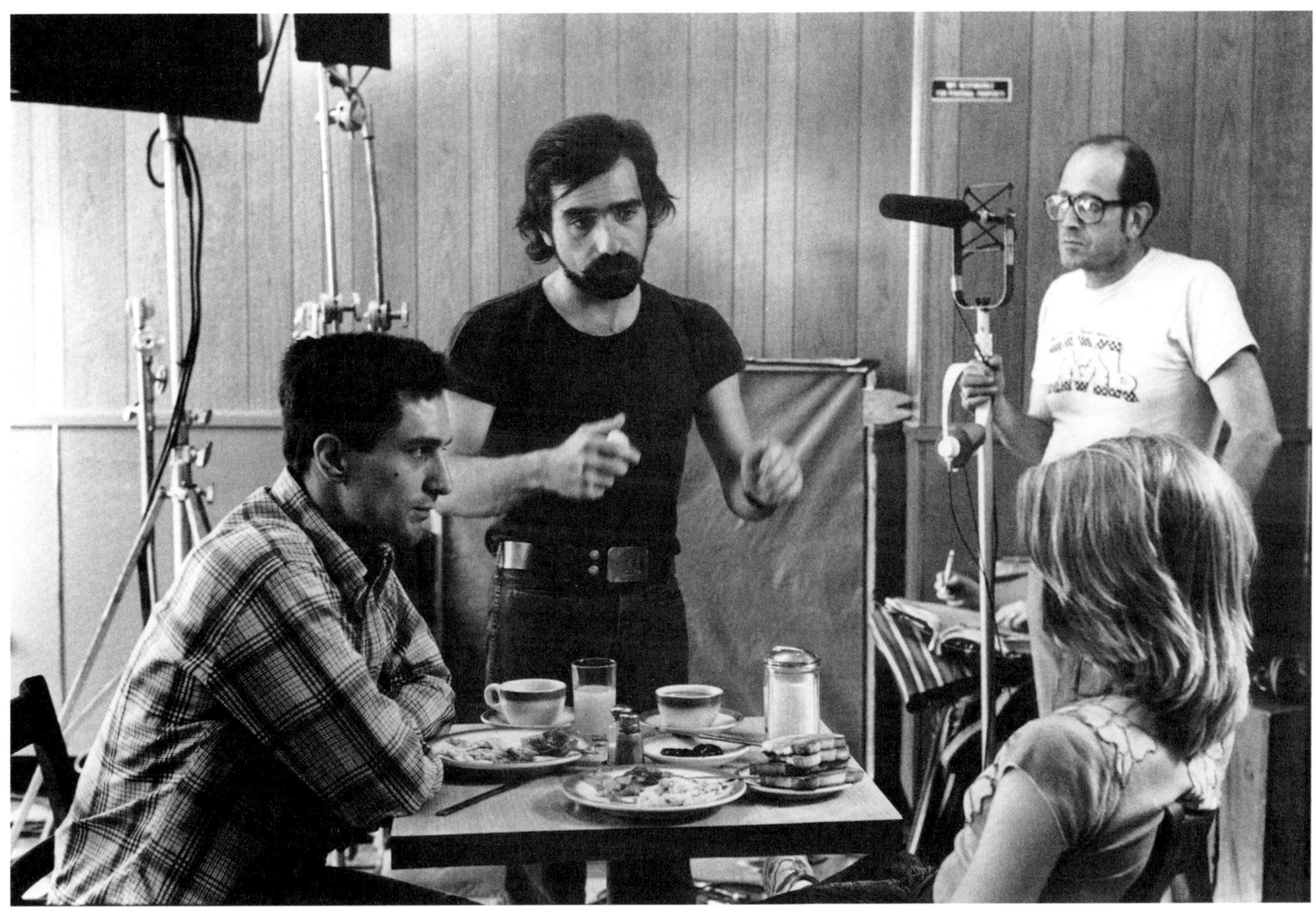

Woody Allen (in tuxedo and sneakers), Diane Keaton (holding his hand), and First Lady Betty Ford at the Uris Theatre for a Martha Graham 50th Anniversary Gala Celebration, June 19, 1975. Allen was there as the escort of Ford, who had once studied under Graham. The highlight of the evening was a new modern dance work, *Lucifer*, choreographed by Graham for Rudolf Nureyev and his longtime partner, Dame Margot Fonteyn, normally classical dancers.

During the production of the film *Taxi Driver*, director Martin Scorsese (center) discusses a scene with actors Robert De Niro and Jodie Foster (back to camera) in a cafe on Third Ave. and East Thirteenth St., July 25, 1975. McDarrah had met and become friendly with Scorsese at the New Jersey family home of photographer Jill Krementz, whose former boyfriend, *Time* critic Jay Cocks, had been Scorsese's New York University film school roommate.

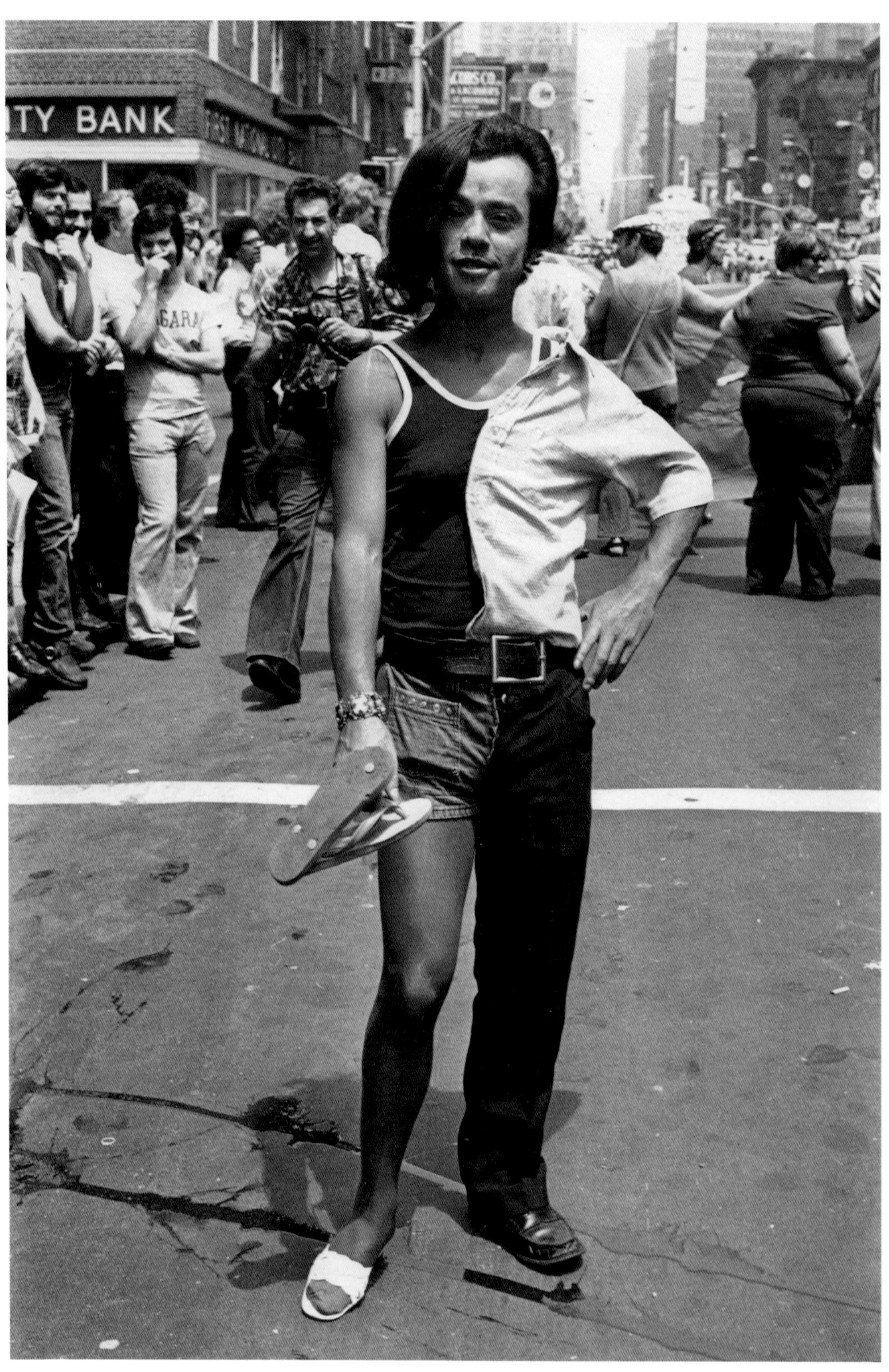

Portrait of a parade-goer at the intersection of West Twenty-Third St. and Sixth Ave. during the Sixth Annual Gay Pride March (Gay Liberation Day), June 29, 1975. One of the other marchers was US Air Force Technical Sergeant Leonard P. Matlovich, a recipient of the Bronze Star and Purple Heart, and the first gay service member to come out in order to challenge the ban on gays in the military.

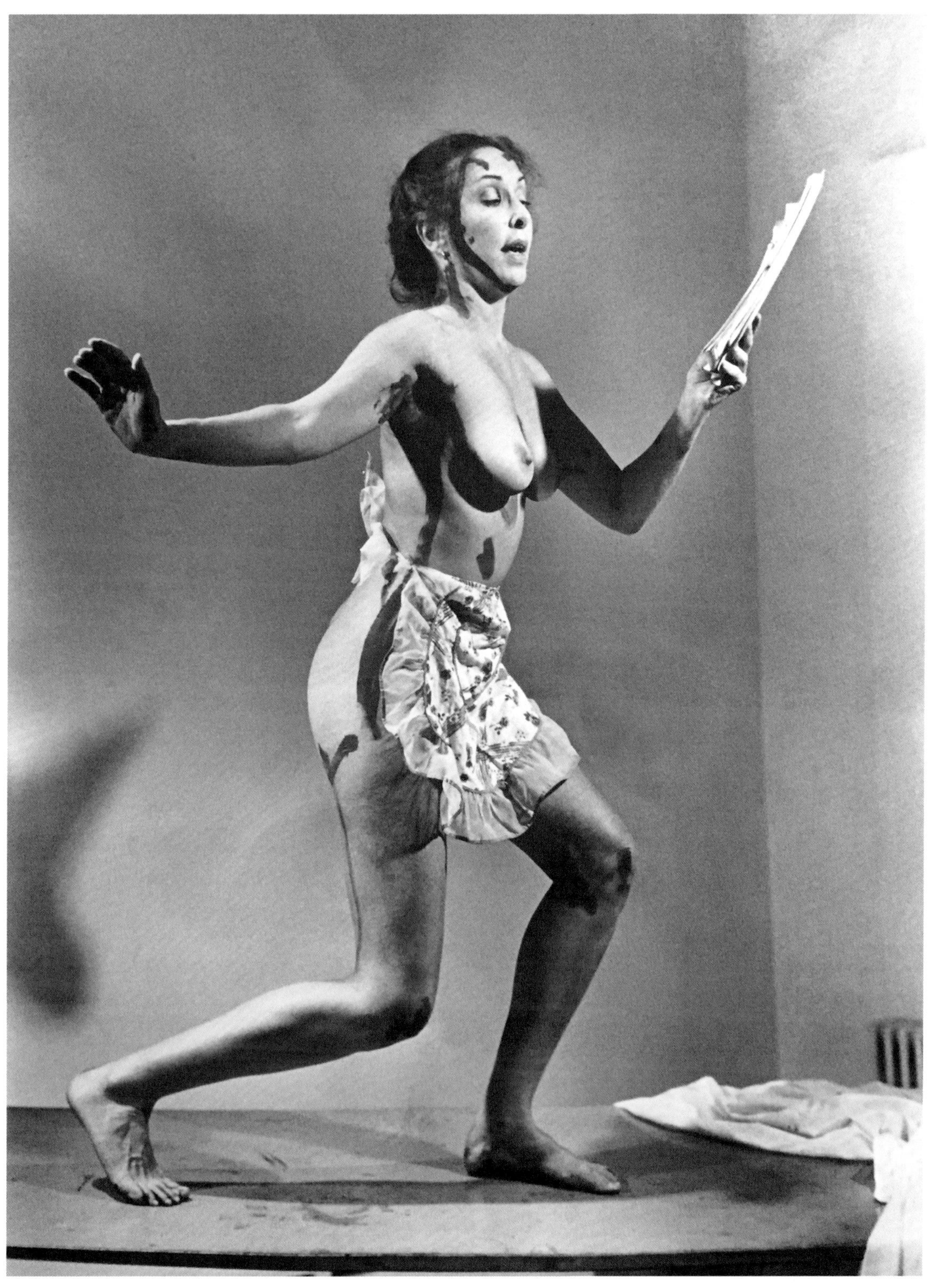

Artist Carolee Schneemann at a private first performance of *Interior Scroll*, at an art show titled *Women Here and Now*, honoring the United Nations' International Women's Year, in East Hampton, August 29, 1975. In this work, she disrobed, climbed onto a table, applied paint to her face and body, and then pulled a small folded scroll out of her vagina and read what was on it, a text relating to criticism of her films.

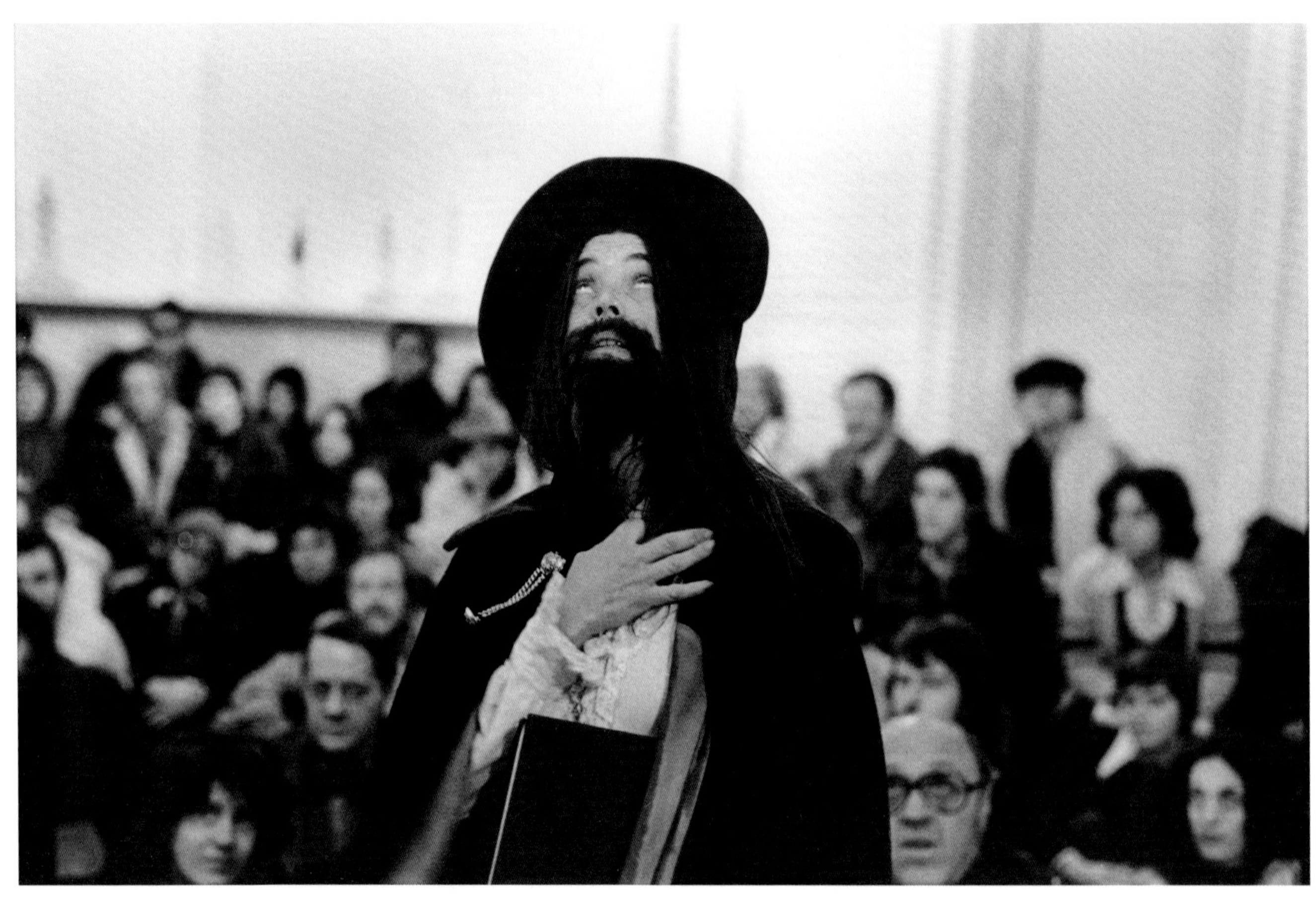

Artist Eleanor Antin in a performance of *Eleanor Antin R.N.* at the Clocktower Gallery, 108 Leonard St., January 24, 1976. In her performances, she created multiple alter egos—including a king, seen here—unimpeded by gender, race, historical era, or other limitations, to explore culture and identity from a feminist viewpoint.

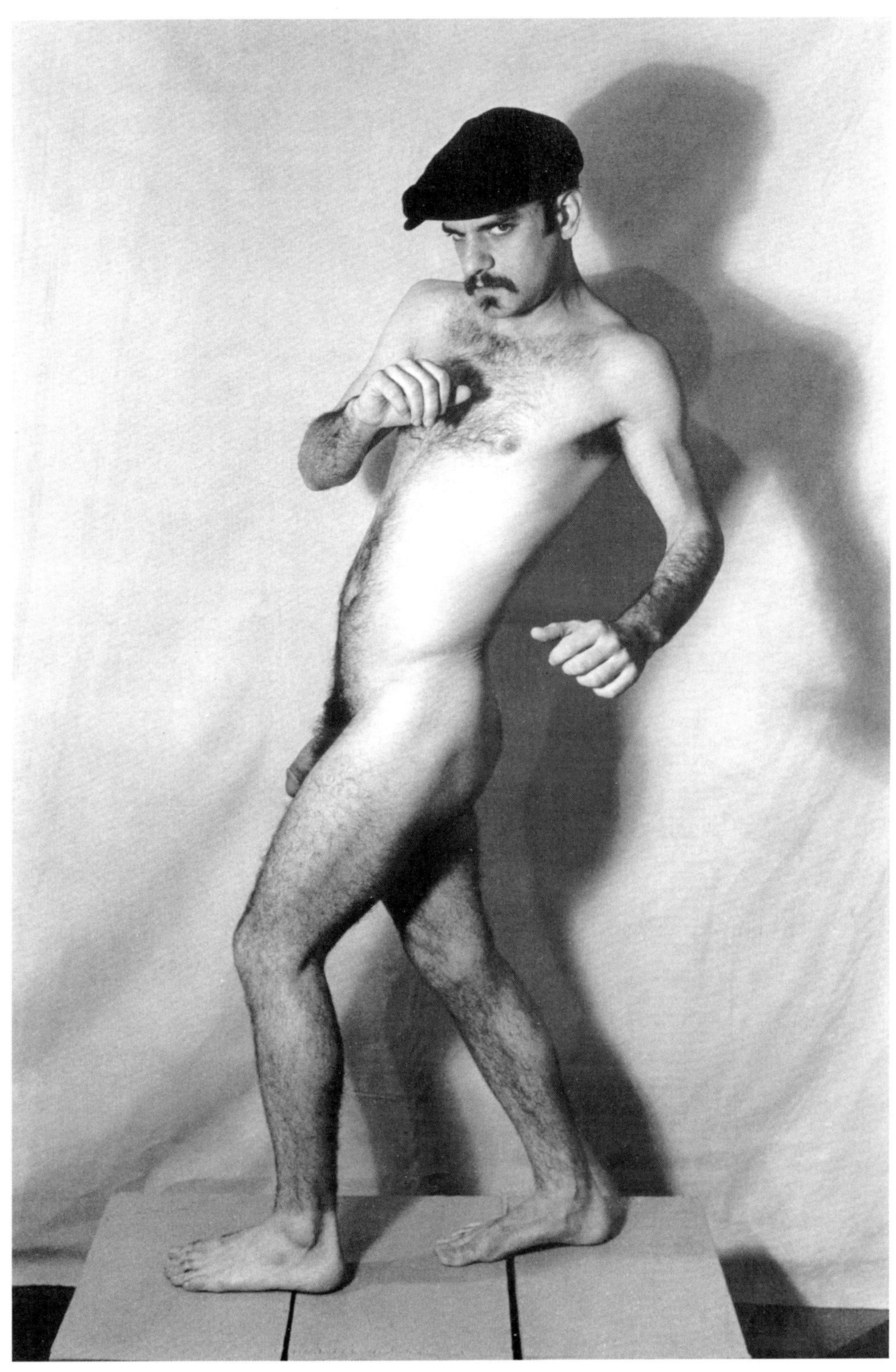

Actor, director, and playwright Charles Ludlam at his Ridiculous Theatrical Company, Sheridan Square, March 13, 1976. He wrote and acted in dozens of plays that were absurdist takes (with cross-dressing) on Gothic novels, classic literature, and popular culture. He died of AIDS in 1987; the street in front of his theater was later renamed Charles Ludlam Lane in his honor.

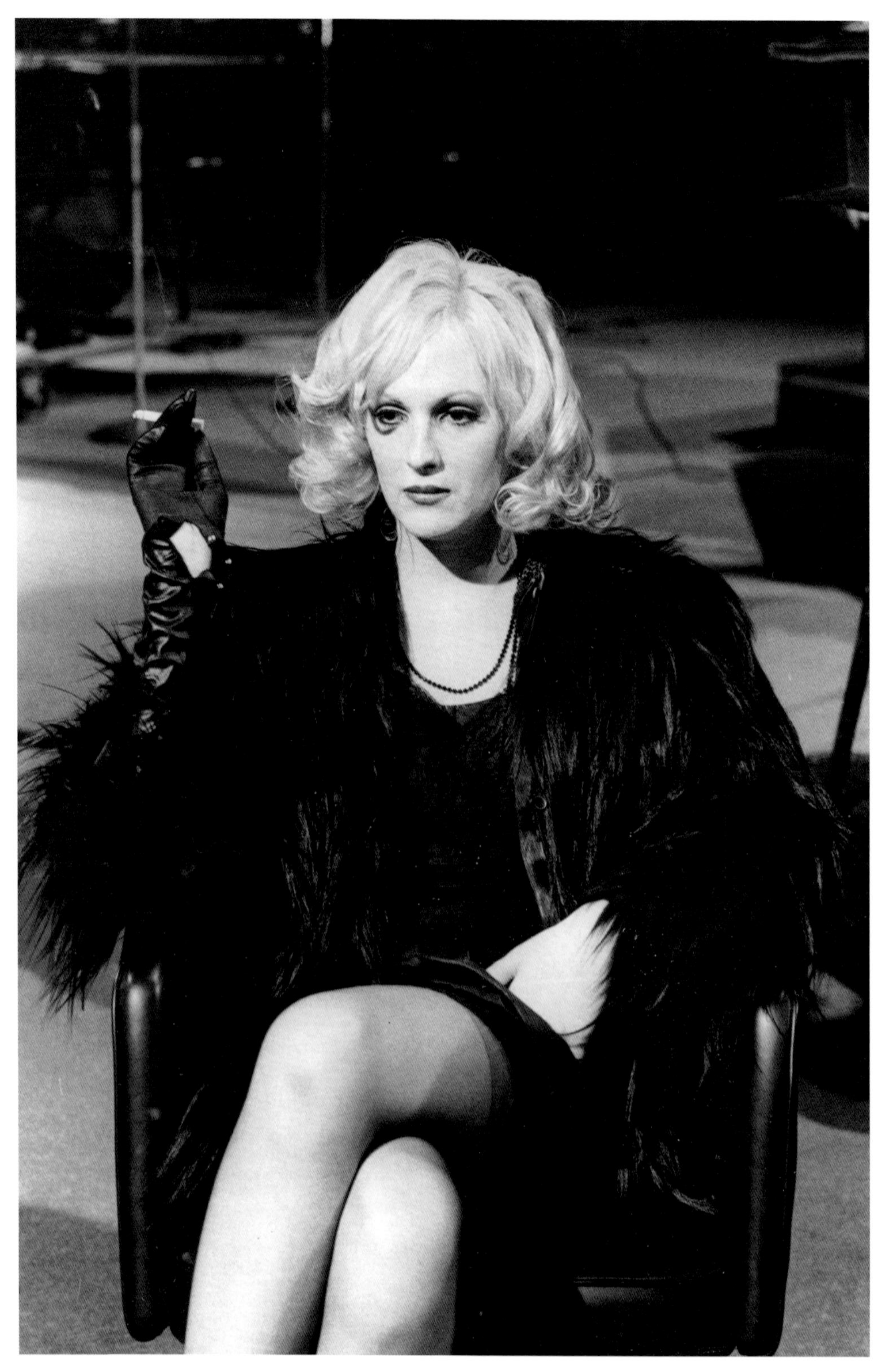

Actress and Warhol superstar Candy Darling (born James Lawrence Slattery) backstage on the set of the *David Susskind Show*, December 7, 1970. Candy, who grew up in Massapequa Park, Long Island, was forever immortalized in the Lou Reed song "Walk on the Wild Side" with the lyrics, "Candy came from out on the island, / In the back room she was everybody's darling...."

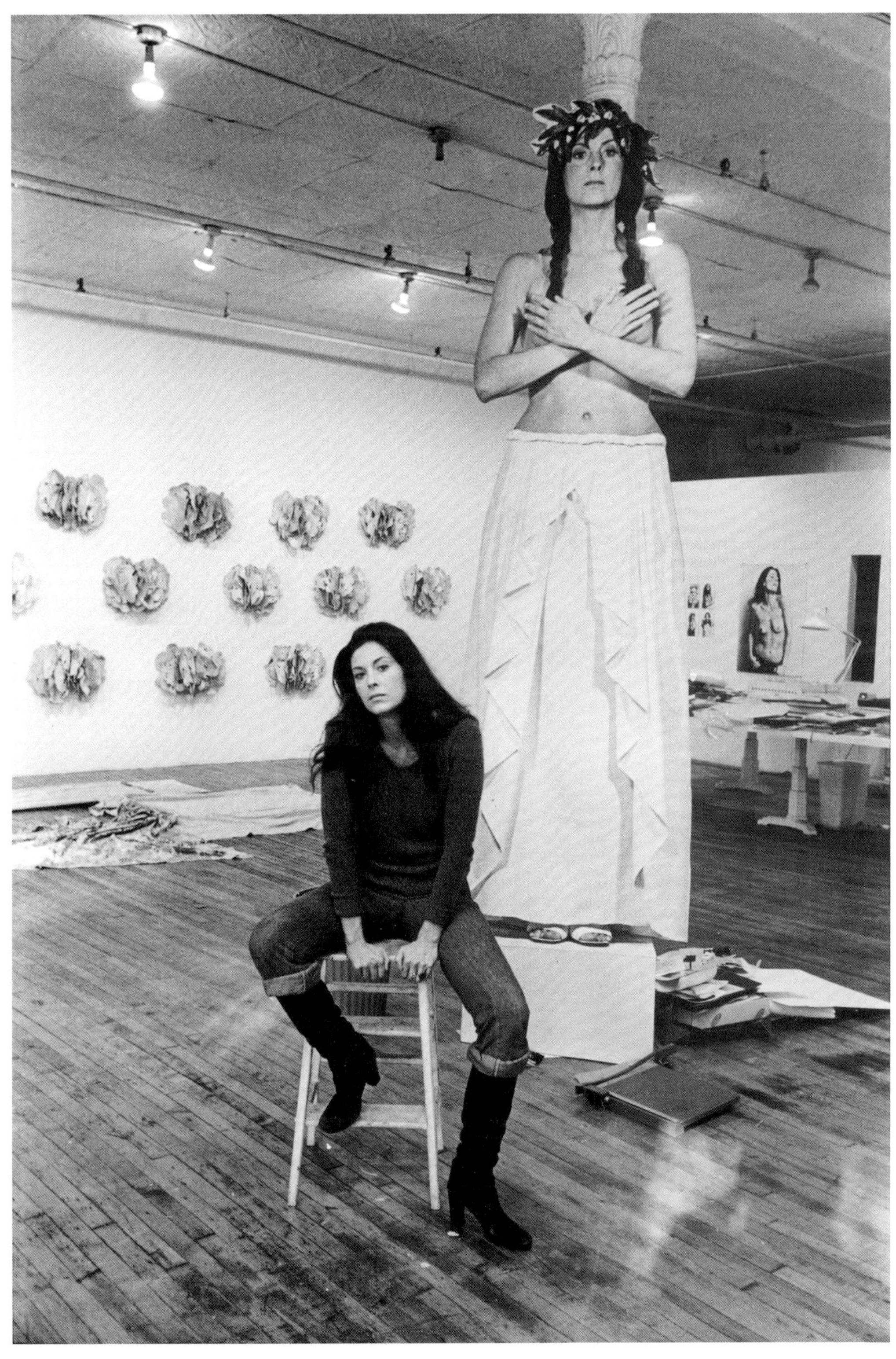

Artist Hannah Wilke in her studio, 62 Greene St., December 28, 1976. She explored feminism and sexuality in painting, sculpture, photography, and video and performance art.

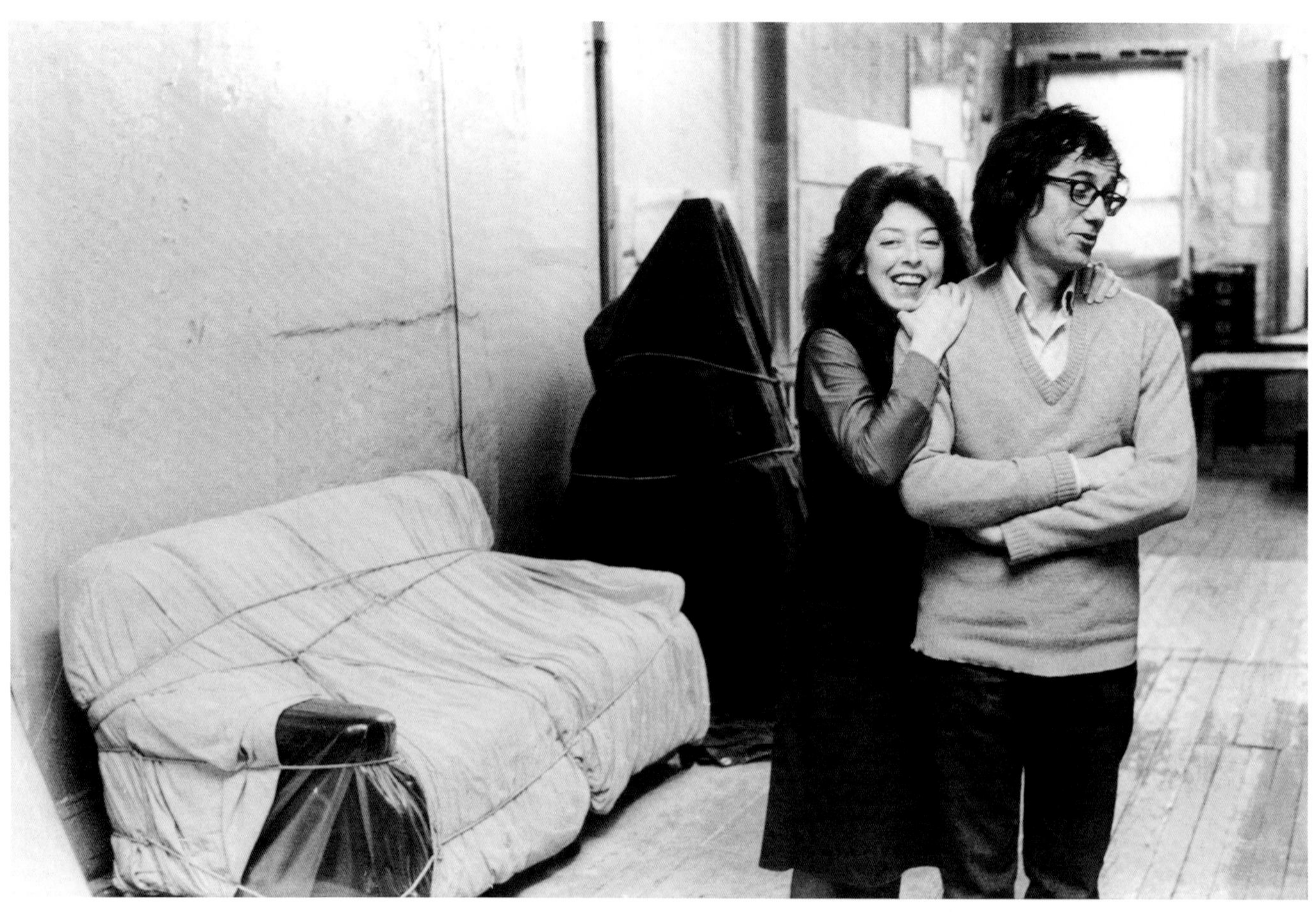

Married artists Christo and Jeanne-Claude in their loft, 48 Howard St., December 29, 1976. The couple created environmental works by wrapping buildings, bridges, landscapes, and other sites in colorful nylon or other material for short periods of time.

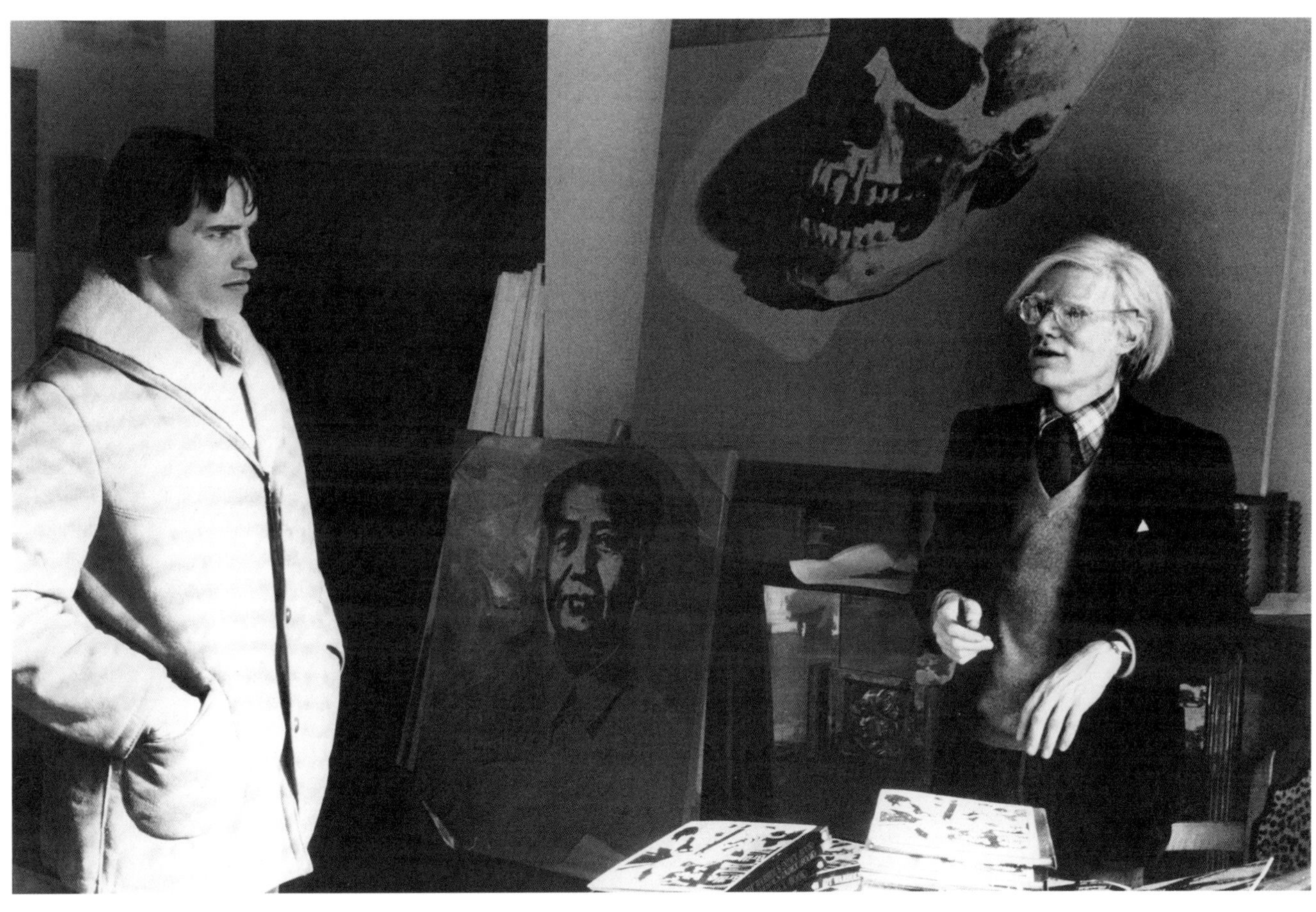

Andy Warhol meets with bodybuilder (and later the governor of California) Arnold Schwarzenegger at the Factory, 860 Broadway, at Union Square and Seventeenth St., January 14, 1977. The meeting resulted in a series of portraits by Warhol in color Polaroid prints.

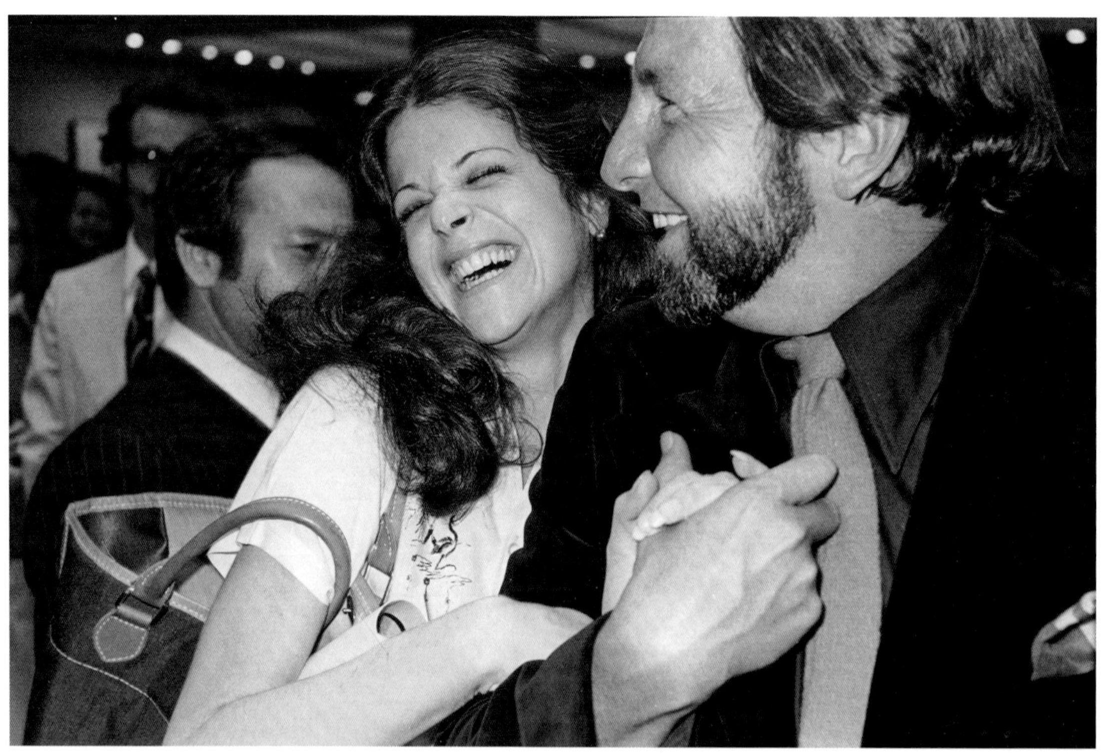

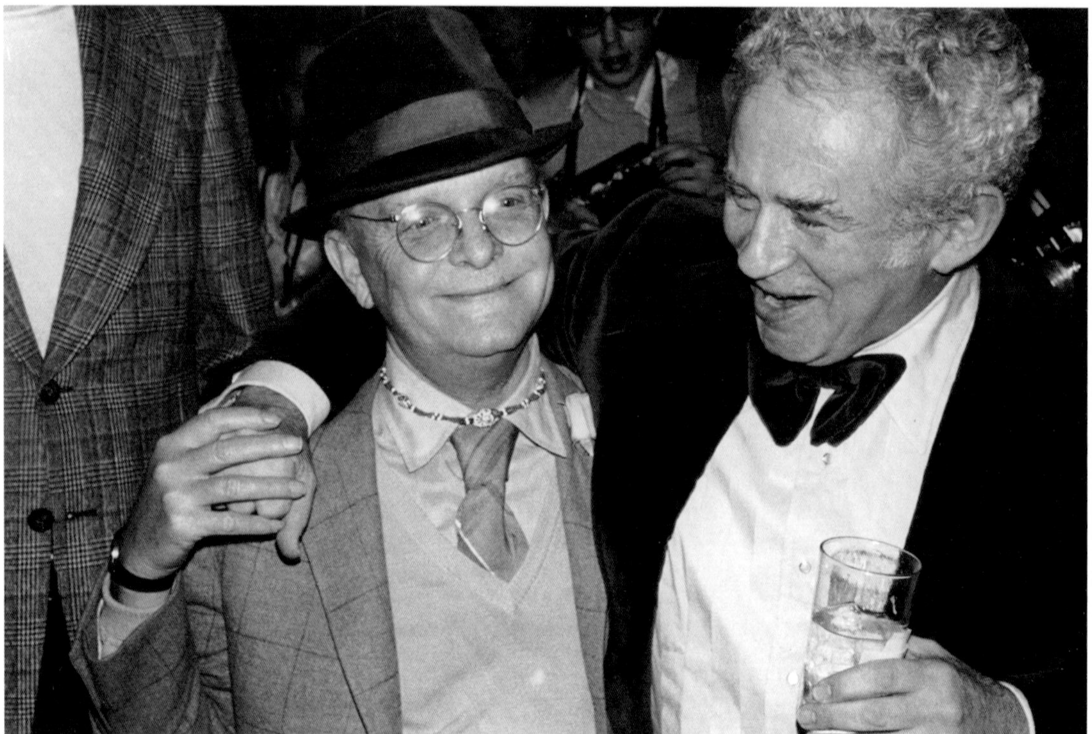

Robert Rauschenberg with comedian and actress Gilda Radner at the opening of a retrospective exhibition of his work at the Museum of Modern Art, March 23, 1977. Radner was one of the seven original cast members of *Saturday Night Live*, which premiered in October 1975.

Truman Capote and Norman Mailer at a book party to celebrate the publication of Dotson Rader's novel *Miracle*, March 21, 1978. In the spirit of New York's intensely competitive postwar literary scene, Capote once said of Mailer, "He has no talent. None, none, none!," and claimed that Mailer had called his "nonfiction novel" *In Cold Blood* a "failure of the imagination," and then gone on to imitate it.

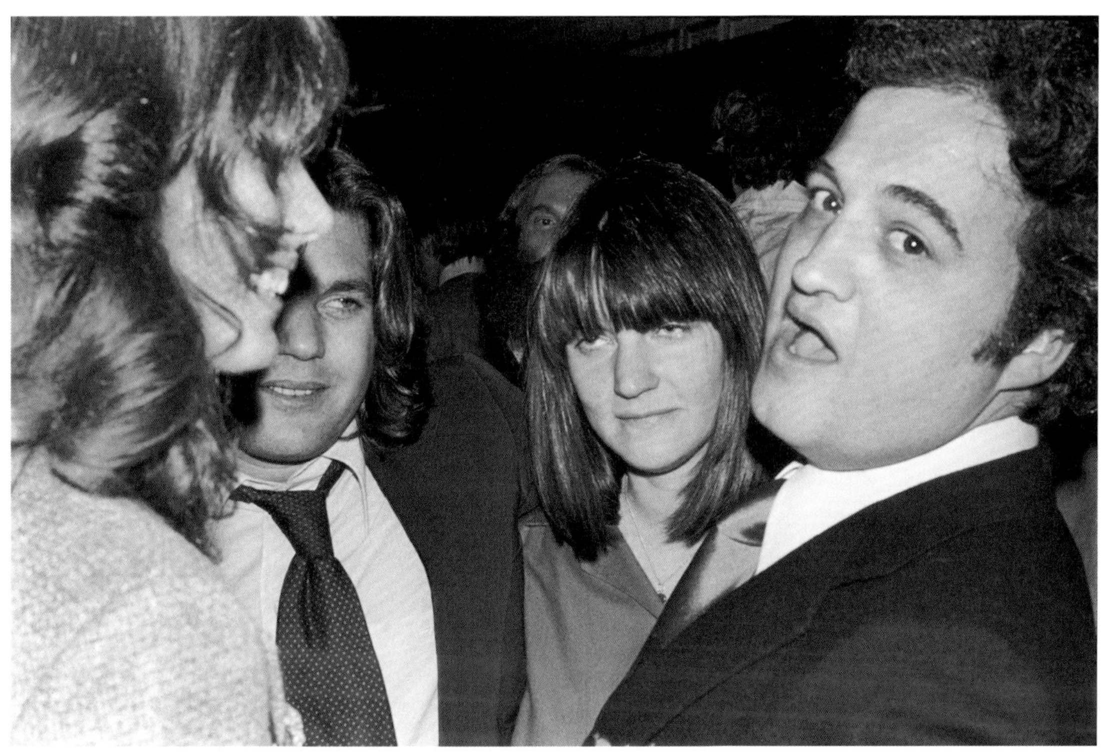

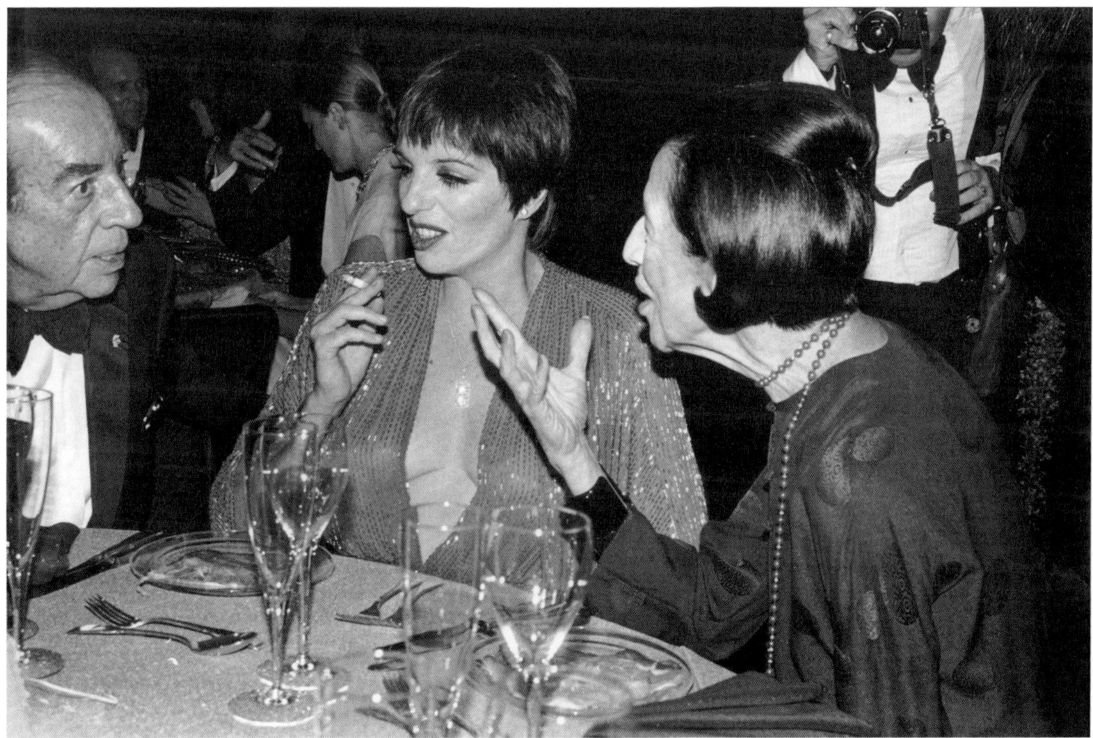

For almost three years after it opened in April 1977, Studio 54 at 254 West Fifty-Fourth St. was the acme of the New York dance club scene, powered by the wattage of its celebrity patrons. Top: Jane Birkin, Jann Wenner, Judith Jacklin, and John Belushi at the club, February 14, 1978. Actor and comedian Belushi was one of the original cast members of *Saturday Night Live*; actor Jacklin was his wife. Actor and singer Birkin was coming to the end of her productive relationship with French singer-songwriter Serge Gainsbourg. Wenner had recently moved *Rolling Stone* magazine to New York City from San Francisco. Bottom: Vincente and Liza Minnelli listen to Diana Vreeland, September 4, 1979. Vincente Minnelli was known for directing classic movie musicals; singer and actor Liza was his daughter with Judy Garland. Vreeland, at this time a consultant for the Costume Institute at the Metropolitan Museum of Art, had been the editor-in-chief of *Vogue*.

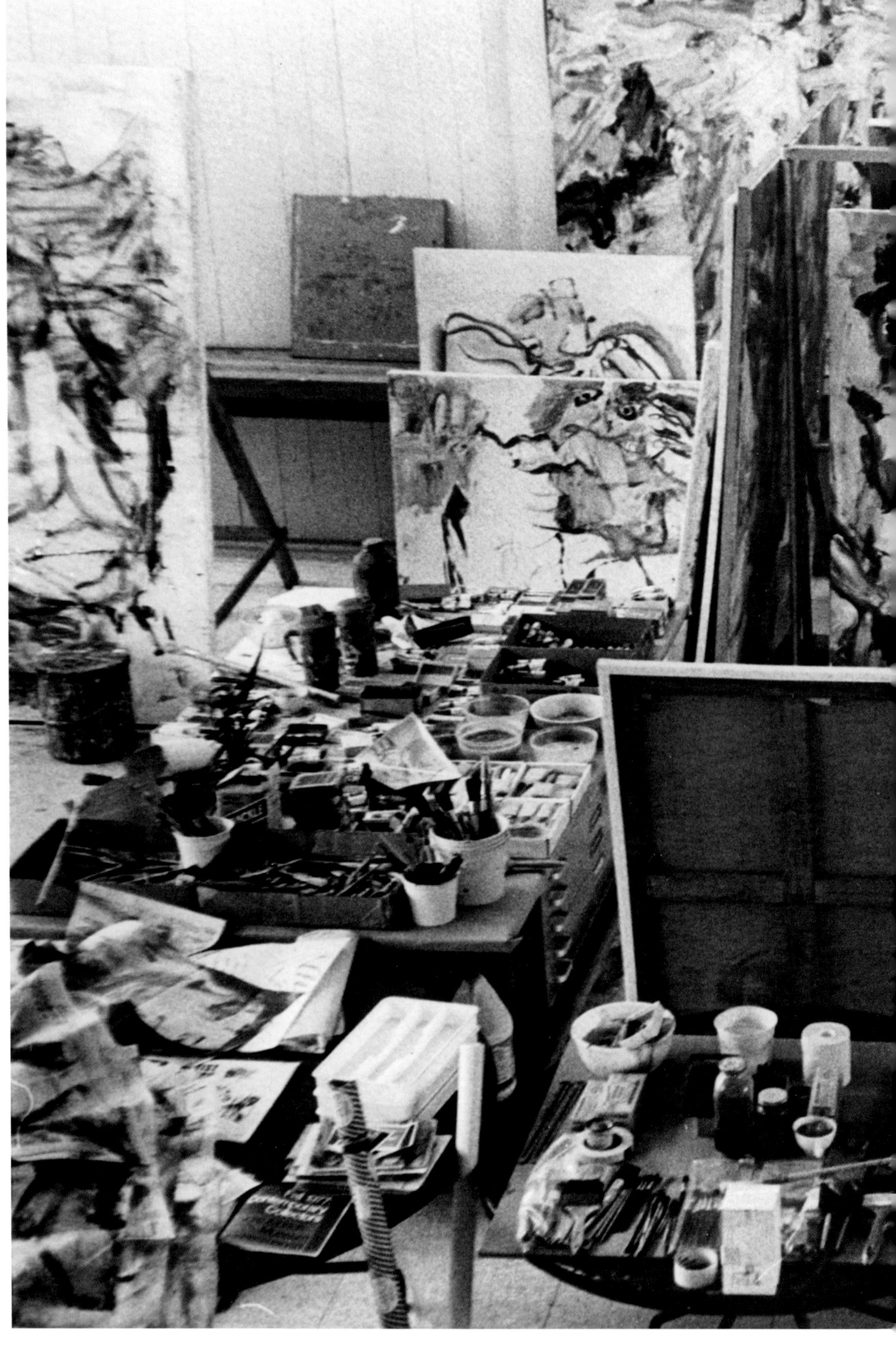

Willem de Kooning in his studio, East Hampton, March 26, 1978. Seventy-four when this photograph was taken, the artist continued to paint though his eighties. He began to suffer the symptoms of Alzheimer's disease in the late 1980s and died in 1997.

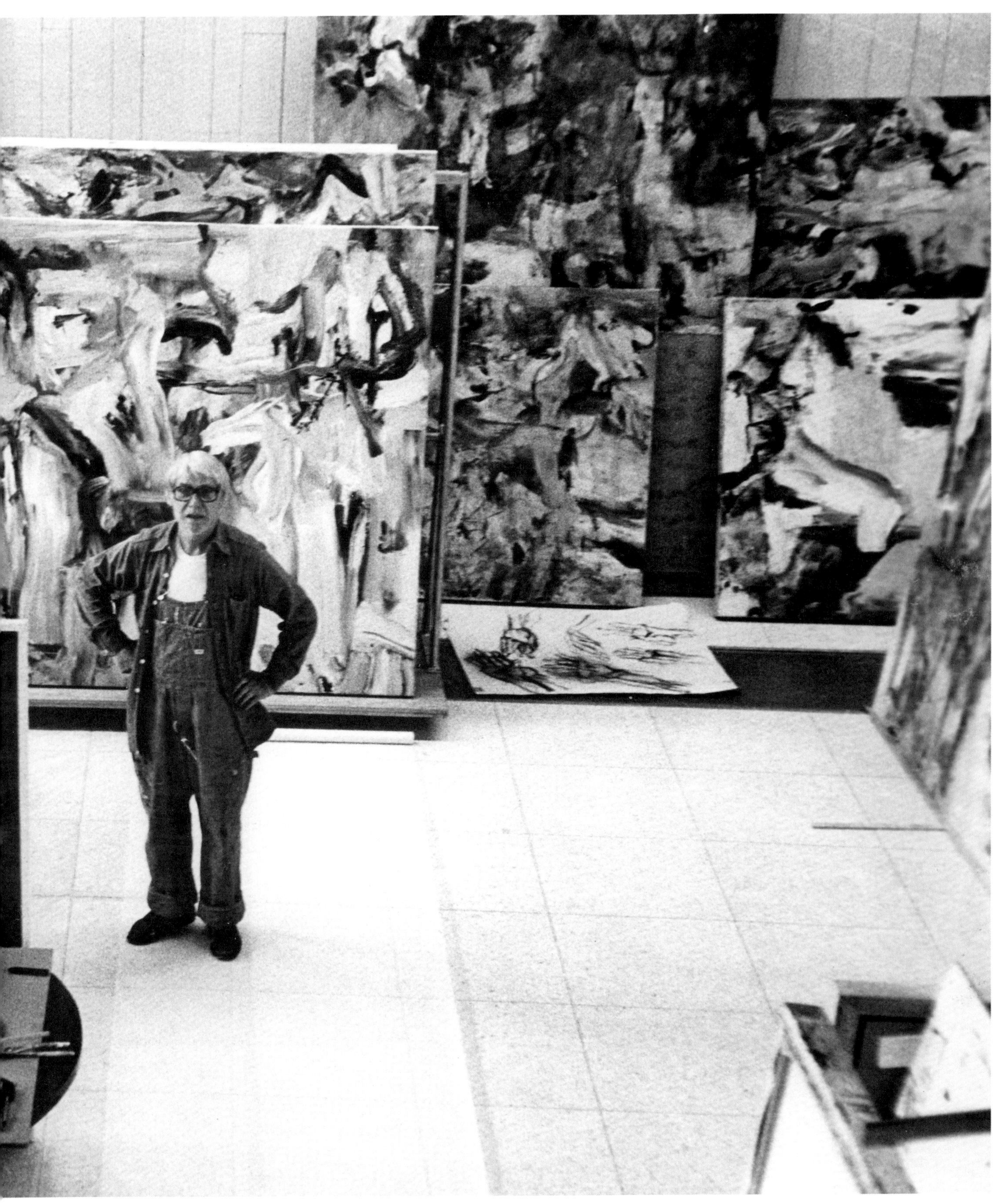

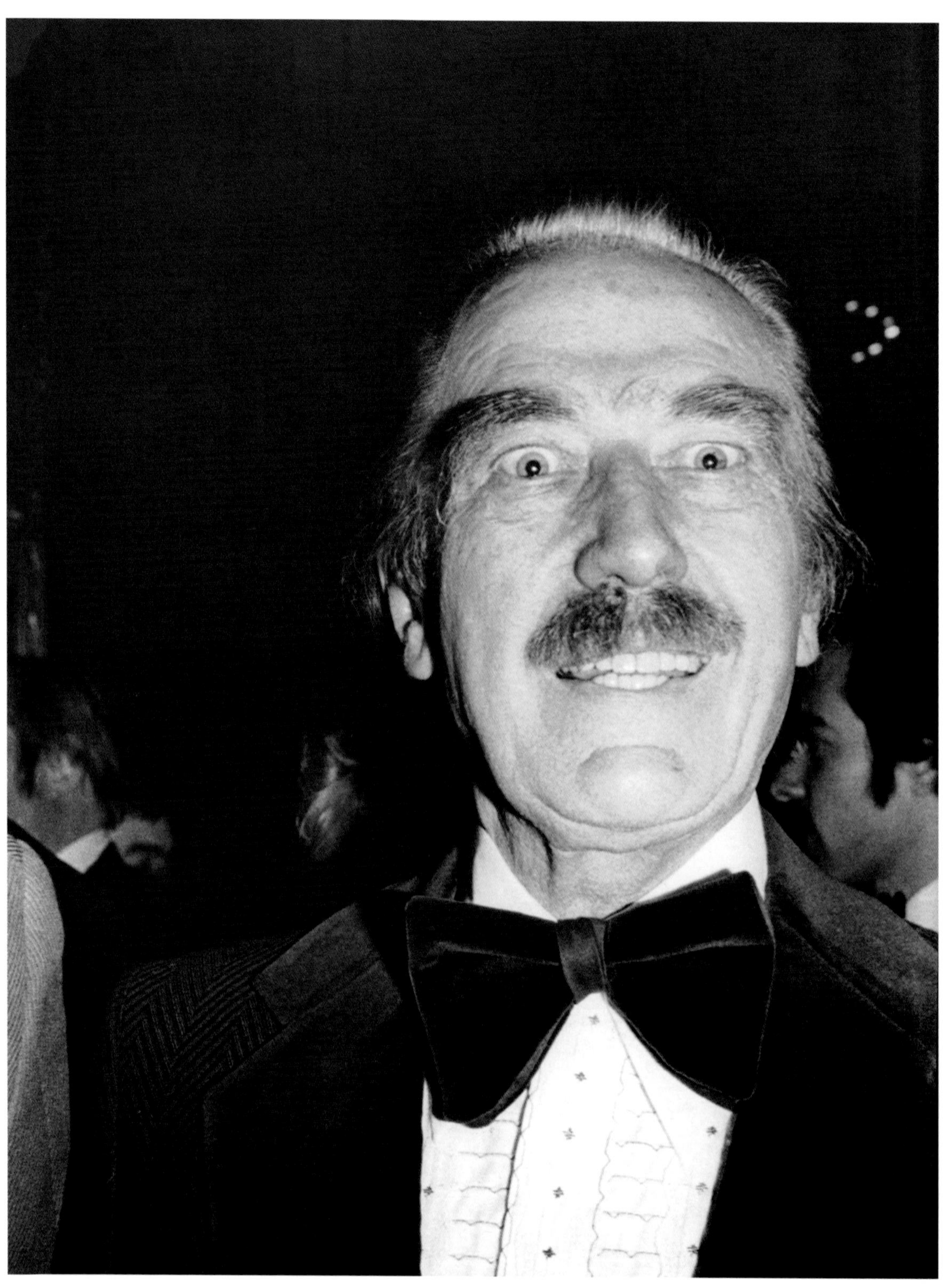

Fred Trump, real estate developer and father of Donald Trump, the forty-fifth president of the United States, at a political fund-raiser, April 2, 1978. Concentrating on Brooklyn and Queens, the elder Trump built and managed thousands of apartments and single-family homes, as well as US Navy barracks near East Coast shipyards during World War II. He was also arrested briefly while apparently taking part in a Ku Klux Klan march in Queens; he was investigated on charges of war profiteering; and he was sued by the US Department of Justice on charges he illegally blocked African Americans from renting his apartments.

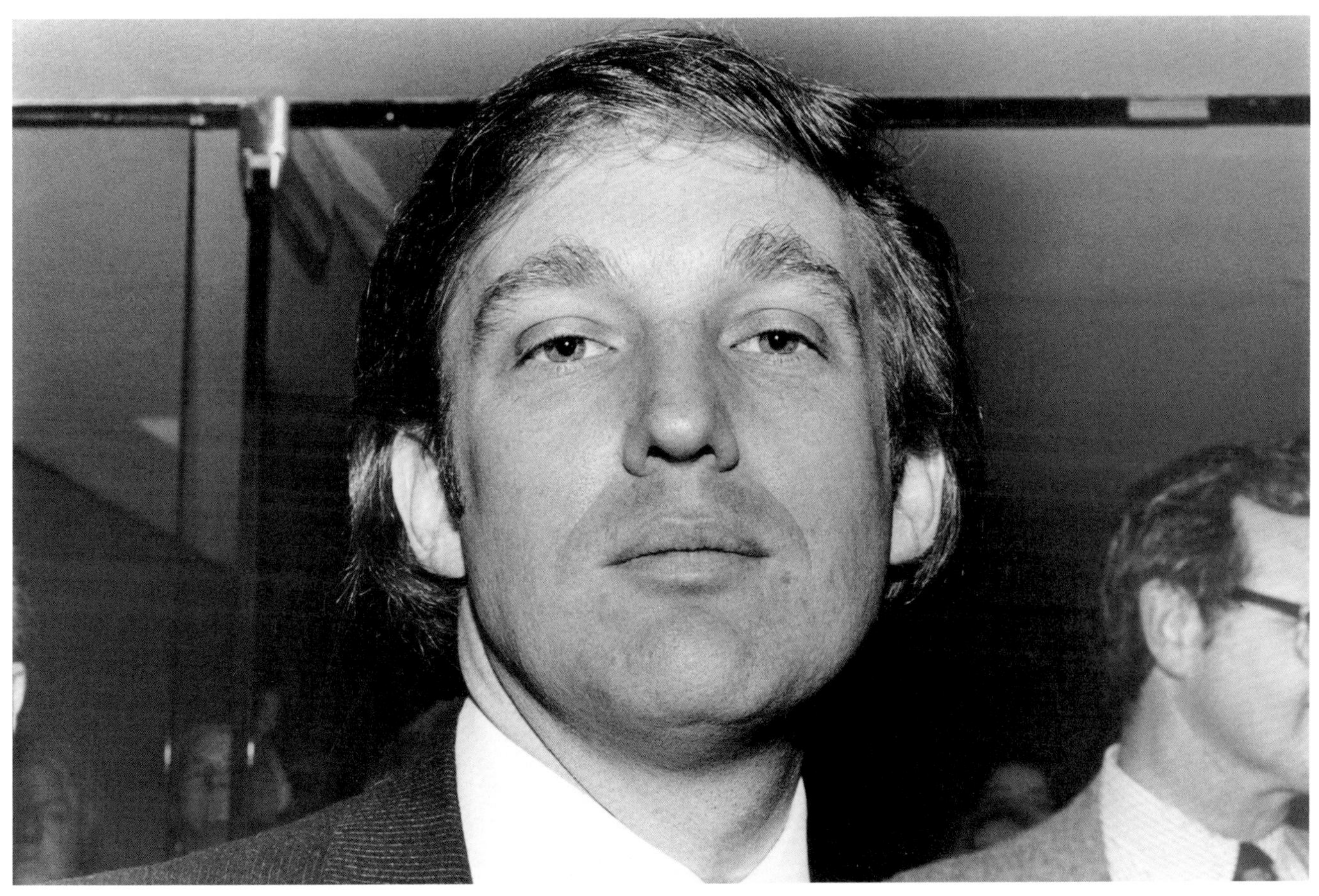

Donald Trump at age thirty-two, February 22, 1979. He joined his father's Trump Management Company in 1968, became company president in 1971, and renamed it the Trump Organization in 1980. Meanwhile, in the mid-seventies, his father gave him what he called "a very small loan"— about $1 million by his account, perhaps as much as $14 million by other accounts—to enter the real estate business in Manhattan.

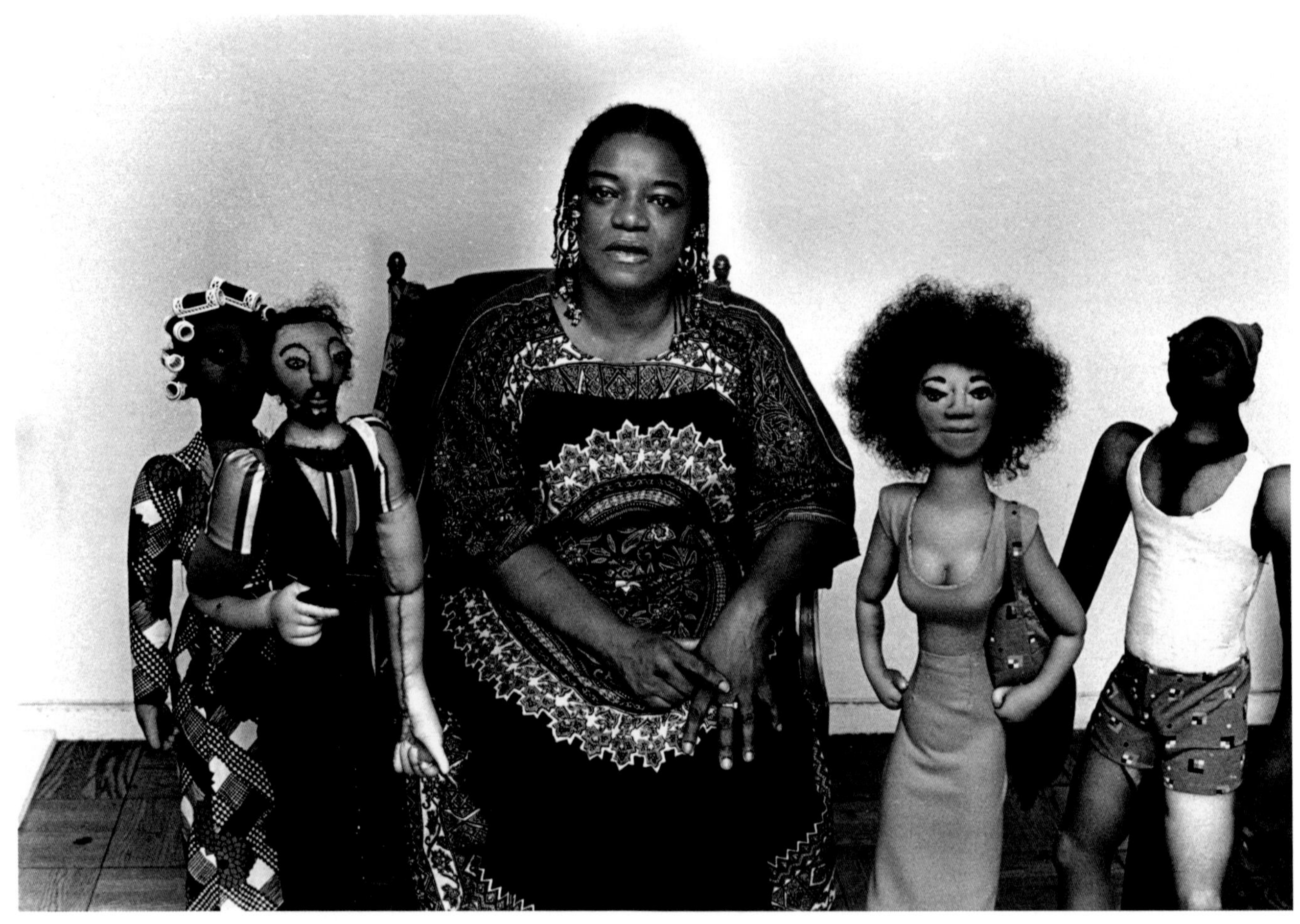

Artist Faith Ringgold poses with her work, August 30, 1978. A storyteller in many mediums, she was best known for her painted narrative quilts.

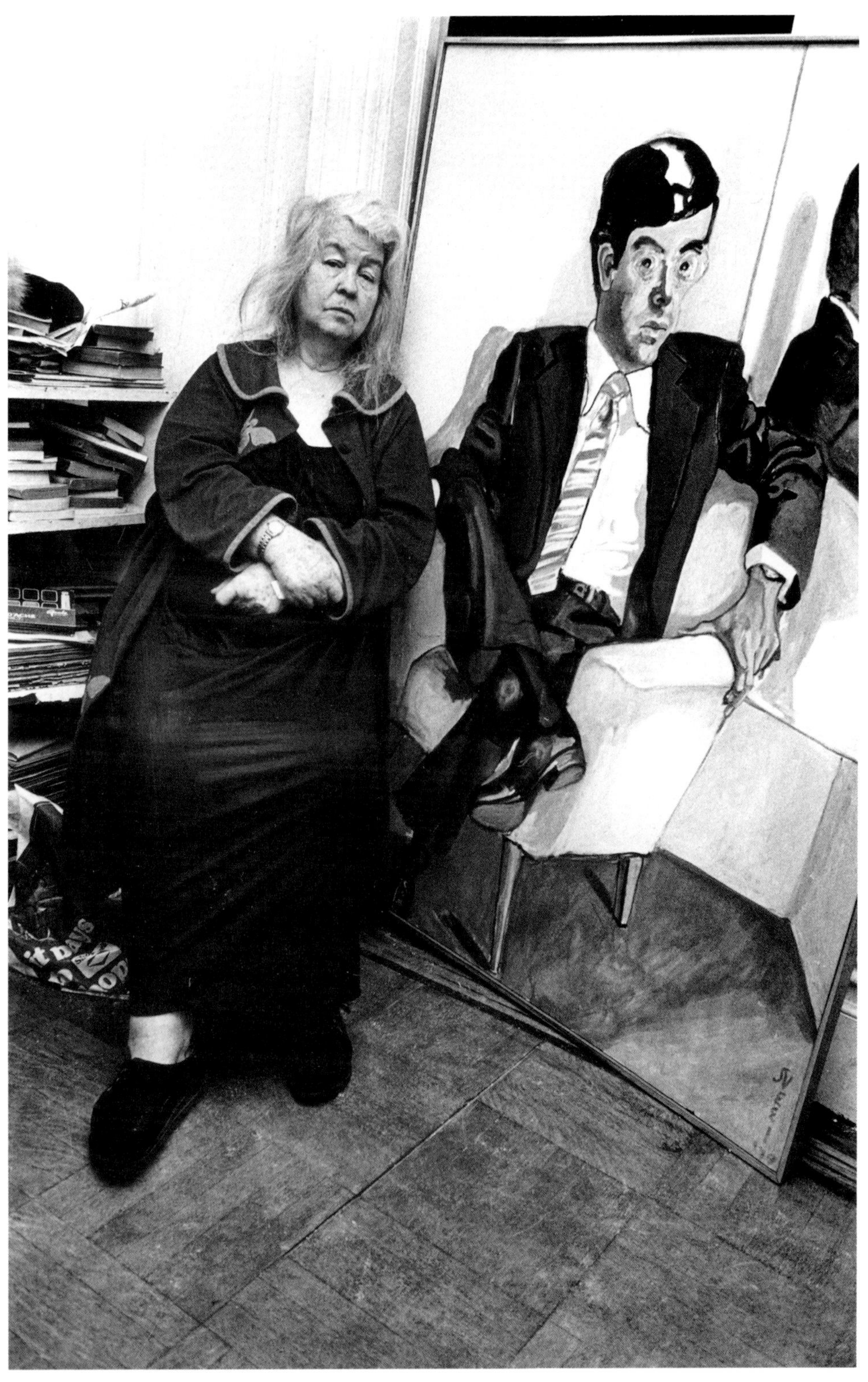

Artist Alice Neel sits next to her portrait of her son, Richard, titled *Richard in the Era of the Corporation*, in her home studio, 21 East 108th St., December 11, 1979. Neel, like de Kooning, was a McDarrah subject over many decades. She died in 1984. Richard Neel became an investment advisor.

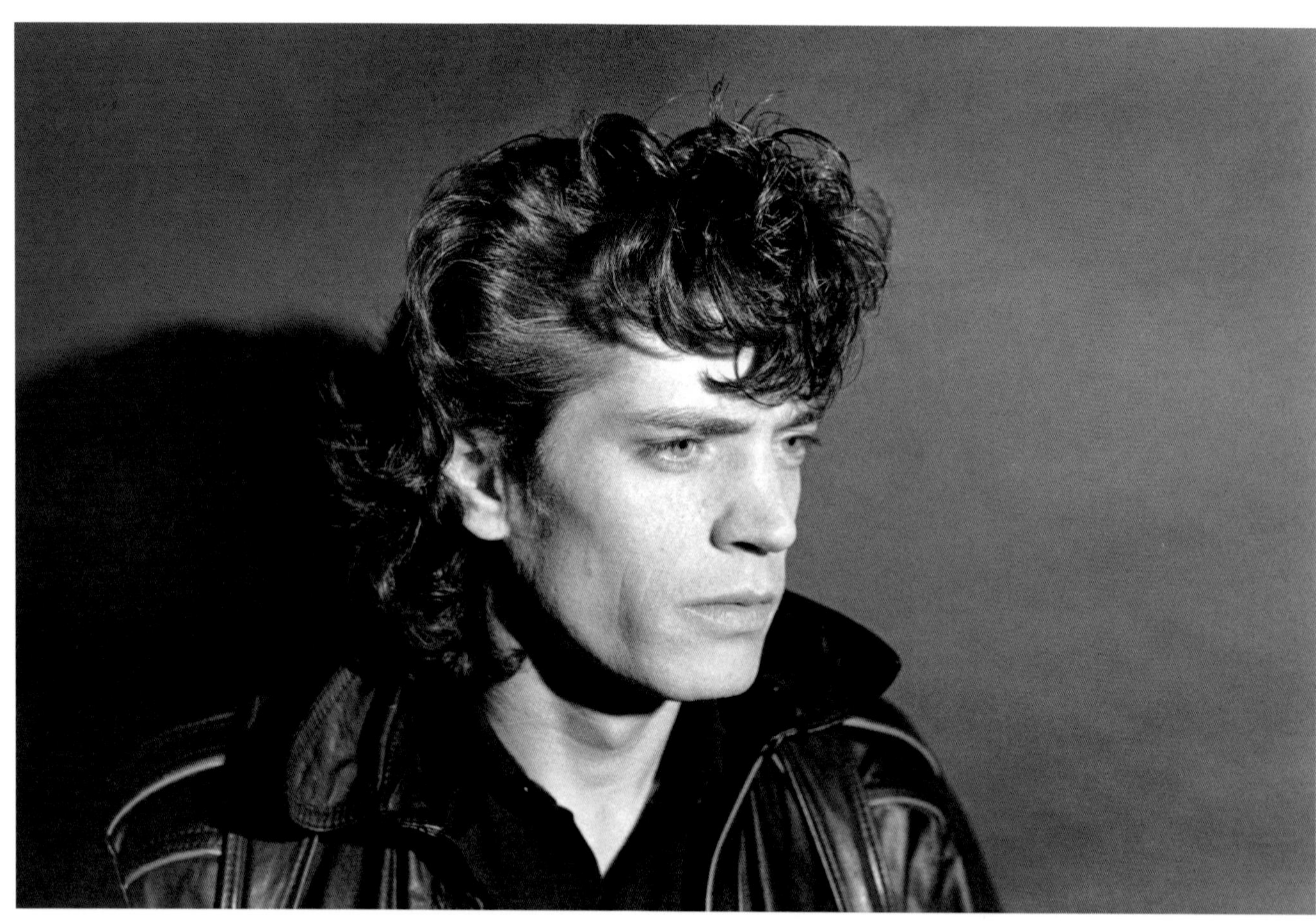

Photographer Robert Mapplethorpe at his 24 Bond St. studio, December 22, 1979. In the next decade, he would be both praised and condemned for his highly stylized black-and-white portraits of nudes—often in sexually explicit poses—in addition to photos of celebrities and other subjects. He died of AIDS on March 9, 1989, at age forty-two.

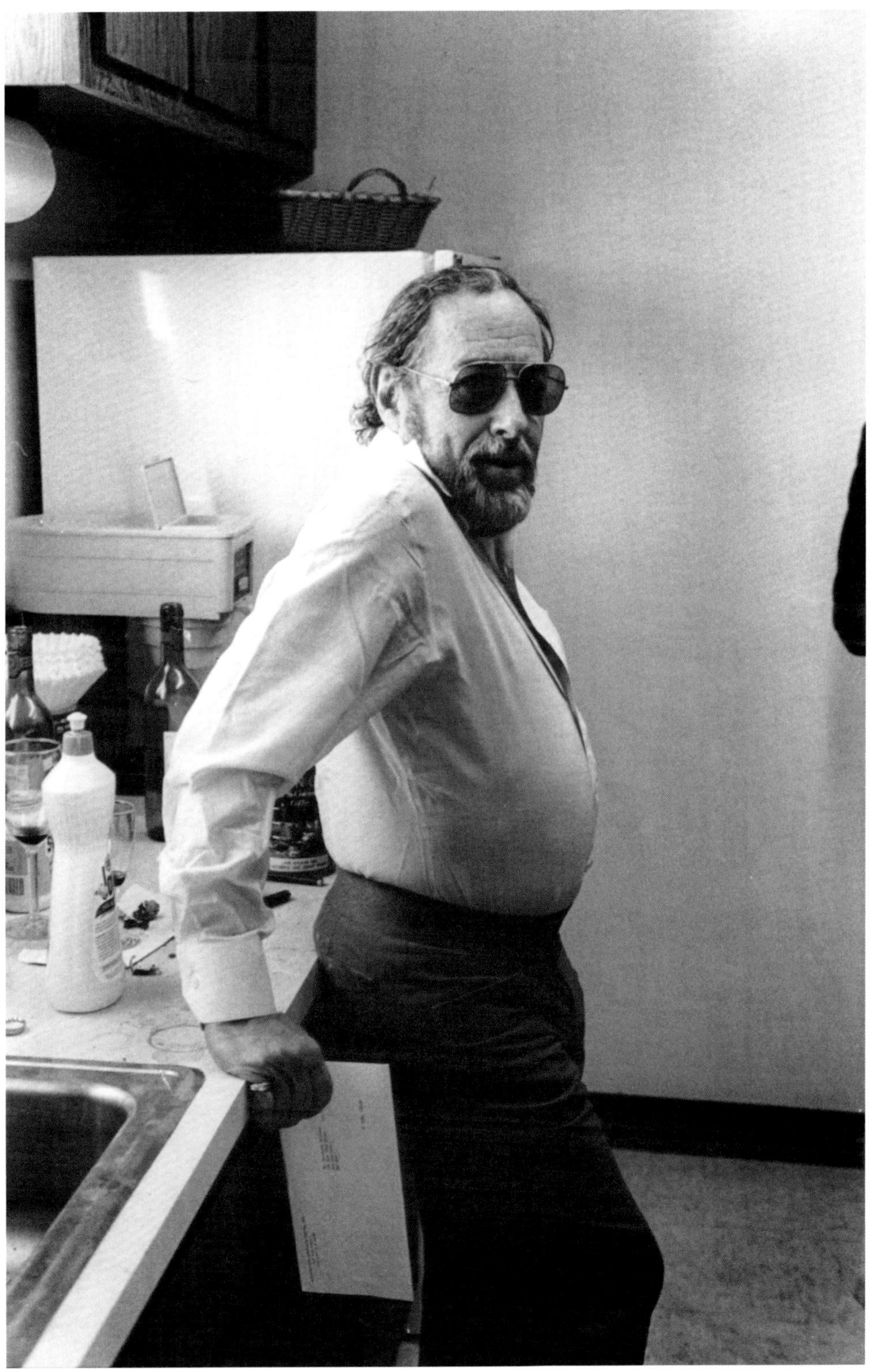

Pulitzer Prize–winning playwright Tennessee Williams leans against the countertop in the kitchen of his apartment in the Hotel Elysée, 60 East Fifty-Fourth St., January 30, 1980. One of America's most honored playwrights, he wrote *The Glass Menagerie*, *A Streetcar Named Desire*, and *Cat on a Hot Tin Roof*, with poetic language and deep empathy for wounded and vulnerable characters. Williams died at the hotel on February 25, 1983.

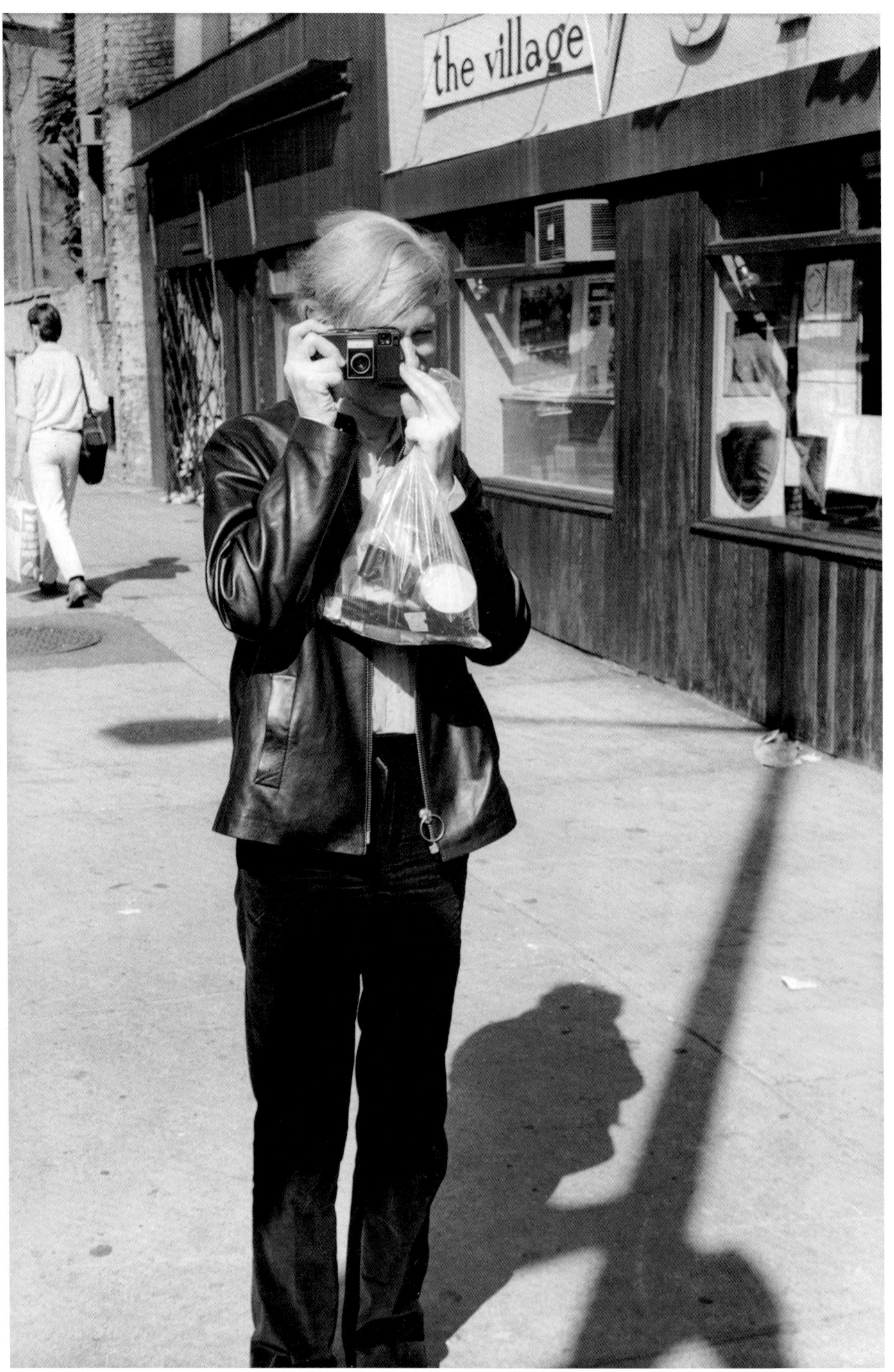

the village

THE PHOTOGRAPHER'S STORY

Andy Warhol photographs the photographer on the sidewalk outside the offices of the *Village Voice* newspaper, 61 Christopher St., New York, September 9, 1968.

"My camera was my diary, my ticket of admission, my way of remembering, preserving, and proving that I had been there when it all happened."

—Fred W. McDarrah

The iconic 1960s counterculture figure Hugh Romney, better known as Wavy Gravy, once said, "If you remember the sixties, then you really weren't there."

Well, Fred W. McDarrah was there, remembered it, and thankfully for us, and for history's sake, he took pictures of what he saw.

And not just during that one tumultuous decade, either.

During his fifty-year association with the *Village Voice*—the world's most famous alternative newspaper and the house organ of the postwar counter-culture—Fred amassed an archive of more than 250,000 images that are an encyclopedic catalog of the people, places, movements, trends, and events of the New York scene spanning the second half of the twentieth century.

Three key things made Fred's career possible: his tireless work ethic, his genuine interest in the world around him, and his being the only staff photographer for the *Village Voice*.

Fred's uncanny ability to be in the right place at the right time for decade upon decade is an example of journalistic instinct and a sense of duty. As the eyes of the reading public, he felt a need to cover it all. He carried his camera with him every time he left the house, even for a trip to the supermarket. You just never knew what you'd see, and he did not want to miss a thing.

He was interested in everything his beloved New York City had to offer. And because it was a kinder, gentler era in many ways, especially regarding access, Fred went to events and could get near people in a way that is simply not possible for photographers today. *C'mon*, one may say after thumbing through the pages here, *look at all those lucky photos!* Who knew to shoot Al Pacino in his first Off-Broadway play, or Philip Glass at NYU's student center, or that painter—it was Franz Kline—in his studio on a shabby stretch of West Fourteenth Street who went on to global fame? Was it all luck? Was Fred lucky to photograph Woody Allen doing standup at the Gaslight on MacDougal Street in 1962, or Bob Dylan at Cafe Wha? less than a month after he arrived in town from Minnesota in 1961? Possibly. But remember, in the course of doing his job, Fred also shot a million other young hopefuls—comics and folkies and writers and artists and politicians who never achieved lasting fame or fortune.

Born in Brooklyn on November 5, 1926, Fred had a sadly typical Depression-era childhood. His parents sent him out to beg for change on the streets. He walked railroad tracks looking for coal that could be brought home to heat the different cold-water flats they lived in for twelve months at a time; families on what was then called "Home Relief" often got one month free rent per year, so the McDarrahs would move annually.

If there was any Christmas present at all, it was an orange. There were visits to foster homes.

His father drank a lot. And he'd stare out the window. Discipline for Fred and his brother, David, was meted out physically, not verbally. He was half-Catholic, half-Protestant, and not observant at all (to the chagrin of his Sunday school teachers at the Central Methodist Episcopal Church on Bushwick Avenue and Madison Street). While Mayflower Compact signer Samuel Fuller was among his ancestors (on his father's side), the only time the word WASP came up in his lifetime was after a bee sting.

He bought his first camera at the 1939 World's Fair in Queens, a Univex, for ninety-nine cents. His mother had a Kodak, the family's only luxury. After leaving Boys High, he served as a US Army paratrooper in Occupied Japan at the end of World War II, camera usually in hand. He chose to be a paratrooper because the pay was fifty dollars more per month than regular army.

When he returned home after the war, he enrolled in a three-month photo course in Baltimore, Maryland. The name of the school and why he picked a school in Baltimore are lost to history.

Afterward he returned to New York and immediately looked to move to Greenwich Village. He found a room for let on the West Side in a railroad flat. The other rooms in the small apartment were occupied by a fellow returning GI named Dan Wolf, and Wolf's mother.

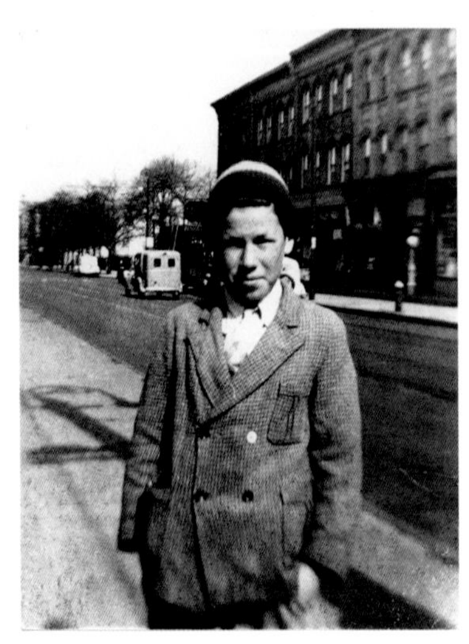

Fred W. McDarrah, self-portrait,
Wilson Ave., Brooklyn, NY
April 13, 1939.

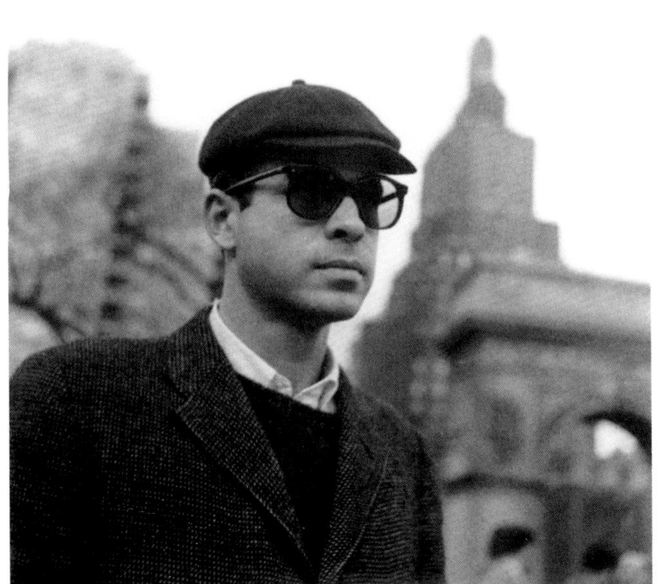

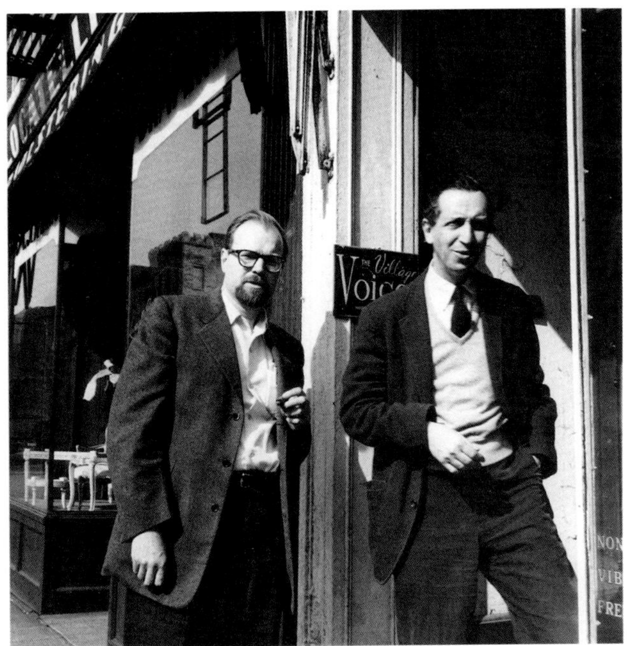

Fred W. McDarrah, Washington Square Park, November 5, 1957.

Village Voice cofounders, publisher Ed Fancher (left) and editor Dan Wolf in front of the paper's first offices at 22 Greenwich Ave., March 16, 1959.

McDarrah enrolled in New York University on the GI Bill, and when he wasn't in class, he began to photograph in Greenwich Village, not because he was assigned to, but because he wanted to.

Why did he even take pictures? He once said he did not feel as talented as some people, especially the artists, writers, and musicians he met and grew to know in bars and coffeehouses, art galleries, and cafés. But he wanted to be part of the emerging Village scene and to document it for people who weren't lucky enough to live where he did and see what he felt he had the privilege to be seeing.

In the summer of 1949, Fred met a painter named William Littlefield on Cape Cod. Littlefield, who came from a wealthy family, had studied in Paris, counted Mrs. John D. Rockefeller among his first patrons, and was a window into a world that Fred, having matriculated on the mean streets of pre-hipster Bushwick, had not previously experienced.

Littlefield brought Fred along to the informal gatherings of "The Club," an artists' association that emerged from late-night talk sessions at the Waldorf Cafeteria, at Sixth Avenue and West Eighth Street, in the late forties. The Club hosted seminars, panels, parties, talks, readings, and other events where artists of the day would share and exchange ideas and opinions, and its activities were central to the creation of the Abstract Expressionist movement. Many of the Club's members lived and worked within a few blocks of its doors: Willem de Kooning, Franz Kline, Ad Reinhardt, James Brooks, Grace Hartigan, Joan

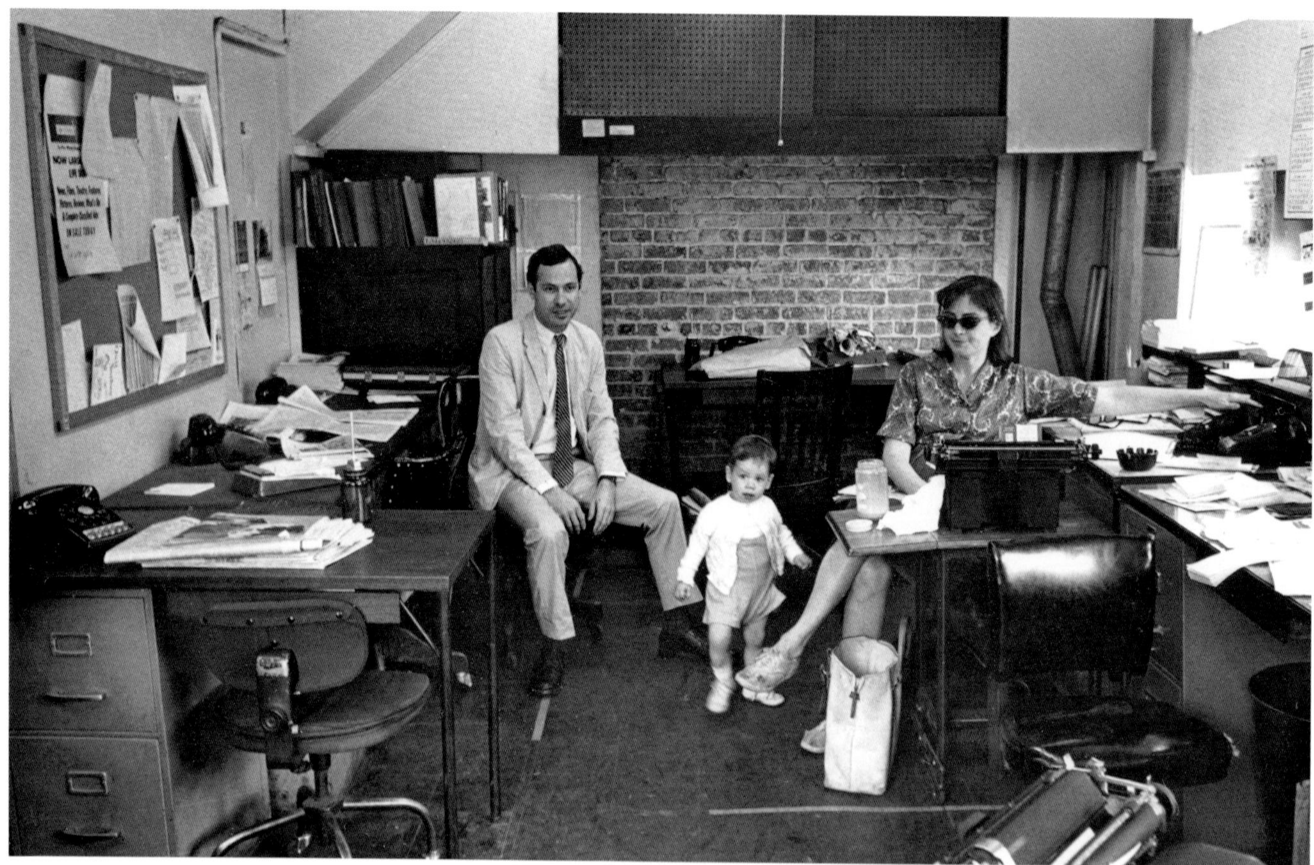

Fred W. McDarrah, Gloria S. McDarrah, and son Timothy S. McDarrah at the *Village Voice* office, 61 Christopher St., June 1, 1963.

Mitchell, Robert Rauschenberg, Jack Tworkov, Alfred Leslie, Milton Resnick, Lee Krasner, Philip Guston, William Baziotes, Robert Motherwell, Nicholas Krushenick, and Adolph Gottlieb. Fred eventually became the Club's volunteer doorman and keeper of the mailing list, cultivating relationships with many of the member artists. Often, he'd have his camera and would unobtrusively document this world he had become a part of.

Meanwhile, Fred's roommate, Dan Wolf, was writing encyclopedia entries for a living and attending the New School, where he had met a psychologist named Ed Fancher while they were both on line (literally, standing on a line; remember this is nearly seventy-five years ago!) to register for a class. Dan and Ed had an epiphany of sorts when they looked at the changing world around them and wondered why there was no newspaper covering it. Oh sure, there were New York newspapers, and plenty of them. But to those papers, culture was the Metropolitan Opera, Carnegie Hall, the Metropolitan Museum of Art, the Fifty-Seventh Street galleries, and other traditional, staid institutions. There was a creative vibrancy below Fourteenth Street, and no one was paying much attention.

So, in 1955, Wolf and Fancher decided to start a newspaper. They just needed some bucks to get it off the ground. Wolf's wife, Rhoda Lazare, had grown up

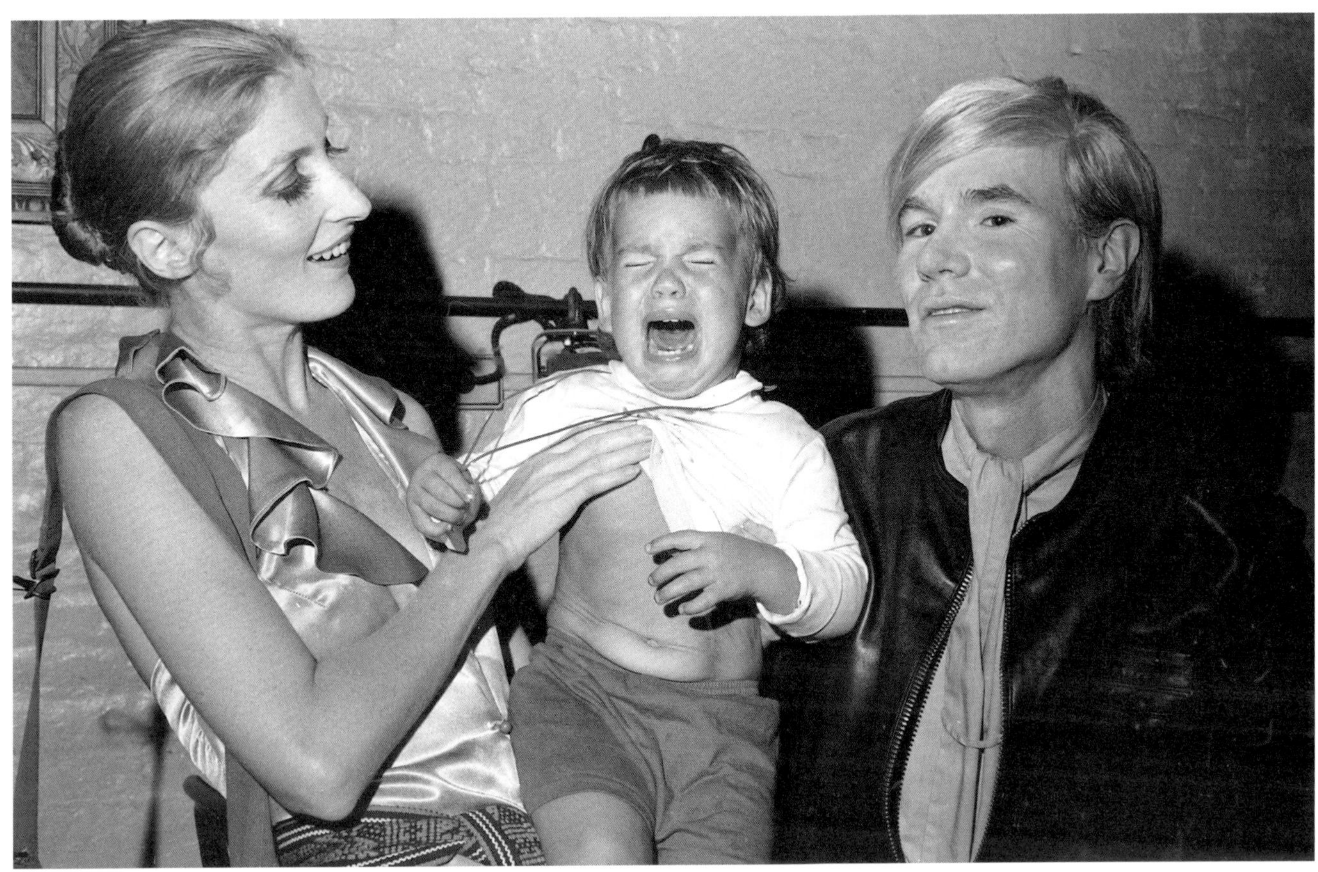

in Brooklyn with a woman named Barbara Mailer, whose brother Norman was then at the top of the cultural wave, still riding his Pulitzer Prize for *The Naked and the Dead*. Wolf and Fancher knew Mailer, that he had an ego and a full bank account. They offered him a weekly column in their new paper, to be called the *Village Voice*, in exchange for ten thousand dollars in seed money. Mailer's column lasted only a few months (he quit after editor and fellow cofounder Jerry Tallmer changed a word in a column from "nuance" to "nuisance"; Mailer's handwritten copy was always a challenge to decipher).

The paper also needed a photographer, and Wolf knew where to find one.

Fred was only mildly interested when Wolf approached him about it. He was focused on a career in advertising; this was the beginning of the "Mad Men" era, and Madison Avenue was glamour. How could anyone pay the bills taking photos?

Wolf assured Fred that there was no need to change his ways. Every week he could just bring in some photos of the events he was going to attend anyway—the art openings, concerts, and poetry readings—and the *Voice* would use some. And since the paper needed money to survive, Fred was welcome to sell ad space as well, which he did.

Fred was to be associated with the paper for the rest of his life. He was for decades, and through a series of owners and editors, the paper's only staff photographer, and he was its first picture editor. He also, presciently, retained the rights to all his photos. Early on, Fred prevailed on Wolf and Fancher to sign a makeshift contract on a piece of yellow legal paper to the effect that Fred and not the paper owned his work, a move that many a photographer of his generation would have had cause to envy.

Thanks to this entrepreneurial spirit, his files were filled with rejected book proposals, story ideas, and failed business plans. The one side business of Fred's that took off came about by happenstance and, ironically, it had nothing to do with his photography. A call came into the *Voice* one day from a Scarsdale matron looking to spice up her society party by having an actual Beat poet come and read some verse. Did Fred know where she might be able to find one?

And so, Rent-A-Beatnik was born. According to a story in the *New York Mirror*, for fifteen dollars the client got one Beat and a half hour of poetry; two hundred dollars bought three Beats, who read poetry, answered questions, played the guitar and, of course, the bongos. One ad that Fred placed in the *Voice* read that the beatnik came to your door "completely equipped: beard, eye shades, old army jacket, levis, frayed shirts, sneakers or sandals (optional). deductions allowed for no beard, baths, shoes, or haircuts. lady beatniks also available, usual garb: all black."

Fred took a small commission and was careful to protect the talent from the clientele. And vice versa. He would not send female Beats to a bachelor party and once turned down a request from a scoutmaster looking to hire, for a speaking engagement, any Beatnik who was also a former Eagle Scout. In that instance, however, the refusal may have simply been because of the sheer impossibility of filling the order.

Fred loved the *Voice* and was proud of the paper, its reporters, the issues it covered, and how they were covered. The paper often seemed to have no editorial direction. But from the first issue its pages were filled with a mix of advocacy and personal journalism that reflected the cultural ferment and political discontent simmering in the intellectual life of the country.

He was involved in all kinds of ways: he wrote film and photo and art reviews, composed scalding letters to the editor when he did not like an article, took press-card photos for all the other staffers on his own time and out of his own pocket, drove car-less reporters to stories, and had *epic* battles on nearly a weekly basis over his photos. "People want to see more pictures!" he'd bellow to Dan Wolf (and later to everyone else at the editor's desk: Tom Morgan, Clay Felker, Marty Gottlieb, Karen Durbin, Tony Ortega, Marianne Partridge, David Schneiderman, Jonathan Larsen, and Robert Friedman).

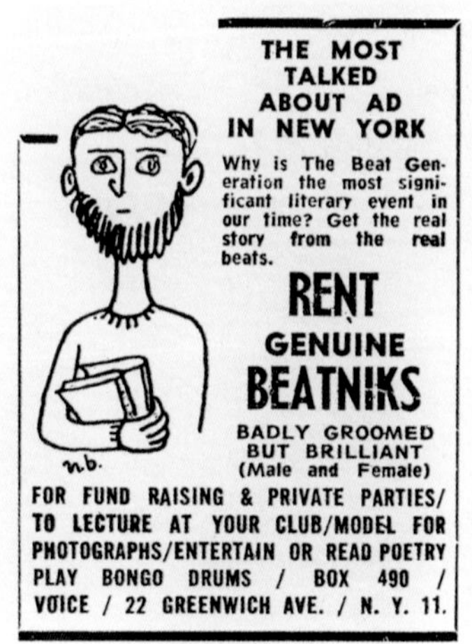

"Rent Genuine Beatniks," an ad that appeared in the *Village Voice*, June 16, 1960.

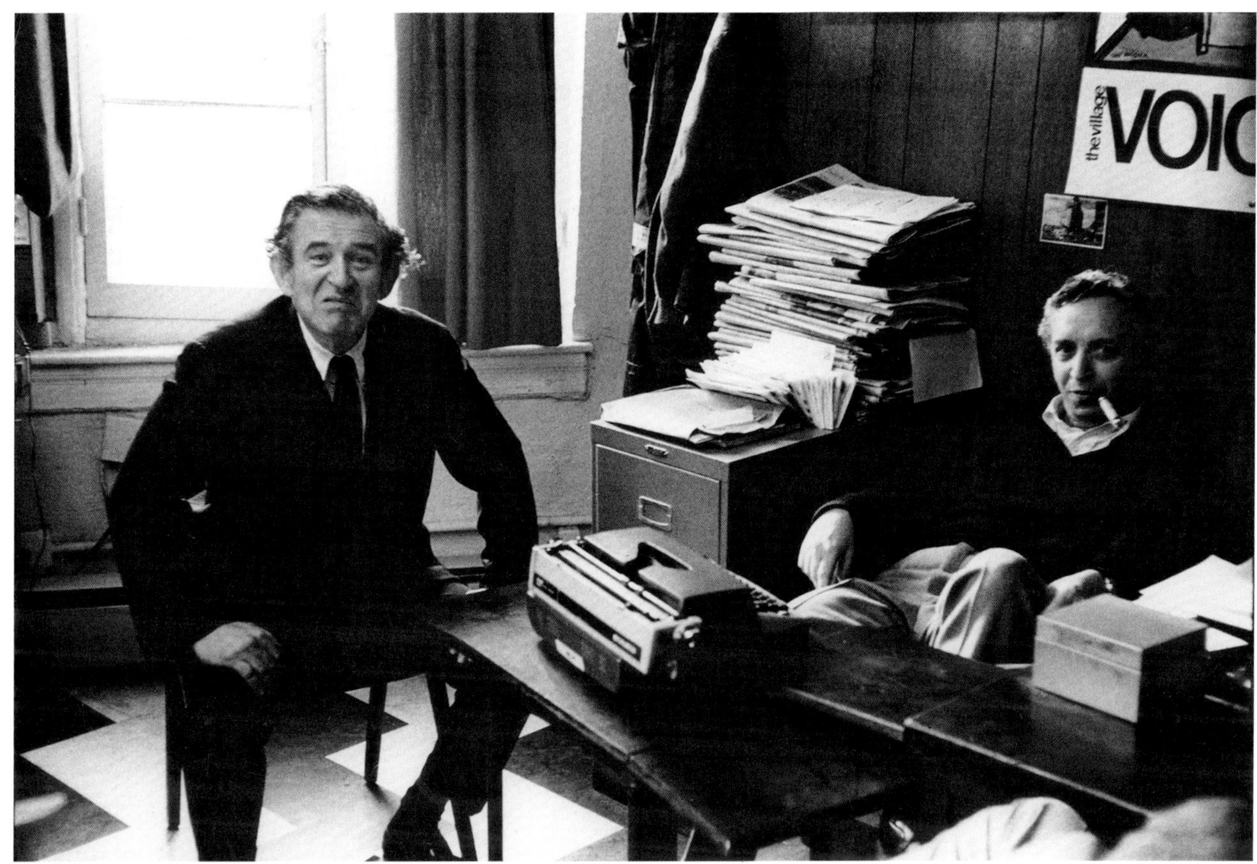

Editor Dan Wolf with author and fellow *Village Voice* cofounder Norman Mailer in the *Voice*'s offices, 61 Christopher St., April 14, 1964.

He'd tussle with the art directors, too. The rat bastards were always cropping photos, dropping type on them, running the photos too small, and not using enough of them.

Despite having no equity in the *Voice*, Fred was thrilled by its growth. By 1967, it was the bestselling weekly newspaper in the United States, with a circulation higher than ninety-five percent of American big-city dailies. Still, there was just one guy taking all the photos. His mailbox at the paper was simply marked "McPhoto."

Fred accompanied writer Robert Christgau to concerts, Mary Perot Nichols and Jack Newfield to City Hall, Howard Smith to the bars, David Bourdon (who first introduced Fred to Warhol) to the galleries, Michael Harrington to protests, Nat Hentoff to symposiums, Andrew Sarris or Jonas Mekas to movie openings, and Jerry Tallmer to Off-Off-Broadway shows. "Fred circled the world of New York politics with me for two decades, responding to every brusque rejection with an irresistible charm and a grin wider than his lens," Wayne Barrett once said.

He never knew which writer he'd be working with when he got up in the morning. A partial list includes John Perreault, Carmen Moore, Frederic

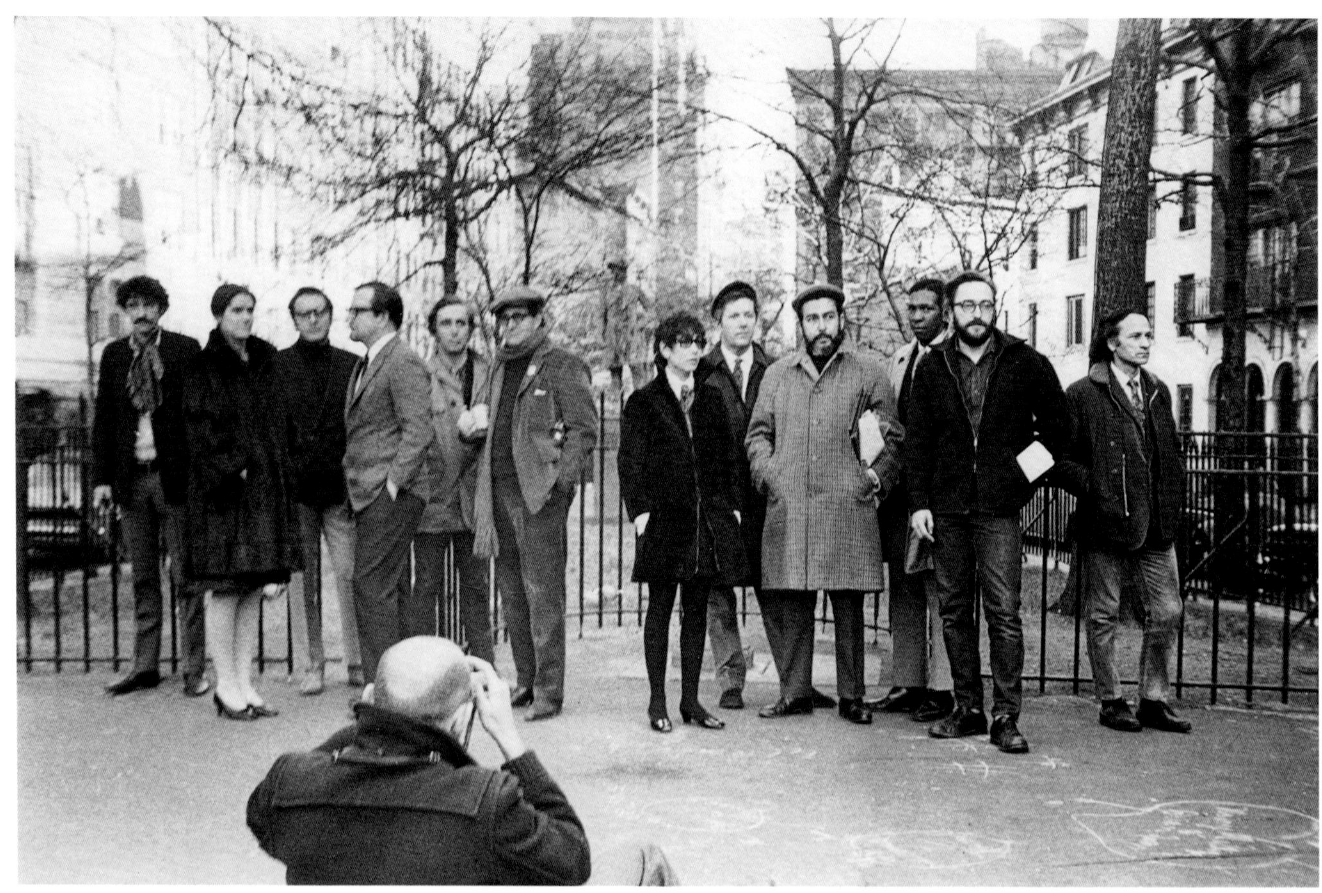

Group portrait of *Village Voice* writers in Christopher Park, across the street from the newspaper's offices, December 21, 1967. From left: Howard Smith, Deborah Jowitt, Michael Zwerin, Joe Flaherty, John Perrault, Danny List, Margot Hentoff, Michael Harrington, Nat Hentoff, Carmen Moore, Ross Wetzsteon, and Jonas Mekas. Photographer Duane Michals is in the foreground, taking the picture.

Morton, Alexander Cockburn, Ellen Frankfort, Gary Giddins, Vivian Gornick, Susan Brownmiller, Sally Kempton, David McReynolds, Jane Kramer, Michael C. D. Macdonald, John Wilcock, Joe Conason, Robin Reisig, Ron Rosenbaum, Leighton Kerner, Eliot Fremont-Smith, James Ridgeway, James Wolcott, Peter Schjeldahl, Stanley Crouch, John Lahr, Howard Blum, Joe Pilati, Mary Breasted, Millie Brower, Paul Cowan, Clark Whelton, Jules Feiffer, Michael Feingold, Joe Flaherty, Jack Goddard, Pete Hamill, Molly Haskell, Blair Sabol, Deborah Jowitt, Letitia Kent, Seymour Krim, Annette Kuhn, Dan List, Anna Mayo, Don McNeill, Arthur Sainer, Phil Tracy, Alan Weitz, Ellen Willis, and Lucy Komisar. By any measure, it was an all-star team. Fred always understood what reporters were looking for to illustrate their stories, and *Voice* reporters loved him for it.

They also loved how he'd never, ever go home from an assignment without getting the shot he came for. "He was really what I would call a reporter-photographer, and he was indomitable," Nat Hentoff once said about his longtime colleague. "Nobody could intimidate him."

"I attended my first press event with Fred…the dedication of the Cube on Astor Place," Lucian Truscott recalled in 2017. "There was a huge press scrum surrounding the city officials who were doing the dedication, including Mayor Lindsay, very photogenic. In the back, a line of old-fashioned video cameras had been set up on raised tripods. In front, maybe thirty or forty reporters pushed and shoved, trying to shout questions or get their shot. I said something to Fred, like, 'How are we going to cover this with such a crowd?' 'Follow me,' he said. He crouched down, and half crouching, half crawling, he made his way quickly between the legs of the reporters and photographers, with me in the same position on his heels. When he got to the front, he popped up, fired off a couple of shots, crouched back down and we made our way through the legs to the back of the scrum. I'd learned how to handle the New York press, Fred style."

Fashion writer Blair Sabol (her dad, Ed Sabol, started NFL Films) said Fred taught her a similar lesson: to get in there. "He used to push me forward at all the shows. I was embarrassed to ask questions or even sit in the front rows.... Fred would find a seat and push me in it. He introduced me to the concept of chutzpah. In the fashion world we were both considered 'downtown disgusting' by Seventh Avenue until suddenly when the *Voice* became 'in,' and we became the 'counterculture darlings.'"

Film critic J. Hoberman: "Fred was free with friendly counsel and fiercely protective of his work, as I learned when I, as *Village Voice* greenhorn, I asked him on behalf of an avant-garde filmmaker friend, if she could use one of his best-known photographs in her movie. Fred lost his smile and gave me an earful. (I considered it career advice.) And he was right, the work he furnished the *Voice* for pennies was only going to grow more valuable. Fred may have been a terrific journalist but, as he'd have been the first to tell you, he wasn't a hippie."

Fred was meticulously organized, which was important as he shot so many different things. And it is incredible to look back at his files and see what a typical week was for him—or a typical day. You can close your eyes and point to a page of his contact sheet catalog and be dazzled by the depth, breadth, and significance of...the whole thing.

On the weekend of March 6, 1959, he photographed the Cedar Tavern with Frank O'Hara and Joe LeSueur inside; a Gaslight poetry reading (with Allen Ginsberg and Peter Orlovsky out on MacDougal Street); and a Robert Motherwell opening at the Sidney Janis Gallery with Willem de Kooning, Irving Sandler, Mark Rothko, Paul Jenkins, Philip Guston, and Franz Kline.

Over one seven-day stretch in January 1968, he took photos of Rudi Gernreich, Norman Mailer, Jane Jacobs, Allen Ginsberg, Yayoi Kusama, Bob Dylan, Arlo Guthrie, Robert Rauschenberg, and A. C. Bhaktivedanta Swami Prabhupada, the guy who started the Hare Krishna movement in Tompkins Square Park the year before. Quite a week. But hardly an unusual one.

Some individual *days* are particularly dazzling. On May 11, 1968, Fred met John and Paul on the tarmac at JFK; the two Beatles had come to town to launch and promote Apple Corps. The same contact sheet has a few images of Timothy Leary at a separate event. And that evening, Fred stopped into the Fillmore East to take a few frames of Jimi Hendrix. Pretty much the crux of the 1960s all captured on one Saturday.

September 27, 1966, was also significant. The contact sheets from that *one day* have Jackie Onassis and the swells at the opening of the Whitney Museum up on East Seventy-Seventh Street and Madison Avenue; John Cage, Steve Paxton, Alex Hay, Robert Whitman, Yvonne Rainer, Billy Klüver, David Tudor, Robert Rauschenberg, Lucinda Childs, Deborah Hay, and Öyvind Fahlström at a Judson Memorial Church press conference to announce the exhibition *9 Evenings: Theatre and Engineering*, a series of programs involving art, industry, and technology; and separately, a couple of frames of Andy Warhol in a tuxedo. Oh yes, Fred's younger son, Patrick McDarrah, was also born that day and there are, between the Warhol and Cage photos, pictures of his wife, Gloria, with their four-year-old son, Timothy, and their new baby at the New York Infirmary (later Beth Israel Hospital) on East Fifteenth Street.

Having grown up in New York, Fred acquired and retained a deep knowledge of the inner working of the city—politically, socially, physically, and culturally— that contributed to his work in unexpected ways.

Take, for example, his memorable May 8, 1967, photo of Robert F. Kennedy walking under a picture of Jesus Christ as the Senator is touring a tenement apartment. After a Senate hearing on Grand Street to evaluate the War on Poverty and a gefilte fish lunch at Ratner's, Kennedy and Senator Jacob K. Javits spent a rainy afternoon walking around the Lower East Side. They stopped at 112 Stanton Street and walked up to a fourth-floor apartment for what was basically a photo op for the assembled TV cameras and reporters.

Typically, Fred was looking for a different angle.

When he saw the slum apartment, he immediately recognized the layout; he had grown up in similarly designed apartments. So he left the press scrum and went to the empty kitchen, where he knew there was an air duct that opened to the hallway where Kennedy would be walking. He reached up and placed his camera in the air duct, on top of a litter of dust bunnies and assorted garbage. Unable to look through the viewfinder—the duct was too high to see over—he simply tilted the lens toward the hallway and waited to hear the press posse with Kennedy approach. Then he'd snap a frame, quickly pull the camera down, advance the film (no motor drives on a 1955 Nikon S2!), and then hold the camera up and snap another frame. Then he'd do it again, and again, and he left hoping that he had a usable picture.

A typical day in the sixties took McDarrah from a preview for an avant-garde art event, the Destruction in Art Symposium, at Judson Memorial Church, featuring Al Hansen, Jon Hendricks, Charlotte Moorman, Hermann Nitsch, Raphael Montañez Ortiz, Nam June Paik, and others, to a Doors concert at the Fillmore East, March 22, 1968.

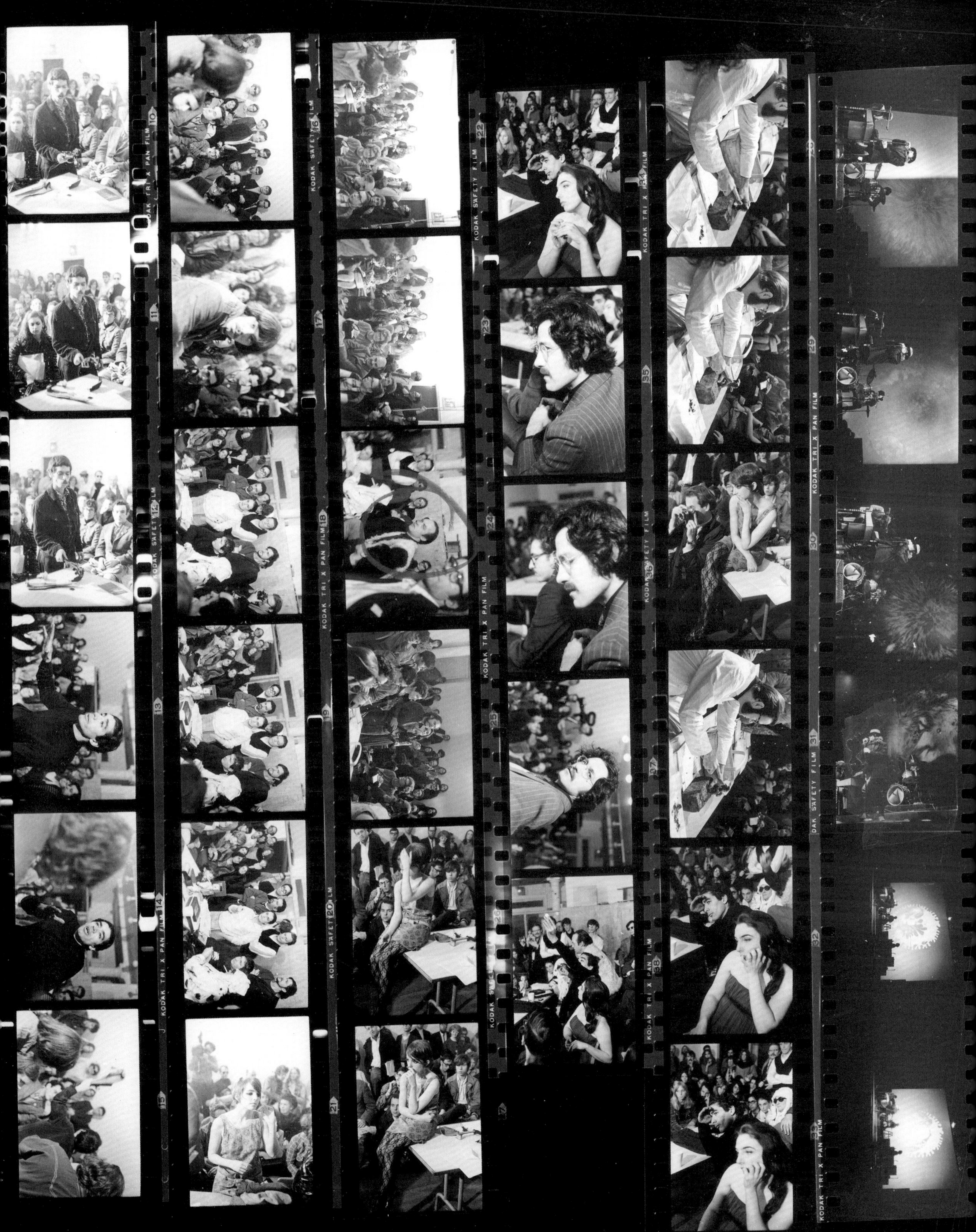

He did.

After his seminal work documenting the Beat literary scene, Fred's archive is especially valuable as a visual record of a special time and place in the history of American art. The entire generation of pop artists—including Roy Lichtenstein, Claes Oldenburg, Tom Wesselmann, Jim Dine, Jasper Johns, Dan Flavin, John Chamberlain, Frank Stella, Donald Judd, Robert Indiana, and James Rosenquist—often sought out Fred for coverage in the *Village Voice*. Warhol would frequently call the house in the early days, hoping Fred would take his photo and use it in the *Voice*, one of the few periodicals giving serious coverage to the Pop genre—and to women artists as well. Fred gave us rare images of Marisol, Eva Hesse, Yayoi Kusama, Carolee Schneemann, Rosalyn Drexler, Hanna Wilke, Niki de Saint Phalle, Helen Frankenthaler, Lee Krasner, Faith Ringgold, Alice Neel, and Marjorie Strider.

Beyond the famous faces, Fred's images are hard-hitting reminders of a controversial era. He generally supported the various social movements he covered, even if he was not of them. His politics were of inclusion and tolerance. In 1993, Allen Ginsberg wrote of Fred, "Though not gay, a hard laboring family man, he's made photo records of gay parades for decades—sign of a real artist's inquisitive sympathy, intelligent democracy." His Stonewall photos in particular exemplify so much about Fred and how he worked.

When Fred got a call from a *Voice* writer who was inside the Stonewall Inn when it was raided in June 1969, he was reluctant to go and take photos. He said, accurately, that cops raiding a gay bar was not that newsworthy, as it happened regularly. However, his sense of duty, and his respect for most of his *Voice* colleagues, especially his friend Arthur Bell (who was the country's first openly gay newspaper columnist), kicked in, and he took nineteen photos of the event that marked the birth of the modern gay rights movement in the United States.

At a twenty-fifth anniversary of Stonewall symposium in 1994, Fred was asked why he took only nineteen photos that evening. "You were at the equivalent of the first shots of the American revolution being fired at Lexington and Concord! Why only nineteen photos?" he was asked.

"Who knew?" he said to laughter. And when you pay your expenses out of your pocket, every image counted, he said. (Fred had, from the beginning, paid for his own film, paper, chemicals, and cameras, and printed—a half bathroom in the family apartment was commandeered as a darkroom—and stored everything at home. That is why many photos in the archive are 5 x 8 inches; he'd cut 8 x 10 inch pieces of photo paper in half to double the amount of available paper to print on.)

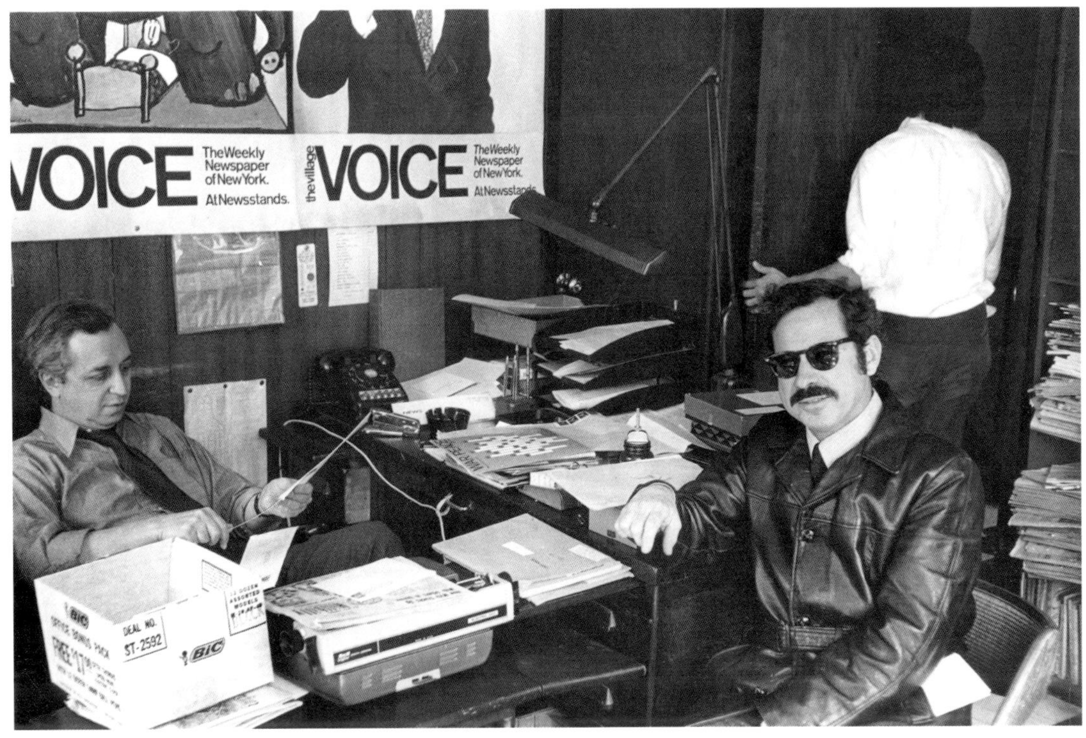

Village Voice editor and cofounder Dan Wolf with Fred W. McDarrah, his post-war housemate, in the *Voice* offices, 61 Christopher St., April 8, 1970.

Fred carried the *Voice* himself through the early seventies, but over time, of course, the photo staff necessarily grew. Fred had a keen eye for talent. His first two staff hires, in 1974, were photographers James Hamilton and Sylvia Plachy (whose son, Adrien Brody, would hang out in the office doing magic tricks for everyone as "The Amazing Adrien"; he later won the Academy Award for best actor in *The Pianist*). Fred's first intern was Harvey Wang, now a respected filmmaker and photographer. Other McPhoto alumni include Marc Asnin, Robin Holland, Tom McGovern, Nevin Shalit, Amy Arbus, Carrie Boretz Keating, Chris Buck, Michel Delsol, Elaine Ellman, Edna Suarez, Lori Grinker, Kristine Larsen, David Lee, Lenore Davis, Pam Duffy, Deborah Feingold, Susan Ferguson, Laura Levine, Andrew Lichtenstein, Sandra Phipps, Keri Pickett, Linda Rosier, Allen Reuben, Coreen Simpson, Doug Vann, Adam Mastoon, Danuta Otfinowski, Carol Halebian, Nick Malter, C. M. Hardt, Catherine McGann, Darren Lew, Meg Handler, Steve Kagan, Pete Kuhns, Steven Mark Needham, Stephen Crichlow, and Donna Day. In 1989, he hired an unknown named Hilton Als to be his assistant. Fred thought he was brilliant. As we all know, the Pulitzer Prize folks agreed when Als, now a *New Yorker* writer, won the criticism award in 2017. "Fred emphasized—to everyone he worked with I think—to value yourself and your work, and to stand up for what is right, no matter how unpopular you may be for it," Als said. "He really didn't care if you liked him. Respected him, yes."

He also knew enough to recognize the value in something unfamiliar. A woman walked into the office one day with a set of hip-hop photos. "That's what's happening these days, huh?" he asked Martha Cooper. "Fred published two landmark photo stories of mine when no one else in New York, or anywhere else, was interested," Cooper said. She is now represented in museums and galleries the world over.

It took a long time for the establishment to grudgingly accept the upstart *Voice*, and for other media outlets and elected officials to belittle the paper was a familiar refrain. Inside the walls of the paper, however, it was a different story. One of Fred's bedrock tenets was to value what the *Voice* did, and that people should value their own work. "If you don't value what you do, then no one else will either. If you don't demand that others value it, too, then why the fuck are you even doing it? Be proud of yourself and what you do."

Like many working photographers of his generation, Fred cheerfully considered himself more photojournalist than artist, but over time, his photos, for both their historical significance and technical achievement, more and more became regarded as fine art. Fred might feel vindicated to some degree were he alive today. He delighted in documenting the socially and culturally disparaged, perhaps feeling a kinship with the outcasts and bohemians he photographed and often befriended. Marginal characters on both sides of the camera who created a vital culture in postwar New York City are now idolized by the young, fêted by high society, studied by academia, discussed in glossy magazines, and portrayed by Hollywood. Fred was one with them.

This was Fred's professional life and legacy, but his camera served him well in one more personal way.

In 1954, Fred applied for a job at Metro Sunday Newspapers, which produced advertising supplements for newspapers. He stapled a photo of himself to his resume. The woman at Metro, Gloria Schoffel, who was tasked to make the new hire, found herself unable to decide among the many similarly qualified young men, mostly returning GIs, who applied for the position. Ruffling through the resumes, she came across the one with a photo attached to it. "He's cute," she thought to herself.

So he was hired. The job didn't last, but Gloria and Fred did.

They got married, had two sons, and were together until his death, on November 6, 2007.

—The Estate of Fred W. McDarrah

ACKNOWLEDGMENTS

A photograph may be worth a thousand words, but since there are no photos in the acknowledgments, we will try to keep the "thank you"s short.

Dan Wolf and Ed Fancher gave Fred an outlet—the pages of the *Village Voice*—and then pretty much left him alone. It worked out. It may have been hard to tell at times, but he was grateful to you both. A lot of other people are, too.

René Aranzamendez and his Getty Images colleagues (especially Mitch Blank and James Bloomfield) have worked endlessly to disseminate more "McPhotos" to more outlets than we ever could have thought possible. No one understands the business better or is easier to work with.

Ken Norwick is one of the nation's leading legal authorities on copyright, intellectual property, and First Amendment law. His advice and guidance to Fred and, since his death, the estate, has been incalculable.

Sean Wilentz found perhaps the only way to rebel against his lefty bookstore-owning family: become an Ivy League professor. Your intro is simply perfect. You have forever defined Fred's unique importance for those who lived through the era and those who find it in his work. Bravo.

Eric Himmel and the Abrams team—designers John Gall and Shawn Dahl; Richard Slovak, who edited the captions; production manager Anet Sirna-Bruder; and managing editors Mary O'Mara and Gabriel Levinson—have made the production of this book a remarkably smooth process. We are thankful to have worked with you on this and are beyond thrilled with the result.

Steve Kasher has been a ceaseless, tireless, fierce, and forceful advocate of Fred's work for decades. This book could not and would not have happened without him and the Steven Kasher Gallery crew: Cassandra Johnson, Elaina Breen, and Patrice Gonzalez. Deep, heartfelt, and sincere thanks, Steve. Now get back to work.

And, finally, thank you to everyone depicted in this book—and those who maybe did not make the cut—and everything they did; for making the bygone Village such an amazing, incredible, creative, exciting, dynamic, stimulating, colorful, exciting, passionate, vibrant place that will forever live on in these photos.

—Timothy, Patrick, and Gloria McDarrah

INDEX

Note: Page numbers in *italics* indicate/include captions.

Picture Editor: Steven Kasher
Designers: John Gall and Shawn Dahl
Production Manager: Anet Sirna-Bruder

Library of Congress Control Number: 2017956797

ISBN: 978-1-4197-2897-6
eISBN: 978-1-68335-212-9

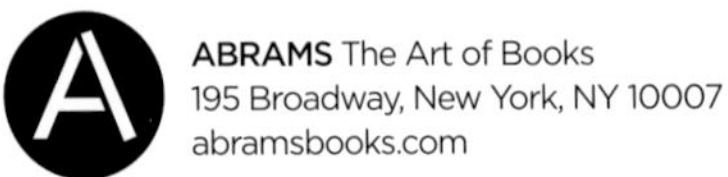
ABRAMS The Art of Books
195 Broadway, New York, NY 10007
abramsbooks.com